Practical mod_perl

Practical mod_perl

Stas Bekman and Eric Cholet

O'REILLY®

Beijing · Cambridge · Farnham · Köln · Paris · Sebastopol · Taipei · Tokyo

Practical mod_perl
by Stas Bekman and Eric Cholet

Published by O'Reilly & Associates, Inc., 1005 Gravenstein Highway North, Sebastopol, CA 95472.

O'Reilly & Associates books may be purchased for educational, business, or sales promotional use. Online editions are also available for most titles (*safari.oreilly.com*). For more information, contact our corporate/institutional sales department: (800) 998-9938 or *corporate@oreilly.com*.

Editor: Linda Mui

Developmental Editor: Rachel Wheeler

Production Editor: Linley Dolby

Cover Designer: Ellie Volckhausen

Interior Designer: Bret Kerr

Printing History:

  May 2003:   First Edition.

ISBN: 0-596-00227-0
[C]

Table of Contents

Part II. mod_perl Performance

Part IV.   Debugging and Troubleshooting

Part V. mod_perl 2.0

Part VI. Appendixes

Preface

mod_perl is an Apache module that builds the power of the Perl programming language directly into the Apache web server. With mod_perl, CGI scripts run as much as 50 times faster, and you can integrate databases with the server, write Apache modules in Perl, embed Perl code directly into Apache configuration files, and even use Perl in server-side includes. With mod_perl, Apache is not only a web server, it is a complete programming platform.

Getting mod_perl running is easy. Tweaking mod_perl and Apache for the best performance and reliability is much more difficult. This book is about building mod_perl, using it, programming with it, and optimizing it.

What You Need to Know

To use this book effectively, you need to be familiar with the day-to-day details of running a web server, and you need to know the Perl programming language. We expect that you have already programmed in the Perl programming language. Having written simple CGI scripts and having experience with setting up the Apache web server are definite pluses. Knowing your way around the operating system is another plus, but not a requirement.

Most examples in the book were done on the Linux operating system, but the examples and discussions should apply equally well to other operating systems, especially other Unix flavors. There is a dedicated section on installing mod_perl on Windows machines in Chapter 2.

Who This Book Is For

This book is not solely about mod_perl web development. It covers two main topics: server administration and programming under mod_perl.

At first, you might think these two topics are unrelated. But in real life, the programmer often needs to know how to build and maintain the server, and the administrator ends up doing much of the programming and tweaking himself.

In this book, administrators will learn:

- How to build and configure the server, with emphasis on improving server performance while keeping memory usage low.

- How to make sure the server is operating nonstop and, in case of malfunction, how to get it back online in no time.

- How to maximize performance by using multiple servers and additional tools such as proxies.

- How to choose the right machine and components. Often the most expensive machine isn't much faster than a cheaper one with more carefully chosen components.

- How to allow users to run custom scripts on a mod_perl server.

As for programmers, the good news is that you can be a capable mod_perl programmer while knowing very little about it. But most of us don't want to stop at being simply capable: we want to develop code that's robust, scalable, and blindingly fast. Here's a taste of the sort of things we cover in this book:

- In CGI, it's often hard to find what's wrong with a CGI script that returns a nondescriptive error message to your browser. You can try the *error_log* file, but with a complex script you have to use the -d switch and call the Perl debugger, which can be difficult for CGI scripts that can't be run from the shell. In Chapter 22, we'll show you how you can run the script in debug mode and control it.

- Alas, mod_perl is picky about coding style—for example, it doesn't like it when you forget to close a file after opening it. But if you ask nicely, it might enter a special mode where it will clean up for you. In Chapter 6, we'll show you how to keep mod_perl happy and keep the *error_log* file small.

- As you may already know, mod_perl is very fast. But with a little effort you can make it even faster. The idea is simple: the more memory (RAM) you have, the more requests you will be able to serve. However, you may be able to serve more requests using the same amount of RAM, thanks to memory sharing. For more information, see Chapter 10.

- With mod_perl, you never need to reinvent the wheel. If you need a so-called "shelf solution," this book includes quite a few copy-and-paste scenarios to inspire you.

- Many programmers use mod_perl in conjunction with databases. We start with the simplest and most basic databases (flat files), continue to Database Management (DBM) implementations, and finally do an in-depth study of relational databases with SQL.

Of course, there's lots more, as you can tell from just the sheer size and weight of the book. This book is filled with gems of information that, taken together, provide a wealth of information on how to work effectively with mod_perl.

How This Book Is Organized

This book has four parts:

Part I: mod_perl Administration
> Part I of this book focuses on the administration of mod_perl: getting it installed, configuring mod_perl and your web site as a whole, performing upgrades, and doing maintenance.

> Chapter 1, *Introducing CGI and mod_perl*

> Chapter 2, *Getting Started Fast*

> Chapter 3, *Installing mod_perl*

> Chapter 4, *mod_perl Configuration*

> Chapter 5, *Web Server Control, Monitoring, Upgrade, and Maintenance*

> Chapter 6, *Coding with mod_perl in Mind*

Part II: mod_perl Performance
> Part II of the book is about how to use mod_perl to its fullest: it covers choosing a hardware platform, writing code, configuring the operating system, and configuring the Apache/mod_perl server itself.

> Chapter 7, *Identifying Your Performance Problems*

> Chapter 8, *Choosing a Platform for the Best Performance*

> Chapter 9, *Essential Tools for Performance Tuning*

> Chapter 10, *Improving Performance with Shared Memory and Proper Forking*

> Chapter 11, *Tuning Performance by Tweaking Apache's Configuration*

> Chapter 12, *Server Setup Strategies*

> Chapter 13, *TMTOWTDI: Convenience and Habit Versus Performance*

> Chapter 14, *Defensive Measures for Performance Enhancement*

> Chapter 15, *Improving Performance Through Build Options*

> Chapter 16, *HTTP Headers for Optimal Performance*

Part III: Databases and mod_perl
> Part III tackles how to integrate databases with mod_perl in the most effective and efficient manner.

> Chapter 17, *Databases Overview*

> Chapter 18, *mod_perl Data-Sharing Techniques*

> Chapter 19, *DBM and mod_perl*

Reference Sections

At the end of almost every chapter in this book, we include lists of resources that give further detail on relevant topics. The references are usually either URLs or book references. Unfortunately, URLs tend to change or disappear over time, so if you read this book some time after it has been published and some of the URLs aren't valid anymore, try to use a search engine such as Google to find the updated link. If you still can't find the listed resource, try to look it up in the Internet archive: *http://www. archive.org/*.

Many chapters refer to the Request For Comments documents (RFCs), which are mirrored by hundreds of Internet sites all around the world and are easy to find. A good starting point is *http://www.rfc-editor.org/*.

Filesystem Conventions

Throughout the book, unless mentioned otherwise, we assume that all the sources are downloaded and built in the directory */home/stas/src/*. If you follow the same convention, you need only to replace *stas* with your username.

As you will learn in Chapter 12, most mod_perl users run one plain Apache server and one mod_perl-enabled Apache server on the same machine. We usually install these into the directories */home/httpd/httpd_docs* and */home/httpd/httpd_perl*, respectively.

Apache and Perl Versions

We have used mod_perl 1.26 and Apache 1.3.24 in most of the examples in this book. You should be able to reproduce all the presented examples with these or later versions of mod_perl and Apache.

We have tested all the examples with Perl 5.6.1. However, most of the examples should work the same under all Perl versions between 5.005_03 and 5.8.0.

At the time of this writing, Apache 2.0 is very young and mod_perl 2.0 is still in development. See Part V for information on mod_perl 2.0. While much of this book should apply to both mod_perl 1.x and mod_perl 2.0, the code has been tested only on mod_perl 1.26.

Typographic Conventions

The following typographic conventions are used in this book:

Italic
> Used for filenames, command names, directory names, and Unix utilities. It is also used for email addresses, URLs, and new terms where they are defined.

`Constant Width`
> Used for code examples and for function, method, variable, and module names.

Command Interpreter Program (Shell) Conventions

When you type a command and press the Enter key to execute this command, it's usually interpreted by some kind of command interpreter program, known as a *shell*. In this book we will use this term when we refer to a command interpreter program.

If you are running your web server on some Unix flavor, it is likely that you are using the C-style shell (e.g., *csh* or *tcsh*) or the Bourne-style shell (e.g., *sh*, *ksh*, or *bash*) for starting programs from the command line. In most examples in this book, it doesn't matter which shell program is used. In places where a different syntax should be used for different shell programs, we will say so.

The following command-line conventions are used in this book:

```
panic% command
```

panic% is a shell prompt when you are logged on as a non-*root* user, usually yourself.

```
panic# command
```

panic# is a shell prompt when you are logged on as *root*. It implies that you have to become a *root* user to run the command. One of the ways to switch to *root* mode is to execute the *su* utility and supply the *root* user password.

Installing Perl Modules

mod_perl and all the various Perl modules and helper utilities mentioned in this book are available via FTP and HTTP from any of the sites on the Comprehensive Perl Archive Network (CPAN) at *http://cpan.org/*. This is a list of several hundred public FTP and HTTP sites that mirror each others' contents on a regular basis.

You can search for and install Perl modules in two ways:

- Manually, by going to *http://search.cpan.org/*, finding the module, then downloading, building, and installing it. You can also browse the modules by categories or authors at *http://cpan.org/*.
- Automatically, by using Andreas Koenig's CPAN shell or (on MS Windows systems) the Perl Package Manager (PPM). These tools allow you to search for available modules and install them with a single command.

Manual Installation

When you download a module manually, it's best to find the one closest to you. You can find a list of CPAN mirrors at *http://mirror.cpan.org/*.

You can download the source packages with your browser, or, if you know the URL of the package, you can use any command tool to do that for you. In this book, we usually use the *lwp-download* perl script (which is bundled with the `libwww-perl` package, by Gisle Aas) as a client. You can use any other utility to download the files from the Internet.

Once you've downloaded the Perl module you want, you'll need to build and install it. Some modules are 100% Perl and can just be copied to the Perl library directory. Others contain some components written in C and need to be compiled.

Let's download the CPAN shell package, which we will use shortly:

```
panic% lwp-download http://www.cpan.org/authors/id/ANDK/CPAN-1.60.tar.gz
Saving to 'CPAN-1.60.tar.gz'...
115 KB received in 2 seconds (56.3 KB/sec)
```

Prerequisites Needed to Install Perl Modules on Windows

While Unix operating systems include standard utilities such as *tar*, *gzip*, and *make*, Windows systems don't. For this reason, you will have to go through some extra steps to ensure that you can install modules from the CPAN under Windows.

We assume here that you are using the ActivePerl distribution from ActiveState.

The first utility needed is *make*. On Windows, such a utility (called *nmake*) is distributed by Microsoft for free. You can download a self-extracting archive from *ftp:// ftp.microsoft.com/Softlib/MSLFILES/nmake15.exe*. When you run this executable, you will have three files: *readme.txt*, *nmake.err*, and *nmake.exe*. Copy these files into a directory in your PATH,* such as *C:\Windows\System*, *C:\Windows*, or even *C:\Perl\ bin*. You will now be able to replace any use of *make* in the examples in this book with *nmake*.

Some examples, and the use of CPAN.pm, also require command-line utilities such as *tar* or *gzip*. There are a number of projects that have ported such tools to Windows—for example, GnuWin32 (*http://gnuwin32.sourceforge.net/*) and UnixUtils (*http://unxutils.sourceforge.net/*). These toolkits allow you to use standard Unix utilities from your Windows command line.

Another option is Cygwin (*http://www.cygwin.com/*), which puts a Unix layer on top of Windows. This allows you to use many Unix-specific applications, but these must run from the Cygwin shell. If you use Cygwin, you should use the normal Unix steps discussed in this book, not any Windows-specific ones.

There is another downside of Windows: compilation tools aren't included. This means that some modules that use C extensions (e.g., mod_perl) can't be installed in the normal way, and you have to get precompiled distributions of them. In such cases, it is a good idea to follow the PPM instructions given later in this Preface, which should allow you to install binary versions of some of the modules discussed here.

Building a Perl Module

Building a Perl module and installing it is simple and usually painless. Perl modules are distributed as *gzip*ped *tar* archives. You can unpack them like this:

```
panic% gunzip -c CPAN-1.60.tar.gz | tar xvf -
CPAN-1.60/
CPAN-1.60/lib/
CPAN-1.60/lib/CPAN/
CPAN-1.60/lib/CPAN/Nox.pm
CPAN-1.60/lib/CPAN/Admin.pm
CPAN-1.60/lib/CPAN/FirstTime.pm
CPAN-1.60/lib/Bundle/
```

---

* To see your PATH, run echo %PATH% from the command line.

```
CPAN-1.60/lib/Bundle/CPAN.pm
CPAN-1.60/lib/CPAN.pm
CPAN-1.60/Todo
CPAN-1.60/ChangeLog
CPAN-1.60/t/
CPAN-1.60/t/loadme.t
CPAN-1.60/t/vcmp.t
CPAN-1.60/MANIFEST
CPAN-1.60/Makefile.PL
CPAN-1.60/cpan
CPAN-1.60/README
```

Or, if you are using a GNU *tar* utility, you can unpack the package in one command:

```
panic% tar zxvf CPAN-1.59.tzr.gz
```

Once the archive has been unpacked, you'll have to enter the newly created directory and issue the *perl Makefile.PL*, *make*, *make test*, and *make install* commands. Together, these will build, test, and install the module:

```
panic% cd CPAN-1.60
panic% perl Makefile.PL
Checking if your kit is complete...
Looks good
Writing Makefile for CPAN

panic% make
cp lib/CPAN/Nox.pm blib/lib/CPAN/Nox.pm
cp lib/Bundle/CPAN.pm blib/lib/Bundle/CPAN.pm
cp lib/CPAN/Admin.pm blib/lib/CPAN/Admin.pm
cp lib/CPAN.pm blib/lib/CPAN.pm
cp lib/CPAN/FirstTime.pm blib/lib/CPAN/FirstTime.pm
cp cpan blib/script/cpan
/usr/bin/perl -I/usr/lib/perl5/5.6.1/i386-linux
              -I/usr/lib/perl5/5.6.1 -MExtUtils::MakeMaker
              -e "MY->fixin(shift)" blib/script/cpan
Manifying blib/man3/CPAN::Nox.3
Manifying blib/man3/Bundle::CPAN.3
Manifying blib/man3/CPAN::Admin.3
Manifying blib/man3/CPAN.3
Manifying blib/man3/CPAN::FirstTime.3

panic% make test
PERL_DL_NONLAZY=1 /usr/bin/perl -Iblib/arch -Iblib/lib
-I/usr/lib/perl5/5.6.1/i386-linux -I/usr/lib/perl5/5.6.1
-e 'use Test::Harness qw(&runtests $verbose);
    $verbose=0; runtests @ARGV;'
t/*.t
t/loadme...........ok
t/vcmp.............ok
All tests successful.
Files=2, Tests=31,  3 wallclock secs ( 1.22 cusr +  0.91 csys =  2.13 CPU)
```

Become *root* if you need to install the module on the whole system:

```
panic% su
<root password>

panic# make install
Installing /usr/lib/perl5/man/man3/CPAN::Nox.3
Installing /usr/lib/perl5/man/man3/Bundle::CPAN.3
Installing /usr/lib/perl5/man/man3/CPAN::Admin.3
Installing /usr/lib/perl5/man/man3/CPAN.3
Installing /usr/lib/perl5/man/man3/CPAN::FirstTime.3
Writing /usr/lib/perl5/5.6.1/i386-linux/auto/CPAN/.packlist
Appending installation info to /usr/lib/perl5/5.6.1/i386-linux/perllocal.pod
```

Using the CPAN Shell

A simpler way to do the same thing is to use Andreas Koenig's wonderful CPAN shell (recent Perl versions come bundled with this module). With it, you can download, build, and install Perl modules from a simple command-line shell. The following illustrates a typical session in which we install the Apache::VMonitor module:

```
panic% perl -MCPAN -e shell

cpan shell -- CPAN exploration and modules installation (v1.60)
ReadLine support enabled

cpan> install Apache::VMonitor
Running install for module Apache::VMonitor
Running make for S/ST/STAS/Apache-VMonitor-0.6.tar.gz
Fetching with LWP:
  http://cpan.org/authors/id/S/ST/STAS/Apache-VMonitor-0.6.tar.gz
Fetching with LWP:
  http://cpan.org/authors/id/S/ST/STAS/CHECKSUMS
Checksum for /root/.cpan/sources/authors/id/S/ST/STAS/Apache-VMonitor-0.6.tar.gz ok
Apache-VMonitor-0.6/
Apache-VMonitor-0.6/README
Apache-VMonitor-0.6/Makefile.PL
Apache-VMonitor-0.6/MANIFEST
Apache-VMonitor-0.6/CHANGES
Apache-VMonitor-0.6/VMonitor.pm

CPAN.pm: Going to build S/ST/STAS/Apache-VMonitor-0.6.tar.gz

Checking for Apache::Scoreboard...ok
Checking for GTop...ok
Checking for Time::HiRes...ok
Checking for mod_perl...ok
Checking if your kit is complete...
Looks good
Writing Makefile for Apache::VMonitor
cp VMonitor.pm blib/lib/Apache/VMonitor.pm
Manifying blib/man3/Apache::VMonitor.3
  /usr/bin/make  -- OK
```

```
Running make test
No tests defined for Apache::VMonitor extension.
  /usr/bin/make test -- OK
Running make install
Installing /usr/lib/perl5/site_perl/5.6.1/Apache/VMonitor.pm
Installing /usr/lib/perl5/man/man3/Apache::VMonitor.3
Writing /usr/lib/perl5/site_perl/5.6.1/i386-linux/auto/Apache/VMonitor/.packlist
Appending installation info to /usr/lib/perl5/5.6.1/i386-linux/perllocal.pod
  /usr/bin/make install UNINST=1 -- OK

cpan> exit
```

Notice that the CPAN shell fetches the *CHECKSUMS* file and verifies that the package hasn't been tampered with.

The latest CPAN module comes with a small utility called *cpan*, which you can use to start the CPAN shell:

```
panic% cpan

cpan shell -- CPAN exploration and modules installation (v1.60)
ReadLine support enabled
```

Using the Perl Package Manager

If you are using ActivePerl on Windows, or the Perl/Apache/mod_perl binary distribution discussed in Chapter 2, you will have access to a handy utility called *ppm*. This program installs Perl modules from archives separate from the CPAN that contain precompiled versions of certain modules.

For first-time configuration, do the following:

```
C:\> ppm
PPM interactive shell (2.1.5) - type 'help' for available commands.
PPM> set repository theoryx5 http://theoryx5.uwinnipeg.ca/cgi-bin/ppmserver?urn:/
PPMServer
PPM> set repository oi http://openinteract.sourceforge.net/ppmpackages/
PPM> set save
PPM> quit
C:\>
```

These steps will allow you to access a number of interesting packages not available from the ActiveState archive (including mod_perl). To see a list of these packages, type search in the PPM interactive shell, or visit *http://openinteract.sourceforge.net/ ppmpackages/* and *http://theoryx5.uwinnipeg.ca/ppmpackages/*.

Now, when you want to install a module, issue the following commands:

```
C:\> ppm
PPM> install Some::Module
PPM> quit
C:\>
```

It's as easy as that! Alternatively, you might want to do it directly:

```
C:\> ppm install Some::Module
```

This will have the same effect.

How to Contact Us

Please address comments and questions concerning this book to the publisher:

O'Reilly & Associates, Inc.
1005 Gravenstein Highway North
Sebastopol, CA 95472
(800) 998-9938 (in the United States or Canada)
(707) 829-0515 (international/local)
(707) 829-0104 (fax)

To comment or ask technical questions about this book, send email to:

bookquestions@oreilly.com

For more information about books, conferences, Resource Centers, and the O'Reilly Network, see the O'Reilly web site at:

http://www.oreilly.com

The web page for this book lists errata, examples, or any additional information. You can access this page at:

http://www.oreilly.com/catalog/pmodperl/

This book also has a companion web site at *http://www.modperlbook.org/*. Here you will find all the source code for the code examples in this book. You will also find announcements, errata, supplementary examples, downloads, and links to other sources of information about Apache, Perl, and Apache module development.

Acknowledgments

Many people have contributed to this book over the long period while it was in the works.

First things first. This book wouldn't exist without Doug MacEachern, creator of mod_perl. Doug's preliminary overview of mod_perl 2.0 was used as the basis of Chapters 24 and 25.

We're also greatly indebted to many people who contributed chapters or appendixes to this book. Andreas Koenig contributed Chapter 16, with helpful corrections, additions, and comments from Ask Björn Hansen, Frank D. Cringle, Mark Kennedy, Doug MacEachern, Tom Hukins, and Wham Bang. Matt Sergeant contributed Appendix E, with helpful comments from Robin Berjon. Andy Wardley contributed Appendix D.

We cannot thank enough the following reviewers, who have reviewed huge portions of the book (or the whole book) and provided good advice: Andreas Koenig, Ged Haywood, Gunther Birznieks, Issac Goldstand, Mark Summerfield, Paul Wilt, Per Einar Ellefsen, Philippe M. Chiasson, and Robin Berjon. Thank you, guys. Without you, this book wouldn't be nearly as useful as it is now.

The following people also contributed much to the book: Aaron Johnson, Ask Björn Hansen, Brian Ingerson, David Landgren, Doug MacEachern, Ed Philips, Geoff Young, Pat Eyler, Perrin Harkins, Philippe Bruhat, Rafael Garcia-Suarez, Stéphane Payrard, Tatsuhiko Miyagawa, and Ken Williams. Thank you all for taking time to improve the book.

Since the book is loosely based on the mod_perl guide, we must acknowledge the following people who have indirectly contributed to the book by helping with the guide (about 200 names!): Aaron Johnson, Ajay Shah, Alexander Farber, Andreas J. Koenig, Andreas Piesk, Andrei A. Voropaev, Andrew Ford, Andrew McNaughton, Anthony D. Ettinger, Artur Zambrzycki, Ask Björn Hansen, Barrie Slaymaker, Bill Moseley, Boris Zentner, Brian Moseley, Carl Hansen, Chad K. Lewis, Chris Nokleberg, Chris Winters, Christof Damian, Christophe Dupre, Cliff Rayman, Craig, Daniel Bohling, Daniel Koch, Daniel W. Burke, Darren Chamberlain, Dave Hodgkinson, Dave Rolsky, David Harris, David Huggins-Daines, David Landgren, David Mitchell, DeWitt Clinton, Dean Fitz, Doug Bagley, Doug Kyle, Doug MacEachern, Drew Taylor, Ed Park, Ed Phillips, Edmund Mergl, Edwin Pratomo, Eric Cholet, Eric Strovink, Evan A. Zacks, Ewan Edwards, Frank Cringle, Frank Schoeters, Garr Updegraff, Ged Haywood, Geoff Crawshaw, Geoffrey S. Young, Gerald Richter, Gerd Knops, Glenn, Greg Cope, Greg Stark, Gunther Birznieks, Hailei Dai, Henrique Pantarotto, Honza Pazdziora, Howard Jones, Hunter Monroe, Ilya Obshadko, Ime Smits, Issac Goldstand, James Furness, James G. Smith, James W. Walden, Jan Peter Hecking, Jason Bodnar, Jason Rhinelander, Jauder Ho, Jay J, Jean-Louis Guenego, Jeff Chan, Jeff Rowe, Jeffrey W. Baker, Jens Heunemann, Jie Gao, Joao Fonseca, Joe Schaefer, Joe Slag, John Armstrong, John Deighan, John Hyland, John Milton, John Walker, Jon Orwant, Jonathan Peterson, Joshua Chamas, Karl Olson, Kavitha, Kees Vonk, Ken Williams, Kenny Gatdula, Kevin Murphy, Kevin Swope, Lance Cleveland, Larry Leszczynski, Leslie Mikesell, Lincoln Stein, Louis Semprini, Lupe Christoph, Mads Toftum, Marc Lehmann, Marcel Grunauer, Mark Mills, Mark Summerfield, Marko van der Puil, Marshall Dudley, Matt Sergeant, Matthew Darwin, Michael Blakeley, Michael Finke, Michael G. Schwern, Michael Hall, Michael Rendell, Michael Schout, Michele Beltrame, Mike Depot, Mike Fletcher, Mike MacKenzie, Mike Miller, Nancy Lin, Nathan Torkington, Nathan Vonnahme, Neil Conway, Nick Tonkin, Oleg Bartunov, Owen Williams, Pascal Eeftinck, Patrick, Paul Buder, Paul Cotter, Pavel Shmidt, Per Einar Ellefsen, Perrin Harkins, Peter Galbavy, Peter Haworth, Peter J. Schoenster, Peter Skov, Philip Jacob, Philip Newton, Radu Greab, Rafael Garcia-Suarez, Ralf Engelschall, Randal L. Schwartz, Randy Harmon, Randy Kobes, Rauznitz Balazs,

Rex Staples, Rich Bowen, Richard A. Wells, Richard Chen, Richard Dice, Richard More, Rick Myers, Robert Mathews, Robin Berjon, Rodger Donaldson, Ron Pero, Roy Nasser, Salve J. Nilsen, Scott Fagg, Scott Holdren, Sean Dague, Shane Nay, Stephane Benoit, Stephen Judd, Steve Fink, Steve Reppucci, Steve Willer, Surat Singh Bhati, Terry West, Thomas Klausner, Tim Bunce, Tim Noll, Todd Finney, Tom Brown, Tom Christiansen, Tom Hughes, Tom Mornini, Tuomas Salo, Tzvetan Stoyanov, Ulrich Neumerkel, Ulrich Pfeifer, Vivek Khera, Ward Vandewege, Wesley Darlington, Will Trillich, Yann Kerhervé, and Yann Ramin. Thank you all!

mod_perl Administration

The first part of this book is about mod_perl administration. Here you'll find everything you need to do to get mod_perl running, from installation to configuration to the nuances of programming in a mod_perl environment.

Chapter 1, *Introducing CGI and mod_perl*, is an introduction to mod_perl and how it works within the Apache framework.

Chapter 2, *Getting Started Fast*, is a whirlwind description of how to get started with mod_perl quickly. Most programmers aren't satisfied just reading a book; they want to start programming right away. This chapter helps you build a working mod_perl environment with minimal fuss.

Chapter 3, *Installing mod_perl*, contains everything we left out of Chapter 2.

Chapter 4, *mod_perl Configuration*, is about how to configure mod_perl for your specific needs.

Chapter 5, *Web Server Control, Monitoring, Upgrade, and Maintenance*, covers how to run a mod_perl-enabled server and keep it running smoothly.

Chapter 6, *Coding with mod_perl in Mind*, contains the essential information for programming under mod_perl.

## CHAPTER 1

Introducing CGI and mod_perl

This chapter provides the foundations on which the rest of the book builds. In this chapter, we give you:

- A history of CGI and the HTTP protocol.
- An explanation of the Apache 1.3 Unix model, which is crucial to understanding how mod_perl 1.0 works.
- An overall picture of mod_perl 1.0 and its development.
- An overview of the difference between the Apache C API, the Apache Perl API (i.e., the mod_perl API), and CGI compatibility. We will also introduce the `Apache::Registry` and `Apache::PerlRun` modules.
- An introduction to the mod_perl API and handlers.

A Brief History of CGI

When the World Wide Web was born, there was only one web server and one web client. The *httpd* web server was developed by the Centre d'Etudes et de Recherche Nucléaires (CERN) in Geneva, Switzerland. *httpd* has since become the generic name of the binary executable of many web servers. When CERN stopped funding the development of *httpd*, it was taken over by the Software Development Group of the National Center for Supercomputing Applications (NCSA). The NCSA also produced Mosaic, the first web browser, whose developers later went on to write the Netscape client.

Mosaic could fetch and view static documents[*] and images served by the *httpd* server. This provided a far better means of disseminating information to large numbers of people than sending each person an email. However, the glut of online resources soon made search engines necessary, which meant that users needed to be able to

---

[*] A static document is one that exists in a constant state, such as a text file that doesn't change.

submit data (such as a search string) and servers needed to process that data and return appropriate content.

Search engines were first implemented by extending the web server, modifying its source code directly. Rewriting the source was not very practical, however, so the NCSA developed the *Common Gateway Interface* (CGI) specification. CGI became a standard for interfacing external applications with web servers and other information servers and generating dynamic information.

A CGI program can be written in virtually any language that can read from STDIN and write to STDOUT, regardless of whether it is interpreted (e.g., the Unix shell), compiled (e.g., C or C++), or a combination of both (e.g., Perl). The first CGI programs were written in C and needed to be compiled into binary executables. For this reason, the directory from which the compiled CGI programs were executed was named *cgi-bin*, and the source files directory was named *cgi-src*. Nowadays most servers come with a preconfigured directory for CGI programs called, as you have probably guessed, *cgi-bin*.

The HTTP Protocol

Interaction between the browser and the server is governed by the *HyperText Transfer Protocol* (HTTP), now an official Internet standard maintained by the World Wide Web Consortium (W3C). HTTP uses a simple request/response model: the client establishes a TCP[*] connection to the server and sends a request, the server sends a response, and the connection is closed. Requests and responses take the form of *messages*. A message is a simple sequence of text lines.

HTTP messages have two parts. First come the *headers*, which hold descriptive information about the request or response. The various types of headers and their possible content are fully specified by the HTTP protocol. Headers are followed by a blank line, then by the message *body*. The body is the actual content of the message, such as an HTML page or a GIF image. The HTTP protocol does not define the content of the body; rather, specific headers are used to describe the content type and its encoding. This enables new content types to be incorporated into the Web without any fanfare.

HTTP is a stateless protocol. This means that requests are not related to each other. This makes life simple for CGI programs: they need worry about only the current request.

The Common Gateway Interface Specification

If you are new to the CGI world, there's no need to worry—basic CGI programming is very easy. Ninety percent of CGI-specific code is concerned with reading data

---

[*] TCP/IP is a low-level Internet protocol for transmitting bits of data, regardless of its use.

submitted by a user through an HTML form, processing it, and returning some response, usually as an HTML document.

In this section, we will show you how easy basic CGI programming is, rather than trying to teach you the entire CGI specification. There are many books and online tutorials that cover CGI in great detail (see *http://hoohoo.ncsa.uiuc.edu/*). Our aim is to demonstrate that if you know Perl, you can start writing CGI scripts almost immediately. You need to learn only two things: how to accept data and how to generate output.

The HTTP protocol makes clients and servers understand each other by transferring all the information between them using headers, where each header is a key-value pair. When you submit a form, the CGI program looks for the headers that contain the input information, processes the received data (e.g., queries a database for the keywords supplied through the form), and—when it is ready to return a response to the client—sends a special header that tells the client what kind of information it should expect, followed by the information itself. The server can send additional headers, but these are optional. Figure 1-1 depicts a typical request-response cycle.

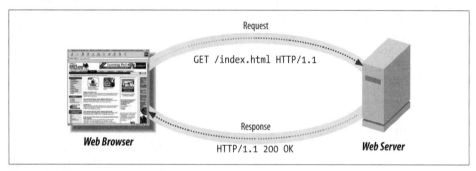

Figure 1-1. Request-response cycle

Sometimes CGI programs can generate a response without needing any input data from the client. For example, a news service may respond with the latest stories without asking for any input from the client. But if you want stories for a specific day, you have to tell the script which day's stories you want. Hence, the script will need to retrieve some input from you.

To get your feet wet with CGI scripts, let's look at the classic "Hello world" script for CGI, shown in Example 1-1.

Example 1-1. "Hello world" script

```
#!/usr/bin/perl -Tw

print "Content-type: text/plain\n\n";
print "Hello world!\n";
```

We start by sending a Content-type header, which tells the client that the data that follows is of plain-text type. *text/plain* is a Multipurpose Internet Mail Extensions (MIME) type. You can find a list of widely used MIME types in the *mime.types* file, which is usually located in the directory where your web server's configuration files are stored.* Other examples of MIME types are *text/html* (text in HTML format) and *video/mpeg* (an MPEG stream).

According to the HTTP protocol, an empty line must be sent after all headers have been sent. This empty line indicates that the actual response data will start at the next line.†

Now save the code in *hello.pl*, put it into a *cgi-bin* directory on your server, make the script executable, and test the script by pointing your favorite browser to:

    http://localhost/cgi-bin/hello.pl

It should display the same output as Figure 1-2.

Figure 1-2. Hello world

A more complicated script involves parsing input data. There are a few ways to pass data to the scripts, but the most commonly used are the GET and POST methods. Let's write a script that expects as input the user's name and prints this name in its response. We'll use the GET method, which passes data in the request URI (uniform resource indicator):

    http://localhost/cgi-bin/hello.pl?username=Doug

When the server accepts this request, it knows to split the URI into two parts: a path to the script (*http://localhost/cgi-bin/hello.pl*) and the "data" part (username=Doug, called the QUERY_STRING). All we have to do is parse the data portion of the URI and extract the key username and value Doug. The GET method is used mostly for hard-coded queries, where no interactive input is needed. Assuming that portions of your

---

* For more information about Internet media types, refer to RFCs 2045, 2046, 2047, 2048, and 2077, accessible from *http://www.rfc-editor.org/*.

† The protocol specifies the end of a line as the character sequence Ctrl-M and Ctrl-J (carriage return and newline). On Unix and Windows systems, this sequence is expressed in a Perl string as \015\012, but Apache also honors \n, which we will use throughout this book. On EBCDIC machines, an explicit \r\n should be used instead.

---

site are dynamically generated, your site's menu might include the following HTML code:

```
<a href="/cgi-bin/display.pl?section=news">News</a><br>
<a href="/cgi-bin/display.pl?section=stories">Stories</a><br>
<a href="/cgi-bin/display.pl?section=links">Links</a><br>
```

Another approach is to use an HTML form, where the user fills in some parameters. The HTML form for the "Hello user" script that we will look at in this section can be either:

```
<form action="/cgi-bin/hello_user.pl" method="POST">
<input type="text" name="username">
<input type="submit">
</form>
```

or:

```
<form action="/cgi-bin/hello_user.pl" method="GET">
<input type="text" name="username">
<input type="submit">
</form>
```

Note that you can use either the GET or POST method in an HTML form. However, POST should be used when the query has side effects, such as changing a record in a database, while GET should be used in simple queries like this one (simple URL links are GET requests).*

Formerly, reading input data required different code, depending on the method used to submit the data. We can now use Perl modules that do all the work for us. The most widely used CGI library is the CGI.pm module, written by Lincoln Stein, which is included in the Perl distribution. Along with parsing input data, it provides an easy API to generate the HTML response.

Our sample "Hello user" script is shown in Example 1-2.

Example 1-2. "Hello user" script

```
#!/usr/bin/perl

use CGI qw(:standard);
my $username = param('username') || "unknown";

print "Content-type: text/plain\n\n";
print "Hello $username!\n";
```

Notice that this script is only slightly different from the previous one. We've pulled in the CGI.pm module, importing a group of functions called :standard. We then used its param( ) function to retrieve the value of the username key. This call will return the

---

* See *Axioms of Web Architecture* at *http://www.w3.org/DesignIssues/Axioms.html#state*.

name submitted by any of the three ways described above (a form using either POST, GET, or a hardcoded name with GET; the last two are essentially the same). If no value was supplied in the request, param( ) returns undef.

```
my $username = param('username') || "unknown";
```

$username will contain either the submitted username or the string "unknown" if no value was submitted. The rest of the script is unchanged—we send the MIME header and print the "Hello $username!" string.*

As we've just mentioned, CGI.pm can help us with output generation as well. We can use it to generate MIME headers by rewriting the original script as shown in Example 1-3.

Example 1-3. "Hello user" script using CGI.pm

```
#!/usr/bin/perl

use CGI qw(:standard);
my $username = param('username') || "unknown";

print header("text/plain");
print "Hello $username!\n";
```

To help you learn how CGI.pm copes with more than one parameter, consider the code in Example 1-4.

Example 1-4. CGI.pm and param() method

```
#!/usr/bin/perl

use CGI qw(:standard);
print header("text/plain");

print "The passed parameters were:\n";
for my $key ( param( ) ) {
    print "$key => ", param($key), "\n";
}
```

Now issue the following request:

```
http://localhost/cgi-bin/hello_user.pl?a=foo&b=bar&c=foobar
```

The browser will display:

```
The passed parameters were:
a => foo
b => bar
c => foobar
```

---

* All scripts shown here generate plain text, not HTML. If you generate HTML output, you have to protect the incoming data from cross-site scripting. For more information, refer to the CERT advisory at *http://www. cert.org/advisories/CA-2000-02.html.*

Separating key=value Pairs

Note that & or ; usually is used to separate the *key=value* pairs. The former is less preferable, because if you end up with a QUERY_STRING of this format:

    id=foo&reg=bar

some browsers will interpret &reg as an SGML entity and encode it as ®. This will result in a corrupted QUERY_STRING:

    id=foo®=bar

You have to encode & as & if it is included in HTML. You don't have this problem if you use ; as a separator:

    id=foo;reg=bar

Both separators are supported by CGI.pm, Apache::Request, and mod_perl's args( ) method, which we will use in the examples to retrieve the request parameters.

Of course, the code that builds QUERY_STRING has to ensure that the values don't include the chosen separator and encode it if it is used. (See RFC2854 for more details.)

Now generate this form:

```
<form action="/cgi-bin/hello_user.pl" method="GET">
<input type="text" name="firstname">
<input type="text" name="lastname">
<input type="submit">
</form>
```

If we fill in only the firstname field with the value Doug, the browser will display:

```
The passed parameters were:
firstname => Doug
lastname =>
```

If in addition the lastname field is MacEachern, you will see:

```
The passed parameters were:
firstname => Doug
lastname => MacEachern
```

These are just a few of the many functions CGI.pm offers. Read its manpage for detailed information by typing perldoc CGI at your command prompt.

We used this long CGI.pm example to demonstrate how simple basic CGI is. You shouldn't reinvent the wheel; use standard tools when writing your own scripts, and you will save a lot of time. Just as with Perl, you can start creating really cool and powerful code from the very beginning, gaining more advanced knowledge over time. There is much more to know about the CGI specification, and you will learn about some of its advanced features in the course of your web development practice. We will cover the most commonly used features in this book.

For now, let CGI.pm or an equivalent library handle the intricacies of the CGI specification, and concentrate your efforts on the core functionality of your code.

Apache CGI Handling with mod_cgi

The Apache server processes CGI scripts via an Apache module called mod_cgi. (See later in this chapter for more information on request-processing phases and Apache modules.) mod_cgi is built by default with the Apache core, and the installation procedure also preconfigures a *cgi-bin* directory and populates it with a few sample CGI scripts. Write your script, move it into the *cgi-bin* directory, make it readable and executable by the web server, and you can start using it right away.

Should you wish to alter the default configuration, there are only a few configuration directives that you might want to modify. First, the ScriptAlias directive:

```
ScriptAlias /cgi-bin/ /home/httpd/cgi-bin/
```

ScriptAlias controls which directories contain server scripts. Scripts are run by the server when requested, rather than sent as documents.

When a request is received with a path that starts with */cgi-bin*, the server searches for the file in the */home/httpd/cgi-bin* directory. It then runs the file as an executable program, returning to the client the generated output, not the source listing of the file.

The other important part of *httpd.conf* specifies how the files in *cgi-bin* should be treated:

```
<Directory /home/httpd/cgi-bin>
    Options FollowSymLinks
    Order allow,deny
    Allow from all
</Directory>
```

The above setting allows the use of symbolic links in the */home/httpd/cgi-bin* directory. It also allows anyone to access the scripts from anywhere.

mod_cgi provides access to various server parameters through environment variables. The script in Example 1-5 will print these environment variables.

Example 1-5. Checking environment variables

```
#!/usr/bin/perl

print "Content-type: text/plain\n\n";
for (keys %ENV) {
    print "$_ => $ENV{$_}\n";
}
```

Save this script as *env.pl* in the directory *cgi-bin* and make it executable and readable by the server (that is, by the username under which the server runs). Point your browser to *http://localhost/cgi-bin/env.pl* and you will see a list of parameters similar to this one:

```
SERVER_SOFTWARE => Server: Apache/1.3.24 (Unix) mod_perl/1.26
                   mod_ssl/2.8.8 OpenSSL/0.9.6
GATEWAY_INTERFACE => CGI/1.1
DOCUMENT_ROOT => /home/httpd/docs
REMOTE_ADDR => 127.0.0.1
SERVER_PROTOCOL => HTTP/1.0
REQUEST_METHOD => GET
QUERY_STRING =>
HTTP_USER_AGENT => Mozilla/5.0 Galeon/1.2.1 (X11; Linux i686; U;) Gecko/0
SERVER_ADDR => 127.0.0.1
SCRIPT_NAME => /cgi-bin/env.pl
SCRIPT_FILENAME => /home/httpd/cgi-bin/env.pl
```

Your code can access any of these variables with $ENV{"somekey"}. However, some variables can be spoofed by the client side, so you should be careful if you rely on them for handling sensitive information. Let's look at some of these environment variables.

```
SERVER_SOFTWARE => Server: Apache/1.3.24 (Unix) mod_perl/1.26
                   mod_ssl/2.8.8 OpenSSL/0.9.6
```

The SERVER_SOFTWARE variable tells us what components are compiled into the server, and their version numbers. In this example, we used Apache 1.3.24, mod_perl 1.26, mod_ssl 2.8.8, and OpenSSL 0.9.6.

```
GATEWAY_INTERFACE => CGI/1.1
```

The GATEWAY_INTERFACE variable is very important; in this example, it tells us that the script is running under mod_cgi. When running under mod_perl, this value changes to CGI-Perl/1.1.

```
REMOTE_ADDR => 127.0.0.1
```

The REMOTE_ADDR variable tells us the remote address of the client. In this example, both client and server were running on the same machine, so the client is localhost (whose IP is 127.0.0.1).

```
SERVER_PROTOCOL => HTTP/1.0
```

The SERVER_PROTOCOL variable reports the HTTP protocol version upon which the client and the server have agreed. Part of the communication between the client and the server is a negotiation of which version of the HTTP protocol to use. The highest version the two can understand will be chosen as a result of this negotiation.

```
REQUEST_METHOD => GET
```

The now-familiar REQUEST_METHOD variable tells us which request method was used (GET, in this case).

```
QUERY_STRING =>
```

The QUERY_STRING variable is also very important. It is used to pass the query parameters when using the GET method. QUERY_STRING is empty in this example, because we didn't pass any parameters.

```
HTTP_USER_AGENT => Mozilla/5.0 Galeon/1.2.1 (X11; Linux i686; U;) Gecko/0
```

The HTTP_USER_AGENT variable contains the user agent specifications. In this example, we are using Galeon on Linux. Note that this variable is very easily spoofed.

Spoofing HTTP_USER_AGENT

If the client is a custom program rather than a widely used browser, it can mimic its bigger brother's signature. Here is an example of a very simple client using the LWP library:

```
#!/usr/bin/perl -w
use LWP::UserAgent;

my $ua  = new LWP::UserAgent;
$ua->agent("Mozilla/5.0 Galeon/1.2.1 (X11; Linux i686; U;) Gecko/0");
my $req = new HTTP::Request('GET', 'http://localhost/cgi-bin/env.pl');

my $res = $ua->request($req);
print $res->content if $res->is_success;
```

This script first creates an instance of a user agent, with a signature identical to Galeon's on Linux. It then creates a request object, which is passed to the user agent for processing. The response content is received and printed.

When run from the command line, the output of this script is strikingly similar to what we obtained with the browser. It notably prints:

```
HTTP_USER_AGENT => Mozilla/5.0 Galeon/1.2.1 (X11; Linux i686; U;) Gecko/0
```

So you can see how easy it is to fool a naïve CGI programmer into thinking we've used Galeon as our client program.

```
SERVER_ADDR => 127.0.0.1
SCRIPT_NAME => /cgi-bin/env.pl
SCRIPT_FILENAME => /home/httpd/cgi-bin/env.pl
```

The SERVER_ADDR, SCRIPT_NAME, and SCRIPT_FILENAME variables tell us (respectively) the server address, the name of the script as provided in the request URI, and the real path to the script on the filesystem.

Now let's get back to the QUERY_STRING parameter. If we submit a new request for *http://localhost/cgi-bin/env.pl?foo=ok&bar=not_ok*, the new value of the query string is displayed:

```
QUERY_STRING => foo=ok&bar=not_ok
```

This is the variable used by CGI.pm and other modules to extract the input data.

Keep in mind that the query string has a limited size. Although the HTTP protocol itself does not place a limit on the length of a URI, most server and client software does. Apache currently accepts a maximum size of 8K (8192) characters for the entire URI. Some older client or proxy implementations do not properly support URIs larger than 255 characters. This is true for some new clients as well—for example, some WAP phones have similar limitations.

Larger chunks of information, such as complex forms, are passed to the script using the POST method. Your CGI script should check the REQUEST_METHOD environment variable, which is set to POST when a request is submitted with the POST method. The script can retrieve all submitted data from the STDIN stream. But again, let CGI.pm or similar modules handle this process for you; whatever the request method, you won't have to worry about it because the key/value parameter pairs will always be handled in the right way.

The Apache 1.3 Server Model

Now that you know how CGI works, let's talk about how Apache implements mod_cgi. This is important because it will help you understand the limitations of mod_cgi and why mod_perl is such a big improvement. This discussion will also build a foundation for the rest of the performance chapters of this book.

Forking

Apache 1.3 on all Unix flavors uses the *forking* model.* When you start the server, a single process, called the *parent process*, is started. Its main responsibility is starting and killing child processes as needed. Various Apache configuration directives let you control how many child processes are spawned initially, the number of spare idle processes, and the maximum number of processes the parent process is allowed to fork.

Each child process has its own lifespan, which is controlled by the configuration directive MaxRequestsPerChild. This directive specifies the number of requests that should be served by the child before it is instructed to step down and is replaced by another process. Figure 1-3 illustrates.

When a client initiates a request, the parent process checks whether there is an idle child process and, if so, tells it to handle the request. If there are no idle processes, the parent checks whether it is allowed to fork more processes. If it is, a new process is forked to handle the request. Otherwise, the incoming request is queued until a child process becomes available to handle it.

---

* In Chapter 24 we talk about Apache 2.0, which introduces a few more server models.

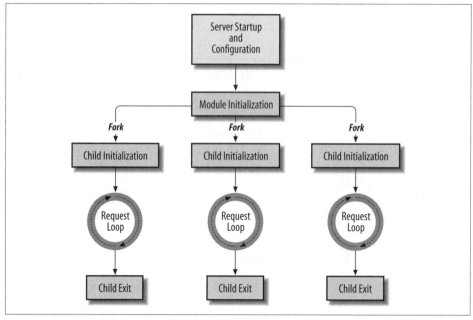

Figure 1-3. The Apache 1.3 server lifecycle

The maximum number of queued requests is configurable by the `ListenBacklog` configuration directive. When this number is reached, a client issuing a new request will receive an error response informing it that the server is unreachable.

This is how requests for static objects, such as HTML documents and images, are processed. When a CGI request is received, an additional step is performed: mod_cgi in the child Apache process forks a new process to execute the CGI script. When the script has completed processing the request, the forked process exits.

CGI Scripts Under the Forking Model

One of the benefits of this model is that if something causes the child process to die (e.g., a badly written CGI script), it won't cause the whole service to fail. In fact, only the client that initiated the request will notice there was a problem.

Many free (and non-free) CGI scripts are badly written, but they still work, which is why no one tries to improve them. Examples of poor CGI programming practices include forgetting to close open files, using uninitialized global variables, ignoring the warnings Perl generates, and forgetting to turn on taint checks (thus creating huge security holes that are happily used by crackers to break into online systems).

Why do these sloppily written scripts work under mod_cgi? The reason lies in the way mod_cgi invokes them: every time a Perl CGI script is run, a new process is forked, and a new Perl interpreter is loaded. This Perl interpreter lives for the span of the request's life, and when the script exits (no matter how), the process and the interpreter exit as well, cleaning up on the way. When a new interpreter is started, it has no history of previous requests. All the variables are created from scratch, and all the files are reopened if needed. Although this detail may seem obvious, it will be of paramount importance when we discuss mod_perl.

Performance Drawbacks of Forking

There are several drawbacks to mod_cgi that triggered the development of improved web technologies. The first problem lies in the fact that a new process is forked and a new Perl interpreter is loaded for each CGI script invocation. This has several implications:

- It adds the overhead of forking, although this is almost insignificant on modern Unix systems.
- Loading the Perl interpreter adds significant overhead to server response times.
- The script's source code and the modules that it uses need to be loaded into memory and compiled each time from scratch. This adds even more overhead to response times.
- Process termination on the script's completion makes it impossible to create persistent variables, which in turn prevents the establishment of persistent database connections and in-memory databases.
- Starting a new interpreter removes the benefit of memory sharing that could be obtained by preloading code modules at server startup. Also, database connections can't be pre-opened at server startup.

Another drawback is limited functionality: mod_cgi allows developers to write only content handlers within CGI scripts. If you need to access the much broader core functionality Apache provides, such as authentication or URL rewriting, you must resort to third-party Apache modules written in C, which sometimes make the production server environment somewhat cumbersome. More components require more administration work to keep the server in a healthy state.

The Development of mod_perl 1.0

Of the various attempts to improve on mod_cgi's shortcomings, mod_perl has proven to be one of the better solutions and has been widely adopted by CGI developers. Doug MacEachern fathered the core code of this Apache module and licensed it under the Apache Software License, which is a certified open source license.

mod_perl does away with mod_cgi's forking by embedding the Perl interpreter into Apache's child processes, thus avoiding the forking mod_cgi needed to run Perl programs. In this new model, the child process doesn't exit when it has processed a request. The Perl interpreter is loaded only once, when the process is started. Since the interpreter is persistent throughout the process's lifetime, all code is loaded and compiled only once, the first time it is needed. All subsequent requests run much faster, because everything is already loaded and compiled. Response processing is reduced to simply running the code, which improves response times by a factor of 10–100, depending on the code being executed.

But Doug's real accomplishment was adding a mod_perl API to the Apache core. This made it possible to write complete Apache modules in Perl, a feat that used to require coding in C. From then on, mod_perl enabled the programmer to handle all phases of request processing in Perl.

The mod_perl API also allows complete server configuration in Perl. This has made the lives of many server administrators much easier, as they now benefit from dynamically generating the configuration and are freed from hunting for bugs in huge configuration files full of similar directives for virtual hosts and the like.[*]

To provide backward compatibility for plain CGI scripts that used to be run under mod_cgi, while still benefiting from a preloaded Perl interpreter and modules, a few special handlers were written, each allowing a different level of proximity to pure mod_perl functionality. Some take full advantage of mod_perl, while others do not.

mod_perl embeds a copy of the Perl interpreter into the Apache *httpd* executable, providing complete access to Perl functionality within Apache. This enables a set of mod_perl-specific configuration directives, all of which start with the string `Perl`. Most, but not all, of these directives are used to specify handlers for various phases of the request.

It might occur to you that sticking a large executable (Perl) into another large executable (Apache) creates a very, very large program. mod_perl certainly makes *httpd* significantly bigger, and you will need more RAM on your production server to be able to run many mod_perl processes. However, in reality, the situation is not as bad as it first appears. mod_perl processes requests much faster, so the number of processes needed to handle the same request rate is much lower relative to the mod_cgi approach. Generally, you need slightly more available memory, but the speed improvements you will see are well worth every megabyte of memory you can add. Techniques that can reduce memory requirements are covered in Chapter 10.

According to *http://netcraft.com/*, as of January 2003, mod_perl has been used on more than four million web sites. Some of these sites have been using mod_perl since its early days. You can see an extensive list of sites that use mod_perl at *http://perl. apache.org/outstanding/sites.html* or *http://perl.apache.org/outstanding/success_stories/*. The latest usage statistics can be viewed at *http://perl.apache.org/outstanding/stats/*.

---

[*] mod_vhost_alias offers similar functionality.

Running CGI Scripts with mod_perl

Since many web application developers are interested in the content delivery phase and come from a CGI background, mod_perl includes packages designed to make the transition from CGI simple and painless. `Apache::PerlRun` and `Apache::Registry` run unmodified CGI scripts, albeit much faster than mod_cgi.[*]

The difference between `Apache::Registry` and `Apache::PerlRun` is that `Apache::Registry` caches all scripts, and `Apache::PerlRun` doesn't. To understand why this matters, remember that if one of mod_perl's benefits is added speed, another is persistence. Just as the Perl interpreter is loaded only once, at child process startup, your scripts are loaded and compiled only once, when they are first used. This can be a double-edged sword: persistence means global variables aren't reset to initial values, and file and database handles aren't closed when the script ends. This can wreak havoc in badly written CGI scripts.

Whether you should use `Apache::Registry` or `Apache::PerlRun` for your CGI scripts depends on how well written your existing Perl scripts are. Some scripts initialize all variables, close all file handles, use taint mode, and give only polite error messages. Others don't.

`Apache::Registry` compiles scripts on first use and keeps the compiled scripts in memory. On subsequent requests, all the needed code (the script and the modules it uses) is already compiled and loaded in memory. This gives you enormous performance benefits, but it requires that scripts be well behaved.

`Apache::PerlRun`, on the other hand, compiles scripts at each request. The script's namespace is flushed and is fresh at the start of every request. This allows scripts to enjoy the basic benefit of mod_perl (i.e., not having to load the Perl interpreter) without requiring poorly written scripts to be rewritten.

A typical problem some developers encounter when porting from mod_cgi to `Apache::Registry` is the use of uninitialized global variables. Consider the following script:

```
use CGI;
$q = CGI->new();
$topsecret = 1 if $q->param("secret") eq 'Muahaha';
# ...
if ($topsecret) {
    display_topsecret_data();
}
else {
    security_alert();
}
```

---

[*] `Apache::RegistryNG` and `Apache::RegistryBB` are two new experimental modules that you may want to try as well.

This script will always do the right thing under mod_cgi: if secret=Muahaha is supplied, the top-secret data will be displayed via display_topsecret_data(), and if the authentication fails, the security_alert() function will be called. This works only because under mod_cgi, all globals are undefined at the beginning of each request.

Under Apache::Registry, however, global variables preserve their values between requests. Now imagine a situation where someone has successfully authenticated, setting the global variable $topsecret to a true value. From now on, anyone can access the top-secret data without knowing the secret phrase, because $topsecret will stay true until the process dies or is modified elsewhere in the code.

This is an example of sloppy code. It will do the right thing under Apache::PerlRun, since all global variables are undefined before each iteration of the script. However, under Apache::Registry and mod_perl handlers, all global variables must be initialized before they can be used.

The example can be fixed in a few ways. It's a good idea to always use the strict mode, which requires the global variables to be declared before they are used:

```
use strict;
use CGI;
use vars qw($top $q);
# init globals
$top = 0;
$q = undef;
# code
$q = CGI->new( );
$topsecret = 1 if $q->param("secret") eq 'Muahaha';
# ...
```

But of course, the simplest solution is to avoid using globals where possible. Let's look at the example rewritten without globals:

```
use strict;
use CGI;
my $q = CGI->new( );
my $topsecret = $q->param("secret") eq 'Muahaha' ? 1 : 0;
# ...
```

The last two versions of the example will run perfectly under Apache::Registry.

Here is another example that won't work correctly under Apache::Registry. This example presents a simple search engine script:

```
use CGI;
my $q = CGI->new( );
print $q->header('text/plain');
my @data = read_data( )
my $pat = $q->param("keyword");
foreach (@data) {
    print if /$pat/o;
}
```

The example retrieves some data using read_data( ) (e.g., lines in the text file), tries to match the keyword submitted by a user against this data, and prints the matching lines. The /o regular expression modifier is used to compile the regular expression only once, to speed up the matches. Without it, the regular expression will be recompiled as many times as the size of the @data array.

Now consider that someone is using this script to search for something inappropriate. Under Apache::Registry, the pattern will be cached and won't be recompiled in subsequent requests, meaning that the next person using this script (running in the same process) may receive something quite unexpected as a result. Oops.

The proper solution to this problem is discussed in Chapter 6, but Apache::PerlRun provides an immediate workaround, since it resets the regular expression cache before each request.

So why bother to keep your code clean? Why not use Apache::PerlRun all the time? As we mentioned earlier, the convenience provided by Apache::PerlRun comes at a price of performance deterioration.

In Chapter 9, we show in detail how to benchmark the code and server configuration. Based on the results of the benchmark, you can tune the service for the best performance. For now, let's just show the benchmark of the short script in Example 1-6.

Example 1-6. readdir.pl

```
use strict;

use CGI ();
use IO::Dir ();

my $q = CGI->new;
print $q->header("text/plain");
my $dir = IO::Dir->new(".");
print join "\n", $dir->read;
```

The script loads two modules (CGI and IO::Dir), prints the HTTP header, and prints the contents of the current directory. If we compare the performance of this script under mod_cgi, Apache::Registry, and Apache::PerlRun, we get the following results:

```
    Mode              Requests/sec
    -----------------------------
    Apache::Registry      473
    Apache::PerlRun       289
    mod_cgi                10
```

Because the script does very little, the performance differences between the three modes are very significant. Apache::Registry thoroughly outperforms mod_cgi, and you can see that Apache::PerlRun is much faster than mod_cgi, although it is still about twice as slow as Apache::Registry. The performance gap usually shrinks a bit as more code is added, as the overhead of fork( ) and code compilation becomes less significant compared to execution times. But the benchmark results won't change significantly.

Jumping ahead, if we convert the script in Example 1-6 into a mod_perl handler, we can reach 517 requests per second under the same conditions, which is a bit faster than Apache::Registry. In Chapter 13, we discuss why running the code under the Apache::Registry handler is a bit slower than using a pure mod_perl content handler.

It can easily be seen from this benchmark that Apache::Registry is what you should use for your scripts to get the most out of mod_perl. But Apache::PerlRun is still quite useful for making an easy transition to mod_perl. With Apache::PerlRun, you can get a significant performance improvement over mod_cgi with minimal effort.

Later, we will see that Apache::Registry's caching mechanism is implemented by compiling each script in its own namespace. Apache::Registry builds a unique package name using the script's name, the current URI, and the current virtual host (if any). Apache::Registry prepends a package statement to your script, then compiles it using Perl's eval function. In Chapter 6, we will show how exactly this is done.

What happens if you modify the script's file after it has been compiled and cached? Apache::Registry checks the file's last-modification time, and if the file has changed since the last compile, it is reloaded and recompiled.

In case of a compilation or execution error, the error is logged to the server's error log, and a server error is returned to the client.

Apache 1.3 Request Processing Phases

To understand mod_perl, you should understand how request processing works within Apache. When Apache receives a request, it processes it in 11 phases. For every phase, a standard default handler is supplied by Apache. You can also write your own Perl handlers for each phase; they will override or extend the default behavior. The 11 phases (illustrated in Figure 1-4) are:

Post-read-request
> This phase occurs when the server has read all the incoming request's data and parsed the HTTP header. Usually, this stage is used to perform something that should be done once per request, as early as possible. Modules' authors usually use this phase to initialize per-request data to be used in subsequent phases.

URI translation
> In this phase, the requested URI is translated to the name of a physical file or the name of a virtual document that will be created on the fly. Apache performs the translation based on configuration directives such as ScriptAlias. This translation can be completely modified by modules such as mod_rewrite, which register themselves with Apache to be invoked in this phase of the request processing.

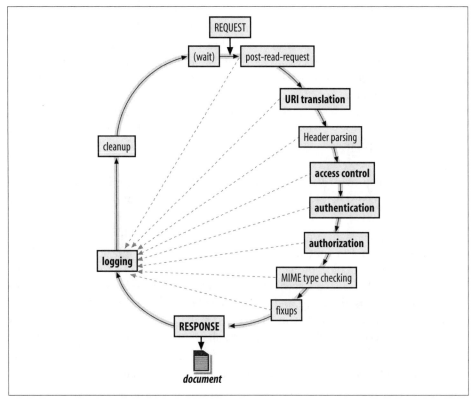

Figure 1-4. Apache 1.3 request processing phases

Header parsing

During this phase, you can examine and modify the request headers and take a special action if needed—e.g., blocking unwanted agents as early as possible.

Access control

This phase allows the server owner to restrict access to specific resources based on various rules, such as the client's IP address or the day of week.

Authentication

Sometimes you want to make sure that a user really is who he claims to be. To verify his identity, challenge him with a question that only he can answer. Generally, the question is a login name and password, but it can be any other challenge that allows you to distinguish between users.

Authorization

The service might have various restricted areas, and you might want to allow the user to access some of these areas. Once a user has passed the authentication process, it is easy to check whether a specific location can be accessed by that user.

MIME type checking

Apache handles requests for different types of files in different ways. For static HTML files, the content is simply sent directly to the client from the filesystem. For CGI scripts, the processing is done by mod_cgi, while for mod_perl programs, the processing is done by mod_perl and the appropriate Perl handler. During this phase, Apache actually decides on which method to use, basing its choice on various things such as configuration directives, the filename's extension, or an analysis of its content. When the choice has been made, Apache selects the appropriate content handler, which will be used in the next phase.

Fixup

This phase is provided to allow last-minute adjustments to the environment and the request record before the actual work in the content handler starts.

Response

This is the phase where most of the work happens. First, the handler that generates the response (a content handler) sends a set of HTTP headers to the client. These headers include the Content-type header, which is either picked by the MIME-type-checking phase or provided dynamically by a program. Then the actual content is generated and sent to the client. The content generation might entail reading a simple file (in the case of static files) or performing a complex database query and HTML-ifying the results (in the case of the dynamic content that mod_perl handlers provide).

This is where mod_cgi, Apache::Registry, and other content handlers run.

Logging

By default, a single line describing every request is logged into a flat file. Using the configuration directives, you can specify which bits of information should be logged and where. This phase lets you hook custom logging handlers—for example, logging into a relational database or sending log information to a dedicated master machine that collects the logs from many different hosts.

Cleanup

At the end of each request, the modules that participated in one or more previous phases are allowed to perform various cleanups, such as ensuring that the resources that were locked but not freed are released (e.g., a process aborted by a user who pressed the Stop button), deleting temporary files, and so on.

Each module registers its cleanup code, either in its source code or as a separate configuration entry.

At almost every phase, if there is an error and the request is aborted, Apache returns an error code to the client using the default error handler (or a custom one, if provided).

Apache 1.3 Modules and the mod_perl 1.0 API

The advantage of breaking up the request process into phases is that Apache gives a programmer the opportunity to "hook" into the process at any of those phases.

Apache has been designed with modularity in mind. A small set of core functions handle the basic tasks of dealing with the HTTP protocol and managing child processes. Everything else is handled by modules. The core supplies an easy way to plug modules into Apache at build time or runtime and enable them at runtime.

Modules for the most common tasks, such as serving directory indexes or logging requests, are supplied and compiled in by default. mod_cgi is one such module. Other modules are bundled with the Apache distribution but are not compiled in by default: this is the case with more specialized modules such as mod_rewrite or mod_proxy. There are also a vast number of third-party modules, such as mod_perl, that can handle a wide variety of tasks. Many of these can be found in the Apache Module Registry (*http://modules.apache.org/*).

Modules take control of request processing at each of the phases through a set of well-defined hooks provided by Apache. The subroutine or function in charge of a particular request phase is called a *handler*. These include authentication handlers such as mod_auth_dbi, as well as content handlers such as mod_cgi. Some modules, such as mod_rewrite, install handlers for more than one request phase.

Apache also provides modules with a comprehensive set of functions they can call to achieve common tasks, including file I/O, sending HTTP headers, or parsing URIs. These functions are collectively known as the Apache Application Programming Interface (API).

Apache is written in C and currently requires that modules be written in the same language. However, as we will see, mod_perl provides the full Apache API in Perl, so modules can be written in Perl as well, although mod_perl must be installed for them to run.

mod_perl 1.0 and the mod_perl API

Like other Apache modules, mod_perl is written in C, registers handlers for request phases, and uses the Apache API. However, mod_perl doesn't directly process requests. Rather, it allows you to write handlers in Perl. When the Apache core yields control to mod_perl through one of its registered handlers, mod_perl dispatches processing to one of the registered Perl handlers.

Since Perl handlers need to perform the same basic tasks as their C counterparts, mod_perl exposes the Apache API through a mod_perl API, which is a set of Perl functions and objects. When a Perl handler calls such a function or method, mod_perl translates it into the appropriate Apache C function.

Perl handlers extract the last drop of performance from the Apache server. Unlike mod_cgi and `Apache::Registry`, they are not restricted to the content generation phase and can be tied to any phase in the request loop. You can create your own custom authentication by writing a `PerlAuthenHandler`, or you can write specialized logging code in a `PerlLogHandler`.

Handlers are not compatible with the CGI specification. Instead, they use the mod_ perl API directly for every aspect of request processing.

mod_perl provides access to the Apache API for Perl handlers via an extensive collection of methods and variables exported by the Apache core. This includes methods for dealing with the request (such as retrieving headers or posted content), setting up the response (such as sending HTTP headers and providing access to configuration information derived from the server's configuration file), and a slew of other methods providing access to most of Apache's rich feature set.

Using the mod_perl API is not limited to mod_perl handlers. `Apache::Registry` scripts can also call API methods, at the price of forgoing CGI compatibility.

We suggest that you refer to the book *Writing Apache Modules with Perl and C*, by Lincoln Stein and Doug MacEachern (O'Reilly), if you want to learn more about API methods.

References

- The CGI specification: *http://hoohoo.ncsa.uiuc.edu/cgi/*
- The HTTP/1.1 standard: *http://www.w3.org/Protocols/rfc2616/rfc2616.html*
- Various information about CGI at the W3C site: *http://www.w3.org/CGI/*
- MIME Media Types: *http://www.ietf.org/rfc/rfc2046.txt*
- The Apache Modules Registry: *http://modules.apache.org/*
- *Writing Apache Modules with Perl and C*, by Lincoln Stein and Doug MacEachern (O'Reilly); selected chapters available online at *http://www.modperl.com/*
- *mod_perl Developer's Cookbook*, by Geoffrey Young, Paul Lindner, and Randy Kobes (Sams Publishing); selected chapters available online at *http://www.modperlcookbook.org/*.
- *CGI Programming with Perl*, by Scott Guelich, Shishir Gundavaram, Gunther Birznieks (O'Reilly)

## CHAPTER 2

Getting Started Fast

This chapter is about getting started with mod_perl, for the very impatient. If all you want is to run your existing CGI scripts in a mod_perl-enabled environment, we'll try to make this as easy for you as possible. Of course, we hope that you'll read the rest of the book too. But first, we want to show you how simple it is to harness the power of mod_perl.

On a decent machine, it should take half an hour or less to compile and configure a mod_perl-based Apache server and get it running. Although there are binary distributions of mod_perl-enabled Apache servers available for various platforms, we recommend that you always build mod_perl from source. It's simple to do (provided you have all the proper tools on your machine), and building from source circumvents possible problems with binary distributions, such as those reported for the RPM packages built for Red Hat Linux.

The mod_perl installation that follows has been tested on many mainstream Unix and Linux platforms. Unless you're using a very nonstandard system, you should have no problems when building the basic mod_perl server.

For Windows users, the simplest solution is to use the binary package available from *http://perl.apache.org/download/binaries.html*. Windows users may skip to the section entitled "Installing mod_perl for Windows."

Before we continue, however, we have one important bit of advice: while you're learning mod_perl, be sure that you experiment on a private machine and not on a production server.

Installing mod_perl 1.0 in Three Steps

You can install mod_perl in three easy steps: obtain the source files required to build mod_perl, build mod_perl, and install it.

Building mod_perl from source requires a machine with basic development tools. In particular, you will need an ANSI-compliant C compiler (such as *gcc*) and the *make* utility. All standard Unix-like distributions include these tools. If a required tool is not already installed, you can install it with the package manager that is provided with the system (*rpm*, *apt*, *yast*, etc.).

A recent version of Perl (5.004 or higher) is also required. Perl is available as an installable package, although most Unix-like distributions will have Perl installed by default. To check that the tools are available and to learn about their version numbers, try:

```
panic% make -v
panic% gcc -v
panic% perl -v
```

If any of these responds with Command not found, the utility will need to be installed.

Once all the tools are in place, the installation can begin. Experienced Unix users will need no explanation of the commands that follow and can simply type them into a terminal window.

Get the source code distrubutions of Apache and mod_perl using your favorite web browser or a command-line client such as *wget* or *lwp-download*. These two distributions are available from *http://www.apache.org/dist/httpd/* and *http://perl.apache.org/dist/*, respectively.

The two packages are named *apache_1.3.xx.tar.gz* and *mod_perl-1.xx.tar.gz*, where *1.3.xx* and *1.xx* should be replaced with the real version numbers of Apache and mod_perl, respectively. Although 2.0 development versions of Apache and mod_perl are available, this book covers the mod_perl 1.0 and Apache 1.3 generation, which were the stable versions when this book was written. See Chapters 24 and 25 for more information on the Apache 2.0 and mod_perl 2.0 generation.

Move the downloaded packages into a directory of your choice (for example, */home/stas/src/*), proceed with the following steps, and mod_perl will be installed:

```
panic% cd /home/stas/src
panic% tar -zvxf apache_1.3.xx.tar.gz
panic% tar -zvxf mod_perl-1.xx.tar.gz
panic% cd mod_perl-1.xx
panic% perl Makefile.PL APACHE_SRC=../apache_1.3.xx/src \
    APACHE_PREFIX=/home/httpd DO_HTTPD=1 USE_APACI=1 EVERYTHING=1
panic% make && make test
panic% su
panic# make install
```

All that remains is to add a few configuration lines to the Apache configuration file (*/usr/local/apache/conf/httpd.conf*), start the server, and enjoy mod_perl.

Installing mod_perl on Unix Platforms

Now let's go over the installation again, this time with each step explained in detail and with some troubleshooting advice. If the build worked and you are in a hurry to boot your new *httpd*, you may skip to the section entitled "Installing mod_perl for Windows."

Before installing Apache and mod_perl, you usually have to become *root* so that the files can be installed in a protected area. However, users without *root* access can still install all files under their home directories by building Apache in an unprivileged location; you need *root* access only to install it. We will talk about the nuances of this approach in Chapter 3.

Obtaining and Unpacking the Source Code

The first step is to obtain the source code distributions of Apache and mod_perl. These distributions can be retrieved from *http://www.apache.org/dist/httpd/* and *http://perl.apache.org/dist/* and are also available from mirror sites. Even if you have the Apache server running on your machine, you'll need its source distribution to rebuild it from scratch with mod_perl.

The source distributions of Apache and mod_perl should be downloaded into a directory of your choice. For the sake of consistency, we assume throughout the book that all builds are being done in the */home/stas/src* directory. Just remember to substitute */home/stas/src* in the examples with the actual path being used.

The next step is to move to the directory containing the source archives:

```
panic% cd /home/stas/src
```

Uncompress and un*tar* both sources. GNU *tar* allows this using a single command per file:

```
panic% tar -zvxf apache_1.3.xx.tar.gz
panic% tar -zvxf mod_perl-1.xx.tar.gz
```

For non-GNU *tar*s, you may need to do this with two steps (which you can combine via a pipe):

```
panic% gzip -dc apache_1.3.xx.tar.gz | tar -xvf -
panic% gzip -dc mod_perl-1.xx.tar.gz | tar -xvf -
```

Linux distributions supply *tar* and *gzip* and install them by default. If your machine doesn't have these utilities already installed, you can get *tar* and *gzip* from *http://www.gnu.org/*, among other sources. The GNU versions are available for every platform that Apache supports.

Building mod_perl

Move into the */home/stas/src/mod_perl-1.xx/* source distribution directory:

```
panic% cd mod_perl-1.xx
```

The next step is to create the *Makefile*. This is no different in principle from the creation of the *Makefile* for any other Perl module.

```
panic% perl Makefile.PL APACHE_SRC=../apache_1.3.xx/src \
   DO_HTTPD=1 USE_APACI=1 EVERYTHING=1
```

mod_perl accepts a variety of parameters. The options specified above will enable almost every feature that mod_perl offers. There are many other options for fine-tuning mod_perl to suit particular circumstances; these are explained in detail in Chapter 3.

Running *Makefile.PL* will cause Perl to check for prerequisites and identify any required software packages that are missing. If it reports missing Perl packages, they will have to be installed before proceeding. Perl modules are available from CPAN (*http://cpan.org/*) and can easily be downloaded and installed.

An advantage of installing mod_perl with the help of the CPAN.pm module is that all the missing modules will be installed with the Bundle::Apache bundle:

```
panic% perl -MCPAN -e 'install("Bundle::Apache")'
```

We will talk in depth about using CPAN.pm in Chapter 3.

Running *Makefile.PL* also transparently executes the *./configure* script from Apache's source distribution directory, which prepares the Apache build configuration files. If parameters must be passed to Apache's *./configure* script, they can be passed as options to *Makefile.PL*. Chapter 3 covers all this in detail.

The *httpd* executable can now be built by using the *make* utility (note that the current working directory is still */home/stas/src/mod_perl-1.xx/*):

```
panic% make
```

This command prepares the mod_perl extension files, installs them in the Apache source tree, and builds the *httpd* executable (the web server itself) by compiling all the required files. Upon completion of the *make* process, the working directory is restored to */home/stas/src/mod_perl-1.xx/*.

Running *make test* will execute various mod_perl tests on the newly built *httpd* executable:

```
panic% make test
```

This command starts the server on a nonstandard port (8529) and tests whether all parts of the built server function correctly. The process will report anything that does not work properly.

Installing mod_perl

Running *make install* completes the installation process by installing all the Perl files required for mod_perl to run. It also installs the mod_perl documentation (manpages). Typically, you need to be *root* to have permission to do this, but another user account can be used if the appropriate options are set on the *perl Makefile.PL* command line (see Chapter 3). To become *root*, use the *su* command.

```
panic% su
panic# make install
```

If you have the proper permissions, you can also chain all three *make* commands into a single command line:

```
panic# make && make test && make install
```

The single-line version simplifies the installation, since there is no need to wait for each command to complete before starting the next one. Of course, if you need to become *root* in order to run *make install*, you'll either need to run *make install* as a separate command or become *root* before running the single-line version.

If you choose the all-in-one approach and any of the *make* commands fail, execution will stop at that point. For example, if *make* alone fails, then *make test* and *make install* will not be attempted. Similarly, if *make test* fails, then *make install* will not be attempted.

Finally, change to the Apache source distribution directory and run *make install* to create the Apache directory tree and install Apache's header files (*.h*), default configuration files (*.conf*), the *httpd* executable, and a few other programs:

```
panic# cd ../apache_1.3.xx
panic# make install
```

Note that, as with a plain Apache installation, any configuration files left from a previous installation will not be overwritten by this process. Although backing up is never unwise, it's not actually necessary to back up the previously working configuration files before the installation.

At the end of the *make install* process, the installation program will list the path to the *apachectl* utility, which you can use to start and stop the server, and the path to the installed configuration files. It is important to write down these pathnames, as they will be needed frequently when maintaining and configuring Apache. On our machines, these two important paths are:

```
/usr/local/apache/bin/apachectl
/usr/local/apache/conf/httpd.conf
```

The mod_perl Apache server is now built and installed. All that needs to be done before it can be run is to edit the configuration file *httpd.conf* and write a test script.

Configuring and Starting the mod_perl Server

Once you have mod_perl installed, you need to configure the server and test it.

The first thing to do is ensure that Apache was built correctly and that it can serve plain HTML files. This helps to minimize the number of possible problem areas:

once you have confirmed that Apache can serve plain HTML files, you know that any problems with mod_perl are related to mod_perl itself.

Apache should be configured just as you would configure it without mod_perl. Use the defaults as suggested, customizing only when necessary. Values that will probably need to be customized are ServerName, Port, User, Group, ServerAdmin, DocumentRoot, and a few others. There are helpful hints preceding each directive in the configuration files themselves, with further information in Apache's documentation. Follow the advice in the files and documentation if in doubt.

When the configuration file has been edited, start the server. One of the ways to start and stop the server is to use the *apachectl* utility. To start the server with *apachectl*, type:

```
panic# /usr/local/apache/bin/apachectl start
```

To stop the server, type:

```
panic# /usr/local/apache/bin/apachectl stop
```

Note that if the server will listen on port 80 or another privileged port,* the user executing *apachectl* must be *root*.

After the server has started, check in the *error_log* file (*/usr/local/apache/logs/error_log*, by default) to see if the server has indeed started. Do not rely on the *apachectl* status reports. The *error_log* should contain something like the following:

```
[Thu Jun 22 17:14:07 2000] [notice] Apache/1.3.12 (Unix)
mod_perl/1.24 configured -- resuming normal operations
```

Now point your browser to *http://localhost/* or *http://example.com/*, as configured with the ServerName directive. If the Port directive has been set with a value other than 80, add this port number to the end of the server name. For example, if the port is 8080, test the server with *http://localhost:8080/* or *http://example.com:8080/*. The "It Worked!" page, which is an *index.html* file that is installed automatically when running *make install* in the Apache source tree, should appear in the browser. If this page does not appear, something went wrong and the contents of the *logs/error_log* file should be checked. The path to the error log file is specified by the ErrorLog directive in *httpd.conf*. (It is usually specified relative to the ServerRoot, so a value of *logs/error_log* usually means */usr/local/apache/logs/error_log* if Apache is installed into */usr/local/apache*.)

If everything works as expected, shut down the server, open *httpd.conf* with a text editor, and scroll to the end of the file. The mod_perl configuration directives are conventionally added to the end of *httpd.conf*. It is possible to place mod_perl's configuration directives anywhere in *httpd.conf*, but adding them at the end seems to work best in practice.

---

* Privileged ports are 0–1023. Only the programs running as *root* are allowed to bind to these.

Assuming that all the scripts that should be executed by the mod_perl-enabled server are located in the */home/stas/modperl* directory, add the following configuration directives:

```
Alias /perl/ /home/stas/modperl/

PerlModule Apache::Registry
<Location /perl/>
    SetHandler perl-script
    PerlHandler Apache::Registry
    Options +ExecCGI
    PerlSendHeader On
    Allow from all
</Location>
```

Save the modified file.

This configuration causes every URI starting with */perl* to be handled by the Apache mod_perl module with the handler from the Perl module `Apache::Registry`.

Installing mod_perl for Windows

Apache runs on many flavors of Unix and Unix-like operating systems. Version 1.3 introduced a port to the Windows family of operating systems, often named Win32 after the name of the common API. Because of the many differences between Unix and Windows, the Win32 port of Apache is still branded as beta quality—it hasn't yet reached the stability and performance levels of the native Unix counterpart.

Another hindrance to using mod_perl on Windows is that current versions of Perl are not thread-safe on Win32. As a consequence, mod_perl calls to the embedded Perl interpreter must be serialized (i.e., executed one at a time). For these reasons, we recommend that mod_perl on Windows be used only for testing purposes, not in production.

Building mod_perl from source on Windows is a bit of a challenge. Development tools such as a C compiler are not bundled with the operating system, and most users expect a point-and-click installation, as with most Windows software. Additionally, all software packages need to be built with the same compiler and compile options. This means building Perl, Apache, and mod_perl from source, which is quite a daunting task.

Fortunately, Randy Kobes maintains a Windows distribution of mod_perl that includes all the necessary tools, including Perl, Apache, and a host of useful CPAN modules. Using this distribution provides an out-of-the-box Apache + mod_perl combo in minutes.

The distribution comes with extensive documentation. Take the time to read it, particularly if you want to install the software in a location different from the default. In the following installation, we'll use the default locations and options.

Here are the steps for installing mod_perl:

1. Download the Windows distribution. Download *perl-win32-bin-x.x.exe* from *http://perl.apache.org/download/binaries.html*. This self-extracting archive yields four directories: *Apache/*, *Perl/*, *openssl/*, and *readmes/*.

2. Install the software. Move the *Apache/* and *Perl/* directories to *C:*. Edit *C:\ AUTOEXEC.BAT* to install the Perl executable directories in your system's search path:

   ```
   SET PATH=C:\Perl\5.6.1\bin;C:\Perl\5.6.1\bin\MSWin32-x86;"%PATH%"
   ```

   Then restart Windows for this change to take effect.

3. Test the Perl installation. Open a DOS prompt window to verify that Perl is installed correctly and learn the version number:

   ```
   C:\> perl -v

   This is perl, v5.6.1 built for MSWin32-x86

   Copyright 1987-2000, Larry Wall
   ```

4. Start Apache. The distribution comes with a ready-made configuration file for mod_perl, which we'll use to start Apache. From the *C:\Apache* directory, start Apache:

   ```
   C:\Apache> apache.exe -f conf\httpd.conf
   ```

   Now, issuing a request for *http://localhost/* displays the usual Apache "It Worked!" page.

5. Test mod_perl. The distribution comes with a preconfigured mod_perl handler and Apache::Registry directory. We can test our mod_perl-enabled server by issuing the following requests:

   ```
   http://localhost/hello
   http://localhost/mod_perl/printenv
   ```

We now have a fully functional mod_perl server. The example scripts described in the rest of this chapter can be used with minor modifications to file paths and URIs. In particular, change all instances of */home/stas* to *C:\Apache*, and change all instances of *http://localhost/perl* to *http://localhost/mod_perl*.

Installing mod_perl with the Perl Package Manager

If you are already a Perl developer on Windows, it is likely that you have ActivePerl (see *http://www.activestate.com/*) installed. In that case, you can get a mod_perl distribution that takes advantage of your existing Perl installation.

First of all, you will need to get the latest Apache distribution. Go to *http://www. apache.org/dist/httpd/binaries/win32/* and get the latest version of *apache_1.3.xx-win32-no_src.msi*, which is a graphical installer. Read the notes on that page about the MSI Binary distribution carefully if you are using Windows NT 4.0 or Windows 9x, as there may be some prerequisites.

There is a lot of documentation at *http://httpd.apache.org/* about installing Apache on Windows, so we won't repeat it here. But for the purposes of this example, let's suppose that your Apache directory is *C:\Apache*, which means you chose *C:* as the installation directory during the installation of Apache, and it created a subdirectory named *Apache* there.

Once Apache is installed, we can install mod_perl. mod_perl is distributed as a *PPM* file, which is the format used by the ActivePerl *ppm* command-line utility. mod_perl isn't available from ActiveState, but it has been made available from a separate archive, maintained by Randy Kobes.* To install mod_perl, do the following from a DOS prompt:

```
C:\> ppm
PPM> install mod_perl
PPM> quit
C:\>
```

When *install mod_perl* completes, a post-installation script will run, asking you where to install *mod_perl.so*, the mod_perl dynamic link library (DLL) that's used by Apache. Look over the suggested path and correct it if necessary, or press Enter if it's correct; it should be the *C:\Apache\modules* directory if you used *C:\Apache* as an installation directory.

Please note that the version of mod_perl provided in that archive is always the latest version of mod_perl compiled against the latest version of Apache, so you will need to make sure you have the latest Apache (of the *1.3.x* series) installed before proceeding. Furthermore, you will need an ActivePerl installation from the 6xx series, based on Perl 5.6.x, or mod_perl won't work.

The next step is to enable mod_perl in your *httpd.conf* file. If you installed Apache in *C:\Apache*, this will be *C:\Apache\conf\httpd.conf*.

Add this line together with any other LoadModule directives:

```
LoadModule perl_module modules/mod_perl.so
```

Furthermore, if you have a ClearModuleList directive in the same file, add the following line with the other AddModule directives:

```
AddModule mod_perl.c
```

For more information, see the Apache documentation for these two directives, and see Chapter 3 for more information on using mod_perl as a dynamic shared object (DSO).

With this installation, you can start Apache as described in its documentation, and try out the examples in this book. However, the mod_perl test scripts cited above

---

* See the Preface for more information about PPM installation.

aren't provided, and you will have to configure mod_perl yourself. See Chapter 4 for more information about configuring mod_perl. For example:

```
Alias /perl/ C:/Apache/perl/

PerlModule Apache::Registry
<Location /perl/>
    SetHandler perl-script
    PerlHandler Apache::Registry
    Options +ExecCGI
    PerlSendHeader On
    Allow from all
</Location>
```

This will allow you to run Apache::Registry scripts placed in the directory *C:\ Apache\perl*. As you may have noticed, we use forward slashes instead of the back-slashes that are used on Windows (i.e., *C:/Apache/perl/* instead of *C:\Apache\perl*), to be compatible with Unix notation.

Preparing the Scripts Directory

Now you have to select a directory where all the mod_perl scripts and modules will be placed. We usually create a directory called *modperl* under our home directory for this purpose (e.g., */home/stas/modperl*), but it is also common to create a directory called *perl* under your Apache server root, such as */usr/local/apache/perl*.

First create this directory if it doesn't yet exist:

```
panic% mkdir /home/stas/modperl
```

Next, set the file permissions. Remember that when scripts are executed from a shell, they are being executed with the permissions of the user's account. Usually, you want to have read, write, and execute access for yourself, but only read and execute permissions for the server. When the scripts are run by Apache, however, the server needs to be able to read and execute them. Apache runs under an account specified by the User directive, typically *nobody*. You can modify the User directive to run the server under your username, for example:

```
User stas
```

Since the permissions on all files and directories should usually be rwx------,* set the directory permissions to:

```
panic% chmod 0700 /home/stas/modperl
```

Now no one but you and the server can access the files in this directory. You should set the same permissions for all the files you place under this directory. †

---

* See the chmod manpage for more information regarding octal modes.

† You don't need to set the x bit for files that aren't going to be executed; mode 0600 is sufficient for those files.

If the server is running under the *nobody* account, you have to set the permissions to `rwxr-xr-x` or 0755 for your files and directories. This is insecure, because other users on the same machine can read your files.

```
panic# chmod 0755  /home/stas/modperl
```

If you aren't running the server with your username, you have to set these permissions for all the files created under this directory so Apache can read and execute them.

In the following examples, we assume that you run the server under your username, and hence we set the scripts' permissions to 0700.

A Sample Apache::Registry Script

One of mod_perl's benefits is that it can run existing CGI scripts written in Perl that were previously used under mod_cgi (the standard Apache CGI handler). Indeed, mod_perl can be used for running CGI scripts without taking advantage of any of mod_perl's special features, while getting the benefit of the potentially huge performance boost. Example 2-1 gives an example of a very simple CGI-style mod_perl script.

Example 2-1. mod_perl_rules1.pl

```
print "Content-type: text/plain\n\n";
print "mod_perl rules!\n";
```

Save this script in the *home/stas/modperl/mod_perl_rules1.pl* file. Notice that the #! line (colloquially known as the *shebang* line) is not needed with mod_perl, although having one causes no problems, as can be seen in Example 2-2.

Example 2-2. mod_perl_rules1.pl with shebang line

```
#!/usr/bin/perl
print "Content-type: text/plain\n\n";
print "mod_perl rules!\n";
```

Now make the script executable and readable by the server, as explained in the previous section:

```
panic% chmod 0700 /home/stas/modperl/mod_perl_rules1.pl
```

The *mod_perl_rules1.pl* script can be tested from the command line, since it is essentially a regular Perl script:

```
panic% perl /home/stas/modperl/mod_perl_rules1.pl
```

This should produce the following output:

```
Content-type: text/plain

mod_perl rules!
```

Make sure the server is running and issue these requests using a browser:

```
http://localhost/perl/mod_perl_rules1.pl
```

If the port being used is not 80 (e.g., 8080), the port number should be included in the URL:

```
http://localhost:8080/perl/mod_perl_rules1.pl
```

Also, the localhost approach will work only if the browser is running on the same machine as the server. If not, use the real server name for this test. For example:

```
http://example.com/perl/mod_perl_rules1.pl
```

The page rendered should be similar to the one in Figure 2-1.

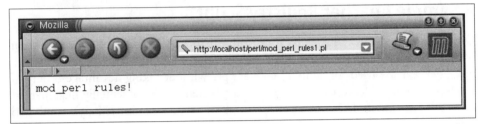

Figure 2-1. Testing the newly configured server

If you see it, congratulations! You have a working mod_perl server.

If something went wrong, go through the installation process again, making sure that none of the steps are missed and that each is completed successfully. You might also look at the *error_log* file for error messages. If this does not solve the problem, Chapter 3 will attempt to salvage the situation.

Jumping a little bit ahead, Example 2-3 shows the same CGI script written with the mod_perl API.

Example 2-3. mod_perl_rules2.pl

```
my $r = Apache->request;
$r->send_http_header('text/plain');
$r->print("mod_perl rules!\n");
```

The mod_perl API needs a request object, $r, to communicate with Apache. The script retrieves this object and uses it to send the HTTP header and print the irrefutable fact about mod_perl's coolness.

This script generates the same output as the previous one.

As you can see, it's not much harder to write your code using the mod_perl API. You need to learn the API, but the concepts are the same. As we will show in the following chapters, usually you will want to use the mod_perl API for better performance or when you need functionality that CGI doesn't provide.

Porting Existing CGI Scripts to mod_perl

Now it's time to move any existing CGI scripts from the */somewhere/cgi-bin* directory to */home/stas/modperl*. Once moved, they should run much faster when requested from the newly configured base URL (*/perl/*). For example, a CGI script called *test.pl* that was previously accessed as */cgi-bin/test.pl* can now be accessed as */perl/test.pl* under mod_perl and the `Apache::Registry` module.

Some of the scripts might not work immediately and may require some minor tweaking or even a partial rewrite to work properly with mod_perl. We will talk in depth about these issues in Chapter 6. Most scripts that have been written with care and developed with warnings enabled and the `strict` pragma* will probably work without any modifications at all.

A quick solution that avoids most rewriting or editing of existing scripts that do not run properly under `Apache::Registry` is to run them under `Apache::PerlRun`. This can be achieved by simply replacing `Apache::Registry` with `Apache::PerlRun` in *httpd.conf*. Put the following configuration directives instead in *httpd.conf* and restart the server:

```
Alias /perl/ /home/stas/modperl/
PerlModule Apache::PerlRun
<Location /perl/>
    SetHandler perl-script
    PerlHandler Apache::PerlRun
    Options ExecCGI
    PerlSendHeader On
    Allow from all
</Location>
```

Almost every script should now run without problems; the few exceptions will almost certainly be due to the few minor limitations that mod_perl or its handlers have, but these are all solvable and covered in Chapter 6.

As we saw in Chapter 1, `Apache::PerlRun` is usually useful while transitioning scripts to run properly under `Apache::Registry`. However, we don't recommend using `Apache::PerlRun` in the long term; although it is significantly faster than mod_cgi, it's still not as fast as `Apache::Registry` and mod_perl handlers.

A Simple mod_perl Content Handler

As we mentioned in the beginning of this chapter, mod_perl lets you run both scripts and handlers. The previous example showed a script, which is probably the most familiar approach to web programming, but the more advanced use of mod_perl

---

* Warnings and `strict` abort your script if you have written sloppy code, so that you won't be surprised by unknown, hidden bugs. Using them is generally considered a good thing in Perl and is *very* important in mod_perl.

involves writing handlers. Have no fear; writing handlers is almost as easy as writing scripts and offers a level of access to Apache's internals that is simply not possible with conventional CGI scripts.

To create a mod_perl handler module, all that is necessary is to wrap the code that would have been the body of a script into a `handler` subroutine, add a statement to return the status to the server when the subroutine has successfully completed, and add a package declaration at the top of the code.

Just as with scripts, the familiar CGI API may be used. Example 2-4 shows an example.

Example 2-4. ModPerl/Rules1.pm

```
package ModPerl::Rules1;
use Apache::Constants qw(:common);

sub handler {
    print "Content-type: text/plain\n\n";
    print "mod_perl rules!\n";
    return OK; # We must return a status to mod_perl
}
1; # This is a perl module so we must return true to perl
```

Alternatively, the mod_perl API can be used. This API provides almost complete access to the Apache core. In the simple example used here, either approach is fine, but when lower-level access to Apache is required, the mod_perl API shown in Example 2-5 must be used.

Example 2-5. ModPerl/Rules2.pm

```
package ModPerl::Rules2;
use Apache::Constants qw(:common);

sub handler {
    my $r = shift;
    $r->send_http_header('text/plain');
    $r->print("mod_perl rules!\n");
    return OK; # We must return a status to mod_perl
}
1; # This is a perl module so we must return true to perl
```

Create a directory called *ModPerl* under one of the directories in @INC (e.g., under */usr/lib/perl5/site_perl/5.6.1*), and put *Rules1.pm* and *Rules2.pm* into it. (Note that you will need *root* access in order to do this.) The files should include the code from the above examples. To find out what the @INC directories are, execute:

```
panic% perl -le 'print join "\n", @INC'
```

On our machine it reports:

```
/usr/lib/perl5/5.6.1/i386-linux
/usr/lib/perl5/5.6.1
```

```
/usr/lib/perl5/site_perl/5.6.1/i386-linux
/usr/lib/perl5/site_perl/5.6.1
/usr/lib/perl5/site_perl
.
```

Therefore, on our machine, we might place the files in the directory */usr/lib/perl5/ site_perl/5.6.1/ModPerl*. By default, when you work as *root*, the files are created with permissions allowing everybody to read them, so here we don't have to adjust the file permissions (the server only needs to be able to read those).

Now add the following snippet to */usr/local/apache/conf/httpd.conf*, to configure mod_perl to execute the `ModPerl::Rules1::handler` subroutine whenever a request to *mod_perl_rules1* is made:

```
PerlModule ModPerl::Rules1
<Location /mod_perl_rules1>
    SetHandler perl-script
    PerlHandler ModPerl::Rules1
    PerlSendHeader On
</Location>
```

Now issue a request to:

```
http://localhost/mod_perl_rules1
```

and, just as with the *mod_perl_rules.pl* scripts, the following should be rendered as a response:

```
mod_perl rules!
```

Don't forget to include the port number if not using port 80 (e.g., *http://localhost: 8080/mod_perl_rules1*); from now on, we will assume you know this.

To test the second module, `ModPerl::Rules2`, add a similar configuration, while replacing all 1s with 2s:

```
PerlModule ModPerl::Rules2
<Location /mod_perl_rules2>
    SetHandler perl-script
    PerlHandler ModPerl::Rules2
</Location>
```

In Chapter 4 we will explain why the `PerlSendHeader` directive is not needed for this particular module.

To test, use the URI:

```
http://localhost/mod_perl_rules2
```

You should see the same response from the server that we saw when issuing a request for the former mod_perl handler.

Is This All We Need to Know About mod_perl?

So do you need to know more about mod_perl? The answer is, "Yes and no."

Just as with Perl, effective scripts can be written even with very little mod_perl knowledge. With the basic unoptimized setup presented in this chapter, visitor counters and guestbooks and any other CGI scripts you use will run much faster and amaze your friends and colleagues, usually without your changing a single line of code.

However, although a 50 times improvement in guestbook response times is great, a very heavy service with thousands of concurrent users will suffer under a delay of even a few milliseconds. You might lose a customer, or even many of them.

When testing a single script with the developer as the only user, squeezing yet another millisecond from the response time seems unimportant. But it becomes a real issue when these milliseconds add up at the production site, with hundreds or thousands of users concurrently generating requests to various scripts on the site. Users are not merciful nowadays. If there is another site that provides the same kind of service significantly faster, chances are that users will switch to the competing site.

Testing scripts on an unloaded machine can be very misleading—everything might seem so perfect. But when they are moved into a production environment, chances are that the scripts will not behave as well as they did on the development box. For example, the production machine may run out of memory on very busy services. In Chapter 10, we will explain how to optimize code to use less memory and how to make as much memory as possible shared.

Debugging is something that some developers prefer not to think about, because the process can be very tedious. Learning how to make the debugging process simpler and more efficient is essential for web programmers. This task can be difficult enough when debugging CGI scripts, but it can be even more complicated with mod_perl. Chapter 21 explains how to approach debugging in the mod_perl environment.

mod_perl has many features unavailable under mod_cgi for working with databases. Some of the most important are persistent database connections. Persistent database connections require a slightly different approach, explained in Chapter 20.

Most web services, especially those aimed at an international audience, must run nonstop, 24×7. But at the same time, new scripts may need to be added and old ones removed, and the server software will need upgrades and security fixes. And if the server goes down, fast recovery is essential. These issues are considered in Chapter 5.

Finally, the most important aspect of mod_perl is the mod_perl API, which allows intervention at any or every stage of request processing. This provides incredible flexibility, allowing the creation of scripts and processes that would simply be impossible with mod_cgi.

There are many more things to learn about mod_perl and web programming in general. The rest of this book will attempt to provide as much information as possible about these and other related matters.

References

- The Apache home page: *http://www.apache.org/.*
- The mod_perl home page: *http://perl.apache.org/.*
- The CPAN home page: *http://cpan.org/*

  CPAN is the Comprehensive Perl Archive Network. Its aim is to contain all the Perl material you will need. The archive is close to a gigabyte in size at the time of this writing, and CPAN is mirrored at more than 100 sites around the world.

- The libwww-perl home page: *http://www.linpro.no/lwp/.*

  The libwww-perl distribution is a collection of Perl modules and programs that provide a simple and consistent programming interface (API) to the World Wide Web. The main focus of the library is to provide classes and functions that facilitate writing WWW clients; thus, libwww-perl is said to be a WWW client library. The library also contains modules that are of more general use, as well as some useful programs.

## CHAPTER 3

Installing mod_perl

In Chapter 2, we presented a basic mod_perl installation. In this chapter, we will talk about various ways in which mod_perl can be installed (using a variety of installation parameters), as well as prepackaged binary installations, and more.

Chapter 2 showed you the following commands to build and install a basic mod_perl-enabled Apache server on almost any standard flavor of Unix.

First, download *http://www.apache.org/dist/httpd/apache_1.3.xx.tar.gz* and *http://perl.apache.org/dist/mod_perl-1.xx.tar.gz*. Then, issue the following commands:

```
panic% cd /home/stas/src
panic% tar xzvf apache_1.3.xx.tar.gz
panic% tar xzvf mod_perl-1.xx.tar.gz
panic% cd mod_perl-1.xx
panic% perl Makefile.PL APACHE_SRC=../apache_1.3.xx/src \
  DO_HTTPD=1 USE_APACI=1 EVERYTHING=1
panic% make && make test
panic# make install
panic# cd ../apache_1.3.xx
panic# make install
```

As usual, replace *1.xx* and *1.3.xx* with the real version numbers of mod_perl and Apache, respectively.

You can then add a few configuration lines to *httpd.conf* (the Apache configuration file), start the server, and enjoy mod_perl. This should work just fine. Why, then, are you now reading a 50-page chapter on installing mod_perl?

You're reading this chapter for the same reason you bought this book. Sure, the instructions above will get you a working version of mod_perl. But the average reader of this book won't want to stop there. If you're using mod_perl, it's because you want to improve the performance of your web server. And when you're concerned with performance, you're always looking for ways to eke a little bit more out of your server. In essence, that's what this book is about: getting the most out of your mod_perl-enabled Apache server. And it all starts at the beginning, with the installation of the software.

In the basic mod_perl installation, the parameter EVERYTHING=1 enables a lot of options for you, whether you actually need them or not. You may want to enable only the required options, to squeeze even more juice out of mod_perl. You may want to build mod_perl as a loadable object instead of compiling it into Apache, so that it can be upgraded without rebuilding Apache itself. You may also want to install other Apache components, such as PHP or mod_ssl, alongside mod_perl.

To accomplish any of these tasks, you will need to understand various techniques for mod_perl configuration and building. You need to know what configuration parameters are available to you and when and how to use them.

As with Perl, in mod_perl simple things are simple. But when you need to accomplish more complicated tasks, you may have to invest some time to gain a deeper understanding of the process. In this chapter, we will take the following route. We'll start with a detailed explanation of the four stages of the mod_perl installation process, then continue on with the different paths each installation might take according to your goal, followed by a few copy-and-paste real-world installation scenarios. Toward the end of the chapter we will show you various approaches that might make the installation easier, by automating most of the steps. Finally, we'll cover some of the general issues that new users might stumble on while installing mod_perl.

Configuring the Source

Before building and installing mod_perl you will have to configure it, as you would configure any other Perl module:

```
panic% perl Makefile.PL [parameters].
```

Perl Installation Requirements

Make sure you have Perl installed! Use the latest stable version, if possible. To determine your version of Perl, run the following command on the command line:

```
panic% perl -v
```

You will need at least Perl Version 5.004. If you don't have it, install it. Follow the instructions in the distribution's *INSTALL* file. The only thing to watch for is that during the configuration stage (while running *./Configure*) you make sure you can dynamically load Perl module extensions. That is, answer YES to the following question:

```
Do you wish to use dynamic loading? [y]
```

In this section, we will explain each of the parameters accepted by the *Makefile.PL* file for mod_perl First, however, lets talk about how the mod_perl configuration dovetails with Apache's configuration. The source configuration mechanism in Apache 1.3 provides four major features (which of course are available to mod_perl):

- Apache modules can use per-module configuration scripts to link themselves into the Apache configuration process. This feature lets you automatically adjust the configuration and build parameters from the Apache module sources. It is triggered by *ConfigStart/ConfigEnd* sections inside *modulename.module* files (e.g., see the file *libperl.module* in the mod_perl distribution).

- The *APache AutoConf-style Interface* (APACI) is the top-level *configure* script from Apache 1.3; it provides a GNU Autoconf-style interface to the Apache configuration process. APACI is useful for configuring the source tree without manually editing any *src/Configuration* files. Any parameterization can be done via command-line options to the *configure* script. Internally, this is just a nifty wrapper over the old *src/Configure* script.

  Since Apache 1.3, APACI is the best way to install mod_perl as cleanly as possible. However, the complete Apache 1.3 source configuration mechanism is available only under Unix at this writing—it doesn't work on Win32.

- *Dynamic shared object* (DSO) support is one of the most interesting features in Apache 1.3. It allows Apache modules to be built as so-called DSOs (usually named *modulename.so*), which can be loaded via the LoadModule directive in Apache's *httpd.conf* file. The benefit is that the modules become part of the *httpd* executable only on demand; they aren't loaded into the address space of the *httpd* executable until the user asks for them to be. The benefits of DSO support are most evident in relation to memory consumption and added flexibility (in that you won't have to recompile your *httpd* each time you want to add, remove, or upgrade a module).

  The DSO mechanism is provided by Apache's mod_so module, which needs to be compiled into the *httpd* binary with:

  ```
  panic% ./configure --enable-module=so
  ```

  The usage of any *--enable-shared* option automatically implies an *--enable-module=so* option, because the bootstrapping module mod_so is always needed for DSO support. So if, for example, you want the module mod_dir to be built as a DSO, you can write:

  ```
  panic% ./configure --enable-shared=dir
  ```

  and the DSO support will be added automatically.

- The *APache eXtension Support* tool (APXS) is a tool from Apache 1.3 that can be used to build an Apache module as a DSO even outside the Apache source tree. APXS is to Apache what MakeMaker and XS are to Perl.* It knows the platform-dependent build parameters for making DSO files and provides an easy way to run the build commands with them.

---

* MakeMaker allows easy, automatic configuration, building, testing, and installation of Perl modules, while XS allows you to call functions implemented in C/C++ from Perl code.

Pros and Cons of Building mod_perl as a DSO

As of Apache 1.3, the configuration system supports two optional features for taking advantage of the modular DSO approach: compilation of the Apache core program into a DSO library for shared usage, and compilation of the Apache modules into DSO files for explicit loading at runtime.

Should you build mod_perl as a DSO? Let's study the pros and cons of this installation method, so you can decide for yourself.

Pros:

- The server package is more flexible because the actual server executable can be assembled at runtime via `LoadModule` configuration commands in *httpd.conf* instead of via `AddModule` commands in the *Configuration* file at build time. This allows you to run different server instances (e.g., standard and SSL servers, or servers with and without mod_perl) with only one Apache installation; the only thing you need is different configuration files (or, by judicious use of `IfDefine`, different startup scripts).

- The server package can easily be extended with third-party modules even after installation. This is especially helpful for vendor package maintainers who can create an Apache core package and additional packages containing extensions such as PHP, mod_perl, mod_fastcgi, etc.

- DSO support allows easier Apache module prototyping, because with the DSO/APXS pair you can work outside the Apache source tree and need only an *apxs -i* command followed by an *apachectl restart* to bring a new version of your currently developed module into the running Apache server.

Cons:

- The DSO mechanism cannot be used on every platform, because not all operating systems support shared libraries.

- The server starts up approximately 20% slower because of the overhead of the symbol-resolving the Unix loader now has to do.

- The server runs approximately 5% slower on some platforms, because position-independent code (PIC) sometimes needs complicated assembler tricks for relative addressing, which are not necessarily as fast as those for absolute addressing.

—continued—

- Because DSO modules cannot be linked against other DSO-based libraries (*ld -lfoo*) on all platforms (for instance, *a.out*-based platforms usually don't provide this functionality, while ELF-based platforms do), you cannot use the DSO mechanism for all types of modules. In other words, modules compiled as DSO files are restricted to use symbols only from the Apache core, from the C library (*libc*) and from any other dynamic or static libraries used by the Apache core, or from static library archives (*libfoo.a*) containing position-independent code. The only way you can use other code is to either make sure the Apache core itself already contains a reference to it, load the code yourself via dlopen( ), or enable the SHARED_CHAIN rule while building Apache (if your platform supports linking DSO files against DSO libraries). This, however, won't be of much significance to you if you're writing modules only in Perl.

- Under some platforms (e.g., many SVR4 systems), there is no way to force the linker to export all global symbols for use in DSOs when linking the Apache *httpd* executable program. But without the visibility of the Apache core symbols, no standard Apache module could be used as a DSO. The only workaround here is to use the SHARED_CORE feature, because in this way the global symbols are forced to be exported. As a consequence, the Apache *src/Configure* script automatically enforces SHARED_CORE on these platforms when DSO features are used in the *Configuration* file or on the *configure* command line.

Together, these four features provide a way to integrate mod_perl into Apache in a very clean and smooth way. No patching of the Apache source tree is usually required, and for APXS support, not even the Apache source tree is needed.

To benefit from the above features, a hybrid build environment was created for the Apache side of mod_perl. See the section entitled "Installation Scenarios for Standalone mod_perl," later in this chapter, for details.

Once the overview of the four building steps is complete, we will return to each of the above configuration mechanisms when describing different installation passes.

Controlling the Build Process

The configuration stage of the build is performed by the command *perl Makefile.PL*, which accepts various parameters. This section covers all of the configuration parameters, grouped by their functionality.

Of course, you should keep in mind that these options are cumulative. We display only one or two options being used at once, but you should use the ones you want to enable all at once, in one call to *perl Makefile.PL*.

APACHE_SRC, DO_HTTPD, NO_HTTPD, PREP_HTTPD

These four parameters are tightly interconnected, as they control the way in which the Apache source is handled.

Typically, when you want mod_perl to be compiled statically with Apache without adding any extra components, you specify the location of the Apache source tree using the APACHE_SRC parameter and use the DO_HTTPD=1 parameter to tell the installation script to build the *httpd* executable:

```
panic% perl Makefile.PL APACHE_SRC=../apache_1.3.xx/src DO_HTTPD=1
```

If no APACHE_SRC is specified, *Makefile.PL* makes an intelligent guess by looking at the directories at the same level as the mod_perl sources and suggesting a directory with the highest version of Apache found there.

By default, the configuration process will ask you to confirm whether the location of the source tree is correct before continuing. If you use DO_HTTPD=1 or NO_HTTPD=1, the first Apache source tree found or the one you specified will be used for the rest of the build process.

If you don't use DO_HTTPD=1, you will be prompted by the following question:

```
Shall I build httpd in ../apache_1.3.xx/src for you?
```

Note that if you set DO_HTTPD=1 but do not use APACHE_SRC=../apache_1.3.xx/src, the first Apache source tree found will be used to configure and build against. Therefore, you should always use an explicit APACHE_SRC parameter, to avoid confusion.

If you don't want to build the *httpd* in the Apache source tree because you might need to add extra third-party modules, you should use NO_HTTPD=1 instead of DO_HTTPD=1. This option will install all the files that are needed to build mod_perl in the Apache source tree, but it will not build *httpd* itself.

PREP_HTTPD=1 is similar to NO_HTTPD=1, but if you set this parameter you will be asked to confirm the location of the Apache source directory even if you have specified the APACHE_SRC parameter.

If you choose not to build the binary, you will have to do that manually. Building an *httpd* binary is covered in an upcoming section. In any case, you will need to run *make install* in the mod_perl source tree so the Perl side of mod_perl will be installed. Note that mod_perl's *make test* won't work until you have built the server.

APACHE_HEADER_INSTALL

When Apache and mod_perl are installed, you may need to build other Perl modules that use Apache C functions, such as HTML::Embperl or Apache::Peek. These modules usually will fail to build if Apache header files aren't installed in the Perl tree. By default, the Apache source header files are installed into the *$Config{sitearchexp}/auto/Apache/include* directory.[*] If you don't want or need

---

[*] *%Config* is defined in the *Config.pm* file in your Perl installation.

these headers to be installed, you can change this behavior by using the `APACHE_HEADER_INSTALL=0` parameter.

`USE_APACI`

The `USE_APACI` parameter tells mod_perl to configure Apache using the flexible APACI. The alternative is the older system, which required a file named *src/Configuration* to be edited manually. To enable APACI, use:

```
panic% perl Makefile.PL USE_APACI=1
```

`APACI_ARGS`

When you use the `USE_APACI=1` parameter, you can tell *Makefile.PL* to pass any arguments you want to the Apache *./configure* utility. For example:

```
panic% perl Makefile.PL USE_APACI=1 \
    APACI_ARGS='--sbindir=/home/httpd/httpd_perl/sbin, \
        --sysconfdir=/home/httpd/httpd_perl/etc'
```

Note that the `APACI_ARGS` argument must be passed as a single long line if you work with a C-style shell (such as *csh* or *tcsh*), as those shells seem to corrupt multi-lined values enclosed inside single quotes.

Of course, if you want the default Apache directory layout but a different root directory (*/home/httpd/httpd_perl/*, in our case), the following is the simplest way to do so:

```
panic% perl Makefile.PL USE_APACI=1 \
    APACI_ARGS='--prefix=/home/httpd/httpd_perl'
```

`ADD_MODULE`

This parameter enables building of built-in Apache modules. For example, to enable the mod_rewrite and mod_proxy modules, you can do the following:

```
panic% perl Makefile.PL ADD_MODULE=proxy,rewrite
```

If you are already using `APACI_ARGS`, you can add the usual Apache *./configure* directives as follows:

```
panic% perl Makefile.PL USE_APACI=1 \
    APACI_ARGS='--enable-module=proxy --enable-module=rewrite'
```

`APACHE_PREFIX`

As an alternative to:

```
APACI_ARGS='--prefix=/home/httpd/httpd_perl'
```

you can use the `APACHE_PREFIX` parameter. When `USE_APACI` is enabled, this attribute specifies the same *--prefix* option.

Additionally, the `APACHE_PREFIX` option automatically executes *make install* in the Apache source directory, which makes the following commands:

```
panic% perl Makefile.PL APACHE_SRC=../apache_1.3.xx/src \
    DO_HTTPD=1 USE_APACI=1 EVERYTHING=1 \
    APACI_ARGS='--prefix=/home/httpd/httpd_perl'
panic% make && make test
panic# make install
panic# cd ../apache_1.3.xx
panic# make install
```

equivalent to these commands:

```
panic% perl Makefile.PL APACHE_SRC=../apache_1.3.xx/src \
    DO_HTTPD=1 USE_APACI=1 EVERYTHING=1 \
    APACHE_PREFIX=/home/httpd/httpd_perl
panic% make && make test
panic# make install
```

PERL_STATIC_EXTS

Normally, if a C code extension is statically linked with Perl, it is listed in *Config.pm*'s *$Config{static_exts}*, in which case mod_perl will also statically link this extension with *httpd*. However, if an extension is statically linked with Perl after it is installed, it will not be listed in *Config.pm*. You can either edit *Config.pm* and add these extensions, or configure mod_perl like this:

```
panic% perl Makefile.PL "PERL_STATIC_EXTS=DBI DBD::Oracle"
```

DYNAMIC

This option tells mod_perl to build the Apache::* API extensions as shared libraries. The default is to link these modules statically with the *httpd* executable. This can save some memory if you use these API features only occasionally. To enable this option, use:

```
panic% perl Makefile.PL DYNAMIC=1
```

USE_APXS

If this option is enabled, mod_perl will be built using the APXS tool. This tool is used to build C API modules in a way that is independent of the Apache source tree. mod_perl will look for the *apxs* executable in the location specified by WITH_APXS; otherwise, it will check the *bin* and *sbin* directories relative to APACHE_PREFIX. To enable this option, use:

```
panic% perl Makefile.PL USE_APXS=1
```

WITH_APXS

This attribute tells mod_perl the location of the *apxs* executable. This is necessary if the binary cannot be found in the command path or in the location specified by APACHE_PREFIX. For example:

```
panic% perl Makefile.PL USE_APXS=1 WITH_APXS=/home/httpd/bin/apxs
```

USE_DSO

This option tells mod_perl to build itself as a DSO. Although this reduces the apparent size of the *httpd* executable on disk, it doesn't actually reduce the memory consumed by each *httpd* process. This is recommended only if you are going to be using the mod_perl API only occasionally, or if you wish to experiment with its features before you start using it in a production environment. To enable this option, use:

```
panic% perl Makefile.PL USE_DSO=1
```

SSL_BASE

When building against a mod_ssl-enabled server, this option will tell Apache where to look for the SSL *include* and *lib* subdirectories. For example:

```
panic% perl Makefile.PL SSL_BASE=/usr/share/ssl
```

PERL_DESTRUCT_LEVEL={1,2}

> When the Perl interpreter shuts down, this level enables additional checks during server shutdown to make sure the interpreter has done proper bookkeeping. The default is 0. A value of 1 enables full destruction, and 2 enables full destruction with checks. This value can also be changed at runtime by setting the environment variable PERL_DESTRUCT_LEVEL. We will revisit this parameter in Chapter 5.

PERL_TRACE

> To enable mod_perl debug tracing, configure mod_perl with the PERL_TRACE option:

```
panic% perl Makefile.PL PERL_TRACE=1
```

> To see the diagnostics, you will also need to set the MOD_PERL_TRACE environment variable at runtime.

> We will use mod_perl configured with this parameter enabled to show a few debugging techniques in Chapter 21.

PERL_DEBUG

> This option builds mod_perl and the Apache server with C source code debugging enabled (the -g switch). It also enables PERL_TRACE, sets PERL_DESTRUCT_LEVEL to 2, and links against the debuggable *libperld* Perl interpreter if one has been installed. You will be able to debug the Apache executable and each of its modules with a source-level debugger, such as the GNU debugger *gdb*. To enable this option, use:

```
panic% perl Makefile.PL PERL_DEBUG=1
```

> We will discuss this option in Chapter 21, as it is extremely useful to track down bugs or report problems.

Activating Callback Hooks

A callback hook (also known simply as a *callback*) is a reference to a subroutine. In Perl, we create subroutine references with the following syntax:

```
$callback = \&subroutine;
```

In this example, $callback contains a reference to the subroutine called subroutine. Another way to create a callback is to use an anonymous subroutine:

```
$callback = sub { 'some code' };
```

Here, $callback contains a reference to the anonymous subroutine. Callbacks are used when we want some action (subroutine call) to occur when some event takes place. Since we don't know exactly when the event will take place, we give the event handler a reference to the subroutine we want to be executed. The handler will call our subroutine at the right time, effectively *calling back* that subroutine.

By default, most of the callback hooks except for PerlHandler, PerlChildInitHandler, PerlChildExitHandler, PerlConnectionApi, and PerlServerApi are turned off. You may enable them via options to *Makefile.PL*.

Here is the list of available hooks and the parameters that enable them. The Apache request prcessing phases were explained in Chapter 1.

```
Directive/Hook              Configuration Option
----------------------------------------------------------
PerlPostReadRequestHandler  PERL_POST_READ_REQUEST
PerlTransHandler            PERL_TRANS
PerlInitHandler             PERL_INIT
PerlHeaderParserHandler     PERL_HEADER_PARSER
PerlAuthenHandler           PERL_AUTHEN
PerlAuthzHandler            PERL_AUTHZ
PerlAccessHandler           PERL_ACCESS
PerlTypeHandler             PERL_TYPE
PerlFixupHandler            PERL_FIXUP
PerlHandler                 PERL_HANDLER
PerlLogHandler              PERL_LOG
PerlCleanupHandler          PERL_CLEANUP
PerlChildInitHandler        PERL_CHILD_INIT
PerlChildExitHandler        PERL_CHILD_EXIT
PerlDispatchHandler         PERL_DISPATCH
```

As with any parameters that are either defined or not, use OPTION_FOO=1 to enable them (e.g., PERL_AUTHEN=1).

To enable all callback hooks, use:

```
ALL_HOOKS=1
```

There are a few more hooks that won't be enabled by default, because they are experimental.

If you are using:

```
panic% perl Makefile.PL EVERYTHING=1 ...
```

it already includes the ALL_HOOKS=1 option.

Activating Standard API Features

The following options enable various standard features of the mod_perl API. While not absolutely needed, they're very handy and there's little penalty in including them. Unless specified otherwise, these options are all disabled by default. The EVERYTHING=1 or DYNAMIC=1 options will enable them en masse. If in doubt, include these.

PERL_FILE_API=1
>   Enables the Apache::File class, which helps with the handling of files under mod_perl.

`PERL_TABLE_API=1`

> Enables the `Apache::Table` class, which provides tied access to the Apache Table structure (used for HTTP headers, among others).

`PERL_LOG_API=1`

> Enables the `Apache::Log` class. This class allows you to access Apache's more advanced logging features.

`PERL_URI_API=1`

> Enables the `Apache::URI` class, which deals with the parsing of URIs in a similar way to the Perl `URI::URL` module, but much faster.

`PERL_UTIL_API=1`

> Enables the `Apache::Util` class, allowing you to use various functions such as HTML escaping or date parsing, but implemented in C.

`PERL_CONNECTION_API=1`

> Enables the `Apache::Connection` class. This class is enabled by default. Set the option to 0 to disable it.

`PERL_SERVER_API=1`

> Enables the `Apache::Server` class. This class is enabled by default. Set the option to 0 to disable it.

Please refer to Lincoln Stein and Doug MacEachern's *Writing Apache Modules with Perl and C* (O'Reilly) for more information about the Apache API.

Enabling Extra Features

mod_perl comes with a number of other features. Most of them are disabled by default. This is the list of features and options to enable them:

- `<Perl>` sections give you a way to configure Apache using Perl code in the *httpd.conf* file itself. See Chapter 4 for more information.

  ```
  panic% perl Makefile.PL PERL_SECTIONS=1 ...
  ```

- With the `PERL_SSI` option, the mod_include module can be extended to include a #perl directive.

  ```
  panic% perl Makefile.PL PERL_SSI=1
  ```

  By enabling `PERL_SSI`, a new #perl element is added to the standard mod_include functionality. This element allows server-side includes to call Perl subroutines directly. This feature works only when mod_perl is not built as a DSO (i.e., when it's built statically).

- If you develop an Apache module in Perl and you want to create custom configuration directives[*] to be recognized in *httpd.conf*, you need to use `Apache::`

---

[*] See Chapters 8 and 9 of *Writing Apache Modules with Perl and C* (O'Reilly).

ModuleConfig and Apache::CmdParms. For these modules to work, you will need to enable this option:

```
panic% perl Makefile.PL PERL_DIRECTIVE_HANDLERS=1
```

- The stacked handlers feature explained in Chapter 4 requires this parameter to be enabled:

```
panic% perl Makefile.PL PERL_STACKED_HANDLERS=1
```

- The method handlers feature discussed in Chapter 4 requires this parameter to be enabled:

```
panic% perl Makefile.PL PERL_METHOD_HANDLERS=1
```

- To enable all phase callback handlers, all API modules, and all miscellaneous features, use the "catch-all" option we used when we first compiled mod_perl:

```
panic% perl Makefile.PL EVERYTHING=1
```

Reusing Configuration Parameters

When you have to upgrade the server, it's sometimes hard to remember what parameters you used in the previous mod_perl build. So it's a good idea to save them in a file.

One way to save parameters is to create a file (e.g., *~/.mod_perl_build_options*) with the following contents:

```
APACHE_SRC=../apache_1.3.xx/src DO_HTTPD=1 USE_APACI=1 \
EVERYTHING=1
```

Then build the server with the following command:

```
panic% perl Makefile.PL `cat ~/.mod_perl_build_options`
panic% make && make test
panic# make install
```

But mod_perl has a standard method to perform this trick. If a file named *makepl_args.mod_perl* is found in the same directory as the mod_perl build location, it will be read in by *Makefile.PL*. Parameters supplied at the command line will override the parameters given in this file.

The *makepl_args.mod_perl* file can also be located in your home directory or in the *../* directory relative to the mod_perl distribution directory. The filename can also start with a dot (*.makepl_args.mod_perl*), so you can keep it nicely hidden along with the rest of the dot files in your home directory. So, *Makefile.PL* will look for the following files (in this order), using the first one it comes across:

```
./makepl_args.mod_perl
../makepl_args.mod_perl
./.makepl_args.mod_perl
../.makepl_args.mod_perl
$ENV{HOME}/.makepl_args.mod_perl
```

For example:

```
panic% ls -1 /home/stas/src
apache_1.3.xx/
makepl_args.mod_perl
mod_perl-1.xx/

panic% cat makepl_args.mod_perl
APACHE_SRC=../apache_1.3.xx/src
DO_HTTPD=1
USE_APACI=1
EVERYTHING=1

panic% cd mod_perl-1.xx
panic% perl Makefile.PL
panic% make && make test
panic# make install
```

Now the parameters from the *makepl_args.mod_perl* file will be used automatically, as if they were entered directly.

In the sample *makepl_args.mod_perl* file in the *eg/* directory of the mod_perl distribution package, you might find a few options enabling some experimental features for you to play with, too!

If you are faced with a compiled Apache and no trace of the parameters used to build it, you can usually still find them if *make clean* was not run on the sources. You will find the Apache-specific parameters in *apache_1.3.xx/config.status* and the mod_perl parameters in *mod_perl-1.xx/apaci/mod_perl.config*.

Discovering Whether a Feature Was Enabled

mod_perl Version 1.25 introduced Apache::MyConfig, which provides access to the various hooks and features set when mod_perl was built. This circumvents the need to set up a live server just to find out if a certain callback hook is available.

To see whether some feature was built in or not, check the %Apache::MyConfig::Setup hash. For example, suppose we install mod_perl with the following options:

```
panic% perl Makefile.PL EVERYTHING=1
```

but the next day we can't remember which callback hooks were enabled. We want to know whether the PERL_LOG callback hook is available. One of the ways to find an answer is to run the following code:

```
panic% perl -MApache::MyConfig -e 'print $Apache::MyConfig::Setup{PERL_LOG}'
```

If it prints 1, that means the PERL_LOG callback hook is enabled (which it should be, as EVERYTHING=1 enables them all).

Another approach is to configure Apache::Status (see Chapter 9) and run *http://localhost/perl-status?hooks* to check for enabled hooks.

If you want to check for the existence of various hooks within your handlers, you can use the script shown in Example 3-1.

Example 3-1. test_hooks.pl

```
use mod_perl_hooks;

for my $hook (mod_perl::hooks()) {
    if (mod_perl::hook($hook)) {
        print "$hook is enabled\n";
    }
    else {
        print "$hook is not enabled\n";
    }
}
```

You can also try to look at the symbols inside the *httpd* executable with the help of *nm(1)* or a similar utility. For example, if you want to see whether you enabled PERL_LOG=1 while building mod_perl, you can search for a symbol with the same name but in lowercase:

```
panic% nm httpd | grep perl_log
08071724 T perl_logger
```

This shows that PERL_LOG=1 was enabled. But this approach will work only if you have an unstripped *httpd* binary. By default, *make install* strips the binary before installing it, thus removing the symbol names to save space. Use the *--without-execstrip ./configure* option to prevent stripping during the *make install* phase. [*]

Yet another approach that will work in most cases is to try to use the feature in question. If it wasn't configured, Apache will give an error message.

Using an Alternative Configuration File

By default, mod_perl provides its own copy of the *Configuration* file to Apache's *configure* utility. If you want to pass it your own version, do this:

```
panic% perl Makefile.PL CONFIG=Configuration.custom
```

where *Configuration.custom* is the pathname of the file *relative* to the Apache source tree you build against.

perl Makefile.PL Troubleshooting

During the configuration (*perl Makefile.PL*) stage, you may encounter some of these problems. To help you avoid them, let's study them, find out why they happened, and discuss how to fix them.

---

[*] You might need the unstripped version for debugging reasons too.

A test compilation with your Makefile configuration failed...

When you see the following error during the *perl Makefile.PL* stage:

```
** A test compilation with your Makefile configuration
** failed. This is most likely because your C compiler
** is not ANSI. Apache requires an ANSI C Compiler, such
** as gcc. The above error message from your compiler
** will also provide a clue.
 Aborting!
```

it's possible that you have a problem with a compiler. It may be improperly installed or not installed at all. Sometimes the reason is that your Perl executable was built on a different machine, and the software installed on your machine is not the same. Generally this happens when you install prebuilt packages, such as *rpm* or *deb*. You may find that the dependencies weren't properly defined in the Perl binary package and you were allowed to install it even though some essential packages were not installed.

The most frequent pitfall is a missing gdbm library (see the next section).

But why guess, when we can actually see the real error message and understand what the real problem is? To get a real error message, edit the Apache *src/Configure* script. Around line 2140, you should see a line like this:

```
if ./helpers/TestCompile sanity; then
```

Add the *-v* option, as follows:

```
if ./helpers/TestCompile -v sanity; then
```

and try again. Now you should get a useful error message.

Missing or misconfigured libgdbm.so

On some Red Hat Linux systems, you might encounter a problem during the *perl Makefile.PL* stage, when Perl was installed from an *rpm* package built with the gdbm library, but `libgdbm` isn't actually installed. If this happens to you, make sure you install it before proceeding with the build process.

You can check how Perl was built by running the *perl -V* command:

```
panic% perl -V | grep libs
```

You should see output similar to this:

```
libs=-lnsl -lndbm -lgdbm -ldb -ldl -lm -lc -lposix -lcrypt
```

Sometimes the problem is even more obscure: you do have `libgdbm` installed, but it's not installed properly. Do this:

```
panic% ls /usr/lib/libgdbm.so*
```

If you get at least three lines, like we do:

```
lrwxrwxrwx   /usr/lib/libgdbm.so -> libgdbm.so.2.0.0
lrwxrwxrwx   /usr/lib/libgdbm.so.2 -> libgdbm.so.2.0.0
-rw-r--r--   /usr/lib/libgdbm.so.2.0.0
```

you are all set. On some installations, the *libgdbm.so* symbolic link is missing, so you get only:

```
lrwxrwxrwx   /usr/lib/libgdbm.so.2 -> libgdbm.so.2.0.0
-rw-r--r--   /usr/lib/libgdbm.so.2.0.0
```

To fix this problem, add the missing symbolic link:

```
panic% cd /usr/lib
panic% ln -s libgdbm.so.2.0.0 libgdbm.so
```

Now you should be able to build mod_perl without any problems.

Note that you might need to prepare this symbolic link as well:

```
lrwxrwxrwx   /usr/lib/libgdbm.so.2 -> libgdbm.so.2.0.0
```

with the command:

```
panic% ln -s libgdbm.so.2.0.0 libgdbm.so.2
```

Of course, if a new version of the libgdbm library was released between the moment we wrote this sentence and the moment you're reading it, you will have to adjust the version numbers. We didn't use the usual *xx.xx* version replacement here, to make it easier to understand how the symbolic links should be set.

About the gdbm, db, and ndbm Libraries

If you need to have the dbm library linked in, you should know that both the gdbm and db libraries offer ndbm emulation, which is the interface that Apache actually uses. So when you build mod_perl, you end up using whichever library was linked first by the Perl compilation. If you build Apache without mod_perl, you end up with whatever appears to be be your ndbm library, which will vary between systems, and especially Linux distributions. So you may have to work a bit to get both Apache and Perl to use the same library, and you are likely to have trouble copying the *dbm* file from one system to another or even using it after an upgrade.

Undefined reference to 'PL_perl_destruct_level'

When manually building mod_perl using the shared library:

```
panic% cd mod_perl-1.xx
panic% perl Makefile.PL PREP_HTTPD=1
panic% make && make test
panic# make install

panic% cd ../apache_1.3.xx
panic% ./configure --with-layout=RedHat --target=perlhttpd
    --activate-module=src/modules/perl/libperl.a
```

you might see the following output:

```
gcc -c  -I./os/unix -I./include   -DLINUX=2 -DTARGET=\"perlhttpd\"
-DUSE_HSREGEX -DUSE_EXPAT -I./lib/expat-lite `./apaci` buildmark.c
gcc  -DLINUX=2 -DTARGET=\"perlhttpd\" -DUSE_HSREGEX -DUSE_EXPAT
-I./lib/expat-lite `./apaci`     \
       -o perlhttpd buildmark.o modules.o modules/perl/libperl.a
modules/standard/libstandard.a main/libmain.a ./os/unix/libos.a ap/libap.a
regex/libregex.a lib/expat-lite/libexpat.a  -lm -lcrypt
modules/perl/libperl.a(mod_perl.o): In function `perl_shutdown':
mod_perl.o(.text+0xf8): undefined reference to `PL_perl_destruct_level'
mod_perl.o(.text+0x102): undefined reference to `PL_perl_destruct_level'
mod_perl.o(.text+0x10c): undefined reference to `PL_perl_destruct_level'
mod_perl.o(.text+0x13b): undefined reference to `Perl_av_undef'
[more errors snipped]
```

This happens when Perl was built statically linked, with no shared libperl.a. Build a dynamically linked Perl (with libperl.a) and the problem will disappear.

Building mod_perl (make)

After completing the configuration, it's time to build the server by simply calling:

```
panic% make
```

The *make* program first compiles the source files and creates a mod_perl library file. Then, depending on your configuration, this library is either linked with *httpd* (statically) or not linked at all, allowing you to dynamically load it at runtime.

You should avoid putting the mod_perl source directory inside the Apache source directory, as this confuses the build process. The best choice is to put both source directories under the same parent directory.

What Compiler Should Be Used to Build mod_perl?

All Perl modules that use C extensions must be compiled using the compiler with which your copy of Perl was built.

When you run *perl Makefile.PL*, a *Makefile* is created. This *Makefile* includes the same compilation options that were used to build Perl itself. They are stored in the Config.pm module and can be displayed with the *Perl -V* command. All these options are reapplied when compiling Perl modules.

If you use a different compiler to build Perl extensions, chances are that the options this compiler uses won't be the same, or they might be interpreted in a completely different way. So the code may not compile, may dump core, or may behave in unexpected ways.

Since Perl, Apache, and third-party modules all work together under mod_perl, it's essential to use the same compiler while building each of the components.

If you compile a non-Perl component separately, you should make sure to use both the same compiler and the same options used to build Perl. You can find much of this information by running *perl -V*.

make Troubleshooting

The following errors are the ones that frequently occur during the *make* process when building mod_perl.

Undefined reference to 'Perl_newAV'

This and similar error messages may show up during the *make* process. Generally it happens when you have a broken Perl installation. If it's installed from a broken *rpm* or another precompiled binary package, build Perl from source or use another properly built binary package. Run *perl -V* to learn what version of Perl you are using and other important details.

Unrecognized format specifier for...

This error is usually reported due to the problems with some versions of the SFIO library. Try to use the latest version to get around this problem or, if you don't really need SFIO, rebuild Perl without this library.

Testing the Server (make test)

After building the server, it's a good idea to test it throughly by calling:

```
panic% make test
```

Fortunately, mod_perl comes with a big collection of tests, which attempt to exercise all the features you asked for at the configuration stage. If any of the tests fails, the *make test* step will fail.

Running *make test* will start the freshly built *httpd* on port 8529 (an unprivileged port), running under the UID (user ID) and GID (group ID) of the *perl Makefile.PL* process. The *httpd* will be terminated when the tests are finished.

To change the default port (8529) used for the tests, do this:

```
panic% perl Makefile.PL PORT=xxxx
```

Each file in the testing suite generally includes more than one test, but when you do the testing, the program will report only how many tests were passed and the total number of tests defined in the test file. To learn which ones failed, run the tests in verbose mode by using the TEST_VERBOSE parameter:

```
panic% make test TEST_VERBOSE=1
```

As of mod_perl v1.23, you can use the environment variables APACHE_USER and APACHE_GROUP to override the default User and Group settings in the *httpd.conf* file used for *make test*. These two variables should be set before the *Makefile* is created to take effect during the testing stage. For example, if you want to set them to *httpd*, you can do the following in the Bourne-style shell:

```
panic% export APACHE_USER=httpd
panic% export APACHE_GROUP=httpd
panic% perl Makefile.PL ...
```

Manual Testing

Tests are invoked by running the *./TEST* script located in the *./t* directory. Use the *-v* option for verbose tests. You might run an individual test like this:

```
panic% perl t/TEST -v modules/file.t
```

or all tests in a test subdirectory:

```
panic% perl t/TEST modules
```

The *TEST* script starts the server before the test is executed. If for some reason it fails to start, use *make start_httpd* to start it manually:

```
panic% make start_httpd
```

To shut down Apache when the testing is complete, use *make kill_httpd*:

```
panic% make kill_httpd
```

make test Troubleshooting

The following sections cover problems that you may encounter during the testing stage.

make test fails

make test requires Apache to be running already, so if you specified NO_HTTPD=1 during the *perl Makefile.PL* stage, you'll have to build *httpd* independently before running *make test*. Go to the Apache source tree and run *make*, then return to the mod_perl source tree and continue with the server testing.

If you get an error like this:

```
still waiting for server to warm up...............not ok
```

you may want to examine the *t/logs/error_log* file, where all the *make test*–stage errors are logged. If you still cannot find the problem or this file is completely empty, you may want to run the test with *strace* (or *truss*) in the following way (assuming that you are located in the root directory of the mod_perl source tree):

```
panic% make start_httpd
panic% strace -f -s1024 -o strace.out -p `cat t/logs/httpd.pid` &
```

```
panic% make run_tests
panic% make kill_httpd
```

where the *strace -f* option tells *strace* to trace child processes as they are created, *-s1024* allows trace strings of a maximum of 1024 characters to be printed (it's 32 by default), *-o* gives the name of the file to which the output should be written, *-p* supplies the PID of the parent process, and *&* puts the job in the background.

When the tests are complete, you can examine the generated *strace.out* file and hopefully find the problem. We talk about creating and analyzing trace outputs in Chapter 21.

mod_perl.c is incompatible with this version of Apache

If you had a stale Apache header layout in one of the *include* paths during the build process, you will see the message "mod_perl.c is incompatible with this version of Apache" when you try to execute *httpd*. Find the file *ap_mmn.h* using *find*, *locate*, or another utility. Delete this file and rebuild Apache. The Red Hat Linux distribution usually installs it in */usr/local/include*.

Before installing mod_perl-enabled Apache from scratch, it's a good idea to remove all the pre-installed Apache modules, and thus save the trouble of looking for files that mess up the build process. For example, to remove the precompiled Apache installed as a Red Hat Package Manager (RPM) package, as *root* you should do:

```
panic# rpm -e apache
```

There may be other RPM packages that depend on the Apache RPM package. You will be notified about any other dependent packages, and you can decide whether to delete them, too. You can always supply the *--nodeps* option to tell the RPM manager to ignore the dependencies.

apt users would do this instead:

```
panic# apt-get remove apache
```

make test......skipping test on this platform

make test may report some tests as *skipped*. They are skipped because you are missing the modules that are needed for these tests to pass. You might want to peek at the contents of each test; you will find them all in the *./t* directory. It's possible that you don't need any of the missing modules to get your work done, in which case you shouldn't worry that the tests are skipped.

If you want to make sure that all tests pass, you will need to figure out what modules are missing from your installation. For example, if you see:

```
modules/cookie......skipping test on this platform
```

you may want to install the Apache::Cookie module. If you see:

```
modules/request.....skipping test on this platform
```

Apache::Request is missing.* If you see:

```
modules/psections...skipping test on this platform
```

Devel::Symdump and Data::Dumper are needed.

Chances are that all of these will be installed if you use CPAN.pm to install Bundle::Apache. We talk about CPAN installations later in this chapter.

make test fails due to misconfigured localhost entry

The *make test* suite uses *localhost* to run the tests that require a network. Make sure you have this entry in */etc/hosts*:

```
127.0.0.1       localhost.localdomain   localhost
```

Also make sure you have the loopback device *lo* configured. If you aren't sure, run:

```
panic% /sbin/ifconfig lo
```

This will tell you whether the loopback device is configured.

Installation (make install)

After testing the server, the last step is to install it. First install all the Perl files (usually as *root*):

```
panic# make install
```

Then go to the Apache source tree and complete the Apache installation (installing the configuration files, *httpd*, and utilities):

```
panic# cd ../apache_1.3.xx
panic# make install
```

Of course, if you have used the APACHE_PREFIX option as explained earlier in this chapter, you can skip this step.

Now the installation should be considered complete. You may now configure your server and start using it.

Manually Building a mod_perl-Enabled Apache

If you want to build *httpd* separately from mod_perl, you should use the NO_HTTPD=1 option during the *perl Makefile.PL* (mod_perl build) stage. Then you will have to configure various things by hand and proceed to build Apache. You shouldn't run *perl Makefile.PL* before following the steps described in this section.

If you choose to manually build mod_perl, there are three things you may need to set up before the build stage:

---

* Apache::Cookie and Apache::Request are both part of the *libapreq* distribution.

mod_perl's Makefile

When *perl Makefile.PL* is executed, *$APACHE_SRC/modules/perl/Makefile* may need to be modified to enable various options (e.g., `ALL_HOOKS=1`).

Optionally, instead of tweaking the options during the *perl Makefile.PL* stage, you can edit *mod_perl-1.xx/src/modules/perl/Makefile* before running *perl Makefile.PL*.

Configuration

Add the following to *apache_1.3.xx/src/Configuration*:

```
AddModule modules/perl/libperl.a
```

We suggest you add this entry at the end of the *Configuration* file if you want your callback hooks to have precedence over core handlers.

Add the following to `EXTRA_LIBS`:

```
EXTRA_LIBS=`perl -MExtUtils::Embed -e ldopts`
```

Add the following to `EXTRA_CFLAGS`:

```
EXTRA_CFLAGS=`perl -MExtUtils::Embed -e ccopts`
```

mod_perl source files

Return to the mod_perl directory and copy the mod_perl source files into the Apache build directory:

```
panic% cp -r src/modules/perl apache_1.3.xx/src/modules/
```

When you are done with the configuration parts, run:

```
panic% perl Makefile.PL NO_HTTPD=1 DYNAMIC=1  EVERYTHING=1 \
    APACHE_SRC=../apache_1.3.xx/src
```

`DYNAMIC=1` enables a build of the shared mod_perl library. Add other options if required.

```
panic# make install
```

Now you may proceed with the plain Apache build process. Note that in order for your changes to the *apache_1.3.xx/src/Configuration* file to take effect, you must run *apache_1.3.xx/src/Configure* instead of the default *apache_1.3.xx/configure* script:

```
panic% cd ../apache_1.3.xx/src
panic% ./Configure
panic% make
panic# make install
```

Installation Scenarios for Standalone mod_perl

When building mod_perl, the mod_perl C source files that have to be compiled into the *httpd* executable usually are copied to the subdirectory *src/modules/perl/* in the Apache source tree. In the past, to integrate this subtree into the Apache build process, a lot of adjustments were done by mod_perl's *Makefile.PL*. *Makefile.PL* was also responsible for the Apache build process.

This approach is problematic in several ways. It is very restrictive and not very clean, because it assumes that mod_perl is the only third-party module that has to be integrated into Apache.

A new hybrid build environment was therefore created for the Apache side of mod_perl, to avoid these problems. It prepares only the *src/modules/perl/* subtree inside the Apache source tree, without adjusting or editing anything else. This way, no conflicts can occur. Instead, mod_perl is activated later (via APACI calls when the Apache source tree is configured), and then it configures itself.

There are various ways to build Apache with the new hybrid build environment (using `USE_APACI=1`):

- Build Apache and mod_perl together, using the default configuration.
- Build Apache and mod_perl separately, allowing you to plug in other third-party Apache modules as needed.
- Build mod_perl as a DSO inside the Apache source tree using APACI.
- Build mod_perl as a DSO outside the Apache source tree with APXS.

The All-in-One Way

If your goal is just to build and install Apache with mod_perl out of their source trees, and you have no interest in further adjusting or enhancing Apache, proceed as we described in Chapter 2:

```
panic% tar xzvf apache_1.3.xx.tar.gz
panic% tar xzvf mod_perl-1.xx.tar.gz
panic% cd mod_perl-1.xx
panic% perl Makefile.PL APACHE_SRC=../apache_1.3.xx/src \
    DO_HTTPD=1 USE_APACI=1 EVERYTHING=1
panic% make && make test
panic# make install
panic# cd ../apache_1.3.xx
panic# make install
```

This builds Apache statically with mod_perl, installs Apache under the default */usr/local/apache* tree, and installs mod_perl into the *site_perl* hierarchy of your existing Perl installation.

Building mod_perl and Apache Separately

However, sometimes you might need more flexibility while building mod_perl. If you build mod_perl into the Apache binary (*httpd*) in separate steps, you'll also have the freedom to include other third-party Apache modules. Here are the steps:

1. Prepare the Apache source tree.

   As before, first extract the distributions:

   ```
   panic% tar xvzf apache_1.3.xx.tar.gz
   panic% tar xzvf mod_perl-1.xx.tar.gz
   ```

2. Install mod_perl's Perl side and prepare the Apache side.

   Next, install the Perl side of mod_perl into the Perl hierarchy and prepare the *src/modules/perl/* subdirectory inside the Apache source tree:

   ```
   panic% cd mod_perl-1.xx
   panic% perl Makefile.PL \
       APACHE_SRC=../apache_1.3.xx/src \
       NO_HTTPD=1    \
       USE_APACI=1   \
       PREP_HTTPD=1 \
       EVERYTHING=1 \
       [...]
   panic% make
   panic# make install
   ```

   The `APACHE_SRC` option sets the path to your Apache source tree, the `NO_HTTPD` option forces this path and only this path to be used, the `USE_APACI` option triggers the new hybrid build environment, and the `PREP_HTTPD` option forces preparation of the *$APACHE_SRC/modules/perl/* tree but no automatic build.

   This tells the configuration process to prepare the Apache side of mod_perl in the Apache source tree, but doesn't touch anything else in it. It then just builds the Perl side of mod_perl and installs it into the Perl installation hierarchy.

   Note that if you use `PREP_HTTPD` as described above, to complete the build you must go into the Apache source directory and run *make* and *make install*.

3. Prepare other third-party modules.

   Now you have a chance to prepare any other third-party modules you might want to include in Apache. For instance, you can build PHP separately, as you did with mod_perl.

4. Build the Apache package.

   Now it's time to build Apache, including the Apache side of mod_perl and any other third-party modules you've prepared:

   ```
   panic% cd apache_1.3.xx
   panic% ./configure \
       --prefix=/path/to/install/of/apache \
       --activate-module=src/modules/perl/libperl.a \
       [...]
   panic% make
   panic# make install
   ```

   You must use the *--prefix* option if you want to change the default target directory of the Apache installation. The *--activate-module* option activates mod_perl for the configuration process and thus also for the build process. If you choose *--prefix=/usr/share/apache*, the Apache directory tree will be installed in */usr/share/apache*.

If you add other third-party components, such as PHP, include a separate *--activate-module* option for each of them. (See the module's documentation for the actual path to which *--activate-module* should point.) For example, for mod_php4:

```
--activate-module=src/modules/php4/libphp4.a
```

Note that the files activated by *--activate-module* do not exist at this time. They will be generated during compilation.

You may also want to go back to the mod_perl source tree and run *make test* (to make sure that mod_perl is working) before running *make install* inside the Apache source tree.

For more detailed examples on building mod_perl with other components, see the section later in this chapter entitled "Building mod_perl with Other Components."

When DSOs Can Be Used

If you want to build mod_perl as a DSO, you must make sure that Perl was built with the system's native `malloc( )`. If Perl was built with its own `malloc( )` and *-Dbincompat5005*, it pollutes the main *httpd* program with *free* and *malloc* symbols. When *httpd* starts or restarts, any references in the main program to *free* and *malloc* become invalid, causing memory leaks and segfaults.

Notice that mod_perl's build system warns about this problem.

With Perl 5.6.0+ this pollution can be prevented by using *-Ubincompat5005* or *-Uusemymalloc* for any version of Perl. However, there's a chance that *-Uusemymalloc* might hurt performance on your platform, so *-Ubincompat5005* is likely a better choice.

If you get the following reports with Perl version 5.6.0+:

```
% perl -V:usemymalloc
usemymalloc='y';
% perl -V:bincompat5005
bincompat5005='define';
```

rebuild Perl with *-Ubincompat5005*.

For pre-5.6.x Perl versions, if you get:

```
% perl -V:usemymalloc
usemymalloc='y';
```

rebuild Perl with *-Uusemymalloc*.

Now rebuild mod_perl.

BUSINESS REPLY MAIL

FIRST CLASS MAIL   PERMIT NO. 80   SEBASTOPOL, CA

Postage will be paid by addressee

O'Reilly & Associates, Inc.
Book Registration
1005 Gravenstein Highway North
Sebastopol, CA 95472-9910

Register Your O'Reilly Book

Register your book with O'Reilly and receive a FREE copy of our latest catalog, email notification of new editions of this book, information about new titles, and special offers available only to registered O'Reilly customers.

Register online at register.oreilly.com or complete and return this postage paid card.

Which book(s) are you registering? Please include title and ISBN # (above bar code on back cover)

Title		ISBN #
Title		ISBN #
Title		ISBN #

Name		
Company/Organization		Job Title
Address		
City	State	Zip/Postal Code	Country
Telephone	Email address	

register.oreilly.com

Part #70071

Building mod_perl as a DSO via APACI

We have already mentioned that the new mod_perl build environment (with USE_
APACI) is a hybrid. What does that mean? It means, for instance, that you can use the
same *src/modules/perl/* configuration to build mod_perl as a DSO or not, without
having to edit any files. To build libperl.so, just add a single option, depending on
which method you used to build mod_perl.

---

libperl.so and libperl.a

The static mod_perl library is called *libperl.a*, and the shared mod_perl library is called
libperl.so. Of course, *libmodperl* would have been a better prefix, but *libperl* was used
because of prehistoric Apache issues. Be careful that you don't confuse mod_perl's *lib-
perl.a* and *libperl.so* files with the ones that are built with the standard Perl installation.

If you choose the "standard" all-in-one way of building mod_perl, add:

```
USE_DSO=1
```

to the *perl Makefile.PL* options.

If you choose to build mod_perl and Apache separately, add:

```
--enable-shared=perl
```

to Apache's *configure* options when you build Apache.

As you can see, whichever way you build mod_perl and Apache, only one additional
option is needed to build mod_perl as a DSO. Everything else is done automatically:
mod_so is automatically enabled, the *Makefiles* are adjusted, and the *install* target
from APACI installs *libperl.so* into the Apache installation tree. Additionally, the
LoadModule and AddModule directives (which dynamically load and insert mod_perl
into *httpd*) are automatically added to *httpd.conf*.

Building mod_perl as a DSO via APXS

We've seen how to build mod_perl as a DSO *inside* the Apache source tree, but there
is a nifty alternative: building mod_perl as a DSO *outside* the Apache source tree via
the new Apache 1.3 support tool called APXS. The advantage is obvious: you can
extend an already installed Apache with mod_perl even if you don't have the sources
(for instance, you may have installed an Apache binary package from your vendor or
favorite distribution).

Here are the build steps:

```
panic% tar xzvf mod_perl-1.xx.tar.gz
panic% cd mod_perl-1.xx
```

```
panic% perl Makefile.PL \
    USE_APXS=1 \
    WITH_APXS=/path/to/bin/apxs \
    EVERYTHING=1 \
    [...]
panic% make && make test
panic# make install
```

This will build the DSO *libperl.so* outside the Apache source tree and install it into the existing Apache hierarchy.

Building mod_perl with Other Components

mod_perl is often used with other components that plug into Apache, such as PHP and SSL. In this section, we'll show you a build combining mod_perl with PHP. We'll also show how to build a secure version of Apache with mod_perl support using each of the SSL options available for Apache today (mod_ssl, Apache-SSL, Stronghold, and Covalent).

Since you now understand how the build process works, we'll present these scenarios without much explanation (unless they involve something we haven't discussed yet).

All these scenarios were tested on a Linux platform. You might need to refer to the specific component's documentation if something doesn't work for you as described here. The intention of this section is not to show you how to install other non-mod_perl components alone, but how to do this in a bundle with mod_perl.

Also, notice that the links we've used are very likely to have changed by the time you read this document. That's why we have used the *x.xx* convention instead of using hardcoded version numbers. Remember to replace the *x.xx* placeholders with the version numbers of the distributions you are going to use. To find out the latest stable version number, visit the components' sites—e.g., if we say *http://perl.apache.org/dist/mod_perl-1.xx.tar.gz*, go to *http://perl.apache.org/download/* to learn the version number of the latest stable release of mod_perl 1, and download the appropriate file.

Unless otherwise noted, all the components install themselves into a default location. When you run *make install*, the installation program tells you where it's going to install the files.

Installing mod_perl with PHP

The following is a simple installation scenario of a combination mod_perl and PHP build for the Apache server. We aren't going to use a custom installation directory, so Apache will use the default */usr/local/apache* directory.

1. Download the latest stable source releases:

   ```
   Apache:   http://www.apache.org/dist/httpd/
   mod_perl: http://perl.apache.org/download/
   PHP:      http://www.php.net/downloads.php
   ```

---

2. Unpack them:

```
panic% tar xvzf mod_perl-1.xx
panic% tar xvzf apache_1.3.xx.tar.gz
panic% tar xvzf php-x.x.xx.tar.gz
```

3. Configure Apache:

```
panic% cd apache_1.3.xx
panic% ./configure
```

4. Build mod_perl:

```
panic% cd ../mod_perl-1.xx
panic% perl Makefile.PL APACHE_SRC=../apache_1.3.xx/src NO_HTTPD=1 \
    USE_APACI=1 PREP_HTTPD=1 EVERYTHING=1
panic% make
```

5. Build mod_php:

```
panic% cd ../php-x.x.xx
panic% ./configure --with-apache=../apache_1.3.xx \
    --with-mysql --enable-track-vars
panic% make
panic# make install
```

(mod_php doesn't come with a *make test* suite, so we don't need to run one.)

6. Reconfigure Apache to use mod_perl and PHP, and then build it:

```
panic% cd ../apache_1.3.xx
panic% ./configure \
    --activate-module=src/modules/perl/libperl.a \
    --activate-module=src/modules/php4/libphp4.a
panic% make
```

Note that if you are building PHP3, you should use *php3/libphp3.a*. Also remember that *libperl.a* and *libphp4.a* do not exist at this time. They will be generated during compilation.

7. Test and install mod_perl:

```
panic% cd ../mod_perl-1.xx
panic% make test
panic# make install
```

8. Complete the Apache installation:

```
panic# cd ../apache_1.3.xx
panic# make install
```

Now when you start the server:

```
panic# /usr/local/apache/bin/apachectl start
```

you should see something like this in *usr/local/apache/logs/error_log*:

```
[Sat May 18 11:10:31 2002] [notice]
Apache/1.3.24 (Unix) PHP/4.2.0 mod_perl/1.26
configured -- resuming normal operations
```

If you need to build mod_ssl as well, make sure that you add the mod_ssl component first (see the next section).

Installing mod_perl with mod_ssl (+openssl)

mod_ssl provides strong cryptography for the Apache 1.3 web server via the Secure Sockets Layer (SSL v2/v3) and Transport Layer Security (TLS v1) protocols. mod_ssl uses the open source SSL/TLS toolkit OpenSSL, which is based on SSLeay, by Eric A. Young and Tim J. Hudson. As in the previous installation scenario, the default installation directory is used in this example.

1. Download the latest stable source releases. For mod_ssl, make sure that the version matches your version of Apache (e.g., get *mod_ssl-2.8.8-1.3.24.tar.gz* if you have Apache 1.3.24).

   ```
   Apache:    http://www.apache.org/dist/httpd/
   mod_perl: http://perl.apache.org/download/
   mod_ssl:   http://www.modssl.org/source/
   openssl:   http://www.openssl.org/source/
   ```

2. Unpack the sources:

   ```
   panic% tar xvzf mod_perl-1.xx.tar.gz
   panic% tar xvzf apache_1.3.xx.tar.gz
   panic% tar xvzf mod_ssl-x.x.x-1.3.xx.tar.gz
   panic% tar xvzf openssl-x.x.x.tar.gz
   ```

3. Configure, build, test, and install *openssl* if it isn't already installed:

   ```
   panic% cd openssl-x.x.x
   panic% ./config
   panic% make && make test
   panic# make install
   ```

   (If you already have the *openssl* development environment installed, you can skip this stage.)

4. Configure mod_ssl:

   ```
   panic% cd mod_ssl-x.x.x-1.3.xx
   panic% ./configure --with-apache=../apache_1.3.xx
   ```

5. Configure, build, test, and install mod_perl:

   ```
   panic% cd ../mod_perl-1.xx
   panic% perl Makefile.PL USE_APACI=1 EVERYTHING=1 \
       DO_HTTPD=1 SSL_BASE=/usr/local/ssl \
       APACHE_SRC=../apache_1.3.xx/src \
       APACI_ARGS='--enable-module=ssl'
   panic% make && make test
   panic# make install
   ```

6. Create an SSL certificate and install Apache and certificate files:

   ```
   panic% cd ../apache_1.3.xx
   panic% make certificate
   panic# make install
   ```

7. Now proceed with the mod_ssl and mod_perl parts of the server configuration in *httpd.conf*. The next chapter provides in-depth information about mod_perl configuration. For mod_ssl configuration, please refer to the mod_ssl documentation available from *http://www.modssl.org/*.

Now when you start the server:

```
panic# /usr/local/apache/bin/apachectl startssl
```

you should see something like this in */usr/local/apache/logs/error_log*:

```
[Fri May 18 11:10:31 2001] [notice]
Apache/1.3.24 (Unix) mod_perl/1.26 mod_ssl/2.8.8
OpenSSL/0.9.6c configured -- resuming normal operations
```

If you used the default configuration, the SSL part won't be loaded if you use *apachectl start* and not *apachectl startssl*.

This scenario also demonstrates the fact that some third-party Apache modules can be added to Apache by just enabling them (as with mod_ssl), while others need to be separately configured and built (as with mod_perl and PHP).

Installing mod_perl with Apache-SSL (+openssl)

Apache-SSL is a secure web server based on Apache and SSLeay/OpenSSL. It is licensed under a BSD-style license, which means that you are free to use it for commercial or non-commercial purposes as long as you retain the copyright notices.

Apache-SSL provides similar functionality to mod_ssl. mod_ssl is what is known as a *split*—i.e., it was originally derived from Apache-SSL but has been extensively redeveloped so the code now bears little relation to the original. We cannot advise you to use one over another—both work fine with mod_perl, so choose whichever you want. People argue about which one to use all the time, so if you are interested in the finer points, you may want to check the mailing list archives of the two projects (*http://www.apache-ssl.org/#Mailing_List* and *http://www.modssl.org/support/*).

To install mod_perl with Apache-SSL:

1. Download the sources. You'll need to have matching Apache-SSL and Apache versions.

   ```
   Apache:      http://www.apache.org/dist/httpd/
   mod_perl:    http://perl.apache.org/download/
   openssl:     http://www.openssl.org/source/
   Apache-SSL:  http://www.apache-ssl.org/#Download
   ```

2. Unpack the sources:

   ```
   panic% tar xvzf mod_perl-1.xx
   panic% tar xvzf apache_1.3.xx.tar.gz
   panic% tar xvzf openssl-x.x.x.tar.gz
   ```

3. Configure and install *openssl*, if necessary:

   ```
   panic% cd openssl-x.x.x
   panic% ./config
   panic% make && make test
   panic# make install
   ```

   If you already have the *openssl* development environment installed, you can skip this stage.

4. Apache-SSL comes as a patch to Apache sources. First unpack the Apache-SSL sources inside the Apache source tree and make sure that the Apache source is clean (in case you've used this source to build Apache before). Then run *./Fix-Patch* and answer y to proceed with the patching of Apache sources:

```
panic% cd apache_1.3.xx
panic% make clean
panic% tar xzvf ../apache_1.3.xx+ssl_x.xx.tar.gz
panic% ./FixPatch
Do you want me to apply the fixed-up Apache-SSL patch for you? [n] y
```

5. Proceed with mod_perl configuration. The notable addition to the usual configuration parameters is that we use the SSL_BASE parameter to point to the directory in which *openssl* is installed:

```
panic% cd ../mod_perl-1.xx
panic% perl Makefile.PL USE_APACI=1 EVERYTHING=1 \
    DO_HTTPD=1 SSL_BASE=/usr/local/ssl \
    APACHE_SRC=../apache_1.3.xx/src
```

6. Build, test, and install mod_perl:

```
panic% make && make test
panic# make install
```

7. Create an SSL certificate and install Apache and the certificate files:

```
panic# cd ../apache_1.3.xx
panic# make certificate
panic# make install
```

8. Now proceed with the configuration of the Apache-SSL and mod_perl parts of the server configuration files before starting the server. Refer to the Apache-SSL documentation to learn how to configure the SSL section of *httpd.conf*.

Now start the server:

```
panic# /usr/local/apache/bin/httpsdctl start
```

Note that by default, Apache-SSL uses *httpsdctl* instead of *apachectl*.

You should see something like this in */usr/local/apache/logs/httpsd_error_log*:

```
[Sat May 18 14:14:12 2002] [notice]
Apache/1.3.24 (Unix) mod_perl/1.26 Ben-SSL/1.48 (Unix)
configured -- resuming normal operations
```

Installing mod_perl with Stronghold

Stronghold is a secure SSL web server for Unix that allows you to give your web site full-strength, 128-bit encryption. It's a commercial product provided by Red Hat. See *http://www.redhat.com/software/apache/stronghold/* for more information.

To install Stronghold:

1. First, build and install Stronghold without mod_perl, following Stronghold's installation procedure.

2. Having done that, download the mod_perl sources:

```
panic% lwp-download http://perl.apache.org/dist/mod_perl-1.xx.tar.gz
```

3. Unpack mod_perl:

```
panic% tar xvzf mod_perl-1.xx.tar.gz
```

4. Configure mod_perl with Stronghold (assuming that you have the Stronghold sources extracted to */usr/local/stronghold*):

```
panic% cd mod_perl-1.xx
panic% perl Makefile.PL APACHE_SRC=/usr/local/stronghold/src \
    DO_HTTPD=1 USE_APACI=1 EVERYTHING=1
```

5. Build mod_perl:

```
panic% make
```

6. Before running *make test*, add your *StrongholdKey* to *t/conf/httpd.conf*. If you are configuring by hand, be sure to edit *src/modules/perl/Makefile* and uncomment the #APACHE_SSL directive.

7. Test and install mod_perl:

```
panic% make test
panic# make install
```

8. Install Stronghold:

```
panic# cd /usr/local/stronghold
panic# make install
```

Note for Solaris 2.5 Users

There has been a report that after building Apache with mod_perl, the the REGEX library that comes with Stronghold produces core dumps. To work around this problem, change the following line in *$STRONGHOLD/src/Configuration*:

```
Rule WANTHSREGEX=default
```

to:

```
Rule WANTHSREGEX=no
```

Now start the server:

```
panic# /usr/local/stronghold/bin/start-server
```

It's possible that the start script will have a different name on your platform.

You should see something like this in */usr/local/stronghold/logs/error_log*:

```
[Sun May 19 11:54:39 2002] [notice]
StrongHold/3.0 Apache/1.3.24 (Unix) mod_perl/1.26
configured -- resuming normal operations
```

Installing mod_perl with the CPAN.pm Interactive Shell

Installation of mod_perl and all the required packages is much easier with the help of the CPAN.pm module, which provides, among other features, a shell interface to the CPAN repository (see the Preface).

First, download the Apache source code and unpack it into a directory (the name of which you will need very soon).

Now execute:

```
panic% perl -MCPAN -eshell
```

You will see the cpan prompt:

```
cpan>
```

All you need to do to install mod_perl is to type:

```
cpan> install mod_perl
```

You will see something like the following:

```
Running make for DOUGM/mod_perl-1.xx.tar.gz
Fetching with LWP:
http://www.cpan.org/authors/id/DOUGM/mod_perl-1.xx.tar.gz

CPAN.pm: Going to build DOUGM/mod_perl-1.xx.tar.gz
```

(As with earlier examples in this book, we use *x.xx* as a placeholder for real version numbers, because these change very frequently.)

CPAN.pm will search for the latest Apache sources and suggest a directory. If the CPAN shell did not find your version of Apache and suggests the wrong directory name, type the name of the directory into which you unpacked Apache:

```
Enter 'q' to stop search
Please tell me where I can find your apache src
[../apache_1.3.xx/src]
```

Answer yes to the following questions, unless you have a good reason not to:

```
Configure mod_perl with /home/stas/src/apache_1.3.xx/src ? [y]
Shall I build httpd in /home/stas/src/apache_1.3.xx/src for you? [y]
```

After you have built mod_perl and Apache, tested mod_perl, and installed its Perl modules, you can quit the CPAN shell and finish the installation. Go to the Apache source root directory and run:

```
cpan> quit
panic% cd /home/stas/src/apache_1.3.xx
panic% make install
```

This will complete the installation by installing Apache's headers and the *httpd* binary into the appropriate directories.

The only caveat of the process we've just described is that you don't have control over the configuration process. But that problem is easy to solve—you can tell CPAN.pm to pass whatever parameters you want to *perl Makefile.PL*. You do this with the *o conf makepl_arg* command:

```
cpan> o conf makepl_arg 'DO_HTTPD=1 USE_APACI=1 EVERYTHING=1'
```

If you had previously set *makepl_arg* to some value, you will probably want to save it somewhere so that you can restore it when you have finished with the mod_perl installation. In that case, type the following command first:

```
cpan> o conf makepl_arg
```

and copy its value somewhere before unsetting the variable.

List all the parameters as if you were passing them to the familiar *perl Makefile.PL*. If you add the APACHE_SRC=/home/stas/src/apache_1.3.xx/src and DO_HTTPD=1 parameters, you will not be asked a single question.

Now proceed with *install mod_perl* as before. When the installation is complete, remember to reset the makepl_arg variable by executing:

```
cpan> o conf makepl_arg ''
```

Note that if there was a previous value, use that instead of ''. You can now install all the modules you want to use with mod_perl. You can install them all at once with a single command:

```
cpan> install Bundle::Apache
```

This will install mod_perl if hasn't already been installed. It will also install many other packages, such as ExtUtils::Embed, MIME::Base64, URI::URL, Digest::MD5, Net::FTP, LWP, HTML::TreeBuilder, CGI, Devel::Symdump, Apache::DB, Tie::IxHash, Data::Dumper, and so on.

Bundling Modules

If you have a system that's already configured with all the Perl modules you use, making your own bundle is a way to replicate them on another system without worrying about binary incompatibilities. To accomplish this, the command *autobundle* can be used on the CPAN shell command line. This command writes a bundle definition file for all modules that are installed for the currently running Perl interpreter.

With the clever bundle file you can then simply say:

```
cpan> install Bundle::my_bundle
```

and, after answering a few questions, go out for a coffee.

Installing mod_perl on Multiple Machines

You may want to build *httpd* once and then copy it to other machines. But the Perl side of mod_perl needs the Apache header files to compile. To avoid dragging and build Apache on all your other machines, there are a few *Makefile* targets in mod_perl to help you out:

```
panic% make tar_Apache
```

This will make a *tar* file (*Apache.tar*) of all the files mod_perl installs in your Perl's *site_perl* directory. You can then unpack this under the *site_perl* directory on another machine:

```
panic% make offsite-tar
```

This will copy all the header files from the Apache source directory against which you configured mod_perl. It will then run *make dist*, which creates a *mod_perl-1.xx.tar.gz* file, ready to unpack on another machine to compile and install the Perl side of mod_perl.

If you really want to make your life easy, you should use one of the more advanced packaging systems. For example, almost all Linux distributions use packaging tools on top of plain *tar.gz*, allowing you to track prerequisites for each package and providing for easy installation, upgrade, and cleanup. One of the most widely used packagers is the Red Hat Package Manager (RPM). See *http://www.rpm.org/* for more information.

Under RPM, all you have to do is prepare a source distribution package (SRPM) and then build a binary release. The binary can be installed on any number of machines in a matter of seconds.

RPM will even work on live production machines. Suppose you have two identical machines (with identical software and hardware, although, depending on your setup, identical hardware may be less critical). Let's say that one is a live server and the other is for development. You build an RPM with a mod_perl binary distribution, install it on the development machine, and make sure that it is working and stable. You can then install the RPM package on the live server without any fear. Make sure that *httpd.conf* is correct, since it generally specifies parameters that are unique to the live machine (for example, the hostname).

When you have installed the package, just restart the server. It's a good idea to keep a package of the previous system, in case something goes wrong. You can then easily remove the installed package and put the old one back in case of problems.

Installation into a Nonstandard Directory

There are situations when you need to install mod_perl-enabled Apache and other components (such as Perl libraries) into nonstandard locations. For example, you might work on a system to which you don't have *root* access, or you might need to install more than one set of mod_perl-enabled Apache and Perl modules on the same machine (usually when a few developers are using the same server and want to have their setups isolated from each other, or when you want to test a few different setups on the same machine).

We have already seen that you can install mod_perl-enabled Apache into different directories on the system (using the APACHE_PREFIX parameter of *Makefile.PL*). Until now, all our scenarios have installed the Perl files that are part of the mod_perl package into the same directory as the system Perl files (usually */usr/lib/perl5*).

Now we are going to show how can you install both the Apache and the Perl files into a nonstandard directory. We'll show a complete installation example using *stas* as a username, assuming that */home/stas* is the home directory of that user.

Installing Perl Modules into a Nonstandard Directory

Before we proceed, let's look at how to install any Perl module into a nonstandard directory. For an example, let's use the package that includes CGI.pm and a few other CGI::* modules.

First, you have to decide where to install the modules. The simplest approach is to simulate the portion of the / filesystem relevant to Perl under your home directory. Actually, we need only two directories:

```
/home/stas/bin
/home/stas/lib
```

We don't have to create them, as they are created automatically when the first module is installed. Ninety-nine percent of the files will go into the *lib* directory. Only occasionally does a module distribution come with Perl scripts that are installed into the *bin* directory, at which time *bin* will be created if it doesn't exist.

As usual, download the package from the CPAN repository (*CGI.pm-x.xx.tar.gz*), unpack it, and *chdir* to the newly created directory.

Now do a standard *perl Makefile.PL* to create the *Makefile*, but this time make use of your nonstandard Perl installation directory instead of the default one:

```
panic% perl Makefile.PL PREFIX=/home/stas
```

Specifying PREFIX=/home/stas is the only part of the installation process that is different from usual. Note that if you don't like how *Makefile.PL* chooses the rest of the directories, or if you are using an older version of it that requires an explicit declaration of all the target directories, you should do this:

```
panic% perl Makefile.PL PREFIX=/home/stas \
    INSTALLPRIVLIB=/home/stas/lib/perl5 \
    INSTALLSCRIPT=/home/stas/bin \
    INSTALLSITELIB=/home/stas/lib/perl5/site_perl \
    INSTALLBIN=/home/stas/bin \
    INSTALLMAN1DIR=/home/stas/lib/perl5/man  \
    INSTALLMAN3DIR=/home/stas/lib/perl5/man3
```

The rest is as usual:

```
panic% make
panic% make test
panic% make install
```

make install installs all the files in the private repository. Note that all the missing directories are created automatically, so you don't need to create them beforehand. Here is what it does (slightly edited):

```
Installing /home/stas/lib/perl5/CGI/Cookie.pm
Installing /home/stas/lib/perl5/CGI.pm
Installing /home/stas/lib/perl5/man3/CGI.3
Installing /home/stas/lib/perl5/man3/CGI::Cookie.3
Writing /home/stas/lib/perl5/auto/CGI/.packlist
Appending installation info to /home/stas/lib/perl5/perllocal.pod
```

If you have to use explicit target parameters instead of a single PREFIX parameter, you will find it useful to create a file called something like *~/.perl_dirs* (where ~ is */home/ stas* in our example), containing:

```
PREFIX=/home/stas \
INSTALLPRIVLIB=/home/stas/lib/perl5 \
INSTALLSCRIPT=/home/stas/bin \
INSTALLSITELIB=/home/stas/lib/perl5/site_perl \
INSTALLBIN=/home/stas/bin \
INSTALLMAN1DIR=/home/stas/lib/perl5/man  \
INSTALLMAN3DIR=/home/stas/lib/perl5/man3
```

From now on, any time you want to install Perl modules locally, simply execute:

```
panic% perl Makefile.PL `cat ~/.perl_dirs`
panic% make
panic% make test
panic% make install
```

Using this technique, you can easily maintain several Perl module repositories. For example, you could have one for production and another for development:

```
panic% perl Makefile.PL `cat ~/.perl_dirs.production`
```

or:

```
panic% perl Makefile.PL `cat ~/.perl_dirs.develop`
```

Finding Modules Installed in Nonstandard Directories

Installing Perl modules into nonstandard directories is only half the battle. We also have to let Perl know what these directories are.

Perl modules are generally placed in four main directories. To find these directories, execute:

```
panic% perl -V
```

The output contains important information about your Perl installation. At the end you will see:

```
Characteristics of this binary (from libperl):
Built under linux
Compiled at Oct 14 2001 17:59:15
@INC:
  /usr/lib/perl5/5.6.1/i386-linux
  /usr/lib/perl5/5.6.1
  /usr/lib/perl5/site_perl/5.6.1/i386-linux
  /usr/lib/perl5/site_perl/5.6.1
  /usr/lib/perl5/site_perl
  .
```

This shows us the content of the Perl special variable @INC, which is used by Perl to look for its modules. It is equivalent to the PATH environment variable, used to find executable programs in Unix shells.

Notice that Perl looks for modules in the . directory too, which stands for the current directory. It's the last entry in the above output.

This example is from Perl Version 5.6.1, installed on our x86 architecture PC running Linux. That's why you see *i386-linux* and *5.6.1*. If your system runs a different version of Perl, or a different operating system, processor, or chipset architecture, then some of the directories will have different names.

All the platform-specific files (such as compiled C files glued to Perl with XS, or some *.h* header files) are supposed to go into the *i386-linux*-like directories. Pure Perl modules are stored in the non-platform-specific directories.

As mentioned earlier, you find the exact directories used by your version of Perl by executing *perl -V* and replacing the global Perl installation's base directory with your home directory. Assuming that we use Perl 5.6.1, in our example the directories are:

```
/home/stas/lib/perl5/5.6.1/i386-linux
/home/stas/lib/perl5/5.6.1
/home/stas/lib/perl5/site_perl/5.6.1/i386-linux
/home/stas/lib/perl5/site_perl/5.6.1
/home/stas/lib/perl5/site_perl
```

There are two ways to tell Perl about the new directories: you can either modify the @INC variable in your scripts or set the PERL5LIB environment variable.

Modifying @INC

Modifying @INC is quite easy. The best approach is to use the lib module (pragma) by adding the following snippet at the top of any of your scripts that require the locally installed modules:

```
use lib qw(/home/stas/lib/perl5/5.6.1/
           /home/stas/lib/perl5/site_perl/5.6.1
           /home/stas/lib/perl5/site_perl
);
```

Another way is to write code to modify @INC explicitly:

```
BEGIN {
    unshift @INC,
        qw(/home/stas/lib/perl5/5.6.1/i386-linux
            /home/stas/lib/perl5/5.6.1
            /home/stas/lib/perl5/site_perl/5.6.1/i386-linux
            /home/stas/lib/perl5/site_perl/5.6.1
            /home/stas/lib/perl5/site_perl
        );
}
```

Note that with the lib module, we don't have to list the corresponding architecture-specific directories—it adds them automatically if they exist (to be exact, when *$dir/ $archname/auto* exists). It also takes care of removing any duplicated entries.

Also, notice that both approaches *prepend* the directories to be searched to @INC. This allows you to install a more recent module into your local repository, which Perl will then use instead of the older one installed in the main system repository.

Both approaches modify the value of @INC at compilation time. The lib module uses the BEGIN block internally.

Using the PERL5LIB environment variable

Now, let's assume the following scenario. We have installed the LWP package in our local repository. Now we want to install another module (e.g., mod_perl), and it has LWP listed in its prerequisites list. We know that we have LWP installed, but when we run *perl Makefile.PL* for the module we're about to install, we're told that we don't have LWP installed.

There is no way for Perl to know that we have some locally installed modules. All it does is search the directories listed in @INC, and because @INC contains only the default four directories (plus the . directory), it cannot find the locally installed LWP package. We cannot solve this problem by adding code to modify @INC, but changing the PERL5LIB environment variable will do the trick.

How to define an environment variable varies according to which shell you use. Bourne-style shell users can split a long line using the backslash (\):

```
panic% export PERL5LIB=/home/stas/lib/perl5/5.6.1:\
/home/stas/lib/perl5/site_perl/5.6.1:\
/home/stas/lib/perl5/site_perl
```

In the C-style shells, however, you'll have to make sure that the value of the PERL5LIB environment variable is specified as one continuous line with no newlines or spaces:

```
panic% setenv PERL5LIB /home/stas/lib/perl5/5.6.1:
/home/stas/lib/perl5/site_perl/5.6.1:
/home/stas/lib/perl5/site_perl
```

(In this example, the lines were split to make them fit on the page.)

As with use lib, Perl automatically prepends the architecture-specific directories to @INC if those exist.

When you have done this, verify the value of the newly configured @INC by executing *perl -V* as before. You should see the modified value of @INC:

```
panic% perl -V

Characteristics of this binary (from libperl):
Built under linux
Compiled at Apr  6 1999 23:34:07
%ENV:
  PERL5LIB="/home/stas/lib/perl5/5.6.1:
  /home/stas/lib/perl5/site_perl/5.6.1:
  /home/stas/lib/perl5/site_perl"
@INC:
  /home/stas/lib/perl5/5.6.1/i386-linux
  /home/stas/lib/perl5/5.6.1
  /home/stas/lib/perl5/site_perl/5.6.1/i386-linux
  /home/stas/lib/perl5/site_perl/5.6.1
  /home/stas/lib/perl5/site_perl
  /usr/lib/perl5/5.6.1/i386-linux
  /usr/lib/perl5/5.6.1
  /usr/lib/perl5/site_perl/5.6.1/i386-linux
  /usr/lib/perl5/site_perl/5.6.1
  /usr/lib/perl5/site_perl
  .
```

When everything works as you want it to, add these commands to your *.tcshrc*, *.bashrc*, *C:\autoexec.bat* or another equivalent file.* The next time you start a shell, the environment will be ready for you to work with the new Perl directories.

Note that if you have a PERL5LIB setting, you don't need to alter the @INC value in your scripts. But if someone else (who doesn't have this setting in the shell) tries to execute your scripts, Perl will fail to find your locally installed modules. This includes *cron* scripts, which *might* use a different shell environment (in which case the PERL5LIB setting won't be available).

The best approach is to have both the PERL5LIB environment variable and the explicit @INC extension code at the beginning of the scripts, as described above.

Using the CPAN.pm Shell with Nonstandard Installation Directories

As we saw previously in this chapter, using the CPAN.pm shell to install mod_perl saves a great deal of time. It does the job for us, even detecting the missing modules

---

* These files are run by the shell at startup and allow you to set environment variables that might be useful every time you use your shell.

listed in prerequisites, fetching them, and installing them. So you might wonder whether you can use CPAN.pm to maintain your local repository as well.

When you start the CPAN interactive shell, it searches first for the user's private configuration file and then for the system-wide one. For example, for a user *stas* and Perl Version 5.6.1, it will search for the following configuration files:

```
/home/stas/.cpan/CPAN/MyConfig.pm
/usr/lib/perl5/5.6.1/CPAN/Config.pm
```

If there is no CPAN shell configured on your system, when you start the shell for the first time it will ask you a dozen configuration questions and then create the *Config.pm* file for you.

If the CPAN shell is already configured system-wide, you should already have a */usr/lib/perl5/5.6.1/CPAN/Config.pm* file. (As always, if you have a different Perl version, the path will include a different version number.) Create the directory for the local configuration file as well:

```
panic% mkdir -p /home/stas/.cpan/CPAN
```

(On many systems, *mkdir -p* creates the whole path at once.)

Now copy the system-wide configuration file to your local one:

```
panic% cp /usr/lib/perl5/5.6.1/CPAN/Config.pm /home/stas/.cpan/CPAN/MyConfig.pm
```

The only thing left is to change the base directory of *.cpan* in your local file to the one under your home directory. On our machine, we replace */root/.cpan* (which is where our system's *.cpan* directory resides) with */home/stas*. Of course, we use Perl to edit the file:

```
panic% perl -pi -e 's|/root|/home/stas|' \
    /home/stas/.cpan/CPAN/MyConfig.pm
```

Now that you have the local configuration file ready, you have to tell it what special parameters you need to pass when executing *perl Makefile.PL*. Open the file in your favorite editor and replace the following line:

```
'makepl_arg' => q[ ],
```

with:

```
'makepl_arg' => q[PREFIX=/home/stas],
```

Now you've finished the configuration. Assuming that you are logged in with the same username used for the local installation (*stas* in our example), start it like this:

```
panic% perl -MCPAN -e shell
```

From now on, any module you try to install will be installed locally. If you need to install some system modules, just become the superuser and install them in the same way. When you are logged in as the superuser, the system-wide configuration file will be used instead of your local one.

If you have used more than just the PREFIX variable, modify *MyConfig.pm* to use the other variables. For example, if you have used these variables during the creation of the *Makefile*:

```
panic% perl Makefile.PL PREFIX=/home/stas \
    INSTALLPRIVLIB=/home/stas/lib/perl5 \
    INSTALLSCRIPT=/home/stas/bin \
    INSTALLSITELIB=/home/stas/lib/perl5/site_perl \
    INSTALLBIN=/home/stas/bin \
    INSTALLMAN1DIR=/home/stas/lib/perl5/man  \
    INSTALLMAN3DIR=/home/stas/lib/perl5/man3
```

replace PREFIX=/home/stas in the line:

```
'makepl_arg' => q[PREFIX=/home/stas],
```

with all the variables from above, so that the line becomes:

```
'makepl_arg' => q[PREFIX=/home/stas \
    INSTALLPRIVLIB=/home/stas/lib/perl5 \
    INSTALLSCRIPT=/home/stas/bin \
    INSTALLSITELIB=/home/stas/lib/perl5/site_perl \
    INSTALLBIN=/home/stas/bin \
    INSTALLMAN1DIR=/home/stas/lib/perl5/man  \
    INSTALLMAN3DIR=/home/stas/lib/perl5/man3
],
```

If you arrange all the above parameters in one line, you can remove the backslashes (\).

Making a Local Apache Installation

Just as with Perl modules, if you don't have the permissions required to install Apache into the system area, you have to install them locally under your home directory. It's almost the same as a plain installation, but you have to run the server listening to a port number greater than 1024 (only *root* processes can listen to lower-numbered ports).

Another important issue you have to resolve is how to add startup and shutdown scripts to the directories used by the rest of the system services. Without *root* access, you won't be able to do this yourself; you'll have to ask your system administrator to assist you.

To install Apache locally, all you have to do is to tell *./configure* in the Apache source directory what target directories to use. If you are following the convention that we use, which makes your home directory look like the / (base) directory, the invocation parameters will be:

```
panic% ./configure --prefix=/home/stas
```

Apache will use the prefix for the rest of its target directories, instead of the default */usr/local/apache*. If you want to see what they are, add the *--show-layout* option before you proceed:

```
panic% ./configure --prefix=/home/stas --show-layout
```

You might want to put all the Apache files under */home/stas/apache*, following Apache's convention:

```
panic% ./configure --prefix=/home/stas/apache
```

If you want to modify some or all of the names of the automatically created directories, use the *--sbindir*, *--sysconfdir*, and *--logfiledir* options:

```
panic% ./configure --prefix=/home/stas/apache \
    --sbindir=/home/stas/apache/sbin        \
    --sysconfdir=/home/stas/apache/conf     \
    --logfiledir=/home/stas/apache/logs
```

Refer to the output of *./configure --help* for all available options.

Also remember that you can start the script only under a user and group to which you belong, so you must set the User and Group directives in *httpd.conf* to appropriate values.

Furthermore, as we said before, the Port directive in *httpd.conf* must be adjusted to use an unused port above 1024, such as 8080. This means that when users need to access the locally installed server, their URLs need to specify the port number (e.g., *http://www.example.com:8080/*). Otherwise, browsers will access the server running on port 80, which isn't the one you installed locally.

Nonstandard mod_perl-Enabled Apache Installation

Now that we know how to install local Apache and Perl modules separately, let's see how to install mod_perl-enabled Apache in our home directory. It's almost as simple as doing each one separately, but there is one wrinkle. We'll talk about it at the end of this section.

Let's say you have unpacked the Apache and mod_perl sources under */home/stas/src* and they look like this:

```
panic% ls /home/stas/src
/home/stas/src/apache_1.3.xx
/home/stas/src/mod_perl-1.xx
```

where *x.xx* are replaced by the real version numbers, as usual. You want the Perl modules from the mod_perl package to be installed under */home/stas/lib/perl5* and the Apache files to go under */home/stas/apache*. The following commands will do that for you:

```
panic% perl Makefile.PL \
    PREFIX=/home/stas \
    APACHE_PREFIX=/home/stas/apache \
    APACHE_SRC=../apache_1.3.xx/src \
    DO_HTTPD=1 \
    USE_APACI=1 \
    EVERYTHING=1
```

```
panic% make && make test && make install
panic% cd ../apache_1.3.xx
panic% make install
```

If you need some parameters to be passed to the *./configure* script, as we saw in the previous section, use `APACI_ARGS`. For example:

```
APACI_ARGS='--sbindir=/home/stas/apache/sbin  \
    --sysconfdir=/home/stas/apache/conf        \
    --logfiledir=/home/stas/apache/logs'
```

Note that the above multiline splitting will work only with Bourne-style shells. C-style shell users will have to list all the parameters on a single line.

Basically, the installation is complete. The only remaining problem is the `@INC` variable. This won't be correctly set if you rely on the `PERL5LIB` environment variable unless you set it explicitly in a startup file that is required before loading any other module that resides in your local repository. A much nicer approach is to use the `lib` pragma, as we saw before, but in a slightly different way—we use it in the startup file and it affects all the code that will be executed under mod_perl handlers. For example:

```
PerlRequire /home/stas/apache/perl/startup.pl
```

where *startup.pl* starts with:

```
use lib qw(/home/stas/lib/perl5/5.6.1/
           /home/stas/lib/perl5/site_perl/5.6.1
           /home/stas/lib/perl5/site_perl
);
```

Note that you can still use the hardcoded `@INC` modifications in the scripts themselves, but be aware that scripts modify `@INC` in `BEGIN` blocks and mod_perl executes the `BEGIN` blocks only when it performs script compilation. As a result, `@INC` will be reset to its original value after the scripts are compiled, and the hardcoded settings will be forgotten.

The only time you can alter the "original" value is during the server configuration stage, either in the startup file or by putting the following line in *httpd.conf*:

```
PerlSetEnv Perl5LIB \
/home/stas/lib/perl5/5.6.1/:/home/stas/lib/perl5/site_perl/5.6.1
```

But the latter setting will be ignored if you use the `PerlTaintcheck` setting, and we hope you do use it. See the *perlrun* manpage for more information.

The rest of the mod_perl configuration can be done just as if you were installing mod_perl as *root*.

Resource Usage

Another important thing to keep in mind is the consumption of system resources. mod_perl is memory-hungry. If you run a lot of mod_perl processes on a public, multiuser machine, most likely the system administrator of this machine will ask you to use fewer resources and may even shut down your mod_perl server and ask you to find another home for it. You have a few options:

- Reduce resource usage as explained in Chapter 21.

- Ask your ISP's system administrator whether she can set up a dedicated machine for you, so that you will be able to install as much memory as you need. If you get a dedicated machine, chances are that you will want to have *root* access, so you may be able to manage the administration yourself. You should also make sure the system administrator is responsible for a reliable electricity supply and a reliable network link. The system administrator should also make sure that the important security patches get applied and the machine is configured to be secure (not to mention having the machine physically protected, so no one will turn off the power or break it).

- The best solution might be to look for another ISP with lots of resources or one that supports mod_perl. You can find a list of these ISPs at *http://perl.apache.org/*.

Nonstandard mod_perl-Enabled Apache Installation with CPAN.pm

Again, CPAN makes installation and upgrades simpler. You have seen how to install a mod_perl-enabled server using CPAN.pm's interactive shell. You have seen how to install Perl modules and Apache locally. Now all you have to do is to merge these techniques.

Assuming that you have configured CPAN.pm to install Perl modules locally, the installation is very simple. Start the CPAN shell, set the arguments to be passed to *perl Makefile.PL* (modify the example setting to suit your needs), and tell CPAN.pm to do the rest for you:

```
panic% perl -MCPAN -eshell
cpan> o conf makepl_arg 'DO_HTTPD=1 USE_APACI=1 EVERYTHING=1 \
      PREFIX=/home/stas APACHE_PREFIX=/home/stas/apache'
cpan> install mod_perl
```

When you use CPAN.pm for local installation, you need to make sure that the value of makepl_arg is restored to its original value after the mod_perl installation is complete, because if you install other Perl modules you probably don't want to pass mod_perl flags to them. The simplest way to do this is to quit the interactive shell and then re-enter it. There is another way to do it without quitting, but it's very cumbersome—if you want to learn about the other option, refer to the CPAN.pm manpage.

How Can I Tell if mod_perl Is Running?

There are several ways to find out if mod_perl is enabled in your version of Apache. In older versions of Apache (versions earlier than 1.3.6), you could check by running *httpd -v*, but that no longer works. Now you should use *httpd -l*.

It is not enough to know that mod_perl is installed—the server needs to be configured for mod_perl as well. Refer to Chapter 4 to learn about mod_perl configuration.

Checking the error_log File

One way to check for mod_perl is to check the *error_log* file for the following message at server startup:

```
[Sat May 18 18:08:01 2002] [notice]
Apache/1.3.24 (Unix) mod_perl/1.26 configured
  -- resuming normal operations
```

Testing by Viewing /perl-status

Assuming that you have configured the `<Location /perl-status>` section in the server configuration file as explained in Chapter 9, fetch *http://www.example.com/perl-status/* using your favorite browser.

You should see something like this:

```
Embedded Perl version 5.6.1 for Apache/1.3.24 (Unix)
mod_perl/1.26 process 50880,
running since Sat May 18 18:08:01 2002
```

Testing via Telnet

Knowing the port you have configured Apache to listen on, you can use `Telnet` to talk directly to it.

Assuming that your mod_perl-enabled server listens to port 8080,[*] telnet to your server at port 8080, type `HEAD / HTTP/1.0`, and then press the Enter key twice:

```
panic% telnet localhost 8080
HEAD / HTTP/1.0
```

You should see a response like this:

```
HTTP/1.1 200 OK
Date: Mon, 06 May 2002 09:49:41 GMT
Server: Apache/1.3.24 (Unix) mod_perl/1.26
```

---

[*] If in doubt, try port 80, which is the standard HTTP port.

```
Connection: close
Content-Type: text/html; charset=iso-8859-1
```

```
Connection closed.
```

The line:

```
Server: Apache/1.3.24 (Unix) mod_perl/1.26
```

confirms that you have mod_perl installed and that its version is 1.26.

Testing via a CGI Script

Another method to test for mod_perl is to invoke a CGI script that dumps the server's environment.

We assume that you have configured the server so that scripts running under the location */perl/* are handled by the Apache::Registry handler and that you have the PerlSendHeader directive set to On.

Copy and paste the script below. Let's say you name it *test.pl* and save it at the root of the CGI scripts, which is mapped directly to the */perl* location of your server.

```
print "Content-type: text/plain\n\n";
print "Server's environment\n";
foreach ( keys %ENV ) {
    print "$_\t$ENV{$_}\n";
}
```

Make it readable and executable by the server (you may need to tune these permissions on a public host):

```
panic% chmod a+rx test.pl
```

Now fetch the URL *http://www.example.com:8080/perl/test.pl* (replacing 8080 with the port your mod_perl-enabled server is listening to). You should see something like this (the output has been edited):

```
SERVER_SOFTWARE Apache/1.3.24 (Unix) mod_perl/1.26
GATEWAY_INTERFACE       CGI-Perl/1.1
DOCUMENT_ROOT    /home/httpd/docs
REMOTE_ADDR      127.0.0.1
[more environment variables snipped]
MOD_PERL         mod_perl/1.21_01-dev
[more environment variables snipped]
```

If you see the that the value of GATEWAY_INTERFACE is CGI-Perl/1.1, everything is OK.

If there is an error, you might have to add a shebang line (#!/usr/bin/perl) as the first line of the CGI script and then try it again. If you see:

```
GATEWAY_INTERFACE       CGI/1.1
```

it means you have configured this location to run under mod_cgi and not mod_perl.

Also note that there is a $ENV{MOD_PERL} environment variable if you run under a mod_perl handler. This variable is set to the mod_perl/1.xx string, where 1.xx is the version number of mod_perl.

Based on this difference, you can write code like this:

```
BEGIN {
    # perl5.004 or better is a must under mod_perl
    require 5.004 if $ENV{MOD_PERL};
}
```

If you develop a generic Perl module aimed at mod_perl, mod_cgi, and other runtime environments, this information comes in handy, because it allows you to do mod_perl-specific things when running under mod_perl. For example, CGI.pm is mod_perl-aware: when CGI.pm knows that it is running under mod_perl, it registers a cleanup handler for its global $Q object, retrieves the query string via Apache->request->args, and does a few other things differently than when it runs under mod_cgi.

Testing via lwp-request

Assuming you have the libwww-perl (LWP) package installed, you can run the following tests. (Most likely you do have it installed, since you need it to pass mod_perl's *make test*.)

```
panic% lwp-request -e -d http://www.example.com
```

This shows you just the headers; the *-d* option disables printing the response content. If you just want to see the server version, try:

```
panic% lwp-request -e -d http://www.example.com | egrep '^Server:'
```

Of course, you should use *http://www.example.com:port_number* if your server is listening to a port other than port 80.

General Notes

This section looks at some other installation issues you may encounter.

How Do I Make the Installation More Secure?

Unix systems usually provide *chroot* or *jail* mechanisms, which allow you to run subsystems isolated from the main system. So if a subsystem gets compromised, the whole system is still safe.

The section titled "Apache" in Chapter 23 includes a few references to articles discussing these mechanisms.

Can I Run mod_perl-Enabled Apache as suExec?

The answer is definitively "no." You can't *suid* a part of a process. mod_perl lives inside the Apache process, so its UID and GID are the same as those of the Apache process.

You have to use mod_cgi if you need this functionality. See Appendix C for other possible solutions.

Should I Rebuild mod_perl if I Have Upgraded Perl?

Yes, you should. You have to rebuild the mod_perl-enabled server, because it has a hardcoded @INC variable. This points to the old Perl and is probably linked to an old libperl library. If for some reason you need to keep the old Perl version around, you can modify @INC in the startup script, but it is better to build afresh to save you from getting into a mess.

mod_auth_dbm Nuances

If you are a mod_auth_dbm or mod_auth_db user, you may need to edit Perl's Config module. When Perl is configured, it attempts to find libraries for ndbm, gdbm, db, etc. for the DB*_File modules. By default, these libraries are linked with Perl and remembered by the Config.pm module. When mod_perl is configured with Apache, the ExtUtils::Embed module requires these libraries to be linked with *httpd* so Perl extensions will work under mod_perl. However, the order in which these libraries are stored in *Config.pm* may confuse mod_auth_db*. If mod_auth_db* does not work with mod_perl, take a look at the order with the following command:

```
panic% perl -V:libs
```

Here's an example:

```
libs='-lnet -lnsl_s -lgdbm -lndbm -ldb -ldld -lm -lc -lndir -lcrypt';
```

If -lgdbm or -ldb is before -lndbm (as it is in the example), edit *Config.pm* and move -lgdbm and -ldb to the end of the list. Here's how to find *Config.pm*:

```
panic% perl -MConfig -e 'print "$Config{archlibexp}/Config.pm\n"'
```

Under Solaris, another solution for building mod_perl- and mod_auth_dbm-enabled Apache is to remove the DBM and NDBM "emulation" from *libgdbm.a*. It seems that Solaris already provides its own DBM and NDBM, and in our installation we found there's no reason to build GDBM with them.

In our *Makefile* for GDBM, we changed:

```
OBJS = $(DBM_OF) $(NDBM_OF) $(GDBM_OF)
```

to:

```
OBJS = $(GDBM_OF)
```

Then rebuild `libgdbm` before building mod_perl-enabled Apache.

References

- Apache Toolbox (*http://apachetoolbox.com/*) provides a means to easily compile Apache with about 60 different Apache modules. It is fully customizable and menu-driven. Everything is compiled from source. It checks for RPMs that might cause problems and uses *wget* to download the source automatically if it's missing.

- Several Apache web server books that discuss the installation details are listed at *http://httpd.apache.org/info/apache_books.html*.

CHAPTER 4

mod_perl Configuration

The next step after building and installing a mod_perl-enabled Apache server is to configure it. This is done in two distinct steps: getting the server running with a standard Apache configuration, and then applying mod_perl-specific configuration directives to get the full benefit out of it.

For readers who haven't previously been exposed to the Apache web server, our discussion begins with standard Apache directives and then continues with mod_perl-specific material.

The *startup.pl* file can be used in many ways to improve performance. We will talk about all these issues later in the book. In this chapter, we discuss the configuration possibilities that the *startup.pl* file gives us.

<Perl> sections are a great time saver if you have complex configuration files. We'll talk about <Perl> sections in this chapter.

Another important issue we'll cover in this chapter is how to validate the configuration file. This is especially important on a live production server. If we break something and don't validate it, the server won't restart. This chapter discusses techniques to prevent validation problems.

At the end of this chapter, we discuss various tips and tricks you may find useful for server configuration, talk about a few security concerns related to server configuration, and finally look at a few common pitfalls people encounter when they misconfigure their servers.

Apache Configuration

Apache configuration can be confusing. To minimize the number of things that can go wrong, it's a good idea to first configure Apache itself without mod_perl. So before we go into mod_perl configuration, let's look at the basics of Apache itself.

Configuration Files

Prior to Version 1.3.4, the default Apache installation used three configuration files: *httpd.conf*, *srm.conf*, and *access.conf*. Although there were historical reasons for having three separate files (dating back to the NCSA server), it stopped mattering which file you used for what a long time ago, and the Apache team finally decided to combine them. Apache Versions 1.3.4 and later are distributed with the configuration directives in a single file, *httpd.conf*. Therefore, whenever we mention a configuration file, we are referring to *httpd.conf*.

By default, *httpd.conf* is installed in the *conf* directory under the server root directory. The default server root is */usr/local/apache/* on many Unix platforms, but it can be any directory of your choice (within reason). Users new to Apache and mod_perl will probably find it helpful to keep to the directory layouts we use in this book.

There is also a special file called *.htaccess*, used for per-directory configuration. When Apache tries to access a file on the filesystem, it will first search for *.htaccess* files in the requested file's parent directories. If found, Apache scans *.htaccess* for further configuration directives, which it then applies only to that directory in which the file was found and its subdirectories. The name *.htaccess* is confusing, because it can contain almost any configuration directives, not just those related to resource access control. Note that if the following directive is in *httpd.conf*:

```
<Directory />
    AllowOverride None
</Directory>
```

Apache will not look for *.htaccess* at all unless `AllowOverride` is set to a value other than `None` in a more specific `<Directory>` section.

.htaccess can be renamed by using the `AccessFileName` directive. The following example configures Apache to look in the target directory for a file called *.acl* instead of *.htaccess*:

```
AccessFileName .acl
```

However, you must also make sure that this file can't be accessed directly from the Web, or else you risk exposing your configuration. This is done automatically for *.ht** files by Apache, but for other files you need to use:

```
<Files .acl>
    Order Allow,Deny
    Deny from all
</Files>
```

Another often-mentioned file is the startup file, usually named *startup.pl*. This file contains Perl code that will be executed at server startup. We'll discuss the *startup.pl* file in greater detail later in this chapter, in the section entitled "The Startup File."

Beware of editing *httpd.conf* without understanding all the implications. Modifying the configuration file and adding new directives can introduce security problems and have performance implications. If you are going to modify anything, read through the documentation beforehand. The Apache distribution comes with an extensive configuration manual. In addition, each section of the distributed configuration file includes helpful comments explaining how each directive should be configured and what the default values are.

If you haven't moved Apache's directories around, the installation program will configure everything for you. You can just start the server and test it. To start the server, use the *apachectl* utility bundled with the Apache distribution. It resides in the same directory as *httpd*, the Apache server itself. Execute:

```
panic% /usr/local/apache/bin/apachectl start
```

Now you can test the server, for example by accessing *http://localhost/* from a browser running on the same host.

Configuration Directives

A basic setup requires little configuration. If you moved any directories after Apache was installed, they should be updated in *httpd.conf*. Here are just a couple of examples:

```
ServerRoot   "/usr/local/apache"
DocumentRoot "/usr/local/apache/docs"
```

You can change the port to which the server is bound by editing the Port directive. This example sets the port to 8080 (the default for the HTTP protocol is 80):

```
Port 8080
```

You might want to change the user and group names under which the server will run. If Apache is started by the user *root* (which is generally the case), the parent process will continue to run as *root*, but its children will run as the user and group specified in the configuration, thereby avoiding many potential security problems. This example uses the *httpd* user and group:

```
User httpd
Group httpd
```

Make sure that the user and group *httpd* already exist. They can be created using *useradd(1)* and *groupadd(1)* or equivalent utilities.

Many other directives may need to be configured as well. In addition to directives that take a single value, there are whole sections of the configuration (such as the <Directory> and <Location> sections) that apply to only certain areas of the web space. The *httpd.conf* file supplies a few examples, and these will be discussed shortly.

<Directory>, <Location>, and <Files> Sections

Let's discuss the basics of the <Directory>, <Location>, and <Files> sections. Remember that there is more to know about them than what we list here, and the rest of the information is available in the Apache documentation. The information we'll present here is just what is important for understanding mod_perl configuration.

Apache considers directories and files on the machine it runs on as *resources*. A particular behavior can be specified for each resource; that behavior will apply to every request for information from that particular resource.

Directives in <Directory> sections apply to specific directories on the host machine, and those in <Files> sections apply only to specific files (actually, groups of files with names that have something in common). <Location> sections apply to specific URIs. Locations are given relative to the document root, whereas directories are given as absolute paths starting from the filesystem root (/). For example, in the default server directory layout where the server root is */usr/local/apache* and the document root is */usr/local/apache/htdocs*, files under the */usr/local/apache/htdocs/pub* directory can be referred to as:

```
<Directory /usr/local/apache/htdocs/pub>
</Directory>
```

or alternatively (and preferably) as:

```
<Location /pub>
</Location>
```

Exercise caution when using <Location> under Win32. The Windows family of operating systems are case-insensitive. In the above example, configuration directives specified for the location */pub* on a case-sensitive Unix machine will not be applied when the request URI is */Pub*. When URIs map to existing files, such as Apache::Registry scripts, it is safer to use the <Directory> or <Files> directives, which correctly canonicalize filenames according to local filesystem semantics.

It is up to you to decide which directories on your host machine are mapped to which locations. This should be done with care, because the security of the server may be at stake. In particular, essential system directories such as */etc/* shouldn't be mapped to locations accessible through the web server. As a general rule, it might be best to organize everything accessed from the Web under your *ServerRoot*, so that it stays organized and you can keep track of which directories are actually accessible.

Locations do not necessarily have to refer to existing physical directories, but may refer to virtual resources that the server creates upon a browser request. As you will see, this is often the case for a mod_perl server.

When a client (browser) requests a resource (URI plus optional arguments) from the server, Apache determines from its configuration whether or not to serve the request, whether to pass the request on to another server, what (if any) authentication and authorization is required for access to the resource, and which module(s) should be invoked to generate the response.

For any given resource, the various sections in the configuration may provide conflicting information. Consider, for example, a <Directory> section that specifies that authorization is required for access to the resource, and a <Files> section that says that it is not. It is not always obvious which directive takes precedence in such cases. This can be a trap for the unwary.

<Directory directoryPath> ... </Directory>

Scope: Can appear in server and virtual host configurations.

<Directory> and </Directory> are used to enclose a group of directives that will apply to only the named directory and its contents, including any subdirectories. Any directive that is allowed in a directory context (see the Apache documentation) may be used.

The path given in the <Directory> directive is either the full path to a directory, or a string containing wildcard characters (also called *globs*). In the latter case, ? matches any single character, * matches any sequence of characters, and [ ] matches character ranges. These are similar to the wildcards used by *sh* and similar shells. For example:

```
<Directory /home/httpd/docs/foo[1-2]>
    Options Indexes
</Directory>
```

will match */home/httpd/docs/foo1* and */home/httpd/docs/foo2*. None of the wildcards will match a / character. For example:

```
<Directory /home/httpd/docs>
    Options Indexes
</Directory>
```

matches */home/httpd/docs* and applies to all its subdirectories.

Matching a regular expression is done by using the <DirectoryMatch regex> ... </DirectoryMatch> or <Directory ~ regex> ... </Directory> syntax. For example:

```
<DirectoryMatch /home/www/.*/public>
    Options Indexes
</DirectoryMatch>
```

will match */home/www/foo/public* but not */home/www/foo/private*. In a regular expression, .* matches any character (represented by .) zero or more times (represented by *). This is entirely different from the shell-style wildcards used by the <Directory> directive. They make it easy to apply a common configuration to a set of public directories. As regular expressions are more flexible than globs, this method provides more options to the experienced user.

If multiple (non–regular expression) <Directory> sections match the directory (or its parents) containing a document, the directives are applied in the order of the shortest match first, interspersed with the directives from any *.htaccess* files. Consider the following configuration:

```
<Directory />
    AllowOverride None
</Directory>

<Directory /home/httpd/docs/>
    AllowOverride FileInfo
</Directory>
```

Let us detail the steps Apache goes through when it receives a request for the file */home/httpd/docs/index.html*:

1. Apply the directive `AllowOverride None` (disabling *.htaccess* files).

2. Apply the directive `AllowOverride FileInfo` for the directory */home/httpd/docs/* (which now enables *.htaccess* in */home/httpd/docs/* and its subdirectories).

3. Apply any directives in the group `FileInfo`, which control document types (`AddEncoding`, `AddLanguage`, `AddType`, etc.—see the Apache documentation for more information) found in */home/httpd/docs/.htaccess*.

<Files filename > ... </Files>

Scope: Can appear in server and virtual host configurations, as well as in *.htaccess* files.

The <Files> directive provides access control by filename and is comparable to the <Directory> and <Location> directives. <Files> should be closed with the corresponding </Files>. The directives specified within this section will be applied to any object with a basename matching the specified filename. (A basename is the last component of a path, generally the name of the file.)

<Files> sections are processed in the order in which they appear in the configuration file, after the <Directory> sections and *.htaccess* files are read, but before <Location> sections. Note that <Files> can be nested inside <Directory> sections to restrict the portion of the filesystem to which they apply. However, <Files> cannot be nested inside <Location> sections.

The filename argument should include a filename or a wildcard string, where ? matches any single character and * matches any sequence of characters, just as with <Directory> sections. Extended regular expressions can also be used, placing a tilde character (~) between the directive and the regular expression. The regular expression should be in quotes. The dollar symbol ($) refers to the end of the string. The pipe character (|) indicates alternatives, and parentheses (()) can be used for grouping. Special characters in extended regular expressions must be escaped with backslashes (\). For example:

```
<Files ~ "\.(pl|cgi)$">
    SetHandler perl-script
    PerlHandler Apache::Registry
    Options +ExecCGI
</Files>
```

would match all the files ending with the *.pl* or *.cgi* extension (most likely Perl scripts). Alternatively, the `<FilesMatch regex>` ... `</FilesMatch>` syntax can be used.

Regular Expressions

There is much more to regular expressions than what we have shown you here. As a Perl programmer, learning to use regular expressions is very important, and what you can learn there will be applicable to your Apache configuration too.

See the *perlretut* manpage and the book *Mastering Regular Expressions* by Jeffrey E. F. Friedl (O'Reilly) for more information.

<Location URI> ... </Location>

Scope: Can appear in server and virtual host configurations.

The `<Location>` directive provides for directive scope limitation by URI. It is similar to the `<Directory>` directive and starts a section that is terminated with the `</Location>` directive.

`<Location>` sections are processed in the order in which they appear in the configuration file, after the `<Directory>` sections, *.htaccess* files, and `<Files>` sections have been interpreted.

The `<Location>` section is the directive that is used most often with mod_perl.

Note that URIs do not have to refer to real directories or files within the filesystem at all; `<Location>` operates completely outside the filesystem. Indeed, it may sometimes be wise to ensure that `<Location>`s do not match real paths, to avoid confusion.

The URI may use wildcards. In a wildcard string, ? matches any single character, * matches any sequences of characters, and [ ] groups characters to match. For regular expression matches, use the `<LocationMatch regex>` ... `</LocationMatch>` syntax.

The `<Location>` functionality is especially useful when combined with the `SetHandler` directive. For example, to enable server status requests (via mod_status) but allow them only from browsers at **.example.com*, you might use:

```
<Location /status>
    SetHandler server-status
```

```
        Order Deny,Allow
        Deny from all
        Allow from .example.com
    </Location>
```

As you can see, the */status* path does not exist on the filesystem, but that doesn't matter because the filesystem isn't consulted for this request—it's passed on directly to mod_status.

Merging <Directory>, <Location>, and <Files> Sections

When configuring the server, it's important to understand the order in which the rules of each section are applied to requests. The order of merging is:

1. `<Directory>` (except for regular expressions) and *.htaccess* are processed simultaneously, with the directives in *.htaccess* overriding `<Directory>`.

2. `<DirectoryMatch>` and `<Directory ~ >` with regular expressions are processed next.

3. `<Files>` and `<FilesMatch>` are processed simultaneously.

4. `<Location>` and `<LocationMatch>` are processed simultaneously.

Apart from `<Directory>`, each group is processed in the order in which it appears in the configuration files. `<Directory>`s (group 1 above) are processed in order from the shortest directory component to the longest (e.g., first / and only then */home/www*). If multiple `<Directory>` sections apply to the same directory, they are processed in the configuration file order.

Sections inside `<VirtualHost>` sections are applied as if you were running several independent servers. The directives inside one `<VirtualHost>` section do not interact with directives in other `<VirtualHost>` sections. They are applied only after processing any sections outside the virtual host definition. This allows virtual host configurations to override the main server configuration.

If there is a conflict, sections found later in the configuration file override those that come earlier.

Subgrouping of <Directory>, <Location>, and <Files> Sections

Let's say that you want all files to be handled the same way, except for a few of the files in a specific directory and its subdirectories. For example, say you want all the files in */home/httpd/docs* to be processed as plain files, but any files ending with *.html* and *.txt* to be processed by the content handler of the Apache::Compress module (assuming that you are already running a mod_perl server):

```
    <Directory /home/httpd/docs>
        <FilesMatch "\.(html|txt)$">
```

```
        PerlHandler +Apache::Compress
    </FilesMatch>
</Directory>
```

The + before Apache::Compress tells mod_perl to load the Apache::Compress module before using it, as we will see later.

Using <FilesMatch>, it is possible to embed sections inside other sections to create subgroups that have their own distinct behavior. Alternatively, you could also use a <Files> section inside an *.htaccess* file.

Note that you can't put <Files> or <FilesMatch> sections inside a <Location> section, but you can put them inside a <Directory> section.

Options Directive Merging

Normally, if multiple Options directives apply to a directory, the most specific one is taken completely; the options are not merged.

However, if all the options on the Options directive are preceded by either a + or - symbol, the options are merged. Any options preceded by + are added to the options currently active, and any options preceded by - are removed.

For example, without any + or - symbols:

```
<Directory /home/httpd/docs>
    Options Indexes FollowSymLinks
</Directory>
<Directory /home/httpd/docs/shtml>
    Options Includes
</Directory>
```

Indexes and FollowSymLinks will be set for */home/httpd/docs/*, but only Includes will be set for the */home/httpd/docs/shtml/* directory. However, if the second Options directive uses the + and - symbols:

```
<Directory /home/httpd/docs>
    Options Indexes FollowSymLinks
</Directory>
<Directory /home/httpd/docs/shtml>
    Options +Includes -Indexes
</Directory>
```

then the options FollowSymLinks and Includes will be set for the */home/httpd/docs/shtml/* directory.

MinSpareServers, MaxSpareServers, StartServers, MaxClients, and MaxRequestsPerChild

MinSpareServers, MaxSpareServers, StartServers, and MaxClients are standard Apache configuration directives that control the number of servers being launched at server startup and kept alive during the server's operation. When Apache starts, it spawns StartServers child processes. Apache makes sure that at any given time there will be at least MinSpareServers but no more than MaxSpareServers idle servers. However, the MinSpareServers rule is completely satisfied only if the total number of live servers is no bigger than MaxClients.

MaxRequestsPerChild lets you specify the maximum number of requests to be served by each child. When a process has served MaxRequestsPerChild requests, the parent kills it and replaces it with a new one. There may also be other reasons why a child is killed, so each child will not necessarily serve this many requests; however, each child will not be allowed to serve more than this number of requests. This feature is handy to gain more control of the server, and especially to avoid child processes growing too big (RAM-wise) under mod_perl.

These five directives are very important for getting the best performance out of your server. The process of tuning these variables is described in great detail in Chapter 11.

mod_perl Configuration

When you have tested that the Apache server works on your machine, it's time to configure the mod_perl part. Although some of the configuration directives are already familiar to you, mod_perl introduces a few new ones.

It's a good idea to keep all mod_perl-related configuration at the end of the configuration file, after the native Apache configuration directives, thus avoiding any confusion.

To ease maintenance and to simplify multiple-server installations, the mod_perl-enabled Apache server configuration system provides several alternative ways to keep your configuration directives in separate places. The Include directive in *httpd.conf* lets you include the contents of other files, just as if the information were all contained in *httpd.conf*. This is a feature of Apache itself. For example, placing all mod_perl-related configuration in a separate file named *conf/mod_perl.conf* can be done by adding the following directive to *httpd.conf*:

```
Include conf/mod_perl.conf
```

If you want to include this configuration conditionally, depending on whether your Apache has been compiled with mod_perl, you can use the IfModule directive :

```
<IfModule mod_perl.c>
  Include conf/mod_perl.conf
</IfModule>
```

mod_perl adds two more directives. <Perl> sections allow you to execute Perl code from within any configuration file at server startup time. Additionally, any file containing a Perl program can be executed at server startup simply by using the PerlRequire or PerlModule directives, as we will show shortly.

Alias Configurations

For many reasons, a server can never allow access to its entire directory hierarchy. Although there is really no indication of this given to the web browser, every path given in a requested URI is therefore a virtual path; early in the processing of a request, the virtual path given in the request must be translated to a path relative to the filesystem root, so that Apache can determine what resource is really being requested. This path can be considered to be a physical path, although it may not physically exist.

For instance, in mod_perl systems, you may *intend* that the translated path does not physically exist, because your module responds when it sees a request for this non-existent path by sending a virtual document. It creates the document on the fly, specifically for that request, and the document then vanishes. Many of the documents you see on the Web (for example, most documents that change their appearance depending on what the browser asks for) do not physically exist. This is one of the most important features of the Web, and one of the great powers of mod_perl is that it allows you complete flexibility to create virtual documents.

The `ScriptAlias` and `Alias` directives provide a mapping of a URI to a filesystem directory. The directive:

```
Alias /foo /home/httpd/foo
```

will map all requests starting with */foo* to the files starting with */home/httpd/foo/*. So when Apache receives a request to *http://www.example.com/foo/test.pl*, the server will map it to the file *test.pl* in the directory */home/httpd/foo/*.

Additionally, `ScriptAlias` assigns all the requests that match the specified URI (i.e., */cgi-bin*) to be executed by mod_cgi.

```
ScriptAlias /cgi-bin /home/httpd/cgi-bin
```

is actually the same as:

```
Alias /cgi-bin /home/httpd/cgi-bin
<Location /cgi-bin>
    SetHandler cgi-script
    Options +ExecCGI
</Location>
```

where the `SetHandler` directive invokes mod_cgi. You shouldn't use the `ScriptAlias` directive unless you want the request to be processed under mod_cgi. Therefore, when configuring mod_perl sections, use `Alias` instead.

Under mod_perl, the `Alias` directive will be followed by a section with at least two directives. The first is the `SetHandler/perl-script` directive, which tells Apache to invoke mod_perl to run the script. The second directive (for example, `PerlHandler`) tells mod_perl which handler (Perl module) the script should be run under, and hence for which phase of the request. Later in this chapter, we discuss the available

Perl*Handlers[*] for the various request phases. A typical mod_perl configuration that will execute the Perl scripts under the `Apache::Registry` handler looks like this:

```
Alias /perl/ /home/httpd/perl/
<Location /perl>
    SetHandler perl-script
    PerlHandler Apache::Registry
    Options +ExecCGI
</Location>
```

The last directive tells Apache to execute the file as a program, rather than return it as plain text.

When you have decided which methods to use to run your scripts and where you will keep them, you can add the configuration directive(s) to *httpd.conf*. They will look like those below, but they will of course reflect the locations of your scripts in your filesystem and the decisions you have made about how to run the scripts:

```
ScriptAlias /cgi-bin/ /home/httpd/cgi-bin/
Alias       /perl/    /home/httpd/perl/
<Location /perl>
    SetHandler perl-script
    PerlHandler Apache::Registry
    Options +ExecCGI
</Location>
```

In the examples above, all requests issued for URIs starting with */cgi-bin* will be served from the directory */home/httpd/cgi-bin/*, and those starting with */perl* will be served from the directory */home/httpd/perl/*.

Running scripts located in the same directory under different handlers

Sometimes you will want to map the same directory to a few different locations and execute each file according to the way it was requested. For example, in the following configuration:

```
# Typical for plain cgi scripts:
ScriptAlias /cgi-bin/  /home/httpd/perl/

# Typical for Apache::Registry scripts:
Alias       /perl/     /home/httpd/perl/

# Typical for Apache::PerlRun scripts:
Alias       /cgi-perl/ /home/httpd/perl/

<Location /perl/>
    SetHandler perl-script
    PerlHandler Apache::Registry
    Options +ExecCGI
</Location>
```

---

[*] When we say `Perl*Handler`, we mean the collection of all Perl handler directives (`PerlHandler`, `PerlAccessHandler`, etc.).

```
<Location /cgi-perl/>
    SetHandler perl-script
    PerlHandler Apache::PerlRun
    Options +ExecCGI
</Location>
```

the following three URIs:

```
http://www.example.com/perl/test.pl
http://www.example.com/cgi-bin/test.pl
http://www.example.com/cgi-perl/test.pl
```

are all mapped to the same file, */home/httpd/perl/test.pl*. If *test.pl* is invoked with the URI prefix */perl*, it will be executed under the Apache::Registry handler. If the prefix is */cgi-bin*, it will be executed under mod_cgi, and if the prefix is */cgi-perl*, it will be executed under the Apache::PerlRun handler.

This means that we can have all our CGI scripts located at the same place in the file-system and call the script in any of three ways simply by changing one component of the URI (*cgi-bin|perl|cgi-perl*).

This technique makes it easy to migrate your scripts to mod_perl. If your script does not seem to work while running under mod_perl, in most cases you can easily call the script in straight mod_cgi mode or under Apache::PerlRun without making any script changes. Simply change the URL you use to invoke it.

Although in the configuration above we have configured all three Aliases to point to the same directory within our filesystem, you can of course have them point to different directories if you prefer.

This should just be a migration strategy, though. In general, it's a bad idea to run scripts in plain mod_cgi mode from a mod_perl-enabled server—the extra resource consumption is wasteful. It is better to run these on a plain Apache server.

<Location /perl> Sections

The <Location> section assigns a number of rules that the server follows when the request's URI matches the location. Just as it is a widely accepted convention to use */cgi-bin* for mod_cgi scripts, it is habitual to use */perl* as the base URI of the Perl scripts running under mod_perl. Let's review the following very widely used <Location> section:

```
Alias /perl/ /home/httpd/perl/
PerlModule Apache::Registry
<Location /perl>
    SetHandler perl-script
    PerlHandler Apache::Registry
    Options +ExecCGI
    Allow from all
    PerlSendHeader On
</Location>
```

This configuration causes all requests for URIs starting with *perl* to be handled by the mod_perl Apache module with the handler from the Apache::Registry Perl module.

Remember the Alias from the previous section? We use the same Alias here. If you use a <Location> that does not have the same Alias, the server will fail to locate the script in the filesystem. You need the Alias setting only if the code that should be executed is located in a file. Alias just provides the URI-to-filepath translation rule.

Sometimes there is no script to be executed. Instead, a method in a module is being executed, as with */perl-status*, the code for which is stored in an Apache module. In such cases, you don't need Alias settings for these <Location>s.

PerlModule is equivalent to Perl's native use( ) function call. We use it to load the Apache::Registry module, later used as a handler in the <Location> section.

Now let's go through the directives inside the <Location> section:

SetHandler perl-script
: The SetHandler directive assigns the mod_perl Apache module to handle the content generation phase.

PerlHandler Apache::Registry
: The PerlHandler directive tells mod_perl to use the Apache::Registry Perl module for the actual content generation.

Options +ExecCGI
: Options +ExecCGI ordinarily tells Apache that it's OK for the directory to contain CGI scripts. In this case, the flag is required by Apache::Registry to confirm that you really know what you're doing. Additionally, all scripts located in directories handled by Apache::Registry must be executable, another check against wayward non-script files getting left in the directory accidentally. If you omit this option, the script either will be rendered as plain text or will trigger a Save As dialog, depending on the client. *

Allow from all
: The Allow directive is used to set access control based on the client's domain or IP adress. The from all setting allows any client to run the script.

PerlSendHeader On
: The PerlSendHeader On line tells mod_perl to intercept anything that looks like a header line (such as Content-Type: text/html) and automatically turn it into a correctly formatted HTTP header the way mod_cgi does. This lets you write scripts without bothering to call the request object's send_http_header( ) method, but it adds a small overhead because of the special handling.

---

* You can use Apache::RegistryBB to skip this and a few other checks.

If you use CGI.pm's header( ) function to generate HTTP headers, you do not need to activate this directive, because CGI.pm detects that it's running under mod_perl and calls send_http_header( ) for you.

You will want to set PerlSendHeader Off for non-parsed headers (*nph*) scripts and generate all the HTTP headers yourself. This is also true for mod_perl handlers that send headers with the send_http_header( ) method, because having PerlSendHeader On as a server-wide configuration option might be a performance hit.

`</Location>`

`</Location>` closes the `<Location>` section definition.

Overriding <Location> Settings

Suppose you have:

```
<Location /foo>
    SetHandler perl-script
    PerlHandler Book::Module
</Location>
```

To remove a mod_perl handler setting from a location beneath a location where a handler is set (e.g., */foo/bar*), just reset the handler like this:

```
<Location /foo/bar>
    SetHandler default-handler
</Location>
```

Now all requests starting with */foo/bar* will be served by Apache's default handler, which serves the content directly.

PerlModule and PerlRequire

As we saw earlier, a module should be loaded before its handler can be used. PerlModule and PerlRequire are the two mod_perl directives that are used to load modules and code. They are almost equivalent to Perl's use( ) and require( ) functions (respectively) and are called from the Apache configuration file. You can pass one or more module names as arguments to PerlModule:

```
PerlModule Apache::DBI CGI DBD::Mysql
```

Generally, modules are preloaded from the startup script, which is usually called *startup.pl*. This is a file containing Perl code that is executed through the PerlRequire directive. For example:

```
PerlRequire /home/httpd/perl/lib/startup.pl
```

A PerlRequire filename can be absolute or relative to the ServerRoot or to a path in @INC.

As with any file with Perl code that gets use( )d or require( )d, it must return a true value. To ensure that this happens, don't forget to add 1; at the end of *startup.pl*.

Perl*Handlers

As mentioned in Chapter 1, Apache specifies 11 phases of the request loop. In order of processing, they are: *Post-read-request*, *URI translation*, *header parsing*, *access control*, *authentication*, *authorization*, *MIME type checking*, *fixup*, *response* (also known as the content handling phase), *logging*, and finally *cleanup*. These are the stages of a request where the Apache API allows a module to step in and do something. mod_perl provides dedicated configuration directives for each of these stages:

```
PerlPostReadRequestHandler
PerlInitHandler
PerlTransHandler
PerlHeaderParserHandler
PerlAccessHandler
PerlAuthenHandler
PerlAuthzHandler
PerlTypeHandler
PerlFixupHandler
PerlHandler
PerlLogHandler
PerlCleanupHandler
```

These configuration directives usually are referred to as Perl*Handler directives. The * in Perl*Handler is a placeholder to be replaced by something that identifies the phase to be handled. For example, PerlLogHandler is the Perl handler that (fairly obviously) handles the logging phase.

In addition, mod_perl adds a few more stages that happen outside the request loop:

PerlChildInitHandler
> Allows your modules to initialize data structures during the startup of the child process.

PerlChildExitHandler
> Allows your modules to clean up during the child process shutdown.
>
> PerlChildInitHandler and PerlChildExitHandler might be used, for example, to allocate and deallocate system resources, pre-open and close database connections, etc. They do not refer to parts of the request loop.

PerlRestartHandler
> Allows you to specify a routine that is called when the server is restarted. Since Apache always restarts itself immediately after it starts, this is a good phase for doing various initializations just before the child processes are spawned.

PerlDispatchHandler
> Can be used to take over the process of loading and executing handler code. Instead of processing the Perl*Handler directives directly, mod_perl will invoke

the routine pointed to by `PerlDispatchHandler` and pass it the Apache request object and a second argument indicating the handler that would ordinarily be invoked to process this phase. So for example, you can write a `PerlDispatchHandler` handler with a logic that will allow only specific code to be executed.

Since most mod_perl applications need to handle only the response phase, in the default compilation, most of the `Perl*Handlers` are disabled. During the *perl Makefile.PL* mod_perl build stage, you must specify whether or not you will want to handle parts of the request loop other than the usual content generation phase. If this is the case, you need to specify which phases, or build mod_perl with the option `EVERYTHING=1`, which enables them all. All the build options are covered in detail in Chapter 3.

Note that it is mod_perl that recognizes these directives, not Apache. They are mod_perl directives, and an ordinary Apache server will not recognize them. If you get error messages about these directives being "perhaps mis-spelled," it is a sure sign that the appropriate part of mod_perl (or the entire mod_perl module!) is missing from your server.

All `<Location>`, `<Directory>`, and `<Files>` sections contain a physical path specification. Like `PerlChildInitHandler` and `PerlChildExitHandler`, the directives `PerlPostReadRequestHandler` and `PerlTransHandler` cannot be used in these sections, nor in *.htaccess* files, because the path translation isn't completed and a physical path isn't known until the end of the translation (`PerlTransHandler`) phase.

`PerlInitHandler` is more of an alias; its behavior changes depending on where it is used. In any case, it is the first handler to be invoked when serving a request. If found outside any `<Location>`, `<Directory>`, or `<Files>` section, it is an alias for `PerlPostReadRequestHandler`. When inside any such section, it is an alias for `PerlHeaderParserHandler`.

Starting with the *header parsing* phase, the requested URI has been mapped to a physical server pathname, and thus `PerlHeaderParserHandler` can be used to match a `<Location>`, `<Directory>`, or `<Files>` configuration section, or to process an *.htaccess* file if such a file exists in the specified directory in the translated path.

`PerlDispatchHandler`, `PerlCleanupHandler`, and `PerlRestartHandler` do not correspond to parts of the Apache API, but allow you to fine-tune the mod_perl API. They are specified *outside* configuration sections.

The Apache documentation and the book *Writing Apache Modules with Perl and C* (O'Reilly) provide in-depth information on the request phases.

The handler( ) Subroutine

By default, the mod_perl API expects a subroutine named handler( ) to handle the request in the registered Perl*Handler module. Thus, if your module implements this subroutine, you can register the handler with mod_perl by just specifying the module name. For example, to set the PerlHandler to Apache::Foo::handler, the following setting would be sufficient:

```
PerlHandler Apache::Foo
```

mod_perl will load the specified module for you when it is first used. Please note that this approach will not preload the module at startup. To make sure it gets preloaded, you have three options:

- You can explicitly preload it with the PerlModule directive:

    ```
    PerlModule Apache::Foo
    ```

- You can preload it in the startup file:

    ```
    use Apache::Foo ( );
    ```

- You can use a nice shortcut provided by the Perl*Handler syntax:

    ```
    PerlHandler +Apache::Foo
    ```

    Note the leading + character. This directive is equivalent to:

    ```
    PerlModule Apache::Foo
    <Location ..>
        ...
        PerlHandler Apache::Foo
    </Location>
    ```

If you decide to give the handler routine a name other than handler( ) (for example, my_handler( )), you must preload the module and explicitly give the name of the handler subroutine:

```
PerlModule Apache::Foo
<Location ..>
    ...
    PerlHandler Apache::Foo::my_handler
</Location>
```

This configuration will preload the module at server startup.

If a module needs to know which handler is currently being run, it can find out with the current_callback( ) method. This method is most useful to PerlDispatchHandlers that take action for certain phases only.

```
if ($r->current_callback eq "PerlLogHandler") {
    $r->warn("Logging request");
}
```

Investigating the Request Phases

Imagine a complex server setup in which many different Perl and non-Perl handlers participate in the request processing, and one or more of these handlers misbehaves. A simple example is one where one of the handlers alters the request record, which breaks the functionality of other handlers. Or maybe a handler invoked first for any given phase of the process returns an unexpected OK status, thus preventing other handlers from doing their job. You can't just add debug statements to trace the offender—there are too many handlers involved.

The simplest solution is to get a trace of all registered handlers for each phase, stating whether they were invoked and what their return statuses were. Once such a trace is available, it's much easier to look only at the players that actually participated, thus narrowing the search path down a potentially misbehaving module.

The Apache::ShowRequest module shows the phases the request goes through, displaying module participation and response codes for each phase. The content response phase is not run, but possible modules are listed as defined. To configure it, just add this snippet to *httpd.conf*:

```
<Location /showrequest>
    SetHandler perl-script
    PerlHandler +Apache::ShowRequest
</Location>
```

To see what happens when you access some URI, add the URI to */showrequest*. Apache::ShowRequest uses PATH_INFO to obtain the URI that should be executed. So, to run */index.html* with Apache::ShowRequest, issue a request for */showrequest/index.html*. For */perl/test.pl*, issue a request for */showrequest/perl/test.pl*.

This module produces rather lengthy output, so we will show only one section from the report generated while requesting */showrequest/index.html*:

```
Running request for /index.html
Request phase: post_read_request
  [snip]
Request phase: translate_handler
    mod_perl ....................DECLINED
    mod_setenvif ................undef
    mod_auth ....................undef
    mod_access ..................undef
    mod_alias ...................DECLINED
    mod_userdir .................DECLINED
    mod_actions .................undef
    mod_imap ....................undef
    mod_asis ....................undef
    mod_cgi .....................undef
    mod_dir .....................undef
    mod_autoindex ...............undef
    mod_include .................undef
    mod_info ....................undef
```

```
        mod_status ..................undef
        mod_negotiation .............undef
        mod_mime ....................undef
        mod_log_config ..............undef
        mod_env .....................undef
        http_core ...................OK
Request phase: header_parser
  [snip]
Request phase: access_checker
  [snip]
Request phase: check_user_id
  [snip]
Request phase: auth_checker
  [snip]
Request phase: type_checker
  [snip]
Request phase: fixer_upper
  [snip]
Request phase: response handler (type: text/html)
        mod_actions .................defined
        mod_include .................defined
        http_core ...................defined
Request phase: logger
  [snip]
```

For each stage, we get a report of what modules could participate in the processing and whether they took any action. As you can see, the content response phase is not run, but possible modules are listed as defined. If we run a mod_perl script, the response phase looks like:

```
Request phase: response handler (type: perl-script)
        mod_perl ....................defined
```

Stacked Handlers

With the mod_perl *stacked handlers* mechanism, it is possible for more than one Perl*Handler to be defined and executed during any stage of a request.

Perl*Handler directives can define any number of subroutines. For example:

```
PerlTransHandler Foo::foo Bar::bar
```

Foo::foo( ) will be executed first and Bar::bar( ) second. As always, if the subroutine's name is handler( ), you can omit it.

With the Apache->push_handlers( ) method, callbacks (handlers) can be added to a stack *at runtime* by mod_perl modules.

Apache->push_handlers( ) takes the callback handler name as its first argument and a subroutine name or reference as its second. For example, let's add two handlers called my_logger1( ) and my_logger2( ) to be executed during the logging phase:

```
use Apache::Constants qw(:common);
sub my_logger1 {
```

```
    #some code here
    return OK;
}
sub my_logger2 {
    #some other code here
    return OK;
}
Apache->push_handlers("PerlLogHandler", \&my_logger1);
Apache->push_handlers("PerlLogHandler", \&my_logger2);
```

You can also pass a reference to an anonymous subroutine. For example:

```
use Apache::Constants qw(:common);

Apache->push_handlers("PerlLogHandler", sub {
    print STDERR "__ANON__ called\n";
    return OK;
});
```

After each request, this stack is erased.

All handlers will be called in turn, unless a handler returns a status other than OK or DECLINED.

To enable this feature, build mod_perl with:

```
panic% perl Makefile.PL PERL_STACKED_HANDLERS=1 [ ... ]
```

or:

```
panic% perl Makefile.PL EVERYTHING=1 [ ... ]
```

To test whether the version of mod_perl you're running can stack handlers, use the Apache->can_stack_handlers method. This method will return a true value if mod_perl was configured with PERL_STACKED_HANDLERS=1, and a false value otherwise.

Let's look at a few real-world examples where this method is used:

- The widely used CGI.pm module maintains a global object for its plain function interface. Since the object is global, under mod_perl it does not go out of scope when the request is completed, and the DESTROY method is never called. Therefore, CGI->new arranges to call the following code if it detects that the module is used in the mod_perl environment:

  ```
  Apache->push_handlers("PerlCleanupHandler", \&CGI::_reset_globals);
  ```

  This function is called during the final stage of a request, resetting CGI.pm's globals before the next request arrives.

- Apache::DCELogin establishes a DCE login context that must exist for the lifetime of a request, so the DCE::Login object is stored in a global variable. Without stacked handlers, users must set the following directive in the configuration file to destroy the context:

  ```
  PerlCleanupHandler Apache::DCELogin::purge
  ```

This is ugly. With stacked handlers, `Apache::DCELogin::handler` can call from within the code:

```
Apache->push_handlers("PerlCleanupHandler", \&purge);
```

- `Apache::DBI`, the persistent database connection module, can pre-open the connection when the child process starts via its connect_on_init( ) function. This function uses push_handlers( ) to add a `PerlChildInitHandler`:

```
Apache->push_handlers(PerlChildInitHandler => \&childinit);
```

Now when the new process gets the first request, it already has the database connection open.

`Apache::DBI` also uses push_handlers( ) to have `PerlCleanupHandler` handle rollbacks if its `AutoCommit` attribute is turned off.

- `PerlTransHandlers` (e.g., `Apache::MsqlProxy`) may decide, based on the URI or some arbitrary condition, whether or not to handle a request. Without stacked handlers, users must configure it themselves.

```
PerlTransHandler Apache::MsqlProxy::translate
PerlHandler      Apache::MsqlProxy
```

`PerlHandler` is never actually invoked unless `translate( )` sees that the request is a proxy request ($r->proxyreq). If it is a proxy request, translate( ) sets $r->handler("perl-script"), and only then will `PerlHandler` handle the request. Now users do not have to specify `PerlHandler Apache::MsqlProxy`, because the translate( ) function can set it with push_handlers( ).

Now let's write our own example using stacked handlers. Imagine that you want to piece together a document that includes footers, headers, etc. without using SSI. The following example shows how to implement it. First we prepare the code as shown in Example 4-1.

Example 4-1. Book/Compose.pm

```perl
package Book::Compose;
use Apache::Constants qw(OK);

sub header {
    my $r = shift;
    $r->send_http_header("text/plain");
    $r->print("header text\n");
    return OK;
}
sub body    {
    shift->print("body text\n");
    return OK;
}
sub footer {
    shift->print("footer text\n");
    return OK;
}
1;
```

The code defines the package Book::Compose, imports the OK constant, and defines three subroutines: header( ) to send the header, body( ) to create and send the actual content, and finally footer( ) to add a standard footer to the page. At the end of each handler we return OK, so the next handler, if any, will be executed.

To enable the construction of the page, we now supply the following configuration:

```
PerlModule Book::Compose
<Location /compose>
    SetHandler perl-script
    PerlHandler Book::Compose::header Book::Compose::body Book::Compose::footer
</Location>
```

We preload the Book::Compose module and construct the PerlHandler directive by listing the handlers in the order in which they should be invoked.[*]

Finally, let's look at the technique that allows parsing the output of another PerlHandler. For example, suppose your module generates HTML responses, but you want the same content to be delivered in plain text at a different location. This is a little trickier, but consider the following:

```
<Location /perl>
    SetHandler perl-script
    PerlHandler Book::HTMLContentGenerator
</Location>
<Location /text>
    SetHandler perl-script
    PerlHandler Book::HTML2TextConvertor Book::HTMLContentGenerator
</Location>
```

Notice that Book::HTML2TextConvertor is listed first. While its handler( ) will be called first, the actual code that does the conversion will run last, as we will explain in a moment. Now let's look at the sample code in Example 4-2.

Example 4-2. Book/HTML2TextConvertor.pm

```
package Book::HTML2TextConvertor;

sub handler {
    my $r = shift;
    untie *STDOUT;
    tie *STDOUT => __PACKAGE__, $r;
}

sub TIEHANDLE {
    my($class, $r) = @_;
    bless { r => $r}, $class;
}
```

---

[*] It may not seem to make sense to use this example, as it would be much simpler to write a single handler to call all three subroutines. But what if the three reside in different modules that are maintained by different authors?

Example 4-2. Book/HTML2TextConvertor.pm (continued)

```
sub PRINT {
    my $self = shift;
    for (@_) {
        # copy it so no 'read-only value modification' will happen
        my $line = $_;
        $line =~ s/<[^>]*>//g; # strip the html <tags>
        $self->{r}->print($line);
    }
}
```

```
1;
```

It untie( )s STDOUT and re-tie( )s it to its own package, so that content printed to STDOUT by the previous content generator in the pipe goes through this module. In the PRINT( ) method, we attempt to strip the HTML tags. Of course, this is only an example; correct HTML stripping actually requires more than one line of code and a quite complex regular expression, but you get the idea.

Perl Method Handlers

If mod_perl was built with:

```
panic% perl Makefile.PL PERL_METHOD_HANDLERS=1 [ ... ]
```

or:

```
panic% perl Makefile.PL EVERYTHING=1 [ ... ]
```

it's possible to write method handlers in addition to function handlers. This is useful when you want to write code that takes advantage of inheritance. To make the handler act as a method under mod_perl, use the $$ function prototype in the handler definition. When mod_perl sees that the handler function is prototyped with $$, it'll pass two arguments to it: the calling object or a class, depending on how it was called, and the Apache request object. So you can write the handler as:

```
sub handler ($$) {
    my($self, $r) = @_;
    # ...
}
```

The configuration is almost as usual. Just use the class name if the default method name handler( ) is used:

```
PerlHandler Book::SubClass
```

However, if you choose to use a different method name, the object-oriented notation should be used:

```
PerlHandler Book::SubClass->my_handler
```

The my_handler( ) method will then be called as a class (static) method.

Also, you can use objects created at startup to call methods. For example:

```
<Perl>
    use Book::SubClass;
    $Book::Global::object = Book::SubClass->new();
</Perl>
...
PerlHandler $Book::Global::object->my_handler
```

In this example, the my_handler( ) method will be called as an instance method on the global object $Book::Global.

PerlFreshRestart

To reload PerlRequire, PerlModule, and other use( )d modules, and to flush the Apache::Registry cache on server restart, add this directive to *httpd.conf*:

```
PerlFreshRestart On
```

You should be careful using this setting. It used to cause trouble in older versions of mod_perl, and some people still report problems using it. If you are not sure if it's working properly, a full stop and restart of the server will suffice.

Starting with mod_perl Version 1.22, PerlFreshRestart is ignored when mod_perl is compiled as a DSO. But it almost doesn't matter, as mod_perl as a DSO will do a full tear-down (calling perl_destruct( )).[*]

PerlSetEnv and PerlPassEnv

In addition to Apache's SetEnv and PassEnv directives, respectively setting and passing shell environment variables, mod_perl provides its own directives: PerlSetEnv and PerlPassEnv.

If you want to globally set an environment variable for the server, you can use the PerlSetEnv directive. For example, to configure the mod_perl tracing mechanism (as discussed in Chapter 21), add this to *httpd.conf*:

```
PerlSetEnv MOD_PERL_TRACE all
```

This will enable full mod_perl tracing.

Normally, PATH is the only shell environment variable available under mod_perl. If you need to rely on other environment variables, you can have mod_perl make those available for your code with PerlPassEnv.

For example, to forward the environment variable HOME (which is usually set to the home of the user who has invoked the server in *httpd.conf*), add:

```
PerlPassEnv HOME
```

---

[*] The parent process would leak several MB on each restart without calling perl_destruct( ).

Once you set the environment variable, it can be accessed via the %ENV hash in Perl (e.g., $ENV{HOME}).

PerlSetEnv and PerlPassEnv work just like the Apache equivalents, except that they take effect in the first phase of the Apache request cycle. The standard Apache directives SetEnv and PassEnv don't affect the environment until the fixup phase, which happens much later, just before content generation. This works for CGI scripts, which aren't run before then, but if you need to set some environment variables and access them in a handler invoked before the response stage, you should use the mod_perl directives. For example, handlers that want to use an Oracle relational database during the authentication phase might need to set the following environment variable (among others) in *httpd.conf*:

```
PerlSetEnv ORACLE_HOME /share/lib/oracle/
```

Note that PerlSetEnv will override the environment variables that were available earlier. For example, we have mentioned that PATH is always supplied by Apache itself. But if you explicitly set:

```
PerlSetEnv PATH /tmp
```

this setting will be used instead of the one set in the shell program.

As with other configuration scoping rules, if you place PerlSetEnv or PerlPassEnv in the scope of the configuration file, it will apply everywhere (unless overridden). If placed into a <Location> section, or another section in the same group, these directives will influence only the handlers in that section.

PerlSetVar and PerlAddVar

PerlSetVar is another directive introduced by mod_perl. It is very similar to PerlSetEnv, but the key/value pairs are stored in an Apache::Table object and retrieved using the dir_config( ) method.

There are two ways to use PerlSetVar. The first is the usual way, as a configuration directive. For example:

```
PerlSetVar foo bar
```

The other way is via Perl code in <Perl> sections:

```
<Perl>
    push @{ $Location{"/"}->{PerlSetVar} }, [ foo => 'bar' ];
</Perl>
```

Now we can retrieve the value of *foo* using the dir_config( ) method:

```
$foo = $r->dir_config('foo');
```

Note that you cannot use the following code in <Perl> sections, which we discuss later in this chapter:

```
<Perl>
    my %foo = (a => 0, b => 1);
```

```
    push @{ $Location{"/"}->{PerlSetVar} }, [ foo => \%foo ];
</Perl>
```

All values are passed to Apache::Table as strings, so you will get a stringified reference to a hash as a value (such as "HASH(0x87a5108)"). This cannot be turned back into the original hash upon retrieval.

However, you can use the PerlAddVar directive to push more values into the variable, emulating arrays. For example:

```
PerlSetVar foo bar
PerlAddVar foo bar1
PerlAddVar foo bar2
```

or the equivalent:

```
PerlAddVar foo bar
PerlAddVar foo bar1
PerlAddVar foo bar2
```

To retrieve the values, use the $r->dir_config->get( ) method:

```
my @foo = $r->dir_config->get('foo');
```

Obviously, you can always turn an array into a hash with Perl, so you can use this directive to pass hashes as well. Consider this example:

```
PerlAddVar foo key1
PerlAddVar foo value1
PerlAddVar foo key2
PerlAddVar foo value2
```

You can then retrieve the hash in this way:

```
my %foo = $r->dir_config->get('foo');
```

Make sure that you use an even number of elements if you store the retrieved values in a hash.

Passing a list or a hash via the PerlAddVar directive in a <Perl> section should be coded in this way:

```
<Perl>
  my %foo = (a => 0, b => 1);
  for (%foo) {
      push @{ $Location{"/"}->{PerlAddVar} }, [ foo => $_ ];
  }
</Perl>
```

Now you get back the hash as before:

```
my %foo = $r->dir_config->get('foo');
```

This might not seem very practical; if you have more complex needs, think about having dedicated configuration files.

Customized configuration directives can also be created for the specific needs of a Perl module. To learn how to create these, please refer to Chapter 8 of *Writing Apache Modules with Perl and C* (O'Reilly), which covers this topic in great detail.

PerlSetupEnv

Certain Perl modules used in CGI code (such as `CGI.pm`) rely on a number of environment variables that are normally set by mod_cgi. For example, many modules depend on `QUERY_STRING`, `SCRIPT_FILENAME`, and `REQUEST_URI`. When the `PerlSetupEnv` directive is turned on, mod_perl provides these environment variables in the same fashion that mod_cgi does. This directive is `On` by default, which means that all the environment variables you are accustomed to being available under mod_cgi are also available under mod_perl.

The process of setting these environment variables adds overhead for each request, whether the variables are needed or not. If you don't use modules that rely on this behavior, you can turn it off in the general configuration and then turn it on in sections that need it (such as legacy CGI scripts):

```
PerlSetupEnv Off
<Location /perl-run>
    SetHandler perl-script
    PerlHandler Apache::PerlRun
    Options +ExecCGI
    PerlSetupEnv On
</Location>
```

You can use mod_perl methods to access the information provided by these environment variables (e.g., `$r->path_info` instead of `$ENV{PATH_INFO}`). For more details, see the explanation in Chapter 11.

PerlWarn and PerlTaintCheck

`PerlWarn` and `PerlTaintCheck` have two possible values, `On` and `Off`. `PerlWarn` turns warnings on and off globally to the whole server, and `PerlTaintCheck` controls whether the server is running with taint checking or not. These two variables are also explained in Chapter 6.

The Startup File

At server startup, before child processes are spawned, you can do much more than just preload modules. You might want to register code that will initialize a database connection for each child when it is forked, tie read-only DBM files, fill in shared caches, etc.

The *startup.pl* file is an ideal place to put code that should be executed when the server starts. Once you have prepared the code, load it in *httpd.conf* before other mod_perl configuration directives with the `PerlRequire` directive:

```
PerlRequire  /home/httpd/perl/lib/startup.pl
```

Be careful with the startup file. Everything run at server initialization is run with *root* privileges if you start the server as *root* (which you have to do unless you choose to run the server on an unprivileged port, numbered 1024 or higher). This means that anyone who has write access to a script or module that is loaded by `PerlModule`, `PerlRequire`, or `<Perl>` sections effectively has *root* access to the system.

A Sample Startup File

Let's look at a real-world startup file. The elements of the file are shown here, followed by their descriptions.

```
use strict;
```

This pragma is worth using in every script longer than half a dozen lines. It will save a lot of time and debugging later.

```
use lib qw(/home/httpd/lib /home/httpd/extra-lib);
```

This permanently adds extra directories to @INC, something that's possible only during server startup. At the end of each request's processing, mod_perl resets @INC to the value it had after the server startup. Alternatively, you can use the PERL5LIB environment variable to add extra directories to @INC.

```
$ENV{MOD_PERL} or die "not running under mod_perl!";
```

This is a sanity check. If mod_perl wasn't properly built, the server startup is aborted.

```
use Apache::Registry ();
use LWP::UserAgent ();
use Apache::DBI ();
use DBI ();
```

Preload the modules that get used by Perl code serving requests. Unless you need the symbols (variables and subroutines) exported by preloaded modules to accomplish something within the startup file, don't import them—it's just a waste of startup time and memory. Instead, use the empty import list ( ) to tell the `import( )` function not to import anything.

```
use Carp ();
$SIG{__WARN__} = \&Carp::cluck;
```

This is a useful snippet to enable extended warnings logged in the *error_log* file. In addition to basic warnings, a trace of calls is added. This makes tracking potential problems a much easier task, since you know who called what.

The only drawback of this method is that it globally overrides the default warning handler behavior—thus, in some places it might be desirable to change the settings locally (for example, with `local $^W=0`, or `no warnings` under Perl 5.6.0 and higher). Usually warnings are turned off on production machines to prevent unnecessary clogging of the *error_log* file if your code is not very clean. Hence, this method is mostly useful in a development environment.

```
use CGI ();
CGI->compile(':all');
```

Some modules, such as CGI.pm, create their subroutines at runtime via AUTOLOAD to improve their loading time. This helps when the module includes many subroutines but only a few are actually used. (Also refer to the AutoSplit manpage.) Since the module is loaded only once with mod_perl, it might be a good idea to precompile all or some of its methods at server startup. This avoids the overhead of compilation at runtime. It also helps share more compiled code between child processes.

CGI.pm's compile() method performs this task. Note that compile() is specific to CGI.pm; other modules that implement this feature may use another name for the compilation method.

As with all modules we preload in the startup file, we don't import symbols from them because they will be lost when they go out of the file's scope.

The following code snippet makes sure that when the child process is spawned, a connection to the database is opened automatically, avoiding this performance hit on the first request:

```
Apache::DBI->connect_on_init
  ("DBI:mysql:database=test;host=localhost",
   "user", "password", {
                         PrintError => 1, # warn() on errors
                         RaiseError => 0, # don't die on error
                         AutoCommit => 1, # commit executes immediately
                        }
  );
```

We discuss this method in detail in Chapter 20.

The file ends with 1; so it can be successfully loaded by Perl.

The entire *startup.pl* file is shown in Example 4-3.

Example 4-3. startup.pl

```
use strict;

use lib qw(/home/httpd/lib /home/httpd/extra-lib);
$ENV{MOD_PERL} or die "not running under mod_perl!";

use Apache::Registry ();
use LWP::UserAgent ();
use Apache::DBI ();
use DBI ();

use Carp ();
$SIG{__WARN__} = \&Carp::cluck;
```

Example 4-3. startup.pl (continued)

```
use CGI ();
CGI->compile(':all');

Apache::DBI->connect_on_init
  ("DBI:mysql:database=test;host=localhost",
   "user", "password", {
                         PrintError => 1, # warn() on errors
                         RaiseError => 0, # don't die on error
                         AutoCommit => 1, # commit executes immediately
                        }
  );
1;
```

Syntax Validation

If the startup file doesn't include any modules that require the mod_perl runtime environment during their loading, you can validate its syntax with:

```
panic% perl -cw /home/httpd/perl/lib/startup.pl
```

The *-c* switch tells Perl to validate only the file's syntax, and the *-w* switch enables warnings.

Apache::DBI is an example of a module that cannot be loaded outside of the mod_perl environment. If you try to load it, you will get the following error message:

```
panic% perl -MApache::DBI -c -e 1
Can't locate object method "module" via package "Apache"
(perhaps you forgot to load "Apache"?) at
/usr/lib/perl5/site_perl/5.6.1/Apache/DBI.pm line 202.
Compilation failed in require.
BEGIN failed--compilation aborted.
```

However, Apache::DBI will work perfectly once loaded from within mod_perl.

What Modules Should Be Added to the Startup File

Every module loaded at server startup will be shared among the server children, saving a lot of RAM on your machine. Usually, we put most of the code we develop into modules and preload them.

You can even preload CGI scripts with Apache::RegistryLoader, as explained in Chapter 10.

The Confusion with use( ) in the Server Startup File

Some people wonder why they need to duplicate use Modulename in the startup file and in the script itself. The confusion arises due to misunderstanding use(). Let's take the POSIX module as an example. When you write:

```
use POSIX qw(setsid);
```

use( ) internally performs two operations:

```
BEGIN {
    require POSIX;
    POSIX->import(qw(setsid));
}
```

The first operation loads and compiles the module. The second calls the module's import( ) method and specifies to import the symbol *setsid* into the caller's namespace. The BEGIN block makes sure that the code is executed as soon as possible, before the rest of the code is even parsed. POSIX, like many other modules, specifies a default export list. This is an especially extensive list, so when you call:

```
use POSIX;
```

about 500 KB worth of symbols gets imported.

Usually, we don't need POSIX or its symbols in the startup file; all we want is to preload it. Therefore, we use an empty list as an argument for use( ):

```
use POSIX ( );
```

so the POSIX::import( ) method won't be even called.

When we want to use the POSIX module in the code, we use( ) it again, but this time no loading overhead occurs because the module has been loaded already. If we want to import something from the module, we supply the list of symbols to load:

```
use POSIX qw(:flock_h);
```

This example loads constants used with the flock( ) function.

Technically, you aren't required to supply the use( ) statement in your handler code if the module has already been loaded during server startup or elsewhere. When writing your code, however, don't assume that the module code has been preloaded. Someday in the future, you or someone else will revisit this code and will not understand how it is possible to use a module's methods without first loading the module itself.

Please refer to the *Exporter* and *perlmod* manpages, and to the section on use( ) in the *perlfunc* manpage for more information about import( ).

Remember that you can always use require( ) to preload the files at server startup if you don't add ( ), because:

```
require Data::Dumper;
```

is the same as:

```
use Data::Dumper ( );
```

except that it's not executed at compile-time.

Apache Configuration in Perl

With <Perl> ... </Perl> sections, you can configure your server entirely in Perl. It's probably not worth it if you have simple configuration files, but if you run many virtual hosts or have complicated setups for any other reason, <Perl> sections become very handy. With <Perl> sections you can easily create the configuration on the fly, thus reducing duplication and easing maintenance.*

To enable <Perl> sections, build mod_perl with:

```
panic% perl Makefile.PL PERL_SECTIONS=1 [ ... ]
```

or with EVERYTHING=1.

Constructing <Perl> Sections

<Perl> sections can contain any and as much Perl code as you wish. <Perl> sections are compiled into a special package called Apache::ReadConfig. mod_perl looks through the symbol table for Apache::ReadConfig for Perl variables and structures to grind through the Apache core configuration gears. Most of the configuration directives can be represented as scalars ($scalar) or arrays (@array). A few directives become hashes.

How do you know which Perl global variables to use? Just take the Apache directive name and prepend either $, @, or % (as shown in the following examples), depending on what the directive accepts. If you misspell the directive, it is silently ignored, so it's a good idea to check your settings.

Since Apache directives are case-insensitive, their Perl equivalents are case-insensitive as well. The following statements are equivalent:

```
$User = 'stas';
$user = 'stas'; # the same
```

Let's look at all possible cases we might encounter while configuring Apache in Perl:

- Directives that accept zero or one argument are represented as scalars. For example, CacheNegotiatedDocs is a directive with no arguments. In Perl, we just assign it an empty string:

```
<Perl>
    $CacheNegotiatedDocs = '';
</Perl>
```

Directives that accept a single value are simple to handle. For example, to configure Apache so that child processes run as user *httpd* and group *httpd*, use:

```
User  = httpd
Group = httpd
```

What if we don't want user and group definitions to be hardcoded? Instead, what if we want to define them on the fly using the user and group with which the server is started? This is easily done with <Perl> sections:

---

* You may also find that mod_macro is useful to simplify the configuration if you have to insert many repetitive configuration snippets.

```
<Perl>
    $User  = getpwuid($>) || $>;
    $Group = getgrgid($)) || $);
</Perl>
```

We use the power of the Perl API to retrieve the data on the fly. $User is set to the name of the effective user ID with which the server was started or, if the name is not defined, the numeric user ID. Similarly, $Group is set to either the symbolic value of the effective group ID or the numeric group ID.

Notice that we've just taken the Apache directives and prepended a $, as they represent scalars.

- Directives that accept more than one argument are represented as arrays or as a space-delimited string. For example, this directive:

```
PerlModule Mail::Send Devel::Peek
```

becomes:

```
<Perl>
    @PerlModule = qw(Mail::Send Devel::Peek);
</Perl>
```

@PerlModule is an array variable, and we assign it a list of modules. Alternatively, we can use the scalar notation and pass all the arguments as a space-delimited string:

```
<Perl>
    $PerlModule = "Mail::Send Devel::Peek";
</Perl>
```

- Directives that can be repeated more than once with different values are represented as arrays of arrays. For example, this configuration:

```
AddEncoding x-compress Z
AddEncoding x-gzip gz tgz
```

becomes:

```
<Perl>
    @AddEncoding = (
        ['x-compress' => qw(Z)],
        ['x-gzip'     => qw(gz tgz)],
    );
</Perl>
```

- Directives that implement a container block, with beginning and ending delimiters such as <Location> ... </Location>, are represented as Perl hashes. In these hashes, the keys are the arguments of the opening directive, and the values are the contents of the block. For example:

```
Alias /private /home/httpd/docs/private
<Location /private>
    DirectoryIndex  index.html index.htm
    AuthType        Basic
    AuthName        "Private Area"
    AuthUserFile    /home/httpd/docs/private/.htpasswd
    Require         valid-user
</Location>
```

These settings tell Apache that URIs starting with *private* are mapped to the physical directory */home/httpd/docs/private/* and will be processed according to the following rules:

— The users are to be authenticated using basic authentication.

— *PrivateArea* will be used as the title of the pop-up box displaying the login and password entry form.

— Only valid users listed in the password file */home/httpd/docs/private/.htpasswd* and who provide a valid password may access the resources under */private/*.

— If the filename is not provided, Apache will attempt to respond with the *index.html* or *index.htm* directory index file, if found.

Now let's see the equivalent <Perl> section:

```
<Perl>
    push @Alias, qw(/private /home/httpd/docs/private);
    $Location{"/private"} = {
        DirectoryIndex => [qw(index.html index.htm)],
        AuthType       => 'Basic',
        AuthName       => '"Private Area"',
        AuthUserFile   => '/home/httpd/docs/private/.htpasswd',
        Require        => 'valid-user',
    };
</Perl>
```

First, we convert the Alias directive into an array @Alias. Instead of assigning, however, we push the values at the end. We do this because it's possible that we have assigned values earlier, and we don't want to overwrite them. Alternatively, you may want to push references to lists, like this:

```
push @Alias, [qw(/private /home/httpd/docs/private)];
```

Second, we convert the Location block, using *private* as a key to the hash %Location and the rest of the block as its value. When the structures are nested, the normal Perl rules apply—that is, arrays and hashes turn into references. Therefore, DirectoryIndex points to an array reference. As shown earlier, we can always replace this array with a space-delimited string:

```
$Location{"/private"} = {
    DirectoryIndex => 'index.html index.htm',
    ...
};
```

Also notice how we specify the value of the AuthName attribute:

```
AuthName => '"Private Area"',
```

The value is quoted twice because Apache expects a single value for this argument, and if we write:

```
AuthName => 'Private Area',
```

<Perl> will pass two values to Apache, "Private" and "Area", and Apache will refuse to start, with the following complaint:

```
[Thu May 16 17:01:20 2002] [error] <Perl>: AuthName takes one
argument, The authentication realm (e.g. "Members Only")
```

- If a block section accepts two or more identical keys (as the <VirtualHost> ... </VirtualHost> section does), the same rules as in the previous case apply, but a reference to an array of hashes is used instead.

In one company, we had to run an Intranet machine behind a NAT/firewall (using the 10.0.0.10 IP address). We decided up front to have two virtual hosts to make both the management and the programmers happy. We had the following simplistic setup:

```
NameVirtualHost 10.0.0.10

<VirtualHost 10.0.0.10>
    ServerName   tech.intranet
    DocumentRoot /home/httpd/docs/tech
    ServerAdmin webmaster@tech.intranet
</VirtualHost>

<VirtualHost 10.0.0.10>
    ServerName   suit.intranet
    DocumentRoot /home/httpd/docs/suit
    ServerAdmin  webmaster@suit.intranet
</VirtualHost>
```

In Perl, we wrote it as follows:

```
<Perl>
    $NameVirtualHost => '10.0.0.10';
    my $doc_root = "/home/httpd/docs";
    $VirtualHost{'10.0.0.10'} = [
        {
          ServerName   => 'tech.intranet',
          DocumentRoot => "$doc_root/tech",
          ServerAdmin  => 'webmaster@tech.intranet',
        },
        {
          ServerName   => 'suit.intranet',
          DocumentRoot => "$doc_root/suit",
          ServerAdmin  => 'webmaster@suit.intranet',
        },
    ];
</Perl>
```

Because normal Perl rules apply, more entries can be added as needed using push( ).* Let's say we want to create a special virtual host for the company's president to show off to his golf partners, but his fancy vision doesn't really fit the purpose of the Intranet site. We just let him handle his own site:

```
push @{ $VirtualHost{'10.0.0.10'} },
    {
      ServerName   => 'president.intranet',
```

---

* For complex configurations with multiple entries, consider using the module Tie::DxHash, which implements a hash that preserves insertion order and allows duplicate keys.

```
    DocumentRoot => "$doc_root/president",
    ServerAdmin  => 'webmaster@president.intranet',
    };
```

- Nested block directives naturally become Perl nested data structures. Let's extend an example from the previous section:

```
<Perl>
    my $doc_root = "/home/httpd/docs";
    push @{ $VirtualHost{'10.0.0.10'} },
        {
        ServerName    => 'president.intranet',
        DocumentRoot  => "$doc_root/president",
        ServerAdmin   => 'webmaster@president.intranet',
        Location      => {
            "/private"    => {
                Options       => 'Indexes',
                AllowOverride => 'None',
                AuthType      => 'Basic',
                AuthName      => '"Do Not Enter"',
                AuthUserFile  => 'private/.htpasswd',
                Require       => 'valid-user',
            },
            "/perlrun" => {
                SetHandler    => 'perl-script',
                PerlHandler   => 'Apache::PerlRun',
                PerlSendHeader => 'On',
                Options       => '+ExecCGI',
            },
        },
    };
</Perl>
```

We have added two Location blocks. The first, */private*, is for the juicy stuff and accessible only to users listed in the president's password file. The second, */perlrun*, is for running dirty Perl CGI scripts, to be handled by the Apache::PerlRun handler.

- <Perl> sections don't provide equivalents for <IfModule> and <IfDefine> containers. Instead, you can use the module( ) and define( ) methods from the Apache package. For example:

```
<IfModule mod_ssl.c>
    Include ssl.conf
</IfModule>
```

can be written as:

```
if (Apache->module("mod_ssl.c")) {
    push @Include, "ssl.conf";
}
```

And this configuration example:

```
<IfDefine SSL>
    Include ssl.conf
</IfDefine>
```

can be written as:

```
if (Apache->define("SSL")) {
    push @Include, "ssl.conf";
}
```

Now that you know how to convert the usual configuration directives to Perl code, there's no limit to what you can do with it. For example, you can put environment variables in an array and then pass them all to the children with a single configuration directive, rather than listing each one via PassEnv or PerlPassEnv:

```
<Perl>
    my @env = qw(MYSQL_HOME CVS_RSH);
    push @PerlPassEnv, \@env;
</Perl>
```

Or suppose you have a cluster of machines with similar configurations and only small distinctions between them. Ideally, you would want to maintain a single configuration file, but because the configurations aren't *exactly* the same (for example, the ServerName directive will have to differ), it's not quite that simple.

<Perl> sections come to the rescue. Now you can have a single configuration file and use the full power of Perl to tweak the local configuration. For example, to solve the problem of the ServerName directive, you might have this <Perl> section:

```
<Perl>
    use Sys::Hostname;
    $ServerName = hostname();
</Perl>
```

and the right machine name will be assigned automatically.

Or, if you want to allow personal directories on all machines except the ones whose names start with *secure*, you can use:

```
<Perl>
    use Sys::Hostname;
    $ServerName = hostname();
    if ($ServerName !~ /^secure/) {
        $UserDir = "public.html";
    }
</Perl>
```

Breaking Out of <Perl> Sections

Behind the scenes, mod_perl defines a package called Apache::ReadConfig in which it keeps all the variables that you define inside the <Perl> sections. So <Perl> sections aren't the only way to use mod_perl to configure the server: you can also place the Perl code in a separate file that will be called during the configuration parsing with either PerlModule or PerlRequire directives, or from within the startup file. All you have to do is to declare the package Apache::ReadConfig before writing any code in this file.

Using the last example from the previous section, we place the code into a file named *apache_config.pl*, shown in *Example 4-4*.

Example 4-4. apache_config.pl

```
package Apache::ReadConfig;

use Sys::Hostname;
$ServerName = hostname();
if ($ServerName !~ /^secure/) {
    $UserDir = "public.html";
}
1;
```

Then we execute it either from *httpd.conf*:

```
PerlRequire /home/httpd/perl/lib/apache_config.pl
```

or from the *startup.pl* file:

```
require "/home/httpd/perl/lib/apache_config.pl";
```

Cheating with Apache->httpd_conf

In fact, you can create a complete configuration file in Perl. For example, instead of putting the following lines in *httpd.conf*:

```
NameVirtualHost         10.0.0.10

<VirtualHost 10.0.0.10>
    ServerName   tech.intranet
    DocumentRoot /home/httpd/httpd_perl/docs/tech
    ServerAdmin webmaster@tech.intranet
</VirtualHost>

<VirtualHost 10.0.0.10>
    ServerName   suit.intranet
    DocumentRoot /home/httpd/httpd_perl/docs/suit
    ServerAdmin webmaster@suit.intranet
</VirtualHost>
```

You can write it in Perl:

```
use Socket;
use Sys::Hostname;
my $hostname = hostname();
(my $domain = $hostname) =~ s/[^.]+\.//;
my $ip = inet_ntoa(scalar gethostbyname($hostname || 'localhost'));
my $doc_root = '/home/httpd/docs';

Apache->httpd_conf(qq{
NameVirtualHost $ip

<VirtualHost $ip>
  ServerName   tech.$domain
```

```
    DocumentRoot $doc_root/tech
    ServerAdmin webmaster\@tech.$domain
  </VirtualHost>

  <VirtualHost $ip>
    ServerName   suit.$domain
    DocumentRoot $doc_root/suit
    ServerAdmin  webmaster\@suit.$domain
  </VirtualHost>
   });
```

First, we prepare the data, such as deriving the domain name and IP address from the hostname. Next, we construct the configuration file in the "usual" way, but using the variables that were created on the fly. We can reuse this configuration file on many machines, and it will work anywhere without any need for adjustment.

Now consider that you have many more virtual hosts with a similar configuration. You have probably already guessed what we are going to do next:

```
use Socket;
use Sys::Hostname;
my $hostname = hostname();
(my $domain = $hostname) =~ s/[^.]+\.//;
my $ip = inet_ntoa(scalar gethostbyname($hostname || 'localhost'));
my $doc_root = '/home/httpd/docs';
my @vhosts = qw(suit tech president);

Apache->httpd_conf("NameVirtualHost $ip");

for my $vh (@vhosts) {
  Apache->httpd_conf(qq{
<VirtualHost $ip>
  ServerName   $vh.$domain
  DocumentRoot $doc_root/$vh
  ServerAdmin webmaster\@$vh.$domain
</VirtualHost>
  });
}
```

In the loop, we create new virtual hosts. If we need to create 100 hosts, it doesn't take a long time—just adjust the @vhosts array.

Declaring Package Names in Perl Sections

Be careful when you declare package names inside <Perl> sections. For example, this code has a problem:

```
<Perl>
    package Book::Trans;
    use Apache::Constants qw(:common);
    sub handler { OK }

    $PerlTransHandler = "Book::Trans";
</Perl>
```

When you put code inside a <Perl> section, by default it goes into the Apache::ReadConfig package, which is already declared for you. This means that the PerlTransHandler we tried to define will be ignored, since it's not a global variable in the Apache::ReadConfig package.

If you define a different package name within a <Perl> section, make sure to close the scope of that package and return to the Apache::ReadConfig package when you want to define the configuration directives. You can do this by either explicitly declaring the Apache::ReadConfig package:

```
<Perl>
    package Book::Trans;
    use Apache::Constants qw(:common);
    sub handler { OK }

    package Apache::ReadConfig;
    $PerlTransHandler = "Book::Trans";
</Perl>
```

or putting the code that resides in a different package into a block:

```
<Perl>
    {
        package Book::Trans;
        use Apache::Constants qw(:common);
        sub handler { OK }
    }

    $PerlTransHandler = "Book::Trans";
</Perl>
```

so that when the block is over, the Book::Trans package's scope is over, and you can use the configuration variables again.

However, it's probably a good idea to use <Perl> sections only to create or adjust configuration directives. If you need to run some other code not related to configuration, it might be better to place it in the startup file or in its own module. Your mileage may vary, of course.

Verifying <Perl> Sections

How do we know whether the configuration made inside <Perl> sections was correct?

First we need to check the validity of the Perl syntax. To do that, we should turn it into a Perl script, by adding #!perl at the top of the section:

```
<Perl>
#!perl
# ... code here ...
__END__
</Perl>
```

Notice that #!perl and __END__ must start from the column zero. Also, the same rules as we saw earlier with validation of the startup file apply: if the <Perl> section includes some modules that can be loaded only when mod_perl is running, this validation is not applicable.

Now we may run:

```
perl -cx httpd.conf
```

If the Perl code doesn't compile, the server won't start. If the Perl code is syntactically correct, but the generated Apache configuration is invalid, <Perl> sections will just log a warning and carry on, since there might be globals in the section that are not intended for the configuration at all.

If you have more than one <Perl> section, you will have to repeat this procedure for each section, to make sure they all work.

To check the Apache configuration syntax, you can use the variable $Apache::Server::StrictPerlSections, added in mod_perl Version 1.22. If you set this variable to a true value:

```
$Apache::Server::StrictPerlSections = 1;
```

then mod_perl will not tolerate invalid Apache configuration syntax and will croak (die) if it encounters invalid syntax. The default value is 0. If you don't set $Apache::Server::StrictPerlSections to 1, you should localize variables unrelated to configuration with my() to avoid errors.

If the syntax is correct, the next thing we need to look at is the parsed configuration as seen by Perl. There are two ways to see it. First, we can dump it at the end of the section:

```
<Perl>
    use Apache::PerlSections ();
    # code goes here
    print STDERR Apache::PerlSections->dump();
</Perl>
```

Here, we load the Apache::PerlSections module at the beginning of the section, and at the end we can use its dump() method to print out the configuration as seen by Perl. Notice that only the configuration created in the section will be seen in the dump. No plain Apache configuration can be found there.

For example, if we adjust this section (parts of which we have seen before) to dump the parsed contents:

```
<Perl>
    use Apache::PerlSections ();
    $User  = getpwuid($>) || $>;
    $Group = getgrgid($)) || $);
    push @Alias, [qw(/private /home/httpd/docs/private)];
    my $doc_root = "/home/httpd/docs";
    push @{ $VirtualHost{'10.0.0.10'} },
```

```
              {
                ServerName   => 'president.intranet',
                DocumentRoot => "$doc_root/president",
                ServerAdmin  => 'webmaster@president.intranet',
                Location     => {
                    "/private"    => {
                        Options       => 'Indexes',
                        AllowOverride => 'None',
                        AuthType      => 'Basic',
                        AuthName      => '"Do Not Enter"',
                        AuthUserFile  => 'private/.htpasswd',
                        Require       => 'valid-user',
                    },
                    "/perlrun" => {
                        SetHandler    => 'perl-script',
                        PerlHandler   => 'Apache::PerlRun',
                        PerlSendHeader => 'On',
                        Options       => '+ExecCGI',
                    },
                },
              },
            };
        print STDERR Apache::PerlSections->dump( );
    </Perl>
```

This is what we get as a dump:

```
    package Apache::ReadConfig;
    #hashes:

    %VirtualHost = (
      '10.0.0.10' => [
        {
          'Location' => {
            '/private' => {
              'AllowOverride' => 'None',
              'AuthType' => 'Basic',
              'Options' => 'Indexes',
              'AuthUserFile' => 'private/.htpasswd',
              'AuthName' => '"Do Not Enter"',
              'Require' => 'valid-user'
            },
            '/perlrun' => {
              'PerlHandler' => 'Apache::PerlRun',
              'Options' => '+ExecCGI',
              'PerlSendHeader' => 'On',
              'SetHandler' => 'perl-script'
            }
          },
          'DocumentRoot' => '/home/httpd/docs/president',
          'ServerAdmin' => 'webmaster@president.intranet',
          'ServerName' => 'president.intranet'
        }
      ]
    );
```

```
#arrays:

@Alias = (
  [
    '/private',
    '/home/httpd/docs/private'
  ]
);

#scalars:

$Group = 'stas';

$User = 'stas';

1;
__END__
```

You can see that the configuration was created properly. The dump places the output into three groups: arrays, hashes, and scalars. The server was started as user *stas*, so the $User and $Group settings were dynamically assigned to the user *stas*.

A different approach to seeing the dump at any time (not only during startup) is to use the Apache::Status module (see Chapter 9). First we store the Perl configuration:

```
<Perl>
    $Apache::Server::SaveConfig = 1;
    # the actual configuration code
</Perl>
```

Now the Apache::ReadConfig namespace (in which the configuration data is stored) will not be flushed, making configuration data available to Perl modules at request time. If the Apache::Status module is configured, you can view it by going to the */perl-status* URI (or another URI that you have chosen) in your browser and selecting "Perl Section Configuration" from the menu. The configuration data should look something like that shown in Figure 4-1.

Since the Apache::ReadConfig namespace is not flushed when the server is started, you can access the configuration values from your code—the data resides in the Apache::ReadConfig package. So if you had the following Perl configuration:

```
<Perl>
    $Apache::Server::SaveConfig = 1;
    $DocumentRoot = "/home/httpd/docs/mine";
</Perl>
```

at request time, you could access the value of $DocumentRoot with the fully qualified name $Apache::ReadConfig::DocumentRoot. But usually you don't need to do this, because mod_perl provides you with an API to access to the most interesting and useful server configuration bits.

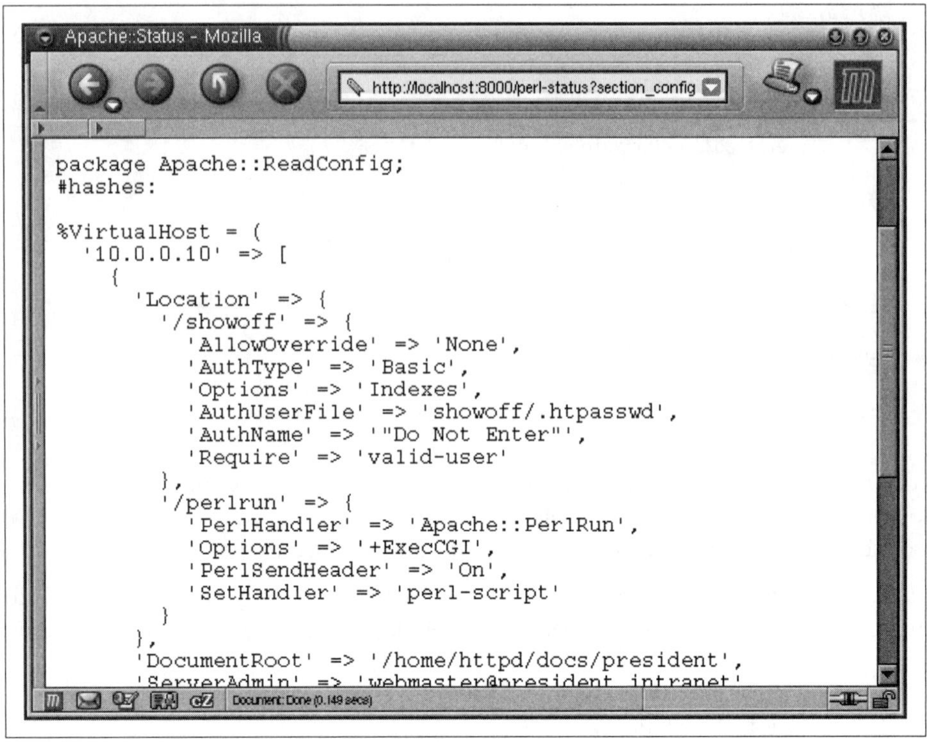

Figure 4-1. <Perl> sections configuration dump

Saving the Perl Configuration

Instead of dumping the generated Perl configuration, you may decide to store it in a file. For example, if you want to store it in *httpd_config.pl*, you can do the following:

```
<Perl>
    use Apache::PerlSections ();
    # code goes here
    Apache::PerlSections->store("httpd_config.pl");
</Perl>
```

You can then require( ) that file in some other <Perl> section. If you have the whole server configuration in Perl, you can start the server using the following trick:

```
panic% httpd -C "PerlRequire httpd_config.pl"
```

Apache will fetch all the configuration directives from *httpd_config.pl*, so you don't need *httpd.conf* at all.

Debugging

If your configuration doesn't seem to do what it's supposed to do, you should debug it. First, build mod_perl with:

```
panic% perl Makefile.PL PERL_TRACE=1 [...]
```

Next, set the environment variable MOD_PERL_TRACE to s (as explained in Chapter 21). Now you should be able to see how the <Perl> section globals are converted into directive string values. For example, suppose you have the following Perl section:

```
<Perl>
    $DocumentRoot = "/home/httpd/docs/mine";
</Perl>
```

If you start the server in single-server mode (e.g., under *bash*):

```
panic% MOD_PERL_TRACE=s httpd -X
```

you will see these lines among the printed trace:

```
...
SVt_PV: $DocumentRoot = `/home/httpd/docs/mine'
handle_command (DocumentRoot /home/httpd/docs/mine): OK
...
```

But what if you mistype the directory name and pass two values instead of a single value? When you start the server, you'll see the following error:

```
...
SVt_PV: $DocumentRoot = `/home/httpd/docs/ mine'
handle_command (DocumentRoot /home/httpd/docs/ mine):
DocumentRoot takes one argument,
Root directory of the document tree
...
```

and of course the error will be logged in the *error_log* file:

```
[Wed Dec 20 23:47:31 2000] [error]
(2)No such file or directory: <Perl>:
DocumentRoot takes one argument,
Root directory of the document tree
```

Validating the Configuration Syntax

Before you restart a server on a live production machine after the configuration has been changed, it's essential to validate that the configuration file is not broken. If the configuration is broken, the server won't restart and users will find your server offline for the time it'll take you to fix the configuration and start the server again.

You can use *apachectl configtest* or *httpd -t* to validate the configuration file without starting the server. You can safely validate the configuration file on a running production server, as long as you run this test before you restart the server with *apachectl restart*. Of course, it is not 100% perfect, but it will reveal any syntax errors you might have made while editing the file.

The validation procedure doesn't just parse the code in *startup.pl*, it executes it too. <Perl> sections invoke the Perl interpreter when reading the configuration files, and PerlRequire and PerlModule do so as well.

Of course, we assume that the code that gets called during this test cannot cause any harm to your running production environment. If you're worried about that, you can prevent the code in the startup script and in <Perl> sections from being executed during the syntax check. If the server configuration is tested with *-Dsyntax_check*:

```
panic% httpd -t -Dsyntax_check
```

you can check in your code whether syntax_check was set with:

```
Apache->define('syntax_check')
```

If, for example, you want to prevent the code in *startup.pl* from being executed, add the following at the top of the code:

```
return if Apache->define('syntax_check');
```

Of course, there is nothing magical about using the string 'syntax_check' as a flag—you can use any other string as well.

The Scope of mod_perl Configuration Directives

Table 4-1 depicts where the various mod_perl configuration directives can be used.

Table 4-1. The Scope of mod_perl configuration directives

Directive	Global	<VirtualHost>	<Directory>
PerlTaintCheck	V		
PerlWarn	V		
PerlFreshRestart	V		
PerlPassEnv	V	V	
PerlRequire	V	V	V
PerlModule	V	V	V
PerlAddVar	V	V	V
PerlSetEnv	V	V	V
PerlSetVar	V	V	V
PerlSetupEnv	V	V	V
PerlSendHeader	V	V	V
<Perl> Sections	V	V	V

The first column represents directives that can appear in the global configuration; that is, outside all sections. Note that PerlTaintCheck, PerlWarn, and PerlFreshRestart can be placed inside <VirtualHost> sections. However, because there's only one Perl interpreter for all virtual hosts and the main server, setting any of these values in one virtual host affects all other servers. Therefore, it's probably a good idea to think of these variables as being allowed only in the global configuration.

The second column represents directives that can appear inside the <VirtualHost> sections.

The third column represents directives that can appear in the <Directory>, <Location>, and <Files> sections and all their regex variants. These mod_perl directives can also appear in .htaccess files.

For example, PerlWarn cannot be used in <Directory> and <VirtualHost> sections. However, PerlSetEnv can be used anywhere, which allows you to provide different behavior in different sections:

```
PerlSetEnv ADMIN_EMAIL webmaster@example.com
<Location /bar/manage/>
    PerlSetEnv ADMIN_EMAIL bar@example.com
</Location>
```

In this example, a handler invoked from /bar/manage/ will see the ADMIN_EMAIL environment variable as bar@example.com, while other handlers configured elsewhere will see ADMIN_EMAIL as the default value, webmaster@example.com.

Apache Restarts Twice

When the server is restarted, the configuration and module initialization phases are called twice before the children are forked. The second restart is done to test that all modules can survive a restart (SIGHUP), in order to ensure that future graceful restarts will work correctly. This is very important if you are going to restart a production server.

You can control what Perl code will be executed on the start or restart by checking the values of $Apache::Server::Starting and $Apache::Server::ReStarting. The former variable is true when the server is starting, and the latter is true when it's restarting.

For example, if you want to be notified when the server starts or restarts, you can do:

```
<Perl>
    email_notify("start")   if $Apache::Server::Starting;
    email_notify("restart") if $Apache::Server::ReStarting;
</Perl>
```

where the function email_notify() (that you have to write) performs the notification. Since Apache restarts itself on start, you will get both notifications when Apache is started, and only one when it's restarted.

The *startup.pl* file and similar files loaded via PerlModule or PerlRequire are compiled only once, because once the module is compiled, it enters the special %INC hash. When Apache restarts, Perl checks whether the module or script in question is already registered in %INC and won't try to compile it again.

Thus, the only code that you might need to protect from running on restart is the code in <Perl> sections. But since <Perl> sections are primarily used for creating on-the-fly configurations, it shouldn't be a problem to run the code more than once.

Enabling Remote Server Configuration Reports

The nifty mod_info Apache module displays the complete server configuration in your browser. In order to use it, you have to compile it in or, if the server was compiled with DSO mode enabled, load it as an object. Then just uncomment the already prepared section in the *httpd.conf* file:

```
<Location /server-info>
    SetHandler server-info
    Order deny,allow
    Deny from all
    Allow from localhost
</Location>
```

Now restart the server and issue the request:

```
http://localhost/server-info
```

We won't show a snapshot of the output here, as it's very lengthy. However, you should know that mod_info is unaware of the configuration created or modified by <Perl> sections or equivalent methods discussed earlier in this chapter.

Tips and Tricks

The following are miscellaneous tips and tricks that might save you lots of time when configuring mod_perl and Apache.

Publishing Port Numbers Other Than 80

If you are using a dual-server setup, with a mod_perl server listening on a high port (e.g., 8080), don't publish the high port number in URLs. Rather, use a proxying rewrite rule in the non-mod_perl server:

```
RewriteEngine     On
RewriteLogLevel   0
RewriteRule       ^/perl/(.*) http://localhost:8080/perl/$1 [P]
ProxyPassReverse  /          http://localhost/
```

In the above example, all the URLs starting with *perl* are rewritten to the backend server, listening on port 8080. The backend server is not directly accessible; it can be reached only through the frontend server.

One of the problems with publishing high port numbers is that Microsoft Internet Explorer (IE) 4.x has a bug when re-posting data to a URL with a nonstandard port (i.e., anything but 80). It drops the port designator and uses port 80 anyway. Hence, your service will be unusable for IE 4.x users.

Another problem is that firewalls will probably have most of the high ports closed, and users behind them will be unable to reach your service if it is running on a blocked port.

Running the Same Script from Different Virtual Hosts

When running under a virtual host, Apache::Registry and other registry family handlers will compile each script into a separate package. The package name includes the name of the virtual host if the variable $Apache::Registry::NameWithVirtualHost is set to 1. This is the default behavior.

Under this setting, two virtual hosts can have two different scripts accessed via the same URI (e.g., */perl/guestbook.pl*) without colliding with each other. Each virtual host will run its own version of the script.

However, if you run a big service and provide a set of identical scripts to many virtual hosts, you will want to have only one copy of each script compiled in memory. By default, each virtual host will create its own copy, so if you have 100 virtual hosts, you may end up with 100 copies of the same script compiled in memory, which is very wasteful. If this is the case, you can override the default behavior by setting the following directive in a startup file or in a <Perl> section:

```
$Apache::Registry::NameWithVirtualHost = 0;
```

But be careful: this makes sense only if you are sure that there are no other scripts with identical URIs but different content on different virtual hosts.

Users of mod_perl v1.15 are encouraged to upgrade to the latest stable version if this problem is encountered—it was solved starting with mod_perl v1.16.

Configuration Security Concerns

Any service open to the Internet at large must take security into account. Large, complex software tends to expose subtle vulnerabilities that attackers can exploit to gain unauthorized access to the server host. Third-party modules or libraries can also contain similarly exploitable bugs. Perl scripts aren't immune either: incorrect untainting and sanitizing of user input can lead to disaster when this input is fed to the open( ) or system( ) functions.

Also, if the same mod_perl server is shared by more than one user, you may need to protect users of the server from each other (see Appendix C).

Using Only Absolutely Necessary Components

The more modules you have enabled in your web server, the more complex the code and interaction between these modules will be. The more complex the code in your web server, the more chances for bugs there are. The more chances for bugs, the more chance there is that some of those bugs may involve security holes.

Before you put the server into production, review the server setup and disable any unused modules. As time goes by, the server enviroment may change and some modules may not be used anymore. Do periodical revisions of your setups and disable modules that aren't in use.

Taint Checking

Make sure to run the server with the following setting in the *httpd.conf* file:

```
PerlTaintCheck On
```

As discussed in Chapter 6, taint checking doesn't ensure that your code is completely safe from external hacks, but it does force you to improve your code to prevent many potential security problems.

Hiding Server Information

We aren't completely sure why the default value of the ServerTokens directive in Apache is Full rather than Minimal. It seems like Full is really useful only for debugging purposes. A probable reason for using ServerTokens Full is publicity: it means that Netcraft (*http://netcraft.com/*) and other similar survey services will count more Apache servers, which is good for all of us. In general, though, you really want to reveal as little information as possible to potential crackers.

Another approach is to modify the *httpd* sources to not reveal any unwanted information, so that all responses return an empty or phony Server: field.

Be aware, however, that there's no security by obscurity (as the old saying goes). Any determined cracker will eventually figure out what version of Apache is running and what third-party modules are built in.

You can see what information is revealed by your server by telneting to it and issuing some request. For example:

```
panic% telnet localhost 8080
Trying 127.0.0.1
Connected to localhost
Escape character is '^]'.
HEAD / HTTP/1.0
```

```
HTTP/1.1 200 OK
Date: Sun, 16 Apr 2000 11:06:25 GMT
Server: Apache/1.3.24 (Unix) mod_perl/1.26 mod_ssl/2.8.8 OpenSSL/0.9.6
[more lines snipped]
```

As you can see, a lot of information is revealed when ServerTokens Full has been specified.

Making the mod_perl Server Inaccessible from the Outside

It is best not to expose mod_perl to the outside world, as it creates a potential security risk by revealing which modules you use and which operating system you are running your web server on. In Chapter 12, we show how to make mod_perl inaccessible directly from the outside by listening only to the request coming from mod_proxy at the local host (127.0.0.1).

Protecting Private Status Locations

It's a good idea to protect your various monitors, such as */perl-status*, by password. The less information you provide for intruders, the harder it will be for them to break in. (One of the biggest helps you can provide for these bad guys is to show them all the scripts you use. If any of these are in the public domain, they can grab the source of the script from the Web, study it, and probably find a few or even many security holes in it.)

Security by obscurity may help to wave away some of the less-determined malicious fellas, but it doesn't really work against a determined intruder. For example, consider the old <Limit> container:

```
<Location /sys-monitor>
    SetHandler perl-script
    PerlHandler Apache::VMonitor
    AuthUserFile /home/httpd/perl/.htpasswd
    AuthGroupFile /dev/null
    AuthName "Server Admin"
    AuthType Basic
    <Limit GET POST>
        require user foo bar
    </Limit>
</Location>
```

Use of the <Limit> container is a leftover from NCSA server days that is still visible in many configuration examples today. In Apache, it will limit the scope of the require directive to the GET and POST request methods. Use of another method will bypass authentication. Since most scripts don't bother checking the request method, content will be served to the unauthenticated users.

For this reason, the Limit directive generally should not be used. Instead, use this secure configuration:

```
<Location /sys-monitor>
    SetHandler perl-script
    PerlHandler Apache::VMonitor
    AuthUserFile /home/httpd/perl/.htpasswd
    AuthGroupFile /dev/null
    AuthName "Server Admin"
    AuthType Basic
    require user foo bar
</Location>
```

The contents of the password file (*/home/httpd/perl/.htpasswd*) are populated by the *htpasswd* utility, which comes bundled with Apache:

```
foo:1SA3h/d27mCp
bar:WbWQhZM3m4kl
```

General Pitfalls

The following are some of the mostly frequently asked questions related to mod_perl configuration issues (and the answers, of course).

My CGI/Perl code is returned as plain text instead of being executed by the web server.
Check your configuration files and make sure that +ExecCGI is turned on in your configurations. + adds an option without resetting any options that were previously set. So this is how the <Location> section might look:

```
<Location /perl>
    SetHandler perl-script
    PerlHandler Apache::Registry
    Options +ExecCGI
    PerlSendHeader On
</Location>
```

My script works under mod_cgi, but when called via mod_perl, I get a Save As prompt.
You probably sent the HTTP header via print( ):

```
print "Content-type: text/html\n\n";
```

If this is the case, you must make sure that you have:

```
PerlSendHeader On
```

in the configuration part of the <Location> section:

```
<Location /perl>
    ...
    PerlSendHeader On
</Location>
```

This adds a little overhead to the output generation, because when this configuration is enabled, mod_perl will parse the output and try to find where the header information ends so it can be converted into a proper HTTP header. It is meant only for mod_cgi emulation with regard to HTTP headers.

Is there a way to provide a different startup.pl file for each individual virtual host?
No. Any virtual host will be able to see the routines from a *startup.pl* file loaded for any other virtual host.

References

- To learn regular expressions for use in <DirectoryMatch> or equivalent sections, the book *Mastering Regular Expressions*, by Jeffrey E. F. Friedl (O'Reilly), may prove to be an invaluable resource.

- Chapters 4 and 8 of *Professional Apache*, by Peter Wainwright (Wrox Press), explain how to configure Apache the way you want and improve Apache's performance.

- Chapter 3 of *Apache: The Definitive Guide*, by Ben Laurie and Peter Laurie (O'Reilly), talks extensively about the Apache configuration process.

- Chapter 8 of *Writing Apache Modules with Perl and C*, by Lincoln Stein and Doug MacEachern (O'Reilly), talks extensively about configuration customization with mod_perl.

- The extensive configuration manual at *http://httpd.apache.org/docs/*.

- mod_macro is a module that allows the definition and use of macros within Apache runtime configuration files. The syntax is a natural extension to Apache HTML-like configuration style. It's very useful if you have to configure many sections (e.g., when you have many virtual hosts) and haven't learned about <Perl> sections yet.

  mod_macro is available from *http://www.cri.ensmp.fr/~coelho/mod_macro/*.

CHAPTER 5

Web Server Control, Monitoring, Upgrade, and Maintenance

This chapter covers everything about administering a running mod_perl server. First, we will explain techniques for starting, restarting, and shutting down the server. As with Perl, there's more than one way to do it, and each technique has different implications for the server itself and the code it runs. A few widely used techniques for operating a server are presented. You may choose to use one of the suggested techniques or develop your own.

Later in the chapter, we give instructions on upgrading and disabling scripts on a live server, using a three-tier scheme, and monitoring and maintaining a web server.

Starting the Server in Multi-Process Mode

To start Apache manually, just run its executable. For example, on our machine, a mod_perl-enabled Apache executable is located at */home/httpd/httpd_perl/httpd_perl*. So to start it, we simply execute:

```
panic% /home/httpd/httpd_perl/bin/httpd_perl
```

This executable accepts a number of optional arguments. To find out what they are (without starting the server), use the *-h* argument:

```
panic% /home/httpd/httpd_perl/bin/httpd_perl -h
```

The most interesting arguments will be covered in the following sections. Any other arguments will be introduced as needed.

Starting the Server in Single-Process Mode

When developing new code, it is often helpful to run the server in single-process mode. This is most often used to find bugs in code that seems to work fine when the server starts, but refuses to work correctly after a few requests have been made. It also helps to uncover problems related to collisions between module names.

Running in single-process mode inhibits the server from automatically running in the background. This allows it to more easily be run under the control of a debugger. The -*X* switch is used to enable this mode:

```
panic% /home/httpd/httpd_perl/bin/httpd_perl -X
```

With the -*X* switch, the server runs in the foreground of the shell, so it can be killed by typing Ctrl-C. You can run it in the background by appending an ampersand:

```
panic% /home/httpd/httpd_perl/bin/httpd_perl -X &
```

Note that in -*X* (single-process) mode, the server will run very slowly when fetching images. Because only one request can be served at a time, requests for images normally done in parallel by the browser will now be serialized, making the page display slower.

Note for Netscape Users

If Netscape is being used as the test browser while the server is running in single-process mode, the HTTP protocol's KeepAlive feature gets in the way. Netscape tries to open multiple connections and keep them all open, as this should be faster for browsing. But because there is only one server process listening, each connection has to time out before the next one succeeds. Turn off KeepAlive in *httpd.conf* to avoid this effect while testing. Assuming you use width and height image size parameters in your HTML files, Netscape will be able to render the page without the images, so you can press the browser's Stop button after a few seconds to speed up page display. It's always good practice to specify width and height image size parameters.

Also note that when running with -*X*, the control messages that the parent server normally writes to *error_log* (e.g., "server started", "server stopped", etc.) will not be written anywhere. *httpd -X* causes the server to handle all requests itself without forking any children, so there is no controlling parent to write the status messages.

Usually Ctrl-C is used to kill a server running in single process mode, but Ctrl-C doesn't constitute a clean shutdown. *httpd.pid* doesn't get removed, so the next time the server is started, the message:

```
[warn] pid file /home/httpd/httpd_perl/logs/httpd.pid
overwritten -- Unclean shutdown of previous Apache run?
```

will appear in *error_log*. You can ignore this warning; there's nothing to worry about.

Using kill to Control Processes

Linux and other Unix-like operating systems support a form of interprocess communication called *signals*. The *kill* command is used to send a signal to a running process. How a process responds to a signal, if it responds at all, depends on the specific signal sent and on the handler set by the process. If you are familiar with Unix signal handling, you will find that Apache adheres to the usual conventions, and you can probably skip this section. This section describes the use of *kill* in relation to Apache for readers who aren't accustomed to working with signals.

The name "kill" is a misnomer; it sounds as if the command is inherently destructive, but *kill* simply sends signals to programs. Only a few signals will actually kill the process by default. Most signals can be caught by the process, which may choose to either perform a specific action or ignore the signal. When a process is in a zombie or uninterruptible sleep( ) state, it might ignore any signals.

The following example will help dispel any fear of using this command. Most people who are familiar with the command line know that pressing Ctrl-C will usually terminate a process running in a console. For example, it is common to execute:

```
panic% tail -f /home/httpd/httpd_perl/logs/error_log
```

to monitor the Apache server's *error_log* file. The only way to stop *tail* is by pressing Ctrl-C in the console in which the process is running. The same result can be achieved by sending the INT (interrupt) signal to this process. For example:

```
panic% kill -INT 17084
```

When this command is run, the *tail* process is aborted, assuming that the process identifier (PID) of the *tail* process is 17084.

Every process running in the system has its own PID. *kill* identifies processes by their PIDs. If *kill* were to use process names and there were two *tail* processes running, it might send the signal to the wrong process. The most common way to determine the PID of a process is to use *ps* to display information about the current processes on the machine. The arguments to this utility vary depending on the operating system. For example, on BSD-family systems, the following command works:

```
panic% ps auxc | grep tail
```

On a System V Unix flavor such as Solaris, the following command may be used instead:

```
panic% ps -eaf | grep tail
```

In the first part of the command, *ps* prints information about all the current processes. This is then piped to a *grep* command that prints lines containing the text "tail". Assuming only one such *tail* process is running, we get the following output:

```
root  17084  0.1  0.1  1112  408  pts/8  S  17:28  0:00  tail
```

The first column shows the username of the account running the process, the second column shows the PID, and the last column shows the name of the command. The other columns vary between operating systems.

Processes are free to ignore almost all signals they receive, and there are cases when they will. Let's run the *less* command on the same *error_log* file:

```
panic% less /home/httpd/httpd_perl/logs/error_log
```

Neither pressing Ctrl-C nor sending the INT signal will kill the process, because the implementers of this utility chose to ignore that signal. The way to kill the process is to type *q*.

Sometimes numerical signal values are used instead of their symbolic names. For example, 2 is normally the numeric equivalent of the symbolic name INT. Hence, these two commands are equivalent on Linux:

```
panic% kill -2 17084
panic% kill -INT 17084
```

On Solaris, the *-s* option is used when working with symbolic signal names:

```
panic% kill -s INT 17084
```

To find the numerical equivalents, either refer to the *signal(7)* manpage, or ask Perl to help you:

```
panic% perl -MConfig -e 'printf "%6s %2d\n", $_, $sig++ \
                    for split / /, $Config{sig_name}'
```

If you want to send a signal to all processes with the same name, you can use *pkill* on Solaris or *killall* on Linux.

kill Signals for Stopping and Restarting Apache

Apache performs certain actions in response to the KILL, TERM, HUP, and USR1 signals (as arguments to *kill*). All Apache system administrators should be familiar with the use of these signals to control the Apache web server.

By referring to the *signal.h* file, we learn the numerical equivalents of these signals:

```
#define SIGHUP    1    /* hangup, generated when terminal disconnects */
#define SIGKILL   9    /* last resort */
#define SIGTERM   15   /* software termination signal */
#define SIGUSR1   30   /* user defined signal 1 */
```

The four types of signal are:

KILL signal: forcefully shutdown
The KILL (9) signal should *never* be used unless absolutely necessary, because it will unconditionally kill Apache, without allowing it to clean up properly. For example, the *httpd.pid* file will not be deleted, and any existing requests will simply be terminated halfway through. Although failure to delete *httpd.pid* is harmless, if code was registered to run upon child exit but was not executed because Apache was sent the KILL signal, you may have problems. For example, a database connection may be closed incorrectly, leaving the database in an inconsistent state.

The three other signals have safe and legitimate uses, and the next sections will explain what happens when each of them is sent to an Apache server process.

It should be noted that these signals should be sent only to the *parent* process, not to any of the child processes. The parent process PID may be found either by using *ps auxc | grep apache* (where it will usually be the lowest-numbered Apache process) or by executing *cat* on the *httpd.pid* file. See "Finding the Right Apache PID," later in this chapter, for more information.

TERM signal: stop now

Sending the TERM signal to the parent causes it to attempt to kill off all its children immediately. Any requests in progress are terminated, and no further requests are accepted. This operation may take tens of seconds to complete. To stop a child, the parent sends it an HUP signal. If the child does not die before a predetermined amount of time, the parent sends a second HUP signal. If the child fails to respond to the second HUP, the parent then sends a TERM signal, and if the child still does not die, the parent sends the KILL signal as a last resort. Each failed attempt to kill a child generates an entry in the *error_log* file.

Before each process is terminated, the Perl cleanup stage happens, in which Perl END blocks and global objects' DESTROY methods are run.

When all child processes have been terminated, all open log files are closed and the parent itself exits.

Unless an explicit signal name is provided, *kill* sends the TERM signal by default. Therefore:

```
panic# kill -TERM 1640
```

and:

```
panic# kill 1640
```

will do the same thing.

HUP signal: restart now

Sending the HUP signal to the parent causes it to kill off its children as if the TERM signal had been sent. That is, any requests in progress are terminated, but the parent does not exit. Instead, the parent rereads its configuration files, spawns a new set of child processes, and continues to serve requests. It is almost equivalent to stopping and then restarting the server.

If the configuration files contain errors when restart is signaled, the parent will exit, so it is important to check the configuration files for errors before issuing a restart. We'll cover how to check for errors shortly.

Using this approach to restart mod_perl-enabled Apache may cause the processes' memory consumption to grow after each restart. This happens when Perl code loaded in memory is not completely torn down, leading to a memory leak.

USR1 signal: gracefully restart now

The USR1 signal causes the parent process to advise the children to exit after serving their current requests, or to exit immediately if they are not serving a request. The parent rereads its configuration files and reopens its log files. As each child dies off, the parent replaces it with a child from the new generation (the new children use the new configuration) and the new child processes begin serving new requests immediately.

The only difference between USR1 and HUP is that USR1 allows the children to complete any current requests prior to terminating. There is no interruption in the service, unlike with the HUP signal, where service is interrupted for the few (and sometimes more) seconds it takes for a restart to complete.

By default, if a server is restarted using the USR1 or the HUP signal and mod_perl is not compiled as a DSO, Perl scripts and modules are not reloaded. To reload modules pulled in via `PerlRequire`, `PerlModule`, or use, and to flush the `Apache::Registry` cache, either completely stop the server and then start it again, or use this directive in *httpd.conf*:

```
PerlFreshRestart On
```

(This directive is not always recommended. See Chapter 22 for further details.)

Speeding Up Apache's Termination and Restart

Restart or termination of a mod_perl server may sometimes take quite a long time, perhaps even tens of seconds. The reason for this is a call to the `perl_destruct()` function during the child exit phase, which is also known as the cleanup phase. In this phase, the Perl END blocks are run and the DESTROY method is called on any global objects that are still around.

Sometimes this will produce a series of messages in the *error_log* file, warning that certain child processes did not exit as expected. This happens when a child process, after a few attempts have been made to terminate it, is still in the middle of `perl_destruct()`. So when you shut down the server, you might see something like this:

```
[warn]   child process 7269 still did not exit,
         sending a SIGTERM
[error]  child process 7269 still did not exit,
         sending a SIGKILL
[notice] caught SIGTERM, shutting down
```

First, the parent process sends the TERM signal to all of its children, without logging a thing. If any of the processes still doesn't quit after a short period, it sends a second TERM, logs the PID of the process, and marks the event as a warning. Finally, if the process still hasn't terminated, it sends the KILL signal, which unconditionaly terminates the process, aborting any operation in progress in the child. This event is logged as an error.

If the mod_perl scripts do not contain any END blocks or DESTROY methods that need to be run during shutdown, or if the ones they have are nonessential, this step can be avoided by setting the PERL_DESTRUCT_LEVEL environment variable to -1. (The -1 value for PERL_DESTRUCT_LEVEL is special to mod_perl.) For example, add this setting to the *httpd.conf* file:

```
PerlSetEnv PERL_DESTRUCT_LEVEL -1
```

What constitutes a significant cleanup? Any change of state outside the current process that cannot be handled by the operating system itself. Committing database transactions and removing the lock on a resource are significant operations, but closing an ordinary file is not. For example, if DBI is used for persistent database connections, Perl's destructors should *not* be switched off.

Finding the Right Apache PID

In order to send a signal to a process, its PID must be known. But in the case of Apache, there are many *httpd* processes running. Which one should be used? The parent process is the one that must be signaled, so it is the parent's PID that must be identified.

The easiest way to find the Apache parent PID is to read the *httpd.pid* file. To find this file, look in the *httpd.conf* file. Open *httpd.conf* and look for the PidFile directive. Here is the line from our *httpd.conf* file:

```
PidFile /home/httpd/httpd_perl/logs/httpd.pid
```

When Apache starts up, it writes its own process ID in *httpd.pid* in a human-readable format. When the server is stopped, *httpd.pid* should be deleted, but if Apache is killed abnormally, *httpd.pid* may still exist even if the process is not running any more.

Of course, the PID of the running Apache can also be found using the *ps(1)* and *grep(1)* utilities (as shown previously). Assuming that the binary is called *httpd_perl*, the command would be:

```
panic% ps auxc | grep httpd_perl
```

or, on System V:

```
panic% ps -ef | grep httpd_perl
```

This will produce a list of all the *httpd_perl* (parent and child) processes. If the server was started by the *root* user account, it will be easy to locate, since it will belong to *root*. Here is an example of the sort of output produced by one of the *ps* command lines given above:

```
root    17309 0.9 2.7 8344 7096 ?  S 18:22 0:00 httpd_perl
nobody  17310 0.1 2.7 8440 7164 ?  S 18:22 0:00 httpd_perl
nobody  17311 0.0 2.7 8440 7164 ?  S 18:22 0:00 httpd_perl
nobody  17312 0.0 2.7 8440 7164 ?  S 18:22 0:00 httpd_perl
```

In this example, it can be seen that all the child processes are running as user *nobody* whereas the parent process runs as user *root*. There is only one *root* process, and this must be the parent process. Any *kill* signals should be sent to this parent process.

If the server is started under some other user account (e.g., when the user does not have *root* access), the processes will belong to that user. The only truly foolproof way to identify the parent process is to look for the process whose parent process ID (PPID) is 1 (use *ps* to find out the PPID of the process).

If you have the GNU tools installed on your system, there is a nifty utility that makes it even easier to discover the parent process. The tool is called *pstree*, and it is very simple to use. It lists all the processes showing the *family* hierarchy, so if we *grep* the output for the wanted process's family, we can see the parent process right away. Running this utility and *grep*ing for *httpd_perl*, we get:

```
panic% pstree -p | grep httpd_perl
 |-httpd_perl(17309)-+-httpd_perl(17310)
 |                   |-httpd_perl(17311)
 |                   |-httpd_perl(17312)
```

And this one is even simpler:

```
panic% pstree -p | grep 'httpd_perl.*httpd_perl'
 |-httpd_perl(17309)-+-httpd_perl(17310)
```

In both cases, we can see that the parent process has the PID 17309.

ps's *f* option, available on many Unix platforms, produces a tree-like report of the processes as well. For example, you can run *ps axfwwww* to get a tree of all processes.

Using apachectl to Control the Server

The Apache distribution comes with a script to control the server called *apachectl*, installed into the same location as the *httpd* executable. For the sake of the examples, let's assume that it is in */home/httpd/httpd_perl/bin/apachectl*.

All the operations that can be performed by using signals can also be performed on the server by using *apachectl*. You don't need to know the PID of the process, as *apachectl* will find this out for itself.

To start *httpd_perl*:

```
panic% /home/httpd/httpd_perl/bin/apachectl start
```

To stop *httpd_perl*:

```
panic% /home/httpd/httpd_perl/bin/apachectl stop
```

To restart *httpd_perl* (if it is running, send HUP; if it is not, just start it):

```
panic% /home/httpd/httpd_perl/bin/apachectl restart
```

Do a graceful restart by sending a USR1 signal, or start it if it's not running:

```
panic% /home/httpd/httpd_perl/bin/apachectl graceful
```

To perform a configuration test:

```
panic% /home/httpd/httpd_perl/bin/apachectl configtest
```

There are other options for *apachectl*. Use the *help* option to see them all.

```
panic% /home/httpd/httpd_perl/bin/apachectl help
```

It is important to remember that *apachectl* uses the PID file, which is specified by the `PidFile` directive in *httpd.conf*. If the PID file is deleted by hand while the server is running, or if the `PidFile` directive is missing or in error, *apachectl* will be unable to stop or restart the server.

Validating Server Configuration

If the configuration file has syntax errors, attempting to restart the server will fail and the server will die. However, if a graceful restart is attempted using *apachectl* and the configuration file contains errors, the server will issue an error message and continue running with the existing configuration. This is because *apachectl* validates the configuration file before issuing the actual restart command when a graceful restart is requested.

Apache provides a method to check the configuration's syntax without actually starting the server. You can run this check at any time, whether or not a server is currently running. The check has two forms, using the *-t* or *-T* options. For example:

```
panic% /home/httpd/httpd_perl/bin/httpd_perl -t
```

-t will verify that the `DocumentRoot` directory exists, whereas *-T* will not. *-T* is most useful when using a configuration file containing a large number of virtual hosts, where verifying the existence of each `DocumentRoot` directory can take a substantial amount of time.

Note that when running this test with a mod_perl server, the Perl code will be executed just as it would be at server startup—that is, from within the *httpd.conf* `<Perl>` sections or a startup file.

Setuid root Startup Scripts

If a group of developers need to be able to start and stop the server, there may be a temptation to give them the *root* password, which is probably not a wise thing to do. The fewer people that know the *root* password, the less likely you will encounter problems. Fortunately, an easy solution to this problem is available on Unix platforms. It is called a *setuid executable* (setuid *root* in this case).

Before continuing, we must stress that this technique should not be used unless it is absolutely necessary. If an improperly written setuid script is used, it may compromise the system by giving *root* privileges to system breakers (crackers).

To be on the safe side, do not deploy the techniques explained in this section. However, if this approach is necessary in a particular situation, this section will address the possible problems and provide solutions to reduce the risks to a minimum.

Introduction to setuid Executables

A setuid executable has the setuid permissions bit set, with the following command:

```
panic% chmod u+s filename
```

This sets the process's effective user ID to that of the file upon execution. Most users have used setuid executables even if they have not realized it. For example, when a user changes his password he executes the *passwd* command, which, among other things, modifies the */etc/passwd* file. In order to change this file, the *passwd* program needs *root* permissions. The *passwd* command has the setuid bit set, so when someone executes this utility, its effective ID becomes the *root* user ID.

Using setuid executables should be avoided as a general practice. The less setuid executables there are in a system, the less likely it is that someone will find a way to break in. One approach that crackers use is to find and exploit unanticipated bugs in setuid executables.

When the executable is setuid to *root*, it is vital to ensure that it does not extend read and write permissions to its group or to the world. Let's take the *passwd* utility as an example. Its permissions are:

```
panic% ls -l /usr/bin/passwd
-r-s--x--x 1 root root 12244 Feb 8 00:20 /usr/bin/passwd
```

The program is group- and world-executable but cannot be read or written by group or world. This is achieved with the following command:

```
panic% chmod 4511 filename
```

The first digit (4) stands for the setuid bit, the second digit (5) is a bitwise-OR of read (4) and executable (1) permissions for the user, and the third and fourth digits set the executable (1) permissions for group and world.

Apache Startup Script's setuid Security

In the situation where several developers need to be able to start and stop an Apache server that is run by the *root* account, setuid access must be available only to this specific group of users. For the sake of this example, let's assume that these developers belong to a group named *apache*. It is important that users who are not *root* or are not part of the *apache* group are unable to execute this script. Therefore, the following commands must be applied to the *apachectl* program:

```
panic% chgrp apache apachectl
panic% chmod 4510  apachectl
```

The execution order is important. If the commands are executed in reverse order, the setuid bit is lost.

The file's permissions now look like this:

```
panic% ls -l apachectl
-r-s--x--- 1 root apache 32 May 13 21:52 apachectl
```

Everything is set. Well, almost...

When Apache is started, Apache and Perl modules are loaded, so code may be executed. Since all this happens with the *root* effective ID, any code is executed as if run by the root user. This means that there is a risk, even though none of the developers has the *root* password—all users in the *apache* group now have an indirect *root* access. For example, if Apache loads some module or executes some code that is writable by any of these users, they can plant code that will allow them to gain shell access to the *root* account.

Of course, if the developers are not trusted, this setuid solution is not the right approach. Although it is possible to try to check that all the files Apache loads are not writable by anyone but *root*, there are so many of them (especially with mod_perl, where many Perl modules are loaded at server startup) that this is a risky approach.

If the developers are trusted, this approach suits the situation. Although there are security concerns regarding Apache startup, once the parent process is loaded, the child processes are spawned as non-*root* processes.

This section has presented a way to allow non-*root* users to start and stop the server. The rest is exactly the same as if they were executing the script as *root* in the first place.

Sample setuid Apache Startup Script

Example 5-1 shows a sample setuid Apache startup script.

Note the line marked *WORKAROUND*, which fixes an obscure error when starting a mod_perl-enabled Apache, by setting the real UID to the effective UID. Without this workaround, a mismatch between the real and the effective UIDs causes Perl to croak on the -*e* switch.

This script depends on using a version of Perl that recognizes and emulates the setuid bits. This script will do different things depending on whether it is named *start_httpd*, *stop_httpd*, or *restart_httpd*; use symbolic links to create the names in the filesystem.

Example 5-1. suid_apache_ctl

```perl
#!/usr/bin/perl -T
use strict;

# These constants will need to be adjusted.
my $PID_FILE = '/home/httpd/httpd_perl/logs/httpd.pid';
my $HTTPD = '/home/httpd/httpd_perl/bin/httpd_perl ';
$HTTPD   .= '-d /home/httpd/httpd_perl';

# These prevent taint checking failures
$ENV{PATH} = '/bin:/usr/bin';
delete @ENV{qw(IFS CDPATH ENV BASH_ENV)};

# This sets the real to the effective ID, and prevents
# an obscure error when starting apache/mod_perl
$< = $>; # WORKAROUND
$( = $) = 0; # set the group to root too

# Do different things depending on our name
my $name = $0;
$name =~ m|([^/]+)$|;

if ($name eq 'start_httpd') {
    system $HTTPD and die "Unable to start HTTPD";
    print "HTTP started.\n";
    exit 0;
}

# extract the process id and confirm that it is numeric
my $pid = `cat $PID_FILE`;
$pid =~ /^(\d+)$/ or die "PID $pid not numeric or not found";
$pid = $1;

if ($name eq 'stop_httpd') {
    kill 'TERM', $pid or die "Unable to signal HTTPD";
    print "HTTP stopped.\n";
    exit 0;
}

if ($name eq 'restart_httpd') {
    kill 'HUP', $pid or die "Unable to signal HTTPD";
    print "HTTP restarted.\n";
    exit 0;
}

# script is named differently
die "Script must be named start_httpd, stop_httpd, or restart_httpd.\n";
```

Preparing for Machine Reboot

When using a non-production development box, it is OK to start and stop the web server by hand when necessary. On a production system, however, it is possible that the machine on which the server is running will have to be rebooted. When the reboot is completed, who is going to remember to start the server? It is easy to forget this task, and what happens if no one is around when the machine is rebooted? (Some OSs will reboot themselves without human intervention in certain situations.)

After the server installation is complete, it is important to remember that a script to perform the server startup and shutdown should be put in a standard system location—for example, /etc/rc.d under Red Hat Linux, or /etc/init.d/apache under Debian GNU/Linux.

This book uses Red Hat-compatible Linux distributions in its examples. Let's step aside for a brief introduction to the System V (SysV) *init* system that many Linux and other Unix flavors use to manage starting and stopping daemons. (A *daemon* is a process that normally starts at system startup and runs in the background until the system goes down.)

The SysV *init* system keeps all its files in the /etc/rc.d/ directory. This directory contains a number of subdirectories:

```
panic% find /etc/rc.d -type d
/etc/rc.d
/etc/rc.d/init.d
/etc/rc.d/rc0.d
/etc/rc.d/rc1.d
/etc/rc.d/rc2.d
/etc/rc.d/rc3.d
/etc/rc.d/rc4.d
/etc/rc.d/rc5.d
/etc/rc.d/rc6.d
```

/etc/rc.d/init.d contains many scripts, one for each service that needs to be started at boot time or when entering a specific runlevel. Common services include networking, file sharing, mail servers, web servers, FTP servers, etc.

When the system boots, the special *init* script runs all scripts for the default runlevel. The default runlevel is specified in the /etc/inittab file. This file contains a line similar to this one:

```
id:3:initdefault:
```

The second column indicates that the default runlevel is 3, which is the default for most server systems. (5 is the default for desktop machines.)

Let's now see how the scripts are run. We'll first look at the contents of the /etc/rc.d/ rc3.d directory:

```
panic% ls -l /etc/rc.d/rc3.d
lrwxrwxrwx 1 root root 13 Jul  1 01:08 K20nfs -> ../init.d/nfs
lrwxrwxrwx 1 root root 18 Jul  1 00:54 K92ipchains -> ../init.d
lrwxrwxrwx 1 root root 17 Jul  1 00:51 S10network -> ../init.d/network
lrwxrwxrwx 1 root root 16 Jul  1 00:51 S30syslog -> ../init.d/syslog
lrwxrwxrwx 1 root root 13 Jul  1 00:52 S40atd -> ../init.d/atd
```

```
lrwxrwxrwx 1 root root 15 Jul  1 00:51 S40crond -> ../init.d/crond
lrwxrwxrwx 1 root root 15 Jul  1 01:13 S91httpd_docs -> ../init.d/httpd_docs
lrwxrwxrwx 1 root root 15 Jul  1 01:13 S91httpd_perl -> ../init.d/httpd_perl
lrwxrwxrwx 1 root root 17 Jul  1 00:51 S95kheader -> ../init.d/kheader
lrwxrwxrwx 1 root root 11 Jul  1 00:51 S99local -> ../rc.local
```

(Only part of the output is shown here, since many services are started and stopped at runlevel 3.)

There are no real files in the directory. Instead, each file is a symbolic link to one of the scripts in the *init.d* directory. The links' names start with a letter (*S* or *K*) and a two-digit number. *S* specifies that the script should be run when the service is started and *K* specifies that the script should be run when the service is stopped. The number following *S* or *K* is there for ordering purposes: *init* will start services in the order in which they appear.

init runs each script with an argument that is either *start* or *stop*, depending on whether the link's name starts with *S* or *K*. Scripts can be executed from the command line; the following command line will stop the *httpd* server:

```
panic# /etc/rc.d/init.d/httpd_perl stop
```

Unfortunately, different Unix flavors implement different *init* systems. Refer to your system's documentation.

Now that we're familiar with how the *init* system works, let's return to our discussion of *apachectl* scripts.

Generally, the simplest solution is to copy the *apachectl* script to the startup directory or, better still, create a symbolic link from the startup directory to the *apachectl* script. The *apachectl* utility is in the same directory as the Apache executable after Apache installation (e.g., */home/httpd/httpd_perl/bin*). If there is more than one Apache server, there will need to be a separate script for each one, and of course they will have to have different names so that they can coexist in the same directory.

On one of our Red Hat Linux machines with two servers, we have the following setup:

```
/etc/rc.d/init.d/httpd_docs
/etc/rc.d/init.d/httpd_perl
/etc/rc.d/rc3.d/S91httpd_docs -> ../init.d/httpd_docs
/etc/rc.d/rc3.d/S91httpd_perl -> ../init.d/httpd_perl
/etc/rc.d/rc6.d/K16httpd_docs -> ../init.d/httpd_docs
/etc/rc.d/rc6.d/K16httpd_perl -> ../init.d/httpd_perl
```

The scripts themselves reside in the */etc/rc.d/init.d* directory. There are symbolic links to these scripts in */etc/rc.d/rc*.d* directories.

When the system starts (runlevel 3), we want Apache to be started when all the services on which it might depend are already running. Therefore, we have used *S91*. If, for example, the mod_perl-enabled Apache issues a connect_on_init( ), the SQL server should be started before Apache.

When the system shuts down (runlevel 6), Apache should be one of the first processes to be stopped—therefore, we have used *K16*. Again, if the server does some cleanup processing during the shutdown event and requires third-party services (e.g., a MySQL server) to be running at the time, it should be stopped before these services.

Notice that it is normal for more than one symbolic link to have the same sequence number.

Under Red Hat Linux and similar systems, when a machine is booted and its runlevel is set to 3 (multiuser plus network), Linux goes into */etc/rc.d/rc3.d/* and executes the scripts to which the symbolic links point with the *start* argument. When it sees *S87httpd_perl*, it executes:

```
/etc/rc.d/init.d/httpd_perl start
```

When the machine is shut down, the scripts are executed through links from the */etc/rc.d/rc6.d/* directory. This time the scripts are called with the *stop* argument, like this:

```
/etc/rc.d/init.d/httpd_perl stop
```

Most systems have GUI utilities to automate the creation of symbolic links. For example, Red Hat Linux includes the *ntsysv* and *tksysv* utilities. These can be used to create the proper symbolic links. Before it is used, the *apachectl* or similar scripts should be put into the *init.d* directory or an equivalent directory. Alternatively, a symbolic link to some other location can be created.

However, it's been reported that sometimes these tools mess up and break things. Therefore, the robust *chkconfig* utility should be used instead. The following example shows how to add an *httpd_perl* startup script to the system using *chkconfig*.

The *apachectl* script may be kept in any directory, as long as it can be the target of a symbolic link. For example, it might be desirable to keep all Apache executables in the same directory (e.g., */home/httpd/httpd_perl/bin*), in which case all that needs to be done is to provide a symbolic link to this file:

```
panic% ln -s /home/httpd/httpd_perl/bin/apachectl /etc/rc.d/init.d/httpd_perl
```

Edit the *apachectl* script to add the following lines after the script's main header:

```
# Comments to support chkconfig on RedHat Linux
# chkconfig: 2345 91 16
# description: mod_perl enabled Apache Server
```

Now the beginning of the script looks like:

```
#!/bin/sh
#
# Apache control script designed to allow an easy command line
# interface to controlling Apache.  Written by Marc Slemko,
# 1997/08/23

# Comments to support chkconfig on Red Hat Linux
# chkconfig: 2345 91 16
# description: mod_perl-enabled Apache Server
```

```
#
# The exit codes returned are:
# ...
```

Adjust the line:

```
# chkconfig: 2345 91 16
```

to suit your situation. For example, the setting used above says the script should be started in levels 2, 3, 4, and 5, that its start priority should be 91, and that its stop priority should be 16.

Now all you need to do is ask *chkconfig* to configure the startup scripts. Before doing so, it is best to check what files and links are in place:

```
panic% find /etc/rc.d | grep httpd_perl
```

```
/etc/rc.d/init.d/httpd_perl
```

This response means that only the startup script itself exists. Now execute:

```
panic% chkconfig --add httpd_perl
```

and repeat the *find* command to see what has changed:

```
panic% find /etc/rc.d | grep httpd_perl
```

```
/etc/rc.d/init.d/httpd_perl
/etc/rc.d/rc0.d/K16httpd_perl
/etc/rc.d/rc1.d/K16httpd_perl
/etc/rc.d/rc2.d/S91httpd_perl
/etc/rc.d/rc3.d/S91httpd_perl
/etc/rc.d/rc4.d/S91httpd_perl
/etc/rc.d/rc5.d/S91httpd_perl
/etc/rc.d/rc6.d/K16httpd_perl
```

The *chkconfig* program has created all the required symbolic links using the startup and shutdown priorities as specified in the line:

```
# chkconfig: 2345 91 16
```

If for some reason it becomes necessary to remove the service from the startup scripts, *chkconfig* can perform the removal of the links automatically:

```
panic% chkconfig --del httpd_perl
```

By running the *find* command once more, you can see that the symbolic links have been removed and only the original file remains:

```
panic% find /etc/rc.d | grep httpd_perl
```

```
/etc/rc.d/init.d/httpd_perl
```

Again, execute:

```
panic% chkconfig --add httpd_perl
```

Note that when using symbolic links, the link name in */etc/rc.d/init.d* is what matters, not the name of the script to which the link points.

Upgrading a Live Server

When you're developing code on a development server, anything goes: modifying the configuration, adding or upgrading Perl modules without checking that they are syntactically correct, not checking that Perl modules don't collide with other modules, adding experimental new modules from CPAN, etc. If something goes wrong, configuration changes can be rolled back (assuming you're using some form of version control), modules can be uninstalled or reinstalled, and the server can be started and stopped as many times as required to get it working.

Of course, if there is more than one developer working on a development server, things can't be quite so carefree. Possible solutions for the problems that can arise when multiple developers share a development server will be discussed shortly.

The most difficult situation is transitioning changes to a live server. However much the changes have been tested on a development server, there is always the risk of breaking something when a change is made to the live server. Ideally, any changes should be made in a way that will go unnoticed by the users, except as new or improved functionality or better performance. No users should be exposed to even a single error message from the upgraded service—especially not the "database busy" or "database error" messages that some high-profile sites seem to consider acceptable.

Live services can be divided into two categories: servers that must be up 24 hours a day and 7 days a week, and servers that can be stopped during non-working hours. The latter generally applies to Intranets of companies with offices located more or less in the same time zone and not scattered around the world. Since the Intranet category is the easier case, let's talk about it first.

Upgrading Intranet Servers

An Intranet server generally serves the company's internal staff by allowing them to share and distribute internal information, read internal email, and perform other similar tasks. When all the staff is located in the same time zone, or when the time difference between sites does not exceed a few hours, there is often no need for the server to be up all the time. This doesn't necessarily mean that no one will need to access the Intranet server from home in the evenings, but it does mean that the server can probably be stopped for a few minutes when it is necessary to perform some maintenance work.

Even if the update of a live server occurs during working hours and goes wrong, the staff will generally tolerate the inconvenience unless the Intranet has become a really mission-critical tool. For servers that *are* mission critical, the following section will describe the least disruptive and safest upgrade approach.

If possible, any administration or upgrades of the company's Intranet server should be undertaken during non-working hours, or, if this is not possible, during the times of least activity (e.g., lunch time). Upgrades that are carried out while users are using the service should be done with a great deal of care.

In very large organizations, upgrades are often scheduled events and employees are notified ahead of time that the service might not be available. Some organizations deem these periods "at-risk" times, when employees are expected to use the service as little as possible and then only for noncritical work. Again, these major updates are generally scheduled during the weekends and late evening hours.

The next section deals with this issue for services that need to be available all the time.

Upgrading 24 × 7 Internet Servers

Internet servers are normally expected to be available 24 hours a day, 7 days a week. E-commerce sites, global B2B (business-to-business) sites, and any other revenue-producing sites may be critical to the companies that run them, and their unavailability could prove to be very expensive. The approach taken to ensure that servers remain in service even when they are being upgraded depends on the type of server in use. There are two categories to consider: *server clusters* and *single servers*.

The server cluster

When a service is very popular, a single machine probably will not be able to keep up with the number of requests the service has to handle. In this situation, the solution is to add more machines and to distribute the load amongst them. From the user's point of view, the use of multiple servers must be completely transparent; users must still have a single access point to the service (i.e., the same single URL) even though there may be many machines with different server names actually delivering the service. The requests must also be properly distributed across the machines: not simply by giving equal numbers of requests to each machine, but rather by giving each machine a load that reflects its actual capabilities, given that not all machines are built with identical hardware. This leads to the need for some smart load-balancing techniques.

All current load-balancing techniques are based on a central machine that dispatches all incoming requests to machines that do the real processing. Think of it as the only entrance into a building with a doorkeeper directing people into different rooms, all of which have identical contents but possibly a different number of clerks. Regardless of what room they're directed to, all people use the entrance door to enter and exit the building, and an observer located outside the building cannot tell what room people are visiting. The same thing happens with the cluster of servers—users send their browsers to URLs, and back come the pages they requested. They remain unaware of the particular machines from which their browsers collected their pages.

No matter what load-balancing technique is used, it should always be straightforward to be able to tell the central machine that a new machine is available or that some machine is not available any more.

How does this long introduction relate to the upgrade problem? Simple. When a particular machine requires upgrading, the dispatching server is told to stop sending requests to that machine. All the requests currently being executed must be left to complete, at which point whatever maintenance and upgrade work is to be done can be carried out. Once the work is complete and has been tested to ensure that everything works correctly, the central machine can be told that it can again send requests to the newly upgraded machine. At no point has there been any interruption of service or any indication to users that anything has occurred. Note that for some services, particularly ones to which users must log in, the wait for all the users to either log out or time out may be considerable. Thus, some sites stop requests to a machine at the end of the working day, in the hope that all requests will have completed or timed out by the morning.

How do we talk to the central machine? This depends on the load-balancing technology that is implemented and is beyond the scope of this book. The references section at the end of this chapter gives a list of relevant online resources.

The single server

It's not uncommon for a popular web site to run on a single machine. It's also common for a web site to run on multiple machines, with one machine dedicated to serving static objects (such as images and static HTML files), another serving dynamically generated responses, and perhaps even a third machine that acts as a dedicated database server.

Therefore, the situation that must be addressed is where just one machine runs the service or where the service is spread over a few machines, with each performing a unique task, such that no machine can be shut down even for a single minute, and leaving the service unavailable for more than five seconds is unacceptable. In this case, two different tasks may be required: upgrading the software on the server (including the Apache server), and upgrading the code of the service itself (i.e., custom modules and scripts).

Upgrading live server components by swapping machines. There are many things that you might need to update on a server, ranging from a major upgrade of the operating system to just an update of a single piece of software (such as the Apache server itself).

One simple approach to performing an upgrade painlessly is to have a backup machine, of similar capacity and identical configuration, that can replace the production machine while the upgrade is happening. It is a good idea to have such a machine handy and to use it whenever major upgrades are required. The two machines must be kept synchronized, of course. (For Unix/Linux users, tools such as *rsync* and *mirror* can be used for synchronization.)

However, it may not be necessary to have a special machine on standby as a backup. Unless the service is hosted elsewhere and you can't switch the machines easily, the development machine is probably the best choice for a backup—all the software and scripts are tested on the development machine as a matter of course, and it probably has a software setup identical to that of the production machine. The development machine might not be as powerful as the live server, but this may well be acceptable for a short period, especially if the upgrade is timed to happen when the site's traffic is fairly quiet. It's much better to have a slightly slower service than to close the doors completely. A web log analysis tool such as *analog* can be used to determine the hour of the day when the server is under the least load.

Switching between the two machines is very simple:

1. Shut down the network on the backup machine.
2. Configure the backup machine to use the same IP address and domain name as the live machine.
3. Shut down the network on the live machine (do not shut down the machine itself!).
4. Start up the network on the backup machine.

When you are certain that the backup server has successfully replaced the live server (that is, requests are being serviced, as revealed by the backup machine's *access_log*), it is safe to switch off the master machine or do any necessary upgrades.

Why bother waiting to check that everything is working correctly with the backup machine? If something goes wrong, the change can immediately be rolled back by putting the known working machine back online. With the service restored, there is time to analyze and fix the problem with the replacement machine before trying it again. Without the ability to roll back, the service may be out of operation for some time before the problem is solved, and users may become frustrated.

We recommend that you practice this technique with two unused machines before using the production boxes.

After the backup machine has been put into service and the original machine has been upgraded, test the original machine. Once the original machine has been passed as ready for service, the server replacement technique described above should be repeated in reverse. If the original machine does not work correctly once returned to service, the backup machine can immediately be brought online while the problems with the original are fixed.

You cannot have two machines configured to use the same IP address, so the first machine must release the IP address by shutting down the link using this IP before the second machine can enable its own link with the same IP address. This leads to a short downtime during the switch. You can use the *heartbeat* utility to automate this process and thus possibly shorten the downtime period. See the references section at the end of this chapter for more information about *heartbeat*.

Upgrading a live server with port forwarding. Using more than one machine to perform an update may not be convenient, or even possible. An alternative solution is to use the port-forwarding capabilities of the host's operating system.

One approach is to configure the web server to listen on an unprivileged port, such as 8000, instead of 80. Then, using a firewalling tool such as *iptables*, *ipchains*, or *ipf-wadm*, redirect all traffic coming for port 80 to port 8000. Keeping a rule like this enabled at all times on a production machine will not noticeably affect performance.

Once this rule is in place, it's a matter of getting the new code in place, adjusting the web server configuration to point to the new location, and picking a new unused port, such as 8001. This way, you can start the "new" server listening on that port and not affect the current setup.

To check that everything is working, you could test the server by accessing it directly by port number. However, this might break links and redirections. Instead, add another port forwarding rule before the first one, redirecting traffic for port 80 from your test machine or network to port 8001.

Once satisfied with the new server, publishing the change is just a matter of changing the port-forwarding rules one last time. You can then stop the now old server and everything is done.

Now you have your primary server listening on port 8001, answering requests coming in through port 80, and nobody will have noticed the change.

Upgrading a live server with prepackaged components. Assuming that the testbed machine and the live server have an identical software installation, consider preparing an upgrade package with the components that must be upgraded. Test this package on the testbed machine, and when it is evident that the package gets installed flawlessly, install it on the live server. Do not build the software from scratch on the live server, because if a mistake is made, it could cause the live server to misbehave or even to fail.

For example, many Linux distributions use the Red Hat Package Manager (RPM) utility, *rpm*, to distribute source and binary packages. It is not necessary for a binary package to include any compiled code (for example, it can include Perl scripts, but it is still called a binary). A binary package allows the new or upgraded software to be used the moment you install it. The *rpm* utility is smart enough to make upgrades (i. e., remove previous installation files, preserve configuration files, and execute appropriate installation scripts).

If, for example, the mod_perl server needs to be upgraded, one approach is to prepare a package on a similarly configured machine. Once the package has been built, tested, and proved satisfactory, it can then be transferred to the live machine. The *rpm* utility can then be used to upgrade the mod_perl server. For example, if the package file is called *mod_perl-1.26-10.i386.rpm*, this command:

```
panic% rpm -Uvh mod_perl-1.26-10.i386.rpm
```

will remove the previous server (if any) and install the new one.

There's no problem upgrading software that doesn't break any dependencies in other packages, as in the above example. But what would happen if, for example, the Perl interpreter needs to be upgraded on the live machine?

If the mod_perl package described earlier was properly prepared, it would specify the packages on which it depends and their versions. So if Perl was upgraded using an RPM package, the *rpm* utility would detect that the upgrade would break a dependency, since the mod_perl package is supposed to work with the previous version of Perl. *rpm* will not allow the upgrade unless forced to.

This is a very important feature of RPM. Of course, it relies on the fact that the person who created the package has set all the dependencies correctly. Do not trust packages downloaded from the Web. If you have to use an RPM package prepared by someone else, get its source, read its specification file, and make doubly sure that it's what you want.

The Perl upgrade task is in fact a very easy problem to solve. Have two packages ready on the development machine: one for Perl and the other for mod_perl, the latter built using the Perl version that is going to be installed. Upload both of them to the live server and install them together. For example:

```
panic% rpm -Uvh mod_perl-1.26-10.i386.rpm perl-5.6.1-5.i386.rpm
```

This should be done as an *atomic* operation—i.e., as a single execution of the *rpm* program. If the installation of the packages is attempted with separate commands, they will both fail, because each of them will break some dependency.

If a mistake is made and checks reveal that a faulty package has been installed, it is easy to roll back. Just make sure that the previous version of the properly packaged software is available. The packages can be downgraded by using the *--force* option—and voilà, the previously working system is restored. For example:

```
panic% rpm -Uvh --force mod_perl-1.26-9.i386.rpm perl-5.6.1-4.i386.rpm
```

Although this example uses the *rpm* utility, other similar utilities exist for various operating systems and distributions. Creating packages provides a simple way of upgrading live systems (and downgrading them if need be). The packages used for any successful upgrade should be kept, because they will become the packages to downgrade to if a subsequent upgrade with a new package fails.

When using a cluster of machines with identical setups, there is another important benefit of prepackaged upgrades. Instead of doing all the upgrades by hand, which could potentially involve dozens or even hundreds of files, preparing a package can save lots of time and will minimize the possibility of error. If the packages are properly written and have been tested thoroughly, it is perfectly possible to make updates to machines that are running live services. (Note that not all operating systems permit the upgrading of running software. For example, Windows does not permit DLLs that are in active use to be updated.)

It should be noted that the packages referred to in this discussion are ones made locally, specifically for the systems to be upgraded, not generic packages downloaded from the Internet. Making local packages provides complete control over what is installed and upgraded and makes upgrades into atomic actions that can be rolled back if necessary. We do not recommend using third-party packaged binaries, as they will almost certainly have been built for a different environment and will not have been fine-tuned for your system.

Upgrading a live server using symbolic links. Yet another alternative is to use symbolic links for upgrades. This concept is quite simple: install a package into some directory and symlink to it. So, if some software was expected in the directory */usr/local/ foo*, you could simply install the first version of the software in the directory */usr/ local/foo-1.0* and point to it from the expected directory:

```
panic# ln -sf /usr/local/foo-1.0 /usr/local/foo
```

If later you want to install a second version of the software, install it into the directory */usr/local/foo-2.0* and change the symbolic link to this new directory:

```
panic# ln -sf /usr/local/foo-2.0 /usr/local/foo
```

Now if something goes wrong, you can always switch back with:

```
panic# ln -sf /usr/local/foo-1.0 /usr/local/foo
```

In reality, things aren't as simple as in this example. It works if you can place all the software components under a single directory, as with the default Apache installation. Everything is installed under a single directory, so you can have:

```
/usr/local/apache-1.3.17
/usr/local/apache-1.3.19
```

and use the symlink */usr/local/apache* to switch between the two versions.

However, if you use a default installation of Perl, files are spread across multiple directories. In this case, it's not easy to use symlinks—you need several of them, and they're hard to keep track of. Unless you automate the symlinks with a script, it might take a while to do a switch, which might mean some downtime. Of course, you can install all the Perl components under a single root, just like the default Apache installation, which simplifies things.

Another complication with upgrading Perl is that you may need to recompile mod_perl and other Perl third-party modules that use XS extensions. Therefore, you probably want to build everything on some other machine, test it, and when ready, just un*tar* everything at once on the production machine and adjust the symbolic links.

Upgrading Perl code. Although new versions of mod_perl and Apache may not be released for months at a time and the need to upgrade them may not be pressing, the handlers and scripts being used at a site may need regular tweaks and changes, and new ones may be added quite frequently.

Of course, the safest and best option is to prepare an RPM (or equivalent) package that can be used to automatically upgrade the system, as explained in the previous section. Once an RPM specification file has been written (a task that might take some effort), future upgrades will be much less time consuming and have the advantage of being very easy to roll back.

But if the policy is to just overwrite files by hand, this section will explain how to do so as safely as possible.

All code should be thoroughly tested on a development machine before it is put on the live server, and both machines must have an identical software base (i.e., the same versions of the operating system, Apache, any software that Apache and mod_perl depend on, mod_perl itself, and all Perl modules). If the versions do not match, code that works perfectly on the development machine might not work on the live server.

For example, we have encountered a problem when the live and development servers were using different versions of the MySQL database server. The new code took advantage of new features added in the version installed on the development machine. The code was tested and shown to work correctly on the development machine, and when it was copied to the live server it seemed to work fine. Only by chance did we discover that scripts did not work correctly when the new features were used.

If the code hadn't worked at all, the problem would have been obvious and been detected and solved immediately, but the problem was subtle. Only after a thorough analysis did we understand that the problem was that we had an older version of the MySQL server on the live machine. This example reminded us that all modifications on the development machine should be logged and the live server updated with all of the modifications, not just the new version of the Perl code for a project.

We solved this particular problem by immediately reverting to the old code, upgrading the MySQL server on the live machine, and then successfully reapplying the new code.

Moving files and restarting the server. Now let's discuss the techniques used to upgrade live server scripts and handlers.

The most common scenario is a live running service that needs to be upgraded with a new version of the code. The new code has been prepared and uploaded to the production server, and the server has been restarted. Unfortunately, the service does not work anymore. What could be worse than that? There is no way back, because the original code has been overwritten with the new but non-working code.

Another scenario is where a whole set of files is being transferred to the live server but some network problem has occurred in the middle, which has slowed things down or totally aborted the transfer. With some of the files old and some new, the service is most likely broken. Since some files were overwritten, you can't roll back to the previously working version of the service.

No matter what file transfer technique is used, be it FTP, NFS, or anything else, live running code should never be directly overwritten during file transfer. Instead, files should be transferred to a temporary directory on the live machine, ready to be moved when necessary. If the transfer fails, it can then be restarted safely.

Both scenarios can be made safer with two approaches. First, do not overwrite working files. Second, use a revision control system such as CVS so that changes to working code can easily be undone if the working code is accidentally overwritten. Revision control will be covered later in this chapter.

We recommend performing all updates on the live server in the following sequence. Assume for this example that the project's code directory is */home/httpd/perl/rel*. When we're about to update the files, we create a new directory, */home/httpd/perl/test*, into which we copy the new files. Then we do some final sanity checks: check that file permissions are readable and executable for the user the server is running under, and run *perl -Tcw* on the new modules to make sure there are no syntax errors in them.

To save some typing, we set up some aliases for some of the *apachectl* commands and for *tail*ing the *error_log* file:

```
panic% alias graceful /home/httpd/httpd_perl/bin/apachectl graceful
panic% alias restart  /home/httpd/httpd_perl/bin/apachectl restart
panic% alias start    /home/httpd/httpd_perl/bin/apachectl start
panic% alias stop     /home/httpd/httpd_perl/bin/apachectl stop
panic% alias err      tail -f /home/httpd/httpd_perl/logs/error_log
```

Finally, when we think we are ready, we do:

```
panic% cd /home/httpd/perl
panic% mv rel old && mv test rel && stop && sleep 3 && restart && err
```

Note that all the commands are typed as a single line, joined by &&, and only at the end should the Enter key be pressed. The && ensures that if any command fails, the following commands will not be executed.

The elements of this command line are:

```
mv rel old &&
```
> Backs up the working directory to *old*, so none of the original code is deleted or overwritten

```
mv test rel &&
```
>   Puts the new code in place of the original

```
stop &&
```
>   Stops the server

```
sleep 3 &&
```
>   Allows the server a few seconds to shut down (it might need a longer sleep)

```
restart &&
```
>   Restarts the server

```
err
```
>   *tail*s the *error_log* file to make sure that everything is OK

If *mv* is overriden by a global alias *mv -i*, which requires confirming every action, you will need to call *mv -f* to override the *-i* option.

When updating code on a remote machine, it's a good idea to prepend *nohup* to the beginning of the command line:

```
panic% nohup mv rel old && mv test rel && stop && sleep 3 && restart && err
```

This approach ensures that if the connection is suddenly dropped, the server will not stay down if the last command that executes is *stop*.

apachectl generates its status messages a little too early. For example, when we execute *apachectl stop*, a message saying that the server has been stopped is displayed, when in fact the server is still running. Similarly, when we execute *apachectl start*, a message is displayed saying that the server has been started, while it is possible that it hasn't yet. In both cases, this happens because these status messages are not generated by Apache itself. Do not rely on them. Rely on the *error_log* file instead, where the running Apache server indicates its real status.

Also note that we use *restart* and not just *start*. This is because of Apache's potentially long stopping times if it has to run lots of destruction and cleanup code on exit. If *start* is used and Apache has not yet released the port it is listening to, the start will fail and the *error_log* will report that the port is in use. For example:

```
Address already in use: make_sock: could not bind to port 8000
```

However, if *restart* is used, *apachectl* will wait for the server to quit and unbind the port and will then cleanly restart it.

Now, what happens if the new modules are broken and the newly restarted server reports problems or refuses to start at all?

The aliased *err* command executes *tail -f* on the *error_log*, so that the failed restart or any other problems will be immediately apparent. The situation can quickly and easily be rectified by returning the system to its pre-upgrade state with this command:

```
panic% mv rel bad && mv old rel && stop && sleep 3 && restart && err
```

This command line moves the new code to the directory *bad*, moves the original code back into the runtime directory *rel*, then stops and restarts the server. Once the server is back up and running, you can analyze the cause of the problem, fix it, and repeat the upgrade again. Usually everything will be fine if the code has been extensively tested on the development server. When upgrades go smoothly, the downtime should be only about 5–10 seconds, and most users will not even notice anything has happened.

Using CVS for code upgrades. The *Concurrent Versions System* (CVS) is an open source version-control system that allows multiple developers to work on code or configuration in a central repository while tracking any changes made. We use it because it's the dominant open source tool, but it's not the only possibility: commercial tools such as Perforce would also work for these purposes.

If you aren't familiar with CVS, you can learn about it from the resources provided at the end of this chapter. CVS is too broad a topic to be covered in this book. Instead, we will concentrate on the CVS techniques that are relevant to our purpose.

Things are much simpler when using CVS for server updates, especially since it allows you to tag each production release. By *tagging* files, we mean having a group of files under CVS control share a common label. Like RCS and other revision-control systems, CVS gives each file its own version number, which allows us to manipulate different versions of this file. But if we want to operate on a group of many files, chances are that they will have different version numbers. Suppose we want to take snapshots of the whole project so we can refer to these snapshots some time in the future, after the files have been modified and their respective version numbers have been changed. We can do this using tags.

To tag the project whose module name is *myproject*, execute the following from any directory on any machine:

```
panic% cvs -rtag PRODUCTION_1_20 myproject
```

Now when the time comes to update the online version, go to the directory on the live machine that needs to be updated and execute:

```
panic% cvs update -dP -r PRODUCTION_1_20
```

The *-P* option to *cvs* prunes empty directories and deleted files, the *-d* option brings in new directories and files (like *cvs checkout* does), and *-r PRODUCTION_1_20* tells CVS to update the current directory recursively to the PRODUCTION_1_20 CVS version of the project.

Suppose that after a while, we have more code updated and we need to make a new release. The currently running version has the tag PRODUCTION_1_20, and the new version has the tag PRODUCTION_1_21. First we tag the files in the current state with a new tag:

```
panic% cvs -rtag PRODUCTION_1_21 myproject
```

and update the live machine:

```
panic% cvs update -dP -r PRODUCTION_1_21
```

Now if there is a problem, we can go back to the previous working version very easily. If we want to get back to version PRODUCTION_1_20, we can run the command:

```
panic% cvs update -dP -r PRODUCTION_1_20
```

As before, the update brings in new files and directories not already present in the local directory (because of the *-dP* options).

Remember that when you use CVS to update the live server, you should avoid making any minor changes to the code on this server. That's because of potential collisions that might happen during the CVS update. If you modify a single line in a single file and then do *cvs update*, and someone else modifies the same line at the same time and commits it just before you do, CVS will try to merge the changes. If they are different, it will see a conflict and insert both versions into the file. CVS leaves it to you to resolve the conflict. If this file is Perl code, it won't compile and it will cause temporal troubles until the conflict is resolved. Therefore, the best approach is to think of live server files as being read-only.

Updating the live code directory should be done only if the update is atomic—i.e., if all files are updated in a very short period of time, and when no network problems can occur that might delay the completion of the file update.

The safest approach is to use CVS in conjunction with the safe code update technique presented previously, by working with CVS in a separate directory. When all files are extracted, move them to the directory the live server uses. Better yet, use symbolic links, as described earlier in this chapter: when you update the code, prepare everything in a new directory and, when you're ready, just change the symlink to point to this new directory. This approach will prevent cases where only a partial update happens because of a network or other problem.

The use of CVS needn't apply exclusively to code. It can be of great benefit for configuration management, too. Just as you want your mod_perl programs to be identical between the development and production servers, you probably also want to keep your *httpd.conf* files in sync. CVS is well suited for this task too, and the same methods apply.

Disabling Scripts and Handlers on a Live Server

Perl programs running on the mod_perl server may be dependent on resources that can become temporarily unavailable when they are being upgraded or maintained. For example, once in a while a database server (and possibly its corresponding DBD module) may need to be upgraded, rendering it unusable for a short period of time.

Using the development server as a temporary replacement is probably the best way to continue to provide service during the upgrade. But if you can't, the service will be unavailable for a while.

Since none of the code that relies on the temporarily unavailable resource will work, users trying to access the mod_perl server will see either the ugly gray "An Error has occurred" message or a customized error message (if code has been added to trap errors and customize the error-reporting facility). In any case, it's not a good idea to let users see these errors, as they will make your web site seem amateurish.

A friendlier approach is to confess to the users that some maintenance work is being undertaken and plead for patience, promising that the service will become fully functional in a few minutes (or however long the scheduled downtime is expected to be).

It is a good idea to be honest and report the real duration of the maintenance operation, not just "we will be back in 10 minutes." Think of a user (or journalist) coming back 20 minutes later and still seeing the same message! Make sure that if the time of resumption of service is given, it is not the system's local time, since users will be visiting the site from different time zones. Instead, we suggest using Greenwich Mean Time (GMT). Most users have some idea of the time difference between their location and GMT, or can find out easily enough. Although GMT is known by programmers as Universal Coordinated Time (UTC), end users may not know what UTC is, so using the older acronym is probably best.

Disabling code running under Apache::Registry

If just a few scripts need to be disabled temporarily, and if they are running under the Apache::Registry handler, a maintenance message can be displayed without messing with the server. Prepare a little script in */home/httpd/perl/down4maintenance.pl*:

```
#!/usr/bin/perl -Tw

use strict;
print "Content-type: text/plain\n\n",
  qq{We regret that the service is temporarily
     unavailable while essential maintenance is undertaken.
     It is expected to be back online from 12:20 GMT.
     Please, bear with us. Thank you!};
```

Let's say you now want to disable the */home/httpd/perl/chat.pl* script. Just do this:

```
panic% mv /home/httpd/perl/chat.pl /home/httpd/perl/chat.pl.orig
panic% ln -s /home/httpd/perl/down4maintenance.pl /home/httpd/perl/chat.pl
```

Of course, the server configuration must allow symbolic links for this trick to work. Make sure that the directive:

```
Options FollowSymLinks
```

is in the <Location> or <Directory> section of *httpd.conf*.

Alternatively, you can just back up the real script and then copy the file over it:

```
panic% cp /home/httpd/perl/chat.pl /home/httpd/perl/chat.pl.orig
panic% cp /home/httpd/perl/down4maintenance.pl /home/httpd/perl/chat.pl
```

Once the maintenance work has been completed, restoring the previous setup is easy. Simply overwrite the symbolic link or the file:

```
panic% mv /home/httpd/perl/chat.pl.orig /home/httpd/perl/chat.pl
```

Now make sure that the script has the current timestamp:

```
panic% touch /home/httpd/perl/chat.pl
```

Apache::Registry will automatically detect the change and use the new script from now on.

This scenario is possible because Apache::Registry checks the modification time of the script before each invocation. If the script's file is more recent than the version already loaded in memory, Apache::Registry reloads the script from disk.

Disabling code running under other handlers

Under non-Apache::Registry handlers, you need to modify the configuration. You must either point all requests to a new location or replace the handler with one that will serve the requests during the maintenance period.

Example 5-2 illustrates a maintenance handler.

Example 5-2. Book/Maintenance.pm

```
package Book::Maintenance;

use strict;
use Apache::Constants qw(:common);

sub handler {
  my $r = shift;
  $r->send_http_header("text/plain");
  print qq{We regret that the service is temporarily
          unavailable while essential maintenance is undertaken.
          It is expected to be back online from 12:20 GMT.
          Please be patient. Thank you!};
  return OK;
}
1;
```

In practice, the maintenance script may well read the "back online" time from a variable set with a PerlSetVar directive in *httpd.conf*, so the script itself need never be changed.

Edit *httpd.conf* and change the handler line from:

```
<Location /perl>
    SetHandler perl-script
```

```
    PerlHandler Book::Handler
    ...
</Location>
```

to:

```
<Location /perl>
    SetHandler perl-script
    #PerlHandler Book::Handler
    PerlHandler Book::Maintenance
    ...
</Location>
```

Now restart the server. Users will be happy to read their email for 10 minutes, knowing that they will return to a much improved service.

Disabling services with help from the frontend server

Many sites use a more complicated setup in which a "light" Apache frontend server serves static content but proxies all requests for dynamic content to the "heavy" mod_perl backend server (see Chapter 12). Those sites can use a third solution to temporarily disable scripts.

Since the frontend machine rewrites all incoming requests to appropriate requests for the backend machine, a change to the RewriteRule is sufficient to take handlers out of service. Just change the directives to rewrite all incoming requests (or a subgroup of them) to a single URI. This URI simply tells users that the service is not available during the maintenance period.

For example, the following RewriteRule rewrites all URIs starting with */perl* to the maintenance URI */control/maintain* on the mod_perl server:

```
RewriteRule ^/perl/(.*)$ http://localhost:8000/control/maintain [P,L]
```

The Book::Maintenance handler from the previous section can be used to generate the response to the URI */control/maintain*.

Make sure that this rule is placed before all the other RewriteRules so that none of the other rules need to be commented out. Once the change has been made, check that the configuration is not broken and restart the server so that the new configuration takes effect. Now the database server can be shut down, the upgrade can be performed, and the database server can be restarted. The RewriteRule that has just been added can be commented out and the Apache server stopped and restarted. If the changes lead to any problems, the maintenance RewriteRule can simply be uncommented while you sort them out.

Of course, all this is error-prone, especially when the maintenance is urgent. Therefore, it can be a good idea to prepare all the required configurations ahead of time, by having different configuration sections and enabling the right one with the help of the IfDefine directive during server startup.

The following configuration will make this approach clear:

```
RewriteEngine On

<IfDefine maintain>
    RewriteRule /perl/  http://localhost:8000/control/maintain [P,L]
</IfDefine>

<IfDefine !maintain>
    RewriteRule ^/perl/(.*)$ http://localhost:8000/$1 [P,L]
    # more directives
</IfDefine>
```

Now enable the maintenance section by starting the server with:

```
panic% httpd -Dmaintain
```

Request URIs starting with */perl/* will be processed by the */control/maintain* handler or script on the mod_perl side.

If the *-Dmaintain* option is not passed, the "normal" configuration will take effect and each URI will be remapped to the mod_perl server as usual.

Of course, if *apachectl* or any other script is used for server control, this new mode should be added so that it will be easy to make the correct change without making any mistakes. When you're in a rush, the less typing you have to do, the better. Ideally, all you'd have to type is:

```
panic% apachectl maintain
```

Which will both shut down the server (if it is running) and start it with the *-Dmaintain* option. Alternatively, you could use:

```
panic% apachectl start_maintain
```

to start the server in maintenance mode. *apachectl graceful* will stop the server and restart it in normal mode.

Scheduled Routine Maintenance

If maintenance tasks can be scheduled when no one is using the server, you can write a simple `PerlAccessHandler` that will automatically disable the server and return a page stating that the server is under maintenance and will be back online at a specified time. When using this approach, you don't need to worry about fiddling with the server configuration when the maintenance hour comes. However, all maintenance must be completed within the given time frame, because once the time is up, the service will resume.

The `Apache::DayLimit` module from *http://www.modperl.com/* is a good example of such a module. It provides options for specifying which day server maintenance occurs. For example, if Sundays are used for maintenance, the configuration for `Apache::DayLimit` is as follows:

```
<Location /perl>
    PerlSetVar ReqDay Sunday
    PerlAccessHandler Apache::DayLimit
</Location>
```

It is very easy to adapt this module to do more advanced filtering. For example, to specify both a day and a time, use a configuration similar to this:

```
<Location /perl>
    PerlSetVar ReqDay     Sunday
    PerlSetVar StartHour  09:00
    PerlSetVar EndHour    11:00
    PerlAccessHandler Apache::DayTimeLimit
</Location>
```

Three-Tier Server Scheme: Development, Staging, and Production

To facilitate transfer from the development server to the production server, the code should be free of any server-dependent variables. This will ensure that modules and scripts can be moved from one directory on the development machine to another directory (possibly in a different path) on the production machine without problems.

If two simple rules are followed, server dependencies can be safely isolated and, as far as the code goes, effectively ignored. First, never use the server name (since development and production machines have different names), and second, never use explicit base directory names in the code. Of course, the code will often need to refer to the server name and directory names, but we can centralize them in server-wide configuration files (as seen in a moment).

By trial and error, we have found that a three-tier (development, staging, and production) scheme works best:

Development

> The development tier might include a single machine or several machines (for example, if there are many developers and each one prefers to develop on his own machine).

Staging

> The staging tier is generally a single machine that is basically identical to the production machine and serves as a backup machine in case the production machine needs an immediate replacement (for example, during maintenance). This is the last station where the code is staged before it is uploaded to the production machine.

> The staging machine does not have to be anywhere near as powerful as the production server if finances are stretched. The staging machine is generally used only for staging; it does not require much processor power or memory since only a few developers are likely to use it simultaneously. Even if several developers are

using it at the same time, the load will be very low, unless of course benchmarks are being run on it along with programs that create a load similar to that on the production server (in which case the staging machine should have hardware identical to that of the production machine).

Production
The production tier might include a single machine or a huge cluster comprising many machines.

You can also have the staging and production servers running on the same machine. This is not ideal, especially if the production server needs every megabyte of memory and every CPU cycle so that it can cope with high request rates. But when a dedicated machine just for staging purposes is prohibitively expensive, using the production server for staging purposes is better than having no staging area at all.

Another possibility is to have the staging environment on the development machine.

So how does this three-tier scheme work?

- Developers write the code on their machines (development tier) and test that it works as expected. These machines should be set up with an environment as similar to the production server as possible. A manageable and simple approach is to have each developer running his own local Apache server on his own machine. If the code relies on a database, the ideal scenario is for each developer to have access to a development database account and server, possibly even on their own machines.

- The pre-release manager installs the code on the staging tier machine and stages it. Whereas developers can change their own *httpd.conf* files on their own machines, the pre-release manager will make the necessary changes on the staging machine in accordance with the instructions provided by the developers.

- The release manager installs the code on the production tier machine(s), tests it, and monitors for a while to ensure that things work as expected.

Of course, on some projects, the developers, the pre-release managers, and the release managers can actually be the same person. On larger projects, where different people perform these roles and many machines are involved, preparing upgrade packages with a packaging tool such as RPM becomes even more important, since it makes it far easier to keep every machine's configuration and software in sync.

Now that we have described the theory behind the three-tier approach, let us see how to have all the code independent of the machine and base directory names.

Although the example shown below is simple, the real configuration may be far more complex; however, the principles apply regardless of complexity, and it is straightforward to build a simple initial configuration into a configuration that is sufficient for more complex environments.

Basically, what we need is the name of the machine, the port on which the server is running (assuming that the port number is not hidden with the help of a proxy server), the root directory of the web server–specific files, the base directories of static objects and Perl scripts, the appropriate relative and full URIs for these base directories, and a support email address. This amounts to 10 variables.

We prepare a minimum of three Local::Config packages, one per tier, each suited to a particular tier's environment. As mentioned earlier, there can be more than one machine per tier and even more than one web server running on the same machine. In those cases, each web server will have its own Local::Config package. The total number of Local::Config packages will be equal to the number of web servers.

For example, for the development tier, the configuration package might look like Example 5-3.

Example 5-3. Local/Config.pm

```
package Local::Config;
use strict;
use constant SERVER_NAME      => 'dev.example.com';
use constant SERVER_PORT      => 8000;
use constant ROOT_DIR         => '/home/userfoo/www';
use constant CGI_BASE_DIR     => '/home/userfoo/www/perl';
use constant DOC_BASE_DIR     => '/home/userfoo/www/docs';
use constant CGI_BASE_URI     => 'http://dev.example.com:8000/perl';
use constant DOC_BASE_URI     => 'http://dev.example.com:8000';
use constant CGI_RELATIVE_URI => '/perl';
use constant DOC_RELATIVE_URI => '';
use constant SUPPORT_EMAIL    => 'stas@example.com';
1;
```

The constants have uppercase names, in accordance with Perl convention.

The configuration shows that the name of the development machine is *dev.example. com*, listening to port 8000. Web server–specific files reside under the */home/userfoo/www* directory. Think of this as a directory *www* that resides under user *userfoo*'s home directory, */home/userfoo*. A developer whose username is *userbar* might use */home/userbar/www* as the development root directory.

If there is another web server running on the same machine, create another Local::Config with a different port number and probably a different root directory.

To avoid duplication of identical parts of the configuration, the package can be rewritten as shown in Example 5-4.

Example 5-4. Local/Config.pm

```
package Local::Config;
use strict;
use constant DOMAIN_NAME   => 'example.com';
use constant SERVER_NAME   => 'dev.' . DOMAIN_NAME;
```

Example 5-4. Local/Config.pm (continued)

```perl
use constant SERVER_PORT      => 8000;
use constant ROOT_DIR         => '/home/userfoo/www';
use constant CGI_BASE_DIR     => ROOT_DIR . '/perl';
use constant DOC_BASE_DIR     => ROOT_DIR . '/docs';
use constant CGI_BASE_URI     => 'http://' . SERVER_NAME . ':' . SERVER_PORT
                                 . '/perl';
use constant DOC_BASE_URI     => 'http://' . SERVER_NAME . ':' . SERVER_PORT;
use constant CGI_RELATIVE_URI => '/perl';
use constant DOC_RELATIVE_URI => '';
use constant SUPPORT_EMAIL    => 'stas@' . DOMAIN_NAME;
1;
```

Reusing constants that were previously defined reduces the risk of making a mistake. In the original file, several lines need to be edited if the server name is changed, but in this new version only one line requires editing, eliminating the risk of your forgetting to change a line further down the file. All the use constant statements are executed at compile time, in the order in which they are specified. The constant pragma ensures that any attempt to change these variables in the code leads to an error, so they can be relied on to be correct. (Note that in certain contexts—e.g., when they're used as hash keys—Perl can misunderstand the use of constants. The solution is to either prepend & or append ( ), so ROOT_DIR would become either &ROOT_DIR or ROOT_DIR( ).)

Now, when the code needs to access the server's global configuration, it needs to refer only to the variables in this module. For example, in an application's configuration file, you can create a dynamically generated configuration, which will change from machine to machine without your needing to touch any code (see Example 5-5).

Example 5-5. App/Foo/Config.pm

```perl
package App::Foo::Config;

use Local::Config ();
use strict;
use vars qw($CGI_URI $CGI_DIR);

# directories and URIs of the App::Foo CGI project
$CGI_URI = $Local::Config::CGI_BASE_URI . '/App/Foo';
$CGI_DIR = $Local::Config::CGI_BASE_DIR . '/App/Foo';
1;
```

Notice that we used fully qualified variable names instead of importing these global configuration variables into the caller's namespace. This saves a few bytes of memory, and since Local::Config will be loaded by many modules, these savings will quickly add up. Programmers used to programming Perl outside the mod_perl environment might be tempted to add Perl's exporting mechanism to Local::Config and thereby save themselves some typing. We prefer not to use Exporter.pm under mod_perl, because we want to save as much memory as possible. (Even though the amount

---

of memory overhead for using an exported name is small, this must be multiplied by the number of concurrent users of the code, which could be hundreds or even thousands on a busy site and could turn a small memory overhead into a large one.)

For the staging tier, a similar `Local::Config` module with just a few changes (as shown in Example 5-6) is necessary.

Example 5-6. Local/Config.pm

```
package Local::Config;
use strict;
use constant DOMAIN_NAME      => 'example.com';
use constant SERVER_NAME      => 'stage.' . DOMAIN_NAME;
use constant SERVER_PORT      => 8000;
use constant ROOT_DIR         => '/home';
use constant CGI_BASE_DIR     => ROOT_DIR . '/perl';
use constant DOC_BASE_DIR     => ROOT_DIR . '/docs';
use constant CGI_BASE_URI     => 'http://' . SERVER_NAME . ':' . SERVER_PORT
                                 . '/perl';
use constant DOC_BASE_URI     => 'http://' . SERVER_NAME . ':' . SERVER_PORT;
use constant CGI_RELATIVE_URI => '/perl';
use constant DOC_RELATIVE_URI => '';
use constant SUPPORT_EMAIL    => 'stage@' . DOMAIN_NAME;
1;
```

We have named our staging tier machine *stage.example.com*. Its root directory is */home*.

The production tier version of `Local/Config.pm` is shown in Example 5-7.

Example 5-7. Local/Config.pm

```
package Local::Config;
use strict;
use constant DOMAIN_NAME      => 'example.com';
use constant SERVER_NAME      => 'www.' . DOMAIN_NAME;
use constant SERVER_PORT      => 8000;
use constant ROOT_DIR         => '/home/';
use constant CGI_BASE_DIR     => ROOT_DIR . '/perl';
use constant DOC_BASE_DIR     => ROOT_DIR . '/docs';
use constant CGI_BASE_URI     => 'http://' . SERVER_NAME . ':' . SERVER_PORT
                                 . '/perl';
use constant DOC_BASE_URI     => 'http://' . SERVER_NAME . ':' . SERVER_PORT;
use constant CGI_RELATIVE_URI => '/perl';
use constant DOC_RELATIVE_URI => '';
use constant SUPPORT_EMAIL    => 'support@' . DOMAIN_NAME;
```

You can see that the setups of the staging and production machines are almost identical. This is only in our example; in reality, they can be very different.

The most important point is that the `Local::Config` module from a machine on one tier must *never* be moved to a machine on another tier, since it will break the code. If locally built packages are used, the `Local::Config` file can simply be excluded—this will help to reduce the risk of inadvertently copying it.

From now on, when modules and scripts are moved between machines, you shouldn't need to worry about having to change variables to accomodate the different machines' server names and directory layouts. All this is accounted for by the `Local::Config` files.

Some developers prefer to run conversion scripts on the moved code that adjust all variables to the local machine. This approach is error-prone, since variables can be written in different ways, and it may result in incomplete adjustment and broken code. Therefore, the conversion approach is not recommended.

Starting a Personal Server for Each Developer

When just one developer is working on a specific server, there are fewer problems, because she can have complete control over the server. However, often a group of developers need to develop mod_perl scripts and modules concurrently on the same machine. Each developer wants to have control over the server: to be able to stop it, run it in single-server mode, restart it, etc. They also want control over the location of log files, configuration settings such as `MaxClients`, and so on.

Each developer might have her own desktop machine, but all development and staging might be done on a single central development machine (e.g., if the developers' personal desktop machines run a different operating system from the one running on the development and production machines).

One workaround for this problem involves having a few versions of the *httpd.conf* file (each having different `Port`, `ErrorLog`, etc. directives) and forcing each developer's server to be started with:

```
panic% httpd_perl -f /path/to/httpd.conf
```

However, this means that these files must be kept synchronized when there are global changes affecting all developers. This can be quite difficult to manage. The solution we use is to have a single *httpd.conf* file and use the *-Dparameter* server startup option to enable a specific section of *httpd.conf* for each developer. Each developer starts the server with his or her username as an argument. As a result, a server uses both the global settings and the developer's private settings.

For example, user *stas* would start his server with:

```
panic% httpd_perl -Dstas
```

In *httpd.conf*, we write:

```
# Personal development server for stas
# stas uses the server running on port 8000
<IfDefine stas>
    Port 8000
```

```
    PidFile /home/httpd/httpd_perl/logs/httpd.pid.stas
    ErrorLog /home/httpd/httpd_perl/logs/error_log.stas
    Timeout 300
    KeepAlive On
    MinSpareServers 2
    MaxSpareServers 2
    StartServers 1
    MaxClients 3
    MaxRequestsPerChild 15
    # let developers to add their own configuration
    # so they can override the defaults
    Include /home/httpd/httpd_perl/conf/stas.conf
</IfDefine>

# Personal development server for eric
# eric uses the server running on port 8001
<IfDefine eric>
    Port 8001
    PidFile /home/httpd/httpd_perl/logs/httpd.pid.eric
    ErrorLog /home/httpd/httpd_perl/logs/error_log.eric
    Timeout 300
    KeepAlive Off
    MinSpareServers 1
    MaxSpareServers 2
    StartServers 1
    MaxClients 5
    MaxRequestsPerChild 0
    Include /home/httpd/httpd_perl/conf/eric.conf
</IfDefine>
```

With this technique, we have separate *error_log* files and full control over server starting and stopping, the number of child processes, and port selection for each server. This saves Eric from having to call Stas several times a day just to warn, "Stas, I'm restarting the server" (a ritual in development shops where all developers are using the same mod_perl server).

With this technique, developers will need to learn the PIDs of their parent *httpd_perl* processes. For user *stas*, this can be found in */home/httpd/httpd_perl/logs/httpd.pid. stas*. To make things even easier, we change the *apachectl* script to do the work for us. We make a copy for each developer, called *apachectl.username*, and change two lines in each script:

```
PIDFILE=/home/httpd/httpd_perl/logs/httpd.pid.username
HTTPD='/home/httpd/httpd_perl/bin/httpd_perl -Dusername'
```

For user *stas*, we prepare a startup script called *apachectl.stas* and change these two lines in the standard *apachectl* script:

```
PIDFILE=/home/httpd/httpd_perl/logs/httpd.pid.stas
HTTPD='/home/httpd/httpd_perl/bin/httpd_perl -Dstas'
```

Now when user *stas* wants to stop the server, he executes:

```
panic% apachectl.stas stop
```

And to start the server, he executes:

```
panic% apachectl.stas start
```

And so on, for all other *apachectl* arguments.

It might seem that we could have used just one *apachectl* and have it determine for itself who executed it by checking the UID. But the setuid bit must be enabled on this script, because starting the server requires *root* privileges. With the setuid bit set, a single *apachectl* script can be used for all developers, but it will have to be modified to include code to read the UID of the user executing it and to use this value when setting developer-specific paths and variables.

The last thing you need to do is to provide developers with an option to run in single-process mode. For example:

```
panic% /home/httpd/httpd_perl/bin/httpd_perl -Dstas -X
```

In addition to making the development process easier, we decided to use relative links in all static documents, including calls to dynamically generated documents. Since each developer's server is running on a different port, we have to make it possible for these relative links to reach the correct port number.

When typing the URI by hand, it's easy. For example, when user *stas*, whose server is running on port 8000, wants to access the relative URI */test/example*, he types *http://www.example.com:8000/test/example* to get the generated HTML page. Now if this document includes a link to the relative URI */test/example2* and *stas* clicks on it, the browser will automatically generate a full request (*http://www.example.com:8000/test/example2*) by reusing the *server:port* combination from the previous request.

Note that all static objects will be served from the same server as well. This may be an acceptable situation for the development environment, but if it is not, a slightly more complicated solution involving the mod_rewrite Apache module will have to be devised.

To use mod_rewrite, we have to configure our *httpd_docs* (light) server with *--enable-module=rewrite* and recompile, or use DSOs and load and enable the module in *httpd.conf*. In the *httpd.conf* file of our *httpd_docs* server, we have the following code:

```
RewriteEngine on

# stas's server
# port = 8000
RewriteCond  %{REQUEST_URI} ^/perl
RewriteCond  %{REMOTE_ADDR} 123.34.45.56
RewriteRule ^(.*)            http://example.com:8000/$1 [P,L]

# eric's server
# port = 8001
RewriteCond  %{REQUEST_URI} ^/perl
RewriteCond  %{REMOTE_ADDR} 123.34.45.57
RewriteRule ^(.*)            http://example.com:8001/$1 [P,L]
```

```
# all the rest
RewriteCond  %{REQUEST_URI} ^/perl
RewriteRule ^(.*)            http://example.com:81/$1 [P]
```

The IP addresses are those of the developer desktop machines (i.e., where they run their web browsers). If an HTML file includes a relative URI such as */perl/test.pl* or even *http://www.example.com/perl/test.pl*, requests for those URIs from user *stas*'s machine will be internally proxied to *http://www.example.com:8000/perl/test.pl*, and requests generated from user *eric*'s machine will be proxied to *http://www.example. com:8001/perl/test.pl*.

Another possibility is to use the REMOTE_USER variable. This requires that all developers be authenticated when they access the server. To do so, change the RewriteRules to match REMOTE_USER in the above example.

Remember, the above setup will work only with relative URIs in the HTML code. If the HTML output by the code uses full URIs including a port other than 80, the requests originating from this HTML code will bypass the light server listening on the default port 80 and go directly to the server and port of the full URI.

Web Server Monitoring

Once the production system is working, you may think that the job is done and the developers can switch to a new project. Unfortunately, in most cases the server will still need to be maintained to make sure that everything is working as expected, to ensure that the web server is always up, and much more. A large part of this job can be automated, which will save time. It will also increase the uptime of the server, since automated processes generally work faster than manual ones. If created properly, automated processes also will always work correctly, whereas human operators are likely to make occassional mistakes.

Interactive Monitoring

When you're getting started, it usually helps to monitor the server interactively. Many different tools are available to do this. We will discuss a few of them now.

When writing automated monitoring tools, you should start by monitoring the tools themselves until they are reliable and stable enough to be left to work by themselves.

Even when everything is automated, you should check at regular intervals that everything is working OK, since a minor change in a single component can silently break the whole monitoring system. A good example is a silent failure of the mail system—if all alerts from the monitoring tools are delivered through email, having no messages from the system does not necessarily mean that everything is OK. If emails alerting about a problem cannot reach the webmaster because of a broken email system, the webmaster will not realize that a problem exists. (Of course, the mailing system should be monitored as well, but then problems must be reported by means other than email. One common solution is to send messages by both email and to a mobile phone's short message service.)

Another very important (albeit often-forgotten) risk time is the post-upgrade period. Even after a minor upgrade, the whole service should be monitored closely for a while.

The first and simplest check is to visit a few pages from the service to make sure that things are working. Of course, this might not suffice, since different pages might use different resources—while code that does not use the database system might work properly, code that does use it might not work if the database server is down.

The second thing to check is the web server's *error_log* file. If there are any problems, they will probably be reported here. However, only obvious syntactic or malfunction bugs will appear here—the subtle bugs that are a result of bad program logic will be revealed only through careful testing (which should have been completed before upgrading the live server).

Periodic system health checking can be done using the *top* utility, which shows free memory and swap space, the machine's CPU load, etc.

Apache::VMonitor—The Visual System and Apache Server Monitor

The Apache::VMonitor module provides even better monitoring functionality than *top*. It supplies all the relevant information that *top* does, plus all the Apache-specific information provided by Apache's mod_status module (request processing time, last request's URI, number of requests served by each child, etc.) In addition, Apache::VMonitor emulates the reporting functions of the *top*, *mount*, and *df* utilities.

Apache::VMonitor has a special mode for mod_perl processes. It also has visual alerting capabilities and a configurable "automatic refresh" mode. A web interface can be used to show or hide all sections dynamically.

The module provides two main viewing modes:

* Multi-processes and overall system status
* Single-process extensive reporting

Prerequisites and configuration

To run Apache::VMonitor, you need to have Apache::Scoreboard installed and configured in *httpd.conf*. Apache::Scoreboard, in turn, requires mod_status to be installed with ExtendedStatus enabled. In *httpd.conf*, add:

```
ExtendedStatus On
```

Turning on extended mode will add a certain overhead to each request's response time. If every millisecond counts, you may not want to use it in production.

You also need `Time::HiRes` and `GTop` to be installed. And, of course, you need a running mod_perl-enabled Apache server.

To enable `Apache::VMonitor`, add the following configuration to *httpd.conf*:

```
<Location /system/vmonitor>
    SetHandler perl-script
    PerlHandler Apache::VMonitor
</Location>
```

The monitor will be displayed when you request *http://localhost/system/vmonitor/*.

You probably want to protect this location from unwanted visitors. If you are accessing this location from the same IP address, you can use a simple host-based authentication:

```
<Location /system/vmonitor>
    SetHandler perl-script
    PerlHandler Apache::VMonitor
    order deny,allow
    deny  from all
    allow from 132.123.123.3
</Location>
```

Alternatively, you may use Basic or other authentication schemes provided by Apache and its extensions.

You should load the module in *httpd.conf*:

```
PerlModule Apache::VMonitor
```

or from the the startup file:

```
use Apache::VMonitor();
```

You can control the behavior of `Apache::VMonitor` by configuring variables in the startup file or inside the `<Perl>` section. To alter the monitor reporting behavior, tweak the following configuration arguments from within the startup file:

```
$Apache::VMonitor::Config{BLINKING} = 1;
$Apache::VMonitor::Config{REFRESH}  = 0;
$Apache::VMonitor::Config{VERBOSE}  = 0;
```

To control what sections are to be displayed when the tool is first accessed, configure the following variables:

```
$Apache::VMonitor::Config{SYSTEM}   = 1;
$Apache::VMonitor::Config{APACHE}   = 1;
$Apache::VMonitor::Config{PROCS}    = 1;
$Apache::VMonitor::Config{MOUNT}    = 1;
$Apache::VMonitor::Config{FS_USAGE} = 1;
```

You can control the sorting of the mod_perl processes report by sorting them by one of the following columns: `pid`, `mode`, `elapsed`, `lastreq`, `served`, `size`, `share`, `vsize`, `rss`, `client`, or `request`. For example, to sort by the process size, use the following setting:

```
$Apache::VMonitor::Config{SORT_BY}  = "size";
```

As the application provides an option to monitor processes other than mod_perl processes, you can define a regular expression to match the relevant processes. For example, to match the process names that include "httpd_docs", "mysql", and "squid", the following regular expression could be used:

```
$Apache::VMonitor::PROC_REGEX = 'httpd_docs|mysql|squid';
```

We will discuss all these configuration options and their influence on the application shortly.

Multi-processes and system overall status reporting mode

The first mode is the one that's used most often, since it allows you to monitor almost all important system resources from one location. For your convenience, you can turn different sections on and off on the report, to make it possible for reports to fit into one screen.

This mode comes with the following features:

Automatic Refresh Mode
> You can tell the application to refresh the report every few seconds. You can preset this value at server startup. For example, to set the refresh to 60 seconds, add the following configuration setting:
> ```
> $Apache::VMonitor::Config{REFRESH} = 60;
> ```
> A 0 (zero) value turns off automatic refresh.
>
> When the server is started, you can always adjust the refresh rate through the user interface.

top Emulation: System Health Report
> Like *top*, this shows the current date/time, machine uptime, average load, and all the system CPU and memory usage levels (CPU load, real memory, and swap partition usage).
>
> The *top* section includes a swap space usage visual alert capability. As we will explain later in this chapter, swapping is very undesirable on production systems. This tool helps to detect abnormal swapping situations by changing the swap report row's color according to the following rules:
> ```
> swap usage                        report color
> -----------------------------------------------------
> 5Mb < swap < 10 MB                light red
> 20% < swap (swapping is bad!)     red
> 70% < swap (almost all used!)     red + blinking (if enabled)
> ```
> Note that you can turn on the blinking mode with:
> ```
> $Apache::VMonitor::Config{BLINKING} = 1;
> ```

The module doesn't alert when swap is being used just a little (< 5 Mb), since swapping is common on many Unix systems, even when there is plenty of free RAM.

If you don't want the system section to be displayed, set:

```
$Apache::VMonitor::Config{SYSTEM} = 0;
```

The default is to display this section.

top Emulation: Apache/mod_perl Processes Status

Like *top*, this emulation gives a report of the processes, but it shows only information relevant to mod_perl processes. The report includes the status of the process (Starting, Reading, Sending, Waiting, etc.), process ID, time since the current request was started, last request processing time, size, and shared, virtual, and resident size. It shows the last client's IP address and the first 64 characters of the request URI.

This report can be sorted by any column by clicking on the name of the column while running the application. The sorting can also be preset with the following setting:

```
$Apache::VMonitor::Config{SORT_BY}  = "size";
```

The valid choices are `pid`, `mode`, `elapsed`, `lastreq`, `served`, `size`, `share`, `vsize`, `rss`, `client`, and `request`.

The section is concluded with a report about the total memory being used by all mod_perl processes as reported by the kernel, plus an extra number approximating the real memory usage when memory sharing is taking place. We discuss this in more detail in Chapter 10.

If you don't want the mod_perl processes section to be displayed, set:

```
$Apache::VMonitor::Config{APACHE} = 0;
```

The default is to display this section.

top Emulation: Any Processes

This section, just like the mod_perl processes section, displays the information as the *top* program would. To enable this section, set:

```
$Apache::VMonitor::Config{PROCS} = 1;
```

The default is not to display this section.

You need to specify which processes are to be monitored. The regular expression that will match the desired processes is required for this section to work. For example, if you want to see all the processes whose names include any of the strings "http", "mysql", or "squid", use the following regular expression:

```
$Apache::VMonitor::PROC_REGEX = 'httpd|mysql|squid';
```

Figure 5-1 visualizes the sections that have been discussed so far. As you can see, the swap memory is heavily used. Although you can't see it here, the swap memory report is colored red.

mount Emulation

This section provides information about mounted filesystems, as if you had called *mount* with no parameters.

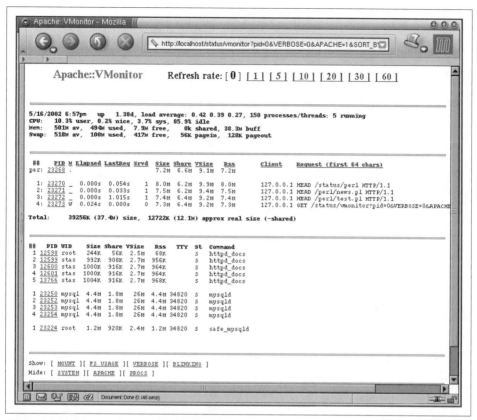

Figure 5-1. Emulation of top, centralized information about mod_perl and selected processes

If you want the *mount* section to be displayed, set:

```
$Apache::VMonitor::Config{MOUNT} = 1;
```

The default is not to display this section.

df Emulation

This section completely reproduces the *df* utility. For each mounted filesystem, it reports the number of total and available blocks for both superuser and user, and usage in percentages. In addition, it reports available and used file inodes in numbers and percentages.

This section can give you a visual alert when a filesystem becomes more than 90% full or when there are less than 10% of free file inodes left. The relevant filesystem row will be displayed in red and in a bold font. A mount point directory will blink if blinking is turned on. You can turn the blinking on with:

```
$Apache::VMonitor::Config{BLINKING} = 1;
```

If you don't want the *df* section to be displayed, set:

```
$Apache::VMonitor::Config{FS_USAGE} = 0;
```

The default is to display this section.

Figure 5-2 presents an example of the report consisting of the last two sections that were discussed (*df* and *mount* emulation), plus the ever-important mod_perl processes report.

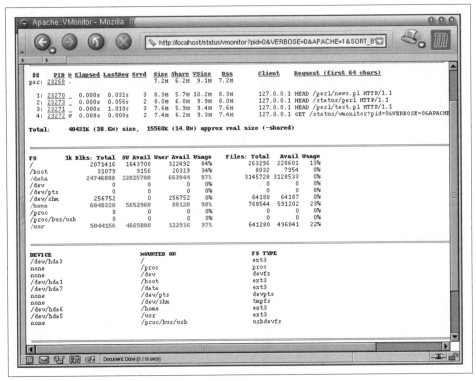

Figure 5-2. Emulation of df, both inodes and blocks

In Figure 5-2, the */mnt/cdrom* and */usr* filesystems are more than 90% full and therefore are colored red. This is normal for */mnt/cdrom*, which is a mounted CD-ROM, but might be critical for the */usr* filesystem, which should be cleaned up or enlarged.

Abbreviations and hints

The report uses many abbreviations that might be new for you. If you enable the VERBOSE mode with:

```
$Apache::VMonitor::Config{VERBOSE} = 1;
```

this section will reveal the full names of the abbreviations at the bottom of the report.

The default is not to display this section.

Single-process extensive reporting system

If you need to get in-depth information about a single process, just click on its PID. If the chosen process is a mod_perl process, the following information is displayed:

- Process type (child or parent), status of the process (Starting, Reading, Sending, Waiting, etc.), and how long the current request has been being processed (or how long the previous request was processed for, if the process is inactive at the moment the report was made).

- How many bytes have been transferred so far, and how many requests have been served per child and per slot. (When the child process quits, it is replaced by a new process running in the same slot.)

- CPU times used by the process: total, utime, stime, cutime, cstime.

For all processes (mod_perl and non-mod_perl), the following information is reported:

- General process information: UID, GID, state, TTY, and command-line arguments

- Memory usage: size, share, VSize, and RSS

- Memory segments usage: text, shared lib, date, and stack

- Memory maps: start-end, offset, device_major:device_minor, inode, perm, and library path

- Sizes of loaded libraries

Just as with the multi-process mode, this mode allows you to automatically refresh the page at the desired intervals.

Figures 5-3, 5-4, and 5-5 show an example report for one mod_perl process.

Automated Monitoring

As we mentioned earlier, the more things are automated, the more stable the server will be. In general, there are three things that we want to ensure:

1. Apache is up and properly serving requests. Remember that it can be running but unable to serve requests (for example, if there is a stale lock and all processes are waiting to acquire it).

2. All the resources that mod_perl relies on are available and working. This might include database engines, SMTP services, NIS or LDAP services, etc.

3. The system is healthy. Make sure that there is no system resource contention, such as a small amount of free RAM, a heavily swapping system, or low disk space.

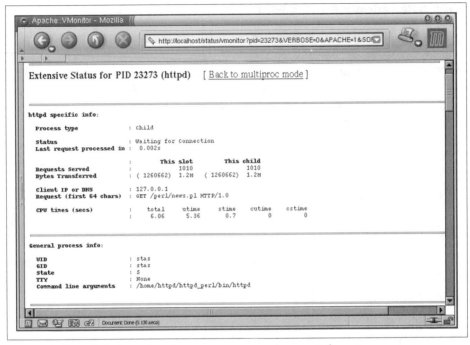

Figure 5-3. Extended information about processes: general process information

None of these categories has a higher priority than the others. A system administrator's role includes the proper functioning of the whole system. Even if the administrator is responsible for just part of the system, she must still ensure that her part does not cause problems for the system as a whole. If any of the above categories is not monitored, the system is not safe.

A specific setup might certainly have additional concerns that are not covered here, but it is most likely that they will fall into one of the above categories.

Before we delve into details, we should mention that all automated tools can be divided into two categories: tools that know how to detect problems and notify the owner, and tools that not only detect problems but also try to solve them, notifying the owner about both the problems and the results of the attempt to solve them.

Automatic tools are generally called *watchdogs*. They can alert the owner when there is a problem, just as a watchdog will bark when something is wrong. They will also try to solve problems themselves when the owner is not around, just as watchdogs will bite thieves when their owners are asleep.

Although some tools can perform corrective actions when something goes wrong without human intervention (e.g., during the night or on weekends), for some problems it may be that only human intervention can resolve the situation. In such cases,

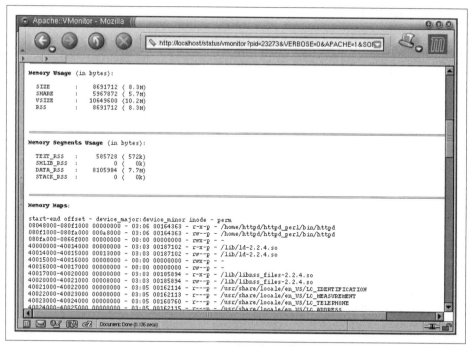

Figure 5-4. Extended information about processes: memory usage and maps

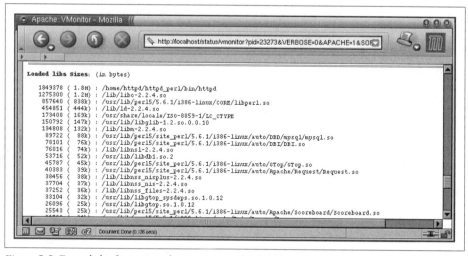

Figure 5-5. Extended information about processes: loaded libraries

the tool should not attempt to do anything at all. For example, if a hardware failure occurs, it is almost certain that a human will have to intervene.

Below are some techniques and tools that apply to each category.

mod_perl server watchdogs

One simple watchdog solution is to use a slightly modified *apachectl* script, which we have called *apache.watchdog*. Call it from *cron* every 30 minutes—or even every minute—to make sure that the server is always up.

The *crontab* entry for 30-minute intervals would read:

```
5,35 * * * * /path/to/the/apache.watchdog >/dev/null 2>&1
```

The script is shown in Example 5-8.

Example 5-8. apache.watchdog

```
--------------------
#!/bin/sh

# This script is a watchdog checking whether
# the server is online.
# It tries to restart the server, and if it is
# down it sends an email alert to the admin.

# admin's email
EMAIL=webmaster@example.com

# the path to the PID file
PIDFILE=/home/httpd/httpd_perl/logs/httpd.pid

# the path to the httpd binary, including any options if necessary
HTTPD=/home/httpd/httpd_perl/bin/httpd_perl

# check for pidfile
if [ -f $PIDFILE ] ; then
    PID=`cat $PIDFILE`

    if kill -0 $PID; then
        STATUS="httpd (pid $PID) running"
        RUNNING=1
    else
        STATUS="httpd (pid $PID?) not running"
        RUNNING=0
    fi
else
    STATUS="httpd (no pid file) not running"
    RUNNING=0
fi

if [ $RUNNING -eq 0 ]; then
    echo "$0 $ARG: httpd not running, trying to start"
    if $HTTPD ; then
        echo "$0 $ARG: httpd started"
        mail $EMAIL -s "$0 $ARG: httpd started" \
            < /dev/null > /dev/null 2>&1
    else
        echo "$0 $ARG: httpd could not be started"
```

Example 5-8. apache.watchdog (continued)

```
        mail $EMAIL -s "$0 $ARG: httpd could not be started" \
            < /dev/null > /dev/null 2>&1
    fi
fi
```

Another approach is to use the Perl LWP module to test the server by trying to fetch a URI served by the server. This is more practical because although the server may be running as a process, it may be stuck and not actually serving any requests—for example, when there is a stale lock that all the processes are waiting to acquire. Failing to get the document will trigger a restart, and the problem will probably go away.

We set a *cron* job to call this LWP script every few minutes to fetch a document generated by a very light script. The best thing, of course, is to call it every minute (the finest resolution *cron* provides). Why so often? If the server gets confused and starts to fill the disk with lots of error messages written to the *error_log*, the system could run out of free disk space in just a few minutes, which in turn might bring the whole system to its knees. In these circumstances, it is unlikely that any other child will be able to serve requests, since the system will be too busy writing to the *error_log* file. Think big—if running a heavy service, adding one more request every minute will have no appreciable impact on the server's load.

So we end up with a *crontab* entry like this:

```
    * * * * * /path/to/the/watchdog.pl > /dev/null
```

The watchdog itself is shown in Example 5-9.

Example 5-9. watchdog.pl

```perl
#!/usr/bin/perl -Tw

# These prevent taint checking failures
$ENV{PATH} = '/bin:/usr/bin';
delete @ENV{qw(IFS CDPATH ENV BASH_ENV)};

use strict;
use diagnostics;

use vars qw($VERSION $ua);
$VERSION = '0.01';

require LWP::UserAgent;

###### Config ########
my $test_script_url = 'http://www.example.com:81/perl/test.pl';
my $monitor_email   = 'root@localhost';
my $restart_command = '/home/httpd/httpd_perl/bin/apachectl restart';
my $mail_program    = '/usr/lib/sendmail -t -n';
#####################

$ua  = LWP::UserAgent->new;
```

Example 5-9. watchdog.pl (continued)

```perl
$ua->agent("$0/watchdog " . $ua->agent);
# Uncomment the following two lines if running behind a firewall
# my $proxy = "http://www-proxy";
# $ua->proxy('http', $proxy) if $proxy;

# If it returns '1' it means that the service is alive, no need to
# continue
exit if checkurl($test_script_url);

# Houston, we have a problem.
# The server seems to be down, try to restart it.
my $status = system $restart_command;

my $message = ($status == 0)
            ? "Server was down and successfully restarted!"
            : "Server is down. Can't restart.";

my $subject = ($status == 0)
            ? "Attention! Webserver restarted"
            : "Attention! Webserver is down. can't restart";

# email the monitoring person
my $to = $monitor_email;
my $from = $monitor_email;
send_mail($from, $to, $subject, $message);

# input:  URL to check
# output: 1 for success, 0 for failure
######################
sub checkurl {
    my($url) = @_;

    # Fetch document
    my $res = $ua->request(HTTP::Request->new(GET => $url));

    # Check the result status
    return 1 if $res->is_success;

    # failed
    return 0;
}

# send email about the problem
######################
sub send_mail {
    my($from, $to, $subject, $messagebody) = @_;

    open MAIL, "|$mail_program"
        or die "Can't open a pipe to a $mail_program :$!\n";

    print MAIL <<__END_OF_MAIL__;
To: $to
```

Example 5-9. watchdog.pl (continued)

```
From: $from
Subject: $subject

$messagebody

--
Your faithful watchdog

__END_OF_MAIL__

    close MAIL or die "failed to close |$mail_program: $!";
}
```

Of course, you may want to replace a call to *sendmail* with `Mail::Send`, `Net::SMTP` code, or some other preferred email-sending technique.

Server Maintenance Chores

It is not enough to have your server and service up and running. The server must be maintained and monitored even when everything seems to be fine. This includes security auditing as well as keeping an eye on the amount of remaining unused disk space, available RAM, the system's load, etc.

If these chores are forgotten, sooner or later the system will crash, either because it has run out of free disk space, all available RAM has been used and the system has started to swap heavily, or it has been broken into. The last issue is much too broad for this book's scope, but the others are quite easily addressed if you follow our advice.

Particular systems might require maintenance chores that are not covered here, but this section highlights some of the most important general tasks.

Handling Log Files

Apache generally logs all the web server access events in the *access_log* file, whereas errors and warnings go into the *error_log* file. The *access_log* file can later be analyzed to report server usage statistics, such as the number of requests made in different time spans, who issued these requests, and much more. The *error_log* file is used to monitor the server for errors and warnings and to prompt actions based on those reports. Some systems do additional logging, such as storing the referrers of incoming requests to find out how users have learned about the site.

The simplest logging technique is to dump the logs into a file opened for appending. With Apache, this is as simple as specifying the logging format and the file to which to log. For example, to log all accesses, use the default directive supplied in *httpd.conf*:

```
LogFormat "%h %l %u %t \"%r\" %>s %b" common
CustomLog /home/httpd/httpd_perl/logs/access_log common
```

This setting will log all server accesses to a file named */home/httpd/httpd_perl/logs/ access_log* using the format specified by the LogFormat directive—in this case, common. Please refer to the Apache documentation for a complete explanation of the various tokens that you can use when specifying log formats. If you're tempted to change the format of the log file, bear in mind that some log analysis tools may expect that only the default or one of a small subset of logging formats is used.

The only risk with log files is their size. It is important to keep log files trimmed. If they are needed for later analysis, they should be rotated and the rotation files should be moved somewhere else so they do not consume disk space. You can usually compress them for storage offline.

The most important thing is to monitor log files for possible sudden explosive growth rates. For example, if a developer makes a mistake in his code running on the mod_perl server and the child processes executing the code start to log thousands of error messages a second, all disk space can quickly be consumed, and the server will cease to function.

Scheduled log file rotation

The first issue is solved by having a process that rotates the logs run by *cron* at certain times (usually off-peak hours, if this term is still valid in the 24-hour global Internet era). Usually, log rotation includes renaming the current log file, restarting the server (which creates a fresh new log file), and compressing and/or moving the rotated log file to a different disk.

For example, if we want to rotate the *access_log* file, we could do:

```
panic% mv access_log access_log.renamed
panic% apachectl graceful
panic% sleep 5
panic% mv access_log.renamed /some/directory/on/another/disk
```

The *sleep* delay is added to make sure that all children complete requests and logging. It's possible that a longer delay is needed. Once the restart is completed, it is safe to use *access_log.renamed*.

There are several popular utilities, such as *rotatelogs* and *cronolog*, that can perform the rotation, although it is also easy to create a basic rotation script. Example 5-10 shows a script that we run from *cron* to rotate our log files.

Example 5-10. logrotate

```
#!/usr/local/bin/perl -Tw

# This script does log rotation. Called from crontab.

use strict;
$ENV{PATH}='/bin:/usr/bin';
delete @ENV{qw(IFS CDPATH ENV BASH_ENV)};
```

Example 5-10. logrotate (continued)

```
### configuration
my @logfiles = qw(access_log error_log);
umask 0;
my $server = "httpd_perl";
my $logs_dir = "/home/httpd/$server/logs";
my $restart_command = "/home/httpd/$server/bin/apachectl restart";
my $gzip_exec = "/usr/bin/gzip -9"; # -9 is maximum compression

my ($sec, $min, $hour, $mday, $mon, $year) = localtime(time);
my $time = sprintf "%0.4d.%0.2d.%0.2d-%0.2d.%0.2d.%0.2d",
                   $year+1900, ++$mon, $mday, $hour, $min, $sec;

chdir $logs_dir;

# rename log files
foreach my $file (@logfiles) {
    rename $file, "$file.$time";
}

# now restart the server so the logs will be restarted
system $restart_command;

# allow all children to complete requests and logging
sleep 5;

# compress log files
foreach my $file (@logfiles) {
    system "$gzip_exec $file.$time";
}
```

As can be seen from the code, the rotated files will include the date and time in their filenames.

Non-scheduled emergency log rotation

As we mentioned earlier, there are times when the web server goes wild and starts to rapidly log lots of messages to the *error_log* file. If no one monitors this, it is possible that in a few minutes all free disk space will be consumed and no process will be able to work normally. When this happens, the faulty server process may cause so much I/O that its sibling processes cannot serve requests.

Although this rarely happens, you should try to reduce the risk of it occurring on your server. Run a monitoring program that checks the log file size and, if it detects that the file has grown too large, attempts to restart the server and trim the log file.

Back when we were using quite an old version of mod_perl, we sometimes had bursts of "Callback called exit" errors showing up in our *error_log*. The file could grow to 300 MB in a few minutes.

Example 5-11 shows a script that should be executed from *crontab* to handle situations like this. This is an emergency solution, not to be used for routine log rotation.

The *cron* job should run every few minutes or even every minute, because if the site experiences this problem, the log files will grow very rapidly. The example script will rotate when *error_log* grows over 100K. Note that this script is still useful when the normal scheduled log-rotation facility is working.

Example 5-11. emergency_rotate.sh

```
#!/bin/sh
S=`perl -e 'print -s "/home/httpd/httpd_perl/logs/error_log"'`;
if [ "$S" -gt 100000 ] ; then
    mv /home/httpd/httpd_perl/logs/error_log \
       /home/httpd/httpd_perl/logs/error_log.old
    /etc/rc.d/init.d/httpd restart
    date | /bin/mail -s "error_log $S kB" admin@example.com
fi
```

Of course, a more advanced script could be written using timestamps and other bells and whistles. This example is just a start, to illustrate a basic solution to the problem in question.

Another solution is to use ready-made tools that are written for this purpose. The *daemontools* package includes a utility called *multilog* that saves the STDIN stream to one or more log files. It optionally timestamps each line and, for each log, includes or excludes lines matching specified patterns. It automatically rotates logs to limit the amount of disk space used. If the disk fills up, it pauses and tries again, without losing any data.

The obvious caveat is that it does not restart the server, so while it tries to solve the log file–handling issue, it does not deal with the problem's real cause. However, because of the heavy I/O induced by the log writing, other server processes will work very slowly if at all. A normal watchdog is still needed to detect this situation and restart the Apache server.

Centralized logging

If you are running more than one server on the same machine, Apache offers the choice of either having a separate set of log files for each server, or using a central set of log files for all servers. If you are running servers on more than one machine, having them share a single log file is harder to achieve, but it is possible, provided that a filesharing system is used (logging into a database, or a special purpose application like *syslog*).

There are a few file-sharing systems that are widely used:

Network File System (NFS)
> NFS is a network file-sharing system. It's a very useful system, when it works. Unfortunately, it breaks too often, which makes it unreliable to use on production systems. NFS is available on most Unix flavors.

Andrew File System (AFS)

AFS is a distributed filesystem that enables cooperating hosts (clients and servers) to efficiently share filesystem resources across both local area and wide area networks. This filesystem is reliable, but it costs money and is available only on the HP, Next, DEC, IBM, SUN, and SGI operating systems. For more information, see *http://www.transarc.com/* and *http://www.angelfire.com/hi/plutonic/afs-faq.html*.

Coda

Coda is a distributed filesystem with its origin in AFS2. It has many features that are very desirable for network filesystems. Coda is platform-independent: you can mix and match servers and clients on any supported platform. As of this writing, it's not clear how stable the system is; some people have reported success using it, but others have had some problems with it. For more information, see *http://www.coda.cs.cmu.edu/*.

Apache permits the location of the file used for logging purposes to be specified, but it also allows you to specify a program to which all logs should be piped. To log to a program, modify the log handler directive (for example, `CustomLog`) to use the logging program instead of specifying an explicit filename:

```
LogFormat "%h %l %u %t \"%r\" %>s %b" common
CustomLog "| /home/httpd/httpd_perl/bin/sqllogger.pl" common
```

Logging into a database is a common solution, because you can do insertions from different machines into a single database. Unless the logger is programmed to send logs to a few databases at once, this solution is not reliable, since a single database constitutes a single failure point. If the database goes down, the logs will be lost. Sending information to one target is called *unicast* (see Figure 5-6), and sending to more than one target is called *multicast* (see Figure 5-7). In the latter case, if one database goes down, the others will still collect the data.

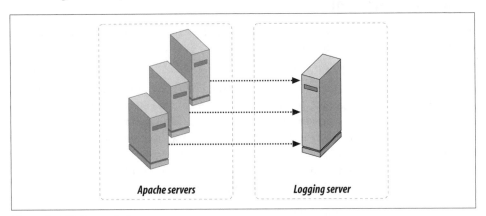

Figure 5-6. Unicast solution

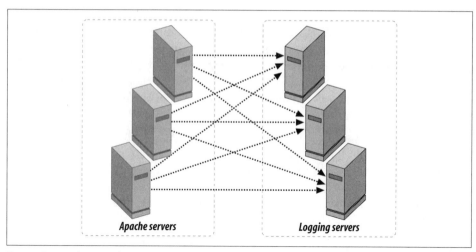

Figure 5-7. Multicast solution

Another solution is to use a centralized logger program based on *syslog(3)* to send all logs to a central location on a master host. *syslog(3)* is not a very scalable solution, because it's slow. It's also unreliable—it uses UDP to send the data, which doesn't ensure that the data will reach its destination. This solution is also unicast: if the master host goes down, the logs will be lost.

One advanced system that provides consolidated logging is mod_log_spread. Based on the group communications toolkit Spread, using IP multicast, mod_log_spread provides reliable, scalable centralized logging whith minimal performance impact on the web servers. For more information, see *http://www.backhand.org/mod_log_spread/*.

Swapping Prevention

Before we delve into swapping process details, let's look briefly at memory components and memory management.

Computer memory is called RAM (Random Access Memory). Reading and writing to RAM is faster than doing the same operations on a hard disk, by around five orders of magnitude (and growing). RAM uses electronic memory cells (transistors) with no moving parts, while hard disks use a rotating magnetic medium. It takes about one tenth of a microsecond to write to RAM but something like ten thousand microseconds to write to hard disk. It is possible to write just one byte (well, maybe one word) to RAM, whereas the minimum that can be written to a disk is often four thousand or eight thousand bytes (a single block). We often refer to RAM as *physical memory*.

A program may take up many thousands of bytes on disk. However, when it is executed normally, only the parts of the code actually needed at the time are loaded into memory. We call these parts *segments*.

Using syslog

The *syslog* solution can be implemented using the following configuration:

```
LogFormat "%h %l %u %t \"%r\" %>s %b" common
CustomLog "| /home/httpd/httpd_perl/bin/syslogger.pl hostnameX" common
```

where a simple *syslogger.pl* can look like this:

```
#!/usr/bin/perl
use Sys::Syslog qw(:DEFAULT setlogsock);

my $hostname = shift || 'localhost';
my $options  = 'ndelay'; # open the connection immediately
my $facility = 'local0'; # one of local0..local7
my $priority = 'info';   # debug|info|notice|warning|err...

setlogsock 'unix';
openlog $hostname, $options, $facility;
while (<>) {
    chomp;
    syslog $priority, $_;
}
closelog;
```

The *syslog* utility needs to know the facility to work with and the logging level. We will use *local0*, one of the special logging facilities reserved for local usage (eight local facilities are available: *local0* through *local7*). We will use the *info* priority level (again, one of eight possible levels: *debug*, *info*, *notice*, *warning*, *err*, *crit*, *alert*, and *emerg*).

Now make the *syslog* utility on the master machine (where all logs are to be stored) log all messages coming from facility *local0* with logging level info to a file of your choice. This is achieved by editing the */etc/syslog.conf* file. For example:

```
local0.info /var/log/web/access_log
```

All other machines forward their logs from facility *local0* to the central machine. Therefore, on all but the master machine, we add the forwarding directive to the */etc/syslog.conf* file (assuming that the master machine's hostname is *masterhost*):

```
local0.info @masterhost
```

We must restart the *syslogd* daemon or send it the HUP kill signal for the changes to take effect before the logger can be used.

On most operating systems, swap memory is used as an extension for RAM and not as a duplication of it. Assuming the operating system you use is one of those, if there is 128 MB of RAM and a 256 MB swap partition, there is a total of 384 MB of memory available. However, the extra (swap) memory should never be taken into consideration when deciding on the maximum number of processes to be run (we will show you why in a moment). The swap partition is also known as *swap space* or *virtual memory*.

The swapping memory can be built from a number of hard disk partitions and swap files formatted to be used as swap memory. When more swap memory is required, as long as there is some free disk space, it can always be extended on demand. (For more information, see the *mkswap* and *swapon* manpages.)

System memory is quantified in units called *memory pages*. Usually the size of a memory page is between 1 KB and 8 KB. So if there is 256 MB of RAM installed on the machine, and the page size is 4 KB, the system has 64,000 main memory pages to work with, and these pages are fast. If there is a 256-MB swap partition, the system can use yet another 64,000 memory pages, but they will be much slower.

When the system is started, all memory pages are available for use by the programs (processes). Unless a program is really small (in which case at any one time the entire program will be in memory), the process running this program uses only a few segments of the program, each segment mapped onto its own memory page. Therefore, only a few memory pages are needed—generally fewer than the program's size might imply.

When a process needs an additional program segment to be loaded into memory, it asks the system whether the page containing this segment is already loaded. If the page is not found, an event known as a "page fault" occurs. This requires the system to allocate a free memory page, go to the disk, and finally read and load the requested segment into the allocated memory page.

If a process needs to bring a new page into physical memory and there are no free physical pages available, the operating system must make room for this page by discarding another page from physical memory.

If the page to be discarded from physical memory came from a binary image or data file and has not been modified, the page does not need to be saved. Instead, it can be discarded, and if the process needs that page again it can be brought back into memory from the image or data file.

However, if the page has been modified, the operating system must preserve the contents of that page so that it can be accessed at a later time. This type of page is known as a *dirty page*, and when it is removed from memory it is saved in a special sort of file called the *swap file*. This process is referred to as *swapping out*.

Accesses to the swap file are very slow compared with the speed of the processor and physical memory, and the operating system must juggle the need to write pages to disk with the need to retain them in memory to be used again.

To try to reduce the probability that a page will be needed just after it has been swapped out, the system may use the LRU (least recently used) algorithm or some similar algorithm.

To summarize the two swapping scenarios, discarding read-only pages incurs little overhead compared with discarding data pages that have been modified, since in the latter case the pages have to be written to a swap partition located on the (very slow) disk. Thus, the fewer memory pages there are that can become dirty, the better will be the machine's overall performance.

But in Perl, both the program code and the program data are seen as data pages by the OS. Both are mapped to the same memory pages. Therefore, a big chunk of Perl code can become dirty when its variables are modified, and when those pages need to be discarded they have to be written to the swap partition.

This leads us to two important conclusions about swapping and Perl:

1. Running the system when there is no free physical memory available hinders performance, because processes' memory pages will be discarded and then reread from disk again and again.

2. Since the majority of the running code is Perl code, in addition to the overhead of reading in the previously discarded pages, there is the additional overhead of saving the dirty pages to the swap partition.

When the system has to swap memory pages in and out, it slows down. This can lead to an accumulation of processes waiting for their turn to run, which further increases processing demands, which in turn slows down the system even more as more memory is required. Unless the resource demand drops and allows the processes to catch up with their tasks and go back to normal memory usage, this ever-worsening spiral can cause the machine to thrash the disk and ultimately to halt.

In addition, it is important to be aware that for better performance, many programs (particularly programs written in Perl) do not return memory pages to the operating system even when they are no longer needed. If some of the memory is freed, it is reused when needed by the process itself, without creating the additional overhead of asking the system to allocate new memory pages. That is why Perl programs tend to grow in size as they run and almost never shrink.

When the process quits, it returns all the memory pages it used to the pool of available pages for other processes to use.

It should now be obvious that a system that runs a web server should never swap. Of course, it is quite normal for a desktop machine to swap, and this is often apparent because everything slows down and sometimes the system starts freezing for short periods. On a personal machine, the solution to swapping is simple: do not start up any new programs for a minute, and try to close down any that are running unnecessarily. This will allow the system to catch up with the load and go back to using just RAM. Unfortunately, this solution cannot be applied to a web server.

In the case of a web server, we have much less control, since it is the remote users who load the machine by issuing requests to the server. Therefore, the server should be configured such that the maximum number of possible processes will be small enough for the system to handle. This is achieved with the MaxClients directive, discussed in Chapter 11. This will ensure that at peak times, the system will not swap.

Remember that for a web server, swap space is an emergency pool, not a resource to be used routinely. If the system is low on memory, either buy more memory or reduce the number of processes to prevent swapping, as discussed in Chapter 14.

However, due to faulty code, sometimes a process might start running in an infinite loop, consuming all the available RAM and using lots of swap memory. In such a situation, it helps if there is a big emergency pool (i.e., lots of swap memory). But the problem must still be resolved as soon as possible, since the pool will not last for long. One solution is to use the Apache::Resource module, described in the next section.

Limiting Resources Used by Apache Child Processes

There are times when we need to prevent processes from excessive consumption of system resources. This includes limiting CPU or memory usage, the number of files that can be opened, and more.

The Apache::Resource module uses the BSD::Resource module, which in turn uses the C function setrlimit() to set limits on system resources.

A resource limit is specified in terms of a soft limit and a hard limit. When a soft limit (for example, CPU time or file size) is exceeded, the process may receive a signal, but it will be allowed to continue execution until it reaches the hard limit (or modifies its resource limit). The rlimit structure is used to specify the hard and soft limits on a resource. (See the *setrlimit* manpage for OS-specific information.)

If the value of variable in rlimit is of the form S:H, S is treated as the soft limit, and H is the hard limit. If the value is a single number, it is used for both soft and hard limits. So if the value is 10:20, the soft limit is 10 and the hard limit is 20, whereas if the value is just 20, both the soft and the hard limits are set to 20.

The most common use of this module is to limit CPU usage. The environment variable PERL_RLIMIT_CPU defines the maximum amount of CPU time the process can use. If it attempts to run longer than this amount, it is killed, no matter what it is doing at the time, be it processing a request or just waiting. This is very useful when there is a bug in the code and a process starts to spin in an infinite loop, using a lot of CPU resources and never completing the request.

The value is measured in seconds. The following example sets the soft limit for CPU usage to 120 seconds (the default is 360):

```
PerlModule Apache::Resource
PerlSetEnv PERL_RLIMIT_CPU 120
```

Although 120 seconds does not sound like a long time, it represents a great deal of work for a modern processor capable of millions of instructions per second. Furthermore, because the child process shares the CPU with other processes, it may be quite some time before it uses all its allotted CPU time, and in all probability it will die from other causes (for example, it may have served all the requests it is permitted to serve before this hard limit is reached).

Of course, we should tell mod_perl to use this module, which is done by adding the following directive to *httpd.conf*:

```
PerlChildInitHandler Apache::Resource
```

There are other resources that we might want to limit. For example, we can limit the data and bstack memory segment sizes (PERL_RLIMIT_DATA and PERL_RLIMIT_STACK), the maximum process file size (PERL_RLIMIT_FSIZE), the core file size (PERL_RLIMIT_CORE), the address space (virtual memory) limit (PERL_RLIMIT_AS), etc. Refer to the *set-rlimit* manpage for other possible resources. Remember to prepend PERL_ to the resource types that are listed in the manpage.

If Apache::Status is configured, it can display the resources set in this way. Remember that Apache::Status must be loaded before Apache::Resource, in order to enable the resources display menu.

To turn on debug mode, set the $Apache::Resource::Debug variable before loading the module. This can be done using a Perl section in *httpd.conf*.

```
<Perl>
    $Apache::Resource::Debug = 1;
    require Apache::Resource;
</Perl>
PerlChildInitHandler Apache::Resource
```

Now view the *error_log* file using *tail -f* and watch the debug messages show up when requests are served.

OS-specific notes

Under certain Linux setups, malloc( ) uses mmap( ) instead of brk( ). This is done to conserve virtual memory—that is, when a program malloc( )s a large block of memory, the block is not actually returned to the program until it is initialized. The old-style brk( ) system call obeyed resource limits on data segment sizes as set in setrlimit( ). mmap( ) does not.

Apache::Resource's defaults put limits on data size and stack size. Linux's current memory-allocation scheme does not honor these limits, so if we just do:

```
PerlSetEnv PERL_RLIMIT_DEFAULTS On
PerlModule Apache::Resource
PerlChildInitHandler Apache::Resource
```

our Apache processes are still free to use as much memory as they like.

However, BSD::Resource also has a limit called RLIMIT_AS (Address Space), which limits the total number of bytes of virtual memory assigned to a process. Fortunately, Linux's memory manager *does* honor this limit.

Therefore, we *can* limit memory usage under Linux with Apache::Resource. Simply add a line to *httpd.conf*:

```
PerlSetEnv PERL_RLIMIT_AS  67108864
```

This example sets hard and soft limits of 64 MB of total address space.

Refer to the `Apache::Resource` and *setrlimit(2)* manpages for more information.

Tracking and Terminating Hanging Processes

Generally, limits should be imposed on mod_perl processes to prevent mayhem if something goes wrong. There is no need to limit processes if the code does not have any bugs, or at least if there is sufficient confidence that the program will never over-consume resources. When there is a risk that a process might hang or start consuming a lot of memory, CPU, or other resources, it is wise to use the `Apache::Resource` module.

But what happens if a process is stuck waiting for some event to occur? Consider a process trying to acquire a lock on a file that can never be satisfied because there is a deadlock. The process just hangs waiting, which means that neither extra CPU nor extra memory is used. We cannot detect and terminate this process using the resource-limiting techniques we just discussed. If there is such a process, it is likely that very soon there will be many more processes stuck waiting for the same or a different event to occur. Within a short time, all processes will be stuck and no new processes will be spawned because the maximum number, as specified by the `MaxClients` directive, has been reached. The service enters a state where it is up but not serving clients.

If a watchdog is run that does not just check that the process is up, but actually issues requests to make sure that the service responds, then there is some protection against a complete service outage. This is because the watchdog will restart the server if the testing request it issues times out. This is a last-resort solution; the ideal is to be able to detect and terminate hanging processes that do not consume many resources (and therefore cannot be detected by the `Apache::Resource` module) as soon as possible, not when the service stops responding to requests, since by that point the quality of service to the users will have been severely degraded.

This is where the `Apache::Watchdog::RunAway` module comes in handy. This module samples all live child processes every `$Apache::Watchdog::RunAway::POLLTIME` seconds. If a process has been serving the same request for more than `$Apache::Watchdog::RunAway::TIMEOUT` seconds, it is killed.

To perform accounting, the `Apache::Watchdog::RunAway` module uses the `Apache::Scoreboard` module, which in turn delivers various items of information about live child processes. Therefore, the following configuration must be added to *httpd.conf*:

```
<Location /scoreboard>
    SetHandler perl-script
    PerlHandler Apache::Scoreboard::send
    order deny,allow
    deny from all
    allow from localhost
</Location>
```

Make sure to adapt the access permission to the local environment. The above configuration allows access to this handler only from the *localhost* server. This setting can be tested by issuing a request for *http://localhost/scoreboard*. However, the returned data cannot be read directly, since it uses a binary format.

We are now ready to configure `Apache::Watchdog::RunAway`. The module should be able to retrieve the information provided by `Apache::Scoreboard`, so we will tell it the URL to use:

```
$Apache::Watchdog::RunAway::SCOREBOARD_URL = "http://localhost/scoreboard";
```

We must decide how many seconds the process is allowed to be busy serving the same request before it is considered a runaway. Consider the slowest clients. Scripts that do file uploading and downloading might take a significantly longer time than normal mod_perl code.

```
$Apache::Watchdog::RunAway::TIMEOUT = 180; # 3 minutes
```

Setting the timeout to 0 will disable the `Apache::Watchdog::RunAway` module entirely.

The rate at which the module polls the server should be chosen carefully. Because of the overhead of fetching the scoreboard data, this is not a module that should be executed too frequently. If the timeout is set to a few minutes, sampling every one or two minutes is a good choice. The following directive specifies the polling interval:

```
$Apache::Watchdog::RunAway::POLLTIME = 60; # 1 minute
```

Just like the timeout value, polling time is measured in seconds.

To see what the module does, enable debug mode:

```
$Apache::Watchdog::RunAway::DEBUG = 1;
```

and watch its log file using the *tail* command.

The following statement allows us to specify the log file's location:

```
$Apache::Watchdog::RunAway::LOG_FILE = "/tmp/safehang.log";
```

This log file is also used for logging information about killed processes, regardless of the value of the $DEBUG variable.

The module uses a lock file in order to prevent starting more than one instance of itself. The default location of this file may be changed using the $LOCK_FILE variable.

```
$Apache::Watchdog::RunAway::LOCK_FILE = "/tmp/safehang.lock";
```

There are two ways to invoke this process: using the Perl functions, or using the bundled utility called *amprapmon* (mnemonic: *ApacheModPerlRunAwayProcessMonitor*).

The following functions are available:

`stop_monitor( )`
> Stops the monitor based on the PID contained in the lock file. Removes the lock file.

start_monitor( )

> Starts the monitor in the current process. Creates the lock file.

start_detached_monitor( )

> Starts the monitor as a forked process (used by *amprapmon*). Creates the lock file.

In order for mod_perl to invoke this process, all that is needed is the start_detached_monitor( ) function. Add the following code to *startup.pl*:

```
use Apache::Watchdog::RunAway( );
Apache::Watchdog::RunAway::start_detached_monitor( );
```

Another approach is to use the *amprapmon* utility. This can be started from the *startup.pl* file:

```
system "amprapmon start";
```

This will fork a new process. If the process is already running, it will just continue to run.

The *amprapmon* utility could instead be started from *cron* or from the command line.

No matter which approach is used, the process will fork itself and run as a daemon process. To stop the daemon, use the following command:

```
panic% amprapmon stop
```

If we want to test this module but have no code that makes processes hang (or we do, but the behavior is not reproducible on demand), the following code can be used to make the process hang in an infinite loop when executed as a script or handler. The code writes "\0" characters to the browser every second, so the request will never time out. The code is shown in Example 5-12.

Example 5-12. hangnow.pl

```
my $r = shift;
$r->send_http_header('text/plain');
print "PID = $$\n";
$r->rflush;
while(1) {
    $r->print("\0");
    $r->rflush;
    sleep 1;
}
```

The code prints the PID of the process running it before it goes into an infinite loop, so that we know which process hangs and whether it gets killed by the Apache::Watchdog::RunAway daemon as it should.

Of course, the watchdog is used only for prevention. If you have a serious problem with hanging processes, you have to debug your code, find the reason for the problem, and resolve it, as discussed in Chapter 21.

Limiting the Number of Processes Serving the Same Resource

To limit the number of Apache children that can simultaneously serve a specific resource, take a look at the Apache mod_throttle_access module.

Throttling access is useful, for example, when a handler uses a resource that places a limitation on concurrent access or that is very CPU-intensive. mod_throttle_access limits the number of concurrent requests to a given URI.

Consider a service providing the following three URIs:

```
/perl/news/
/perl/webmail/
/perl/morphing/
```

The response times of the first two URIs are critical, since people want to read the news and their email interactively. The third URI is a very CPU- and RAM-intensive image-morphing service, provided as a bonus to the users. Since we do not want users to abuse this service, we have to set some limit on the number of concurrent requests for this resource. If we do not, the other two critical resources may have their performance degraded.

When compiled or loaded into Apache and enabled, mod_throttle_access makes the MaxConcurrentReqs directive available. For example, the following setting:

```
<Location "/perl/morphing">
    <Limit PUT GET POST>
        MaxConcurrentReqs 10
    </Limit>
</Location>
```

will allow only 10 concurrent PUT, GET, HEAD (as implied by GET), or POST requests for the URI */perl/morphing* to be processed at any given time. The other two URIs in our example remain unlimited.

Limiting the Request-Rate Speed (Robot Blocking)

Web services generally welcome search engine robots, also called *spiders*. Search engine robots are programs that query the site and index its documents for a search engine.

Most indexing robots are polite and pause between requests. However, some search engine robots behave very badly, issuing too many requests too often, thus slowing down the service for human users. While everybody wants their sites to be indexed by search engines, it is really annoying when an initially welcomed spider gives the server a hard time, eventually becoming an unwanted spider.

A common remedy for keeping impolite robots off a site is based on an AccessHandler that checks the name of the robot and disallows access to the server if it is listed in the robot blacklist. For an example of such an `AccessHandler`, see the `Apache::BlockAgent` module, available from *http://www.modperl.com/*.

Unfortunately, some robots have learned to work around this blocking technique, masquerading as human users by using user agent strings identifying them as conventional browsers. This prevents us from blocking just by looking at the robot's name—we have to be more sophisticated and beat the robots by turning their own behavior against them. Robots work much faster than humans, so we can gather statistics over a period of time, and when we detect too many requests issued too fast from a specific IP, this IP can be blocked.

The `Apache::SpeedLimit` module, also available from *http://www.modperl.com/*, provides this advanced filtering technique.

There might be a problem with proxy servers, however, where many users browse the Web via a single proxy. These users are seen from the outside world (and from our sites) as coming from the proxy's single IP address or from one of a small set of IP addresses. In this case, `Apache::SpeedLimit` cannot be used, since it might block legitimate users and not just robots. However, we could modify the module to ignore specific IP addresses that we designate as acceptable.

Stonehenge::Throttle

Randal Schwartz wrote `Stonehenge::Throttle` for one of his *Linux Magazine* columns. This module does CPU percentage–based throttling. The module looks at the recent CPU usage over a given window for a given IP. If the percentage exceeds a threshold, a 503 error and a correct `Retry-After:` header are sent, telling for how long access from this IP is banned. The documentation can be found at *http://www.stonehenge.com/merlyn/LinuxMag/col17.html*, and the source code is available at *http://www.stonehenge.com/merlyn/LinuxMag/col17.listing.txt*.

Spambot Trap

Neil Gunton has developed a Spambot Trap (*http://www.neilgunton.com/spambot_trap/*) that keeps robots harvesting email addresses away from your web content. One of the important components of the trap is the *robots.txt* file, which is a standard mechanism for controlling which agents can reach your site and which areas can be browsed. This is an advisory mechanism, so if the agent doesn't follow the standard it will simply ignore the rules of the house listed in this file. For more information, refer to the W3C specification at *http://www.w3.org/TR/html401/appendix/notes.html#h-B.4.1.1*.

References

- "Stopping and Restarting Apache," from the Apache documentation: *http://httpd.apache.org/docs/stopping.html*.
- RPM resources:
  — The Red Hat Package Manager web site: *http://www.rpm.org/*.
  — *Maximum RPM*, by Ed Bailey (Red Hat Press).
  — "RPM-HOWTO," by Donnie Barnes: *http://www.rpm.org/support/RPM-HOWTO.html*.
- CVS (Concurrent Versions System) resources:
  — *http://www.cvshome.org/* is the home of the CVS project and includes a plethora of documentation. Of special interest is the *Cederqvist*, the official CVS manual, available at *http://www.cvshome.org/docs/manual/*.
  — *Open Source Development with CVS*, by Karl Fogel (Coriolis, Inc.). Most of the book is available online at *http://cvsbook.red-bean.com/*.
  — CVS Quick Reference Card: *http://www.refcards.com/about/cvs.html*.
- daemontools, a collection of tools for managing Unix services: *http://cr.yp.to/daemontools.html*.
- Log collecting and processing tools: *http://www.apache-tools.com/search.jsp?keys=log*.
- *cronolog*, a log file–rotation program for the Apache web server: *http://www.cronolog.org/*.
- mod_log_spread, which provides reliable distributed logging for Apache *http://www.backhand.org/mod_log_spread/*.
- Spread, a wide area group communication system: *http://www.spread.org/*.
- Recall, an open source library for writing distributed, fault-tolerant, replicated storage servers. A Recall-based server will allow you to save and access data even in the presence of machine failures. See *http://www.fault-tolerant.org/recall/*.
- Chapters 2, 4, 9, 11, and 28 in *UNIX System Administration Handbook*, by Evi Nemeth, Garth Snyder, Scott Seebass, and Trent H. Hein (Prentice Hall).
- Chapters 4 and 5 in *Optimizing UNIX for Performance*, by Amir H. Majidimehr (Prentice Hall).
- To learn more about memory management, refer to a book that deals with operating system theory, and especially with the operating systems used on web server machines.

A good starting point is one of the classic textbooks used in operating system courses. For example:

— *Operating System Concepts*, by Abraham Silberschatz and Peter Baer Galvin (John Wiley & Sons, Inc.).

— *Applied Operating System Concepts*, by Abraham Silberschatz, Peter Baer Galvin, and Greg Gagne (John Wiley & Sons, Inc.).

— *Design of the Unix Operating System*, by Maurice Bach (Prentice Hall).

The Memory Management Reference at *http://www.xanalys.com/software_tools/mm/* is also very helpful.

- mod_throttle_access: *http://www.fremen.org/apache/mod_throttle_access.html*.
- mod_backhand, which provides load balancing for Apache: *http://www.backhand.org/mod_backhand/*.
- The High-Availability Linux Project, the definitive guide to load-balancing techniques: *http://www.linux-ha.org/*.

  The Heartbeat project is a part of the HA Linux project.

- *lbnamed*, a load-balancing name server written in Perl: *http://www.stanford.edu/~riepel/lbnamed/* or *http://www.stanford.edu/~schemers/docs/lbnamed/lbnamed.html*.
- "Network Address Translation and Networks: Virtual Servers (Load Balancing)": *http://www.suse.de/~mha/linux-ip-nat/diplom/node4.html#SECTION00043100000000000000*.
- Linux Virtual Server Project: *http://www.linuxvirtualserver.org/*.
- Linux and port forwarding: *http://www.netfilter.org/ipchains/* or *http://www.netfilter.org/*.
- "Efficient Support for P-HTTP in Cluster-Based Web Servers," by Mohit Aron and Willy Zwaenepoel, in Proceedings of the USENIX 1999 Annual Technical Conference, Monterey, CA, June 1999: *http://www.cs.rice.edu/~druschel/usenix99lard.ps.gz* or *http://www.usenix.org/publications/library/proceedings/usenix99/full_papers/aron/aron_html/*.
- IP filter: *http://coombs.anu.edu.au/~avalon/*. The latest IP filter includes some simple load-balancing code that allows a round-robin distribution onto several machines via *ipnat*.
- Perl modules available from *http://www.modperl.com/book/source* (not on CPAN):

  — `Apache::BlockAgent`, which allows you to block impolite web agents.

  — `Apache::SpeedLimit`, which allows you to limit indexing robots' speed.

## CHAPTER 6

Coding with mod_perl in Mind

This is the most important chapter of this book. In this chapter, we cover all the nuances the programmer should know when porting an existing CGI script to work under mod_perl, or when writing one from scratch.

This chapter's main goal is to teach the reader how to think in mod_perl. It involves showing most of the mod_perl peculiarities and possible traps the programmer might fall into. It also shows you some of the things that are impossible with vanilla CGI but easily done with mod_perl.

Before You Start to Code

There are three important things you need to know before you start your journey in a mod_perl world: how to access mod_perl and related documentation, and how to develop your Perl code when the strict and warnings modes are enabled.

Accessing Documentation

mod_perl doesn't tolerate sloppy programming. Although we're confident that you're a talented, meticulously careful programmer whose programs run perfectly every time, you still might want to tighten up some of your Perl programming practices.

In this chapter, we include discussions that rely on prior knowledge of some areas of Perl, and we provide short refreshers where necessary. We assume that you can already program in Perl and that you are comfortable with finding Perl-related information in books and Perl documentation. There are many Perl books that you may find helpful. We list some of these in the reference sections at the end of each chapter.

If you prefer the documentation that comes with Perl, you can use either its online version (start at *http://www.perldoc.com/* or *http://theoryx5.uwinnipeg.ca/CPAN/perl/*) or the *perldoc* utility, which provides access to the documentation installed on your system.

To find out what Perl manpages are available, execute:

```
panic% perldoc perl
```

For example, to find what functions Perl has and to learn about their usage, execute:

```
panic% perldoc perlfunc
```

To learn the syntax and to find examples of a specific function, use the *-f* flag and the name of the function. For example, to learn more about open( ), execute:

```
panic% perldoc -f open
```

The *perldoc* supplied with Perl versions prior to 5.6.0 presents the information in POD (Plain Old Documentation) format. From 5.6.0 onwards, the documentation is shown in manpage format.

You may find the *perlfaq* manpages very useful, too. To find all the FAQs (Frequently Asked Questions) about a function, use the *-q* flag. For example, to search through the FAQs for the open( ) function, execute:

```
panic% perldoc -q open
```

This will show you all the relevant *question* and *answer* sections.

Finally, to learn about *perldoc* itself, refer to the *perldoc* manpage:

```
panic% perldoc perldoc
```

The documentation available through *perldoc* provides good information and examples, and should be able to answer most Perl questions that arise.

Chapter 23 provides more information about mod_perl and related documentation.

The strict Pragma

We're sure you already do this, but it's absolutely essential to start all your scripts and modules with:

```
use strict;
```

It's especially important to have the strict pragma enabled under mod_perl. While it's not required by the language, its use cannot be too strongly recommended. It will save you a great deal of time. And, of course, clean scripts will still run under mod_cgi!

In the rare cases where it is necessary, you can turn off the strict pragma, or a part of it, inside a block. For example, if you want to use symbolic references (see the *perlref* manpage) inside a particular block, you can use no strict 'refs';, as follows:

```
use strict;
{
    no strict 'refs';
    my $var_ref = 'foo';
    $$var_ref = 1;
}
```

Starting the block with no strict 'refs'; allows you to use symbolic references in the rest of the block. Outside this block, the use of symbolic references will trigger a runtime error.

Enabling Warnings

It's also important to develop your code with Perl reporting every possible relevant warning. Under mod_perl, you can turn this mode on globally, just like you would by using the -w command-line switch to Perl. Add this directive to *httpd.conf*:

```
PerlWarn On
```

In Perl 5.6.0 and later, you can also enable warnings only for the scope of a file, by adding:

```
use warnings;
```

at the top of your code. You can turn them off in the same way as strict for certain blocks. See the *warnings* manpage for more information.

We will talk extensively about warnings in many sections of the book. Perl code written for mod_perl should run without generating any warnings with both the strict and warnings pragmas in effect (that is, with use strict and PerlWarn On or use warnings).

Warnings are almost always caused by errors in your code, but on some occasions you may get warnings for totally legitimate code. That's part of why they're warnings and not errors. In the unlikely event that your code really does reveal a spurious warning, it is possible to switch off the warning.

Exposing Apache::Registry Secrets

Let's start with some simple code and see what can go wrong with it. This simple CGI script initializes a variable $counter to 0 and prints its value to the browser while incrementing it:

```perl
#!/usr/bin/perl -w
use strict;

print "Content-type: text/plain\n\n";

my $counter = 0;

for (1..5) {
    increment_counter();
}

sub increment_counter {
    $counter++;
    print "Counter is equal to $counter !\n";
}
```

When issuing a request to */perl/counter.pl* or a similar script, we would expect to see the following output:

```
Counter is equal to 1 !
Counter is equal to 2 !
Counter is equal to 3 !
Counter is equal to 4 !
Counter is equal to 5 !
```

And in fact that's what we see when we execute this script for the first time. But let's reload it a few times.... After a few reloads, the counter suddenly stops counting from 1. As we continue to reload, we see that it keeps on growing, but not steadily, starting almost randomly at 10, 10, 10, 15, 20..., which makes no sense at all!

```
Counter is equal to 6 !
Counter is equal to 7 !
Counter is equal to 8 !
Counter is equal to 9 !
Counter is equal to 10 !
```

We saw two anomalies in this very simple script:

- Unexpected increment of our counter over 5
- Inconsistent growth over reloads

The reason for this strange behavior is that although $counter is incremented with each request, it is never reset to 0, even though we have this line:

```
my $counter = 0;
```

Doesn't this work under mod_perl?

The First Mystery: Why Does the Script Go Beyond 5?

If we look at the *error_log* file (we *did* enable warnings), we'll see something like this:

```
Variable "$counter" will not stay shared
at /home/httpd/perl/counter.pl line 13.
```

This warning is generated when a script contains a named (as opposed to an anonymous) nested subroutine that refers to a lexically scoped (with my( )) variable defined outside this nested subroutine.

Do you see a nested named subroutine in our script? We don't! What's going on? Maybe it's a bug in Perl? But wait, maybe the Perl interpreter sees the script in a different way! Maybe the code goes through some changes before it actually gets executed? The easiest way to check what's actually happening is to run the script with a debugger.

Since we must debug the script when it's being executed by the web server, a normal debugger won't help, because the debugger has to be invoked from within the web server. Fortunately, we can use Doug MacEachern's Apache::DB module to debug our script. While `Apache::DB` allows us to debug the code interactively (as we will show in Chapter 21), we will use it noninteractively in this example.

To enable the debugger, modify the *httpd.conf* file in the following way:

```
PerlSetEnv PERLDB_OPTS "NonStop=1 LineInfo=/tmp/db.out AutoTrace=1 frame=2"
PerlModule Apache::DB
<Location /perl>
    PerlFixupHandler Apache::DB
    SetHandler perl-script
    PerlHandler Apache::Registry
    Options ExecCGI
    PerlSendHeader On
</Location>
```

We have added a debugger configuration setting using the `PERLDB_OPTS` environment variable, which has the same effect as calling the debugger from the command line. We have also loaded and enabled `Apache::DB` as a `PerlFixupHandler`.

In addition, we'll load the `Carp` module, using `<Perl>` sections (this could also be done in the *startup.pl* file):

```
<Perl>
    use Carp;
</Perl>
```

After applying the changes, we restart the server and issue a request to */perl/counter.pl*, as before. On the surface, nothing has changed; we still see the same output as before. But two things have happened in the background:

- The file */tmp/db.out* was written, with a complete trace of the code that was executed.

- Since we have loaded the `Carp` module, the *error_log* file now contains the real code that was actually executed. This is produced as a side effect of reporting the "Variable "$counter" will not stay shared at..." warning that we saw earlier.

Here is the code that was actually executed:

```
package Apache::ROOT::perl::counter_2epl;
use Apache qw(exit);
sub handler {
    BEGIN {
        $^W = 1;
    };
    $^W = 1;

    use strict;

    print "Content-type: text/plain\n\n";

    my $counter = 0;
```

```
        for (1..5) {
            increment_counter( );
        }

        sub increment_counter {
            $counter++;
            print "Counter is equal to $counter !\n";
        }
    }
```

Note that the code in *error_log* wasn't indented—we've indented it to make it obvious that the code was wrapped inside the handler( ) subroutine.

From looking at this code, we learn that every Apache::Registry script is cached under a package whose name is formed from the Apache::ROOT:: prefix and the script's URI (*/perl/counter.pl*) by replacing all occurrences of / with :: and . with _2e. That's how mod_perl knows which script should be fetched from the cache on each request—each script is transformed into a package with a unique name and with a single subroutine named handler( ), which includes all the code that was originally in the script.

Essentially, what's happened is that because increment_counter( ) is a subroutine that refers to a lexical variable defined outside of its scope, it has become a *closure*. Closures don't normally trigger warnings, but in this case we have a nested subroutine. That means that the first time the enclosing subroutine handler( ) is called, both subroutines are referring to the same variable, but after that, increment_counter( ) will keep its own copy of $counter (which is why $counter is not *shared*) and increment its own copy. Because of this, the value of $counter keeps increasing and is never reset to 0.

If we were to use the diagnostics pragma in the script, which by default turns terse warnings into verbose warnings, we would see a reference to an inner (nested) subroutine in the text of the warning. By observing the code that gets executed, it is clear that increment_counter( ) is a named nested subroutine since it gets defined inside the handler( ) subroutine.

Any subroutine defined in the body of the script executed under Apache::Registry becomes a nested subroutine. If the code is placed into a library or a module that the script require( )s or use( )s, this effect doesn't occur.

For example, if we move the code from the script into the subroutine run( ), place the subroutines in the *mylib.pl* file, save it in the same directory as the script itself, and require( ) it, there will be no problem at all.[*] Examples 6-1 and 6-2 show how we spread the code across the two files.

Example 6-1. mylib.pl

```
my $counter;
sub run {
    $counter = 0;
```

---

[*] Don't forget the 1; at the end of the library, or the require( ) call might fail.

Example 6-1. mylib.pl (continued)

```
    for (1..5) {
        increment_counter( );
    }
}
sub increment_counter {
    $counter++;
    print "Counter is equal to $counter !\n";
}
1;
```

Example 6-2. counter.pl

```
use strict;
require "./mylib.pl";
print "Content-type: text/plain\n\n";
run( );
```

This solution is the easiest and fastest way to solve the nested subroutine problem. All you have to do is to move the code into a separate file, by first wrapping the initial code into some function that you later call from the script, and keeping the lexically scoped variables that could cause the problem out of this function.

As a general rule, it's best to put all the code in external libraries (unless the script is very short) and have only a few lines of code in the main script. Usually the main script simply calls the main function in the library, which is often called init( ) or run( ). This way, you don't have to worry about the effects of named nested subroutines.

As we will show later in this chapter, however, this quick solution might be problematic on a different front. If you have many scripts, you might try to move more than one script's code into a file with a similar filename, like *mylib.pl*. A much cleaner solution would be to spend a little bit more time on the porting process and use a fully qualified package, as in Examples 6-3 and 6-4.

Example 6-3. Book/Counter.pm

```
package Book::Counter;

my $counter = 0;

sub run {
    $counter = 0;
    for (1..5) {
        increment_counter( );
    }
}

sub increment_counter {
    $counter++;
    print "Counter is equal to $counter !<BR>\n";
}
```

Example 6-3. Book/Counter.pm (continued)

```
1;
__END__
```

Example 6-4. counter-clean.pl

```
use strict;
use Book::Counter;

print "Content-type: text/plain\n\n";
Book::Counter::run( );
```

As you can see, the only difference is in the package declaration. As long as the package name is unique, you won't encounter any collisions with other scripts running on the same server.

Another solution to this problem is to change the lexical variables to global variables. There are two ways global variables can be used:

- Using the vars pragma. With the use strict 'vars' setting, global variables can be used after being declared with vars. For example, this code:

  ```
  use strict;
  use vars qw($counter $result);
  # later in the code
  $counter = 0;
  $result  = 1;
  ```

  is similar to this code if use strict is not used:

  ```
  $counter = 0;
  $result  = 1;
  ```

  However, the former style of coding is much cleaner, because it allows you to use global variables by declaring them, while avoiding the problem of misspelled variables being treated as undeclared globals.

  The only drawback to using vars is that each global declared with it consumes more memory than the undeclared but fully qualified globals, as we will see in the next item.

- Using fully qualified variables. Instead of using $counter, we can use $Foo::counter, which will place the global variable $counter into the package Foo. Note that we don't know which package name Apache::Registry will assign to the script, since it depends on the location from which the script will be called. Remember that globals must always be initialized before they can be used.

Perl 5.6.x also introduces a third way, with the our( ) declaration. our( ) can be used in different scopes, similar to my( ), but it creates global variables.

Finally, it's possible to avoid this problem altogether by always passing the variables as arguments to the functions (see Example 6-5).

Example 6-5. counter2.pl

```perl
#!/usr/bin/perl -w
use strict;

print "Content-type: text/plain\n\n";

my $counter = 0;

for (1..5) {
    $counter = increment_counter($counter);
}

sub increment_counter {
    my $counter = shift;

    $counter++;
    print "Counter is equal to $counter !\n";

    return $counter;
}
```

In this case, there is no variable-sharing problem. The drawback is that this approach adds the overhead of passing and returning the variable from the function. But on the other hand, it ensures that your code is doing the right thing and is not dependent on whether the functions are wrapped in other blocks, which is the case with the Apache::Registry handlers family.

When Stas (one of the authors of this book) had just started using mod_perl and wasn't aware of the nested subroutine problem, he happened to write a pretty complicated registration program that was run under mod_perl. We will reproduce here only the interesting part of that script:

```perl
use CGI;
$q = CGI->new;
my $name = $q->param('name');
print_response();

sub print_response {
    print "Content-type: text/plain\n\n";
    print "Thank you, $name!";
}
```

Stas and his boss checked the program on the development server and it worked fine, so they decided to put it in production. Everything seemed to be normal, but the boss decided to keep on checking the program by submitting variations of his profile using *The Boss* as his username. Imagine his surprise when, after a few successful submissions, he saw the response *"Thank you, Stas!"* instead of *"Thank you, The Boss!"*

After investigating the problem, they learned that they had been hit by the nested subroutine problem. Why didn't they notice this when they were trying the software on their development server? We'll explain shortly.

To conclude this first mystery, remember to keep the warnings mode On on the development server and to watch the *error_log* file for warnings.

The Second Mystery—Inconsistent Growth over Reloads

Let's return to our original example and proceed with the second mystery we noticed. Why have we seen inconsistent results over numerous reloads?

What happens is that each time the parent process gets a request for the page, it hands the request over to a child process. Each child process runs its own copy of the script. This means that each child process has its own copy of $counter, which will increment independently of all the others. So not only does the value of each $counter increase independently with each invocation, but because different children handle the requests at different times, the increment seems to grow inconsistently. For example, if there are 10 *httpd* children, the first 10 reloads might be correct (if each request went to a different child). But once reloads start reinvoking the script from the child processes, strange results will appear.

Moreover, requests can appear at random since child processes don't always run the same requests. At any given moment, one of the children could have served the same script more times than any other, while another child may never have run it.

Stas and his boss didn't discover the aforementioned problem with the user registration system before going into production because the *error_log* file was too crowded with warnings continuously logged by multiple child processes.

To immediately recognize the problem visually (so you can see incorrect results), you need to run the server as a single process. You can do this by invoking the server with the *-X* option:

```
panic% httpd -X
```

Since there are no other servers (children) running, you will get the problem report on the second reload.

Enabling the warnings mode (as explained earlier in this chapter) and monitoring the *error_log* file will help you detect most of the possible errors. Some warnings can become errors, as we have just seen. You should check every reported warning and eliminate it, so it won't appear in *error_log* again. If your *error_log* file is filled up with hundreds of lines on every script invocation, you will have difficulty noticing and locating real problems, and on a production server you'll soon run out of disk space if your site is popular.

Namespace Issues

If your service consists of a single script, you will probably have no namespace problems. But web services usually are built from many scripts and handlers. In the following sections, we will investigate possible namespace problems and their solutions. But first we will refresh our understanding of two special Perl variables, @INC and %INC.

The @INC Array

Perl's @INC array is like the PATH environment variable for the shell program. Whereas PATH contains a list of directories to search for executable programs, @INC contains a list of directories from which Perl modules and libraries can be loaded.

When you use( ), require( ), or do( ) a filename or a module, Perl gets a list of directories from the @INC variable and searches them for the file it was requested to load. If the file that you want to load is not located in one of the listed directories, you must tell Perl where to find the file. You can either provide a path relative to one of the directories in @INC or provide the absolute path to the file.

The %INC Hash

Perl's %INC hash is used to cache the names of the files and modules that were loaded and compiled by use( ), require( ), or do( ) statements. Every time a file or module is successfully loaded, a new key-value pair is added to %INC. The key is the name of the file or module as it was passed to one of the three functions we have just mentioned. If the file or module was found in any of the @INC directories (except "."), the file-names include the full path. Each Perl interpreter, and hence each process under mod_perl, has its own private %INC hash, which is used to store information about its compiled modules.

Before attempting to load a file or a module with use( ) or require( ), Perl checks whether it's already in the %INC hash. If it's there, the loading and compiling are not performed. Otherwise, the file is loaded into memory and an attempt is made to compile it. Note that do( ) loads the file or module unconditionally—it does not check the %INC hash. We'll look at how this works in practice in the following examples.

First, let's examine the contents of @INC on our system:

```
panic% perl -le 'print join "\n", @INC'
/usr/lib/perl5/5.6.1/i386-linux
/usr/lib/perl5/5.6.1
/usr/lib/perl5/site_perl/5.6.1/i386-linux
/usr/lib/perl5/site_perl/5.6.1
/usr/lib/perl5/site_perl
.
```

Notice . (the current directory) as the last directory in the list.

Let's load the module strict.pm and see the contents of %INC:

```
panic% perl -le 'use strict; print map {"$_ => $INC{$_}"} keys %INC'
strict.pm => /usr/lib/perl5/5.6.1/strict.pm
```

Since strict.pm was found in the */usr/lib/perl5/5.6.1/* directory and */usr/lib/perl5/5.6.1/* is a part of @INC, %INC includes the full path as the value for the key strict.pm.

Let's create the simplest possible module in */tmp/test.pm*:

```
1;
```

This does absolutely nothing, but it returns a true value when loaded, which is enough to satisfy Perl that it loaded correctly. Let's load it in different ways:

```
panic% cd /tmp
panic% perl -e 'use test; \
      print map { "$_ => $INC{$_}\n" } keys %INC'
test.pm => test.pm
```

Since the file was found in . (the directory the code was executed from), the relative path is used as the value. Now let's alter @INC by appending */tmp*:

```
panic% cd /tmp
panic% perl -e 'BEGIN { push @INC, "/tmp" } use test; \
      print map { "$_ => $INC{$_}\n" } keys %INC'
test.pm => test.pm
```

Here we still get the relative path, since the module was found first relative to ".". The directory */tmp* was placed after . in the list. If we execute the same code from a different directory, the "." directory won't match:

```
panic% cd /
panic% perl -e 'BEGIN { push @INC, "/tmp" } use test; \
      print map { "$_ => $INC{$_}\n" } keys %INC'
test.pm => /tmp/test.pm
```

so we get the full path. We can also prepend the path with unshift( ), so that it will be used for matching before ".". We will get the full path here as well:

```
panic% cd /tmp
panic% perl -e 'BEGIN { unshift @INC, "/tmp" } use test; \
      print map { "$_ => $INC{$_}\n" } keys %INC'
test.pm => /tmp/test.pm
```

The code:

```
BEGIN { unshift @INC, "/tmp" }
```

can be replaced with the more elegant:

```
use lib "/tmp";
```

This is almost equivalent to our BEGIN block and is the recommended approach.

These approaches to modifying @INC can be labor intensive: moving the script around in the filesystem might require modifying the path.

Name Collisions with Modules and Libraries

In this section, we'll look at two scenarios with failures related to namespaces. For the following discussion, we will always look at a single child process.

A first faulty scenario

It is impossible to use two modules with identical names on the same server. Only the first one found in a use( ) or a require( ) statement will be loaded and compiled. All subsequent requests to load a module with the same name will be skipped, because Perl will find that there is already an entry for the requested module in the %INC hash.

Let's examine a scenario in which two independent projects in separate directories, *projectA* and *projectB*, both need to run on the same server. Both projects use a module with the name MyConfig.pm, but each project has completely different code in its MyConfig.pm module. This is how the projects reside on the filesystem (all located under the directory */home/httpd/perl*):

```
projectA/MyConfig.pm
projectA/run.pl
projectB/MyConfig.pm
projectB/run.pl
```

Examples 6-6, 6-7, 6-8, and 6-9 show some sample code.

Example 6-6. projectA/run.pl

```
use lib qw(.);
use MyConfig;
print "Content-type: text/plain\n\n";
print "Inside project: ", project_name( );
```

Example 6-7. projectA/MyConfig.pm

```
sub project_name { return 'A'; }
1;
```

Example 6-8. projectB/run.pl

```
use lib qw(.);
use MyConfig;
print "Content-type: text/plain\n\n";
print "Inside project: ", project_name( );
```

Example 6-9. projectB/MyConfig.pm

```
sub project_name { return 'B'; }
1;
```

Both projects contain a script, *run.pl*, which loads the module MyConfig.pm and prints an *indentification* message based on the project_name( ) function in the MyConfig.pm module. When a request to */perl/projectA/run.pl* is issued, it is supposed to print:

```
Inside project: A
```

Similarly, */perl/projectB/run.pl* is expected to respond with:

```
Inside project: B
```

When tested using single-server mode, only the first one to run will load the MyConfig.pm module, although both *run.pl* scripts call use MyConfig. When the second script is run, Perl will skip the use MyConfig; statement, because MyConfig.pm is already located in %INC. Perl reports this problem in the *error_log*:

```
Undefined subroutine
&Apache::ROOT::perl::projectB::run_2epl::project_name called at
/home/httpd/perl/projectB/run.pl line 4.
```

This is because the modules didn't declare a package name, so the project_name( ) subroutine was inserted into *projectA/run.pl*'s namespace, Apache::ROOT::perl:: projectB::run_2epl. Project B doesn't get to load the module, so it doesn't get the subroutine either!

Note that if a library were used instead of a module (for example, config.pl instead of MyConfig.pm), the behavior would be the same. For both libraries and modules, a file is loaded and its filename is inserted into %INC.

A second faulty scenario

Now consider the following scenario:

```
project/MyConfig.pm
project/runA.pl
project/runB.pl
```

Now there is a single project with two scripts, *runA.pl* and *runB.pl*, both trying to load the same module, MyConfig.pm, as shown in Examples 6-10, 6-11, and 6-12.

Example 6-10. project/MyConfig.pm

```
sub project_name { return 'Super Project'; }
1;
```

Example 6-11. project/runA.pl

```
use lib qw(.);
use MyConfig;
print "Content-type: text/plain\n\n";
print "Script A\n";
print "Inside project: ", project_name( );
```

Example 6-12. project/runB.pl

```
use lib qw(.);
use MyConfig;
print "Content-type: text/plain\n\n";
print "Script B\n";
print "Inside project: ", project_name( );
```

This scenario suffers from the same problem as the previous two-project scenario: only the first script to run will work correctly, and the second will fail. The problem occurs because there is no package declaration here.

We'll now explore some of the ways we can solve these problems.

A quick but ineffective hackish solution

The following solution should be used only as a short term bandage. You can force reloading of the modules either by fiddling with %INC or by replacing use( ) and require( ) calls with do( ).

If you delete the module entry from the %INC hash before calling require( ) or use( ), the module will be loaded and compiled again. See Example 6-13.

Example 6-13. project/runA.pl

```
BEGIN {
    delete $INC{"MyConfig.pm"};
}
use lib qw(.);
use MyConfig;
print "Content-type: text/plain\n\n";
print "Script A\n";
print "Inside project: ", project_name( );
```

Apply the same fix to *runB.pl*.

Another alternative is to force module reload via do( ), as seen in Example 6-14.

Example 6-14. project/runA.pl forcing module reload by using do() instead of use()

```
use lib qw(.);
do "MyConfig.pm";
print "Content-type: text/plain\n\n";
print "Script B\n";
print "Inside project: ", project_name( );
```

Apply the same fix to *runB.pl*.

If you needed to import( ) something from the loaded module, call the import( ) method explicitly. For example, if you had:

```
use MyConfig qw(foo bar);
```

now the code will look like:

```
do "MyConfig.pm";
MyConfig->import(qw(foo bar));
```

Both presented solutions are ultimately ineffective, since the modules in question will be reloaded on each request, slowing down the response times. Therefore, use these only when a very quick fix is needed, and make sure to replace the hack with one of the more robust solutions discussed in the following sections.

A first solution

The first faulty scenario can be solved by placing library modules in a subdirectory structure so that they have different path prefixes. The new filesystem layout will be:

```
projectA/ProjectA/MyConfig.pm
projectA/run.pl
projectB/ProjectB/MyConfig.pm
projectB/run.pl
```

The *run.pl* scripts will need to be modified accordingly:

```
use ProjectA::MyConfig;
```

and:

```
use ProjectB::MyConfig;
```

However, if later on we want to add a new script to either of these projects, we will hit the problem described by the second problematic scenario, so this is only half a solution.

A second solution

Another approach is to use a full path to the script, so the latter will be used as a key in %INC:

```
require "/home/httpd/perl/project/MyConfig.pm";
```

With this solution, we solve both problems but lose some portability. Every time a project moves in the filesystem, the path must be adjusted. This makes it impossible to use such code under version control in multiple-developer environments, since each developer might want to place the code in a different absolute directory.

A third solution

This solution makes use of package-name declaration in the require( )d modules. For example:

```
package ProjectA::Config;
```

Similarly, for *ProjectB*, the package name would be ProjectB::Config.

Each package name should be unique in relation to the other packages used on the same *httpd* server. %INC will then use the unique package name for the key instead of the filename of the module. It's a good idea to use at least two-part package names for your private modules (e.g., MyProject::Carp instead of just Carp), since the latter will collide with an existing standard package. Even though a package with the same name may not exist in the standard distribution now, in a later distribution one may come along that collides with a name you've chosen.

What are the implications of package declarations? Without package declarations in the modules, it is very convenient to use( ) and require( ), since all variables and subroutines from the loaded modules will reside in the same package as the script itself. Any of them can be used as if it was defined in the same scope as the script itself. The downside of this approach is that a variable in a module might conflict with a variable in the main script; this can lead to hard-to-find bugs.

With package declarations in the modules, things are a bit more complicated. Given that the package name is PackageA, the syntax PackageA::project_name( ) should be used to call a subroutine project_name( ) from the code using this package. Before the package declaration was added, we could just call project_name( ). Similarly, a global variable $foo must now be referred to as $PackageA::foo, rather than simply as $foo. Lexically defined variables (declared with my( )) inside the file containing PackageA will be inaccessible from outside the package.

You can still use the unqualified names of global variables and subroutines if these are imported into the namespace of the code that needs them. For example:

```
use MyPackage qw(:mysubs sub_b $var1 :myvars);
```

Modules can export any global symbols, but usually only subroutines and global variables are exported. Note that this method has the disadvantage of consuming more memory. See the perldoc Exporter manpage for information about exporting other variables and symbols.

Let's rewrite the second scenario in a truly clean way. This is how the files reside on the filesystem, relative to the directory /home/httpd/perl:

```
project/MyProject/Config.pm
project/runA.pl
project/runB.pl
```

Examples 6-15, 6-16, and 6-17 show how the code will look.

Example 6-15. project/MyProject/Config.pm

```
package MyProject::Config
sub project_name { return 'Super Project'; }
1;
```

Example 6-16. project/runB.pl

```
use lib qw(.);
use MyProject::Config;
print "Content-type: text/plain\n\n";
print "Script B\n";
print "Inside project: ", MyProject::Config::project_name( );
```

Example 6-17. project/runA.pl

```
use lib qw(.);
use MyProject::Config;
print "Content-type: text/plain\n\n";
print "Script A\n";
print "Inside project: ", MyProject::Config::project_name( );
```

As you can see, we have created the *MyProject/Config.pm* file and added a package declaration at the top of it:

```
package MyProject::Config
```

Now both scripts load this module and access the module's subroutine, project_name( ), with a fully qualified name, MyProject::Config::project_name( ).

See also the *perlmodlib* and *perlmod* manpages.

From the above discussion, it also should be clear that you cannot run development and production versions of the tools using the same Apache server. You have to run a dedicated server for each environment. If you need to run more than one development environment on the same server, you can use Apache::PerlVINC, as explained in Appendix B.

Perl Specifics in the mod_perl Environment

In the following sections, we discuss the specifics of Perl's behavior under mod_perl.

exit( )

Perl's core exit( ) function shouldn't be used in mod_perl code. Calling it causes the mod_perl process to exit, which defeats the purpose of using mod_perl. The Apache::exit( ) function should be used instead. Starting with Perl Version 5.6.0, mod_perl overrides exit( ) behind the scenes using CORE::GLOBAL::, a new *magical* package.

The CORE:: Package

CORE:: is a special package that provides access to Perl's built-in functions. You may need to use this package to override some of the built-in functions. For example, if you want to override the exit( ) built-in function, you can do so with:

```
use subs qw(exit);
exit( ) if $DEBUG;
sub exit { warn "exit( ) was called"; }
```

Now when you call exit( ) in the same scope in which it was overridden, the program won't exit, but instead will just print a warning "exit( ) was called". If you want to use the original built-in function, you can still do so with:

```
# the 'real' exit
CORE::exit( );
```

Apache::Registry and Apache::PerlRun override exit( ) with Apache::exit( ) behind the scenes; therefore, scripts running under these modules don't need to be modified to use Apache::exit( ).

If `CORE::exit( )` is used in scripts running under mod_perl, the child will exit, but the current request won't be logged. More importantly, a proper exit won't be performed. For example, if there are some database handles, they will remain open, causing costly memory and (even worse) database connection leaks.

If the child process needs to be killed, `Apache::exit(Apache::Constants::DONE)` should be used instead. This will cause the server to exit gracefully, completing the logging functions and protocol requirements.

If the child process needs to be killed cleanly after the request has completed, use the `$r->child_terminate` method. This method can be called anywhere in the code, not just at the end. This method sets the value of the `MaxRequestsPerChild` configuration directive to 1 and clears the `keepalive` flag. After the request is serviced, the current connection is broken because of the `keepalive` flag, which is set to false, and the parent tells the child to cleanly quit because `MaxRequestsPerChild` is smaller than or equal to the number of requests served.

In an `Apache::Registry` script you would write:

```
Apache->request->child_terminate;
```

and in *httpd.conf*:

```
PerlFixupHandler "sub { shift->child_terminate }"
```

You would want to use the latter example only if you wanted the child to terminate every time the registered handler was called. This is probably not what you want.

You can also use a post-processing handler to trigger child termination. You might do this if you wanted to execute your own cleanup code before the process exits:

```
my $r = shift;
$r->post_connection(\&exit_child);

sub exit_child {
    # some logic here if needed
    $r->child_terminate;
}
```

This is the code that is used by the `Apache::SizeLimit` module, which terminates processes that grow bigger than a preset quota.

die( )

die( ) is usually used to abort the flow of the program if something goes wrong. For example, this common idiom is used when opening files:

```
open FILE, "foo" or die "Cannot open 'foo' for reading: $!";
```

If the file cannot be opened, the script will die( ): script execution is aborted, the reason for death is printed, and the Perl interpreter is terminated.

You will hardly find any properly written Perl scripts that don't have at least one die( ) statement in them.

CGI scripts running under mod_cgi exit on completion, and the Perl interpreter exits as well. Therefore, it doesn't matter whether the interpreter exits because the script died by natural death (when the last statement in the code flow was executed) or was aborted by a die( ) statement.

Under mod_perl, we don't want the process to quit. Therefore, mod_perl takes care of it behind the scenes, and die( ) calls don't abort the process. When die( ) is called, mod_perl logs the error message and calls Apache::exit( ) instead of CORE:: die( ). Thus, the script stops, but the process doesn't quit. Of course, we are talking about the cases where the code calling die( ) is not wrapped inside an exception handler (e.g., an eval { } block) that traps die( ) calls, or the $SIG{__DIE__} sighandler, which allows you to override the behavior of die( ) (see Chapter 21). The reference section at the end of this chapter mentions a few exception-handling modules available from CPAN.

Global Variable Persistence

Under mod_perl a child process doesn't exit after serving a single request. Thus, global variables persist inside the same process from request to request. This means that you should be careful not to rely on the value of a global variable if it isn't initialized at the beginning of each request. For example:

```
# the very beginning of the script
use strict;
use vars qw($counter);
$counter++;
```

relies on the fact that Perl interprets an undefined value of $counter as a zero value, because of the increment operator, and therefore sets the value to 1. However, when the same code is executed a second time in the same process, the value of $counter is not undefined any more; instead, it holds the value it had at the end of the previous execution in the same process. Therefore, a cleaner way to code this snippet would be:

```
use strict;
use vars qw($counter);
$counter = 0;
$counter++;
```

In practice, you should avoid using global variables unless there really is no alternative. Most of the problems with global variables arise from the fact that they keep their values across functions, and it's easy to lose track of which function modifies the variable and where. This problem is solved by localizing these variables with local( ). But if you are already doing this, using lexical scoping (with my( )) is even better because its scope is clearly defined, whereas localized variables are seen and can be modified from anywhere in the code. Refer to the *perlsub* manpage for more details. Our example will now be written as:

```
use strict;
my $counter = 0;
$counter++;
```

Note that it is a good practice to both declare and initialize variables, since doing so will clearly convey your intention to the code's maintainer.

You should be especially careful with Perl special variables, which cannot be lexically scoped. With special variables, local( ) must be used. For example, if you want to read in a whole file at once, you need to undef( ) the input record separator. The following code reads the contents of an entire file in one go:

```
open IN, $file or die $!;
$/ = undef;
$content = <IN>; # slurp the whole file in
close IN;
```

Since you have modified the special Perl variable $/ globally, it'll affect any other code running under the same process. If somewhere in the code (or any other code running on the same server) there is a snippet reading a file's content line by line, relying on the default value of $/ (\n), this code will work incorrectly. Localizing the modification of this special variable solves this potential problem:

```
{
  local $/; # $/ is undef now
  $content = <IN>; # slurp the whole file in
}
```

Note that the localization is enclosed in a block. When control passes out of the block, the previous value of $/ will be restored automatically.

STDIN, STDOUT, and STDERR Streams

Under mod_perl, both STDIN and STDOUT are tied to the socket from which the request originated. If, for example, you use a third-party module that prints some output to STDOUT when it shouldn't (for example, control messages) and you want to avoid this, you must temporarily redirect STDOUT to */dev/null*. You will then have to restore STDOUT to the original handle when you want to send a response to the client. The following code demonstrates a possible implementation of this workaround:

```
{
    my $nullfh = Apache::gensym( );
    open $nullfh, '>/dev/null' or die "Can't open /dev/null: $!";
    local *STDOUT = $nullfh;
    call_something_thats_way_too_verbose( );
    close $nullfh;
}
```

The code defines a block in which the STDOUT stream is localized to print to /dev/null. When control passes out of this block, STDOUT gets restored to the previous value.

STDERR is tied to a file defined by the ErrorLog directive. When native *syslog* support is enabled, the STDERR stream will be redirected to /dev/null.

Redirecting STDOUT into a Scalar Variable

Sometimes you encounter a black-box function that prints its output to the default file handle (usually STDOUT) when you would rather put the output into a scalar. This is very relevant under mod_perl, where STDOUT is tied to the Apache request object. In this situation, the IO::String package is especially useful. You can re-tie( ) STDOUT (or any other file handle) to a string by doing a simple select( ) on the IO::String object. Call select( ) again at the end on the original file handle to re-tie( ) STDOUT back to its original stream:

```
my $str;
my $str_fh = IO::String->new($str);

my $old_fh = select($str_fh);
black_box_print( );
select($old_fh) if defined $old_fh;
```

In this example, a new IO::String object is created. The object is then selected, the black_box_print( ) function is called, and its output goes into the string object. Finally, we restore the original file handle, by re-select( )ing the originally selected file handle. The $str variable contains all the output produced by the black_box_print( ) function.

print( )

Under mod_perl, CORE::print( ) (using either STDOUT as a filehandle argument or no filehandle at all) will redirect output to Apache::print( ), since the STDOUT file handle is tied to Apache. That is, these two are functionally equivalent:

```
print "Hello";
$r->print("Hello");
```

Apache::print( ) will return immediately without printing anything if $r->connection->aborted returns true. This happens if the connection has been aborted by the client (e.g., by pressing the Stop button).

There is also an optimization built into Apache::print( ): if any of the arguments to this function are scalar references to strings, they are automatically dereferenced. This avoids needless copying of large strings when passing them to subroutines. For example, the following code will print the actual value of $long_string:

```
my $long_string = "A" x 10000000;
$r->print(\$long_string);
```

To print the reference value itself, use a double reference:

```
$r->print(\\$long_string);
```

When Apache::print( ) sees that the passed value is a reference, it dereferences it once and prints the real reference value:

```
SCALAR(0x8576e0c)
```

Formats

The interface to file handles that are linked to variables with Perl's tie( ) function is not yet complete. The format( ) and write( ) functions are missing. If you configure Perl with sfio, write( ) and format( ) should work just fine.

Instead of format( ), you can use printf( ). For example, the following formats are equivalent:

```
format    printf
---------------
##.##     %2.2f
####.##   %4.2f
```

To print a string with fixed-length elements, use the printf( ) format %n.ms where n is the length of the field allocated for the string and m is the maximum number of characters to take from the string. For example:

```
printf "[%5.3s][%10.10s][%30.30s]\n",
       12345, "John Doe", "1234 Abbey Road"
```

prints:

```
[  123][  John Doe][               1234 Abbey Road]
```

Notice that the first string was allocated five characters in the output, but only three were used because $m=5$ and $n=3$ (%5.3s). If you want to ensure that the text will always be correctly aligned without being truncated, n should always be greater than or equal to m.

You can change the alignment to the left by adding a minus sign (-) after the %. For example:

```
printf "[%-5.5s][%-10.10s][%-30.30s]\n",
       123, "John Doe", "1234 Abbey Road"
```

prints:

```
[123  ][John Doe  ][1234 Abbey Road               ]
```

You can also use a plus sign (+) for the right-side alignment. For example:

```
printf "[%+5s][%+10s][%+30s]\n",
       123, "John Doe", "1234 Abbey Road"
```

prints:

```
[  123][  John Doe][               1234 Abbey Road]
```

Another alternative to format( ) and printf( ) is to use the Text::Reform module from CPAN.

In the examples above we've printed the number *123* as a string (because we used the %s format specifier), but numbers can also be printed using numeric formats. See *perldoc -f sprintf* for full details.

Output from System Calls

The output of system( ), exec( ), and open(PIPE,"|program") calls will not be sent to the browser unless Perl was configured with sfio. To learn if your version of Perl is sfio-enabled, look at the output of the *perl -V* command for the *useperlio* and *d_sfio* strings.

You can use backticks as a possible workaround:

```
print `command here`;
```

But this technique has very poor performance, since it forks a new process. See the discussion about forking in Chapter 10.

BEGIN blocks

Perl executes BEGIN blocks as soon as possible, when it's compiling the code. The same is true under mod_perl. However, since mod_perl normally compiles scripts and modules only once, either in the parent process or just once per child, BEGIN blocks are run only once. As the *perlmod* manpage explains, once a BEGIN block has run, it is immediately undefined. In the mod_perl environment, this means that BEGIN blocks will not be run during the response to an incoming request unless that request happens to be the one that causes the compilation of the code. However, there are cases when BEGIN blocks will be rerun for each request.

BEGIN blocks in modules and files pulled in via require( ) or use( ) will be executed:

- Only once, if pulled in by the parent process.
- Once per child process, if not pulled in by the parent process.
- One additional time per child process, if the module is reloaded from disk by Apache::StatINC.
- One additional time in the parent process on each restart, if PerlFreshRestart is On.
- On every request, if the module with the BEGIN block is deleted from %INC, before the module's compilation is needed. The same thing happens when do( ) is used, which loads the module even if it's already loaded.

BEGIN blocks in Apache::Registry scripts will be executed:

- Only once, if pulled in by the parent process via Apache::RegistryLoader.
- Once per child process, if not pulled in by the parent process.
- One additional time per child process, each time the script file changes on disk.
- One additional time in the parent process on each restart, if pulled in by the parent process via Apache::RegistryLoader and PerlFreshRestart is On.

Note that this second list is applicable only to the scripts themselves. For the modules used by the scripts, the previous list applies.

END Blocks

As the *perlmod* manpage explains, an END subroutine is executed when the Perl interpreter exits. In the mod_perl environment, the Perl interpreter exits only when the child process exits. Usually a single process serves many requests before it exits, so END blocks cannot be used if they are expected to do something at the end of each request's processing.

If there is a need to run some code after a request has been processed, the $r->register_cleanup() function should be used. This function accepts a reference to a function to be called during the PerlCleanupHandler phase, which behaves just like the END block in the normal Perl environment. For example:

```
$r->register_cleanup(sub { warn "$$ does cleanup\n" });
```

or:

```
sub cleanup { warn "$$ does cleanup\n" };
$r->register_cleanup(\&cleanup);
```

will run the registered code at the end of each request, similar to END blocks under mod_cgi.

As you already know by now, Apache::Registry handles things differently. It does execute all END blocks encountered during compilation of Apache::Registry scripts at the end of each request, like mod_cgi does. That includes any END blocks defined in the packages use()d by the scripts.

If you want something to run only once in the parent process on shutdown and restart, you can use register_cleanup() in *startup.pl*:

```
warn "parent pid is $$\n";
Apache->server->register_cleanup(
    sub { warn "server cleanup in $$\n" });
```

This is useful when some server-wide cleanup should be performed when the server is stopped or restarted.

CHECK and INIT Blocks

The CHECK and INIT blocks run when compilation is complete, but before the program starts. CHECK can mean "checkpoint," "double-check," or even just "stop." INIT stands for "initialization." The difference is subtle: CHECK blocks are run just after the compilation ends, whereas INIT blocks are run just before the runtime begins (hence, the -c command-line flag to Perl runs up to CHECK blocks but not INIT blocks).

Perl calls these blocks only during perl_parse( ), which mod_perl calls once at startup time. Therefore, CHECK and INIT blocks don't work in mod_perl, for the same reason these don't:

```
panic% perl -e 'eval qq(CHECK { print "ok\n" })'
panic% perl -e 'eval qq(INIT  { print "ok\n" })'
```

$^T and time( )

Under mod_perl, processes don't quit after serving a single request. Thus, $^T gets initialized to the server startup time and retains this value throughout the process's life. Even if you don't use this variable directly, it's important to know that Perl refers to the value of $^T internally.

For example, Perl uses $^T with the -M, -C, or -A file test operators. As a result, files created after the child server's startup are reported as having a negative age when using those operators. -M returns the age of the script file relative to the value of the $^T special variable.

If you want to have -M report the file's age relative to the current request, reset $^T, just as in any other Perl script. Add the following line at the beginning of your scripts:

```
local $^T = time;
```

You can also do:

```
local $^T = $r->request_time;
```

The second technique is better performance-wise, as it skips the time( ) system call and uses the timestamp of the request's start time, available via the $r->request_time method.

If this correction needs to be applied to a lot of handlers, a more scalable solution is to specify a fixup handler, which will be executed during the fixup stage:

```
sub Apache::PerlBaseTime::handler {
    $^T = shift->request_time;
    return Apache::Constants::DECLINED;
}
```

and then add the following line to *httpd.conf*:

```
PerlFixupHandler Apache::PerlBaseTime
```

Now no modifications to the content-handler code and scripts need to be performed.

Command-Line Switches

When a Perl script is run from the command line, the shell invokes the Perl interpreter via the #!/bin/perl directive, which is the first line of the script (sometimes referred to as the *shebang line*). In scripts running under mod_cgi, you may use Perl switches as described in the *perlrun* manpage, such as -w, -T, or -d. Under the Apache::Registry handlers family, all switches except -w are ignored (and use of the -T switch triggers a warning). The support for -w was added for backward compatibility with mod_cgi.

Most command-line switches have special Perl variable equivalents that allow them to be set/unset in code. Consult the *perlvar* manpage for more details.

mod_perl provides its own equivalents to -w and -T in the form of configuration directives, as we'll discuss presently.

Finally, if you still need to set additional Perl startup flags, such as -d and -D, you can use the PERL5OPT environment variable. Switches in this variable are treated as if they were on every Perl command line. According to the *perlrun* manpage, only the -[DIMUdmw] switches are allowed.

Warnings

There are three ways to enable warnings:

Globally to all processes
> In *httpd.conf*, set:
>
> ```
> PerlWarn On
> ```
>
> You can then fine-tune your code, turning warnings off and on by setting the $^W variable in your scripts.

Locally to a script
> Including the following line:
>
> ```
> #!/usr/bin/perl -w
> ```
>
> will turn warnings on for the scope of the script. You can turn them off and on in the script by setting the $^W variable, as noted above.

Locally to a block
> This code turns warnings on for the scope of the block:
>
> ```
> {
>     local $^W = 1;
>     # some code
> }
> # $^W assumes its previous value here
> ```

This turns warnings off:

```
{
    local $^W = 0;
    # some code
}
# $^W assumes its previous value here
```

If $^W isn't properly localized, this code will affect the current request and all subsequent requests processed by this child. Thus:

```
$^W = 0;
```

will turn the warnings off, no matter what.

If you want to turn warnings on for the scope of the whole file, as in the previous item, you can do this by adding:

```
local $^W = 1;
```

at the beginning of the file. Since a file is effectively a block, file scope behaves like a block's curly braces ({ }), and local $^W at the start of the file will be effective for the whole file.

While having warnings mode turned on is essential for a development server, you should turn it globally off on a production server. Having warnings enabled introduces a non-negligible performance penalty. Also, if every request served generates one warning, and your server processes millions of requests per day, the *error_log* file will eat up all your disk space and the system won't be able to function normally anymore.

Perl 5.6.x introduced the warnings pragma, which allows very flexible control over warnings. This pragma allows you to enable and disable groups of warnings. For example, to enable only the syntax warnings, you can use:

```
use warnings 'syntax';
```

Later in the code, if you want to disable syntax warnings and enable signal-related warnings, you can use:

```
no  warnings 'syntax';
use warnings 'signal';
```

But usually you just want to use:

```
use warnings;
```

which is the equivalent of:

```
use warnings 'all';
```

If you want your code to be really clean and consider all warnings as errors, Perl will help you to do that. With the following code, any warning in the lexical scope of the definition will trigger a fatal error:

```
use warnings FATAL => 'all';
```

Of course, you can fine-tune the groups of warnings and make only certain groups of warnings fatal. For example, to make only closure problems fatal, you can use:

```
use warnings FATAL => 'closure';
```

Using the warnings pragma, you can also disable warnings locally:

```
{
  no warnings;
  # some code that would normally emit warnings
}
```

In this way, you can avoid some warnings that you are aware of but can't do anything about.

For more information about the warnings pragma, refer to the *perllexwarn* manpage.

Taint mode

Perl's *-T* switch enables *taint mode*. In taint mode, Perl performs some checks on how your program is using the data passed to it. For example, taint checks prevent your program from passing some external data to a system call without this data being explicitly checked for nastiness, thus avoiding a fairly large number of common security holes. If you don't force all your scripts and handlers to run under taint mode, it's more likely that you'll leave some holes to be exploited by malicious users. (See Chapter 23 and the *perlsec* manpage for more information. Also read the re pragma's manpage.)

Since the *-T* switch can't be turned on from within Perl (this is because when Perl is running, it's already too late to mark *all* external data as tainted), mod_perl provides the `PerlTaintCheck` directive to turn on taint checks globally. Enable this mode with:

```
PerlTaintCheck On
```

anywhere in *httpd.conf* (though it's better to place it as early as possible for clarity).

For more information on taint checks and how to untaint data, refer to the *perlsec* manpage.

Compiled Regular Expressions

When using a regular expression containing an interpolated Perl variable that you are confident will not change during the execution of the program, a standard speed-optimization technique is to add the */o* modifier to the regex pattern. This compiles the regular expression once, for the entire lifetime of the script, rather than every time the pattern is executed. Consider:

```
my $pattern = '^\d+$'; # likely to be input from an HTML form field
foreach (@list) {
    print if /$pattern/o;
}
```

This is usually a big win in loops over lists, or when using the grep( ) or map( ) operators.

In long-lived mod_perl scripts and handlers, however, the variable may change with each invocation. In that case, this memorization can pose a problem. The first request processed by a fresh mod_perl child process will compile the regex and perform the search correctly. However, all subsequent requests running the same code in the same process will use the memorized pattern and not the fresh one supplied by users. The code will appear to be broken.

Imagine that you run a search engine service, and one person enters a search keyword of her choice and finds what she's looking for. Then another person who happens to be served by the same process searches for a different keyword, but unexpectedly receives the same search results as the previous person.

There are two solutions to this problem.

The first solution is to use the eval q// construct to force the code to be evaluated each time it's run. It's important that the eval block covers the entire processing loop, not just the pattern match itself.

The original code fragment would be rewritten as:

```
my $pattern = '^\d+$';
eval q{
    foreach (@list) {
        print if /$pattern/o;
    }
}
```

If we were to write this:

```
foreach (@list) {
    eval q{ print if /$pattern/o; };
}
```

the regex would be compiled for every element in the list, instead of just once for the entire loop over the list (and the /o modifier would essentially be useless).

However, watch out for using strings coming from an untrusted origin inside eval—they might contain Perl code dangerous to your system, so make sure to sanity-check them first.

This approach can be used if there is more than one pattern-match operator in a given section of code. If the section contains only one regex operator (be it m// or s///), you can rely on the property of the *null pattern*, which reuses the last pattern seen. This leads to the second solution, which also eliminates the use of eval.

The above code fragment becomes:

```
my $pattern = '^\d+$';
"0" =~ /$pattern/; # dummy match that must not fail!
foreach (@list) {
    print if //;
}
```

The only caveat is that the dummy match that boots the regular expression engine *must* succeed—otherwise the pattern will not be cached, and the // will match everything. If you can't count on fixed text to ensure the match succeeds, you have two options.

If you can guarantee that the pattern variable contains no metacharacters (such as *, +, ^, $, \d, etc.), you can use the dummy match of the pattern itself:

```
$pattern =~ /\Q$pattern\E/; # guaranteed if no metacharacters present
```

The \Q modifier ensures that any special regex characters will be escaped.

If there is a possibility that the pattern contains metacharacters, you should match the pattern itself, or the nonsearchable \377 character, as follows:

```
"\377" =~ /$pattern|^\377$/; # guaranteed if metacharacters present
```

Matching patterns repeatedly

Another technique may also be used, depending on the complexity of the regex to which it is applied. One common situation in which a compiled regex is usually more efficient is when you are matching any one of a group of patterns over and over again.

To make this approach easier to use, we'll use a slightly modified helper routine from Jeffrey Friedl's book *Mastering Regular Expressions* (O'Reilly):

```perl
sub build_match_many_function {
    my @list = @_;
    my $expr = join '||',
        map { "\$_[0] =~ m/\$list[$_]/o" } (0..$#list);
    my $matchsub = eval "sub { $expr }";
    die "Failed in building regex @list: $@" if $@;
    return $matchsub;
}
```

This function accepts a list of patterns as an argument, builds a match regex for each item in the list against $_[0], and uses the logical || (OR) operator to stop the matching when the first match succeeds. The chain of pattern matches is then placed into a string and compiled within an anonymous subroutine using eval. If eval fails, the code aborts with die( ); otherwise, a reference to this subroutine is returned to the caller.

Here is how it can be used:

```perl
my @agents = qw(Mozilla Lynx MSIE AmigaVoyager lwp libwww);
my $known_agent_sub = build_match_many_function(@agents);

while (<ACCESS_LOG>) {
    my $agent = get_agent_field($_);
    warn "Unknown Agent: $agent\n"
        unless $known_agent_sub->($agent);
}
```

This code takes lines of log entries from the *access_log* file already opened on the ACCESS_LOG file handle, extracts the agent field from each entry in the log file, and tries to match it against the list of known agents. Every time the match fails, it prints a warning with the name of the unknown agent.

An alternative approach is to use the qr// operator, which is used to compile a regex. The previous example can be rewritten as:

```
my @agents = qw(Mozilla Lynx MSIE AmigaVoyager lwp libwww);
my @compiled_re = map qr/$_/, @agents;

while (<ACCESS_LOG>) {
    my $agent = get_agent_field($_);
    my $ok = 0;
    for my $re (@compiled_re) {
        $ok = 1, last if /$re/;
    }
    warn "Unknown Agent: $agent\n"
        unless $ok;
}
```

In this code, we compile the patterns once before we use them, similar to build_match_many_function( ) from the previous example, but now we save an extra call to a subroutine. A simple benchmark shows that this example is about 2.5 times faster than the previous one.

Apache::Registry Specifics

The following coding issues are relevant only for scripts running under the Apache::Registry content handler and similar handlers, such as Apache::PerlRun. Of course, all of the mod_perl specifics described earlier apply as well.

__END__ and __DATA__ Tokens

An Apache::Registry script cannot contain __END__ or __DATA__ tokens, because Apache::Registry wraps the original script's code into a subroutine called handler( ), which is then called. Consider the following script, accessed as */perl/test.pl*:

```
print "Content-type: text/plain\n\n";
print "Hi";
```

When this script is executed under Apache::Registry, it becomes wrapped in a handler( ) subroutine, like this:

```
package Apache::ROOT::perl::test_2epl;
use Apache qw(exit);
sub handler {
    print "Content-type: text/plain\n\n";
    print "Hi";
}
```

If we happen to put an __END__ tag in the code, like this:

```
print "Content-type: text/plain\n\n";
print "Hi";
__END__
Some text that wouldn't be normally executed
```

it will be turned into:

```
package Apache::ROOT::perl::test_2epl;
use Apache qw(exit);
sub handler {
    print "Content-type: text/plain\n\n";
    print "Hi";
    __END__
    Some text that wouldn't be normally executed
}
```

When issuing a request to */perl/test.pl*, the following error will then be reported:

```
Missing right bracket at .... line 4, at end of line
```

Perl cuts everything after the __END__ tag. Therefore, the subroutine handler( )'s closing curly bracket is not seen by Perl. The same applies to the __DATA__ tag.

Symbolic Links

Apache::Registry caches the script in the package whose name is constructed from the URI from which the script is accessed. If the same script can be reached by different URIs, which is possible if you have used symbolic links or aliases, the same script will be stored in memory more than once, which is a waste.

For example, assuming that you already have the script at */home/httpd/perl/news/news.pl*, you can create a symbolic link:

```
panic% ln -s /home/httpd/perl/news/news.pl /home/httpd/perl/news.pl
```

Now the script can be reached through both URIs, */news/news.pl* and */news.pl*. This doesn't really matter until the two URIs get advertised and users reach the same script from the two of them.

Now start the server in single-server mode and issue a request to both URIs:

```
http://localhost/perl/news/news.pl
http://localhost/perl/news.pl
```

To reveal the duplication, you should use the Apache::Status module. Among other things, it shows all the compiled Apache::Registry scripts (using their respective packages). If you are using the default configuration directives, you should either use this URI:

```
http://localhost/perl-status?rgysubs
```

or just go to the main menu at:

```
http://localhost/perl-status
```

and click on the "Compiled Registry Scripts" menu item.

If the script was accessed through the two URIs, you will see the output shown in Figure 6-1.

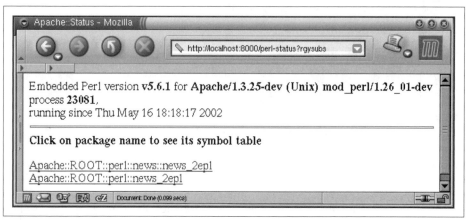

Figure 6-1. Compiled Registry Scripts output

You can usually spot this kind of problem by running a link checker that goes recursively through all the pages of the service by following all links, and then using Apache::Status to find the symlink duplicates (without restarting the server, of course). To make it easier to figure out what to look for, first find all symbolic links. For example, in our case, the following command shows that we have only one symlink:

```
panic% find /home/httpd/perl -type l
/home/httpd/perl/news.pl
```

So now we can look for that symlink in the output of the Compiled Registry Scripts section.

Notice that if you perform the testing in multi-server mode, some child processes might show only one entry or none at all, since they might not serve the same requests as the others.

Return Codes

Apache::Registry normally assumes a return code of *OK (200)* and sends it for you. If a different return code needs to be sent, $r->status( ) can be used. For example, to send the return code 404 (*Not Found*), you can use the following code:

```
use Apache::Constants qw(NOT_FOUND);
$r->status(NOT_FOUND);
```

If this method is used, there is no need to call $r->send_http_header( ) (assuming that the PerlSendHeader Off setting is in effect).

Transition from mod_cgi Scripts to Apache Handlers

If you don't need to preserve backward compatibility with mod_cgi, you can port mod_cgi scripts to use mod_perl-specific APIs. This allows you to benefit from features not available under mod_cgi and gives you better performance for the features available under both. We have already seen how easily Apache::Registry turns scripts into handlers before they get executed. The transition to handlers is straightforward in most cases.

Let's see a transition example. We will start with a mod_cgi-compatible script running under Apache::Registry, transpose it into a Perl content handler without using any mod_perl-specific modules, and then convert it to use the Apache::Request and Apache::Cookie modules that are available only in the mod_perl environment.

Starting with a mod_cgi-Compatible Script

Example 6-18 shows the original script's code.

Example 6-18. cookie_script.pl

```
use strict;
use CGI;
use CGI::Cookie;
use vars qw($q $switch $status $sessionID);

init();
print_header();
print_status();

sub init {
    $q = new CGI;
    $switch = $q->param("switch") ? 1 : 0;
    my %cookies = CGI::Cookie->fetch;
    $sessionID = exists $cookies{'sessionID'}
        ? $cookies{'sessionID'}->value
        : '';

    # 0 = not running, 1 = running
    $status = $sessionID ? 1 : 0;
    # switch status if asked to
    $status = !$status if $switch;

    if ($status) {
        # preserve sessionID if it exists or create a new one
        $sessionID ||= generate_sessionID() if $status;
    } else {
        # delete the sessionID
        $sessionID = '';
    }
```

Example 6-18. cookie_script.pl (continued)

```
}

sub print_header {
    my $c = CGI::Cookie->new(
        -name    => 'sessionID',
        -value   => $sessionID,
        -expires => '+1h'
    );

    print $q->header(
        -type   => 'text/html',
        -cookie => $c
    );
}

# print the current Session status and a form to toggle the status
sub print_status {

    print qq{<html><head><title>Cookie</title></head><body>};

    print "<B>Status:</B> ",
        $status
            ? "Session is running with ID: $sessionID"
            : "No session is running";


    # change status form
    my $button_label = $status ? "Stop" : "Start";
    print qq{<hr>
        <form>
          <input type=submit name=switch value=" $button_label ">
        </form>
            };

    print qq{</body></html>};

}

# A dummy ID generator
# Replace with a real session ID generator
#########################
sub generate_sessionID {
    return scalar localtime;
}
```

The code is very simple. It creates a session when you press the Start button and deletes it when you pressed the Stop button. The session is stored and retrieved using cookies.

We have split the code into three subroutines. init( ) initializes global variables and parses incoming data. print_header( ) prints the HTTP headers, including the cookie

---

header. Finally, print_status( ) generates the output. Later, we will see that this logical separation will allow an easy conversion to Perl content-handler code.

We have used a few global variables, since we didn't want to pass them from function to function. In a big project, you should be very restrictive about what variables are allowed to be global, if any. In any case, the init( ) subroutine makes sure all these variables are reinitialized for each code reinvocation.

We have used a very simple generate_sessionID( ) function that returns a current date-time string (e.g., Wed Apr 12 15:02:23 2000) as a session ID. You'll want to replace this with code that generates a unique and unpredictable session ID each time it is called.

Converting into a Perl Content Handler

Let's now convert this script into a content handler. There are two parts to this task: first configure Apache to run the new code as a Perl handler, then modify the code itself.

First we add the following snippet to *httpd.conf*:

```
PerlModule Book::Cookie
<Location /test/cookie>
    SetHandler perl-script
    PerlHandler Book::Cookie
</Location>
```

and restart the server.

When a request whose URI starts with */test/cookie* is received, Apache will execute the Book::Cookie::handler( ) subroutine (which we will look at presently) as a content handler. We made sure we preloaded the Book::Cookie module at server startup with the PerlModule directive.

Now we modify the script itself. We copy its contents to the file *Cookie.pm* and place it into one of the directories listed in @INC. In this example, we'll use */home/httpd/perl*, which we added to @INC. Since we want to call this package Book::Cookie, we'll put *Cookie.pm* into the */home/httpd/perl/Book/* directory.

The changed code is in Example 6-19. As the subroutines were left unmodified from the original script, they aren't reproduced here (so you'll see the differences more clearly.)

Example 6-19. Book/Cookie.pm

```
package Book::Cookie;
use Apache::Constants qw(:common);

use strict;
use CGI;
use CGI::Cookie;
```

Example 6-19. Book/Cookie.pm

```
use vars qw($q $switch $status $sessionID);

sub handler {
    my $r = shift;

    init();
    print_header();
    print_status();

    return OK;
}

# all subroutines unchanged

1;
```

Two lines have been added to the beginning of the code:

```
package Book::Cookie;
use Apache::Constants qw(:common);
```

The first line declares the package name, and the second line imports constants commonly used in mod_perl handlers to return status codes. In our case, we use the OK constant only when returning from the handler() subroutine.

The following code is left unchanged:

```
use strict;
use CGI;
use CGI::Cookie;
use vars qw($q $switch $status $sessionID);
```

We add some new code around the subroutine calls:

```
sub handler {
    my $r = shift;

    init();
    print_header();
    print_status();

    return OK;
}
```

Each content handler (and any other handler) should begin with a subroutine called handler(). This subroutine is called when a request's URI starts with */test/cookie*, as per our configuration. You can choose a different subroutine name—for example, execute()—but then you must explicitly specify that name in the configuration directives in the following way:

```
PerlModule Book::Cookie
<Location /test/cookie>
    SetHandler perl-script
    PerlHandler Book::Cookie::execute
</Location>
```

We will use the default name, handler( ).

The handler( ) subroutine is just like any other subroutine, but generally it has the following structure:

```
sub handler {
    my $r = shift;

    # the code

    # status (OK, DECLINED or else)
    return OK;
}
```

First, we retrieve a reference to the request object by shifting it from @_ and assigning it to the $r variable. We'll need this a bit later.

Second, we write the code that processes the request.

Third, we return the status of the execution. There are many possible statuses; the most commonly used are OK and DECLINED. OK tells the server that the handler has completed the request phase to which it was assigned. DECLINED means the opposite, in which case another handler will process this request. Apache::Constants exports these and other commonly used status codes.

In our example, all we had to do was to wrap the three calls:

```
init( );
print_header( );
print_status( );
```

inside the handler( ) skeleton:

```
sub handler {
    my $r = shift;

    return OK;
}
```

Last, we need to add 1; at the end of the module, as we do with any Perl module. This ensures that PerlModule doesn't fail when it tries to load Book::Cookie.

To summarize, we took the original script's code and added the following seven lines:

```
package Book::Cookie;
use Apache::Constants qw(:common);

sub handler {
    my $r = shift;

    return OK;
}
1;
```

and we now have a fully-fledged Perl content handler.

Converting to use the mod_perl API and mod_perl-Specific Modules

Now that we have a complete PerlHandler, let's convert it to use the mod_perl API and mod_perl-specific modules. First, this may give us better performance where the internals of the API are implemented in C. Second, this unleashes the full power of Apache provided by the mod_perl API, which is only partially available in the mod_cgi-compatible modules.

We are going to replace CGI.pm and CGI::Cookie with their mod_perl-specific equivalents: Apache::Request and Apache::Cookie, respectively. These two modules are written in C with the XS interface to Perl, so code that uses these modules heavily runs much faster.

Apache::Request has an API similar to CGI's, and Apache::Cookie has an API similar to CGI::Cookie's. This makes porting straightforward. Essentially, we just replace:

```
use CGI;
$q = new CGI;
```

with:

```
use Apache::Request ( );
$q = Apache::Request->new($r);
```

And we replace:

```
use CGI::Cookie ( );
my $cookie = CGI::Cookie->new(...)
```

with:

```
use Apache::Cookie ( );
my $cookie = Apache::Cookie->new($r, ...);
```

Example 6-20 is the new code for Book::Cookie2.

Example 6-20. Book/Cookie2.pm

```
package Book::Cookie2;
use Apache::Constants qw(:common);

use strict;
use Apache::Request ( );
use Apache::Cookie ( );
use vars qw($r $q $switch $status $sessionID);

sub handler {
    $r = shift;

    init( );
    print_header( );
    print_status( );

    return OK;
```

Example 6-20. Book/Cookie2.pm (continued)

```perl
}

sub init {

    $q = Apache::Request->new($r);
    $switch = $q->param("switch") ? 1 : 0;

    my %cookies = Apache::Cookie->fetch;
    $sessionID = exists $cookies{'sessionID'}
        ? $cookies{'sessionID'}->value : '';

    # 0 = not running, 1 = running
    $status = $sessionID ? 1 : 0;
    # switch status if asked to
    $status = !$status if $switch;

    if ($status) {
        # preserve sessionID if it exists or create a new one
        $sessionID ||= generate_sessionID() if $status;
    } else {
        # delete the sessionID
        $sessionID = '';
    }
}

sub print_header {
    my $c = Apache::Cookie->new(
        $r,
        -name    => 'sessionID',
        -value   => $sessionID,
        -expires => '+1h');

    # Add a Set-Cookie header to the outgoing headers table
    $c->bake;

    $r->send_http_header('text/html');
}

# print the current Session status and a form to toggle the status
sub print_status {

    print qq{<html><head><title>Cookie</title></head><body>};

    print "<B>Status:</B> ",
        $status
            ? "Session is running with ID: $sessionID"
            : "No session is running";

    # change status form
    my $button_label = $status ? "Stop" : "Start";
    print qq{<hr>
      <form>
```

Example 6-20. Book/Cookie2.pm (continued)

```
            <input type=submit name=switch value=" $button_label ">
        </form>
            };

    print qq{</body></html>};

}

# replace with a real session ID generator
sub generate_sessionID {
    return scalar localtime;
}

1;
```

The only other changes are in the print_header( ) function. Instead of passing the cookie code to CGI's header( ) function to return a proper HTTP header, like this:

```
    print $q->header(
        -type   => 'text/html',
        -cookie => $c);
```

we do it in two stages. First, the following line adds a Set-Cookie header to the outgoing headers table:

```
    $c->bake;
```

Then this line sets the Content-Type header to *text/html* and sends out the whole HTTP header:

```
    $r->send_http_header('text/html');
```

The rest of the code is unchanged.

The last thing we need to do is add the following snippet to *httpd.conf*:

```
    PerlModule Book::Cookie2
    <Location /test/cookie2>
        SetHandler perl-script
        PerlHandler Book::Cookie2
    </Location>
```

Now the magic URI that will trigger the above code execution will be one starting with */test/cookie2*. We save the code in the file */home/httpd/perl/Book/Cookie2.pm*, since we have called this package Book::Cookie2.

As you've seen, converting well-written CGI code into mod_perl handler code is straightforward. Taking advantage of mod_perl-specific features and modules is also generally simple. Very little code needs to be changed to convert a script.

Note that to make the demonstration simple to follow, we haven't changed the style of the original package. But by all means consider doing that when porting real code: use lexicals instead of globals, apply mod_perl API functions where applicable, etc.

Loading and Reloading Modules

You often need to reload modules in development and production environments. mod_perl tries hard to avoid unnecessary module reloading, but sometimes (especially during the development process) we want some modules to be reloaded when modified. The following sections discuss issues related to module loading and reloading.

The @INC Array Under mod_perl

Under mod_perl, @INC can be modified only during server startup. After each request, mod_perl resets @INC's value to the one it had before the request.

If mod_perl encounters a statement like the following:

```
use lib qw(foo/bar);
```

it modifies @INC only for the period during which the code is being parsed and compiled. Afterward, @INC is reset to its original value. Therefore, the only way to change @INC permanently is to modify it at server startup.

There are two ways to alter @INC at server startup:

- In the configuration file, with:

    ```
    PerlSetEnv PERL5LIB /home/httpd/perl
    ```

    or:

    ```
    PerlSetEnv PERL5LIB /home/httpd/perl:/home/httpd/mymodules
    ```

- In the *startup.pl* file:

    ```
    use lib qw(/home/httpd/perl /home/httpd/mymodules);
    1;
    ```

    As always, the startup file needs to be loaded from *httpd.conf*:

    ```
    PerlRequire /path/to/startup.pl
    ```

To make sure that you have set @INC correctly, configure perl-status into your server, as explained in Chapter 21. Follow the "Loaded Modules" item in the menu and look at the bottom of the generated page, where the contents of @INC are shown:

```
@INC =
/home/httpd/mymodules
/home/httpd/perl
/usr/lib/perl5/5.6.1/i386-linux
/usr/lib/perl5/5.6.1
/usr/lib/perl5/site_perl/5.6.1/i386-linux
/usr/lib/perl5/site_perl/5.6.1
/usr/lib/perl5/site_perl
.
/home/httpd/httpd_perl/
/home/httpd/httpd_perl/lib/perl
```

As you can see in our setup, we have two custom directories prepended at the beginning of the list. The rest of the list contains standard directories from the Perl distribution, plus the *$ServerRoot* and *$ServerRoot/lib/perl* directories appended at the end (which mod_perl adds automatically).

Reloading Modules and Required Files

When working with mod_cgi, you can change the code and rerun the CGI script from your browser to see the changes. Since the script isn't cached in memory, the server starts up a new Perl interpreter for each request, which loads and recompiles the script from scratch. The effects of any changes are immediate.

The situation is different with mod_perl, since the whole idea is to get maximum performance from the server. By default, the server won't spend time checking whether any included library modules have been changed. It assumes that they weren't, thus saving the time it takes to stat( ) the source files from any modules and libraries you use( ) and require( ) in your script.

If the scripts are running under Apache::Registry, the only check that is performed is to see whether your main script has been changed. If your scripts do not use( ) or require( ) any other Perl modules or packages, there is nothing to worry about. If, however, you are developing a script that includes other modules, the files you use( ) or require( ) aren't checked for modification, and you need to do something about that.

There are a couple of techniques to make a mod_perl-enabled server recognize changes in library modules. They are discussed in the following sections.

Restarting the server

The simplest approach is to restart the server each time you apply some change to your code. Restarting techniques are covered in Chapter 5. After restarting the server about 50 times, you will tire of it and look for other solutions.

Using Apache::StatINC

Help comes from the Apache::StatINC module. When Perl pulls in a file with require( ), it stores the full pathname as a value in the global hash %INC with the filename as the key. Apache::StatINC looks through %INC and immediately reloads any file that has been updated on the disk.

To enable this module, add these two lines to *httpd.conf*:

```
PerlModule Apache::StatINC
PerlInitHandler Apache::StatINC
```

To be sure it really works, turn on debug mode on your development system by adding `PerlSetVar StatINCDebug On` to your configuration file. You end up with something like this:

```
PerlModule Apache::StatINC
PerlInitHandler Apache::StatINC
<Location /perl>
    SetHandler perl-script
    PerlHandler Apache::Registry
    Options ExecCGI
    PerlSendHeader On
    PerlSetVar StatINCDebug On
</Location>
```

Be aware that only the modules located in @INC are reloaded on change, and you can change @INC only before the server has been started (in the startup file).

Note the following trap: because ".", the current directory, is in @INC, Perl knows how to require( ) files with pathnames relative to the current script's directory. After the code has been parsed, however, the server doesn't remember the path. So if the code loads a module `MyModule` located in the directory of the script and this directory is not in @INC, you end up with the following entry in %INC:

```
'MyModule.pm' => 'MyModule.pm'
```

When `Apache::StatINC` tries to check whether the file has been modified, it won't be able to find the file, since *MyModule.pm* is not in any of the paths in @INC. To correct this problem, add the module's location path to @INC at server startup.

Using Apache::Reload

`Apache::Reload` is a newer module that comes as a drop-in replacement for `Apache::StatINC`. It provides extra functionality and is more flexible.

To make `Apache::Reload` check all the loaded modules on each request, just add the following line to *httpd.conf*:

```
PerlInitHandler Apache::Reload
```

To reload only specific modules when these get changed, three alternatives are provided: registering the module implicitly, registering the module explicitly, and setting up a dummy file to *touch* whenever you want the modules reloaded.

To use implicit module registration, turn off the `ReloadAll` variable, which is on by default:

```
PerlInitHandler Apache::Reload
PerlSetVar ReloadAll Off
```

and add the following line to every module that you want to be reloaded on change:

```
use Apache::Reload;
```

Alternatively, you can explicitly specify modules to be reloaded in *httpd.conf*:

```
PerlInitHandler Apache::Reload
PerlSetVar ReloadModules "Book::Foo Book::Bar Foo::Bar::Test"
```

Note that these are split on whitespace, but the module list *must* be in quotes, or Apache will try to parse the parameter list itself.

You can register groups of modules using the metacharacter *:

```
PerlSetVar ReloadModules "Foo::* Bar::*"
```

In the above example, all modules starting with `Foo::` and `Bar::` will become registered. This feature allows you to assign all the modules in a project using a single pattern.

The third option is to set up a file that you can *touch* to cause the reloads to be performed:

```
PerlSetVar ReloadTouchFile /tmp/reload_modules
```

Now when you're happy with your changes, simply go to the command line and type:

```
panic% touch /tmp/reload_modules
```

If you set this, and don't *touch* the file, the reloads won't happen (regardless of how the modules have been registered).

This feature is very convenient in a production server environment, but compared to a full restart, the benefits of preloaded modules memory-sharing are lost, since each child will get its own copy of the reloaded modules.

Note that `Apache::Reload` might have a problem with reloading single modules containing multiple packages that all use pseudo-hashes. The solution: don't use pseudo-hashes. Pseudo-hashes will be removed from newer versions of Perl anyway.

Just like with `Apache::StatInc`, if you have modules loaded from directories that are not in `@INC`, `Apache::Reload` will fail to find the files. This is because `@INC` is reset to its original value even if it gets temporarily modified in the script. The solution is to extend `@INC` at server startup to include all the directories from which you load files that aren't in the standard `@INC` paths.

Using dynamic configuration files

Sometimes you may want an application to monitor its own configuration file and reload it when it is altered. But you don't want to restart the server for these changes to take effect. The solution is to use dynamic configuration files.

Dynamic configuration files are especially useful when you want to provide administrators with a configuration tool that modifies an application on the fly. This approach eliminates the need to provide shell access to the server. It can also prevent typos, because the administration program can verify the submitted modifications.

It's possible to get away with `Apache::Reload` and still have a similar small overhead for the `stat()` call, but this requires the involvement of a person who can modify *httpd.conf* to configure `Apache::Reload`. The method described next has no such requirement.

Writing configuration files.   We'll start by describing various approaches to writing configuration files, and their strengths and weaknesses.

If your configuration file contains only a few variables, it doesn't matter how you write the file. In practice, however, configuration files often grow as a project develops. This is especially true for projects that generate HTML files, since they tend to demand many easily configurable settings, such as the location of headers, footers, templates, colors, and so on.

A common approach used by CGI programmers is to define all configuration variables in a separate file. For example:

```
$cgi_dir   = '/home/httpd/perl';
$cgi_url   = '/perl';
$docs_dir  = '/home/httpd/docs';
$docs_url  = '/';
$img_dir   = '/home/httpd/docs/images';
$img_url   = '/images';
# ... many more config params here ...
$color_hint   = '#777777';
$color_warn   = '#990066';
$color_normal = '#000000';
```

The use `strict`; pragma demands that all variables be declared. When using these variables in a mod_perl script, we must declare them with use `vars` in the script, so we start the script with:

```
use strict;
use vars qw($cgi_dir $cgi_url $docs_dir $docs_url
            # ... many more config params here ....
            $color_hint  $color_warn $color_normal
            );
```

It is a nightmare to maintain such a script, especially if not all features have been coded yet—we have to keep adding and removing variable names. Since we're writing clean code, we also start the configuration file with use `strict`;, so we have to list the variables with use `vars` here as well—a second list of variables to maintain. Then, as we write many different scripts, we may get name collisions between configuration files.

The solution is to use the power of Perl's packages and assign a unique package name to each configuration file. For example, we might declare the following package name:

```
package Book::Config0;
```

Now each configuration file is isolated into its own namespace. But how does the script use these variables? We can no longer just require( ) the file and use the variables, since they now belong to a different package. Instead, we must modify all our scripts to use the configuration variables' fully qualified names (e.g., referring to $Book::Config0::cgi_url instead of just $cgi_url).

You may find typing fully qualified names tedious, or you may have a large repository of legacy scripts that would take a while to update. If so, you'll want to import the required variables into any script that is going to use them. First, the configuration package has to export those variables. This entails listing the names of all the variables in the @EXPORT_OK hash. See Example 6-21.

Example 6-21. Book/Config0.pm

```
package Book::Config0;
use strict;

BEGIN {
  use Exporter ();

  @Book::HTML::ISA       = qw(Exporter);
  @Book::HTML::EXPORT    = qw( );
  @Book::HTML::EXPORT_OK = qw($cgi_dir $cgi_url $docs_dir $docs_url
                            # ... many more config params here ....
                            $color_hint $color_warn $color_normal);
}

use vars qw($cgi_dir $cgi_url $docs_dir $docs_url
          # ... many more config params here ....
          $color_hint  $color_warn $color_normal
          );

$cgi_dir  = '/home/httpd/perl';
$cgi_url  = '/perl';
$docs_dir = '/home/httpd/docs';
$docs_url = '/';
$img_dir  = '/home/httpd/docs/images';
$img_url  = '/images';
# ... many more config params here ...
$color_hint   = "#777777";
$color_warn   = "#990066";
$color_normal = "#000000";
```

A script that uses this package will start with this code:

```
    use strict;
    use Book::Config0 qw($cgi_dir $cgi_url $docs_dir $docs_url
                        # ... many more config params here ....
                        $color_hint  $color_warn $color_normal
                        );
    use vars          qw($cgi_dir $cgi_url $docs_dir $docs_url
                        # ... many more config params here ....
                        $color_hint  $color_warn $color_normal
                        );
```

Whoa! We now have to update at least three variable lists when we make a change in naming of the configuration variables. And we have only one script using the configuration file, whereas a real-life application often contains many different scripts.

There's also a performance drawback: exported variables add some memory overhead, and in the context of mod_perl this overhead is multiplied by the number of server processes running.

There are a number of techniques we can use to get rid of these problems. First, variables can be grouped in named groups called *tags*. The tags are later used as arguments to the import( ) or use( ) calls. You are probably familiar with:

```
use CGI qw(:standard :html);
```

We can implement this quite easily, with the help of export_ok_tags( ) from Exporter. For example:

```
BEGIN {
  use Exporter ();
  use vars qw( @ISA @EXPORT @EXPORT_OK %EXPORT_TAGS );
  @ISA        = qw(Exporter);
  @EXPORT     = ();
  @EXPORT_OK  = ();

  %EXPORT_TAGS = (
      vars => [qw($firstname $surname)],
      subs => [qw(reread_conf untaint_path)],
  );
  Exporter::export_ok_tags('vars');
  Exporter::export_ok_tags('subs');
}
```

In the script using this configuration, we write:

```
use Book::Config0 qw(:subs :vars);
```

Subroutines are exported exactly like variables, since symbols are what are actually being exported. Notice we don't use export_tags( ), as it exports the variables automatically without the user asking for them (this is considered bad style). If a module automatically exports variables with export_tags(), you can avoid unnecessary imports in your script by using this syntax:

```
use Book::Config0 ();
```

You can also go even further and group tags into other named groups. For example, the :all tag from CGI.pm is a group tag of all other groups. It requires a little more effort to implement, but you can always save time by looking at the solution in CGI. pm's code. It's just a matter of an extra code to expand all the groups recursively.

As the number of variables grows, however, your configuration will become unwieldy. Consider keeping all the variables in a single hash built from references to other scalars, anonymous arrays, and hashes. See Example 6-22.

Example 6-22. Book/Config1.pm

```
package Book::Config1;
use strict;

BEGIN {
  use Exporter ();

  @Book::Config1::ISA       = qw(Exporter);
  @Book::Config1::EXPORT    = qw( );
  @Book::Config1::EXPORT_OK = qw(%c);
}

use vars qw(%c);

%c = (
    dir => {
        cgi  => '/home/httpd/perl',
        docs => '/home/httpd/docs',
        img  => '/home/httpd/docs/images',
      },
    url => {
        cgi  => '/perl',
        docs => '/',
        img  => '/images',
      },
    color => {
        hint   => '#777777',
        warn   => '#990066',
        normal => '#000000',
        },
  );
```

Good Perl style suggests keeping a comma at the end of each list. This makes it easy to add new items at the end of a list.

Our script now looks like this:

```
use strict;
use Book::Config1 qw(%c);
use vars          qw(%c);
print "Content-type: text/plain\n\n";
print "My url docs root: $c{url}{docs}\n";
```

The whole mess is gone. Now there is only one variable to worry about.

The one small downside to this approach is auto-vivification. For example, if we write $c{url}{doc} by mistake, Perl will silently create this element for us with the value undef. When we use strict;, Perl will tell us about any misspelling of this kind for a simple scalar, but this check is not performed for hash elements. This puts the onus of responsibility back on us, since we must take greater care.

The benefits of the hash approach are significant. Let's make it even better by getting rid of the Exporter stuff completely, removing all the exporting code from the configuration file. See Example 6-23.

Example 6-23. Book/Config2.pm

```
package Book::Config2;
use strict;
use vars qw(%c);

%c = (
   dir => {
       cgi  => '/home/httpd/perl',
       docs => '/home/httpd/docs',
       img  => '/home/httpd/docs/images',
     },
   url => {
       cgi  => '/perl',
       docs => '/',
       img  => '/images',
     },
   color => {
        hint   => '#777777',
        warn   => '#990066',
        normal => '#000000',
       },
 );
```

Our script is modified to use fully qualified names for the configuration variables it uses:

```
use strict;
use Book::Config2 ();
print "Content-type: text/plain\n\n";
print "My url docs root: $Book::Config2::c{url}{docs}\n";
```

To save typing and spare the need to use fully qualified variable names, we'll use a magical Perl feature to alias the configuration variable to a script's variable:

```
use strict;
use Book::Config2 ();
use vars qw(%c);
*c = \%Book::Config2::c;
print "Content-type: text/plain\n\n";
print "My url docs root: $c{url}{docs}\n";
```

We've aliased the *c glob with a reference to the configuration hash. From now on, %Book::Config2::c and %c refer to the same hash for all practical purposes.

One last point: often, redundancy is introduced in configuration variables. Consider:

```
$cgi_dir  = '/home/httpd/perl';
$docs_dir = '/home/httpd/docs';
$img_dir  = '/home/httpd/docs/images';
```

It's obvious that the base path *home/httpd* should be moved to a separate variable, so only that variable needs to be changed if the application is moved to another location on the filesystem.

```
$base      = '/home/httpd';
$cgi_dir  = "$base/perl";
$docs_dir = "$base/docs";
$img_dir  = "$docs_dir/images";
```

This cannot be done with a hash, since we cannot refer to its values before the definition is completed. That is, this will not work:

```
%c = (
    base => '/home/httpd',
    dir => {
        cgi  => "$c{base}/perl",
        docs => "$c{base}/docs",
        img  => "$c{base}{docs}/images",
    },
);
```

But nothing stops us from adding additional variables that are lexically scoped with my( ). The following code is correct:

```
my $base = '/home/httpd';
%c = (
    dir => {
        cgi  => "$base/perl",
        docs => "$base/docs",
        img  => "$base/docs/images",
    },
);
```

We've learned how to write configuration files that are easy to maintain, and how to save memory by avoiding importing variables in each script's namespace. Now let's look at reloading those files.

Reloading configuration files. First, lets look at a simple case, in which we just have to look after a simple configuration file like the one below. Imagine a script that tells you who is the patch pumpkin of the current Perl release.* (*Pumpkin* is a whimsical term for the person with exclusive access to a virtual "token" representing a certain authority, such as applying patches to a master copy of some source.)

```
use CGI ();
use strict;

my $firstname = "Jarkko";
my $surname = "Hietaniemi";
my $q = CGI->new;
```

---

* These are the recent pumpkins: Chip Salzenberg for 5.004, Gurusamy Sarathy for 5.005 and 5.6, Jarkko Hietaniemi for 5.8, Hugo van der Sanden for 5.10.

```
print $q->header(-type=>'text/html');
print $q->p("$firstname $surname holds the patch pumpkin" .
            "for this Perl release.");
```

The script is very simple: it initializes the CGI object, prints the proper HTTP header, and tells the world who the current patch pumpkin is. The name of the patch pumpkin is a hardcoded value.

We don't want to modify the script every time the patch pumpkin changes, so we put the $firstname and $surname variables into a configuration file:

```
$firstname = "Jarkko";
$surname = "Hietaniemi";
1;
```

Note that there is no package declaration in the above file, so the code will be evaluated in the caller's package or in the main:: package if none was declared. This means that the variables $firstname and $surname will override (or initialize) the variables with the same names in the caller's namespace. This works for global variables only—you cannot update variables defined lexically (with my( )) using this technique.

Let's say we have started the server and everything is working properly. After a while, we decide to modify the configuration. How do we let our running server know that the configuration was modified without restarting it? Remember, we are in production, and a server restart can be quite expensive. One of the simplest solutions is to poll the file's modification time by calling stat( ) before the script starts to do real work. If we see that the file was updated, we can force a reconfiguration of the variables located in this file. We will call the function that reloads the configuration reread_conf( ) and have it accept the relative path to the configuration file as its single argument.

Apache::Registry executes a chdir( ) to the script's directory before it starts the script's execution. So if your CGI script is invoked under the Apache::Registry handler, you can put the configuration file in the same directory as the script. Alternatively, you can put the file in a directory below that and use a path relative to the script directory. However, you have to make sure that the file will be found, somehow. Be aware that do( ) searches the libraries in the directories in @INC.

```
use vars qw(%MODIFIED);
sub reread_conf {
    my $file = shift;
    return unless defined $file;
    return unless -e $file and -r _;
    my $mod = -M _;
    unless (exists $MODIFIED{$file} and $MODIFIED{$file} == $mod) {
        unless (my $result = do $file) {
            warn "couldn't parse $file: $@" if $@;
            warn "couldn't read $file: $!" unless defined $result;
            warn "couldn't run $file"      unless          $result;
        }
        $MODIFIED{$file} = $mod; # Update the MODIFICATION times
    }
}
```

Notice that we use the == comparison operator when checking the file's modification timestamp, because all we want to know is whether the file was changed or not.

When the require( ), use( ), and do( ) operators successfully return, the file that was passed as an argument is inserted into %INC. The hash element key is the name of the file, and the element's value is the file's path. When Perl sees require( ) or use( ) in the code, it first tests %INC to see whether the file is already there and thus loaded. If the test returns true, Perl saves the overhead of code rereading and recompiling; however, calling do( ) will load or reload the file regardless of whether it has been previously loaded.

We use do( ), not require( ), to reload the code in this file because although do( ) behaves almost identically to require( ), it reloads the file unconditionally. If do( ) cannot read the file, it returns undef and sets $! to report the error. If do( ) can read the file but cannot compile it, it returns undef and sets an error message in $@. If the file is successfully compiled, do( ) returns the value of the last expression evaluated.

The configuration file can be broken if someone has incorrectly modified it. Since we don't want the whole service using that file to be broken that easily, we trap the possible failure to do( ) the file and ignore the changes by resetting the modification time. If do( ) fails to load the file, it might be a good idea to send an email about the problem to the system administrator.

However, since do( ) updates %INC like require( ) does, if you are using Apache::StatINC it will attempt to reload this file before the reread_conf( ) call. If the file doesn't compile, the request will be aborted. Apache::StatINC shouldn't be used in production anyway (because it slows things down by stat( )ing all the files listed in %INC), so this shouldn't be a problem.

Note that we assume that the entire purpose of this function is to reload the configuration if it was changed. This is fail-safe, because if something goes wrong we just return without modifying the server configuration. The script should not be used to initialize the variables on its first invocation. To do that, you would need to replace each occurrence of return( ) and warn( ) with die( ).

We've used the above approach with a huge configuration file that was loaded only at server startup and another little configuration file that included only a few variables that could be updated by hand or through the web interface. Those variables were initialized in the main configuration file. If the webmaster breaks the syntax of this dynamic file while updating it by hand, it won't affect the main (write-protected) configuration file and won't stop the proper execution of the programs. In the next section, we will see a simple web interface that allows us to modify the configuration file without the risk of breaking it.

Example 6-24 shows a sample script using our reread_conf( ) subroutine.

Example 6-24. reread_conf.pl

```perl
use vars qw(%MODIFIED $firstname $surname);
use CGI ();
use strict;

my $q = CGI->new;
print $q->header(-type => 'text/plain');
my $config_file = "./config.pl";
reread_conf($config_file);
print $q->p("$firstname $surname holds the patch pumpkin" .
            "for this Perl release.");

sub reread_conf {
    my $file = shift;
    return unless defined $file;
    return unless -e $file and -r _;
    my $mod = -M _;
    unless ($MODIFIED{$file} and $MODIFIED{$file} == $mod) {
        unless (my $result = do $file) {
            warn "couldn't parse $file: $@" if $@;
            warn "couldn't read $file: $!"  unless defined $result;
            warn "couldn't run $file"       unless $result;
        }
        $MODIFIED{$file} = $mod; # Update the MODIFICATION time
    }
}
```

You should be using (stat $file)[9] instead of -M $file if you are modifying the $^T variable. This is because -M returns the modification time relative to the Perl interpreter startup time, set in $^T. In some scripts, it can be useful to reset $^T to the time of the script invocation with "local $^T = time()". That way, -M and other -X file status tests are performed relative to the script invocation time, not the time the process was started.

If your configuration file is more sophisticated—for example, if it declares a package and exports variables—the above code will work just as well. Variables need not be import()ed again: when do() recompiles the script, the originally imported variables will be updated with the values from the reloaded code.

Dynamically updating configuration files. The CGI script below allows a system administrator to dynamically update a configuration file through a web interface. This script, combined with the code we have just seen to reload the modified files, gives us a system that is dynamically reconfigurable without having to restart the server. Configuration can be performed from any machine that has a browser.

Let's say we have a configuration file like the one in Example 6-25.

Example 6-25. Book/MainConfig.pm

```
package Book::MainConfig;

use strict;
use vars qw(%c);

%c = (
    name     => "Larry Wall",
    release  => "5.000",
    comments => "Adding more ways to do the same thing :)",

    other    => "More config values",

    colors   => { foreground => "black",
                    background => "white",
                },

    machines => [qw( primary secondary tertiary )],

);
```

We want to make the variables name, release, and comments dynamically config-urable. We'll need a web interface with an input form that allows modifications to these variables. We'll also need to update the configuration file and propagate the changes to all the currently running processes.

Let's look at the main stages of the implementation:

1. Create a form with preset current values of the variables.
2. Let the administrator modify the variables and submit the changes.
3. Validate the submitted information (numeric fields should hold numbers within a given range, etc.).
4. Update the configuration file.
5. Update the modified value in the current process's memory.
6. Display the form as before with the (possibly changed) current values.

The only part that seems hard to implement is a configuration file update, for a cou-ple of reasons. If updating the file breaks it, the whole service won't work. If the file is very big and includes comments and complex data structures, parsing the file can be quite a challenge.

So let's simplify the task. If all we want is to update a few variables, why don't we create a tiny configuration file containing just those variables? It can be modified through the web interface and overwritten each time there is something to be changed, so that we don't have to parse the file before updating it. If the main config-uration file is changed, we don't care, because we don't depend on it any more.

The dynamically updated variables will be duplicated in the main file and the dynamic file. We do this to simplify maintenance. When a new release is installed,

---

the dynamic configuration file won't exist—it will be created only after the first update. As we just saw, the only change in the main code is to add a snippet to load this file if it exists and was changed.

This additional code must be executed after the main configuration file has been loaded. That way, the updated variables will override the default values in the main file. See Example 6-26.

Example 6-26. manage_conf.pl

```
# remember to run this code in taint mode
use strict;
use vars qw($q %c $dynamic_config_file %vars_to_change %validation_rules);

use CGI ();

use lib qw(.);
use Book::MainConfig ();
*c = \%Book::MainConfig::c;

$dynamic_config_file = "./config.pl";

# load the dynamic configuration file if it exists, and override the
# default values from the main configuration file
do $dynamic_config_file if -e $dynamic_config_file and -r _;

# fields that can be changed and their captions
%vars_to_change =
  (
   'name'     => "Patch Pumpkin's Name",
   'release'  => "Current Perl Release",
   'comments' => "Release Comments",
  );

# each field has an associated regular expression
# used to validate the field's content when the
# form is submitted
%validation_rules =
  (
   'name'     => sub { $_[0] =~ /^[\w\s\.]+$/;   },
   'release'  => sub { $_[0] =~ /^\d+\.[\d_]+$/; },
   'comments' => sub { 1;                        },
  );

# create the CGI object, and print the HTTP and HTML headers
$q = CGI->new;
print $q->header(-type=>'text/html'),
      $q->start_html();

# We always rewrite the dynamic config file, so we want all the
# variables to be passed, but to save time we will only check
# those variables that were changed.  The rest will be retrieved from
# the 'prev_*' values.
```

Example 6-26. manage_conf.pl (continued)

```perl
my %updates = ( );
foreach (keys %vars_to_change) {
    # copy var so we can modify it
    my $new_val = $q->param($_) || '';

    # strip a possible ^M char (Win32)
    $new_val =~ s/\cM//g;

    # push to hash if it was changed
    $updates{$_} = $new_val
        if defined $q->param("prev_" . $_)
            and $new_val ne $q->param("prev_" . $_);
}

# Note that we cannot trust the previous values of the variables
# since they were presented to the user as hidden form variables,
# and the user could have mangled them. We don't care: this can't do
# any damage, as we verify each variable by rules that we define.

# Process if there is something to process. Will not be called if
# it's invoked the first time to display the form or when the form
# was submitted but the values weren't modified (we'll know by
# comparing with the previous values of the variables, which are
# the hidden fields in the form).

process_changed_config(%updates) if %updates;

show_modification_form( );

# update the config file, but first validate that the values are
# acceptable
sub process_changed_config {
    my %updates = @_;

    # we will list here all variables that don't validate
    my %malformed = ( );

    print $q->b("Trying to validate these values<br>");
    foreach (keys %updates) {
        print "<dt><b>$_</b> => <pre>$updates{$_}</pre>";

        # now we have to handle each var to be changed very carefully,
        # since this file goes immediately into production!
        $malformed{$_} = delete $updates{$_}
            unless $validation_rules{$_}->($updates{$_});

    }

    if (%malformed) {
        print $q->hr,
            $q->p($q->b(qq{Warning! These variables were changed
                            to invalid values. The original
```

Example 6-26. manage_conf.pl (continued)

```
                              values will be kept.})
                ),
        join ",<br>",
                map { $q->b($vars_to_change{$_}) . " : $malformed{$_}\n"
                    } keys %malformed;
    }

    # Now complete the vars that weren't changed from the
    # $q->param('prev_var') values
    map { $updates{$_} = $q->param('prev_' . $_)
            unless exists $updates{$_} } keys %vars_to_change;

    # Now we have all the data that should be written into the dynamic
    # config file

    # escape single quotes "'" while creating a file
    my $content = join "\n",
        map { $updates{$_} =~ s/(['\\])/\\$1/g;
              '$c{' . $_ . "} = '" . $updates{$_} . "';\n"
            } keys %updates;

    # add '1;' to make require() happy
    $content .= "\n1;";

    # keep the dummy result in $res so it won't complain
    eval {my $res = $content};
    if ($@) {
        print qq{Warning! Something went wrong with config file
                generation!<p> The error was :</p> <br><pre>$@</pre>};
        return;
    }

    print $q->hr;

    # overwrite the dynamic config file
    my $fh = Apache::gensym();
    open $fh, ">$dynamic_config_file.bak"
        or die "Can't open $dynamic_config_file.bak for writing: $!";
    flock $fh, 2; # exclusive lock
    seek $fh, 0, 0; # rewind to the start
    truncate $fh, 0; # the file might shrink!
    print $fh $content;
    close $fh;

    # OK, now we make a real file
    rename "$dynamic_config_file.bak", $dynamic_config_file
        or die "Failed to rename: $!";

    # rerun it to update variables in the current process! Note that
    # it won't update the variables in other processes. Special
    # code that watches the timestamps on the config file will do this
    # work for each process. Since the next invocation will update the
```

Example 6-26. manage_conf.pl (continued)

```
        # configuration anyway, why do we need to load it here? The reason
        # is simple: we are going to fill the form's input fields with
        # the updated data.
        do $dynamic_config_file;

}

sub show_modification_form {

    print $q->center($q->h3("Update Form"));

    print $q->hr,
        $q->p(qq{This form allows you to dynamically update the current
            configuration. You don't need to restart the server in
            order for changes to take an effect}
            );

    # set the previous settings in the form's hidden fields, so we
    # know whether we have to do some changes or not
    $q->param("prev_$_", $c{$_}) for keys %vars_to_change;

    # rows for the table, go into the form
    my @configs = ( );

    # prepare text field entries
    push @configs,
        map {
          $q->td( $q->b("$vars_to_change{$_}:") ),
          $q->td(
            $q->textfield(
                -name      => $_,
                -default   => $c{$_},
                -override  => 1,
                -size      => 20,
                -maxlength => 50,
                )
          ),
        } qw(name release);

    # prepare multiline textarea entries
    push @configs,
        map {
          $q->td( $q->b("$vars_to_change{$_}:") ),
          $q->td(
            $q->textarea(
                -name     => $_,
                -default  => $c{$_},
                -override => 1,
                -rows     => 10,
                -columns  => 50,
                -wrap     => "HARD",
                )
```

Example 6-26. manage_conf.pl (continued)

```
        ),
    } qw(comments);

print $q->startform(POST => $q->url), "\n",
    $q->center(
        $q->table(map {$q->Tr($_), "\n",} @configs),
        $q->submit('', 'Update!'), "\n",
    ),
    map ({$q->hidden("prev_" . $_, $q->param("prev_".$_)) . "\n" }
        keys %vars_to_change), # hidden previous values
    $q->br, "\n",
    $q->endform, "\n",
    $q->hr, "\n",
    $q->end_html;
}
```

For example, on July 19 2002, Perl 5.8.0 was released. On that date, Jarkko Hietaniemi exclaimed:

```
The pumpking is dead! Long live the pumpking!
```

Hugo van der Sanden is the new pumpking for Perl 5.10. Therefore, we run *manage_conf.pl* and update the data. Once updated, the script overwrites the previous *config.pl* file with the following content:

```
$c{release}  =  '5.10';

$c{name}  =  'Hugo van der Sanden';

$c{comments}  =  'Perl rules the world!';

1;
```

Instead of crafting your own code, you can use the CGI::QuickForm module from CPAN to make the coding less tedious. See Example 6-27.

Example 6-27. manage_conf.pl

```
use strict;
use CGI qw( :standard :html3 ) ;
use CGI::QuickForm;
use lib qw(.);
use Book::MainConfig ();
*c = \%Book::MainConfig::c;

my $TITLE = 'Update Configuration';
show_form(
    -HEADER => header . start_html( $TITLE ) . h3( $TITLE ),
    -ACCEPT => \&on_valid_form,
    -FIELDS => [
        {
            -LABEL      => "Patch Pumpkin's Name",
```

Example 6-27. manage_conf.pl (continued)

```
                 -VALIDATE   => sub { $_[0] =~ /^[\w\s\.]+$/;   },
                 -default    => $c{name},
        },
        {
                 -LABEL      => "Current Perl Release",
                 -VALIDATE   => sub { $_[0] =~ /^\d+\.[\d_]+$/; },
                 -default    => $c{release},
        },
        {
                 -LABEL      => "Release Comments",
                 -default    => $c{comments},
        },
        ],
    );

sub on_valid_form {
    # save the form's values
}
```

That's it. show_form( ) creates and displays a form with a submit button. When the user submits, the values are checked. If all the fields are valid, on_valid_form( ) is called; otherwise, the form is re-presented with the errors highlighted.

Handling the "User Pressed Stop Button" Case

When a user presses the Stop or Reload button, the current socket connection is broken (aborted). It would be nice if Apache could always immediately detect this event. Unfortunately, there is no way to tell whether the connection is still valid unless an attempt to read from or write to the connection is made.

Note that no detection technique will work if the connection to the backend mod_perl server is coming from a frontend mod_proxy (as discussed in Chapter 12). This is because mod_proxy doesn't break the connection to the backend when the user has aborted the connection.

If the reading of the request's data is completed and the code does its processing without writing anything back to the client, the broken connection won't be noticed. When an attempt is made to send at least one character to the client, the broken connection will be noticed and the SIGPIPE signal (Broken Pipe) will be sent to the process. The program can then halt its execution and perform all its cleanup requirements.

Prior to Apache 1.3.6, SIGPIPE was handled by Apache. Currently, Apache does not handle SIGPIPE, but mod_perl takes care of it.

Under mod_perl, $r->print (or just print( )) returns a true value on success and a false value on failure. The latter usually happens when the connection is broken.

If you want behavior similar to the old SIGPIPE (as it was before Apache version 1.3.6), add the following configuration directive:

```
PerlFixupHandler Apache::SIG
```

When Apache's SIGPIPE handler is used, Perl may be left in the middle of its eval( ) context, causing bizarre errors when subsequent requests are handled by that child. When Apache::SIG is used, it installs a different SIGPIPE handler that rewinds the context to make sure Perl is in a normal state before the new request is served, preventing these bizarre errors. But in general, you don't need to use Apache::SIG.

If you use Apache::SIG and you would like to log when a request was canceled by a SIGPIPE in your Apache *access_log*, you must define a custom LogFormat in your *httpd.conf*. For example:

```
PerlFixupHandler Apache::SIG
LogFormat "%h %l %u %t \"%r\" %s %b %{SIGPIPE}e"
```

If the server has noticed that the request was canceled via a SIGPIPE, the log line will end with 1. Otherwise, it will just be a dash. For example:

```
127.0.0.1 - - [09/Jan/2001:10:27:15 +0100]
"GET /perl/stopping_detector.pl HTTP/1.0" 200 16 1
127.0.0.1 - - [09/Jan/2001:10:28:18 +0100]
"GET /perl/test.pl HTTP/1.0"              200 10 -
```

Detecting Aborted Connections

Now let's use the knowledge we have acquired to trace the execution of the code and watch all the events as they happen. Let's take a simple Apache::Registry script that purposely hangs the server process, like the one in Example 6-28.

Example 6-28. stopping_detector.pl

```
my $r = shift;
$r->send_http_header('text/plain');

print "PID = $$\n";
$r->rflush;

while (1) {
    sleep 1;
}
```

The script gets a request object $r by shift( )ing it from the @_ argument list (passed by the handler( ) subroutine that was created on the fly by Apache::Registry). Then the script sends a Content-Type header telling the client that we are going to send a plain-text response.

Next, the script prints out a single line telling us the ID of the process that handled the request, which we need to know in order to run the tracing utility. Then we flush Apache's STDOUT buffer. If we don't flush the buffer, we will never see this information printed (our output is shorter than the buffer size used for print( ), and the script intentionally hangs, so the buffer won't be auto-flushed).*

Then we enter an infinite while loop that does nothing but sleep( ), emulating code that doesn't generate any output. For example, it might be a long-running mathematical calculation, a database query, or a search for extraterrestrial life.

Running *strace -p PID*, where *PID* is the process ID as printed on the browser, we see the following output printed every second:

```
rt_sigprocmask(SIG_BLOCK, [CHLD], [ ], 8)   = 0
rt_sigaction(SIGCHLD, NULL, {SIG_DFL}, 8)   = 0
rt_sigprocmask(SIG_SETMASK, [ ], NULL, 8)   = 0
nanosleep({1, 0}, {1, 0})                   = 0
time([978969822])                           = 978969822
time([978969822])                           = 978969822
```

Alternatively, we can run the server in single-server mode. In single-server mode, we don't need to print the process ID, since the PID is the process of the single mod_perl process that we're running. When the process is started in the background, the shell program usually prints the PID of the process, as shown here:

```
panic% httpd -X &
[1] 20107
```

Now we know what process we have to attach to with *strace* (or a similar utility):

```
panic% strace -p 20107
rt_sigprocmask(SIG_BLOCK, [CHLD], [ ], 8)   = 0
rt_sigaction(SIGCHLD, NULL, {SIG_DFL}, 8)   = 0
rt_sigprocmask(SIG_SETMASK, [ ], NULL, 8)   = 0
nanosleep({1, 0}, {1, 0})                   = 0
time([978969822])                           = 978969822
time([978969822])                           = 978969822
```

We see the same output as before.

Let's leave *strace* running and press the Stop button. Did anything change? No, the same system calls trace is printed every second, which means that Apache didn't detect the broken connection.

Now we are going to write \0 (NULL) characters to the client in an attempt to detect the broken connection as soon as possible after the Stop button is pressed. Since these are NULL characters, they won't be seen in the output. Therefore, we modify the loop code in the following way:

---

* Buffering is used to reduce the number of system calls (which do the actual writing) and therefore improve performance. When the buffer (usually a few kilobytes in size) is getting full, it's flushed and the data is written.

```
while (1) {
    $r->print("\0");
    last if $r->connection->aborted;
    sleep 1;
}
```

We add a print( ) statement to print a NULL character, then we check whether the connection was aborted, with the help of the $r->connection->aborted method. If the connection is broken, we break out of the loop.

We run this script and run *strace* on it as before, but we see that it still doesn't work—the script doesn't stop when the Stop button is pressed.

The problem is that we aren't flushing the buffer. The NULL characters won't be printed until the buffer is full and is autoflushed. Since we want to try writing to the connection pipe all the time, we add an $r->rflush( ) call. Example 6-29 is a new version of the code.

Example 6-29. stopping_detector2.pl

```
my $r = shift;
$r->send_http_header('text/plain');

print "PID = $$\n";
$r->rflush;

while (1) {
    $r->print("\0");
    $r->rflush;
    last if $r->connection->aborted;
    sleep 1;
}
```

After starting the *strace* utility on the running process and pressing the Stop button, we see the following output:

```
rt_sigprocmask(SIG_BLOCK, [CHLD], [ ], 8)  = 0
rt_sigaction(SIGCHLD, NULL, {SIG_DFL}, 8) = 0
rt_sigprocmask(SIG_SETMASK, [ ], NULL, 8)  = 0
nanosleep({1, 0}, {1, 0})               = 0
time([978970895])                       = 978970895
alarm(300)                              = 0
alarm(0)                                = 300
write(3, "\0", 1)                       = -1 EPIPE (Broken pipe)
--- SIGPIPE (Broken pipe) ---
chdir("/usr/src/httpd_perl")            = 0
select(4, [3], NULL, NULL, {0, 0})      = 1 (in [3], left {0, 0})
time(NULL)                              = 978970895
write(17, "127.0.0.1 - - [08/Jan/2001:19:21"..., 92) = 92
gettimeofday({978970895, 554755}, NULL) = 0
times({tms_utime=46, tms_stime=5, tms_cutime=0,
  tms_cstime=0}) = 8425400
close(3)                                = 0
```

```
rt_sigaction(SIGUSR1, {0x8099524, [ ], SA_INTERRUPT|0x4000000},
  {SIG_IGN}, 8) = 0alarm(0)                                      = 0
rt_sigprocmask(SIG_BLOCK, NULL, [ ], 8)  = 0
rt_sigaction(SIGALRM, {0x8098168, [ ], SA_RESTART|0x4000000},
  {0x8098168, [ ], SA_INTERRUPT|0x4000000}, 8) = 0
fcntl(18, F_SETLKW, {type=F_WRLCK, whence=SEEK_SET,
  start=0, len=0}) = 0
```

Apache detects the broken pipe, as you can see from this snippet:

```
write(3, "\0", 1)                              = -1 EPIPE (Broken pipe)
--- SIGPIPE (Broken pipe) ---
```

Then it stops the script and does all the cleanup work, such as access logging:

```
write(17, "127.0.0.1 - - [08/Jan/2001:19:21"..., 92) = 92
```

where 17 is a file descriptor of the opened *access_log* file.

The Importance of Cleanup Code

Cleanup code is a critical issue with aborted scripts. For example, what happens to locked resources, if there are any? Will they be freed or not? If not, scripts using these resources and the same locking scheme might hang forever, waiting for these resources to be freed.

And what happens if a file was opened and never closed? In some cases, this might lead to a file-descriptor leakage. In the long run, many leaks of this kind might make your system unusable: when all file descriptors are used, the system will be unable to open new files.

First, let's take a step back and recall what the problems and solutions for these issues are under mod_cgi. Under mod_cgi, the resource-locking issue is a problem only if you use external lock files and use them for lock indication, instead of using flock( ). If the script running under mod_cgi is aborted between the lock and the unlock code, and you didn't bother to write cleanup code to remove old, dead locks, you're in big trouble.

The solution is to place the cleanup code in an END block:

```
END {
    # code that ensures that locks are removed
}
```

When the script is aborted, Perl will run the END block while shutting down.

If you use flock( ), things are much simpler, since all opened files will be closed when the script exits. When the file is closed, the lock is removed as well—all the locked resources are freed. There are systems where flock( ) is unavailable; on those systems, you can use Perl's emulation of this function.

With mod_perl, things can be more complex when you use global variables as file-handles. Because processes don't exit after processing a request, files won't be closed unless you explicitly close( ) them or reopen them with the open( ) call, which first closes the file. Let's see what problems we might encounter and look at some possible solutions.

Critical section

First, we want to take a little detour to discuss the "critical section" issue. Let's start with a resource-locking scheme. A schematic representation of a proper locking technique is as follows:

1. Lock a resource

   <critical section starts>

2. Do something with the resource

   <critical section ends>

3. Unlock the resource

If the locking is exclusive, only one process can hold the resource at any given time, which means that all the other processes will have to wait. The code between the locking and unlocking functions cannot be interrupted and can therefore become a service bottleneck. That's why this code section is called critical. Its execution time should be as short as possible.

Even if you use a shared locking scheme, in which many processes are allowed to concurrently access the resource, it's still important to keep the critical section as short as possible, in case a process requires an exclusive lock.

Example 6-30 uses a shared lock but has a poorly designed critical section.

Example 6-30. critical_section_sh.pl

```
use Fcntl qw(:flock);
use Symbol;

my $fh = gensym;
open $fh, "/tmp/foo" or die $!;

# start critical section
flock $fh, LOCK_SH;  # shared lock, appropriate for reading
seek $fh, 0, 0;
my @lines = <$fh>;
for (@lines) {
    print if /foo/;
}
close $fh; # close unlocks the file
# end critical section
```

The code opens the file for reading, locks and rewinds it to the beginning, reads all the lines from the file, and prints out the lines that contain the string "foo".

The gensym( ) function imported by the Symbol module creates an anonymous glob data structure and returns a reference to it. Such a glob reference can be used as a file or directory handle. Therefore, it allows lexically scoped variables to be used as file-handles.

Fcntl imports file-locking symbols, such as LOCK_SH, LOCK_EX, and others with the :flock group tag, into the script's namespace. Refer to the Fcntl manpage for more information about these symbols.

If the file being read is big, it will take a relatively long time for this code to complete printing out the lines. During this time, the file remains open and locked with a shared lock. While other processes may access this file for reading, any process that wants to modify the file (which requires an exclusive lock) will be blocked waiting for this section to complete.

We can optimize the critical section as follows. Once the file has been read, we have all the information we need from it. To make the example simpler, we've chosen to just print out the matching lines. In reality, the code might be much longer.

We don't need the file to be open while the loop executes, because we don't access it inside the loop. Closing the file before we start the loop will allow other processes to obtain exclusive access to the file if they need it, instead of being blocked for no reason.

Example 6-31 is an improved version of the previous example, in which we only read the contents of the file during the critical section and process it afterward, without creating a possible bottleneck.

Example 6-31. critical_section_sh2.pl

```
use Fcntl qw(:flock);
use Symbol;

my $fh = gensym;
open $fh, "/tmp/foo" or die $!;

# start critical section
flock $fh, LOCK_SH;
seek $fh, 0, 0;
my @lines = <$fh>;
close $fh; # close unlocks the file
# end critical section

for (@lines) {
    print if /foo/;
}
```

Example 6-32 is a similar example that uses an exclusive lock. The script reads in a file and writes it back, prepending a number of new text lines to the head of the file.

Example 6-32. critical_section_ex.pl

```perl
use Fcntl qw(:flock);
use Symbol;

my $fh = gensym;
open $fh, "+>>/tmp/foo" or die $!;

# start critical section
flock $fh, LOCK_EX;
seek $fh, 0, 0;
my @add_lines =
  (
    qq{Complete documentation for Perl, including FAQ lists,\n},
    qq{should be found on this system using 'man perl' or\n},
    qq{'perldoc perl'. If you have access to the Internet, point\n},
    qq{your browser at http://www.perl.com/, the Perl Home Page.\n},
  );

my @lines = (@add_lines, <$fh>);
seek $fh, 0, 0;
truncate $fh, 0;
print $fh @lines;
close $fh; # close unlocks the file
# end critical section
```

Since we want to read the file, modify it, and write it back without anyone else changing it in between, we open it for reading and writing with the help of "+>>" and lock it with an exclusive lock. You cannot safely accomplish this task by opening the file first for reading and then reopening it for writing, since another process might change the file between the two events. (You could get away with "+<" as well; please refer to the *perlfunc* manpage for more information about the open( ) function.)

Next, the code prepares the lines of text it wants to prepend to the head of the file and assigns them and the content of the file to the @lines array. Now we have our data ready to be written back to the file, so we seek( ) to the start of the file and truncate( ) it to zero size. Truncating is necessary when there's a chance the file might shrink. In our example, the file always grows, so in this case there is actually no need to truncate it; however, it's good practice to always use truncate( ), as you never know what changes your code might undergo in the future, and truncate( ) doesn't significantly affect performance.

Finally, we write the data back to the file and close it, which unlocks it as well.

Did you notice that we created the text lines to be prepended as close to the place of usage as possible? This complies with good "locality of code" style, but it makes the critical section longer. In cases like this, you should sacrifice style in order to make the critical section as short as possible. An improved version of this script with a shorter critical section is shown in Example 6-33.

Example 6-33. critical_section_ex2.pl

```perl
use Fcntl qw(:flock);
use Symbol;

my @lines =
  (
    qq{Complete documentation for Perl, including FAQ lists,\n},
    qq{should be found on this system using 'man perl' or\n},
    qq{'perldoc perl'. If you have access to the Internet, point\n},
    qq{your browser at http://www.perl.com/, the Perl Home Page.\n},
  );

my $fh = gensym;
open $fh, "+>>/tmp/foo" or die $!;

# start critical section
flock $fh, LOCK_EX;
seek $fh, 0, 0;
push @lines, <$fh>;

seek $fh, 0, 0;
truncate $fh, 0;
print $fh @lines;
close $fh; # close unlocks the file
# end critical section
```

There are two important differences. First, we prepared the text lines to be prepended *before* the file is locked. Second, rather than creating a new array and copying lines from one array to another, we appended the file directly to the @lines array.

Safe resource locking and cleanup code

Now let's get back to this section's main issue, safe resource locking. If you don't make a habit of closing all files that you open, you may encounter many problems (unless you use the Apache::PerlRun handler, which does the cleanup for you). An open file that isn't closed can cause file-descriptor leakage. Since the number of file descriptors available is finite, at some point you will run out of them and your service will fail. This will happen quite fast on a heavily used server.

You can use system utilities to observe the opened and locked files, as well as the processes that have opened (and locked) the files. On FreeBSD, use the *fstat* utility. On many other Unix flavors, use *lsof*. On systems with a */proc* filesystem, you can see the opened file descriptors under */proc/PID/fd/*, where PID is the actual process ID.

However, file-descriptor leakage is nothing compared to the trouble you will give yourself if the code terminates and the file remains locked. Any other process requesting a lock on the same file (or resource) will wait indefinitely for it to become unlocked. Since this will not happen until the server reboots, all processes trying to use this resource will hang.

Example 6-34 is an example of such a terrible mistake.

Example 6-34. flock.pl

```
use Fcntl qw(:flock);
open IN, "+>>filename" or die "$!";
flock IN, LOCK_EX;
# do something
# quit without closing and unlocking the file
```

Is this safe code? No—we forgot to close the file. So let's add the close( ), as in Example 6-35.

Example 6-35. flock2.pl

```
use Fcntl qw(:flock);
open IN, "+>>filename" or die "$!";
flock IN, LOCK_EX;
# do something
close IN;
```

Is it safe code now? Unfortunately, it is not. If the user aborts the request (for example, by pressing the browser's Stop or Reload buttons) during the critical section, the script will be aborted before it has had a chance to close( ) the file, which is just as bad as if we forgot to close it.

In fact, if the same process runs the same code again, an open( ) call will close( ) the file first, which will unlock the resource. This is because IN is a global variable. But it's quite possible that the process that created the lock will not serve the same request for a while, since it might be busy serving other requests. During that time, the file will be locked for other processes, making them hang. So relying on the same process to reopen the file is a bad idea.

This problem happens only if you use global variables as file handles. Example 6-36 has the same problem.

Example 6-36. flock3.pl

```
use Fcntl qw(:flock);
use Symbol ( );
use vars qw($fh);
$fh = Symbol::gensym( );
open $fh, "+>>filename" or die "$!";
flock $fh, LOCK_EX;
# do something
close $fh;
```

$fh is still a global variable, and therefore the code using it suffers from the same problem.

The simplest solution to this problem is to always use lexically scoped variables (created with my( )). The lexically scoped variable will always go out of scope (assuming that it's not used in a closure, as explained in the beginning of this chapter), whether the script gets aborted before close( ) is called or you simply forgot to close( ) the file. Therefore, if the file was locked, it will be closed and unlocked. Example 6-37 is a good version of the code.

Example 6-37. flock4.pl

```
use Fcntl qw(:flock);
use Symbol ();
my $fh = Symbol::gensym( );
open $fh, "+>>filename" or die "$!";
flock $fh, LOCK_EX;
# do something
close $fh;
```

If you use this approach, please don't conclude that you don't have to close files anymore because they are automatically closed for you. Not closing files is bad style and should be avoided.

Note also that Perl 5.6 provides a Symbol.pm-like functionality as a built-in feature, so you can write:

```
open my $fh, ">/tmp/foo" or die $!;
```

and $fh will be automatically vivified as a valid filehandle. You don't need to use Symbol::gensym and Apache::gensym anymore, if backward compatibility is not a requirement.

You can also use IO::* modules, such as IO::File or IO::Dir. These are much bigger than the Symbol module (as a matter of fact, these modules use the Symbol module themselves) and are worth using for files or directories only if you are already using them for the other features they provide. Here is an example of their usage:

```
use IO::File;
use IO::Dir;
my $fh = IO::File->new(">filename");
my $dh = IO::Dir->new("dirname");
```

Alternatively, there are also the lighter FileHandle and DirHandle modules.

If you still have to use global filehandles, there are a few approaches you can take to clean up in the case of abnormal script termination.

If you are running under Apache::Registry and friends, the END block will perform the cleanup work for you. You can use END in the same way for scripts running under mod_cgi, or in plain Perl scripts. Just add the cleanup code to this block, and you are safe.

For example, if you work with DBM files, it's important to flush the DBM buffers by calling a sync( ) method:

```
END {
    # make sure that the DB is flushed
```

```
    $dbh->sync();
}
```

Under mod_perl, the above code will work only for `Apache::Registry` and `Apache::PerlRun` scripts. Otherwise, execution of the `END` block is postponed until the process terminates. If you write a handler in the mod_perl API, use the `register_cleanup()` method instead. It accepts a reference to a subroutine as an argument. You can rewrite the DBM synchronization code in this way:

```
$r->register_cleanup(sub { $dbh->sync() });
```

This will work under `Apache::Registry` as well.

Even better would be to check whether the client connection has been aborted. Otherwise, the cleanup code will always be executed, and for normally terminated scripts, this may not be what you want. To perform this check, use:

```
$r->register_cleanup(
    # make sure that the DB is flushed
    sub {
        $dbh->sync() if Apache->request->connection->aborted();
    }
);
```

Or, if using an `END` block, use:

```
END {
    # make sure that the DB is flushed
    $dbh->sync() if Apache->request->connection->aborted();
}
```

Note that if you use `register_cleanup()`, it should be called at the beginning of the script or as soon as the variables you want to use in this code become available. If you use it at the end of the script, and the script happens to be aborted before this code is reached, no cleanup will be performed.

For example, `CGI.pm` registers a cleanup subroutine in its `new()` method:

```
sub new {
    # code snipped
    if ($MOD_PERL) {
        Apache->request->register_cleanup(\&CGI::_reset_globals);
        undef $NPH;
    }
    # more code snipped
}
```

Another way to register a section of cleanup code for mod_perl API handlers is to use `PerlCleanupHandler` in the configuration file:

```
<Location /foo>
    SetHandler perl-script
    PerlHandler        Apache::MyModule
    PerlCleanupHandler Apache::MyModule::cleanup()
    Options ExecCGI
</Location>
```

`Apache::MyModule::cleanup` performs the cleanup.

Handling Server Timeout Cases and Working with $SIG{ALRM}

Similar to the case where a user aborts the script execution by pressing the Stop button, the browser itself might abort the script if it hasn't returned any output after a certain timeout period (usually a few minutes).

Sometimes scripts perform very long operations that might take longer than the client's timeout.

This can happen when performing full searches of a large database with no full search support. Another example is a script interacting with external applications whose prompt reponse time isn't guaranteed. Consider a script that retrieves a page from another site and does some processing on it before it gets presented to the user. Obviously, nothing guarantees that the page will be retrieved fast, if at all.

In this situation, use $SIG{ALRM} to prevent the timeouts:

```
my $timeout = 10; # seconds
eval {
  local $SIG{ALRM} =
      sub { die "Sorry, timed out. Please try again\n" };
  alarm $timeout;
  # some operation that might take a long time to complete
  alarm 0;
};
die $@ if $@;
```

In this code, we run the operation that might take a long time to complete inside an eval block. First we initialize a localized ALRM signal handler, which resides inside the special %SIG hash. If this handler is triggered, it will call die( ), and the eval block will be aborted. You can then do what you want with it—in our example, we chose to abort the execution of the script. In most cases, you will probably want to report to the user that the operation has timed out.

The actual operation is placed between two alarm( ) calls. The first call starts the clock, and the second cancels it. The clock is running for 10 seconds in our example. If the second alarm( ) call doesn't occur within 10 seconds, the SIGALRM signal is sent and the handler stored in $SIG{ALRM} is called. In our case, this will abort the eval block.

If the operation between the two alarm( )s completes in under 10 seconds, the alarm clock is stopped and the eval block returns successfully, without triggering the ALRM handler.

Notice that only one timer can be used at a given time. alarm( )'s returned value is the amount of time remaining in the previous timer. So you can actually roughly measure the execution time as a side effect.

It is usually a mistake to intermix alarm( ) and sleep( ) calls. sleep( ) may be internally implemented in your system with alarm( ), which will break your original alarm( ) settings, since every new alarm( ) call cancels the previous one.

Finally, the actual time resolution may be imprecise, with the timeout period being accurate to plus or minus one second. You may end up with a timeout that varies between 9 and 11 seconds. For granularity finer than one second, you can use Perl's four-argument version of select( ), leaving the first three arguments undefined. Other techniques exist, but they will not help with the task in question, in which we use alarm( ) to implement timeouts.

Generating Correct HTTP Headers

An HTTP response header consists of at least two fields: HTTP response and MIME-type header Content-Type:

```
HTTP/1.0 200 OK
Content-Type: text/plain
```

After adding a newline, you can start printing the content. A more complete response includes the date timestamp and server type. For example:

```
HTTP/1.0 200 OK
Date: Tue, 10 Apr 2001 03:01:36 GMT
Server: Apache/1.3.19 (Unix) mod_perl/1.25
Content-Type: text/plain
```

To notify clients that the server is configured with KeepAlive Off, clients must be told that the connection will be closed after the content has been delivered:

```
Connection: close
```

There can be other headers as well, such as caching control headers and others specified by the HTTP protocol. You can code the response header with a single print( ) statement:

```
print qq{HTTP/1.1 200 OK
  Date: Tue, 10 Apr 2001 03:01:36 GMT
  Server: Apache/1.3.19 (Unix) mod_perl/1.25
  Connection: close
  Content-Type: text/plain

};
```

or with a "here"-style print( ):

```
print <<'EOT';
  HTTP/1.1 200 OK
  Date: Tue, 10 Apr 2001 03:01:36 GMT
```

```
Server: Apache/1.3.19 (Unix) mod_perl/1.25
Connection: close
Content-type: text/plain

EOT
```

Don't forget to include two newlines at the end of the HTTP header. With the help of `Apache::Util::ht_time( )`, you can get the right timestamp string for the `Date:` field.

If you want to send non-default headers, use the `header_out( )` method. For example:

```
$r->header_out("X-Server" => "Apache Next Generation 10.0");
$r->header_out("Date" => "Tue, 10 Apr 2001 03:01:36 GMT");
```

When the headers setting is completed, the `send_http_header( )` method will flush the headers and add a newline to designate the start of the content.

```
$r->send_http_header;
```

Some headers have special aliases. For example:

```
$r->content_type('text/plain');
```

is the same as:

```
$r->header_out("Content-Type" => "text/plain");
```

but additionally sets some internal flags used by Apache. Whenever special-purpose methods are available, you should use those instead of setting the header directly.

A typical handler looks like this:

```
use Apache::Constants qw(OK);
$r->content_type('text/plain');
$r->send_http_header;
return OK if $r->header_only;
```

To be compliant with the HTTP protocol, if the client issues an HTTP `HEAD` request rather than the usual `GET`, we should send only the HTTP header, the document body. When Apache receives a `HEAD` request, `header_only( )` returns true. Therefore, in our example the handler returns immediately after sending the headers.

In some cases, you can skip the explicit content-type setting if Apache figures out the right MIME type based on the request. For example, if the request is for an HTML file, the default *text/html* will be used as the content type of the response. Apache looks up the MIME type in the *mime.types* file. You can always override the default content type.

The situation is a little bit different with `Apache::Registry` and similar handlers. Consider a basic CGI script:

```
print "Content-type: text/plain\n\n";
print "Hello world";
```

By default, this won't work, because it looks like normal text, and no HTTP headers are sent. You may wish to change this by adding:

```
PerlSendHeader On
```

in the Apache::Registry <Location> section of your configuration. Now the response line and common headers will be sent in the same way they are by mod_cgi. Just as with mod_cgi, even if you set PerlSendHeader On, the script still needs to send the MIME type and a terminating double newline:

```
print "Content-type: text/html\n\n";
```

The PerlSendHeader On directive tells mod_perl to intercept anything that looks like a header line (such as Content-Type: text/plain) and automatically turn it into a correctly formatted HTTP header, much like CGI scripts running under mod_cgi. This feature allows you to keep your CGI scripts unmodified.

You can use $ENV{PERL_SEND_HEADER} to find out whether PerlSendHeader is On or Off.

```
if ($ENV{PERL_SEND_HEADER}) {
    print "Content-type: text/html\n\n";
}
else {
    my $r = Apache->request;
    $r->content_type('text/html');
    $r->send_http_header;
}
```

Note that you can always use the code in the else part of the above example, whether the PerlSendHeader directive is On or Off.

If you use CGI.pm's header( ) function to generate HTTP headers, you do not need to activate this directive because CGI.pm detects *mod_perl* and calls send_http_header( ) for you.

There is no free lunch—you get the mod_cgi behavior at the expense of the small but finite overhead of parsing the text that is sent. Note that mod_perl makes the assumption that individual headers are not split across print( ) statements.

The Apache::print( ) routine must gather up the headers that your script outputs in order to pass them to $r->send_http_header. This happens in src/modules/perl/ Apache.xs (print( )) and Apache/Apache.pm (send_cgi_header( )). There is a shortcut in there—namely, the assumption that each print( ) statement contains one or more complete headers. If, for example, you generate a Set-Cookie header using multiple print( ) statements, like this:

```
print "Content-type: text/plain\n";
print "Set-Cookie: iscookietext\; ";
print "expires=Wednesday, 09-Nov-1999 00:00:00 GMT\; ";
print "path=\/\; ";
print "domain=\.mmyserver.com\; ";
print "\n\n";
print "Hello";
```

the generated Set-Cookie header is split over a number of print( ) statements and gets lost. The above example won't work! Try this instead:

```
my $cookie = "Set-Cookie: iscookietext\; ";
$cookie .= "expires=Wednesday, 09-Nov-1999 00:00:00 GMT\; ";
$cookie .= "path=\/\; ";
$cookie .= "domain=\.mmyserver.com\; ";
print "Content-type: text/plain\n",
print "$cookie\n\n";
print "Hello";
```

Using special-purpose cookie generator modules (for example, Apache::Cookie or CGI::Cookie) is an even cleaner solution.

Sometimes when you call a script you see an ugly "Content-Type: text/html" displayed at the top of the page, and often the HTML content isn't rendered correctly by the browser. As you have seen above, this generally happens when your code sends the headers twice.

If you have a complicated application in which the header might be sent from many different places depending on the code logic, you might want to write a special subroutine that sends a header and keeps track of whether the header has already been sent. You can use a global variable to flag that the header has already been sent, as shown in Example 6-38.

Example 6-38. send_header.pl

```
use strict;
use vars qw($header_printed);
$header_printed = 0;

print_header("text/plain");
print "It worked!\n";
print_header("text/plain");

sub print_header {
    return if $header_printed;

    my $type = shift || "text/html";
    $header_printed = 1;
    my $r = Apache->request;
    $r->content_type($type);
    $r->send_http_header;
}
1;
```

$header_printed serves as a Boolean variable, specifying whether the header was sent or not. It gets initialized to false (0) at the beginning of each code invocation. Note that the second invocation of print_header( ) within the same request will immediately return, since $header_printed will become true after print_header( ) is executed for the first time in the same request.

You can continue to improve this subroutine even further to handle additional headers, such as cookies.

Method Handlers: The Browse and See, Browse and View Example

Let's look at an example of the method-handler concepts presented in Chapter 4. Suppose you need to implement a handler that allows browsing the files in the document root and beneath. Directories should be browsable (so you can move up and down the directory tree), but files should not be viewable (so you can see the available files, but you cannot click to view them).

So let's write a simple file browser. We know what customers are like, so we suspect that the customer will ask for similar customized modules pretty soon. To avoid having to duplicate our work later, we decide to start writing a base class whose methods can easily be overridden as needed. Our base class is called Apache::BrowseSee.

We start the class by declaring the package and using the strict pragma:

```
package Apache::BrowseSee;
use strict;
```

Next, we import common constants (e.g., OK, NOT_FOUND, etc.), load the File::Spec::Functions and File::Basename modules, and import a few path-manipulation functions that we are going to use:

```
use Apache::Constants qw(:common);
use File::Spec::Functions qw(catdir canonpath curdir updir);
use File::Basename 'dirname';
```

Now let's look at the functions. We start with the simple constructor:

```
sub new { bless {}, shift;}
```

The real entry point, the handler, is prototyped as ($$). The handler starts by instantiating its object, if it hasn't already been done, and storing the $r object, so we don't need to pass it to the functions as an argument:

```
sub handler ($$) {
    my($self, $r) = @_;
    $self = $self->new unless ref $self;
    $self->{r} = $r;
```

Next we retrieve the path_info element of the request record:

```
    $self->{dir} = $r->path_info || '/';
```

For example, if the request was /browse/foo/bar, where /browse is the location of the handler, the path_info element will be /foo/bar. The default value / is used when the path is not specified.

Then we reset the entries for *dirs* and *files*:

```
$self->{dirs}  = { };
$self->{files} = { };
```

This is needed because it's possible that the $self object is created outside the handler (e.g., in the startup file) and may persist between requests.

Now an attempt to fetch the contents of the directory is made:

```
eval { $self->fetch( ) };
return NOT_FOUND if $@;
```

If the fetch( ) method dies, the error message is assigned to $@ and we return NOT_FOUND. You may choose to approach it differently and return an error message explaining what has happened. You may also want to log the event before returning:

```
warn($@), return NOT_FOUND if $@;
```

Normally this shouldn't happen, unless a user messes with the arguments (something you should always be on the lookout for, because they *will* do it).

When the fetch( ) function has completed successfully, all that's left is to send the HTTP header and start of the HTML via the head( ) method, render the response, send the end of the HTML via tail( ),* and finally to return the OK constant to tell the server that the request has been fully answered:

```
$self->head;
$self->render;
$self->tail;

return OK;
}
```

The response is generated by three functions. The head( ) method is a very simple one—it sends the HTTP header text/html and prints an HTML preamble using the current directory name as a title:

```
sub head {
    my $self = shift;
    $self->{r}->send_http_header("text/html");
    print "<html><head><title>Dir: $self->{dir}</title><head><body>";
}
```

The tail( ) method finishes the HTML document:

```
sub tail {
    my $self = shift;
    print "</body></html>";
}
```

---

* This could perhaps be replaced by a templating system. See Appendix D for more information about the Template Toolkit.

The fetch( ) method reads the contents of the directory stored in the object's *dir* attribute (relative to the document root) and then sorts the contents into two groups, directories and files:

```
sub fetch {
    my $self = shift;
    my $doc_root = Apache->document_root;
    my $base_dir = canonpath( catdir($doc_root, $self->{dir}));

    my $base_entry = $self->{dir} eq '/' ? '' : $self->{dir};
    my $dh = Apache::gensym( );
    opendir $dh, $base_dir or die "Cannot open $base_dir: $!";
    for (readdir $dh) {
        next if $_ eq curdir( );  # usually '.'

        my $full_dir = catdir $base_dir, $_;
        my $entry = "$base_entry/$_";
        if (-d $full_dir) {
            if ($_ eq updir( )) { # '..'
                $entry = dirname $self->{dir};
                next if catdir($base_dir, $entry) eq $doc_root;
            }
            $self->{dirs}{$_} = $entry;
        }
        else {
            $self->{files}{$_} = $entry;
        }
    }
    closedir $dh;
}
```

By using canonpath( ), we make sure that nobody messes with the path_info element, by eliminating successive slashes and "/."s on Unix and taking appropriate actions on other operating systems. It's important to use File::Spec and other cross-platform functions when developing applications.

While looping through the directory entries, we skip over the current directory entry using the curdir( ) function imported from File::Spec::Functions (which is equivalent to . on Unix) and handle the parent directory entry specially by matching the updir( ) function (which is equivalent to .. on Unix). The function dirname( ) gives us the parent directory, and afterward we check that this directory is different from the document root. If it's the same, we skip this entry.

Note that since we use the path_info element to pass the directory relative to the document root, we rely on Apache to handle the case when users try to mess with the URL and add .. to reach files they aren't supposed to reach.

Finally, let's look at the render( ) method:

```
sub render {
    my $self = shift;
    print "<p>Current Directory: <i>$self->{dir}</i><br>";
```

```
    my $location = $self->{r}->location;
    print qq{<a href="$location$self->{dirs}{$_}">$_</a><br>}
        for sort keys %{ $self->{dirs} || {} };
    print qq{$_<br>}
        for sort keys %{ $self->{files} || {} };
}
```

The render( ) method actually takes the files and directories prepared in the fetch( )
method and displays them to the user. First the name of the current directory is displayed, followed by the directories and finally the files. Since the module should
allow browsing of directories, we hyperlink them. The files aren't linked, since we
are in "see but don't touch" mode.[*]

Finally, we finish the package with 1; to make sure that the module will be successfully loaded. The __END__ token allows us to put various notes and POD documentation after the program, where Perl won't complain about them.

```
    1;
    __END__
```

Example 6-39 shows how the whole package looks.

Example 6-39. Apache/BrowseSee.pm

```
package Apache::BrowseSee;
use strict;

use Apache::Constants qw(:common);
use File::Spec::Functions qw(catdir canonpath curdir updir);
use File::Basename 'dirname';

sub new { bless {}, shift;}

sub handler ($$) {
    my($self, $r) = @_;
    $self = $self->new unless ref $self;

    $self->{r}     = $r;
    $self->{dir}   = $r->path_info || '/';
    $self->{dirs}  = {};
    $self->{files} = {};

    eval { $self->fetch() };
    return NOT_FOUND if $@;

    $self->head;
    $self->render;
    $self->tail;
```

---

[*] In your real code you should also escape HTML- and URI-unsafe characters in the filenames (e.g., <, >, &,
", ', etc.) by using the Apache::Util::escape_html and Apache::Util::escape_uri functions.

Example 6-39. Apache/BrowseSee.pm (continued)

```perl
    return OK;
}

sub head {
    my $self = shift;
    $self->{r}->send_http_header("text/html");
    print "<html><head><title>Dir: $self->{dir}</title><head><body>";
}

sub tail {
    my $self = shift;
    print "</body></html>";
}

sub fetch {
    my $self = shift;
    my $doc_root = Apache->document_root;
    my $base_dir = canonpath( catdir($doc_root, $self->{dir}));

    my $base_entry = $self->{dir} eq '/' ? '' : $self->{dir};
    my $dh = Apache::gensym( );
    opendir $dh, $base_dir or die "Cannot open $base_dir: $!";
    for (readdir $dh) {
        next if $_ eq curdir( );

        my $full_dir = catdir $base_dir, $_;
        my $entry = "$base_entry/$_";
        if (-d $full_dir) {
            if ($_ eq updir( )) {
                $entry = dirname $self->{dir};
                next if catdir($base_dir, $entry) eq $doc_root;
            }
            $self->{dirs}{$_} = $entry;
        }
        else {
            $self->{files}{$_} = $entry;
        }
    }
    closedir $dh;
}

sub render {
    my $self = shift;
    print "Current Directory: <i>$self->{dir}</i><br>";

    my $location = $self->{r}->location;
    print qq{<a href="$location$self->{dirs}{$_}">$_</a><br>}
        for sort keys %{ $self->{dirs} || {} };
    print qq{$_<br>}
        for sort keys %{ $self->{files} || {} };
}
```

Example 6-39. Apache/BrowseSee.pm (continued)

```
1;
__END__
```

This module should be saved as *Apache/BrowseSee.pm* and placed into one of the directories in @INC. For example, if */home/httpd/perl* is in your @INC, you can save it in */home/httpd/perl/Apache/BrowseSee.pm*.

To configure this module, we just add the following snippet to *httpd.conf*:

```
PerlModule Apache::BrowseSee
<Location /browse>
    SetHandler perl-script
    PerlHandler Apache::BrowseSee->handler
</Location>
```

Users accessing the server from */browse* can now browse the contents of your server from the document root and beneath but cannot view the contents of the files (see Figure 6-2).

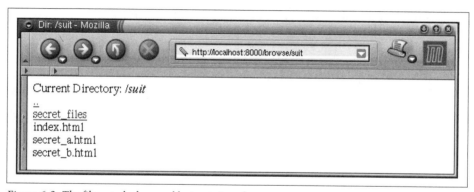

Figure 6-2. The files can be browsed but not viewed

Now let's say that as soon as we get the module up and running, the client comes back and tells us he would like us to implement a very similar application, except that files should now be viewable (clickable). This is because later he wants to allow only authorized users to read the files while letting everybody see what he has to offer.

We knew that was coming, remember? Since we are lazy and it's not exciting to write the same code again and again, we will do the minimum amount of work while still keeping the client happy. This time we are going to implement the Apache:: BrowseRead module:

```
package Apache::BrowseRead;
use strict;
use base qw(Apache::BrowseSee);
```

We place the new module into *Apache/BrowseRead.pm*, declare a new package, and tell Perl that this package inherits from Apache::BrowseSee using the base pragma. The last line is roughly equivalent to:

```
BEGIN {
    require Apache::BrowseSee;
    @Apache::BrowseRead::ISA = qw(Apache::BrowseSee);
}
```

Since this class is going to do the same job as Apache::BrowseSee, apart from rendering the file listings differently, all we have to do is override the render( ) method:

```
sub render {
    my $self = shift;
    print "<p>Current Directory: <i>$self->{dir}</i><br>";

    my $location = $self->{r}->location;
    print qq{<a href="$location$self->{dirs}{$_}">$_</a><br>}
        for sort keys %{ $self->{dirs} || {} };
    print  qq{<a href="$self->{files}{$_}">$_</a><br>}
        for sort keys %{ $self->{files} || {} };
}
```

As you can see, the only difference here is that we link to the real files now.

We complete the package as usual with 1; and __END__:

```
1;
__END__
```

Example 6-40 shows the whole package.

Example 6-40. Apache/BrowseRead.pm

```
package Apache::BrowseRead;
use strict;
use base qw(Apache::BrowseSee);

sub render {
    my $self = shift;
    print "<p>Current Directory: <i>$self->{dir}</i><br>";

    my $location = $self->{r}->location;
    print qq{<a href="$location$self->{dirs}{$_}">$_</a><br>}
        for sort keys %{ $self->{dirs} || {} };
    print  qq{<a href="$self->{files}{$_}">$_</a><br>}
        for sort keys %{ $self->{files} || {} };
}
1;
__END__
```

Finally, we should add a new configuration section in *httpd.conf*:

```
PerlModule Apache::BrowseRead
<Location /read>
    SetHandler perl-script
    PerlHandler Apache::BrowseRead->handler
</Location>
```

Now, when accessing files through */read*, we can browse and view the contents of the files (see Figure 6-3). Once we add some authentication/authorization methods, we will have a server where everybody can browse, but only privileged users can read.

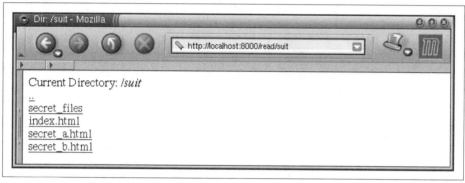

Figure 6-3. The files can be browsed and read

You might be wondering why you would write a special module to do something Apache itself can already do for you. First, this was an example on using method handlers, so we tried to keep it simple while showing some real code. Second, this example can easily be adapted and extended—for example, it can handle virtual files that don't exist on the filesystem but rather are generated on the fly and/or fetched from the database, and it can easily be changed to do whatever *you* (or your client) want to do, instead of what Apache allows.

References

- "Just the FAQs: Coping with Scoping," an article by Mark-Jason Dominus about how Perl handles variables and namespaces, and the difference between use vars( ) and my( ): *http://www.plover.com/~mjd/perl/FAQs/Namespaces.html*.

- It's important to know how to perform exception handling in Perl code. Exception handling is a general Perl technique; it's not mod_perl-specific. Further information is available in the documentation for the following modules:

    — `Error.pm`, by Graham Barr.

    — `Exception::Class` and `Devel::StackTrace`, by Dave Rolsky.

— Try.pm, by Tony Olekshy, available at *http://www.avrasoft.com/perl6/try6-ref5.txt*.

— There is also a great deal of information concerning error handling in the mod_perl online documentation (e.g., *http://perl.apache.org/docs/general/perl_reference/perl_reference.html*).

• Perl Module Mechanics: *http://world.std.com/~swmcd/steven/perl/module_mechanics.html*.

This page describes the mechanics of creating, compiling, releasing, and maintaining Perl modules, which any mod_perl developer planning on sharing code with others will find useful.

mod_perl Performance

This section explains the details of tuning mod_perl and the scripts running under it, so you can squeeze every ounce of power from your server. Performance tuning is a very complex task requiring a lot of understanding and experience, but once you acquire this knowledge you can make magic with your server.

This part of the book would have been much shorter if we had limited ourselves to telling only the facts, without any investigation details. We decided to do the opposite. We show you different areas that we think might be good to investigate in order to improve performance; we show the code under test, the way it was executed, and the results of the test, and we analyze these results and provide conclusions. Each case demonstrates some aspect of the performance-improvement process, so when you complete this part of the book, you will be able to conduct similar tests and decide what's the best on your own.

This section contains the following chapters:

Chapter 7, *Identifying Your Performance Problems*, helps you track down exactly where your performance problems are.

Chapter 8, *Choosing a Platform for the Best Performance*, gives you some guidelines on how to determine that you're using the right hardware and operating system. There's no point spending your time tweaking the configuration of mod_perl if the problem actually lies in the platform you're running on.

Chapter 9, *Essential Tools for Performance Tuning*, introduces you to existing tools to analyze your performance and talks about developing your own tools.

Chapter 10, *Improving Performance with Shared Memory and Proper Forking*, explains how shared memory and forking affect the performance of mod_perl and what you can do about it.

Chapter 11, *Tuning Performance by Tweaking Apache's Configuration*, covers the *httpd.conf* file and how it can be modified to improve the performance of mod_perl-enabled Apache.

Chapter 12, *Server Setup Strategies*, discusses techniques for setting up your mod_perl-enabled Apache server in conjunction with other modules and other services.

Chapter 13, *TMTOWTDI: Convenience and Habit Versus Performance*, discusses the trade-offs involved in various coding techniques.

Chapter 14, *Defensive Measures for Performance Enhancement*, is about how to keep memory usage from spiraling out of control.

Chapter 15, *Improving Performance Through Build Options*, talks about decisions you make when building Apache and mod_perl from source that can affect performance.

Chapter 16, *HTTP Headers for Optimal Performance*, gives some guidance on how HTTP headers can be used to speed up web transactions.

## CHAPTER 7

Identifying Your Performance Problems

You have been assigned to improve the performance of your company's web service. The hardest thing is to get started. How should you tackle this task? And how do you sort out the insignificant issues and identify those that will make a difference once resolved?

In this chapter, we look at this problem from different angles. Only after you understand the problem should you start looking for solutions. Don't search for a solution before the problem has been precisely identified, or you'll end up wasting a lot of time concentrating on trivial issues. Instead, try to identify where you can make the biggest difference in performance.

Note that in this book, we use the term "web service" to mean the whole aggregate that provides the service: the machine, the network, and the software. Don't confuse this with web services such as SOAP and XML-RPC.

Looking at the Big Picture

To make the user's web-browsing experience as painless as possible, every effort must be made to wring the last drop of performance from the server. Many factors affect web site usability, but one of the most important is speed. (This applies to any web server, not just Apache.)

How do we measure the speed of a server? Since the user (and not the computer) is the one that interacts with the web site, one good speed measurement is the time that elapses between the moment the user clicks on a link or presses a Submit button, and the time when the resulting page is fully rendered in his browser.

The requests and resulting responses are broken into packets. Each packet has to make its own way from one machine to another, perhaps passing through many interconnection nodes. We must measure the time starting from when the request's first packet leaves our user's machine to when the reply's last packet arrives back there.

A request may be made up of several packets, and a response may contain a few hundred (typical for a GET request). Remember that the Internet standard for Maximum Transmission Unit (MTU), which is the size of a TCP/IP packet, is 576 bytes. While the packet size can be 1,500 bytes or more, if it crosses a network where the MTU is 576, it will be broken into smaller packets.

It is also possible that a request will be made up of many more packets than its response (typical for a POST request where an uploaded file is followed by a short confirmation response). Therefore, it is important to optimize the handling of both the input and the output.

A web server is only one of the entities the packets see on their journey. If we follow them from browser to server and back again, they may travel via different routes through many different entities. For example, here is the route the packets may go through to reach *perl.apache.org* from our machine:

```
% /usr/sbin/traceroute -n perl.apache.org

traceroute to perl.apache.org (63.251.56.142), 30 hops max, 38 byte packets
 1   10.0.0.1          0.847 ms     1.827 ms     0.817 ms
 2   165.21.104.1      7.628 ms    11.271 ms    12.646 ms
 3   165.21.78.37      8.613 ms     7.882 ms    12.479 ms
 4   202.166.127.28   10.131 ms     8.686 ms    12.163 ms
 5   203.208.145.125   9.033 ms     7.281 ms     9.930 ms
 6   203.208.172.30  225.319 ms   231.167 ms   234.747 ms
 7   203.208.172.46  252.473 ms          *     252.602 ms
 8   198.32.176.29   250.532 ms   251.693 ms   226.962 ms
 9   207.136.163.125 232.632 ms   231.504 ms   232.019 ms
10   206.132.110.98  225.417 ms   224.801 ms   252.480 ms
11   206.132.110.138 254.443 ms   225.056 ms   259.674 ms
12   64.209.88.54    227.754 ms   226.362 ms   253.664 ms
13   63.251.63.71    252.921 ms   252.573 ms   258.014 ms
14   64.125.132.18   237.191 ms   234.256 ms  *
15   63.251.56.142   254.539 ms   252.895 ms   253.895 ms
```

As you can see, the packets travel through 14 gateways before they reach *perl.apache. org*. Each of the hops between these gateways may slow down the packet.

Before they are processed by the server, the packets may have to go through proxy servers, and if the request contains more than one packet, packets might arrive at the server by different routes and at different times. It is possible that some packets may arrive out of order, causing some that arrive earlier to have to wait for other packets before they can be reassembled into a chunk of the request message that can then be read by the server. The whole process is then repeated in the opposite direction as response packets travel back to the browser.

Even if you work hard to fine-tune your web server's performance, a slow Network Interface Card (NIC) or a slow network connection from your server might defeat it all. That is why it is important to think about the big picture and to be aware of possible bottlenecks between your server and the Web.

Of course, there is little you can do if the user has a slow connection. You might tune your scripts and web server to process incoming requests ultra quickly, so you will need only a small number of working servers, but even then you may find that the server processes are all busy waiting for slow clients to accept their responses.

There are techniques to cope with this. For example, you can compress the response before delivery. If you are delivering a pure text response, *gzip* compression will reduce the size of the sent text by two to five times.

You should analyze all the components involved when you try to create the best service for your users, not just the web server or the code that the web server executes.

```
          -----
            |
      A web service is
    like     a     car,
    if       one    of the
  parts or mechanisms  is  broken
  the car may ~ not ~  run  smoothly;
  it can even stop dead if pushed too
    far without  first  fixing  it.
      \___/           \___/
```

If you want to have success in the web service business, you should start worrying about the client's browsing experience, not only how good your code benchmarks are.

Asking the Right Questions

There is much more to the web service than writing the code, and firing the server to crunch this code. But before you specify a set of questions that will lead you to the coverage of the whole mechanism and not just a few of its components, it is hard to know what issues are to be checked, what components are to be watched, and what software is to be monitored. The better questions you ask, the better coverage you should have.

Let's raise a few questions and look at some possible answers.

Q: *How long does it take to process each request? What is the request distribution?*

A: Obviously you will have more than one script and handler, and each one might be called in different modes; the amount of processing to be done may be different in every case. Therefore, you should attempt to benchmark your code, using all the modes in which it can be executed. It is good to learn the average case, as well as to learn the edges—the worst and best cases.

It is also very important to find out the distribution of different requests relative to the total number of requests. You might have only two handlers: one very slow and the other very fast. If you optimize for the average case without finding out the request distribution, you might end up under-optimizing your server, if in fact the slow request handler has a much higher call rate than the fast one. Or you might have your server over-optimized, if the slow handler is used much less frequently than the fast handler.

Remember that users can never be trusted not to do unexpected things such as uploading huge core dump files, messing with HTML forms, and supplying parameters and values you didn't consider. Which leads us to two things. First, it is not enough to test the code with automatic offline benchmarking, because chances are you will forget a few possible scenarios. You should try to log the requests and their execution times on the live server and watch the real picture. Secondly, after everything has been optimized, you should add a safety margin so your server won't be rendered unusable when heavily hit by the worst-case usage load.

Q: *How many requests can the server process simultaneously?*

A: The number of simultaneous requests you can handle is equal to the number of web server processes you can afford to run. This all translates to the amount of main memory (RAM) available to the web server. Note that we are not talking about the amount of RAM installed on your machine, since this number is misleading. Each machine is running many processes in addition to the web server processes. Most of these don't consume a lot of memory, but some do. It is possible that your web servers share the available RAM with big memory consumers such as SQL engines or proxy servers. The first step is to figure out what is the real amount of memory dedicated to your web server.

Q: *How many simultaneous requests is the site expected to service? What is the expected request rate?*

A: This question sounds similar to the previous one, but it is different in essence. You should know your server's abilities, but you also need to have a realistic estimate of the expected request rate.

Are you really expecting eight million hits per day? What is the expected peak load, and what kind of response time do you need to guarantee? Doing market research would probably help to identify the potential request rates, and the code you develop should be written in a scalable way, to allow you to add a few more machines to accommodate the possibility of rising demand.

Remember that whatever statistics you gathered during your last service analysis might change drastically when your site gains popularity. When you get a very high hit rate, in most cases the resource requirements grow exponentially, not linearly!

Also remember that whenever you apply code changes it is possible that the new code will be more resource-hungry than the previous code. The best case is when the new code requires fewer resources, but generally this is not the case.

If you machine runs the service perfectly well under normal loads, but the load is subject to occasional peaks—e.g., a product announcement or a special offer—it is possible to maintain performance without changing the web service at all. For example, some services can be switched off temporarily to cope with a peak. Also avoid running heavy, non-urgent processes (backups, cron jobs, etc.) during the peak times.

Q:	*Who are the users?*

A:	Just as it is important for a public speaker to know her audience in order to provide a successful presentation and deliver the right points, it is important to know who your users are and what can be expected from them.

If you are administering an Intranet web service (internal to a company, publicly inaccessible), you can tell what connection speed most of your users have, the number of possible users, and therefore the maximum request rate. You can be sure that the service will not gain a sudden popularity that will drive the demand rate up exponentially. Since there are a known number of users in your company, you know the expected limit. You can optimize the Intranet web service for high-speed connections, but don't forget that some users might connect to the Intranet with a slower dial-up connection. Also, you probably know at what hours your users will use the service (unless your company has branches all over the world, which requires 24-hour server availability) and can optimize service during those hours.

If you are administering an Internet web service, your knowledge of your audience is very limited. Depending on your target audience, it can be possible to learn about usage patterns and obtain some numerical estimates of the possible demands. You can either attempt to do the research by yourself or hire professionals to do this work for you. There are companies who release various survey reports available for purchase.

Once your service is running in the ideal way, know what to expect by keeping up with the server statistics. This will allow you to identify possible growth trends. Certainly, most web services cannot stand the so-called *Slashdot Effect*, which happens when some very popular news service (Slashdot, for instance) releases an exotic report on your service and suddenly all readers of this news service are trying to hit your site. The effect can be a double-edged sword: on one side you gain free advertising, but on the other side your server may not be able to withstand the suddenly increased load. If that's the case, most clients may not succeed in getting through.

Just as with the Intranet server, it is possible that your users are all located in a given time zone (e.g., for a particular country-specific service), in which case you know that hardly any users will be hitting your service in the early morning. The peak will probably occur during late evening and early night hours, and you can optimize your service during these times.

Q:	*How can we protect ourselves from the Slashdot Effect?*

A:	Use mod_throttle. mod_throttle allows you to limit the use of your server based on different metrics, configurable per vhost/location/file. For example, you can limit requests for the URL */old_content* to a maximum of four connections per second. Using mod_throttle will help you prioritize different parts of your server, allowing smart use of limited bandwidth and limiting the effect of spikes.

Q: *Does load balancing help in this area?*

A: Yes. Load balancing, using mod_backhand, Cisco LocalDirector, or similar products, lets you wring the most performance out of your servers by spreading the load across a group of servers.

Q: *How can we deal with the situation where we can afford only a limited amount of bandwidth but some of the service's content is large (e.g., streaming media or large files)?*

A: mod_bandwidth is a module for the Apache web server that enables the setting of server-wide or per-connection bandwidth limits, based on the directory, size of files, and remote IP/domain.

Also see Akamai, which allows you to cache large content in regionally specific areas (e.g., east/west coast in the U.S.).

The given list of questions is in no way complete, and each specific project will have a different set of questions and answers. Some will be retained from project to project; others will be replaced by new ones. Remember that this is not a one-size-fits-all glove. While partial functionality can generally be optimized using the same method, you will have to go through this question-and-answer process each time from scratch if you want to achieve the best performance.

References

- *http://slashdot.org/* is a site for geeks with news interesting to geeks. It has become very popular and gathers large crowds of people who read the posted articles and participate in various discussions. When a news story posted on this site appeals to a large number of Slashdot readers, the site mentioned in the news story often suddenly becomes a new mecca during the day the story was posted and the next few days. If the site's owner has just a small machine and never expected to gain such popularity in so little time, the server is generally unable to supply the demand and often dies. This is known as the Slashdot Effect.
- *Web Performance Tuning*, by Patrick Killelea (O'Reilly).
- The mod_throttle home page: *http://www.snert.com/Software/mod_throttle/*.
- The mod_bandwidth home page: *http://www.cohprog.com/mod_bandwidth.html*.
- The mod_backhand home page: *http://www.backhand.org/mod_backhand/*.

## CHAPTER 8

Choosing a Platform for the Best Performance

Before you start to optimize your code and server configuration, you need to consider the demands that will be placed on the hardware and the operating system. There is no point in investing a lot of time and money in configuration tuning and code optimizing only to find that your server's performance is poor because you did not choose a suitable platform in the first place.

Because hardware platforms and operating systems are developing rapidly, the following advisory discussion must be in general terms, without mentioning specific vendors' names.

Choosing the Right Operating System

This section discusses the characteristics and features you should be looking for to support a mod_perl-enabled Apache server. When you know what you want from your OS, you can go out and find it. Visit the web sites of the operating systems that interest you. You can gauge users' opinions by searching the relevant discussions in newsgroup and mailing-list archives. Deja (*http://deja.com/*) and eGroups (*http://egroups.com/*) are good examples. However, your best shot is probably to ask other mod_perl users.

mod_perl Support for the Operating System

Clearly, before choosing an OS, you will want to make sure that mod_perl even *runs* on it! As you will have noticed throughout this book, mod_perl 1.x is traditionally a Unix-centric solution. Although it also runs on Windows, there are several limitations related to its implementation.

The problem is that Apache on Windows uses a multithreaded implementation, due to the fact that Windows can't use the multi-process scheme deployed on Unix platforms. However, when mod_perl (and thereby the Perl runtime) is built into the

Apache process, it *cannot* run multithreaded, because before Version 5.8.0 the Perl runtime wasn't thread-safe.

What does this mean for you? Well, essentially it means that your Apache process will be able to serve only *one request at a time*, just like when using *httpd -X*. Of course, this becomes a severe performance hit, making you unable to have more than one user receiving a page at a time. The situation is resolved in mod_perl 2.0, however, thanks to advances in both Apache and Perl, as described in Chapter 24. Furthermore, you can still use mod_perl on Windows for development, although you should follow the considerations below when choosing the production OS.

Stability and Robustness

Probably the most important features in an OS are stability and robustness. You are in an Internet business. You do not keep normal 9 A.M. to 5 P.M. working hours like many conventional businesses you know. You are open 24 hours a day. You cannot afford to be offline, because your customers will go shop at another service like yours (unless you have a monopoly). If the OS of your choice crashes every day, first do a little investigation. There might be a simple reason that you can find and fix. However, there are OSes that won't work unless you reboot them twice a day. You don't want to use an OS of this kind, no matter how good the OS's vendor sales department is. Do not follow flush advertisements—follow developers' advice instead.

Generally, people who have used an OS for some time can tell you a lot about its stability. Ask them. Try to find people who are doing similar things to what you are planning to do; they may even be using the same software. There are often compatibility issues to resolve, and you may need to become familiar with patching and compiling your OS.

Good Memory Management

You want an OS with a good memory-management implementation. Some OSes are well known as memory hogs. The same code can use twice as much memory on one OS compared to another. If the size of the mod_perl process is 10 MB and you have tens of these processes running, it definitely adds up!

Avoiding Memory Leaks

Some OSes and/or their libraries (e.g., C runtime libraries) suffer from memory leaks. A *leak* is when some process requests a chunk of memory for temporary storage but then does not subsequently release it. The chunk of memory then won't be available for any purpose until the process that requested it dies. You cannot afford such leaks. A single mod_perl process sometimes serves thousands of requests before it terminates; if a leak occurs on every request, the memory demands could become huge. Of course, your code can be the cause of the memory leaks as well, but that's easy to detect and solve. Certainly, you can reduce the number of requests to be served over the process's life, but that can degrade performance. When you have so many performance concerns to think about, do you *really* want to be using faulty code that's not under your control?

Memory-Sharing Capabilities

You want an OS with good memory-sharing capabilities. If you preload the Perl modules and scripts at server startup, they are shared between the spawned children (at least for part of a process's life—memory pages can become "dirty" and cease to be shared). This feature can vastly reduce memory consumption. Therefore, you don't want an OS that doesn't have memory-sharing capabilities.

The Real Cost of Support

If you are in a big business, you probably do not mind paying another $1,000 for some fancy OS with bundled support. But if your resources are low, you will look for cheaper or free OSes. Free does not mean bad. In fact, it can be quite the opposite—some of the free OSes have the best support available.

This is easy to understand—most people are not rich and will try to use a cheaper or free OS first if it does the work for them. If it fits their needs, they will keep using it and eventually come to know it well enough to be able to provide support for others in trouble. Why would they do this for free? One reason is the spirit of the first days of the Internet, when there was no commercial Internet and people helped each other because someone else had helped them first. We were there, we were touched by that spirit, and we are keen to keep that spirit alive.

Nevertheless, we are living in a material world, and our bosses pay us to keep the systems running. So if you feel that you cannot provide the support yourself and you do not trust the available free resources, you must pay for an OS backed by a company to which you can turn in case of problems. Insufficient support has often been characterized as an important drawback of open source products, and in the past it may have been the main reason for many companies to choose a commercial product.

Luckily, in recent years many companies have realized how good the open source products are and started to provide official support for these products. So your suggestion of using an open source operating system cannot be dismissed solely on the basis of lacking vendor support; most likely you will be able to find commercial support just like with any other commercial OS vendor!

Also remember that the less money you spend on an OS and software, the more you will be able to spend on faster and stronger hardware. Of course, for some companies money is a non-issue, but there are many companies for which it is a major concern.

Discontinued Products

You might find yourself in a position where you have invested a lot of time and money into developing some proprietary software that is bundled with the OS you chose (say, writing a mod_perl handler that takes advantage of some proprietary features of the OS and that will not run on any other OS). Things are under control, the performance is great, and you sing with happiness on your way to work. Then, one day, the company that supplies your beloved OS goes bankrupt (not unlikely nowadays), or they produce a newer, incompatible version and decide not to support the old one (it happens all the time). You are stuck with their early masterpiece, no support, and no source code! What are you going to do? Invest more money into porting the software to another OS?

The OSes in this hazard group tend to be developed by a single company or organization, so free and open source OSes are probably less susceptible to this kind of problem. Their development is usually distributed between many companies and developers, so if a person who developed a really important part of the kernel loses interest in continuing, someone else usually will pick up the work and carry on. Of course, if some better project shows up tomorrow, developers might migrate there and finally drop the development, but in practice people are often given support on older versions and helped to migrate to current versions. Development tends to be more incremental than revolutionary, so upgrades are less traumatic, and there is usually plenty of notice of the forthcoming changes so that you have time to plan for them.

Of course, with the open source OSes you have the source code, too. You can always have a go at maintaining it yourself, but do not underestimate the amount of work involved.

Keeping Up with OS Releases

Actively developed OSes generally try to keep pace with the latest technology developments and continually optimize the kernel and other parts of the OS to become better and faster. Nowadays, the Internet and networking in general are the hottest topics for system developers. Sometimes a simple OS upgrade to the latest stable version can save you an expensive hardware upgrade. Also, remember that when you buy new hardware, chances are that the latest software will make the most of it.

If a new product supports an old one by virtue of backward compatibility with previous products of the same family, you might not reap all the benefits of the new product's features. You might get almost the same functionality for much less money if you were to buy an older model of the same product.

Choosing the Right Hardware

Sometimes the most expensive machine is not the one that provides the best performance. Your demands on the platform hardware are based on many aspects and affect many components. Let's discuss some of them.

This discussion relies on the specific definitions of various hardware and operating-system terms. Although you may be familiar with the terms below, we have explicitly provided definitions to make sure there is no ambiguity when we discuss the hardware strategies.

Cluster

> A group of machines connected together to perform one big or many small computational tasks in a reasonable time. Clustering can also be used to provide failover, where if one machine fails, its processes are transferred to another without interruption of service. And you may be able to take one of the machines down for maintenance (or an upgrade) and keep your service running—the main server simply will not dispatch the requests to the machine that was taken down.

Load balancing

> Say that users are given the name of one of your machines, but it cannot stand the heavy load. You can use a clustering approach to distribute the load over a number of machines (which gives you the advantages of clustering, too). The central server, which users access initially when they type the name of your service into their browsers, works as a dispatcher. It redirects requests to other machines, and sometimes the central server also collects the results and returns them to the users.

Network Interface Card (NIC)

> A hardware component that allows your machine to connect to the network. It sends and receives packets. NICs come in different speeds, varying from 10 MBps to 10 GBps and faster. The most widely used NIC type is the one that implements the Ethernet networking protocol.

Random Access Memory (RAM)

> The memory that you have in your computer (comes in units of 8 MB, 16 MB, 64 MB, 256 MB, etc.).

Redundant Array of Inexpensive Disks (RAID)

> An array of physical disks, usually treated by the operating system as one single disk, and often forced to appear that way by the hardware. The reason for using RAID is often simply to achieve a high data-transfer rate, but it may also be to get adequate disk capacity or high reliability. *Redundancy* means that the system is capable of continued operation even if a disk fails. There are various types of RAID arrays and several different approaches to implementing them. Some systems provide protection against failure of more than one drive and some ("hot-swappable") systems allow a drive to be replaced without even stopping the OS.

Machine Strength Demands According to Expected Site Traffic

If you are building a fan site and you want to amaze your friends with a mod_perl guestbook, any old 486 machine could do it. But if you are in a serious business, it is very important to build a scalable server. If your service is successful and becomes popular, the traffic could double every few days, and you should be ready to add more resources to keep up with the demand. While we can define the web server scalability more precisely, the important thing is to make sure that you can add more power to your web server(s) without investing much additional money in software development (you will need a little software effort to connect your servers, if you add more of them). This means that you should choose hardware and OSes that can talk to other machines and become part of a cluster.

On the other hand, if you prepare for a lot of traffic and buy a monster to do the work for you, what happens if your service doesn't prove to be as successful as you thought it would be? Then you've spent too much money, and meanwhile faster processors and other hardware components have been released, so you lose.

Wisdom and prophecy, that's all it takes. :)

A Single Strong Machine Versus Many Weaker Machines

Let's start with a claim that a four-year-old processor is still very powerful and can be put to good use. Now let's say that for a given amount of money you can probably buy either one new, very strong machine or about 10 older but very cheap machines. We claim that with 10 old machines connected into a cluster, by deploying load balancing, you will be able to serve about five times more requests than with a single new machine.

Why is that? Generally the performance improvement on a new machine is marginal, while the price is much higher. Ten machines will do faster disk I/O than one single machine, even if the new disk is quite a bit faster. Yes, you have more administration overhead, but there is a chance that you will have it anyway, for in a short time the new machine you have just bought might not be able to handle the load. Then you will have to purchase more equipment and think about how to implement load balancing and web server filesystem distribution anyway.

Why are we so convinced? Look at the busiest services on the Internet: search engines, webmail servers, and the like—most of them use a clustering approach. You may not always notice it, because they hide the real implementation details behind proxy servers, but they do.

Getting a Fast Internet Connection

You have the best hardware you can get, but the service is still crawling. What's wrong? Make sure you have a fast Internet connection—not necessarily as fast as your ISP claims it to be, but as fast as it should be. The ISP might have a very good connection to the Internet but put many clients on the same line. If these are heavy clients, your traffic will have to share the same line and your throughput will suffer. Think about a dedicated connection and make sure it is truly dedicated. Don't trust the ISP, check it!

Another issue is connection latency. Latency defines the number of milliseconds it takes for a packet to travel to its final destination. This issue is really important if you have to do interactive work (via *ssh* or a similar protocol) on some remote machine, since if the latency is big (400+ ms) it's really hard to work. It is less of an issue for web services, since it influences only the first packet. The rest of the packets arrive without any extra delay.

The idea of having a connection to "the Internet" is a little misleading. Many web hosting and colocation companies have large amounts of bandwidth but still have poor connectivity. The public exchanges, such as MAE-East and MAE-West, frequently become overloaded, yet many ISPs depend on these exchanges.

Private peering is a solution used by the larger backbone operators. No longer exchanging traffic among themselves at the public exchanges, each implements private interconnections with each of the others. Private peering means that providers can exchange traffic much quicker.

Also, if your web site is of global interest, check that the ISP has good global connectivity. If the web site is going to be visited mostly by people in a certain country or region, your server should probably be located there.

Bad connectivity can directly influence your machine's performance. Here is a story one of the developers told on the mod_perl mailing list:

> What relationship has 10% packet loss on one upstream provider got to
> do with machine memory ?
>
> Yes.. a lot. For a nightmare week, the box was located downstream of a
> provider who was struggling with some serious bandwidth problems of
> his own... people were connecting to the site via this link, and
> packet loss was such that retransmits and TCP stalls were keeping
> httpd heavies around for much longer than normal.. instead of blasting
> out the data at high or even modem speeds, they would be stuck at
> 1k/sec or stalled out... people would press stop and refresh, httpds
> would take 300 seconds to timeout on writes to no-one.. it was a
> nightmare. Those problems didn't go away till I moved the box to a
> place closer to some decent backbones.

Note that with a proxy, this only keeps a lightweight httpd tied up, assuming the page is small enough to fit in the buffers. If you are a busy internet site you always have some slow clients. This is a difficult thing to simulate in benchmark testing, though.

Tuning I/O Performance

If your service is I/O-bound (i.e., does a lot of read/write operations to disk) you need a very fast disk, especially when using a relational database. Don't spend the money on a fancy video card and monitor! A cheap card and a 14-inch monochrome monitor are perfectly adequate for a web server—you will probably access it by *telnet* or *ssh* most of the time anyway. Look for hard disks with the best price/performance ratio. Of course, ask around and avoid disks that have a reputation for headcrashes and other disasters.

Consider RAID or similar systems when you want to improve I/O's throughput (performance) and the reliability of the stored data, and of course if you have an enormous amount of data to store.

OK, you have a fast disk—so what's next? You need a fast disk controller. There may be a controller embedded on your computer's motherboard. If the controller is not fast enough, you should buy a faster one. Don't forget that it may be necessary to disable the original controller.

How Much Memory Is Enough?

How much RAM do you need? Nowadays, chances are that you will hear: "Memory is cheap, the more you buy the better." But how much is enough? The answer is pretty straightforward: *you do not want your machine to swap!* When the CPU needs to write something into memory, but memory is already full, it takes the least frequently used memory pages and swaps them out to disk. This means you have to bear the time penalty of writing the data to disk. If another process then references some of the data that happens to be on one of the pages that has just been swapped out, the CPU swaps it back in again, probably swapping out some other data that will be needed very shortly by some other process. Carried to the extreme, the CPU and disk start to thrash hopelessly in circles, without getting any real work done. The less RAM there is, the more often this scenario arises. Worse, you can exhaust swap space as well, and then your troubles really start.

How do you make a decision? You know the highest rate at which your server expects to serve pages and how long it takes on average to serve one. Now you can calculate how many server processes you need. If you know the maximum size to which your servers can grow, you know how much memory you need. If your OS supports memory sharing, you can make best use of this feature by preloading the modules and scripts at server startup, so you will need less memory than you have calculated.

Do not forget that other essential system processes need memory as well, so you should not only plan for the web server but also take into account the other players. Remember that requests can be queued, so you can afford to let your client wait for a few moments until a server is available to serve it. Most of the time your server will not have the maximum load, but you should be ready to bear the peaks. You need to reserve at least 20% of free memory for peak situations. Many sites have crashed a few moments after a big scoop about them was posted and an unexpected number of requests suddenly arrived. If you are about to announce something cool, be aware of the possible consequences.

Getting a Fault-Tolerant CPU

Make sure that the CPU is operating within its specifications. Many boxes are shipped with incorrect settings for CPU clock speed, power supply voltage, etc. Sometimes a if cooling fan is not fitted, it may be ineffective because a cable assembly fouls the fan blades. Like faulty RAM, an overheating processor can cause all kinds of strange and unpredictable things to happen. Some CPUs are known to have bugs that can be serious in certain circumstances. Try not to get one of them.

Detecting and Avoiding Bottlenecks

You might use the most expensive components but still get bad performance. Why? Let me introduce an annoying word: bottleneck.

A machine is an aggregate of many components. Almost any one of them may become a bottleneck. If you have a fast processor but a small amount of RAM, the RAM will probably be the bottleneck. The processor will be underutilized, and it will often be waiting for the kernel to swap the memory pages in and out, because memory is too small to hold the busiest pages.

If you have a lot of memory, a fast processor, and a fast disk, but a slow disk controller, the disk controller will be the bottleneck. The performance will still be bad, and you will have wasted money.

A slow NIC can cause a bottleneck as well and make the whole service run slowly. This is a most important component, since web servers are much more often network-bound than they are disk-bound (i.e., they have more network traffic than disk utilization).

Solving Hardware Requirement Conflicts

It may happen that the combination of software components you find yourself using gives rise to conflicting requirements for the optimization of tuning parameters. If you can separate the components onto different machines you may find that this approach (a kind of clustering) solves the problem, at much less cost than buying faster hardware, because you can tune the machines individually to suit the tasks they should perform.

For example, if you need to run a relational database engine and a mod_perl server, it can be wise to put the two on different machines, since an RDBMS needs a very fast disk while mod_perl processes need lots of memory. Placing the two on different machines makes it easy to optimize each machine separately and satisfy each software component's requirements in the best way.

References

- For more information about RAID, see the Disk-HOWTO, Module-HOWTO, and Parallel-Processing-HOWTO, available from the Linux Documentation Project and its mirrors (*http://www.tldp.org/docs.html#howto*).

- For more information about clusters and high-availability setups, see:

  High-Availability Linux Project, the definitive guide to load-balancing techniques: *http://www.linux-ha.org/*

  Linux Virtual Server Project: *http://www.linuxvirtualserver.org/*

  mod_backhand, which provides load balancing for Apache: *http://www.backhand.org/mod_backhand/*

  lbnamed, a load balancing name server written in Perl: *http://www.stanford.edu/~riepel/lbnamed/*, *http://www.stanford.edu/~riepel/lbnamed/bof.talk/*, or *http://www.stanford.edu/~schemers/docs/lbnamed/lbnamed.html*

- Chapters 11 to 18 of *Web Performance Tuning*, by Patrick Killelea (O'Reilly).

- Chapters 2 and 12 in *Optimizing UNIX for Performance*, by Amir H. Majidimehr (Prentice Hall).

- Chapter 9 ("Tuning Apache and mod_perl") in *mod_perl Developer's Cookbook*, by Geoffrey Young, Paul Lindner, and Randy Kobes (Sams Publishing).

Essential Tools for Performance Tuning

To be able to improve the performance of your system you need a prior understanding of what can be improved, how it can be improved, how much it can be improved, and, most importantly, what impact the improvement will have on the overall performance of your system. You need to be able to identify those things that, after you have done your best to improve them, will yield substantial benefits for the overall system performance. Concentrate your efforts on them, and avoid wasting time on improvements that give little overall gain.

If you have a small application it may be possible to detect places that could be improved simply by inspecting the code. On the other hand, if you have a large application, or many applications, it's usually impossible to do the detective work with the naked eye. You need observation instruments and measurement tools. These belong to the benchmarking and code-profiling categories.

It's important to understand that in the majority of the benchmarking tests that we will execute, we will not be looking at absolute results. Few machines will have exactly the same hardware and software setup, so this kind of comparison would usually be misleading, and in most cases we will be trying to show which coding approach is preferable, so the hardware is almost irrelevant.

Rather than looking at absolute results, we will be looking at the differences between two or more result sets run on the same machine. This is what you should do; you shouldn't try to compare the absolute results collected here with the results of those same benchmarks on your own machines.

In this chapter we will present a few existing tools that are widely used; we will apply them to example code snippets to show you how performance can be measured, monitored, and improved; and we will give you an idea of how you can develop your own tools.

Server Benchmarking

As web service developers, the most important thing we should strive for is to offer the user a fast, trouble-free browsing experience. Measuring the response rates of our servers under a variety of load conditions and benchmark programs helps us to do this.

A benchmark program may consume significant resources, so you cannot find the real times that a typical user will wait for a response from your service by running the benchmark on the server itself. Ideally you should run it from a different machine. A benchmark program is unlike a typical user in the way it generates requests. It should be able to emulate multiple concurrent users connecting to the server by generating many concurrent requests. We want to be able to tell the benchmark program what load we want to emulate—for example, by specifying the number or rate of requests to be made, the number of concurrent users to emulate, lists of URLs to request, and other relevant arguments.

ApacheBench

ApacheBench (*ab*) is a tool for benchmarking your Apache HTTP server. It is designed to give you an idea of the performance that your current Apache installation can give. In particular, it shows you how many requests per second your Apache server is capable of serving. The *ab* tool comes bundled with the Apache source distribution, and like the Apache web server itself, it's free.

Let's try it. First we create a test script, as shown in Example 9-1.

Example 9-1. simple_test.pl

```
my $r = shift;
$r->send_http_header('text/plain');
print "Hello\n";
```

We will simulate 10 users concurrently requesting the file *simple_test.pl* through *http://localhost/perl/simple_test.pl*. Each simulated user makes 500 requests. We generate 5,000 requests in total:

```
panic% ./ab -n 5000 -c 10 http://localhost/perl/simple_test.pl

Server Software:        Apache/1.3.25-dev
Server Hostname:        localhost
Server Port:            8000

Document Path:          /perl/simple_test.pl
Document Length:        6 bytes

Concurrency Level:      10
Time taken for tests:   5.843 seconds
Complete requests:      5000
Failed requests:        0
```

```
Broken pipe errors:       0
Total transferred:        810162 bytes
HTML transferred:         30006 bytes
Requests per second:      855.72 [#/sec] (mean)
Time per request:         11.69 [ms] (mean)
Time per request:         1.17 [ms] (mean, across all concurrent requests)
Transfer rate:            138.66 [Kbytes/sec] received

Connnection Times (ms)
              min  mean[+/-sd] median   max
Connect:        0    1    1.4      0     17
Processing:     1   10   12.9      7    208
Waiting:        0    9   13.0      7    208
Total:          1   11   13.1      8    208
```

Most of the report is not very interesting to us. What we really care about are the *Requests per second* and *Connection Times* results:

Requests per second
> The number of requests (to our test script) the server was able to serve in one second

Connect and Waiting times
> The amount of time it took to establish the connection and get the first bits of a response

Processing time
> The server response time—i.e., the time it took for the server to process the request and send a reply

Total time
> The sum of the Connect and Processing times

As you can see, the server was able to respond on average to 856 requests per second. On average, it took no time to establish a connection to the server both the client and the server are running on the same machine and 10 milliseconds to process each request. As the code becomes more complicated you will see that the processing time grows while the connection time remains constant. The latter isn't influenced by the code complexity, so when you are working on your code performance, you care only about the processing time. When you are benchmarking the overall service, you are interested in both.

Just for fun, let's benchmark a similar script, shown in Example 9-2, under mod_cgi.

Example 9-2. simple_test_mod_cgi.pl

```
#!/usr/bin/perl
print "Content-type: text/plain\n\n";
print "Hello\n";
```

The script is configured as:

```
ScriptAlias /cgi-bin/ /usr/local/apache/cgi-bin/

panic% /usr/local/apache/bin/ab -n 5000 -c 10 \
http://localhost/cgi-bin/simple_test_mod_cgi.pl
```

We will show only the results that interest us:

```
Requests per second:    156.40 [#/sec] (mean)
Time per request:        63.94 [ms] (mean)
```

Now, when essentially the same script is executed under mod_cgi instead of mod_perl, we get 156 requests per second responded to, not 856.

ApacheBench can generate KeepAlives, GET (default) and POST requests, use *Basic Authentication*, send cookies and custom HTTP headers. The version of *Apache-Bench* released with Apache version 1.3.20 adds SSL support, generates *gnuplot* and CSV output for postprocessing, and reports median and standard deviation values.

HTTPD::Bench::ApacheBench, available from CPAN, provides a Perl interface for *ab*.

httperf

httperf is another tool for measuring web server performance. Its input and reports are different from the ones we saw while using *ApacheBench*. This tool's manpage includes an in-depth explanation of all the options it accepts and the results it generates. Here we will concentrate on the input and on the part of the output that is most interesting to us.

With *httperf* you cannot specify the concurrency level; instead, you have to specify the connection opening rate (*--rate*) and the number of calls (*--num-call*) to perform on each opened connection. To compare the results we received from *ApacheBench* we will use a connection rate slightly higher than the number of requests responded to per second reported by *ApacheBench*. That number was 856, so we will try a rate of 860 (*--rate 860*) with just one request per connection (*--num-call 1*). As in the previous test, we are going to make 5,000 requests (*--num-conn 5000*). We have set a timeout of 60 seconds and allowed *httperf* to use as many ports as it needs (*--hog*).

So let's execute the benchmark and analyze the results:

```
panic% httperf --server localhost --port 80 --uri /perl/simple_test.pl \
--hog --rate 860 --num-conn 5000 --num-call 1 --timeout 60

Maximum connect burst length: 11

Total: connections 5000 requests 5000 replies 5000 test-duration 5.854 s

Connection rate: 854.1 conn/s (1.2 ms/conn, <=50 concurrent connections)
Connection time [ms]: min 0.8 avg 23.5 max 226.9 median 20.5 stddev 13.7
Connection time [ms]: connect 4.0
Connection length [replies/conn]: 1.000
```

```
Request rate: 854.1 req/s (1.2 ms/req)
Request size [B]: 79.0

Reply rate [replies/s]: min 855.6 avg 855.6 max 855.6 stddev 0.0 (1 samples)
Reply time [ms]: response 19.5 transfer 0.0
Reply size [B]: header 184.0 content 6.0 footer 2.0 (total 192.0)
Reply status: 1xx=0 2xx=5000 3xx=0 4xx=0 5xx=0

CPU time [s]: user 0.33 system 1.53 (user 5.6% system 26.1% total 31.8%)
Net I/O: 224.4 KB/s (1.8*10^6 bps)

Errors: total 0 client-timo 0 socket-timo 0 connrefused 0 connreset 0
Errors: fd-unavail 0 addrunavail 0 ftab-full 0 other 0
```

As before, we are mostly interested in the average *Reply rate*—855, almost exactly the same result reported by *ab* in the previous section. Notice that when we tried *--rate 900* for this particular setup, the reported request rate went down drastically, since the server's performance gets worse when there are more requests than it can handle.

http_load

http_load is yet another utility that does web server load testing. It can simulate a 33.6 Kbps modem connection (*-throttle*) and allows you to provide a file with a list of URLs that will be fetched randomly. You can specify how many parallel connections to run (*-parallel N*) and the number of requests to generate per second (*-rate N*). Finally, you can tell the utility when to stop by specifying either the test time length (*-seconds N*) or the total number of fetches (*-fetches N*).

Again, we will try to verify the results reported by *ab* (claiming that the script under test can handle about 855 requests per second on our machine). Therefore we run *http_load* with a rate of 860 requests per second, for 5 seconds in total. We invoke is on the file *urls*, containing a single URL:

```
http://localhost/perl/simple_test.pl
```

Here is the generated output:

```
panic% http_load -rate 860 -seconds 5 urls
4278 fetches, 325 max parallel, 25668 bytes, in 5.00351 seconds
6 mean bytes/connection
855 fetches/sec, 5130 bytes/sec
msecs/connect: 20.0881 mean, 3006.54 max, 0.099 min
msecs/first-response: 51.3568 mean, 342.488 max, 1.423 min
HTTP response codes:
  code 200 -- 4278
```

This application also reports almost exactly the same response-rate capability: 855 requests per second. Of course, you may think that it's because we have specified a rate close to this number. But no, if we try the same test with a higher rate:

```
panic% http_load -rate 870 -seconds 5 urls
4045 fetches, 254 max parallel, 24270 bytes, in 5.00735 seconds
```

```
6 mean bytes/connection
807.813 fetches/sec, 4846.88 bytes/sec
msecs/connect: 78.4026 mean, 3005.08 max, 0.102 min
```

we can see that the performance goes down—it reports a response rate of only 808 requests per second.

The nice thing about this utility is that you can list a few URLs to test. The URLs that get fetched are chosen randomly from the specified file.

Note that when you provide a file with a list of URLs, you must make sure that you don't have empty lines in it. If you do, the utility will fail and complain:

```
./http_load: unknown protocol -
```

Other Web Server Benchmark Utilities

The following are also interesting benchmarking applications implemented in Perl:

HTTP::WebTest
> The HTTP::WebTest module (available from CPAN) runs tests on remote URLs or local web files containing Perl, JSP, HTML, JavaScript, etc. and generates a detailed test report.

HTTP::Monkeywrench
> HTTP::Monkeywrench is a test-harness application to test the integrity of a user's path through a web site.

Apache::Recorder *and* HTTP::RecordedSession
> Apache::Recorder (available from CPAN) is a mod_perl handler that records an HTTP session and stores it on the web server's filesystem. HTTP::RecordedSession reads the recorded session from the filesystem and formats it for playback using HTTP::WebTest or HTTP::Monkeywrench. This is useful when writing acceptance and regression tests.

Many other benchmark utilities are available both for free and for money. If you find that none of these suits your needs, it's quite easy to roll your own utility. The easiest way to do this is to write a Perl script that uses the LWP::Parallel::UserAgent and Time::HiRes modules. The former module allows you to open many parallel connections and the latter allows you to take time samples with microsecond resolution.

Perl Code Benchmarking

If you want to benchmark your Perl code, you can use the Benchmark module. For example, let's say that our code generates many long strings and finally prints them out. We wonder what is the most efficient way to handle this task—we can try to concatenate the strings into a single string, or we can store them (or references to them) in an array before generating the output. The easiest way to get an answer is to try each approach, so we wrote the benchmark shown in Example 9-3.

Example 9-3. strings_benchmark.pl

```perl
use Benchmark;
use Symbol;
my $fh = gensym;

open $fh, ">/dev/null" or die $!;

my($one, $two, $three) = map { $_ x 4096 } 'a'..'c';

timethese(100_000, {
    ref_array => sub {
        my @a;
        push @a, \($one, $two, $three);
        my_print(@a);
    },
    array => sub {
        my @a;
        push @a, $one, $two, $three;
        my_print(@a);
    },
    concat => sub {
        my $s;
        $s .= $one;
        $s .= $two;
        $s .= $three;
        my_print($s);
    },
});
sub my_print {
    for (@_) {
        print $fh ref($_) ? $$_ : $_;
    }
}
```

As you can see, we generate three big strings and then use three anonymous functions to print them out. The first one (ref_array) stores the references to the strings in an array. The second function (array) stores the strings themselves in an array. The third function (concat) concatenates the three strings into a single string. At the end of each function we print the stored data. If the data structure includes references, they are first dereferenced (relevant for the first function only). We execute each subtest 100,000 times to get more precise results. If your results are too close and are below 1 CPU clocks, you should try setting the number of iterations to a bigger number. Let's execute this benchmark and check the results:

```
panic% perl strings_benchmark.pl
Benchmark: timing 100000 iterations of array, concat, ref_array...
     array:  2 wallclock secs ( 2.64 usr +  0.23 sys =  2.87 CPU)
    concat:  2 wallclock secs ( 1.95 usr +  0.07 sys =  2.02 CPU)
 ref_array:  3 wallclock secs ( 2.02 usr +  0.22 sys =  2.24 CPU)
```

First, it's important to remember that the reported wallclock times can be misleading and thus should not be relied upon. If during one of the subtests your computer was more heavily loaded than during the others, it's possible that this particular subtest will take more wallclocks to complete, but this doesn't matter for our purposes. What matters is the CPU clocks, which tell us the exact amount of CPU time each test took to complete. You can also see the fraction of the CPU allocated to *usr* and *sys*, which stand for the user and kernel (system) modes, respectively. This tells us what proportions of the time the subtest has spent running code in user mode and in kernel mode.

Now that you know how to read the results, you can see that concatenation outperforms the two array functions, because concatenation only has to grow the size of the string, whereas array functions have to extend the array and, during the print, iterate over it. Moreover, the array method also creates a string copy before appending the new element to the array, which makes it the slowest method of the three.

Let's make the strings much smaller. Using our original code with a small correction:

```
my($one, $two, $three) = map { $_ x 8 } 'a'..'c';
```

we now make three strings of 8 characters, instead of 4,096. When we execute the modified version we get the following picture:

```
Benchmark: timing 100000 iterations of array, concat, ref_array...
     array:  1 wallclock secs ( 1.59 usr +  0.01 sys =  1.60 CPU)
    concat:  1 wallclock secs ( 1.16 usr +  0.04 sys =  1.20 CPU)
 ref_array:  2 wallclock secs ( 1.66 usr +  0.05 sys =  1.71 CPU)
```

Concatenation still wins, but this time the array method is a bit faster than ref_array, because the overhead of taking string references before pushing them into an array and dereferencing them afterward during print( ) is bigger than the overhead of making copies of the short strings.

As these examples show, you should benchmark your code by rewriting parts of the code and comparing the benchmarks of the modified and original versions.

Also note that benchmarks can give different results under different versions of the Perl interpreter, because each version might have built-in optimizations for some of the functions. Therefore, if you upgrade your Perl interpreter, it's best to benchmark your code again. You may see a completely different result.

Another Perl code benchmarking method is to use the Time::HiRes module, which allows you to get the runtime of your code with a fine-grained resolution of the order of microseconds. Let's compare a few methods to multiply two numbers (see Example 9-4).

Example 9-4. hires_benchmark_time.pl

```
use Time::HiRes qw(gettimeofday tv_interval);
my %subs = (
    obvious => sub {
        $_[0] * $_[1]
    },
    decrement => sub {
```

Example 9-4. hires_benchmark_time.pl (continued)

```
        my $a = shift;
        my $c = 0;
        $c += $_[0] while $a--;
        $c;
    },
);

for my $x (qw(10 100)) {
    for my $y (qw(10 100)) {
        for (sort keys %subs) {
            my $start_time = [ gettimeofday ];
            my $z = $subs{$_}->($x,$y);
            my $end_time = [ gettimeofday ];
            my $elapsed = tv_interval($start_time,$end_time);
            printf "%-9.9s: Doing %3.d * %3.d = %5.d took %f seconds\n",
                $_, $x, $y, $z, $elapsed;
        }
        print "\n";
    }
}
```

We have used two methods here. The first (obvious) is doing the normal multiplication, $z=$x*$y. The second method is using a trick of the systems where there is no built-in multiplication function available; it uses only the addition and subtraction operations. The trick is to add $x for $y times (as you did in school before you learned multiplication).

When we execute the code, we get:

```
panic% perl hires_benchmark_time.pl
decrement: Doing  10 *  10 =   100 took 0.000064 seconds
obvious  : Doing  10 *  10 =   100 took 0.000016 seconds

decrement: Doing  10 * 100 =  1000 took 0.000029 seconds
obvious  : Doing  10 * 100 =  1000 took 0.000013 seconds

decrement: Doing 100 *  10 =  1000 took 0.000098 seconds
obvious  : Doing 100 *  10 =  1000 took 0.000013 seconds

decrement: Doing 100 * 100 = 10000 took 0.000093 seconds
obvious  : Doing 100 * 100 = 10000 took 0.000012 seconds
```

Note that if the processor is very fast or the OS has a coarse time-resolution granularity (i.e., cannot count microseconds) you may get zeros as reported times. This of course shouldn't be the case with applications that do a lot more work.

If you run this benchmark again, you will notice that the numbers will be slightly different. This is because the code measures absolute time, not the real execution time (unlike the previous benchmark using the Benchmark module).

You can see that doing 10*100 as opposed to 100*10 results in quite different results for the decrement method. When the arguments are 10*100, the code performs the *add 100* operation only 10 times, which is obviously faster than the second invocation, 100*10, where the code performs the *add 10* operation 100 times. However, the normal multiplication takes a constant time.

Let's run the same code using the Benchmark module, as shown in Example 9-5.

Example 9-5. hires_benchmark.pl

```
use Benchmark;
my %subs = (
    obvious => sub {
        $_[0] * $_[1]
    },
    decrement => sub {
        my $a = shift;
        my $c = 0;
        $c += $_[0] while $a--;
        $c;
    },
);

for my $x (qw(10 100)) {
    for my $y (qw(10 100)) {
        print "\nTesting $x*$y\n";
        timethese(300_000, {
            obvious   => sub {$subs{obvious}->($x, $y)  },
            decrement => sub {$subs{decrement}->($x, $y)},
        });
    }
}
```

Now let's execute the code:

```
panic% perl hires_benchmark.pl
Testing 10*10
Benchmark: timing 300000 iterations of decrement, obvious...
  decrement:  4 wallclock secs ( 4.27 usr +  0.09 sys =  4.36 CPU)
    obvious:  1 wallclock secs ( 0.91 usr +  0.00 sys =  0.91 CPU)

Testing 10*100
Benchmark: timing 300000 iterations of decrement, obvious...
  decrement:  5 wallclock secs ( 3.74 usr +  0.00 sys =  3.74 CPU)
    obvious:  0 wallclock secs ( 0.87 usr +  0.00 sys =  0.87 CPU)

Testing 100*10
Benchmark: timing 300000 iterations of decrement, obvious...
  decrement: 24 wallclock secs (24.41 usr +  0.00 sys = 24.41 CPU)
    obvious:  2 wallclock secs ( 0.86 usr +  0.00 sys =  0.86 CPU)
```

```
Testing 100*100
Benchmark: timing 300000 iterations of decrement, obvious...
 decrement: 23 wallclock secs (23.64 usr +  0.07 sys = 23.71 CPU)
    obvious:  0 wallclock secs ( 0.80 usr +  0.00 sys =  0.80 CPU)
```

You can observe exactly the same behavior, but this time using the average CPU clocks collected over 300,000 tests and not the absolute time collected over a single sample. Obviously, you can use the Time::HiRes module in a benchmark that will execute the same code many times to report a more precise runtime, similar to the way the Benchmark module reports the CPU time.

However, there are situations where getting the average speed is not enough. For example, if you're testing some code with various inputs and calculate only the average processing times, you may not notice that for some particular inputs the code is very ineffective. Let's say that the average is 0.72 seconds. This doesn't reveal the possible fact that there were a few cases when it took 20 seconds to process the input. Therefore, getting the variance[*] in addition to the average may be important. Unfortunately Benchmark.pm cannot provide such results—system timers are rarely good enough to measure fast code that well, even on single-user systems, so you must run the code thousands of times to get any significant CPU time. If the code is slow enough that each single execution can be measured, most likely you can use the profiling tools.

Process Memory Measurements

A very important aspect of performance tuning is to make sure that your applications don't use too much memory. If they do, you cannot run many servers, and therefore in most cases, under a heavy load the overall performance will be degraded. The code also may leak memory, which is even worse, since if the same process serves many requests and more memory is used after each request, after a while all the RAM will be used and the machine will start swapping (i.e., using the swap partition). This is a very undesirable situation, because when the system starts to swap, the performance will suffer badly. If memory consumption grows without bound, it will eventually lead to a machine crash.

The simplest way to figure out how big the processes are and to see whether they are growing is to watch the output of the *top(1)* or *ps(1)* utilities.

For example, here is the output of *top(1)*:

```
8:51am  up 66 days,  1:44,  1 user,  load average: 1.09, 2.27, 2.61
  95 processes: 92 sleeping, 3 running, 0 zombie, 0 stopped
  CPU states: 54.0% user,  9.4% system,  1.7% nice, 34.7% idle
```

---

[*] See Chapter 15 in the book *Mastering Algorithms with Perl*, by Jon Orwant, Jarkko Hietaniemi, and John Macdonald (O'Reilly). Of course, there are gazillions of statistics-related books and resources on the Web; *http://mathforum.org/* and *http://mathworld.wolfram.com/* are two good starting points for anything that has to do with mathematics.

```
Mem:   387664K av, 309692K used,   77972K free, 111092K shrd,   70944K buff
Swap: 128484K av,  11176K used, 117308K free                   170824K cached

  PID USER PRI NI  SIZE   RSS SHARE STAT LIB %CPU %MEM    TIME COMMAND
29225 nobody 0  0  9760  9760  7132 S        0 12.5  2.5  0:00 httpd_perl
29220 nobody 0  0  9540  9540  7136 S        0  9.0  2.4  0:00 httpd_perl
29215 nobody 1  0  9672  9672  6884 S        0  4.6  2.4  0:01 httpd_perl
29255 root   7  0  1036  1036   824 R        0  3.2  0.2  0:01 top
  376 squid  0  0 15920   14M   556 S      0  1.1  3.8 209:12 squid
29227 mysql  5  5  1892  1892   956 S N      0  1.1  0.4  0:00 mysqld
29223 mysql  5  5  1892  1892   956 S N      0  0.9  0.4  0:00 mysqld
29234 mysql  5  5  1892  1892   956 S N      0  0.9  0.4  0:00 mysqld
```

This starts with overall information about the system and then displays the most active processes at the given moment. So, for example, if we look at the *httpd_perl* processes, we can see the size of the resident (RSS) and shared (SHARE) memory segments.* This sample was taken on a production server running Linux.

But of course we want to see all the apache/mod_perl processes, and that's where *ps(1)* comes in. The options of this utility vary from one Unix flavor to another, and some flavors provide their own tools. Let's check the information about mod_perl processes:

```
panic% ps -o pid,user,rss,vsize,%cpu,%mem,ucomm -C httpd_perl
  PID USER       RSS   VSZ %CPU %MEM COMMAND
29213 root      8584 10264  0.0  2.2 httpd_perl
29215 nobody    9740 11316  1.0  2.5 httpd_perl
29216 nobody    9668 11252  0.7  2.4 httpd_perl
29217 nobody    9824 11408  0.6  2.5 httpd_perl
29218 nobody    9712 11292  0.6  2.5 httpd_perl
29219 nobody    8860 10528  0.0  2.2 httpd_perl
29220 nobody    9616 11200  0.5  2.4 httpd_perl
29221 nobody    8860 10528  0.0  2.2 httpd_perl
29222 nobody    8860 10528  0.0  2.2 httpd_perl
29224 nobody    8860 10528  0.0  2.2 httpd_perl
29225 nobody    9760 11340  0.7  2.5 httpd_perl
29235 nobody    9524 11104  0.4  2.4 httpd_perl
```

Now you can see the resident (RSS) and virtual (VSZ) memory segments (and the shared memory segment if you ask for it) of all mod_perl processes. Please refer to the *top(1)* and *ps(1)* manpages for more information.

You probably agree that using *top(1)* and *ps(1)* is cumbersome if you want to use memory-size sampling during the benchmark test. We want to have a way to print memory sizes during program execution at the desired places. The GTop module, which is a Perl glue to the libgtop library, is exactly what we need for that task.

You are fortunate if you run Linux or any of the BSD flavors, as the libgtop C library from the GNOME project is supported on those platforms. This library provides an

---

* You can tell *top* to sort the entries by memory usage by pressing *M* while viewing the *top* screen.

API to access various system-wide and process-specific information. (Some other operating systems also support libgtop.)

With GTop, if we want to print the memory size of the current process we'd just execute:

```
use GTop ();
print GTop->new->proc_mem($$)->size;
```

$$ is the Perl special variable that gives the process ID (PID) of the currently running process.

If you want to look at some other process and you have the necessary permission, just replace $$ with the other process's PID and you can peek inside it. For example, to check the shared size, you'd do:

```
print GTop->new->proc_mem($$)->share;
```

Let's try to run some tests:

```
panic% perl -MGTop -e 'my $g = GTop->new->proc_mem($$); \
  printf "%5.5s => %d\n",$_,$g->$_() for qw(size share vsize rss)'

 size => 1519616
share => 1073152
vsize => 2637824
  rss => 1515520
```

We have just printed the memory sizes of the process: the real, the shared, the virtual, and the resident (not swapped out).

There are many other things GTop can do for you—please refer to its manpage for more information. We are going to use this module in our performance tuning tips later in this chapter, so you will be able to exercise it a lot.

If you are running a true BSD system, you may use BSD::Resource::getrusage instead of GTop. For example:

```
print "used memory = ".(BSD::Resource::getrusage)[2]."\n"
```

For more information, refer to the BSD::Resource manpage.

The Apache::VMonitor module, with the help of the GTop module, allows you to watch all your system information using your favorite browser, from anywhere in the world, without the need to *telnet* to your machine. If you are wondering what information you can retrieve with GTop, you should look at Apache::VMonitor, as it utilizes a large part of the API GTop provides.

Apache::Status and Measuring Code Memory Usage

The Apache::Status module allows you to peek inside the Perl interpreter in the Apache web server. You can watch the status of the Perl interpreter: what modules and Registry scripts are compiled in, the content of variables, the sizes of the subroutines, and more.

To configure this module you should add the following section to your *httpd.conf* file:

```
<Location /perl-status>
    SetHandler perl-script
    PerlHandler +Apache::Status
</Location>
```

and restart Apache.

Now when you access the location *http://localhost:8000/perl-status* you will see a menu (shown in Figure 9-1) that leads you into various sections that will allow you to explore the innards of the Perl interpreter.

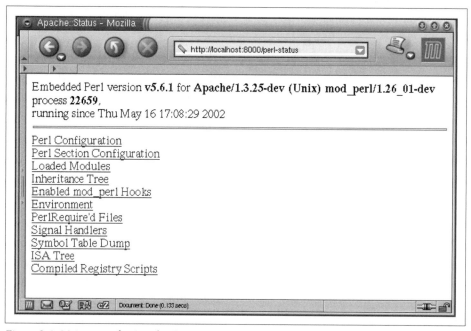

Figure 9-1. Main menu for Apache::Status

When you use this module for debugging, it's best to run the web server in single-server mode (*httpd -X*). If you don't you can get confused, because various child processes might show different information. It's simpler to work with a single process.

To enable the Apache::Status modules to present more exotic information, make sure that the following modules are installed: Data::Dumper, Apache::Peek, Devel::Peek, B::LexInfo, B::Deparse, B::Terse, and B::TerseSize. Some of these modules are bundled with Perl; others should be installed by hand.

When you have the aforementioned modules installed, add these directives to your *httpd.conf* file:

```
PerlSetVar StatusOptionsAll On
PerlSetVar StatusDumper On
PerlSetVar StatusPeek On
PerlSetVar StatusLexInfo On
PerlSetVar StatusDeparse On
PerlSetVar StatusDeparseOptions "-p -sC"
PerlSetVar StatusTerse On
PerlSetVar StatusTerseSize On
PerlSetVar StatusTerseSizeMainSummary On
```

and restart Apache. Alternatively, if you enable all the options, you can use the option StatusOptionsAll to replace all the options that can be On or Off, so you end up with just these two lines:

```
PerlSetVar StatusOptionsAll On
PerlSetVar StatusDeparseOptions "-p -sC"
```

When you explore the contents of the compiled Perl module or Registry script, at the bottom of the screen you will see a Memory Usage link. When you click on it, you will be presented with a list of funtions in the package. For each function, the size and the number of OP codes will be shown.

For example, let's create a module that prints the contents of the %ENV hash. This module is shown in Example 9-6.

Example 9-6. Book/DumpEnv.pm

```
package Book::DumpEnv;
use strict;
use Apache::Constants qw(:common);
sub handler {
    shift->send_http_header('text/plain');
    print map {"$_ => $ENV{$_}\n"} keys %ENV;
    return OK;
}
1;
```

Now add the following to *httpd.conf*:

```
<Location /dumpenv>
    SetHandler perl-script
    PerlHandler +Book::DumpEnv
</Location>
```

Restart the server in single-server mode (*httpd -X*), request the URL *http://localhost:8000/dumpenv*, and you will see that the contents of %ENV are displayed.

Now it's time to peek inside the Book::DumpEnv package inside the Perl interpreter. Issue the request to *http://localhost:8000/perl-status*, click on the "Loaded Modules" menu item, and locate Book::DumpEnv on the displayed page. Click on it to request a page at the URI *http://localhost:8000/perl-status?Book::DumpEnv*. You will see the screen shown in Figure 9-2.

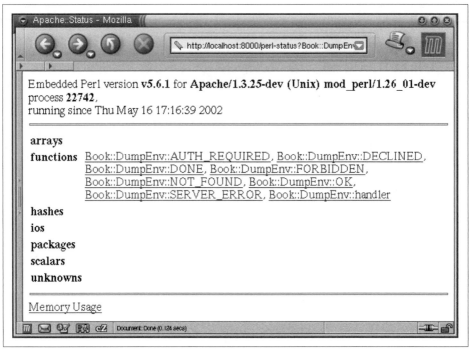

Figure 9-2. Data structures compiled in the module

You can see seven functions that were imported with:

```
use Apache::Constants qw(:common);
```

and a single function that we have created, called handler. No other Perl variable types were created in the package Book::DumpEnv.

Now click on the "Memory Usage" link at the bottom of the page. The screen shown in Figure 9-3 will be rendered.

So you can see that Book::DumpEnv takes 3,427 bytes in memory, whereas the handler function takes 2,362 bytes.

Is this all? No, we can go even further inside the code and learn the syntax tree size (i.e., what opcodes construct each line of the source code and how many bytes each source-code line consumes). If we click on handler we will see the syntax tree of this function, and how much memory each Perl OPcode and line of code take. For example, in Figure 9-4 we can see that line 7, which corresponds to this source-code line in *Book/DumpEnv.pm*:

```
7:    return OK;
```

takes up 136 bytes of memory.

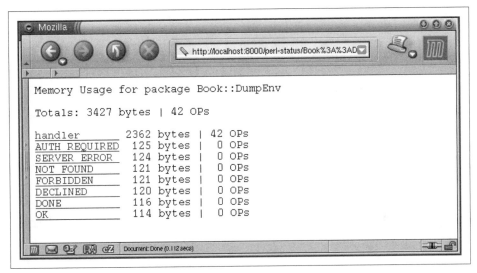

Figure 9-3. Book::DumpEnv memory usage

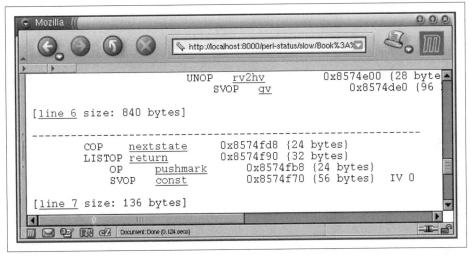

Figure 9-4. Per line and Perl OPcode memory usage

We found the corresponding source-code line by clicking the "line 7" hyperlink shown in Figure 9-4, which displays the source code of the module with the relevant line highlighted (see Figure 9-5).

Now you should be able to to find out how much memory each subroutine or even each individual source line of Perl code consumes. This will allow you to optimize memory usage by comparing several implemenations of the same algorithm and choosing the one that consumes the smallest amount of memory.

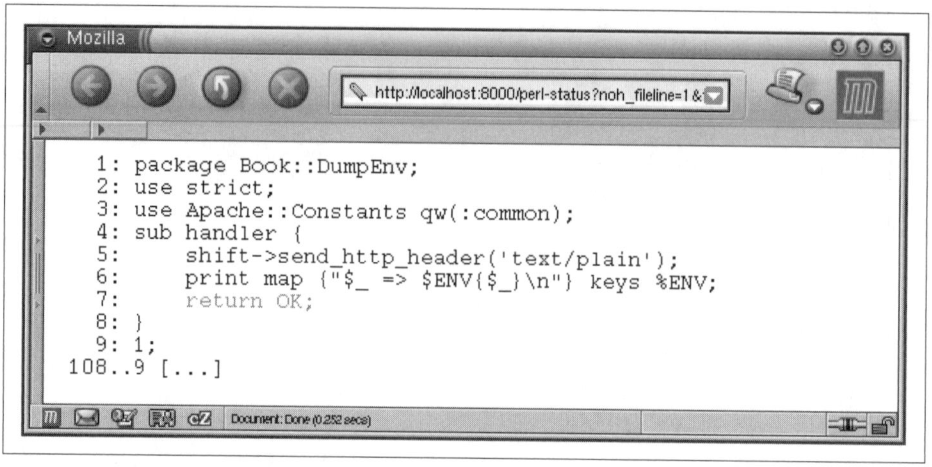
Mozilla
http://localhost:8000/perl-status?noh_fileline=1&
1: package Book::DumpEnv;
2: use strict;
3: use Apache::Constants qw(:common);
4: sub handler {
5:     shift->send_http_header('text/plain');
6:     print map {"$_ => $ENV{$_}\n"} keys %ENV;
7:     return OK;
8: }
9: 1;
108..9 [...]
Document: Done (0.252 secs)

Figure 9-5. Source code corresponding to the OPcodes

Code Profiling Techniques

The profiling process helps you to determine which subroutines (or just snippets of code) take longest to execute and which subroutines are called most often. You will probably want to optimize these.

When do you need to profile your code? You do that when you suspect that some part of your code is called very often and maybe there is a need to optimize it, which could significantly improve the overall performance.

Profiling with Devel::DProf

`Devel::DProf` collects information on the execution time of a Perl script and of the subroutines in that script.

Let's take for example the `diagnostics` pragma and measure the impact of its usage on the program compilation and execution speed. This pragma extends the terse diagnostics normally emitted by both the Perl compiler and the Perl interpreter, augmenting them with the more verbose and endearing descriptions found in the *perldiag* manpage. We have claimed that this pragma should not be used on a production server. We are going to use `Devel::DProf` to explain our claim.

We will run a benchmark, once with diagnostics enabled and once disabled, on a subroutine called `test_code()`.

The code inside the subroutine does either a lexical or a numeric comparison of two strings. It assigns one string to another if the condition tests true, but the condition is always false. To demonstrate the `diagnostics` pragma overhead, the comparison operator that we use in Example 9-7 is intentionally wrong. It should be a string comparison (eq), and we use a numeric one (= =).

Example 9-7. bench_diagnostics.pl

```perl
use Benchmark;
use diagnostics;
use strict;

my $count = 50000;

disable diagnostics;
my $t1 = timeit($count,\&test_code);

enable  diagnostics;
my $t2 = timeit($count,\&test_code);

print "Off: ",timestr($t1),"\n";
print "On : ",timestr($t2),"\n";

sub test_code {
    my ($a, $b) = qw(foo bar);
    my $c;
    if ($a == $b) {
        $c = $a;
    }
}
```

For only a few lines of code we get:

```
Off:  1 wallclock secs ( 0.81 usr +  0.00 sys =  0.81 CPU)
On : 13 wallclock secs (12.54 usr +  0.01 sys = 12.55 CPU)
```

With diagnostics enabled, the subroutine test_code( ) is 16 times slower (12.55/0.81: remember that we're talking in CPU time, not wallclock seconds) than with diagnostics disabled!

Now let's fix the comparison the way it should be, by replacing == with eq, so we get:

```perl
my ($a, $b) = qw(foo bar);
my $c;
if ($a eq $b) {
    $c = $a;
}
```

and run the same benchmark again:

```
Off:  1 wallclock secs ( 0.57 usr +  0.00 sys =  0.57 CPU)
On :  1 wallclock secs ( 0.56 usr +  0.00 sys =  0.56 CPU)
```

Now there is no overhead at all. The diagnostics pragma slows things down only when warnings are generated.

After we have verified that using the diagnostics pragma might add a big overhead to execution runtime, let's use code profiling to understand why this happens. We use Devel::DProf to profile the code shown in Example 9-8.

Example 9-8. diagnostics.pl

```perl
use diagnostics;

test_code();
sub test_code {
    my($a, $b) = qw(foo bar);
    my $c;
    if ($a == $b) {
        $c = $a;
    }
}
```

Run it with the profiler enabled, and then create the profiling statistics with the help of *dprofpp*:

```
panic% perl -d:DProf diagnostics.pl
panic% dprofpp

Total Elapsed Time = 0.342236 Seconds
  User+System Time = 0.335420 Seconds
Exclusive Times
%Time ExclSec CumulS #Calls sec/call Csec/c  Name
 92.1  0.309  0.358      1  0.3089 0.3578  main::BEGIN
 14.9  0.050  0.039   3161  0.0000 0.0000  diagnostics::unescape
 2.98  0.010  0.010      2  0.0050 0.0050  diagnostics::BEGIN
 0.00  0.000 -0.000      2  0.0000      -  Exporter::import
 0.00  0.000 -0.000      2  0.0000      -  Exporter::export
 0.00  0.000 -0.000      1  0.0000      -  Config::BEGIN
 0.00  0.000 -0.000      1  0.0000      -  Config::TIEHASH
 0.00  0.000 -0.000      2  0.0000      -  Config::FETCH
 0.00  0.000 -0.000      1  0.0000      -  diagnostics::import
 0.00  0.000 -0.000      1  0.0000      -  main::test_code
 0.00  0.000 -0.000      2  0.0000      -  diagnostics::warn_trap
 0.00  0.000 -0.000      2  0.0000      -  diagnostics::splainthis
 0.00  0.000 -0.000      2  0.0000      -  diagnostics::transmo
 0.00  0.000 -0.000      2  0.0000      -  diagnostics::shorten
 0.00  0.000 -0.000      2  0.0000      -  diagnostics::autodescribe
```

It's not easy to see what is responsible for this enormous overhead, even if `main::BEGIN` seems to be running most of the time. To get the full picture we must see the OPs tree, which shows us who calls whom, so we run:

```
panic% dprofpp -T
```

The output is:

```
main::BEGIN
  diagnostics::BEGIN
    Exporter::import
       Exporter::export
  diagnostics::BEGIN
    Config::BEGIN
    Config::TIEHASH
    Exporter::import
```

```
       Exporter::export
  Config::FETCH
  Config::FETCH
  diagnostics::unescape
  ....................
  3159 times [diagnostics::unescape] snipped
  ....................
  diagnostics::unescape
  diagnostics::import
diagnostics::warn_trap
  diagnostics::splainthis
     diagnostics::transmo
     diagnostics::shorten
     diagnostics::autodescribe
main::test_code
  diagnostics::warn_trap
    diagnostics::splainthis
       diagnostics::transmo
       diagnostics::shorten
       diagnostics::autodescribe
  diagnostics::warn_trap
    diagnostics::splainthis
       diagnostics::transmo
       diagnostics::shorten
      diagnostics::autodescribe
```

So we see that 2 executions of diagnostics::BEGIN and 3,161 of diagnostics::unescape are responsible for most of the running overhead.

If we comment out the diagnostics module, we get:

```
Total Elapsed Time = 0.079974 Seconds
  User+System Time = 0.059974 Seconds
Exclusive Times
%Time ExclSec CumulS #Calls sec/call Csec/c  Name
 0.00   0.000 -0.000      1  0.0000       -  main::test_code
```

It is possible to profile code running under mod_perl with the Devel::DProf module, available on CPAN. However, you must have PerlChildExitHandler enabled during the mod_perl build process. When the server is started, Devel::DProf installs an END block to write the *tmon.out* file. This block will be called at server shutdown. Here is how to start and stop a server with the profiler enabled:

```
panic% setenv PERL5OPT -d:DProf
panic% httpd -X -d `pwd` &
... make some requests to the server here ...
panic% kill `cat logs/httpd.pid`
panic% unsetenv PERL5OPT
panic% dprofpp
```

The Devel::DProf package is a Perl code profiler. It will collect information on the execution time of a Perl script and of the subroutines in that script (remember that print( ) and map( ) are just like any other subroutines you write, but they come bundled with Perl!).

Another approach is to use `Apache::DProf`, which hooks `Devel::DProf` into mod_perl. The `Apache::DProf` module will run a `Devel::DProf` profiler inside the process and write the *tmon.out* file in the directory *$ServerRoot/logs/dprof/$$* (make sure that it's writable by the server!) when the process is shut down (where *$$* is the PID of the process). All it takes to activate this module is to modify *httpd.conf*.

You can test for a command-line switch in *httpd.conf*. For example, to test if the server was started with *-DPERLDPROF*, use:

```
<Location /perl>
    SetHandler perl-script
    PerlHandler Apache::Registry
    <IfDefine PERLDPROF>
        PerlModule Apache::DProf
    </IfDefine>
</Location>
```

And to activate profiling, use:

```
panic% httpd -X -DPERLDPROF &
```

Remember that any `PerlHandler` that was pulled in before `Apache::DProf` in the *httpd. conf* or *startup.pl* file will not have code-debugging information inserted. To run *dprofpp*, *chdir* to *$ServerRoot/logs/dprof/$$*[*] and run:

```
panic% dprofpp
```

Use the command-line options for *dropfpp(1)* if a nondefault output is desired, as explained in the *dropfpp* manpage. You might especially want to look at the *-r* switch to display wallclock times (more relevant in a web-serving environment) and the *-l* switch to sort by number of subroutine calls.

If you are running Perl 5.6.0 or higher, take a look at the new module `Devel::Profiler` (Version 0.04 as of this writing), which is supposed to be a drop-in replacement for `Apache::DProf`, with improved functionality and stability.

Profiling with Devel::SmallProf

The `Devel::SmallProf` profiler is focused on the time taken for a program run on a line-by-line basis. It is called "small" because it's supposed to impose very little extra load on the machine (speed- and memory-wise) while profiling the code.

Let's take a look at the simple example shown in Example 9-9.

Example 9-9. table_gen.pl

```
for (1..1000) {
    my @rows = ( );
    push @rows, Tr(  map { td($_) } 'a'..'d' );
```

---

[*] Look up the `ServerRoot` directive's value in *httpd.conf* to figure out what your $ServerRoot is.

Example 9-9. table_gen.pl (continued)

```
    push @rows, Tr( map { td($_) } 'e'..'h' );
    my $var = table(@rows);
}
sub table { my @rows  = @_;    return "<table>\n@rows</table>\n";}
sub Tr    { my @cells = @_;    return "<tr>@cells</tr>\n";       }
sub td    { my $cell  = shift; return "<td>$cell</td>";         }
```

It creates the same HTML table in $var, with the cells of the table filled with single letters. The functions table( ), Tr( ), and td( ) insert the data into appropriate HTML tags. Notice that we have used Tr( ) and not tr( ), since the latter is a built-in Perl function, and we have used the same function name as in CGI.pm that does the same thing. If we print $var we will see something like this:

```
<table>
<tr><td>a</td> <td>b</td> <td>c</td> <td>d</td></tr>
<tr><td>e</td> <td>f</td> <td>g</td> <td>h</td></tr>
</table>
```

We have looped a thousand times through the same code in order to get a more precise speed measurement. If the code runs very quickly we won't be able to get any meaningful results from just one loop.

If we run this code with Devel::SmallProf:

```
panic% perl -d:SmallProf table_gen.pl
```

we get the following output in the autogenerated *smallprof.out* file:

```
count wall tm  cpu time line
 1001 0.003855 0.030000    1:  for (1..1000) {
 1000 0.004823 0.040000    2:      my @rows = ( );
 5000 0.272651 0.410000    3:      push @rows, Tr( map { td($_) }
 5000 0.267107 0.360000    4:      push @rows, Tr( map { td($_) }
 1000 0.067115 0.120000    5:      my $var = table(@rows);
    0 0.000000 0.000000    6:  }
 3000 0.033798 0.080000    7:  sub table { my @rows  = @_;    return
 6000 0.078491 0.120000    8:  sub Tr    { my @cells = @_;    return
24000 0.267353 0.490000    9:  sub td    { my $cell  = shift; return
    0 0.000000 0.000000   10:
```

We can see in the *CPU time* column that Perl spends most of its time in the td( ) function; it's also the code that's visited by Perl the most times. In this example we could find this out ourselves without much effort, but if the code is longer it will be harder to find the lines of code where Perl spends most of its time. So we sort the output by the third column as a numerical value, in descending order:

```
panic% sort -k 3nr,3 smallprof.out | less
24000 0.267353 0.490000    9:  sub td    { my $cell  = shift; return
 5000 0.272651 0.410000    3:      push @rows, Tr( map { td($_) }
 5000 0.267107 0.360000    4:      push @rows, Tr( map { td($_) }
 1000 0.067115 0.120000    5:      my $var = table(@rows);
 6000 0.078491 0.120000    8:  sub Tr    { my @cells = @_;    return
 3000 0.033798 0.080000    7:  sub table { my @rows  = @_;    return
```

```
1000 0.004823 0.040000    2:       my @rows = ( );
1001 0.003855 0.030000    1:   for (1..1000) {
```

According to the Devel::SmallProf manpage, the wallclock's measurements are fairly accurate (we suppose that they're correct on an unloaded machine), but CPU clock time is always more accurate. That's because if it takes more than one CPU time slice for a directive to complete, the time that some other process uses CPU is counted in the wallclock counts. Since the load on the same machine may vary greatly from moment to moment, it's possible that if we rerun the same test a few times we will get inconsistent results.

Let's try to improve the td( ) function and at the same time the Tr( ) and table( ) functions. We will not copy the passed arguments, but we will use them directly in all three functions. Example 9-10 shows the new version of our script.

Example 9-10. table_gen2.pl

```
for (1..1000) {
    my @rows = ( );
    push @rows, Tr( map { td($_) } 'a'..'d' );
    push @rows, Tr( map { td($_) } 'e'..'h' );
    my $var = table(@rows);
}
sub table { return "<table>\n@_</table>\n";}
sub Tr    { return "<tr>@_</tr>\n";        }
sub td    { return "<td>@_</td>";          }
```

Now let's rerun the code with the profiler:

```
panic% perl -d:SmallProf table_gen2.pl
```

The results are much better now—only 0.34 CPU clocks are spent in td( ), versus 0.49 in the earlier run:

```
panic% sort -k 3nr,3 smallprof.out | less
 5000 0.279138 0.400000   4:       push @rows, Tr(  map { td($_) }
16000 0.241350 0.340000   9:   sub td    { return "<td>@_</td>";          }
 5000 0.269940 0.320000   3:       push @rows, Tr(  map { td($_) }
 4000 0.050050 0.130000   8:   sub Tr    { return "<tr>@_</tr>\n";        }
 1000 0.065324 0.080000   5:       my $var = table(@rows);
 1000 0.006650 0.010000   2:       my @rows = ( );
 2000 0.020314 0.030000   7:   sub table{ return "<table>\n@_</table>\n";}
 1001 0.006165 0.030000   1:   for (1..1000) {
```

You will also notice that Devel::SmallProf reports that the functions were executed different numbers of times in the two runs. That's because in our original example all three functions had two statements on each line, but in the improved version they each had only one. Devel::SmallProf looks at the code after it's been parsed and optimized by Perl—thus, if some optimizations took place, it might not be exactly the same as the code that you wrote.

In most cases you will probably find `Devel::DProf` more useful than `Devel::SmallProf`, as it allows you to analyze the code by subroutine and not by line.

Just as there is the `Apache::DProf` equivalent for `Devel::DProf`, there is the `Apache::SmallProf` equivalent for `Devel::SmallProf`. It uses a configuration similar to `Apache::DProf`—i.e., it is registered as a `PerlFixupHandler`—but it also requires `Apache::DB`. Therefore, to use it you should add the following configuration to *httpd.conf*:

```
<Perl>
    if (Apache->define('PERLSMALLPROF')) {
        require Apache::DB;
        Apache::DB->init;
    }
</Perl>

<Location /perl>
    SetHandler perl-script
    PerlHandler Apache::Registry
    <IfDefine PERLSMALLPROF>
        PerlFixupHandler Apache::SmallProf
    </IfDefine>
</Location>
```

Now start the server:

```
panic% httpd -X -DPERLSMALLPROF &
```

This will activate `Apache::SmallProf::handler` during the request. As a result, the profile files will be written to the *$ServerRoot/logs/smallprof/* directory. Unlike with `Devel::SmallProf`, the profile is split into several files based on package name. For example, if `CGI.pm` was used, one of the generated profile files will be called *CGI.pm.prof*.

References

- The diagnostics pragma is a part of the Perl distribution. See *perldoc diagnostics* for more information about the program, and *perldoc perldiag* for Perl diagnostics; this is the source of this pragma's information.
- *ab(1)* (ApacheBench) comes bundled with the Apache web server and is available from *http://httpd.apache.org/*.
- *httperf(1)* is available from *http://www.hpl.hp.com/personal/David_Mosberger./httperf.html*.
- *http_load(1)* is available from *http://www.acme.com/software/http_load/*.
- BenchWeb (*http://www.netlib.org/benchweb/*) is a good starting point for finding information about computer system performance benchmarks, benchmark results, and benchmark code.

- The libgtop library (*ftp://ftp.gnome.org/pub/GNOME/stable/sources/gtop/*) is a part of the GNOME project (*http://www.gnome.org/*). Also try *http://fr.rpmfind. net/linux/rpm2html/search.php?query=libgtop*.

- Chapter 3 of *Web Performance Tuning*, by Patrick Killelea (O'Reilly).

- Chapter 9 of *mod_perl Developer's Cookbook*, by Geoffrey Young, Paul Lindner, and Randy Kobes (Sams).

CHAPTER 10

Improving Performance with Shared Memory and Proper Forking

In this chapter we will talk about two issues that play an important role in optimizing server performance: sharing memory and forking.

Firstly, mod_perl Apache processes can become quite large, and it is therefore very important to make sure that the memory used by the Apache processes is shared between them as much as possible.

Secondly, if you need the Apache processes to fork new processes, it is important to perform the fork( ) calls in the proper way.

Sharing Memory

The sharing of memory is a very important factor. If your OS supports it (and most sane systems do), a lot of memory can be saved by sharing it between child processes. This is possible only when code is preloaded at server startup. However, during a child process's life, its memory pages tend to become unshared. Here is why.

There is no way to make Perl allocate memory so that (dynamic) variables land on different memory pages from constants or the rest of your code (which is really just data to the Perl interpreter), so the *copy-on-write* effect (explained in a moment) will hit almost at random.

If many modules are preloaded, you can trade off the memory that stays shared against the time for an occasional fork of a new Apache child by tuning the MaxRequestsPerChild Apache directive. Each time a child reaches this upper limit and dies, it will release its unshared pages. The new child will have to be forked, but it will share its fresh pages until it writes on them (when some variable gets modified).

The ideal is a point where processes usually restart before too much memory becomes unshared. You should take some measurements, to see if it makes a real difference and to find the range of reasonable values. If you have success with this tuning, bear in mind that the value of MaxRequestsPerChild will probably be specific to your situation and may change with changing circumstances.

349

It is very important to understand that the goal is not necessarily to have the highest MaxRequestsPerChild that you can. Having a child serve 300 requests on precompiled code is already a huge overall speedup. If this value also provides a substantial memory saving, that benefit may outweigh using a higher MaxRequestsPerChild value.

A newly forked child inherits the Perl interpreter from its parent. If most of the Perl code is preloaded at server startup, then most of this preloaded code is inherited from the parent process too. Because of this, less RAM has to be written to create the process, so it is ready to serve requests very quickly.

During the life of the child, its memory pages (which aren't really its own to start with—it uses the parent's pages) gradually get *dirty*—variables that were originally inherited and shared are updated or modified—and *copy-on-write* happens. This reduces the number of shared memory pages, thus increasing the memory requirement. Killing the child and spawning a new one allows the new child to use the pristine shared memory of the parent process.

The recommendation is that MaxRequestsPerChild should not be too large, or you will lose some of the benefit of sharing memory. With memory sharing in place, you can run many more servers than without it. In Chapter 11 we will devise a formula to calculate the optimum value for the MaxClients directive when sharing is taking place.

As we mentioned in Chapter 9, you can find the size of the shared memory by using the *ps(1)* or *top(1)* utilities, or by using the GTop module:

```
use GTop ();
print "Shared memory of the current process: ",
    GTop->new->proc_mem($$)->share, "\n";

print "Total shared memory: ",
    GTop->new->mem->share, "\n";
```

Calculating Real Memory Usage

We have shown how to measure the size of the process's shared memory, but we still want to know what the real memory usage is. Obviously this cannot be calculated simply by adding up the memory size of each process, because that wouldn't account for the shared memory.

On the other hand, we cannot just subtract the shared memory size from the total size to get the real memory-usage numbers, because in reality each process has a different history of processed requests, which makes different memory pages dirty; therefore, different processes have different memory pages shared with the parent process.

So how do we measure the real memory size used by all running web-server processes? It is a difficult task—probably too difficult to make it worthwhile to find the exact number—but we have found a way to get a fair approximation.

This is the calculation technique that we have devised:

1. Calculate all the unshared memory, by summing up the difference between shared and system memory of each process. To calculate a difference for a single process, use:

```
use GTop;
my $proc_mem = GTop->new->proc_mem($$);
my $diff     = $proc_mem->size - $proc_mem->share;
print "Difference is $diff bytes\n";
```

2. Add the system memory use of the parent process, which already includes the shared memory of all other processes.

Figure 10-1 helps to visualize this.

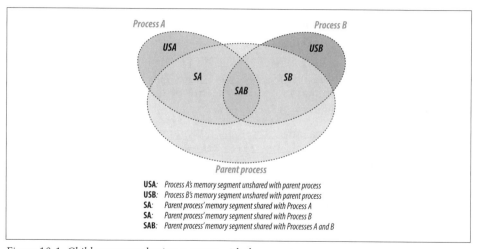

Figure 10-1. Child processes sharing memory with the parent process

The Apache::VMonitor module uses this technique to display real memory usage. In fact, it makes no separation between the parent and child processes. They are all counted indifferently using the following code:

```
use GTop ();
my $gtop = GTop->new;
my ($parent_pid, @child_pids) = some_code();
# add the parent proc memory size
my $total_real = $gtop->proc_mem($parent_pid)->size;
# add the unshared memory sizes
for my $pid (@child_pids) {
    my $proc_mem = $gtop->proc_mem($pid);
    $total_real += $proc_mem->size - $proc_mem->share;
}
```

Now $total_real contains approximately the amount of memory really used.

This method has been verified in the following way. We calculate the real memory used using the technique described above. We then look at the system memory report for the total memory usage. We then stop Apache and look at the total memory usage for a second time. We check that the system memory usage report indicates that the total memory used by the whole system has gone down by about the same number that we've calculated.

Note that some OSes do smart memory-page caching, so you may not see the memory usage decrease immediately when you stop the server, even though it is actually happening. Also, if your system is swapping, it's possible that your swap memory was used by the server as well as the real memory. Therefore, to get the verification right you should use a tool that reports real memory usage, cached memory, and swap memory. For example, on Linux you can use the *free* command. Run this command before and after stopping the server, then compare the numbers reported in the column called *free*.

Based on this logic we can devise a formula for calculating the maximum possible number of child processes, taking into account the shared memory. From now on, instead of adding the memory size of the parent process, we are going to add the maximum shared size of the child processes, and the result will be approximately the same. We do that approximation because the size of the parent process is usually unknown during the calculation.

Therefore, the formula to calculate the maximum number of child processes with minimum shared memory size of Min_Shared_RAM_per_Child MB that can run simultaneously on a machine that has a total RAM of Total_RAM MB available for the web server, and knowing the maximum process size, is:

$$MaxClients = \frac{Total\_RAM - Min\_Shared\_RAM\_per\_Child}{Max\_Process\_Size - Min\_Shared\_RAM\_per\_Child}$$

which can also be rewritten as:

$$MaxClients = \frac{Total\_RAM - Shared\_RAM\_per\_Child}{Max\_UnShared\_RAM\_per\_Child}$$

since the denominator is really the maximum possible amount of a child process's unshared memory.

In Chapter 14 we will see how we can enforce the values used in calculation during runtime.

Memory-Sharing Validation

How do you find out if the code you write is shared between processes or not? The code should remain shared, except when it is on a memory page used by variables that change. As you know, a variable becomes unshared when a process modifies its value, and so does the memory page it resides on, because the memory is shared in memory-page units.

Sometimes you have variables that use a lot of memory, and you consider their usage read-only and expect them to be shared between processes. However, certain operations that seemingly don't modify the variable values do modify things internally, causing the memory to become unshared.

Imagine that you have a 10 MB in-memory database that resides in a single variable, and you perform various operations on it and want to make sure that the variable is still shared. For example, if you do some regular expression (regex)–matching processing on this variable and you want to use the pos( ) function, will it make the variable unshared or not? If you access the variable once as a numerical value and once as a string value, will the variable become unshared?

The Apache::Peek module comes to the rescue.

Variable unsharing caused by regular expressions

Let's write a module called Book::MyShared, shown in Example 10-1, which we will preload at server startup so that all the variables of this module are initially shared by all children.

Example 10-1. Book/MyShared.pm

```
package Book::MyShared;
use Apache::Peek;

my $readonly = "Chris";

sub match    { $readonly =~ /\w/g;              }
sub print_pos { print "pos: ",pos($readonly),"\n";}
sub dump      { Dump($readonly);                }
1;
```

This module declares the package Book::MyShared, loads the Apache::Peek module and defines the lexically scoped $readonly variable. In most instances, the $readonly variable will be very large (perhaps a huge hash data structure), but here we will use a small variable to simplify this example.

The module also defines three subroutines: match( ), which does simple character matching; print_pos( ), which prints the current position of the matching engine inside the string that was last matched; and finally dump( ), which calls the Apache::Peek module's Dump( ) function to dump a raw Perl representation of the $readonly variable.

Now we write a script (Example 10-2) that prints the process ID (PID) and calls all three functions. The goal is to check whether pos( ) makes the variable dirty and therefore unshared.

Example 10-2. share_test.pl

```
use Book::MyShared;
print "Content-type: text/plain\n\n";
print "PID: $$\n";
Book::MyShared::match();
Book::MyShared::print_pos();
Book::MyShared::dump();
```

Before you restart the server, in *httpd.conf*, set:

```
MaxClients 2
```

for easier tracking. You need at least two servers to compare the printouts of the test program. Having more than two can make the comparison process harder.

Now open two browser windows and issue requests for this script in each window, so that you get different PIDs reported in the two windows and so that each process has processed a different number of requests for the *share_test.pl* script.

In the first window you will see something like this:

```
PID: 27040
pos: 1
SV = PVMG(0x853db20) at 0x8250e8c
  REFCNT = 3
  FLAGS = (PADBUSY,PADMY,SMG,POK,pPOK)
  IV = 0
  NV = 0
  PV = 0x8271af0 "Chris"\0
  CUR = 5
  LEN = 6
  MAGIC = 0x853dd80
    MG_VIRTUAL = &vtbl_mglob
    MG_TYPE = 'g'
    MG_LEN = 1
```

And in the second window:

```
PID: 27041
pos: 2
SV = PVMG(0x853db20) at 0x8250e8c
  REFCNT = 3
  FLAGS = (PADBUSY,PADMY,SMG,POK,pPOK)
  IV = 0
  NV = 0
  PV = 0x8271af0 "Chris"\0
  CUR = 5
  LEN = 6
  MAGIC = 0x853dd80
    MG_VIRTUAL = &vtbl_mglob
    MG_TYPE = 'g'
    MG_LEN = 2
```

All the addresses of the supposedly large data structure are the same (0x8250e8c and 0x8271af0)—therefore, the variable data structure is almost completely shared. The only difference is in the SV.MAGIC.MG_LEN record, which is not shared. This record is used to track where the last m//g match left off for the given variable, (e.g., by pos( )) and therefore it cannot be shared. See the *perlre* manpage for more information.

Given that the $readonly variable is a big one, its value is still shared between the processes, while part of the variable data structure is nonshared. The nonshared part is almost insignificant because it takes up very little memory space.

If you need to compare more than one variable, doing it by hand can be quite time consuming and error prone. Therefore, it's better to change the test script to dump the Perl datatypes into files (e.g., */tmp/dump.$$*, where *$$* is the PID of the process). Then you can use the *diff(1)* utility to see whether there is some difference.

Changing the dump( ) function to write the information to a file will do the job. Notice that we use Devel::Peek and not Apache::Peek, so we can easily reroute the STDERR stream into a file. In our example, when Devel::Peek tries to print to STDERR, it actually prints to our file. When we are done, we make sure to restore the original STDERR file handle.

The resulting code is shown in Example 10-3.

Example 10-3. Book/MyShared2.pm

```
package Book::MyShared2;
use Devel::Peek;

my $readonly = "Chris";

sub match     { $readonly =~ /\w/g;                }
sub print_pos { print "pos: ",pos($readonly),"\n";}
sub dump {
    my $dump_file = "/tmp/dump.$$";
    print "Dumping the data into $dump_file\n";
    open OLDERR, ">&STDERR";
    open STDERR, ">$dump_file" or die "Can't open $dump_file: $!";
    Dump($readonly);
    close STDERR ;
    open STDERR, ">&OLDERR";
}
1;
```

Now we modify our script to use the modified module, as shown in Example 10-4.

Example 10-4. share_test2.pl

```
use Book::MyShared2;
print "Content-type: text/plain\n\n";
print "PID: $$\n";
Book::MyShared2::match( );
Book::MyShared2::print_pos( );
Book::MyShared2::dump( );
```

Now we can run the script as before (with `MaxClients 2`). Two dump files will be created in the directory */tmp*. In our test these were created as */tmp/dump.1224* and */tmp/dump.1225*. When we run *diff(1)*:

```
panic% diff -u /tmp/dump.1224 /tmp/dump.1225
12c12
-        MG_LEN = 1
+        MG_LEN = 2
```

we see that the two padlists (of the variable `$readonly`) are different, as we observed before, when we did a manual comparison.

If we think about these results again, we come to the conclusion that there is no need for two processes to find out whether the variable gets modified (and therefore unshared). It's enough just to check the data structure twice, before the script was executed and again afterward. We can modify the `Book::MyShared2` module to dump the padlists into a different file after each invocation and then to run *diff(1)* on the two files.

Suppose you have some lexically scoped variables (i.e., variables declared with `my()`) in an `Apache::Registry` script. If you want to watch whether they get changed between invocations inside one particular process, you can use the `Apache::RegistryLexInfo` module. It does exactly that: it takes a snapshot of the padlist before and after the code execution and shows the difference between the two. This particular module was written to work with `Apache::Registry` scripts, so it won't work for loaded modules. Use the technique we described above for any type of variables in modules and scripts.

Another way of ensuring that a scalar is read-only and therefore shareable is to use either the `constant` pragma or the `readonly` pragma, as shown in Example 10-5. But then you won't be able to make calls that alter the variable even a little, such as in the example that we just showed, because it will be a true constant variable and you will get a compile-time error if you try this.

Example 10-5. Book/Constant.pm

```
package Book::Constant;
use constant readonly => "Chris";

sub match     { readonly =~ /\w/g;              }
sub print_pos { print "pos: ",pos(readonly),"\n";}
1;

panic% perl -c Book/Constant.pm

Can't modify constant item in match position at Book/Constant.pm
line 5, near "readonly)"
Book/Constant.pm had compilation errors.
```

However, the code shown in Example 10-6 is OK.

Example 10-6. Book/Constant1.pm

```
package Book::Constant1;
use constant readonly => "Chris";

sub match { readonly =~ /\w/g; }
1;
```

It doesn't modify the variable flags at all.

Numerical versus string access to variables

Data can get unshared on read as well—for example, when a numerical variable is accessed as a string. Example 10-7 shows some code that proves this.

Example 10-7. numerical_vs_string.pl

```
#!/usr/bin/perl -w

use Devel::Peek;
my $numerical = 10;
my $string    = "10";
$|=1;

dump_numerical();
read_numerical_as_numerical();
dump_numerical();
read_numerical_as_string();
dump_numerical();

dump_string();
read_string_as_numerical();
dump_string();
read_string_as_string();
dump_string();

sub read_numerical_as_numerical {
    print "\nReading numerical as numerical: ", int($numerical), "\n";
}
sub read_numerical_as_string {
    print "\nReading numerical as string: ", "$numerical", "\n";
}
sub read_string_as_numerical {
    print "\nReading string as numerical: ", int($string), "\n";
}
sub read_string_as_string {
    print "\nReading string as string: ", "$string", "\n";
}
sub dump_numerical {
    print "\nDumping a numerical variable\n";
    Dump($numerical);
}
sub dump_string {
    print "\nDumping a string variable\n";
```

Example 10-7. numerical_vs_string.pl (continued)

```
    Dump($string);
}
```

The test script defines two lexical variables: a number and a string. Perl doesn't have strong data types like C does; Perl's scalar variables can be accessed as strings and numbers, and Perl will try to return the equivalent numerical value of the string if it is accessed as a number, and vice versa. The initial internal representation is based on the initially assigned value: a numerical value* in the case of $numerical and a string value† in the case of $string.

The script accesses $numerical as a number and then as a string. The internal representation is printed before and after each access. The same test is performed with a variable that was initially defined as a string ($string).

When we run the script, we get the following output:

```
    Dumping a numerical variable
    SV = IV(0x80e74c0) at 0x80e482c
      REFCNT = 4
      FLAGS = (PADBUSY,PADMY,IOK,pIOK)
      IV = 10

    Reading numerical as numerical: 10

    Dumping a numerical variable
    SV = PVNV(0x810f960) at 0x80e482c
      REFCNT = 4
      FLAGS = (PADBUSY,PADMY,IOK,NOK,pIOK,pNOK)
      IV = 10
      NV = 10
      PV = 0

    Reading numerical as string: 10

    Dumping a numerical variable
    SV = PVNV(0x810f960) at 0x80e482c
      REFCNT = 4
      FLAGS = (PADBUSY,PADMY,IOK,NOK,POK,pIOK,pNOK,pPOK)
      IV = 10
      NV = 10
      PV = 0x80e78b0 "10"\0
      CUR = 2
      LEN = 28

    Dumping a string variable
    SV = PV(0x80cb87c) at 0x80e8190
```

---

* IV, for signed integer value, or a few other possible types for floating-point and unsigned integer representations.

† PV, for pointer value (SV is already taken by a scalar data type)

```
  REFCNT = 4
  FLAGS = (PADBUSY,PADMY,POK,pPOK)
  PV = 0x810f518 "10"\0
  CUR = 2
  LEN = 3

Reading string as numerical: 10

Dumping a string variable
SV = PVNV(0x80e78d0) at 0x80e8190
  REFCNT = 4
  FLAGS = (PADBUSY,PADMY,NOK,POK,pNOK,pPOK)
  IV = 0
  NV = 10
  PV = 0x810f518 "10"\0
  CUR = 2
  LEN = 3

Reading string as string: 10

Dumping a string variable
SV = PVNV(0x80e78d0) at 0x80e8190
  REFCNT = 4
  FLAGS = (PADBUSY,PADMY,NOK,POK,pNOK,pPOK)
  IV = 0
  NV = 10
  PV = 0x810f518 "10"\0
  CUR = 2
  LEN = 3
```

We know that Perl does the conversion from one type to another on the fly, and that's where the variables get modified—during the automatic conversion behind the scenes. From this simple test you can see that variables may change internally when accessed in different contexts. Notice that even when a numerical variable is accessed as a number for the first time, its internals change, as Perl has intialized its PV and NV fields (the string and floating-point represenations) and adjusted the FLAGS fields.

From this example you can clearly see that if you want your variables to stay shared and there is a chance that the same variable will be accessed both as a string and as a numerical value, you have to access this variable as a numerical and as a string, as in the above example, before the fork happens (e.g., in the startup file). This ensures that the variable will be shared if no one modifies its value. Of course, if some other variable in the same page happens to change its value, the page will become unshared anyway.

Preloading Perl Modules at Server Startup

As we just explained, to get the code-sharing effect, you should preload the code before the child processes get spawned. The right place to preload modules is at server startup.

You can use the `PerlRequire` and `PerlModule` directives to load commonly used modules such as `CGI.pm` and `DBI` when the server is started. On most systems, server children will be able to share the code space used by these modules. Just add the following directives into *httpd.conf*:

```
PerlModule CGI
PerlModule DBI
```

An even better approach is as follows. First, create a separate startup file. In this file you code in plain Perl, loading modules like this:

```
use DBI ();
use Carp ();
1;
```

(When a module is loaded, it may export symbols to your package namespace by default. The empty parentheses ( ) after a module's name prevent this. Don't forget this, unless you need some of these in the startup file, which is unlikely. It will save you a few more kilobytes of memory.)

Next, `require()` this startup file in *httpd.conf* with the `PerlRequire` directive, placing the directive before all the other mod_perl configuration directives:

```
PerlRequire /path/to/startup.pl
```

As usual, we provide some numbers to prove the theory. Let's conduct a memory-usage test to prove that preloading reduces memory requirements.

To simplify the measurement, we will use only one child process. We will use these settings in *httpd.conf*:

```
MinSpareServers 1
MaxSpareServers 1
StartServers 1
MaxClients 1
MaxRequestsPerChild 100
```

We are going to use *memuse.pl* (shown in Example 10-8), an `Apache::Registry` script that consists of two parts: the first one loads a bunch of modules (most of which aren't going to be used); the second reports the memory size and the shared memory size used by the single child process that we start, and the difference between the two, which is the amount of unshared memory.

Example 10-8. memuse.pl

```
use strict;
use CGI ();
use DB_File ();
use LWP::UserAgent ();
use Storable ();
use DBI ();
use GTop ();
```

Example 10-8. memuse.pl (continued)

```
my $r = shift;
$r->send_http_header('text/plain');
my $proc_mem = GTop->new->proc_mem($$);
my $size  = $proc_mem->size;
my $share = $proc_mem->share;
my $diff  = $size - $share;
printf "%10s %10s %10s\n", qw(Size Shared Unshared);
printf "%10d %10d %10d (bytes)\n", $size, $share, $diff;
```

First we restart the server and execute this CGI script with none of the above modules preloaded. Here is the result:

```
Size       Shared    Unshared
4706304   2134016   2572288 (bytes)
```

Now we take the following code:

```
use strict;
use CGI ();
use DB_File ();
use LWP::UserAgent ();
use Storable ();
use DBI ();
use GTop ();
1;
```

and copy it into the *startup.pl* file. The script remains unchanged. We restart the server (now the modules are preloaded) and execute it again. We get the following results:

```
Size       Shared    Unshared
4710400   3997696   712704 (bytes)
```

Let's put the two results into one table:

```
Preloading    Size     Shared   Unshared
--------------------------------------------
Yes          4710400   3997696    712704 (bytes)
No           4706304   2134016   2572288 (bytes)
--------------------------------------------
Difference      4096   1863680  -1859584
```

You can clearly see that when the modules weren't preloaded, the amount of shared memory was about 1,864 KB smaller than in the case where the modules were preloaded.

Assuming that you have 256 MB dedicated to the web server, if you didn't preload the modules, you could have 103 servers:

```
268435456 = X * 2572288 + 2134016

X = (268435456 - 2134016) / 2572288 = 103
```

(Here we have used the formula that we devised earlier in this chapter.)

Now let's calculate the same thing with the modules preloaded:

```
268435456 = X * 712704 + 3997696

X = (268435456 - 3997696) / 712704 = 371
```

You can have almost four times as many servers!!!

Remember, however, that memory pages get dirty, and the amount of shared memory gets smaller with time. We have presented the ideal case, where the shared memory stays intact. Therefore, in use, the real numbers will be a little bit different.

Since you will use different modules and different code, obviously in your case it's possible that the process sizes will be bigger and the shared memory smaller, and vice versa. You probably won't get the same ratio we did, but the example certainly shows the possibilities.

Preloading Registry Scripts at Server Startup

Suppose you find yourself stuck with self-contained Perl CGI scripts (i.e., all the code placed in the CGI script itself). You would like to preload modules to benefit from sharing the code between the children, but you can't or don't want to move most of the stuff into modules. What can you do?

Luckily, you can preload scripts as well. This time the Apache::RegistryLoader module comes to your aid. Apache::RegistryLoader compiles Apache::Registry scripts at server startup.

For example, to preload the script */perl/test.pl*, which is in fact the file */home/httpd/perl/test.pl*, you would do the following:

```
use Apache::RegistryLoader ();
Apache::RegistryLoader->new->handler("/perl/test.pl",
                        "/home/httpd/perl/test.pl");
```

You should put this code either in <Perl> sections or in a startup script.

But what if you have a bunch of scripts located under the same directory and you don't want to list them one by one? Then the File::Find module will do most of the work for you.

The script shown in Example 10-9 walks the directory tree under which all Apache::Registry scripts are located. For each file with the extension *.pl*, it calls the Apache::RegistryLoader::handler( ) method to preload the script in the parent server. This happens before Apache pre-forks the child processes.

Example 10-9. startup_preload.pl

```
use File::Find qw(finddepth);
use Apache::RegistryLoader ();
{
    my $scripts_root_dir = "/home/httpd/perl/";
```

Example 10-9. startup_preload.pl (continued)

```
    my $rl = Apache::RegistryLoader->new;
    finddepth(
        sub {
            return unless /\.pl$/;
            my $url = $File::Find::name;
            $url =~ s|$scripts_root_dir/?|/|;
            warn "pre-loading $url\n";
            # preload $url
            my $status = $rl->handler($url);
            unless($status == 200) {
                warn "pre-load of '$url' failed, status=$status\n";
            }
        },
        $scripts_root_dir
    );
}
```

Note that we didn't use the second argument to handler( ) here, as we did in the first example. To make the loader smarter about the URI-to-filename translation, you might need to provide a trans( ) function to translate the URI to a filename. URI-to-filename translation normally doesn't happen until an HTTP request is received, so the module is forced to do its own translation. If the filename is omitted and a trans( ) function is not defined, the loader will try to use the URI relative to the ServerRoot.

A simple trans( ) function can be something like this:

```
sub mytrans {
    my $uri = shift;
    $uri =~ s|^/perl/|/home/httpd/perl/|;
    return $uri;
}
```

You can easily derive the right translation by looking at the Alias directive. The above mytrans( ) function matches our Alias:

```
Alias /perl/ /home/httpd/perl/
```

After defining the URI-to-filename translation function, you should pass it during the creation of the Apache::RegistryLoader object:

```
my $rl = Apache::RegistryLoader->new(trans => \&mytrans);
```

We won't show any benchmarks here, since the effect is just like preloading modules. However, we will use this technique later in this chapter, when we will need to have a fair comparison between PerlHandler code and Apache::Registry scripts. This will require both the code and the scripts to be preloaded at server startup.

Module Initialization at Server Startup

It's important to preload modules and scripts at server startup. But for some modules this isn't enough, and you have to prerun their initialization code to get more memory pages shared. Usually you will find information about specific modules in their respective manpages. We will present a few examples of widely used modules where the code needs to be initialized.

Initializing DBI.pm

The first example is the DBI module. DBI works with many database drivers from the DBD:: category (e.g., DBD::mysql). If you want to minimize memory use after Apache forks its children, it's not enough to preload DBI—you must initialize DBI with the driver(s) that you are going to use (usually a single driver is used). Note that you should do this only under mod_perl and other environments where sharing memory is very important. Otherwise, you shouldn't initialize drivers.

You probably already know that under mod_perl you should use the Apache::DBI module to get persistent database connections (unless you open a separate connection for each user). Apache::DBI automatically loads DBI and overrides some of its methods. You should continue coding as if you had loaded only the DBI module.

As with preloading modules, our goal is to find the configuration that will give the smallest difference between the shared and normal memory reported, and hence the smallest total memory usage.

To simplify the measurements, we will again use only one child process. We will use these settings in *httpd.conf*:

```
MinSpareServers 1
MaxSpareServers 1
StartServers 1
MaxClients 1
MaxRequestsPerChild 100
```

We always preload these modules:

```
use Gtop();
use Apache::DBI(); # preloads DBI as well
```

We are going to run memory benchmarks on five different versions of the *startup.pl* file:

Version 1
> Leave the file unmodified.

Version 2
> Install the MySQL driver (we will use the MySQL RDBMS for our test):
> ```
> DBI->install_driver("mysql");
> ```
> It's safe to use this method—as with use(), if it can't be installed, it will die().

Version 3
> Preload the MySQL driver module:
> ```
> use DBD::mysql;
> ```

Version 4

Tell Apache::DBI to connect to the database when the child process starts (ChildInitHandler). No driver is preloaded before the child is spawned!

```
Apache::DBI->connect_on_init('DBI:mysql:test::localhost', "", "",
    {
        PrintError => 1, # warn( ) on errors
        RaiseError => 0, # don't die on error
        AutoCommit => 1, # commit executes
        # immediately
    }
) or die "Cannot connect to database: $DBI::errstr";
```

Version 5

Use both connect_on_init( ) from version 4 and install_driver( ) from version 2.

The Apache::Registry test script that we have used is shown in Example 10-10.

Example 10-10. preload_dbi.pl

```perl
use strict;
use GTop ( );
use DBI ( );

my $dbh = DBI->connect("DBI:mysql:test::localhost", "", "",
    {
        PrintError => 1, # warn( ) on errors
        RaiseError => 0, # don't die on error
        AutoCommit => 1, # commit executes immediately
    }
) or die "Cannot connect to database: $DBI::errstr";

my $r = shift;
$r->send_http_header('text/plain');

my $do_sql = "SHOW TABLES";
my $sth = $dbh->prepare($do_sql);
$sth->execute( );
my @data = ( );
while (my @row = $sth->fetchrow_array) {
    push @data, @row;
}
print "Data: @data\n";
$dbh->disconnect( ); # NOOP under Apache::DBI

my $proc_mem = GTop->new->proc_mem($$);
my $size  = $proc_mem->size;
my $share = $proc_mem->share;
my $diff  = $size - $share;
printf "%8s %8s %8s\n", qw(Size Shared Unshared);
printf "%8d %8d %8d (bytes)\n", $size, $share, $diff;
```

The script opens a connection to the database *test* and issues a query to learn what tables the database has. Ordinarily, when the data is collected and printed the connection would be closed, but Apache::DBI overrides thsi with an empty method. After processing the data, the memory usage is printed. You will already be familiar with that part of the code.

Here are the results of the five tests. The server was restarted before each new test. We have sorted the results by the *Unshared* column.

1. After the first request:

```
Test type                                    Size     Shared   Unshared
--------------------------------------------------------------
(2) install_driver                           3465216  2621440  843776
(5) install_driver & connect_on_init 3461120  2609152  851968
(3) preload driver                           3465216  2605056  860160
(1) nothing added                            3461120  2494464  966656
(4) connect_on_init                          3461120  2482176  978944
```

2. After the second request (all the subsequent requests showed the same results):

```
Test type                                    Size     Shared   Unshared
--------------------------------------------------------------
(2) install_driver                           3469312  2609152  860160
(5) install_driver & connect_on_init 3481600  2605056  876544
(3) preload driver                           3469312  2588672  880640
(1) nothing added                            3477504  2482176  995328
(4) connect_on_init                          3481600  2469888  1011712
```

What do we conclude from analyzing this data? First we see that only after a second reload do we get the final memory footprint for the specific request in question (if you pass different arguments, the memory usage will be different).

But both tables show the same pattern of memory usage. We can clearly see that the real winner is version 2, where the MySQL driver was installed. Since we want to have a connection ready for the first request made to the freshly spawned child process, we generally use version 5. This uses somewhat more memory but has almost the same number of shared memory pages. Version 3 preloads only the driver, which results in less shared memory. Having nothing initialized (version 1) and using only the connect_on_init( ) method (version 4) gave the least shared memory. The former is a little bit better than the latter, but both are significantly worse than the first two.

Notice that the smaller the value of the *Unshared* column, the more processes you can have using the same amount of RAM. If we compare versions 2 and 4 of the script, assuming for example that we have 256 MB of memory dedicated to mod_perl processes, we get the following numbers.

Version 2:

$$N = \frac{268435456 - 2609152}{860160} = 309$$

Version 4:

$$N = \frac{268435456 - 2469888}{1011712} = 262$$

As you can see, there are 17% more child processes with version 2.

Initializing CGI.pm

CGI.pm is a big module that by default postpones the compilation of its methods until they are actually needed, thus making it possible to use it under a slow mod_cgi handler without adding a big startup overhead. That's not what we want under mod_perl—if you use CGI.pm, in addition to preloading the module at server startup, you should precompile the methods that you are going to use. To do that, simply call the compile( ) method:

```
use CGI;
CGI->compile(':all');
```

You should replace the tag group :all with the real tags and group tags that you are going to use if you want to optimize memory usage.

We are going to compare the shared-memory footprint using a script that is backward compatible with mod_cgi. You can improve the performance of this kind of script as well, but if you really want fast code, think about porting it to use Apache:: Request* for the CGI interface and some other module for your HTML generation.

The Apache::Registry script that we are going to use to make the comparison is shown in Example 10-11.

Example 10-11. preload_cgi_pm.pl

```
use strict;
use CGI ( );
use GTop ( );

my $q = new CGI;
print $q->header('text/plain');
print join "\n", map {"$_ => ".$q->param($_) } $q->param;
print "\n";

my $proc_mem = GTop->new->proc_mem($$);
my $size  = $proc_mem->size;
my $share = $proc_mem->share;
my $diff  = $size - $share;
printf "%8s %8s %8s\n", qw(Size Shared Unshared);
printf "%8d %8d %8d (bytes)\n", $size, $share, $diff;
```

The script initializes the CGI object, sends the HTTP header, and then prints any arguments and values that were passed to it. At the end, as usual, we print the memory usage.

---

* Apache::Request is significantly faster than CGI.pm because its methods for processing a request's arguments are written in C.

Again, we are going to use a single child process. Here is part of our *httpd.conf* file:

```
MinSpareServers 1
MaxSpareServers 1
StartServers 1
MaxClients 1
MaxRequestsPerChild 100
```

We always preload the Gtop module:

```
use Gtop ();
```

We are going to run memory benchmarks on three different versions of the *startup.pl* file:

Version 1

Leave the file unmodified.

Version 2

Preload CGI.pm:

```
use CGI ();
```

Version 3

Preload CGI.pm and precompile the methods that we are going to use in the script:

```
use CGI ();
CGI->compile(qw(header param));
```

Here are the results of the three tests, sorted by the *Unshared* column. The server was restarted before each new test.

1. After the first request:

```
Test type                          Size      Shared    Unshared
----------------------------------------------------------------
(3) preloaded & methods+compiled   3244032   2465792    778240
(2) preloaded                      3321856   2326528    995328
(1) not preloaded                  3321856   2146304   1175552
```

2. After the second request (the subsequent request showed the same results):

```
Test type                          Size      Shared    Unshared
----------------------------------------------------------------
(3) preloaded & methods+compiled   3248128   2445312    802816
(2) preloaded                      3325952   2314240   1011712
(1) not preloaded                  3325952   2134016   1191936
```

Since the memory usage stabilized after the second request, we are going to look at the second table. By comparing the first (not preloaded) and the second (preloaded) versions, we can see that preloading adds about 180 KB (2314240 – 2134016 bytes) of shared memory size, which is the result we expect from most modules. However, by comparing the second (preloaded) and the third (preloaded and precompiled methods) options, we can see that by precompiling methods, we gain 207 KB (1011712 – 802816 bytes) more of shared memory. And we have used only a few methods (the header method loads a few more methods transparently for the user).

The gain grows as more of the used methods are precompiled. If you use CGI.pm's functional interface, all of the above applies as well.

Even in our very simple case using the same formula, what do we see? Let's again assume that we have 256 MB dedicated for mod_perl.

Version 1:

$$N = \frac{268435456 - 2134016}{1191936} = 223$$

Version 3:

$$N = \frac{268435456 - 2445312}{802816} = 331$$

If we preload CGI.pm and precompile a few methods that we use in the test script, we can have 50% more child processes than when we don't preload and precompile the methods that we are going to use.

Note that CGI.pm Versions 3.x are supposed to be much less bloated, but make sure to test your code as we just demonstrated.

Memory Preallocation

Perl reuses allocated memory whenever possible. With Devel::Peek we can actually see this happening by peeking at the variable data structure. Consider the simple code in Example 10-12.

Example 10-12. realloc.pl

```
use Devel::Peek;

foo() for 1..2;

sub foo {
    my $sv;
    Dump $sv;
    print "----\n";
    $sv = 'x' x 100_000;
    $sv = "";
    Dump $sv;
    print "\n\n";
}
```

The code starts by loading the Devel::Peek module and calling the function foo() twice in the for loop.

The foo() function declares a lexically scoped variable, $sv (scalar value). Then it dumps the $sv data structure and prints a separator, assigns a string of 100,000 x characters to $sv, assigns it to an empty string, and prints the $sv data structure again. At the end, a separator of two empty lines is printed.

Let's observe the output generated by this code:

```
SV = NULL(0x0) at 0x80787c0
  REFCNT = 1
  FLAGS = (PADBUSY,PADMY)
----
SV = PV(0x804c6c8) at 0x80787c0
  REFCNT = 1
  FLAGS = (PADBUSY,PADMY,POK,pPOK)
  PV = 0x8099d98 ""\0
  CUR = 0
  LEN = 100001


SV = PV(0x804c6c8) at 0x80787c0
  REFCNT = 1
  FLAGS = (PADBUSY,PADMY)
  PV = 0x8099d98 ""\0
  CUR = 0
  LEN = 100001
----
SV = PV(0x804c6c8) at 0x80787c0
  REFCNT = 1
  FLAGS = (PADBUSY,PADMY,POK,pPOK)
  PV = 0x8099d98 ""\0
  CUR = 0
  LEN = 100001
```

In this output, we are interested in the values of PV—the memory address of the string value, and LEN—the length of the allocated memory.

When foo( ) is called for the first time and the $sv data structure is dumped for the first time, we can see that no data has yet been assigned to it. The second time the $sv data structure is dumped, we can see that while $sv contains an empty string, its data structure still kept all the memory allocated for the long string.

Notice that $sv is declared with my( ), so at the end of the function foo( ) it goes out of scope (i.e., it is destroyed). To our surprise, when we observe the output from the second call to foo( ), we discover that when $sv is declared at the beginning of foo( ), it reuses the data structure from the previously destroyed $sv variable—the PV field contains the same memory address and the LEN field is still 100,101 characters long.

If we had asked for a longer memory chunk during the second invocation, Perl would have called realloc( ) and a new chunk of memory would have been allocated.

Therefore, if you have some kind of buffering variable that will grow over the processes life, you may want to preallocate the memory for this variable. For example, if you know a variable $Book::Buffer::buffer may grow to the size of 100,000 characters, you can preallocate the memory in the following way:

```
package Book::Buffer;

my $buffer;
sub prealloc { $buffer = ' ' x 100_000; $buffer = ""; 0;}
```

```
# ...
1;
```

You should load this module during the `PerlChildInitHandler`. In *startup.pl*, insert:

```
use Book::Buffer;
Apache->push_handlers(PerlChildInitHandler => \&Book::Buffer::prealloc);
```

so each child will allocate its own memory for the variable. When `$Book::Buffer::buffer` starts growing at runtime, no time will be wasted on memory reallocation as long as the preallocated memory is sufficient.

Forking and Executing Subprocesses from mod_perl

When you fork Apache, you are forking the entire Apache server, lock, stock and barrel. Not only are you duplicating your Perl code and the Perl interpreter, but you are also duplicating all the core routines and whatever modules you have used in your server—for example, mod_ssl, mod_rewrite, mod_log, mod_proxy, and mod_speling (no, that's not a typo!). This can be a large overhead on some systems, so wherever possible, it's desirable to avoid forking under mod_perl.

Modern operating systems have a light version of `fork( )`, optimized to do the absolute minimum of memory-page duplication, which adds little overhead when called. This fork relies on the *copy-on-write* technique. The gist of this technique is as follows: the parent process's memory pages aren't all copied immediately to the child's space on `fork( )`ing; this is done later, when the child or the parent modifies the data in the shared memory pages.

If you need to call a Perl program from your mod_perl code, it's better to try to convert the program into a module and call it as a function without spawning a special process to do that. Of course, if you cannot do that or the program is not written in Perl, you have to call the program via `system( )` or an equivalent function, which spawns a new process. If the program is written in C, you can try to write some Perl glue code with help of the Inline, XS, or SWIG architectures. Then the program will be executed as a Perl subroutine and avoid a `fork( )` call.

Also by trying to spawn a subprocess, you might be trying to do the wrong thing. If you just want to do some post-processing after sending a response to the browser, look into the `PerlCleanupHandler` directive. This allows you to do exactly that. If you just need to run some cleanup code, you may want to register this code during the request processing via:

```
my $r = shift;
$r->register_cleanup(\&do_cleanup);
sub do_cleanup{ #some clean-up code here }
```

But when a lengthy job needs to be done, there is not much choice but to use fork( ). You cannot just run such a job within an Apache process, since firstly it will keep the Apache process busy instead of letting it do the job it was designed for, and secondly, unless it is coded so as to detach from the Apache processes group, if Apache should happen to be stopped the lengthy job might be terminated as well.

In the following sections, we'll discuss how to properly spawn new processes under mod_perl.

Forking a New Process

The typical way to call fork( ) under mod_perl is illustrated in Example 10-13.

Example 10-13. fork1.pl

```
defined (my $kid = fork) or die "Cannot fork: $!\n";
if ($kid) {
    # Parent runs this block
}
else {
    # Child runs this block
    # some code comes here
    CORE::exit(0);
}
# possibly more code here usually run by the parent
```

When using fork( ), you should check its return value, since a return of undef it means that the call was unsuccessful and no process was spawned. This can happen for example, when the system is already running too many processes and cannot spawn new ones.

When the process is successfully forked, the parent receives the PID of the newly spawned child as a returned value of the fork( ) call and the child receives 0. Now the program splits into two. In the above example, the code inside the first block after if will be executed by the parent, and the code inside the first block after else will be executed by the child.

It's important not to forget to explicitly call exit( ) at the end of the child code when forking. If you don't and there is some code outside the if...else block, the child process will execute it as well. But under mod_perl there is another nuance—you must use CORE::exit( ) and not exit( ), which would be automatically overriden by Apache::exit( ) if used in conjunction with Apache::Registry and similar modules. You want the spawned process to quit when its work is done, or it'll just stay alive, using resources and doing nothing.

The parent process usually completes its execution and returns to the pool of free servers to wait for a new assignment. If the execution is to be aborted earlier for some reason, you should use Apache::exit() or die(). In the case of Apache::Registry or Apache::PerlRun handlers, a simple exit() will do the right thing.

Freeing the Parent Process

In the child code, you must also close all the pipes to the connection socket that were opened by the parent process (i.e., STDIN and STDOUT) and inherited by the child, so the parent will be able to complete the request and free itself for serving other requests. If you need the STDIN and/or STDOUT streams, you should reopen them. You may need to close or reopen the STDERR file handle, too. As inherited from its parent, it's opened to append to the *error_log* file, so the chances are that you will want to leave it untouched.

Under mod_perl, the spawned process also inherits the file descriptor that's tied to the socket through which all the communications between the server and the client pass. Therefore, you need to free this stream in the forked process. If you don't, the server can't be restarted while the spawned process is still running. If you attempt to restart the server, you will get the following error:

```
[Mon May 20 23:04:11 2002] [crit]
(98)Address already in use: make_sock:
    could not bind to address 127.0.0.1 port 8000
```

Apache::SubProcess comes to help, providing a method called cleanup_for_exec() that takes care of closing this file descriptor.

The simplest way to free the parent process is to close the STDIN, STDOUT, and STDERR streams (if you don't need them) and untie the Apache socket. If the mounted partition is to be unmounted at a later time, in addition you may want to change the current directory of the forked process to / so that the forked process won't keep the mounted partition busy.

To summarize all these issues, here is an example of a fork that takes care of freeing the parent process (Example 10-14).

Example 10-14. fork2.pl

```
use Apache::SubProcess;
defined (my $kid = fork) or die "Cannot fork: $!\n";
if ($kid) {
    # Parent runs this block
}
else {
    # Child runs this block
    $r->cleanup_for_exec(); # untie the socket
    chdir '/' or die "Can't chdir to /: $!";
    close STDIN;
    close STDOUT;
    close STDERR;
```

Example 10-14. fork2.pl (continued)

```
    # some code goes here

    CORE::exit(0);
}
# possibly more code here usually run by the parent
```

Of course, the real code should be placed between freeing the parent code and the child process termination.

Detaching the Forked Process

Now what happens if the forked process is running and we decide that we need to restart the web server? This forked process will be aborted, because when the parent process dies during the restart, it will kill its child processes as well. In order to avoid this, we need to detach the process from its parent session by opening a new session with help of a setsid( ) system call (provided by the POSIX module). This is demonstrated in Example 10-15.

Example 10-15. fork3.pl

```
use POSIX 'setsid';

defined (my $kid = fork) or die "Cannot fork: $!\n";
if ($kid) {
    # Parent runs this block
}
else {
    # Child runs this block
    setsid or die "Can't start a new session: $!";
    # ...
}
```

Now the spawned child process has a life of its own, and it doesn't depend on the parent any more.

Avoiding Zombie Processes

Normally, every process has a parent. Many processes are children of the init process, whose PID is 1. When you fork a process, you must wait( ) or waitpid( ) for it to finish. If you don't wait( ) for it, it becomes a zombie.

A zombie is a process that doesn't have a parent. When the child quits, it reports the termination to its parent. If no parent wait( )s to collect the exit status of the child, it gets confused and becomes a ghost process that can be seen as a process but not killed. It will be killed only when you stop the parent process that spawned it.

Generally, the *ps(1)* utility displays these processes with the <defunc> tag, and you may see the zombies counter increment when using *top()*. These zombie processes can take up system resources and are generally undesirable.

The proper way to do a fork, to avoid zombie processes, is shown in Example 10-16.

Example 10-16. fork4.pl

```
my $r = shift;
$r->send_http_header('text/plain');

defined (my $kid = fork) or die "Cannot fork: $!";
if ($kid) {
    waitpid($kid,0);
    print "Parent has finished\n";
}
else {
    # do something
    CORE::exit(0);
}
```

In most cases, the only reason you would want to fork is when you need to spawn a process that will take a long time to complete. So if the Apache process that spawns this new child process has to wait for it to finish, you have gained nothing. You can neither wait for its completion (because you don't have the time to) nor continue, because if you do you will get yet another zombie process. This is called a *blocking call*, since the process is blocked from doing anything else until this call gets completed.

The simplest solution is to ignore your dead children. Just add this line before the fork( ) call:

```
$SIG{CHLD} = 'IGNORE';
```

When you set the CHLD (SIGCHLD in C) signal handler to 'IGNORE', all the processes will be collected by the init process and therefore will be prevented from becoming zombies. This doesn't work everywhere, but it has been proven to work at least on Linux.

Note that you cannot localize this setting with local( ). If you try, it won't have the desired effect.

The latest version of the code is shown in Example 10-17.

Example 10-17. fork5.pl

```
my $r = shift;
$r->send_http_header('text/plain');

$SIG{CHLD} = 'IGNORE';

defined (my $kid = fork) or die "Cannot fork: $!\n";
if ($kid) {
    print "Parent has finished\n";
```

Example 10-17. fork5.pl (continued)

```
}
else {
    # do something time-consuming
    CORE::exit(0);
}
```

Note that the `waitpid( )` call is gone. The `$SIG{CHLD} = 'IGNORE';` statement protects us from zombies, as explained above.

Another solution (more portable, but slightly more expensive) is to use a double fork approach, as shown in Example 10-18.

Example 10-18. fork6.pl

```
my $r = shift;
$r->send_http_header('text/plain');

defined (my $kid = fork) or die "Cannot fork: $!\n";
if ($kid) {
    waitpid($kid,0);
}
else {
    defined (my $grandkid = fork) or die "Kid cannot fork: $!\n";
    if ($grandkid) {
        CORE::exit(0);
    }
    else {
        # code here
        # do something long lasting
        CORE::exit(0);
    }
}
```

Grandkid becomes a child of `init`—i.e., a child of the process whose PID is 1.

Note that the previous two solutions do allow you to determine the exit status of the process, but in our example, we don't care about it.

Yet another solution is to use a different SIGCHLD handler:

```
use POSIX 'WNOHANG';
$SIG{CHLD} = sub { while( waitpid(-1,WNOHANG)>0 ) {} };
```

This is useful when you `fork( )` more than one process. The handler could call `wait( )` as well, but for a variety of reasons involving the handling of stopped processes and the rare event in which two children exit at nearly the same moment, the best technique is to call `waitpid( )` in a tight loop with a first argument of `-1` and a second argument of `WNOHANG`. Together these arguments tell `waitpid( )` to reap the next child that's available and prevent the call from blocking if there happens to be no child ready for reaping. The handler will loop until `waitpid( )` returns a negative number or zero, indicating that no more reapable children remain.

While testing and debugging code that uses one of the above examples, you might want to write debug information to the *error_log* file so that you know what's happening.

Read the *perlipc* manpage for more information about signal handlers.

A Complete Fork Example

Now let's put all the bits of code together and show a well-written example that solves all the problems discussed so far. We will use an Apache::Registry script for this purpose. Our script is shown in Example 10-19.

Example 10-19. proper_fork1.pl

```perl
use strict;
use POSIX 'setsid';
use Apache::SubProcess;

my $r = shift;
$r->send_http_header("text/plain");

$SIG{CHLD} = 'IGNORE';
defined (my $kid = fork) or die "Cannot fork: $!\n";
if ($kid) {
    print "Parent $$ has finished, kid's PID: $kid\n";
}
else {
    $r->cleanup_for_exec(); # untie the socket
    chdir '/'                or die "Can't chdir to /: $!";
    open STDIN, '/dev/null'  or die "Can't read /dev/null: $!";
    open STDOUT, '>/dev/null' or die "Can't write to /dev/null: $!";
    open STDERR, '>/tmp/log'  or die "Can't write to /tmp/log: $!";
    setsid                   or die "Can't start a new session: $!";

    my $oldfh = select STDERR;
    local $| = 1;
    select $oldfh;
    warn "started\n";

    # do something time-consuming
    sleep 1, warn "$_\n" for 1..20;
    warn "completed\n";

    CORE::exit(0); # terminate the process
}
```

The script starts with the usual declaration of strict mode, then loads the POSIX and Apache::SubProcess modules and imports the setsid() symbol from the POSIX package.

The HTTP header is sent next, with the Content-Type of text/plain. To avoid zombies, the parent process gets ready to ignore the child, and the fork is called.

The if condition evaluates to a true value for the parent process and to a false value for the child process; therefore, the first block is executed by the parent and the second by the child.

The parent process announces its PID and the PID of the spawned process, and finishes its block. If there is any code outside the if statement, it will be executed by the parent as well.

The child process starts its code by disconnecting from the socket, changing its current directory to /, and opening the STDIN and STDOUT streams to /dev/null (this has the effect of closing them both before opening them). In fact, in this example we don't need either of these, so we could just close( ) both. The child process completes its disengagement from the parent process by opening the STDERR stream to /tmp/log, so it can write to that file, and creates a new session with the help of setsid( ). Now the child process has nothing to do with the parent process and can do the actual processing that it has to do. In our example, it outputs a series of warnings, which are logged to /tmp/log:

```
my $oldfh = select STDERR;
local $| = 1;
select $oldfh;
warn "started\n";
# do something time-consuming
sleep 1, warn "$_\n" for 1..20;
warn "completed\n";
```

We set $|=1 to unbuffer the STDERR stream, so we can immediately see the debug output generated by the program. We use the keyword local so that buffering in other processes is not affected. In fact, we don't really need to unbuffer output when it is generated by warn( ). You want it if you use print( ) to debug.

Finally, the child process terminates by calling:

```
CORE::exit(0);
```

which makes sure that it terminates at the end of the block and won't run some code that it's not supposed to run.

This code example will allow you to verify that indeed the spawned child process has its own life, and that its parent is free as well. Simply issue a request that will run this script, see that the process starts writing warnings to the file /tmp/log, and issue a complete server stop and start. If everything is correct, the server will successfully restart and the long-term process will still be running. You will know that it's still running if the warnings are still being written into /tmp/log. If Apache takes a long time to stop and restart, you may need to raise the number of warnings to make sure that you don't miss the end of the run.

If there are only five warnings to be printed, you should see the following output in the */tmp/log* file:

```
started
1
2
3
4
5
completed
```

Starting a Long-Running External Program

What happens if we cannot just run Perl code from the spawned process? We may have a compiled utility, such as a program written in C, or a Perl program that cannot easily be converted into a module and thus called as a function. In this case, we have to use system( ), exec( ), qx( ) or `` (backticks) to start it.

When using any of these methods, and when taint mode is enabled, we must also add the following code to untaint the PATH environment variable and delete a few other insecure environment variables. This information can be found in the *perlsec* manpage.

```
$ENV{'PATH'} = '/bin:/usr/bin';
delete @ENV{'IFS', 'CDPATH', 'ENV', 'BASH_ENV'};
```

Now all we have to do is reuse the code from the previous section.

First we move the core program into the *external.pl* file, then we add the shebang line so that the program will be executed by Perl, tell the program to run under taint mode (*-T*), possibly enable *warnings* mode (*-w*), and make it executable. These changes are shown in Example 10-20.

Example 10-20. external.pl

```
#!/usr/bin/perl -Tw

open STDIN, '/dev/null'   or die "Can't read /dev/null: $!";
open STDOUT, '>/dev/null' or die "Can't write to /dev/null: $!";
open STDERR, '>/tmp/log'  or die "Can't write to /tmp/log: $!";

my $oldfh = select STDERR;
local $| = 1;
select $oldfh;
warn "started\n";
# do something time-consuming
sleep 1, warn "$_\n" for 1..20;
warn "completed\n";
```

Now we replace the code that we moved into the external program with a call to exec( ) to run it, as shown in Example 10-21.

Example 10-21. proper_fork_exec.pl

```perl
use strict;
use POSIX 'setsid';
use Apache::SubProcess;

$ENV{'PATH'} = '/bin:/usr/bin';
delete @ENV{'IFS', 'CDPATH', 'ENV', 'BASH_ENV'};

my $r = shift;
$r->send_http_header("text/html");

$SIG{CHLD} = 'IGNORE';

defined (my $kid = fork) or die "Cannot fork: $!\n";
if ($kid) {
    print "Parent has finished, kid's PID: $kid\n";
}
else {
    $r->cleanup_for_exec();  # untie the socket
    chdir '/'                or die "Can't chdir to /: $!";
    open STDIN, '/dev/null'  or die "Can't read /dev/null: $!";
    open STDOUT, '>/dev/null' or die "Can't write to /dev/null: $!";
    open STDERR, '>&STDOUT'  or die "Can't dup stdout: $!";
    setsid                   or die "Can't start a new session: $!";

    exec "/home/httpd/perl/external.pl" or die "Cannot execute exec: $!";
}
```

Notice that exec( ) never returns unless it fails to start the process. Therefore you shouldn't put any code after exec( )—it will not be executed in the case of success. Use system( ) or backticks instead if you want to continue doing other things in the process. But then you probably will want to terminate the process after the program has finished, so you will have to write:

```perl
system "/home/httpd/perl/external.pl"
    or die "Cannot execute system: $!";
CORE::exit(0);
```

Another important nuance is that we have to close all STD streams in the forked process, even if the called program does that.

If the external program is written in Perl, you can pass complicated data stuctures to it using one of the methods to serialize and then restore Perl data. The Storable and FreezeThaw modules come in handy. Let's say that we have a program called *master.pl* (Example 10-22) calling another program called *slave.pl* (Example 10-23).

Example 10-22. master.pl

```perl
# we are within the mod_perl code
use Storable ();
my @params = (foo => 1, bar => 2);
```

Example 10-22. master.pl (continued)

```
my $params = Storable::freeze(\@params);
exec "./slave.pl", $params or die "Cannot execute exec: $!";
```

Example 10-23. slave.pl

```
#!/usr/bin/perl -w
use Storable ();
my @params = @ARGV ? @{ Storable::thaw(shift)||[] } : ();
# do something
```

As you can see, *master.pl* serializes the @params data structure with Storable::freeze and passes it to *slave.pl* as a single \argument. *slave.pl* recovers it with Storable::thaw, by shifting the first value of the @ARGV array (if available). The FreezeThaw module does a very similar thing.

Starting a Short-Running External Program

Sometimes you need to call an external program and you cannot continue before this program completes its run (e.g., if you need it to return some result). In this case, the fork solution doesn't help. There are a few ways to execute such a program. First, you could use system( ):

```
system "perl -e 'print 5+5'"
```

You would never call the Perl interperter for doing a simple calculation like this, but for the sake of a simple example it's good enough.

The problem with this approach is that we cannot get the results printed to STDOUT. That's where backticks or qx( ) can help. If you use either:

```
my $result = `perl -e 'print 5+5'`;
```

or:

```
my $result = qx{perl -e 'print 5+5'};
```

the whole output of the external program will be stored in the $result variable.

Of course, you can use other solutions, such as opening a pipe (|) to the program if you need to submit many arguments. And there are more evolved solutions provided by other Perl modules, such as IPC::Open2 and IPC::Open3, that allow you to open a process for reading, writing, and error handling.

Executing system( ) or exec( ) in the Right Way

The Perl exec( ) and system( ) functions behave identically in the way they spawn a program. Let's use system( ) as an example. Consider the following code:

```
system("echo", "Hi");
```

Perl will use the first argument as a program to execute, find the echo executable along the search path, invoke it directly, and pass the string "Hi" as an argument.

Note that Perl's system( ) is not the same as the standard *libc* system(3) call.

If there is more than one argument to system( ) or exec( ), or the argument is an array with more than one element in it, the arguments are passed directly to the C-level functions. When the argument is a single scalar or an array with only a single scalar in it, it will first be checked to see if it contains any shell metacharacters (e.g., *, ?). If there are any, the Perl interpreter invokes a real shell program (*/bin/sh -c* on Unix platforms). If there are no shell metacharacters in the argument, it is split into words and passed directly to the C level, which is more efficient.

In other words, only if you do:

```
system "echo *"
```

will Perl actually exec( ) a copy of */bin/sh* to parse your command, which may incur a slight overhead on certain OSes.

It's especially important to remember to run your code with taint mode enabled when system( ) or exec( ) is called using a single argument. There can be bad consequences if user input gets to the shell without proper laundering first. Taint mode will alert you when such a condition happens.

Perl will try to do the most efficient thing no matter how the arguments are passed, and the additional overhead may be incurred only if you need the shell to expand some metacharacters before doing the actual call.

References

- *Mastering Regular Expressions*, by Jeffrey E. F. Friedl (O'Reilly).
- Chapters 2 and 4 in *Operating Systems: Design And Implementation*, by Andrew S. Tanenbaum and Albert S. Woodhull (Prentice Hall).
- Chapter 4 in *Modern Operating Systems*, by Andrew S. Tanenbaum (Prentice Hall).
- Chapters 7 and 9 in *Design of the UNIX Operating System*, by Maurice J. Bach (Prentice Hall).
- Chapter 9 ("Tuning Apache and mod_perl") in *mod_perl Developer's Cookbook*, by Geoffrey Young, Paul Lindner, and Randy Kobes (Sams Publishing).
- The Solaris memory system, sizing, tools, and architecture: *http://www.sun.com/sun-on-net/performance/vmsizing.pdf*.
- Refer to the *Unix Programming Frequently Asked Questions* to learn more about fork( ) and related system calls: *http://www.erlenstar.demon.co.uk/unix/faq_toc.html*.

Tuning Performance by Tweaking Apache's Configuration

When you implement mod_perl on your system, it's very important to go through the default configuration file (*httpd.conf*), because most of the default settings were designed without mod_perl in mind. Some variables (such as MaxClients) should be adapted to the capabilities of your system, while some (such as KeepAlive, in many cases) should be disabled, because although they can improve performance for a plain Apache server, they can reduce performance for a mod_perl server.

Correct configuration of the MinSpareServers, MaxSpareServers, StartServers, MaxClients, and MaxRequestsPerChild parameters is very important. If they are too low, you will under-use the system's capabilities. If they are too high, it is likely that the server will bring the machine to its knees.

The KeepAlive directive improves the performance of a plain Apache server by saving the TCP handshake if the client requests more than one object from your server. But you don't want this option to be enabled under mod_perl, since it will keep a large mod_perl process tied to the client and do nothing while waiting for the timeout to occur.

We will talk about these and other issues in the following sections.

Setting the MaxClients Directive

It's important to specify MaxClients on the basis of the resources your machine has. The MaxClients directive sets the limit on the number of simultaneous requests that can be supported. No more than this number of child server processes will be created. To configure more than 256 clients, you must edit the HARD_SERVER_LIMIT entry in *httpd.h* and recompile Apache.

With a plain Apache server, it doesn't matter much if you run many child processes—the processes are about 1 MB each (most of it shared), so they don't eat a lot of RAM. The situation is different with mod_perl, where the processes can easily grow to 10 MB and more. For example, if you have MaxClients set to 50, the memory usage becomes 50×10 MB = 500 MB.* Do you have 500 MB of RAM dedicated to the mod_perl server?

With a high MaxClients, if you get a high load the server will try to serve all requests immediately. Your CPU will have a hard time keeping up, and if the child size multiplied by the number of running children is larger than the total available RAM, your server will start swapping. The swapping will slow down everything, which will lead to more swapping, slowing down everything even more, until eventually the machine will die. It's important that you take pains to ensure that swapping does not normally happen. Swap space is an emergency pool, not a resource to be used routinely. If you are low on memory and you badly need it, buy it. Memory is cheap.

We want the value of MaxClients to be as small as possible, because in this way we can limit the resources used by the server's children. Since we can restrict each child's process size, as discussed later, the calculation of MaxClients is straightforward:

$$MaxClients = \frac{\text{Total RAM dedicated to the web server}}{\text{Max childs process size}}$$

So if we have 400 MB for the mod_perl server to use, we can set MaxClients to 40 if we know that each child is limited to 10 MB of memory.

You may be wondering what will happen to your server if there are more concurrent users than MaxClients. This situation is pointed out by the following warning message in the *error_log* file:

```
[Sat May 18 13:40:35 2002] [error] server reached MaxClients setting,
consider raising the MaxClients setting
```

Technically there is no problem—any connection attempts over the MaxClients limit will normally be queued, up to a number based on the ListenBacklog directive. When a child process is freed at the end of a different request, the next waiting connection will be served.

But it is an error, because clients are being put in the queue rather than getting served immediately, despite the fact that they do not get an error response. The error can be allowed to persist to balance available system resources and response time, but sooner or later you will need to get more RAM so you can start more child processes. The best approach is to prevent this situation from arising in the first place, and if it keeps on happening you should start worrying about it.

In Chapter 10 we showed that when memory sharing is available, the approximate real memory used can be calculated by adding up all the unshared memory of the client processes plus the memory of the parent process, or, if the latter is unknown, the maximum shared memory size of a single child process, which is smaller than the

---

* Of course, you also have to take into account the shared memory usage, as described in Chapter 10.

memory size of the parent process but good enough for our calculations. We have also devised the following formula:

$$MaxClients = \frac{Total\_RAM - Min\_Shared\_RAM\_per\_Child}{Max\_Process\_Size - Min\_Shared\_RAM\_per\_Child}$$

where `Total_RAM` is of course the estimated total RAM available to the web server.

Let's perform some calculations, first with sharing in place:

```
Total_RAM                 = 500Mb
Max_Process_Size          = 10Mb
Min_Shared_RAM_per_Child  =  4Mb
```

$$MaxClients = \frac{500 - 4}{10 - 4} = 82$$

then with no sharing in place:

$$MaxClients = \frac{500}{10} = 50$$

With sharing in place, if your numbers are similar to the ones in our example, you can have 64% more servers without buying more RAM (82 compared to 50).

If you improve sharing and the sharing level is maintained throughout the child's life, you might get:

```
Total_RAM             = 500Mb
Max_Process_Size      = 10Mb
Shared_RAM_per_Child  =  8Mb
```

$$MaxClients = \frac{500 - 8}{10 - 8} = 246$$

Here we have 392% more servers (246 compared to 50)!

There is one more nuance to remember. The number of requests per second that your server can serve won't grow linearly when you raise the value of `MaxClients`. Assuming that you have a lot of RAM available and you try to set `MaxClients` as high as possible, you will find that you eventually reach a point where increasing the `MaxClients` value will not improve performance.

The more clients that are running, the more CPU time will be required and the fewer CPU time slices each process will receive. The response latency (the time to respond to a request) will grow, so you won't see the expected improvement. Let's explore these issues.

The test handler that we have used is shown in Example 11-1. You can see that it does mostly CPU-intensive computations.

Example 11-1. Book/HandlerBenchmark.pm

```
package Book::HandlerBenchmark;
use Apache::Constants qw(:common);
sub handler {
    $r = shift;
    $r->send_http_header('text/html');
    $r->print("Hello");
    my $x = 100;
    my $y = log ($x ** 100) for (0..100);
    return OK;
}
1;
```

Here's the configuration section to enable this handler:

```
PerlModule Book::HandlerBenchmark
<Location /benchmark_handler_middle>
    SetHandler perl-script
    PerlHandler Book::HandlerBenchmark
</Location>
```

Now we will run the benchmark for different values of MaxClients. The results are:

```
MaxClients | avtime completed failed    rps
------------------------------------------------
       100 |    333     50000      0     755
       125 |    340     50000      0     780
       150 |    342     50000      0     791
       175 |    338     50000      0     783
       200 |    339     50000      0     785
       225 |    365     50000      0     760
       250 |    402     50000      0     741
------------------------------------------------

Non-varying sub-test parameters:
------------------------------------------------
MaxRequestsPerChild : 0
StartServers        : 100
Concurrency         : 300
Number of requests  : 50000
------------------------------------------------
```

Figure 11-1 depicts requests per second versus MaxClients. Looking at this figure, you can see that with a concurrency level of 300, the performance is almost identical for MaxClients values of 150 and 200, but it goes down for the value of 100 (not enough processes) and are even worse for the value of 250 (too many processes competing over CPU cycles). Note that we have kept the server fully loaded, since the number of concurrent requests was always higher than the number of available processes, which means that some requests were queued rather than responded to immediately. When the number of processes went above 200, more and more time was spent by the processes in the sleep state and context switching, enlarging the latency of response generation. On the other hand, with only 100 available processes, the CPU was not fully loaded and we had plenty of memory available. You can see that in our case, a MaxClients value of 150 is close to optimal.[*]

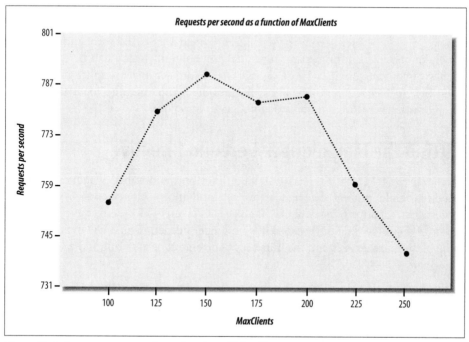

Figure 11-1. Requests per second as a function of MaxClients

This leads us to an interesting discovery, which we can summarize in the following way: increasing your RAM might not improve the performance if your CPU is already fully loaded with the current number of processes. In fact, if you start more processes, you will get a degradation in performance. On the other hand, if you decide to upgrade your machine with a very powerful CPU but you don't add enough memory, the machine will use swap memory or the CPU will be under-used; in any case, the performance will be poor. Whenever you opt for a more powerful CPU, you must always budget for enough extra memory to ensure that the CPU's greater processing power is fully utilized. It is generally best to add more memory in the first place to see if that helps with performance problems (assuming you follow our tuning advice as well).

To discover the right configuration for your server, you should run benchmarks on a machine with identical hardware to the one that you are going to use in production. Try to simulate the probable loads your machine will experience. Remember that the

---

[*] When we tried the same benchmark on different machines with a much stronger CPU and more memory, we saw different results. So we would like to stress again that the optimal configuration choices for a given application and load pattern may vary from machine to machine.

load will be variable, and plan accordingly. Experiment with the configuration parameters under different loads to discover the optimal balance of CPU and RAM use for your machine. When you change the processor or add RAM, retest the configuration to see how to change the settings to get the best from the new hardware.

You can tune your machine using reports like the one in our example, by analyzing either the requests per second (*rps*) column, which shows the throughput of your server, or the average processing time (*avtime*) column, which can be seen as the latency of your server. Take more samples to build nicer linear graphs, and pick the value of MaxClients where the curve reaches a maximum value for a throughput graph or reaches the minimum value for a latency graph.

Setting the MaxRequestsPerChild Directive

The MaxRequestsPerChild directive sets the limit on the number of requests that an individual child process can handle during its lifetime. After MaxRequestsPerChild requests, the child process will die. If MaxRequestsPerChild is zero, the process will live until the server kills it (because it is no longer needed, which will depend on the value of MinSpareServers and the number of current requests) or until the server itself is stopped.

Setting MaxRequestsPerChild to a non-zero limit solves some memory-leakage problems caused by sloppy programming practices and bugs, whereby a child process consumes a little more memory after each request. In such cases, and where the directive is left unbounded, after a certain number of requests the children will use up all the available memory and the server will die from memory starvation. Note that sometimes standard system libraries leak memory too, especially on operating systems with bad memory management.

If this is your situation you may want to set MaxRequestsPerChild to a small number. This will allow the system to reclaim the memory that a greedy child process has consumed when it exits after MaxRequestsPerChild requests.

But beware—if you set this number too low, you will lose some of the speed bonus you get from mod_perl. Consider using Apache::PerlRun if the leakage is in the CGI script that you run. This handler flushes all the memory used by the script after each request. It does, however, reduce performance, since the script's code will be loaded and recompiled for each request, so you may want to compare the loss in performance caused by Apache::PerlRun with the loss caused by memory leaks and accept the lesser of the evils.

Another approach is to use the memory usage–limiting modules, Apache::SizeLimit or Apache::GTopLimit. If you use either of these modules, you shouldn't need to set MaxRequestPerChild (i.e., you can set it to 0), although for some developers, using both in combination does the job. These modules also allow you to control the maximum unshared and minimum shared memory sizes. We discuss these modules in Chapter 14.

Setting MinSpareServers, MaxSpareServers, and StartServers

With mod_perl enabled, it might take as much as 20 seconds from the time you start the server until it is ready to serve incoming requests. This delay depends on the OS, the number of preloaded modules, and the process load of the machine. It's best to set StartServers and MinSpareServers to high numbers, so that if you get a high load just after the server has been restarted, the fresh servers will be ready to serve requests immediately.

To maximize the benefits of mod_perl, you don't want to kill servers when they are idle; rather, you want them to stay up and available to handle new requests immediately. We think an ideal configuration is to set MinSpareServers and MaxSpareServers to similar (or even the same) values. Having MaxSpareServers close to MaxClients will completely use all of your resources (if MaxClients has been chosen to take full advantage of the resources) and make sure that at any given moment your system will be capable of responding to requests with the maximum speed (assuming that the number of concurrent requests is not higher than MaxClients—otherwise, some requests will be put on hold).

If you keep a small number of servers active most of the time, keep StartServers low. Keep it low especially if MaxSpareServers is also low, as if there is no load Apache will kill its children before they have been utilized at all. If your service is heavily loaded, make StartServers close to MaxClients, and keep MaxSpareServers equal to MaxClients.

If your server performs other work besides running the mod_perl-enabled server—for example, an SQL server—make MinSpareServers low so the memory of unused children will be freed when the load is light. If your server's load varies (i.e., you get loads in bursts) and you want fast responses for all clients at any time, you will want to make it high, so that new children will be respawned in advance and able to handle bursts of requests.

For MaxSpareServers, the logic is the same as for MinSpareServers—low if you need the machine for other tasks, high if it's a host dedicated to mod_perl servers and you want a minimal delay between the request and the response.

KeepAlive

If your mod_perl server's *httpd.conf* file includes the following directives:

```
KeepAlive On
MaxKeepAliveRequests 100
KeepAliveTimeout 15
```

you have a real performance penalty, since after completing the processing for each request, the process will wait for `KeepAliveTimeout` seconds before closing the connection and will therefore not be serving other requests during this time. With this configuration you will need many more concurrent processes on a server with high traffic.

If you use the mod_status or `Apache::VMonitor` server status reporting tools, you will see a process in *K* state when it's in `KeepAlive` state.

You will probably want to switch this feature off:

```
KeepAlive Off
```

The other two directives don't matter if `KeepAlive` is `Off`.

However, you might consider enabling `KeepAlive` if the client's browser needs to request more than one object from your mod_perl server for a single HTML page. If this is the situation, by setting `KeepAlive On`, for every object rendered in the HTML page on the client's browser you save the HTTP connection overhead for all requests but the first one.

For example, if the only thing your mod_perl server does is process ads, and each of your pages has 10 or more banner ads (which is not uncommon today), your server will work more efficiently if a single process serves them all during a single connection. However, your client will see a slightly slower response, since the banners will be brought one at a time and not concurrently, as is the case if each <img> tag opens a separate connection.

SSL connections benefit the most from `KeepAlive` if you don't configure the server to cache session IDs. See the mod_ssl documentation for how to do this.

You have probably followed our advice to send all the requests for static objects to a plain Apache (proxy/accelerator) server. Since most pages include more than one unique static image, you should keep the default `KeepAlive` setting of the non-mod_perl server (i.e., keep it `On`). It will probably also be a good idea to reduce the `KeepAliveTimeout` to 1 or 2 seconds—a client is going to send a new request on the `KeepAlive` connection immediately, and the first bits of the request should reach the server within this limit, so wait only for the maximum latency of a modem connection plus a little bit more.

Another option is for the proxy/accelerator to keep the connection open to the client but make individual connections to the server, read the responses, buffer them for sending to the client, and close the server connection. Obviously, you would make new connections to the server as required by the client's requests.

PerlSetupEnv

By default, `PerlSetupEnv` is `On`, but `PerlSetupEnv Off` is another optimization you should consider.

mod_perl modifies the environment to make it appear as if the script were being called under the CGI protocol. For example, the $ENV{QUERY_STRING} environment variable is initialized with the contents of $r->args( ), and the value returned by $r-> server_hostname( ) is put into $ENV{SERVER_NAME}.

But populating %ENV is expensive. Those who have moved to the mod_perl API no longer need this duplicated data and can improve performance by turning it off. Scripts using the CGI.pm module require PerlSetupEnv On because that module relies on the environment created by mod_cgi. This is yet another reason why we recommend using the Apache::Request module in preference to CGI.pm.

Note that you can still set environment variables when PerlSetupEnv is Off. For example, say you use the following configuration:

```
PerlSetupEnv Off
PerlModule Apache::RegistryNG
<Location /perl>
    PerlSetEnv TEST hi
    SetHandler perl-script
    PerlHandler Apache::RegistryNG
    Options +ExecCGI
</Location>
```

Now issue a request for the script shown in Example 11-2.

Example 11-2. setupenvoff.pl

```
use Data::Dumper;
my $r = Apache->request( );
$r->send_http_header('text/plain');
print Dumper \%ENV;
```

You should see something like this:

```
$VAR1 = {
          'GATEWAY_INTERFACE' => 'CGI-Perl/1.1',
          'MOD_PERL' => 'mod_perl/1.26',
          'PATH' => '/bin:/usr/bin:/usr... snipped ...',
          'TEST' => 'hi'
        };
```

Note that we got the value of the TEST environment variable we set in *httpd.conf*.

Reducing the Number of stat( ) Calls Made by Apache

If (using *truss*, *strace*, or another tool available for your OS) you watch the system calls that your mod_perl server makes while processing a request, you will notice that a few stat( ) calls are made, and these are quite expensive. For example, if you have your DocumentRoot set to */home/httpd/docs* and you fetch *http://localhost/perl-status*, you will see:

```
[snip]
stat("/home/httpd/docs/perl-status", 0xbffff8cc) = -1
                    ENOENT (No such file or directory)
stat("/home/httpd/docs", {st_mode=S_IFDIR|0755,
                                st_size=1024, ...}) = 0
[snip]
```

If you have some dynamic content and your virtual relative URI is looks like */news/ perl/mod_perl/summary* (i.e., there is no such directory on the web server—the path components are used only for requesting a specific report), this will generate five stat( ) calls before the DocumentRoot is reached and the search is stopped. You will see something like this:

```
stat("/home/httpd/docs/news/perl/mod_perl/summary", 0xbffff744) = -1
                    ENOENT (No such file or directory)
stat("/home/httpd/docs/news/perl/mod_perl",        0xbffff744) = -1
                    ENOENT (No such file or directory)
stat("/home/httpd/docs/news/perl",                 0xbffff744) = -1
                    ENOENT (No such file or directory)
stat("/home/httpd/docs/news",                      0xbffff744) = -1
                    ENOENT (No such file or directory)
stat("/home/httpd/docs",
                    {st_mode=S_IFDIR|0755, st_size=1024, ...})  =  0
```

How expensive are these calls? Let's use the Time::HiRes module to find out.

The script in Example 11-3, which you should run on the command line, takes a time sample at the beginning, then does a million stat( ) calls to a nonexistent file, samples the time at the end, and prints the average time it took to make a single stat( ) call.

Example 11-3. stat_call_sample.pl

```
use Time::HiRes qw(gettimeofday tv_interval);
my $calls = 1_000_000;

my $start_time = [ gettimeofday ];

stat "/foo" for 1..$calls;

my $end_time = [ gettimeofday ];
my $avg = tv_interval($start_time,$end_time) / $calls;
print "The average execution time: $avg seconds\n";
```

Before we actually run the script we should distinguish between two different scenarios. When the server is idle, the time between the first and the last system call will be much shorter than the same time measured on a loaded system. This is because on an idle system, a process can use the CPU very often, whereas on a loaded system, lots of processes compete for CPU time and each process has to wait longer to get the same amount of CPU time.

So first we run the above code on an unloaded system:

```
panic% perl stat_call_sample.pl
The average execution time: 4.209645e-06 seconds
```

Here it takes about four microseconds to execute a stat( ) call. Now we'll start a CPU-intensive process in one console (make sure to kill the process afterward!). The following code keeps the CPU busy all the time:

```
panic% perl -e '1 while 1'
```

And now we run the *stat_call_sample.pl* script in another console:

```
panic% perl stat_call_sample.pl
The average execution time: 8.777301e-06 seconds
```

You can see that the average time has doubled (about eight microseconds). This is intuitive, since there were two processes competing for CPU resources. Now if we run four occurrences of the above code:

```
panic% perl -e '1**1 while 1' &
panic% perl -e '1**1 while 1' &
panic% perl -e '1**1 while 1' &
panic% perl -e '1**1 while 1' &
```

and run our script in parallel with these processes, we get:

```
panic% perl stat_call_sample.pl
2.0853558e-05 seconds
```

So the average stat( ) system call is five times longer now (about 20 microseconds). Now if you have 50 mod_perl processes that keep the CPU busy all the time, the stat( ) call will be 50 times slower and it'll take 0.2 milliseconds to complete a series of calls. If you have five redundant calls, as in the *strace* example above, they add up to one millisecond. If you have more processes constantly consuming CPU resources, this time adds up. Now multiply this time by the number of processes that you have and you get a few seconds lost. For some services this loss is insignificant, while for others it could be very significant.

So why does Apache do all these redundant stat( ) calls? The reason is the default installed TransHandler. One solution would be to supply our own, which would be smart enough not to look for this virtual path and would immediately return OK. In cases where you have a virtual host that serves only dynamically generated documents, you can override the default PerlTransHandler with the following one:

```
PerlModule Apache::Constants
<VirtualHost 10.10.10.10:80>
    ...
    PerlTransHandler Apache::Constants::OK
    ...
</VirtualHost>
```

The `Apache::Constants::OK` constant (which is actually a subroutine) is used here as a handler that does nothing but finish the translation phase by returning `OK`. By skipping the default translation handler, which tries to find a filesystem component that matches the given URI, you save the redundant `stat( )` calls!

As you see, it affects only this specific virtual host. Remember that `PerlTransHandler` cannot appear inside a specific `<Location>` or similar section, because the request has not yet been associated with a particular file or directory.

As we will show next, Apache's default `TransHandler` may perform several `stat( )` calls when the request is served by a virtual resource that doesn't reside on the filesystem. Things get worse when Apache is configured to look for *.htaccess* files, adding many redundant `open( )` calls.

Let's start with the following simple configuration and try to reduce the number of redundant system calls to a minimum:

```
DocumentRoot "/home/httpd/docs"
<Directory />
    AllowOverride All
</Directory>
<Location /foo/test>
    SetHandler perl-script
    PerlHandler Apache::Foo
</Location>
```

The above configuration causes the Perl `handler( )` defined in `Apache::Foo` to be executed when we make a request to */foo/test*. Notice that in the test setup there is no real file to be executed and no *.htaccess* file.

Using the above configuration, the system calls trace may look as follows:

```
stat("/home/httpd/docs/foo/test", 0xbffff8fc) = -1 ENOENT
  (No such file or directory)
stat("/home/httpd/docs/foo",        0xbffff8fc) = -1 ENOENT
  (No such file or directory)
stat("/home/httpd/docs",
  {st_mode=S_IFDIR|0755, st_size=1024, ...}) = 0
open("/.htaccess", O_RDONLY)                = -1 ENOENT
  (No such file or directory)
open("/home/.htaccess", O_RDONLY)           = -1 ENOENT
  (No such file or directory)
open("/home/httpd/.htaccess", O_RDONLY)     = -1 ENOENT
  (No such file or directory)
open("/home/httpd/docs/.htaccess", O_RDONLY) = -1 ENOENT
  (No such file or directory)
stat("/home/httpd/docs/test", 0xbffff774)   = -1 ENOENT
  (No such file or directory)
stat("/home/httpd/docs",
  {st_mode=S_IFDIR|0755, st_size=1024, ...}) = 0
```

Now we modify the `<Directory>` entry and add `AllowOverride None`, which, among other things, tells Apache not to search for *.htaccess* files:

```
<Directory />
    AllowOverride None
</Directory>
```

After restarting the server and issuing a request to */foo/test*, we see that the four open( ) calls for *.htaccess* have gone. The remaining system calls are:

```
stat("/home/httpd/docs/foo/test", 0xbffff8fc) = -1 ENOENT
  (No such file or directory)
stat("/home/httpd/docs/foo",      0xbffff8fc) = -1 ENOENT
  (No such file or directory)
stat("/home/httpd/docs",
  {st_mode=S_IFDIR|0755, st_size=1024, ...}) = 0
stat("/home/httpd/docs/test", 0xbffff774)  = -1 ENOENT
  (No such file or directory)
stat("/home/httpd/docs",
  {st_mode=S_IFDIR|0755, st_size=1024, ...}) = 0
```

Next, let's try to shortcut the *foo* location with:

```
Alias /foo/ /
```

which makes Apache look for the file in the / directory and not under */home/httpd/ docs/foo*. Let's restart the server and try again:

```
stat("/test", 0xbffff8fc) = -1 ENOENT (No such file or directory)
```

Now we've got only one `stat( )` call left!

Let's replace the `Alias` setting we have just added with:

```
PerlModule Apache::Constants
PerlTransHandler Apache::Constants::OK
```

as explained earlier. When we issue the request, we see no remaining `stat( )` calls. This technique works if you serve content using only mod_perl handlers, since CGI scripts and other files won't be looked for on the filesystem now. Also, since the default translation handler is now skipped, `$r->filename` now won't be set.

If you want to serve both mod_perl handlers and real files, you will have to write your own `PerlTransHandler` to handle requests as desired. For example, the following `PerlTransHandler` will not look up the file on the filesystem if the URI starts with */foo*—the handler will return `DECLINED` and the default `PerlTransHandler` will be used:

```
PerlTransHandler 'sub { return shift->uri( ) =~ m|^/foo| \
                    ? Apache::Constants::OK \
                    : Apache::Constants::DECLINED; }'
```

Let's see the same configuration using a `<Perl>` section and a dedicated package (see Example 11-4).

Example 11-4. perl_section.conf

```
<Perl>
  package Book::Trans;
  use Apache::Constants qw(:common);
  sub handler {
      my $r = shift;
      return OK if $r->uri() =~ m|^/foo|;
      return DECLINED;
  }

  package Apache::ReadConfig;
  $PerlTransHandler = "Book::Trans";
</Perl>
```

Here we have defined the Book::Trans package and implemented the handler( ) function. Then we have assigned this handler to the PerlTransHandler.

You can move the code in the module into an external file (e.g., *Book/Trans.pm*) and configure the PerlTransHandler with:

```
PerlTransHandler Book::Trans
```

in the normal way (no <Perl> section required).

Now we'll run some benchmarks to test the solutions described above, both individually and in groups. To make the difference in the number of stat( ) calls more prominent, we will use a very light handler that just prints something out.

The module that we have used is shown in Example 11-5.

Example 11-5. Book/News.pm

```
package Book::News;
use Apache::Constants qw(:common);
sub handler {
    my $r = shift;
    my $uri = $r->uri;
    my @sections = split "/", $uri;
    # in a real handler you'd do some DB lookup and return the story:
    # my $story = get_story(@sections);
    $r->send_http_header('text/plain');
    print "Story matching @sections\n";
    return OK;
}
1;
```

This is the URI we have used for testing:

```
/news/perl/mod_perl/summary
```

Notice that the URI is long enough to generate many stat( ) calls with the default Apache configuration.

This is the main configuration:

```
<Location /news>
    SetHandler perl-script
    PerlHandler +Book::News
</Location>
```

Now we try different configurations and see how they influence performance. Each configuration is listed with a tag in parentheses that is used as a key in the table and explanation that follows.

1. (*default*) Nothing was added:

   ```
   <Directory />
       AllowOverride All
   </Directory>
   ```

2. (*noht*) Prevent *.htaccess* lookup:

   ```
   <Directory />
       AllowOverride None
   </Directory>
   ```

3. (*alias*) Location alias shortcutting:

   ```
   Alias /news /
   ```

4. (*trans*) Using a nondefault TransHandler:

   ```
   <Perl>
       package Book::Trans;
       use Apache::Constants qw(:common);
       sub handler {
           my $r = shift;
           return OK if $r->uri() =~ m|^/news|;
           return DECLINED;
       }

       package Apache::ReadConfig;
       $PerlTransHandler = "Book::Trans";
   </Perl>
   ```

The results, sorted by the requests per second (*rps*) rate, are:

```
Options     | avtime completed failed   rps
----------- |------------------------------
noht+alias  |    27     5000       0    996
noht+trans  |    29     5000       0    988
trans       |    29     5000       0    975
alias       |    28     5000       0    974
noht        |    32     5000       0    885
default     |    34     5000       0    827
```

with static arguments:

```
Concurrency        : 30
Number of requests : 5000
```

The concurrency and connections don't matter here; we are concerned with the relative rather than the absolute numbers.

Figure 11-2 depicts these results.

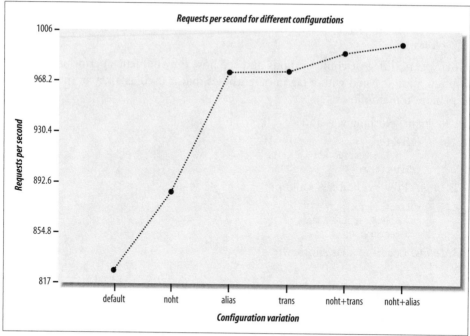

Figure 11-2. Results of the four solutions

Preventing *.htaccess* lookup (*noht*) improved the performance by about 8% (885 versus 827). Using alias shortcutting (*alias*) or a nondefault TransHandler (*trans*) gave even more of a performance boost: since for a long URI like the one in our example, each directory generates a few stat( ) and open( ) system calls, the speedup was around 15% compared to the standard configuration (*default*). Grouping the prevention of *.htaccess* lookup (*noht*) plus one of the techniques that don't look for the nonexistent file in the filesystem (*alias* or *trans*) gave a performance boost of about 18% (996 versus 827).

As we have seen, the number of pseudo-subdirectories is in direct proportion to the number of stat( ) and open( ) system calls that are made. To prove this, let's use the standard configuration (*default*) and benchmark three URIs with a different number of sections (directories), without counting the first section (*/news*):

```
Sections  URI
--------------------------------------------
1         /news/perl
3         /news/perl/mod_perl/summary
5         /news/perl/mod_perl/summary/foo/bar
```

The results are what we expected:

```
Sections | avtime completed failed    rps
---------------------------------------------------
       1 |    33      5000       0     849
       3 |    34      5000       0     829
       5 |    35      5000       0     801
---------------------------------------------------
```

Each of the two sections add an extra millisecond to the average processing and connection time, which reduces performance by about 25 requests per second.

It's important to read the figures cautiously. Improving performance by 20% simply by adding a few configuration directives is not likely to be achieved in practice. In our test code we used a very light handler, which did nothing but send a few lines of text without doing any processing. When you use real code, whose runtime is not 30–40 milliseconds but 300–400 milliseconds, the improvement of 7 milliseconds on average (as we saw between the standard configuration (*default*), giving 34 ms, and the combination of *noht* and *alias*, giving 27 ms) might be insignificant. The tuning we've discussed here is important mostly for servers that serve millions of requests per day and where every millisecond counts.

But even if your server has a light load, you can still make it a little bit faster. Use a benchmark on the real code and see whether you win something or not.

Symbolic Links Lookup

The two options FollowSymLinks and SymLinksIfOwnerMatch are designed for the user's security. Unless FollowSymLinks is enabled, symbolic links will not be followed by the server. If SymLinksIfOwnerMatch is enabled, the server will follow symbolic links only when the target file or directory is owned by the same user as the link. Note that the two options are ignored if set within a <Location> block.

This protection costs a little overhead for each request. Wherever in your URL-space you *do not* have this setting:

```
Options FollowSymLinks
```

or you *do* have this setting:

```
Options SymLinksIfOwnerMatch
```

Apache will have to issue an extra call to lstat( ) per directory segment in the path to the file. For example, if you have:

```
DocumentRoot /home/httpd/docs
<Directory />
    Options SymLinksIfOwnerMatch
</Directory>
```

and a request is made for the URI *index.html*, Apache will perform lstat() on these three directories and one file:

```
/home
/home/httpd
/home/httpd/docs
/home/httpd/docs/index.html
```

The deeper the file is located in the filesystem, the more lstat() system calls will be made. The results of these lstat() calls are never cached, so they will occur for every single request. If you really want the symbolic-links security checking, you can do something like this:

```
DocumentRoot /home/httpd/docs
<Directory />
    Options FollowSymLinks
</Directory>
<Directory /home/httpd/docs>
    Options -FollowSymLinks +SymLinksIfOwnerMatch
</Directory>
```

This at least avoids the extra checks for the DocumentRoot path. Note that you'll need to add similar sections if you have any Alias or RewriteRule paths outside of your document root. For highest performance, and no symbolic link protection, set the FollowSymLinks option everywhere, and never set the SymLinksIfOwnerMatch option.

Disabling DNS Resolution

You should make sure that your *httpd.conf* file has this setting:

```
HostnameLookups Off
```

This is the default.

If this directive is set to On (or even worse, Double), Apache will try to use DNS resolution to translate the client's IP address into its hostname for every single request.

The problem is that there are many servers with broken reverse DNS, which means that resolution will never succeed, but it might take a significant time for the lookup attempt to time out. The web page will not be served before the lookup has either succeeded or timed out, because it's assumed that if you have this feature enabled you want to know the hostname from which the request came. Consequently Apache won't run any script or handler until the lookup attempt has concluded.

Moreover, you can end up with a hostname that is completely useless and gives you far less information than the IP address would. To avoid this problem you can enable:

```
HostnameLookups Double
```

which does a reverse lookup, then a forward lookup on what it gets to make sure that the IP address is not being spoofed. However, this double lookup makes it even slower.

If you need DNS names in some CGI script or handler, you should use gethostbyname( ) or its equivalents.

In addition to having HostnameLookups turned off, you should avoid using hostname-based access control and use IP-based access control instead. If you have a setting like this:

```
<Location /perl-status>
    ...
    Order deny, allow
    Deny  from all
    Allow from www.example.com
</Location>
```

the server will have to perform a double reverse DNS lookup for each incoming IP address to make sure it matches the domain name listed in the Allow directive and is not being spoofed. Of course, in our example this will happen only for requests for URIs starting with /perl-status.

This is another way to do the authorization based on the IP address:

```
<Location /perl-status>
    ...
    Order deny, allow
    Deny  from all
    Allow from 128.9.176.32
</Location>
```

Note that since some IP addresses map to multiple hosts (multiple CNAME records), this solution will not always do what you want.

Response Compressing

Have you ever served a huge HTML file (e.g., a file bloated with JavaScript code) and wondered how you could send it compressed, thus dramatically cutting down the download times? After all, Java applets can be compressed into a jar and benefit from faster download times. Why can't we do the same with plain text files (HTML, Java-Script, etc.)? Plain text can often be compressed by a factor of 10.

Apache::GzipChain can help you with this task. If a client (browser) understands *gzip* encoding, this module compresses the output and sends it downstream. The client decompresses the data upon receiving it and renders the HTML as if it was fetching uncompressed HTML. Furthermore, this module is used as a filter, thanks to Apache::OutputChain, and can therefore compress not only static files but also dynamic content created from your handlers or scripts.

For example, to compress all HTML files on the fly, do this:

```
<Files *.html>
    SetHandler perl-script
    PerlHandler Apache::OutputChain Apache::GzipChain Apache::PassFile
</Files>
```

Browsers are supposed to declare that they can handle compressed input by setting the Accept-Encoding header. Unfortunately, many browsers cannot handle it, even if they claim that they can. Apache::GzipChain keeps a list of user agents, and also looks at the User-Agent header to check for browsers known to accept compressed output.

As an example, if you want to return compressed files that will in addition pass through the Embperl module, you would write:

```
<Location /test>
    SetHandler perl-script
    PerlHandler Apache::OutputChain Apache::GzipChain \
                Apache::EmbperlChain Apache::PassFile
</Location>
```

Watch the *access_log* file to see how many bytes were actually sent, and compare that with the bytes sent using a regular configuration.

Notice that the rightmost PerlHandler must be a content producer. Here we are using Apache::PassFile, but you can use any module that creates output.

Alternatively, you may want to try Apache::Compress, which is compatible with Apache::Filter and is covered in Appendix B. To compress only outgoing static files, you can look at the mod_gzip and mod_deflate modules for Apache.

The cool thing about these modules is that they don't require any modification of the code. To enable or disable them, only *httpd.conf* has to be tweaked.

References

- Apache Performance Notes: *http://httpd.apache.org/docs/misc/perf-tuning.html.*
- OS-specific hints on running a high-performance web server: *http://httpd.apache.org/docs/misc/perf.html.*
- "The Case for Persistent-Connection HTTP," by Jeffrey C. Mogul: *http://www.research.compaq.com/wrl/techreports/abstracts/95.4.html.*

  This paper discusses the pros and cons of persistent-connection HTTP, in particular talking about KeepAlive.
- Chapter 9 ("Tuning Apache and mod_perl) in *mod_perl Developer's Cookbook,* by Geoffrey Young, Paul Lindner, and Randy Kobes (Sams Publishing).

## CHAPTER 12

Server Setup Strategies

Since the first day mod_perl was available, users have adopted various techniques that make the best of mod_perl by deploying it in combination with other modules and tools. This chapter presents the theory behind these useful techniques, their pros and cons, and of course detailed installation and configuration notes so you can easily reproduce the presented setups.

This chapter will explore various ways to use mod_perl, running it in parallel with other web servers as well as coexisting with proxy servers.

mod_perl Deployment Overview

There are several different ways to build, configure, and deploy your mod_perl-enabled server. Some of them are:

1. One big binary (for mod_perl) and one configuration file.

2. Two binaries (one big one for mod_perl and one small one for static objects, such as images) and two configuration files.

3. One DSO-style Apache binary and two configuration files. The first configuration file is used for the plain Apache server (equivalent to a static build of Apache); the second configuration file is used for the heavy mod_perl server, by loading the mod_perl DSO loadable object using the same binary.

4. Any of the above plus a reverse proxy server in *httpd* accelerator mode.

If you are new to mod_perl and just want to set up your development server quickly, we recommend that you start with the first option and work on getting your feet wet with Apache and mod_perl. Later, you can decide whether to move to the second option, which allows better tuning at the expense of more complicated administration, to the third option (the more state-of-the-art DSO system), or to the fourth option, which gives you even more power and flexibility. Here are some of the things to consider.

1. The first option will kill your production site if you serve a lot of static data from large (4–15 MB) web server processes. On the other hand, while testing you will have no other server interaction to mask or add to your errors.

2. The second option allows you to tune the two servers individually, for maximum performance. However, you need to choose whether to run the two servers on multiple ports, multiple IPs, etc., and you have the burden of administering more than one server. You also have to deal with proxying or complicated links to keep the two servers synchronized.

3. With DSO, modules can be added and removed without recompiling the server, and their code is even shared among multiple servers.

    You can compile just once and yet have more than one binary, by using different configuration files to load different sets of modules. The different Apache servers loaded in this way can run simultaneously to give a setup such as that described in the second option above.

    The downside is that you are dealing with a solution that has weak documentation, is still subject to change, and, even worse, might cause some subtle bugs. It is still somewhat platform-specific, and your mileage may vary.

    Also, the DSO module (mod_so) adds size and complexity to your binaries.

4. The fourth option (proxy in *httpd* accelerator mode), once correctly configured and tuned, improves the performance of any of the above three options by caching and buffering page results. This should be used once you have mastered the second or third option, and is generally the preferred way to deploy a mod_perl server in a production environment.

If you are going to run two web servers, you have the following options:

Two machines

Serve the static content from one machine and the dynamic content from another. You will have to adjust all the links in the generated HTML pages: you cannot use relative references (e.g., */images/foo.gif*) for static objects when the page is generated by the dynamic-content machine, and conversely you can't use relative references to dynamic objects in pages served by the static server. In these cases, fully qualified URIs are required.

Later we will explore a frontend/backend strategy that solves this problem.

The drawback is that you must maintain two machines, and this can get expensive. Still, for extremely large projects, this is the best way to go. When the load is high, it can be distributed across more than two machines.

One machine and two IP addresses

If you have only one machine but two IP addresses, you may tell each server to bind to a different IP address, with the help of the BindAddress directive in *httpd. conf*. You still have the problem of relative links here (solutions to which will be presented later in this chapter). As we will show later, you can use the 127.0.0.1

address for the backend server if the backend connections are proxied through the frontend.

One machine, one IP address, and two ports

Finally, the most widely used approach uses only one machine and one NIC, but binds the two servers to two different ports. Usually the static server listens on the default port 80, and the dynamic server listens on some other, nonstandard port.

Even here the problem of relative links is still relevant, since while the same IP address is used, the port designators are different, which prevents you from using relative links for both contents. For example, a URL to the static server could be *http://www.example.com/images/nav.png*, while the dynamic page might reside at *http://www.example.com:8000/perl/script.pl*. Once again, the solutions are around the corner.

Standalone mod_perl-Enabled Apache Server

The first and simplest scenario uses a straightforward, standalone, mod_perl-enabled Apache server, as shown in Figure 12-1. Just take your plain Apache server and add mod_perl, like you would add any other Apache module. Continue to run it at the port it was using before. You probably want to try this before you proceed to more sophisticated and complex techniques. This is the standard installation procedure we described in Chapter 3.

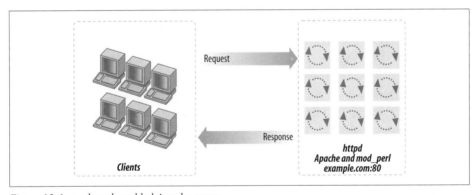

Figure 12-1. mod_perl-enabled Apache server

A standalone server gives you the following advantages:

Simplicity

You just follow the installation instructions, configure it, restart the server, and you are done.

No network changes

You do not have to worry about using additional ports, as we will see later.

Speed

You get a very fast server for dynamic content, and you see an enormous speedup compared to mod_cgi, from the first moment you start to use it.

The disadvantages of a standalone server are as follows:

- The process size of a mod_perl-enabled Apache server might be huge (maybe 4 MB at startup and growing to 10 MB or more, depending on how you use it) compared to a typical plain Apache server (about 500 KB). Of course, if memory sharing is in place, RAM requirements will be smaller.

  You probably have a few dozen child processes. The additional memory requirements add up in direct relation to the number of child processes. Your memory demands will grow by an order of magnitude, but this is the price you pay for the additional performance boost of mod_perl. With memory being relatively inexpensive nowadays, the additional cost is low—especially when you consider the dramatic performance boost mod_perl gives to your services with every 100 MB of RAM you add.

  While you will be happy to have these monster processes serving your scripts with monster speed, you should be very worried about having them serve static objects such as images and HTML files. Each static request served by a mod_perl-enabled server means another large process running, competing for system resources such as memory and CPU cycles. The real overhead depends on the static object request rate. Remember that if your mod_perl code produces HTML code that includes images, each of these will produce another static object request. Having another plain web server to serve the static objects solves this unpleasant problem. Having a proxy server as a frontend, caching the static objects and freeing the mod_perl processes from this burden, is another solution. We will discuss both later.

- Another drawback of this approach is that when serving output to a client with a slow connection, the huge mod_perl-enabled server process (with all of its system resources) will be tied up until the response is completely written to the client. While it might take a few milliseconds for your script to complete the request, there is a chance it will still be busy for a number of seconds or even minutes if the request is from a client with a slow connection. As with the previous drawback, a proxy solution can solve this problem. We'll discuss proxies more later.

  Proxying dynamic content is not going to help much if all the clients are on a fast local net (for example, if you are administering an Intranet). On the contrary, it can decrease performance. Still, remember that some of your Intranet users might work from home through slow modem links.

If you are new to mod_perl, this is probably the best way to get yourself started.

And of course, if your site is serving only mod_perl scripts (and close to zero static objects), this might be the perfect choice for you!

Before trying the more advanced setup techniques we are going to talk about now, it's probably a good idea to review the simpler straightforward installation and configuration techniques covered in Chapters 3 and 4. These will get you started with the standard deployment discussed here.

One Plain and One mod_perl-Enabled Apache Server

As mentioned earlier, when running scripts under mod_perl you will notice that the *httpd* processes consume a huge amount of virtual memory—from 5 MB–15 MB, and sometimes even more. That is the price you pay for the enormous speed improvements under mod_perl, mainly because the code is compiled once and needs to be cached for later reuse. But in fact less memory is used if memory sharing takes place. Chapter 14 covers this issue extensively.

Using these large processes to serve static objects such as images and HTML documents is overkill. A better approach is to run two servers: a very light, plain Apache server to serve static objects and a heavier, mod_perl-enabled Apache server to serve requests for dynamically generated objects. From here on, we will refer to these two servers as *httpd_docs* (vanilla Apache) and *httpd_perl* (mod_perl-enabled Apache). This approach is depicted in Figure 12-2.

The advantages of this setup are:

- The heavy mod_perl processes serve only dynamic requests, so fewer of these large servers are deployed.
- MaxClients, MaxRequestsPerChild, and related parameters can now be optimally tuned for both the *httpd_docs* and *httpd_perl* servers (something we could not do before). This allows us to fine-tune the memory usage and get better server performance.

  Now we can run many lightweight *httpd_docs* servers and just a few heavy *httpd_perl* servers.

The disadvantages are:

- The need for two configuration files, two sets of controlling scripts (startup/ shutdown), and watchdogs.
- If you are processing log files, you will probably have to merge the two separate log files into one before processing them.

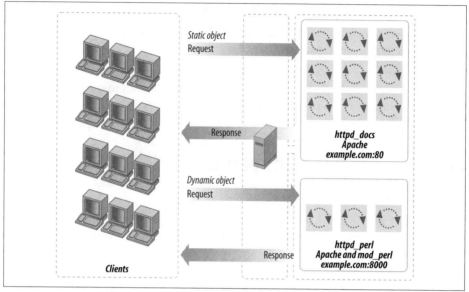

Figure 12-2. Standalone and mod_perl-enabled Apache servers

- Just as in the one-server approach, we still have the problem of a mod_perl process spending its precious time serving slow clients when the processing portion of the request was completed a long time ago. (Deploying a proxy, covered in the next section, solves this problem.)

  As with the single-server approach, this is not a major disadvantage if you are on a fast network (i.e., an Intranet). It is likely that you do not want a buffering server in this case.

Note that when a user browses static pages and the base URL in the browser's location window points to the static server (for example *http://www.example.com/index.html*), all relative URLs (e.g., <a href="/main/download.html">) are being served by the plain Apache server. But this is not the case with dynamically generated pages. For example, when the base URL in the location window points to the dynamic server (e.g., *http://www.example.com:8000/perl/index.pl*), all relative URLs in the dynamically generated HTML will be served by heavy mod_perl processes.

You must use fully qualified URLs, not relative ones. *http://www.example.com/icons/arrow.gif* is a full URL, while *icons/arrow.gif* is a relative one. Using <base href="http://www.example.com/"> in the generated HTML is another way to handle this problem. Also, the *httpd_perl* server could rewrite the requests back to *httpd_docs* (much slower) and you still need the attention of the heavy servers.

This is not an issue if you hide the internal port implementations, so the client sees only one server running on port 80, as explained later in this chapter.

Choosing the Target Installation Directories Layout

If you're going to run two Apache servers, you'll need two complete (and different) sets of configuration, log, and other files. In this scenario we'll use a dedicated root directory for each server, which is a personal choice. You can choose to have both servers living under the same root, but this may cause problems since it requires a slightly more complicated configuration. This decision would allow you to share some directories, such as *include* (which contains Apache headers), but this can become a problem later, if you decide to upgrade one server but not the other. You will have to solve the problem then, so why not avoid it in the first place?

First let's prepare the sources. We will assume that all the sources go into the */home/stas/src* directory. Since you will probably want to tune each copy of Apache separately, it is better to use two separate copies of the Apache source for this configuration. For example, you might want only the *httpd_docs* server to be built with the mod_rewrite module.

Having two independent source trees will prove helpful unless you use dynamically shared objects (covered later in this chapter).

Make two subdirectories:

```
panic% mkdir /home/stas/src/httpd_docs
panic% mkdir /home/stas/src/httpd_perl
```

Next, put the Apache source into the */home/stas/src/httpd_docs* directory (replace *1.3.x* with the version of Apache that you have downloaded):

```
panic% cd /home/stas/src/httpd_docs
panic% tar xvzf ~/src/apache_1.3.x.tar.gz
```

Now prepare the *httpd_perl* server sources:

```
panic% cd /home/stas/src/httpd_perl
panic% tar xvzf ~/src/apache_1.3.x.tar.gz
panic% tar xvzf ~/src/modperl-1.xx.tar.gz

panic% ls -l
drwxr-xr-x  8 stas  stas 2048 Apr 29 17:38 apache_1.3.x/
drwxr-xr-x  8 stas  stas 2048 Apr 29 17:38 modperl-1.xx/
```

We are going to use a default Apache directory layout and place each server directory under its dedicated directory. The two directories are:

```
/home/httpd/httpd_perl/
/home/httpd/httpd_docs/
```

We are using the user *httpd*, belonging to the group *httpd*, for the web server. If you don't have this user and group created yet, add them and make sure you have the correct permissions to be able to work in the */home/httpd* directory.

Configuration and Compilation of the Sources

Now we proceed to configure and compile the sources using the directory layout we have just described.

Building the httpd_docs server

The first step is to configure the source:

```
panic% cd /home/stas/src/httpd_docs/apache_1.3.x
panic% ./configure --prefix=/home/httpd/httpd_docs \
    --enable-module=rewrite --enable-module=proxy
```

We need the mod_rewrite and mod_proxy modules, as we will see later, so we tell *./configure* to build them in.

You might also want to add *--layout*, to see the resulting directories' layout without actually running the configuration process.

Next, compile and install the source:

```
panic% make
panic# make install
```

Rename *httpd* to *httpd_docs*:

```
panic% mv /home/httpd/httpd_docs/bin/httpd \
    /home/httpd/httpd_docs/bin/httpd_docs
```

Now modify the *apachectl* utility to point to the renamed *httpd* via your favorite text editor or by using Perl:

```
panic% perl -pi -e 's|bin/httpd|bin/httpd_docs|' \
    /home/httpd/httpd_docs/bin/apachectl
```

Another approach would be to use the *--target* option while configuring the source, which makes the last two commands unnecessary.

```
panic% ./configure --prefix=/home/httpd/httpd_docs \
    --target=httpd_docs \
    --enable-module=rewrite --enable-module=proxy
panic% make
panic# make install
```

Since we told *./configure* that we want the executable to be called *httpd_docs* (via *--target=httpd_docs*), it performs all the naming adjustments for us.

The only thing that you might find unusual is that *apachectl* will now be called *httpd_docsctl* and the configuration file *httpd.conf* will now be called *httpd_docs.conf*.

We will leave the decision making about the preferred configuration and installation method to the reader. In the rest of this guide we will continue using the regular names that result from using the standard configuration and the manual executable name adjustment, as described at the beginning of this section.

Building the httpd_perl server

Now we proceed with the source configuration and installation of the *httpd_perl* server.

```
panic% cd /home/stas/src/httpd_perl/mod_perl-1.xx
```

```
panic% perl Makefile.PL \
    APACHE_SRC=../apache_1.3.x/src \
    DO_HTTPD=1 USE_APACI=1 EVERYTHING=1 \
    APACHE_PREFIX=/home/httpd/httpd_perl \
    APACI_ARGS='--prefix=/home/httpd/httpd_perl'
```

If you need to pass any other configuration options to Apache's *./configure*, add them after the *--prefix* option. For example:

```
APACI_ARGS='--prefix=/home/httpd/httpd_perl \
            --enable-module=status'
```

Notice that just like in the *httpd_docs* configuration, you can use *--target=httpd_perl*. Note that this option has to be the very last argument in APACI_ARGS; otherwise *make test* tries to run *httpd_perl*, which fails.

Now build, test, and install *httpd_perl*.

```
panic% make && make test
panic# make install
```

Upon installation, Apache puts a stripped version of *httpd* at */home/httpd/httpd_perl/ bin/httpd*. The original version, which includes debugging symbols (if you need to run a debugger on this executable), is located at */home/stas/src/httpd_perl/apache_1.3.x/ src/httpd*.

Now rename *httpd* to *httpd_perl*:

```
panic% mv /home/httpd/httpd_perl/bin/httpd \
    /home/httpd/httpd_perl/bin/httpd_perl
```

and update the *apachectl* utility to drive the renamed *httpd*:

```
panic% perl -p -i -e 's|bin/httpd|bin/httpd_perl|' \
    /home/httpd/httpd_perl/bin/apachectl
```

Configuration of the Servers

When we have completed the build process, the last stage before running the servers is to configure them.

Basic httpd_docs server configuration

Configuring the *httpd_docs* server is a very easy task. Open */home/httpd/httpd_docs/ conf/httpd.conf* in your favorite text editor and configure it as you usually would.

Now you can start the server with:

```
/home/httpd/httpd_docs/bin/apachectl start
```

Basic httpd_perl server configuration

Now we edit the */home/httpd/httpd_perl/conf/httpd.conf* file. The first thing to do is to set a Port directive—it should be different from that used by the plain Apache server (Port 80), since we cannot bind two servers to the same port number on the same IP address. Here we will use 8000. Some developers use port 81, but you can bind to ports below 1024 only if the server has *root* permissions. Also, if you are running on a multiuser machine, there is a chance that someone already uses that port, or will start using it in the future, which could cause problems. If you are the only user on your machine, you can pick any unused port number, but be aware that many organizations use firewalls that may block some of the ports, so port number choice can be a controversial topic. Popular port numbers include 80, 81, 8000, and 8080. In a two-server scenario, you can hide the nonstandard port number from firewalls and users by using either mod_proxy's ProxyPass directive or a proxy server such as Squid.

Now we proceed to the mod_perl-specific directives. It's a good idea to add them all at the end of *httpd.conf*, since you are going to fiddle with them a lot in the early stages.

First, you need to specify where all the mod_perl scripts will be located. Add the following configuration directive:

```
# mod_perl scripts will be called from
Alias /perl /home/httpd/httpd_perl/perl
```

From now on, all requests for URIs starting with */perl* will be executed under mod_perl and will be mapped to the files in the directory */home/httpd/httpd_perl/perl*.

Now configure the */perl* location:

```
PerlModule Apache::Registry

<Location /perl>
    #AllowOverride None
    SetHandler perl-script
    PerlHandler Apache::Registry
    Options ExecCGI
    PerlSendHeader On
    Allow from all
</Location>
```

This configuration causes any script that is called with a path prefixed with */perl* to be executed under the Apache::Registry module and as a CGI script (hence the ExecCGI—if you omit this option, the script will be printed to the user's browser as plain text or will possibly trigger a "Save As" window).

This is only a very basic configuration. Chapter 4 covers the rest of the details.

Once the configuration is complete, it's a time to start the server with:

```
/home/httpd/httpd_perl/bin/apachectl start
```

One Light Non-Apache and One mod_perl-Enabled Apache Server

If the only requirement from the light server is for it to serve static objects, you can get away with non-Apache servers, which have an even smaller memory footprint and even better speed. Most of these servers don't have the configurability and flexibility provided by the Apache web server, but if those aren't required, you might consider using one of these alternatives as a server for static objects. To accomplish this, simply replace the Apache web server that was serving the static objects with another server of your choice.

Among the small memory–footprint and fast-speed servers, *thttpd* is one of the best choices. It runs as a multithreaded single process and consumes about 250K of memory. You can find more information about this server at *http://www.acme.com/software/thttpd/*. This site also includes a very interesting web server performance comparison chart (*http://www.acme.com/software/thttpd/benchmarks.html*).

Another good choice is the kHTTPd web server for Linux. kHTTPd is different from other web servers in that it runs from within the Linux kernel as a module (device-driver). kHTTPd handles only static (file-based) web pages; it passes all requests for non-static information to a regular user space web server such as Apache. For more information, see *http://www.fenrus.demon.nl/*.

Boa is yet another very fast web server, whose primary design goals are speed and security. According to *http://www.boa.org/*, Boa is capable of handling several thousand hits per second on a 300-MHz Pentium and dozens of hits per second on a lowly 20-MHz 386/SX.

Adding a Proxy Server in httpd Accelerator Mode

We have already presented a solution with two servers: one plain Apache server, which is very light and configured to serve static objects, and the other with mod_perl enabled (very heavy) and configured to serve mod_perl scripts and handlers. We named them *httpd_docs* and *httpd_perl*, respectively.

In the dual-server setup presented earlier, the two servers coexist at the same IP address by listening to different ports: *httpd_docs* listens to port 80 (e.g., *http://www.example.com/images/test.gif*) and *httpd_perl* listens to port 8000 (e.g., *http://www.example.com:8000/perl/test.pl*). Note that we did not write *http://www.example.com:80*

for the first example, since port 80 is the default port for the HTTP service. Later on, we will change the configuration of the *httpd_docs* server to make it listen to port 81.

This section will attempt to convince you that you should really deploy a proxy server in *httpd* accelerator mode. This is a special mode that, in addition to providing the normal caching mechanism, accelerates your CGI and mod_perl scripts by taking the responsibility of pushing the produced content to the client, thereby freeing your mod_perl processes. Figure 12-3 shows a configuration that uses a proxy server, a standalone Apache server, and a mod_perl-enabled Apache server.

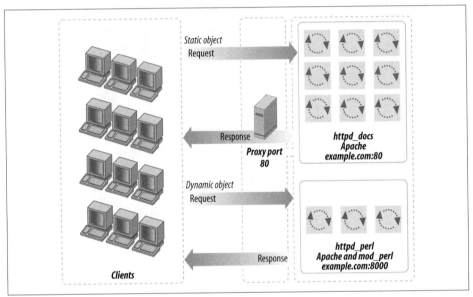

Figure 12-3. A proxy server, standalone Apache, and mod_perl-enabled Apache

The advantages of using the proxy server in conjunction with mod_perl are:

- You get all the benefits of the usual use of a proxy server that serves static objects from the proxy's cache. You get less I/O activity reading static objects from the disk (the proxy serves the most "popular" objects from RAM—of course you benefit more if you allow the proxy server to consume more RAM), and since you do not wait for the I/O to be completed, you can serve static objects much faster.

- You get the extra functionality provided by *httpd* accelerator mode, which makes the proxy server act as a sort of output buffer for the dynamic content. The mod_perl server sends the entire response to the proxy and is then free to deal with other requests. The proxy server is responsible for sending the response to the browser. This means that if the transfer is over a slow link, the mod_perl server is not waiting around for the data to move.

- This technique allows you to hide the details of the server's implementation. Users will never see ports in the URLs (more on that topic later). You can have a few boxes serving the requests and only one serving as a frontend, which spreads the jobs between the servers in a way that you can control. You can actually shut down a server without the user even noticing, because the frontend server will dispatch the jobs to other servers. This is called *load balancing*—it's too big an issue to cover here, but there is plenty of information available on the Internet (refer to the References section at the end of this chapter).

- For security reasons, using an *httpd* accelerator (or a proxy in *httpd* accelerator mode) is essential because it protects your internal server from being directly attacked by arbitrary packets. The *httpd* accelerator and internal server communicate only expected HTTP requests, and usually only specific URI namespaces get proxied. For example, you can ensure that only URIs starting with */perl/* will be proxied to the backend server. Assuming that there are no vulnerabilities that can be triggered via some resource under */perl*, this means that only your public "bastion" accelerating web server can get hosed in a successful attack—your backend server will be left intact. Of course, don't consider your web server to be impenetrable because it's accessible only through the proxy. Proxying it reduces the number of ways a cracker can get to your backend server; it doesn't eliminate them all.

  Your server will be effectively impenetrable if it listens only on ports on your *localhost* (127.0.0.1), which makes it impossible to connect to your backend machine from the outside. But you don't need to connect from the outside anymore, as you will see when you proceed to this technique's implementation notes.

  In addition, if you use some sort of access control, authentication, and authorization at the frontend server, it's easy to forget that users can still access the backend server directly, bypassing the frontend protection. By making the backend server directly inaccessible you prevent this possibility.

Of course, there are drawbacks. Luckily, these are not functionality drawbacks—they are more administration hassles. The disadvantages are:

- You have another daemon to worry about, and while proxies are generally stable, you have to make sure to prepare proper startup and shutdown scripts, which are run at boot and reboot as appropriate. This is something that you do once and never come back to again. Also, you might want to set up the *crontab* to run a watchdog script that will make sure that the proxy server is running and restart it if it detects a problem, reporting the problem to the administrator on the way. Chapter 5 explains how to develop and run such watchdogs.

- Proxy servers can be configured to be light or heavy. The administrator must decide what gives the highest performance for his application. A proxy server such as Squid is light in the sense of having only one process serving all requests, but it can consume a lot of memory when it loads objects into memory for faster service.

- If you use the default logging mechanism for all requests on the front- and back-end servers, the requests that will be proxied to the backend server will be logged twice, which makes it tricky to merge the two log files, should you want to. Therefore, if all accesses to the backend server are done via the frontend server, it's the best to turn off logging of the backend server.

If the backend server is also accessed directly, bypassing the frontend server, you want to log only the requests that don't go through the frontend server. One way to tell whether a request was proxied or not is to use mod_proxy_add_forward, presented later in this chapter, which sets the HTTP header X-Forwarded-For for all proxied requests. So if the default logging is turned off, you can add a custom PerlLogHandler that logs only requests made directly to the backend server.

If you still decide to log proxied requests at the backend server, they might not contain all the information you need, since instead of the real remote IP of the user, you will always get the IP of the frontend server. Again, mod_proxy_add_forward, presented later, provides a solution to this problem.

Let's look at a real-world scenario that shows the importance of the proxy *httpd* accelerator mode for mod_perl.

First let's explain an abbreviation used in the networking world. If someone claims to have a 56-kbps connection, it means that the connection is made at 56 kilobits per second (~56,000 bits/sec). It's not 56 kilobytes per second, but 7 kilobytes per second, because 1 byte equals 8 bits. So don't let the merchants fool you—your modem gives you a 7 kilobytes-per-second connection at most, not 56 kilobytes per second, as one might think.

Another convention used in computer literature is that 10 Kb usually means 10 kilobits and 10 KB means 10 kilobytes. An uppercase B generally refers to bytes, and a lowercase b refers to bits (K of course means kilo and equals 1,024 or 1,000, depending on the field in which it's used). Remember that the latter convention is not followed everywhere, so use this knowledge with care.

In the typical scenario (as of this writing), users connect to your site with 56-kbps modems. This means that the speed of the user's network link is 56/8 = 7 KB per second. Let's assume an average generated HTML page to be of 42 KB and an average mod_perl script to generate this response in 0.5 seconds. How many responses could this script produce during the time it took for the output to be delivered to the user? A simple calculation reveals pretty scary numbers:

$$(42KB)/(0.5s \times 7KB/s) = 12$$

Twelve other dynamic requests could be served at the same time, if we could let mod_perl do only what it's best at: generating responses.

This very simple example shows us that we need only one-twelfth the number of children running, which means that we will need only one-twelfth of the memory.

But you know that nowadays scripts often return pages that are blown up with Java-Script and other code, which can easily make them 100 KB in size. Can you calculate what the download time for a file that size would be?

Furthermore, many users like to open multiple browser windows and do several things at once (e.g., download files and browse graphically heavy sites). So the speed of 7 KB/sec we assumed before may in reality be 5–10 times slower. This is not good for your server.

Considering the last example and taking into account all the other advantages that the proxy server provides, we hope that you are convinced that despite a small administration overhead, using a proxy is a good thing.

Of course, if you are on a very fast local area network (LAN) (which means that all your users are connected from this network and not from the outside), the big benefit of the proxy buffering the output and feeding a slow client is gone. You are probably better off sticking with a straight mod_perl server in this case.

Two proxy implementations are known to be widely used with mod_perl: the Squid proxy server and the mod_proxy Apache module. We'll discuss these in the next sections.

The Squid Server and mod_perl

To give you an idea of what Squid is, we will reproduce the following bullets from Squid's home page (*http://www.squid-cache.org/*):

Squid is...

- A full-featured web proxy cache
- Designed to run on Unix systems
- Free, open source software
- The result of many contributions by unpaid volunteers
- Funded by the National Science Foundation

Squid supports...

- Proxying and caching of HTTP, FTP, and other URLs
- Proxying for SSL
- Cache hierarchies
- ICP, HTCP, CARP, and Cache Digests
- Transparent caching
- WCCP (Squid v2.3)
- Extensive access controls
- *httpd* server acceleration

- SNMP
- Caching of DNS lookups

Pros and Cons

The advantages of using Squid are:

- Caching of static objects. These are served much faster, assuming that your cache size is big enough to keep the most frequently requested objects in the cache.

- Buffering of dynamic content. This takes the burden of returning the content generated by mod_perl servers to slow clients, thus freeing mod_perl servers from waiting for the slow clients to download the data. Freed servers immediately switch to serve other requests; thus, your number of required servers goes down dramatically.

- Nonlinear URL space/server setup. You can use Squid to play some tricks with the URL space and/or domain-based virtual server support.

The disadvantages are:

- Buffering limit. By default, Squid buffers in only 16 KB chunks, so it will not allow mod_perl to complete immediately if the output is larger. (READ_AHEAD_GAP, which is 16 KB by default, can be enlarged in *defines.h* if your OS allows that.)

- Speed. Squid is not very fast when compared with the plain file-based web servers available today. Only if you are using a lot of dynamic features, such as with mod_perl, is there a reason to use Squid, and then only if the application and the server are designed with caching in mind.

- Memory usage. Squid uses quite a bit of memory. It can grow three times bigger than the limit provided in the configuration file.

- HTTP protocol level. Squid is pretty much an HTTP/1.0 server, which seriously limits the deployment of HTTP/1.1 features, such as KeepAlives.

- HTTP headers, dates, and freshness. The Squid server might give out stale pages, confusing downstream/client caches. This might happen when you update some documents on the site—Squid will continue serve the old ones until you explicitly tell it which documents are to be reloaded from disk.

- Stability. Compared to plain web servers, Squid is not the most stable.

The pros and cons presented above indicate that you might want to use Squid for its dynamic content–buffering features, but only if your server serves mostly dynamic requests. So in this situation, when performance is the goal, it is better to have a plain Apache server serving static objects and Squid proxying only the mod_perl-enabled server. This means that you will have a triple server setup, with frontend Squid proxying the backend light Apache server and the backend heavy mod_perl server.

Light Apache, mod_perl, and Squid Setup Implementation Details

You will find the installation details for the Squid server on the Squid web site (*http://www.squid-cache.org/*). In our case it was preinstalled with Mandrake Linux. Once you have Squid installed, you just need to modify the default *squid.conf* file (which on our system was located at */etc/squid/squid.conf*), as we will explain now, and you'll be ready to run it.

Before working on Squid's configuration, let's take a look at what we are already running and what we want from Squid.

Previously we had the *httpd_docs* and *httpd_perl* servers listening on ports 80 and 8000, respectively. Now we want Squid to listen on port 80 to forward requests for static objects (plain HTML pages, images, and so on) to the port to which the *httpd_docs* server listens, and dynamic requests to *httpd_perl*'s port. We also want Squid to collect the generated responses and deliver them to the client. As mentioned before, this is known as *httpd* accelerator mode in proxy dialect.

We have to reconfigure the *httpd_docs* server to listen to port 81 instead, since port 80 will be taken by Squid. Remember that in our scenario both copies of Apache will reside on the same machine as Squid. The server configuration is illustrated in Figure 12-4.

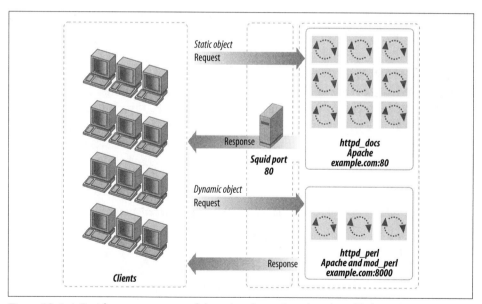

Figure 12-4. A Squid proxy server, standalone Apache, and mod_perl-enabled Apache

A proxy server makes all the magic behind it transparent to users. Both Apache servers return the data to Squid (unless it was already cached by Squid). The client never sees the actual ports and never knows that there might be more than one server running. Do not confuse this scenario with mod_rewrite, where a server redirects the request somewhere according to the rewrite rules and forgets all about it (i.e., works as a one-way dispatcher, responsible for dispatching the jobs but not for collecting the results).

Squid can be used as a straightforward proxy server. ISPs and big companies generally use it to cut down the incoming traffic by caching the most popular requests. However, we want to run it in *httpd* accelerator mode. Two configuration directives, httpd_accel_host and httpd_accel_port, enable this mode. We will see more details shortly.

If you are currently using Squid in the regular proxy mode, you can extend its functionality by running both modes concurrently. To accomplish this, you can extend the existing Squid configuration with *httpd* accelerator mode's related directives or you can just create a new configuration from scratch.

Let's go through the changes we should make to the default configuration file. Since the file with default settings (*/etc/squid/squid.conf*) is huge (about 60 KB) and we will not alter 95% of its default settings, our suggestion is to write a new configuration file that includes the modified directives.*

First we want to enable the redirect feature, so we can serve requests using more than one server (in our case we have two: the *httpd_docs* and *httpd_perl* servers). So we specify httpd_accel_host as virtual. (This assumes that your server has multiple interfaces—Squid will bind to all of them.)

```
httpd_accel_host virtual
```

Then we define the default port to which the requests will be sent, unless they're redirected. We assume that most requests will be for static documents (also, it's easier to define redirect rules for the mod_perl server because of the URI that starts with */perl* or similar). We have our *httpd_docs* listening on port 81:

```
httpd_accel_port 81
```

And Squid listens to port 80:

```
http_port 80
```

We do not use icp (icp is used for cache sharing between neighboring machines, which is more relevant in the proxy mode):

```
icp_port 0
```

hierarchy_stoplist defines a list of words that, if found in a URL, cause the object to be handled directly by the cache. Since we told Squid in the previous directive that

---

* The configuration directives we use are correct for Squid Cache Version 2.4STABLE1. It's possible that the configuration directives might change in new versions of Squid.

we aren't going to share the cache between neighboring machines, this directive is irrelevant. In case you do use this feature, make sure to set this directive to something like:

```
hierarchy_stoplist /cgi-bin /perl
```

where */cgi-bin* and */perl* are aliases for the locations that handle the dynamic requests.

Now we tell Squid not to cache dynamically generated pages:

```
acl QUERY urlpath_regex /cgi-bin /perl
no_cache deny QUERY
```

Please note that the last two directives are controversial ones. If you want your scripts to be more compliant with the HTTP standards, according to the HTTP specification, the headers of your scripts should carry the caching directives: Last-Modified and Expires.

What are they for? If you set the headers correctly, there is no need to tell the Squid accelerator *not* to try to cache anything. Squid will not bother your mod_perl servers a second time if a request is (a) cacheable and (b) still in the cache. Many mod_perl applications will produce identical results on identical requests if not much time has elapsed between the requests. So your Squid proxy might have a hit ratio of 50%, which means that the mod_perl servers will have only half as much work to do as they did before you installed Squid (or mod_proxy).

But this is possible only if you set the headers correctly. Refer to Chapter 16 to learn more about generating the proper caching headers under mod_perl. In the case where only the scripts under */perl/caching-unfriendly* are not caching-friendly, fix the above setting to be:

```
acl QUERY urlpath_regex /cgi-bin /perl/caching-unfriendly
no_cache deny QUERY
```

If you are lazy, or just have too many things to deal with, you can leave the above directives the way we described. Just keep in mind that one day you will want to reread this section to squeeze even more power from your servers without investing money in more memory and better hardware.

While testing, you might want to enable the debugging options and watch the log files in the directory */var/log/squid/*. But make sure to turn debugging off in your production server. Below we show it commented out, which makes it disabled, since it's disabled by default. Debug option 28 enables the debugging of the access-control routes; for other debug codes, see the documentation embedded in the default configuration file that comes with Squid.

```
# debug_options 28
```

We need to provide a way for Squid to dispatch requests to the correct servers. Static object requests should be redirected to *httpd_docs* unless they are already cached, while requests for dynamic documents should go to the *httpd_perl* server. The configuration:

```
redirect_program /usr/lib/squid/redirect.pl
redirect_children 10
redirect_rewrites_host_header off
```

tells Squid to fire off 10 redirect daemons at the specified path of the redirect daemon and (as suggested by Squid's documentation) disables rewriting of any Host: headers in redirected requests. The redirection daemon script is shown later, in Example 12-1.

The maximum allowed request size is in kilobytes, which is mainly useful during PUT and POST requests. A user who attempts to send a request with a body larger than this limit receives an "Invalid Request" error message. If you set this parameter to 0, there will be no limit imposed. If you are using POST to upload files, then set this to the largest file's size plus a few extra kilobytes:

```
request_body_max_size 1000 KB
```

Then we have access permissions, which we will not explain here. You might want to read the documentation, so as to avoid any security problems.

```
acl all src 0.0.0.0/0.0.0.0
acl manager proto cache_object
acl localhost src 127.0.0.1/255.255.255.255
acl myserver src 127.0.0.1/255.255.255.255
acl SSL_ports port 443 563
acl Safe_ports port 80 81 8080 81 443 563
acl CONNECT method CONNECT

http_access allow manager localhost
http_access allow manager myserver
http_access deny manager
http_access deny !Safe_ports
http_access deny CONNECT !SSL_ports
# http_access allow all
```

Since Squid should be run as a non-*root* user, you need these settings:

```
cache_effective_user squid
cache_effective_group squid
```

if you are invoking Squid as *root*. The user *squid* is usually created when the Squid server is installed.

Now configure a memory size to be used for caching:

```
cache_mem 20 MB
```

The Squid documentation warns that the actual size of Squid can grow to be three times larger than the value you set.

You should also keep pools of allocated (but unused) memory available for future use:

```
memory_pools on
```

(if you have the memory available, of course—otherwise, turn it off).

Now tighten the runtime permissions of the cache manager CGI script (*cachemgr.cgi*, which comes bundled with Squid) on your production server:

```
cachemgr_passwd disable shutdown
```

If you are not using this script to manage the Squid server remotely, you should disable it:

```
cachemgr_passwd disable all
```

Put the redirection daemon script at the location you specified in the redirect_ program parameter in the configuration file, and make it executable by the web server (see Example 12-1).

Example 12-1. redirect.pl

```
#!/usr/bin/perl -p
BEGIN { $|=1 }
s|www.example.com(?::81)?/perl/|www.example.com:8000/perl/|;
```

The regular expression in this script matches all the URIs that include either the string "www.example.com/perl/" or the string "www.example.com:81/perl/" and replaces either of these strings with "www.example.com:8080/perl". No matter whether the regular expression worked or not, the $_ variable is automatically printed, thanks to the *-p* switch.

You must disable buffering in the redirector script. $|=1; does the job. If you do not disable buffering, STDOUT will be flushed only when its buffer becomes full—and its default size is about 4,096 characters. So if you have an average URL of 70 characters, only after about 59 (4,096/70) requests will the buffer be flushed and will the requests finally reach the server. Your users will not wait that long (unless you have hundreds of requests per second, in which case the buffer will be flushed very frequently because it'll get full very fast).

If you think that this is a very ineffective way to redirect, you should consider the following explanation. The redirector runs as a daemon; it fires up *N* redirect daemons, so there is no problem with Perl interpreter loading. As with mod_perl, the Perl interpreter is always present in memory and the code has already been compiled, so the redirect is very fast (not much slower than if the redirector was written in C). Squid keeps an open pipe to each redirect daemon; thus, the system calls have no overhead.

Now it is time to restart the server:

```
/etc/rc.d/init.d/squid restart
```

Now the Squid server setup is complete.

If on your setup you discover that port 81 is showing up in the URLs of the static objects, the solution is to make both the Squid and *httpd_docs* servers listen to the same port. This can be accomplished by binding each one to a specific interface (so they are listening to different sockets). Modify *httpd_docs/conf/httpd.conf* as follows:

```
Port 80
BindAddress 127.0.0.1
Listen 127.0.0.1:80
```

Now the *httpd_docs* server is listening only to requests coming from the local server. You cannot access it directly from the outside. Squid becomes a gateway that all the packets go through on the way to the *httpd_docs* server.

Modify *squid.conf* as follows:

```
http_port example.com:80
tcp_outgoing_address 127.0.0.1
httpd_accel_host 127.0.0.1
httpd_accel_port 80
```

It's important that *http_port* specifies the external hostname, which doesn't map to 127.0.0.1, because otherwise the *httpd_docs* and Squid server cannot listen to the same port on the same address.

Now restart the Squid and *httpd_docs* servers (it doesn't matter which one you start first), and voilà—the port number is gone.

You must also have the following entry in the file */etc/hosts* (chances are that it's already there):

```
127.0.0.1 localhost.localdomain localhost
```

Now if your scripts are generating HTML including fully qualified self references, using 8000 or the other port, you should fix them to generate links to point to port 80 (which means not using the port at all in the URI). If you do not do this, users will bypass Squid and will make direct requests to the mod_perl server's port. As we will see later, just like with *httpd_docs*, the *httpd_perl* server can be configured to listen only to requests coming from *localhost* (with Squid forwarding these requests from the outside). Then users will not be able to bypass Squid.

The whole modified *squid.conf* file is shown in Example 12-2.

Example 12-2. squid.conf

```
http_port example.com:80
tcp_outgoing_address 127.0.0.1
httpd_accel_host 127.0.0.1
httpd_accel_port 80

icp_port 0

acl QUERY urlpath_regex /cgi-bin /perl
no_cache deny QUERY

# debug_options 28
```

Example 12-2. squid.conf (continued)

```
redirect_program /usr/lib/squid/redirect.pl
redirect_children 10
redirect_rewrites_host_header off

request_body_max_size 1000 KB

acl all src 0.0.0.0/0.0.0.0
acl manager proto cache_object
acl localhost src 127.0.0.1/255.255.255.255
acl myserver src 127.0.0.1/255.255.255.255
acl SSL_ports port 443 563
acl Safe_ports port 80 81 8080 8081 443 563
acl CONNECT method CONNECT

http_access allow manager localhost
http_access allow manager myserver
http_access deny manager
http_access deny !Safe_ports
http_access deny CONNECT !SSL_ports
# http_access allow all

cache_effective_user squid
cache_effective_group squid

cache_mem 20 MB

memory_pools on

cachemgr_passwd disable shutdown
```

mod_perl and Squid Setup Implementation Details

When one of the authors was first told about Squid, he thought: "Hey, now I can drop the *httpd_docs* server and have just Squid and the *httpd_perl* servers. Since all static objects will be cached by Squid, there is no more need for the light *httpd_docs* server."

But he was a wrong. Why? Because there is still the overhead of loading the objects into the Squid cache the first time. If a site has many static objects, unless a huge chunk of memory is devoted to Squid, they won't all be cached, and the heavy mod_perl server will still have the task of serving these objects.

How do we measure the overhead? The difference between the two servers is in memory consumption; everything else (e.g., I/O) should be equal. So you have to estimate the time needed to fetch each static object for the first time at a peak period, and thus the number of additional servers you need for serving the static objects. This will allow you to calculate the additional memory requirements. This amount can be significant in some installations.

So on our production servers we have decided to stick with the Squid, *httpd_docs*, and *httpd_perl* scenario, where we can optimize and fine-tune everything. But if in your case there are almost no static objects to serve, the *httpd_docs* server is definitely redundant; all you need are the mod_perl server and Squid to buffer the output from it.

If you want to proceed with this setup, install mod_perl-enabled Apache and Squid. Then use a configuration similar to that in the previous section, but without *httpd_docs* (see Figure 12-5). Also, you do not need the redirector any more, and you should specify httpd_accel_host as a name of the server instead of virtual. Because you do not redirect, there is no need to bind two servers on the same port, so you also don't need the Bind or Listen directives in *httpd.conf*.

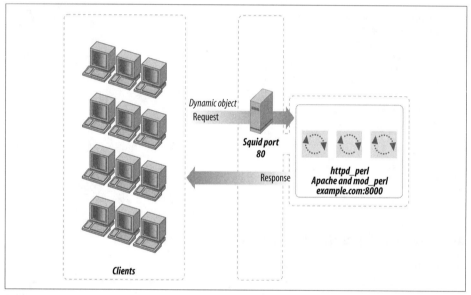

Figure 12-5. A Squid proxy server and mod_perl-enabled Apache

The modified configuration for this simplified setup is given in Example 12-3 (see the explanations in the previous section).

Example 12-3. squid2.conf

```
httpd_accel_host example.com
httpd_accel_port 8000
http_port 80
icp_port 0

acl QUERY urlpath_regex /cgi-bin /perl
no_cache deny QUERY

# debug_options 28
```

Example 12-3. squid2.conf (continued)

```
# redirect_program /usr/lib/squid/redirect.pl
# redirect_children 10
# redirect_rewrites_host_header off

request_body_max_size 1000 KB

acl all src 0.0.0.0/0.0.0.0
acl manager proto cache_object
acl localhost src 127.0.0.1/255.255.255.255
acl myserver src 127.0.0.1/255.255.255.255
acl SSL_ports port 443 563
acl Safe_ports port 80 81 8080 8081 443 563
acl CONNECT method CONNECT

http_access allow manager localhost
http_access allow manager myserver
http_access deny manager
http_access deny !Safe_ports
http_access deny CONNECT !SSL_ports
# http_access allow all

cache_effective_user squid
cache_effective_group squid

cache_mem 20 MB

memory_pools on

cachemgr_passwd disable shutdown
```

Apache's mod_proxy Module

Apache's mod_proxy module implements a proxy and cache for Apache. It implements proxying capabilities for the following protocols: FTP, CONNECT (for SSL), HTTP/0.9, HTTP/1.0, and HTTP/1.1. The module can be configured to connect to other proxy modules for these and other protocols.

mod_proxy is part of Apache, so there is no need to install a separate server—you just have to enable this module during the Apache build process or, if you have Apache compiled as a DSO, you can compile and add this module after you have completed the build of Apache.

A setup with a mod_proxy-enabled server and a mod_perl-enabled server is depicted in Figure 12-6.

We do not think the difference in speed between Apache's mod_proxy and Squid is relevant for most sites, since the real value of what they do is buffering for slow client connections. However, Squid runs as a single process and probably consumes fewer system resources.

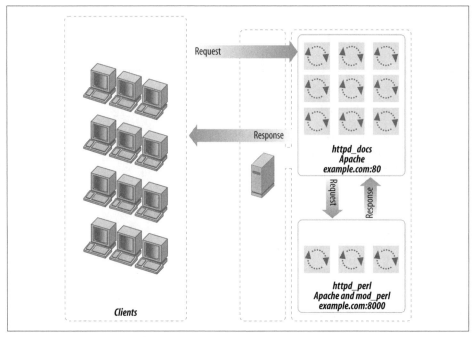

Figure 12-6. mod_proxy-enabled Apache and mod_perl-enabled Apache

The trade-off is that mod_rewrite is easy to use if you want to spread parts of the site across different backend servers, while mod_proxy knows how to fix up redirects containing the backend server's idea of the location. With Squid you can run a redirector process to proxy to more than one backend, but there is a problem in fixing redirects in a way that keeps the client's view of both server names and port numbers in all cases.

The difficult case is where you have DNS aliases that map to the same IP address, you want them redirected to port 80 (although the server is on a different port), and you want to keep the specific name the browser has already sent so that it does not change in the client's browser's location window.

The advantages of mod_proxy are:

- No additional server is needed. We keep the plain one plus one mod_perl-enabled Apache server. All you need is to enable mod_proxy in the *httpd_docs* server and add a few lines to the *httpd.conf* file.

    ```
    ProxyPass        /perl/ http://localhost:81/perl/
    ProxyPassReverse /perl/ http://localhost:81/perl/
    ```

The ProxyPass directive triggers the proxying process. A request for *http://example. com/perl/* is proxied by issuing a request for *http://localhost:81/perl/* to the mod_perl server. mod_proxy then sends the response to the client. The URL rewriting is transparent to the client, except in one case: if the mod_perl server issues a redirect, the URL to redirect to will be specified in a Location header in the response. This is where ProxyPassReverse kicks in: it scans Location headers from the responses it gets from proxied requests and rewrites the URL before forwarding the response to the client.

- It buffers mod_perl output like Squid does.
- It does caching, although you have to produce correct Content-Length, Last-Modified, and Expires HTTP headers for it to work. If some of your dynamic content does not change frequently, you can dramatically increase performance by caching it with mod_proxy.
- ProxyPass happens before the authentication phase, so you do not have to worry about authenticating twice.
- Apache is able to accelerate secure HTTP requests completely, while also doing accelerated HTTP. With Squid you have to use an external redirection program for that.
- The latest mod_proxy module (for Apache 1.3.6 and later) is reported to be very stable.

Concepts and Configuration Directives

In the following explanation, we will use *www.example.com* as the main server users access when they want to get some kind of service and *backend.example.com* as the machine that does the heavy work. The main and backend servers are different; they may or may not coexist on the same machine.

We'll use the mod_proxy module built into the main server to handle requests to *www.example.com*. For the sake of this discussion it doesn't matter what functionality is built into the *backend.example.com* server—obviously it'll be mod_perl for most of us, but this technique can be successfully applied to other web programming languages (PHP, Java, etc.).

ProxyPass

You can use the ProxyPass configuration directive to map remote hosts into the URL space of the local server; the local server does not act as a proxy in the conventional sense, but appears to be a mirror of the remote server.

Let's explore what this rule does:

```
ProxyPass   /perl/ http://backend.example.com/perl/
```

When a user initiates a request to *http://www.example.com/perl/foo.pl*, the request is picked up by mod_proxy. It issues a request for *http://backend.example.com/perl/foo.pl* and forwards the response to the client. This reverse proxy process is mostly transparent to the client, as long as the response data does not contain absolute URLs.

One such situation occurs when the backend server issues a redirect. The URL to redirect to is provided in a Location header in the response. The backend server will use its own ServerName and Port to build the URL to redirect to. For example, mod_dir will redirect a request for *http://www.example.com/somedir/* to *http://backend.example.com/somedir/* by issuing a redirect with the following header:

```
Location: http://backend.example.com/somedir/
```

Since ProxyPass forwards the response unchanged to the client, the user will see *http://backend.example.com/somedir/* in her browser's location window, instead of *http://www.example.com/somedir/*.

You have probably noticed many examples of this from real-life web sites you've visited. Free email service providers and other similar heavy online services display the login or the main page from their main server, and then when you log in you see something like *x11.example.com*, then *w59.example.com*, etc. These are the backend servers that do the actual work.

Obviously this is not an ideal solution, but since users don't usually care about what they see in the location window, you can sometimes get away with this approach. In the following section we show a better solution that solves this issue and provides even more useful functionalities.

ProxyPassReverse

This directive lets Apache adjust the URL in the Location header on HTTP redirect responses. This is essential when Apache is used as a reverse proxy to avoid bypassing the reverse proxy because of HTTP redirects on the backend servers. It is generally used in conjunction with the ProxyPass directive to build a complete frontend proxy server.

```
ProxyPass        /perl/  http://backend.example.com/perl/
ProxyPassReverse /perl/  http://backend.example.com/perl/
```

When a user initiates a request to *http://www.example.com/perl/foo*, the request is proxied to *http://backend.example.com/perl/foo*. Let's say the backend server responds by issuing a redirect for *http://backend.example.com/perl/foo/* (adding a trailing slash). The response will include a Location header:

```
Location: http://backend.example.com/perl/foo/
```

ProxyPassReverse on the frontend server will rewrite this header to:

```
Location: http://www.example.com/perl/foo/
```

This happens completely transparently. The end user is never aware of the URL rewrites happening behind the scenes.

Note that this ProxyPassReverse directive can also be used in conjunction with the proxy pass-through feature of mod_rewrite, described later in this chapter.

Security issues

Whenever you use mod_proxy you need to make sure that your server will not become a proxy for freeriders. Allowing clients to issue proxy requests is controlled by the ProxyRequests directive. Its default setting is Off, which means proxy requests are handled only if generated internally (by ProxyPass or RewriteRule...[P] directives). Do not use the ProxyRequests directive on your reverse proxy servers.

Knowing the Proxypassed Connection Type

Let's say that you have a frontend server running mod_ssl, mod_rewrite, and mod_proxy. You want to make sure that your user is using a secure connection for some specific actions, such as login information submission. You don't want to let the user log in unless the request was submitted through a secure port.

Since you have to proxypass the request between the frontend and backend servers, you cannot know where the connection originated. The HTTP headers cannot reliably provide this information.

A possible solution for this problem is to have the mod_perl server listen on two different ports (e.g., 8000 and 8001) and have the mod_rewrite proxy rule in the regular server redirect to port 8000 and the mod_rewrite proxy rule in the SSL virtual host redirect to port 8001. Under the mod_perl server, use $r->connection->port or the environment variable PORT to tell if the connection is secure.

Buffering Feature

In addition to correcting the URI on its way back from the backend server, mod_proxy, like Squid, also provides buffering services that benefit mod_perl and similar heavy modules. The buffering feature allows mod_perl to pass the generated data to mod_proxy and move on to serve new requests, instead of waiting for a possibly slow client to receive all the data.

Figure 12-7 depicts this feature.

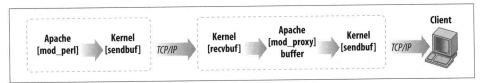

Figure 12-7. mod_proxy buffering

mod_perl streams the generated response into the kernel send buffer, which in turn goes into the kernel receive buffer of mod_proxy via the TCP/IP connection. mod_proxy then streams the file into the kernel send buffer, and the data goes to the client over the TCP/IP connection. There are four buffers between mod_perl and the client: two kernel send buffers, one receive buffer, and finally the mod_proxy user space buffer. Each of those buffers will take the data from the previous stage, as long as the buffer is not full. Now it's clear that in order to immediately release the mod_perl process, the generated response should fit into these four buffers.

If the data doesn't fit immediately into all buffers, mod_perl will wait until the first kernel buffer is emptied partially or completely (depending on the OS implementation) and then place more data into it. mod_perl will repeat this process until the last byte has been placed into the buffer.

The kernel's receive buffers (*recvbuf*) and send buffers (*sendbuf*) are used for different things: the receive buffers are for TCP data that hasn't been read by the application yet, and the send buffers are for application data that hasn't been sent over the network yet. The kernel buffers actually seem smaller than their declared size, because not everything goes to actual TCP/IP data. For example, if the size of the buffer is 64 KB, only about 55 KB or so can actually be used for data. Of course, the overhead varies from OS to OS.

It might not be a very good idea to increase the kernel's receive buffer too much, because you could just as easily increase mod_proxy's user space buffer size and get the same effect in terms of buffering capacity. Kernel memory is *pinned* (not swappable), so it's harder on the system to use a lot of it.

The user space buffer size for mod_proxy seems to be fixed at 8 KB, but changing it is just a matter of replacing HUGE_STRING_LEN with something else in *src/modules/proxy/proxy_http.c* under the Apache source distribution.

mod_proxy's receive buffer is configurable by the ProxyReceiveBufferSize parameter. For example:

```
ProxyReceiveBufferSize 16384
```

will create a buffer 16 KB in size. ProxyReceiveBufferSize must be bigger than or equal to 512 bytes. If it's not set or is set to 0, the system default will be used. The number it's set to should be an integral multiple of 512. ProxyReceiveBufferSize cannot be bigger than the kernel receive buffer size; if you set the value of ProxyReceiveBufferSize larger than this size, the default value will be used (a warning will be printed in this case by mod_proxy).

You can modify the source code to adjust the size of the server's internal read-write buffers by changing the definition of IOBUFSIZE in *include/httpd.h*.

Unfortunately, you cannot set the kernel buffers' sizes as large as you might want because there is a limit to the available physical memory and OSes have their own upper limits on the possible buffer size. To increase the physical memory limits, you have to add more RAM. You can change the OS limits as well, but these procedures are very specific to OSes. Here are some of the OSes and the procedures to increase their socket buffer sizes:

Linux

For 2.2 kernels, the maximum limit for receive buffer size is set in */proc/sys/net/core/rmem_max* and the default value is in */proc/sys/net/core/rmem_default*. If you want to increase the *rcvbuf* size above 65,535 bytes, the default maximum value, you have to first raise the absolute limit in */proc/sys/net/core/rmem_max*. At runtime, execute this command to raise it to 128 KB:

```
panic# echo 131072 > /proc/sys/net/core/rmem_max
```

You probably want to put this command into */etc/rc.d/rc.local* (or elsewhere, depending on the operating system and the distribution) or a similar script that is executed at server startup, so the change will take effect at system reboot.

For the 2.2.5 kernel, the maximum and default values are either 32 KB or 64 KB. You can also change the default and maximum values during kernel compilation; for that, you should alter the SK_RMEM_DEFAULT and SK_RMEM_MAX definitions, respectively. (Since kernel source files tend to change, use the *grep(1)* utility to find the files.)

The same applies for the write buffers. You need to adjust */proc/sys/net/core/wmem_max* and possibly the default value in */proc/sys/net/core/wmem_default*. If you want to adjust the kernel configuration, you have to adjust the SK_WMEM_DEFAULT and SK_WMEM_MAX definitions, respectively.

FreeBSD

Under FreeBSD it's possible to configure the kernel to have bigger socket buffers:

```
panic# sysctl -w kern.ipc.maxsockbuf=2621440
```

Solaris

Under Solaris this upper limit is specified by the tcp_max_buf parameter; its default value is 256 KB.

This buffering technique applies only to *downstream data* (data coming from the origin server to the proxy), not to upstream data. When the server gets an incoming stream, because a request has been issued, the first bits of data hit the mod_perl server immediately. Afterward, if the request includes a lot of data (e.g., a big POST request, usually a file upload) and the client has a slow connection, the mod_perl process will stay tied, waiting for all the data to come in (unless it decides to abort the request for some reason). Falling back on mod_cgi seems to be the best solution for specific scripts whose major function is receiving large amounts of upstream data. Another alternative is to use yet another mod_perl server, which will be dedicated to file uploads only, and have it serve those specific URIs through correct proxy configuration.

Closing Lingering Connections with lingerd

Because of some technical complications in TCP/IP, at the end of each client connection, it is not enough for Apache to close the socket and forget about it; instead, it needs to spend about one second *lingering* (waiting) on the client.*

lingerd is a daemon (service) designed to take over the job of properly closing network connections from an HTTP server such as Apache and immediately freeing it to handle new connections.

lingerd can do an effective job only if HTTP KeepAlives are turned off. Since Keep-Alives are useful for images, the recommended setup is to serve dynamic content with mod_perl-enabled Apache and lingerd, and static content with plain Apache.

With a lingerd setup, we don't have the proxy (we don't want to use lingerd on our *httpd_docs* server, which is also our proxy), so the buffering chain we presented earlier for the proxy setup is much shorter here (see Figure 12-8).

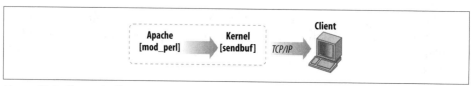

Figure 12-8. Shorter buffering chain

Hence, in this setup it becomes more important to have a big enough kernel send buffer.

With lingerd, a big enough kernel send buffer, and KeepAlives off, the job of spoon-feeding the data to a slow client is done by the OS kernel in the background. As a result, lingerd makes it possible to serve the same load using considerably fewer Apache processes. This translates into a reduced load on the server. It can be used as an alternative to the proxy setups we have seen so far.

For more information about lingerd, see *http://www.iagora.com/about/software/lingerd/*.

Caching Feature

Apache does caching as well. It's relevant to mod_perl only if you produce proper headers, so your scripts' output can be cached. See the Apache documentation for more details on the configuration of this capability.

To enable caching, use the CacheRoot directive, specifying the directory where cache files are to be saved:

```
CacheRoot /usr/local/apache/cache
```

* More details can be found at *http://httpd.apache.org/docs/misc/fin_wait_2.html*.

Make sure that directory is writable by the user under which *httpd* is running.

The CacheSize directive sets the desired space usage in kilobytes:

```
CacheSize 50000    # 50 MB
```

Garbage collection, which enforces the cache size, is set in hours by the CacheGcInterval. If unspecified, the cache size will grow until disk space runs out. This setting tells mod_proxy to check that your cache doesn't exceed the maximum size every hour:

```
CacheGcInterval 1
```

CacheMaxExpire specifies the maximum number of hours for which cached documents will be retained without checking the origin server:

```
CacheMaxExpire 72
```

If the origin server for a document did not send an expiry date in the form of an Expires header, then the CacheLastModifiedFactor will be used to estimate one by multiplying the factor by the time the document was last modified, as supplied in the Last-Modified header.

```
CacheLastModifiedFactor 0.1
```

If the content was modified 10 hours ago, mod_proxy will assume an expiration time of $10 \times 0.1 = 1$ hour. You should set this according to how often your content is updated.

If neither Last-Modified nor Expires is present, the CacheDefaultExpire directive specifies the number of hours until the document is expired from the cache:

```
CacheDefaultExpire 24
```

Build Process

To build mod_proxy into Apache, just add *--enable-module=proxy* during the Apache *./configure* stage. Since you will probably need mod_rewrite's capability as well, enable it with *--enable-module=rewrite*.

mod_rewrite Examples

In the mod_proxy and mod_perl servers scenario, ProxyPass was used to redirect all requests to the mod_perl server by matching the beginning of the relative URI (e.g., */perl*). What should you do if you want everything, except files with *.gif*, *.cgi*, and similar extensions, to be proxypassed to the mod_perl server? (These other files are to be served by the light Apache server, which carries the mod_proxy module.)

The following example locally handles all requests for files with extensions *.gif*, *.jpg*, *.png*, *.css*, *.txt*, and *.cgi* and relative URIs starting with */cgi-bin* (e.g., if you want some scripts to be executed under mod_cgi), and rewrites everything else to the mod_perl server. That is, first handle locally what you want to handle locally, then hand off everything else to the backend guy. Notice that we assume that there are no static HTML files. If you have any of those, adjust the rules to handle HTML files as well.

```
RewriteEngine On
# handle static files and traditional CGIs directly
RewriteRule \.(gif|jpg|png|css|txt|cgi)$ - [last]
RewriteRule ^/cgi-bin - [last]
# pass off everything but images to the heavy-weight server via proxy
RewriteRule ^/(.*)$ http://localhost:4077/$1 [proxy]
```

This is the configuration of the logging facilities:

```
RewriteLogLevel 1
RewriteLog "| /home/httpd/httpd_docs/bin/rotatelogs \
/home/httpd/httpd_docs/logs/r_log 86400"
```

It says to log all the rewrites through the Unix process pipe to the *rotatelogs* utility, which will rotate the logs every 24 hours (86,400 seconds).

As another example, here's how to redirect all those Internet Explorer 5 (IE5) requests for *favicon.ico* to a central image:

```
RewriteRule .*favicon.ico /wherever/favicon.ico [passthrough]
```

The passthrough flag tells mod_rewrite to set the URI of the request to the value of the rewritten filename */whatever/favicon.ico*, so that any other rewriting directives, such as Alias, still apply.

Here's a quick way to make dynamic pages look static:

```
RewriteRule ^/wherever/([a-zA-Z]+).html /perl/$1.pl [passthrough]
```

passthrough is used again so that the URI is properly rewritten and any ScriptAlias or other directives applying to */perl* will be carried out.

Instead of keeping all your Perl scripts in */perl* and your static content everywhere else, you could keep your static content in special directories and keep your Perl scripts everywhere else. You can still use the light/heavy Apache separation approach described earlier, with a few minor modifications.

In the light Apache's *httpd.conf* file, turn rewriting on:

```
RewriteEngine On
```

Now list all directories that contain only static objects. For example, if the only directories relative to DocumentRoot are */images* and */style*, you can set the following rule:

```
RewriteRule ^/(images|style) - [last]
```

The [last] flag means that the rewrite engine should stop if it has a match. This is necessary because the very last rewrite rule proxies everything to the heavy server:

```
RewriteRule ^/(.*) http://www.example.com:8080/$1 [proxy]
```

This line is the difference between a server for which static content is the default and one for which dynamic (Perlish) content is the default.

You should also add the reverse rewrite rule, as before:

```
ProxyPassReverse / http://www.example.com/
```

so that the user doesn't see the port number :8000 in the browser's location window in cases where the heavy server issues a redirect.

It is possible to use *localhost* in the RewriteRule above if the heavy and light servers are on the same machine. So if we sum up the above setup, we get:

```
RewriteEngine On
RewriteRule ^/(images|style) - [last]
RewriteRule ^/(.*) http://www.example.com:8000/$1 [proxy]
ProxyPassReverse / http://www.example.com/
```

In the next example, we use mod_rewrite's env flag to set an environment variable only for proxied requests. This variable can later be used by other directives.

```
RewriteRule ^/(images|style) - [last]
RewriteRule ^/(.*) http://www.example.com:8000/$1 [env=dyn:1,proxy]
ProxyPassReverse / http://www.example.com/
```

We could use this environment variable to turn off logging for dynamic requests:

```
LogFormat "%h %l %u %t \"%r\" %>s %b" common
CustomLog logs/access_log common env=!dyn
```

This comes in handy when using an authentication module on the mod_perl server, such as Apache::AuthenDBI. Authenticated user credentials we're interested in logging are available only in the backend server. This technique is most useful when virtual hosts are used: logging can be turned on in the mod_perl server for this specific virtual host only.

Getting the Remote Server IP in the Backend Server in the Proxy Setup

When using the proxy setup to boost performance, you might face the problem that the remote IP always seems to be 127.0.0.1, which is your proxy's IP. To solve that issue, Ask Bjoern Hansen has written the mod_proxy_add_forward module,[*] which can be aded to the frontend Apache server. It sets the X-Forwarded-For header when doing a ProxyPass, similar to what Squid can do. This header contains the IP address of the client connecting to the proxy, which you can then access in the mod_perl-enabled server. You won't need to compile anything into the backend server.

---

[*] See the References section at the end of this chapter for download information.

To enable this module you have to recompile the frontend server with the following options:

```
panic% ./configure \
    --with-layout=Apache \
    --activate-module=src/modules/extra/mod_proxy_add_forward.c \
    --enable-module=proxy_add_forward \
    ... other options ...
```

Adjust the location of *mod_proxy_add_forward.c* if needed.

In the backend server you can use the handler in Example 12-4 to automatically correct $r->connection->remote_ip.

Example 12-4. Book/ProxyRemoteAddr.pm

```
package Book::ProxyRemoteAddr;

use Apache::Constants qw(OK);
use strict;

sub handler {
    my $r = shift;

    # we'll only look at the X-Forwarded-For header if the request
    # comes from our proxy at localhost
    return OK unless ($r->connection->remote_ip eq "127.0.0.1") &&
        $r->header_in('X-Forwarded-For');

    # Select last value in the chain -- original client's IP
    if (my ($ip) = $r->headers_in->{'X-Forwarded-For'} =~ /([^,\s]+)$/) {
        $r->connection->remote_ip($ip);
    }

    return OK;
}
1;
```

Next, enable this handler in the backend's *httpd.conf* file:

```
PerlPostReadRequestHandler Book::ProxyRemoteAddr
```

and the right thing will happen transparently for your scripts: for Apache::Registry or Apache::PerlRun scripts, you can access the remote IP through $ENV{REMOTE_ADDR}, and for other handlers you can use $r->connection->remote_ip.

Generally, you shouldn't trust the X-Forwarded-For header. You should only rely on the X-Forwarded-For header from proxies you control yourself—this is why the recommended handler we have just presented checks whether the request really came from 127.0.0.1 before changing remote_ip. If you know how to spoof a cookie, you've probably got the general idea of making HTTP headers and can spoof the X-Forwarded-For header as well. The only address you can count on as being a reliable value is the one from $r->connection->remote_ip.

Frontend/Backend Proxying with Virtual Hosts

This section explains a configuration setup for proxying your backend mod_perl servers when you need to use virtual hosts.

Virtual Host Flavors

Apache supports three flavors of virtual hosts:

IP-based virtual hosts
> In this form, each virtual host uses its own IP address. Under Unix, multiple IP addresses are assigned to the same network interface using the *ifconfig* utility. These additional IP addresses are sometimes called *virtual addresses* or *IP aliases*. IP-based virtual hosting is the oldest form of virtual hosting. Due to the supposed increasing scarcity of IP addresses and ensuing difficulty in obtaining large network blocks in some parts of the world, IP-based virtual hosting is now less preferred than name-based virtual hosting.

Name-based virtual hosts
> Name-based virtual hosts share a single IP address. Apache dispatches requests to the appropriate virtual host by examining the Host: HTTP header field. This field's value is the hostname extracted from the requested URI. Although this header is mandatory for HTTP 1.1 clients, it has also been widely used by HTTP 1.0 clients for many years.

Port-based virtual hosts
> In this setup, all virtual hosts share the same IP address, but each uses its own unique port number. As we'll discuss in the next section, port-based virtual hosts are mostly useful for backend servers not directly accessible from Internet clients.

Mixed flavors
> It is perfectly possible to mix the various virtual host flavors in one server.

Dual-Server Virtual Host Configuration

In the dual-server setup, which virtual host flavor is used on the frontend (reverse proxy) server is irrelevant. When running a large number of virtual hosts, it is generally preferable to use name-based virtual hosts, since they share a single IP address. HTTP clients have been supporting this since 1995.

SSL-enabled sites cannot use this scheme, however. This is because when using SSL, all HTTP traffic is encrypted, and this includes the request's Host: header. This header is unavailable until the SSL handshake has been performed, and that in turn requires that the request has been dispatched to the appropriate virtual host, because the SSL handshake depends on that particular host's SSL certificate. For this reason, each SSL-enabled virtual host needs its own, unique IP address. You can still use name-based virtual hosts along with SSL-enabled virtual hosts in the same configuration file, though.

For the backend mod_perl-enabled server, we recommend using port-based virtual hosts using the IP address 127.0.0.1 (*localhost*). This enforces the fact that this server is accessible only from the frontend server and not directly by clients.

Virtual Hosts and Main Server Interaction

When using virtual hosts, any configuration directive outside of a `<VirtualHost>` container is applied to a virtual host called the *main server*, which plays a special role. First, it acts as the default host when you're using name-based virtual hosts and a request can't be mapped to any of the configured virtual hosts (for example, if no `Host:` header is provided). Secondly, many directives specified for the main server are merged with directives provided in `<VirtualHost>` containers. In other words, virtual hosts inherit properties from the main server. This allows us to specify default behaviors that will apply to all virtual hosts, while still allowing us to override these behaviors for specific virtual hosts.

In the following example, we use the `PerlSetupEnv` directive to turn off environment population for all virtual hosts, except for the *www.example.com* virtual host, which needs it for its legacy CGI scripts running under `Apache::Registry`:

```
PerlSetupEnv Off

Listen 8001
<VirtualHost 127.0.0.1:8001>
    ServerName www.example.com
    PerlSetupEnv On
</VirtualHost>
```

Frontend Server Configuration

The following example illustrates the use of name-based virtual hosts. We define two virtual hosts, *www.example.com* and *www.example.org*, which will reverse-proxy dynamic requests to ports 8001 and 8002 on the backend mod_perl-enabled server.

```
Listen          192.168.1.2:80
NameVirtualHost 192.168.1.2:80
```

Replace 192.168.1.2 with your server's public IP address.

```
LogFormat "%v %h %l %u %t \"%r\" %s %b \"%{Referer}i\" \"%{User-agent}i\""
```

The log format used is the Common Log Format prefixed with %v, a token representing the name of the virtual host. Using a combined log common to all virtual hosts uses fewer system resources. The log file can later be split into seperate files according to the prefix, using *splitlog* or an equivalent program.

The following are global options for mod_rewrite shared by all virtual hosts:

```
RewriteLogLevel      0
RewriteRule \.(gif|jpg|png|txt|html)$ - [last]
```

This turns off the mod_rewrite module's logging feature and makes sure that the frontend server will handle files with the extensions *.gif*, *.jpg*, *.png*, *.txt*, and *.html* internally.

If your server is configured to run traditional CGI scripts (under mod_cgi) as well as mod_perl CGI programs, it would be beneficial to configure the frontend server to run the traditional CGI scripts directly. This can be done by altering the (gif|jpg|png|txt|html) rewrite rule to add cgi if all your mod_cgi scripts have the *.cgi* extension, or by adding a new rule to handle all */cgi-bin/* locations internally.

The virtual hosts setup is straightforward:

```
##### www.example.com
<VirtualHost 192.168.1.2:80>
    ServerName       www.example.com
    ServerAdmin      webmaster@example.com
    DocumentRoot     /home/httpd_docs/htdocs/www.example.com

    RewriteEngine    on
    RewriteOptions   'inherit'
    RewriteRule      ^/(perl/.*)$     http://127.0.0.1:8001/$1    [P,L]
    ProxyPassReverse / http://www.example.com/
</VirtualHost>

##### www.example.org
<VirtualHost 192.168.1.2:80>
    ServerName       www.example.org
    ServerAdmin      webmaster@example.org
    DocumentRoot     /home/httpd_docs/htdocs/www.example.org

    RewriteEngine    on
    RewriteOptions   'inherit'
    RewriteRule      ^/(perl/.*)$     http://127.0.0.1:8002/$1    [P,L]
    ProxyPassReverse / http://www.example.org/
</VirtualHost>
```

The two virtual hosts' setups differ in the `DocumentRoot` and `ProxyPassReverse` settings and in the backend ports to which they rewrite.

Backend Server Configuration

This section describes the configuration of the backend server.

The backend server listens on the loopback (*localhost*) interface:

```
BindAddress          127.0.0.1
```

In this context, the following directive does not specify a listening port:

```
Port                 80
```

Rather, it indicates which port the server should advertise when issuing a redirect.

The following global mod_perl settings are shared by all virtual hosts:

```
##### mod_perl settings
PerlRequire                     /home/httpd/perl/startup.pl
PerlFixupHandler                Apache::SizeLimit
PerlPostReadRequestHandler      Book::ProxyRemoteAddr
PerlSetupEnv                    Off
```

As explained earlier, we use the Book::ProxyRemoteAddr handler to get the *real* remote IP addresses from the proxy.

We can then proceed to configure the virtual hosts themselves:

```
##### www.example.com
Listen 8001
<VirtualHost 127.0.0.1:8001>
```

The Listen directive specifies the port to listen on. A connection to that port will be matched by this <VirtualHost> container.

The remaining configuration is straightforward:

```
ServerName  www.example.com
ServerAdmin webmaster@example.com

<Location /perl>
    SetHandler perl-script
    PerlHandler Apache::Registry
    Options +ExecCGI
</Location>

<Location /perl-status>
    SetHandler perl-script
    PerlHandler Apache::Status
</Location>

    </VirtualHost>
```

We configure the second virtual host in a similar way:

```
##### www.example.org
Listen 8002
<VirtualHost 127.0.0.1:8002>
    ServerName  www.example.org
    ServerAdmin webmaster@example.org

    <Location /perl>
        SetHandler perl-script
        PerlHandler Apache::Registry
        Options +ExecCGI
    </Location>

</VirtualHost>
```

You may need to specify the DocumentRoot setting in each virtual host if there is any need for it.

HTTP Authentication with Two Servers and a Proxy

In a setup with one frontend server that proxies to a backend mod_perl server, authentication should be performed entirely on one of the servers: don't mix and match frontend- and backend-based authentication for the same URI.

File-based basic authentication (performed by mod_auth) is best done on the frontend server. Only authentication implemented by mod_perl handlers, such as Apache::AuthenDBI, should be performed on the backend server. mod_proxy will proxy all authentication headers back and forth, making the frontend Apache server unaware of the authentication process.

When One Machine Is Not Enough for Your RDBMS DataBase and mod_perl

Imagine a scenario where you start your business as a small service providing a web site. After a while your business becomes very popular, and at some point you realize that it has outgrown the capacity of your machine. Therefore, you decide to upgrade your current machine with lots of memory, a cutting-edge, super-expensive CPU, and an ultra-fast hard disk. As a result, the load goes back to normal—but not for long. Demand for your services keeps on growing, and just a short time after you've upgraded your machine, once again it cannot cope with the load. Should you buy an even more powerful and very expensive machine, or start looking for another solution? Let's explore the possible solutions for this problem.

A typical web service consists of two main software components: the database server and the web server.

A typical user-server interaction consists of accepting the query parameters entered into an HTML form and submitted to the web server by a user, converting these parameters into a database query, sending it to the database server, accepting the results of the executed query, formatting them into a nice HTML page, and sending it to a user's Internet browser or another application that created the request (e.g., a mobile phone with WAP browsing capabilities). This process is depicted in Figure 12-9.

This schema is known as a *three-tier architecture* in the computing world. In a three-tier architecture, you split up several processes of your computing solution between different machines:

Tier 1

The client, who will see the data on its screen and can give instructions to modify or process the data. In our case, an Internet browser.

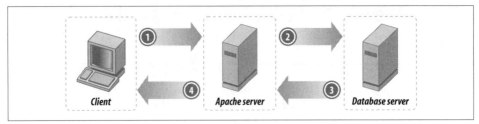

Figure 12-9. Typical user-server interaction

Tier 2

The application server, which does the actual processing of the data and sends it back to the client. In our case, a mod_perl-enabled Apache server.

Tier 3

The database server, which stores and retrieves all the data for the application server.

We are interested only in the second and the third tiers; we don't specify user machine requirements, since mod_perl is all about server-side programming. The only thing the client should be able to do is to render the generated HTML from the response, which any simple browser will do.

Server Requirements

Let's first look at what kind of software the web and database servers are, what they need to run fast, and what implications they have on the rest of the system software.

The three important machine components are the hard disk, the amount of RAM, and the CPU type. Typically, the mod_perl server is mostly RAM-hungry, while the SQL database server mostly needs a very fast hard disk. Of course, if your mod_perl process reads a lot from the disk (a quite infrequent phenomenon) you will need a fast disk too. And if your database server has to do a lot of sorting of big tables and do lots of big table joins, it will need a lot of RAM too.

If we specified average virtual requirements for each machine, that's what we'd get.

An "ideal" mod_perl machine would have:

HD

Low-end (no real I/O, mostly logging)

RAM

The more, the better

CPU

Medium to high (according to needs)

An "ideal" database server machine would have:

HD
> High-end

RAM
> Large amounts (for big joins, sorting of many records), small amounts otherwise

CPU
> Medium to high (according to needs)

The Problem

With the database and the web server on the same machine, you have conflicting interests.

During peak loads, Apache will spawn more processes and use RAM that the database server might have been using, or that the kernel was using on its behalf in the form of a cache. You will starve your database of resources at the time when it needs those resources the most.

Disk I/O contention produces the biggest time issue. Adding another disk won't cut I/O times, because the database is the only thing that does I/O—mod_perl processes have all their code loaded in memory (we are talking about code that does pure Perl and SQL processing). Thus, it's clear that the database is I/O- and CPU-bound (it's RAM-bound only if there are big joins to make), while mod_perl is mostly CPU- and memory-bound.

There is a problem, but it doesn't mean that you cannot run the application and the web servers on the same machine. There is a very high degree of parallelism in modern PC architecture. The I/O hardware is helpful here. The machine can do many things while a SCSI subsystem is processing a command or the network hardware is writing a buffer over the wire.

If a process is not runnable (that is, it is blocked waiting for I/O or something else), it is not using significant CPU time. The only CPU time that will be required to maintain a blocked process is the time it takes for the operating system's scheduler to look at the process, decide that it is still not runnable, and move on to the next process in the list. This is hardly any time at all. If there are two processes, one of which is blocked on I/O and the other of which is CPU-bound, the blocked process is getting 0% CPU time, the runnable process is getting 99.9% CPU time, and the kernel scheduler is using the rest.

The Solution

The solution is to add another machine, which allows a setup where both the database and the web server run on their own dedicated machines.

This solution has the following advantages:

Flexible hardware requirements

It allows you to scale two requirements independently.

If your *httpd* processes are heavily weighted with respect to RAM consumption, you can easily add another machine to accommodate more *httpd* processes, without changing your database machine.

If your database is CPU-intensive but your *httpd* doesn't need much CPU time, you can get a low-end machine for the *httpd* and a high-end machine with a very fast CPU for the database server.

Scalability

Since your web server doesn't depend on the database server location any more, you can add more web servers hitting the same database server, using the existing infrastructure.

Database security

Once you have multiple web server boxes, the backend database becomes a single point of failure, so it's a good idea to shield it from direct Internet access— something that is harder to do when the web and database servers reside on the same machine.

It also has the following disadvantages:

Network latency

A database request from a web server to a database server running on the same machine uses Unix sockets, not the TCP/IP sockets used when the client submits the query from another machine. Unix sockets are very fast, since all the communications happen within the same box, eliminating network delays. TCP/IP socket communication totally depends on the quality and the speed of the network that connects the two machines.

Basically, you can have almost the same client-server speed if you install a very fast and dedicated network between the two machines. It might impose a cost of additional NICs, but that cost is probably insignificant compared to the speed improvement you gain.

Even the normal network that you have would probably fit as well, because the network delays are probably much smaller than the time it takes to execute the query. In contrast to the previous paragraph, you really want to test the added overhead here, since the network can be quite slow, especially at peak hours.

How do you know what overhead is a significant one? All you have to measure is the average time spent in the web server and the database server. If either of the two numbers is at least 20 times bigger than the added overhead of the network, you are all set.

To give you some numbers, if your query takes about 20 milliseconds to process and only 1 millisecond to deliver the results, it's good. If the delivery takes about half of the time the processing takes, you should start considering switching to a faster and/or dedicated network.

The consequences of a slow network can be quite bad. If the network is slow, mod_perl processes remain open, waiting for data from the database server, and eat even more RAM as new child processes pop up to handle new requests. So the overall machine performance can be worse than it was originally, when you had just a single machine for both servers.

Three Machine Model

Since we are talking about using a dedicated machine for each server, you might consider adding a third machine to do the proxy work; this will make your setup even more flexible, as it will enable you to proxypass all requests not just to one mod_perl-running box, but to many of them. This will enable you to do load balancing if and when you need it.

Generally, the proxy machine can be very light when it serves just a little traffic and mainly proxypasses to the mod_perl processes. Of course, you can use this machine to serve the static content; the hardware requirement will then depend on the number of objects you have to serve and the rate at which they are requested.

Figure 12-10 illustrates the three machine model.

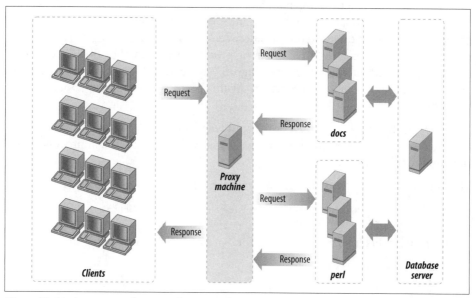

Figure 12-10. A proxy machine, machine(s) with mod_perl-enabled Apache, and the database server machine

Running More than One mod_perl Server on the Same Machine

Let's assume that you have two different sets of code that have little or nothing in common—different Perl modules, no code sharing. Typical numbers can be 4 MB of unshared* and 4 MB of shared memory for each code set, plus 3 MB of shared basic mod_perl stuff—which makes each process 17 MB in size when the two code sets are loaded. Let's also assume that we have 251 MB of RAM dedicated to the web server (Total_RAM):

```
Shared_RAM_per_Child :   11MB
Max_Process_Size     :   17MB
Total_RAM            :  251MB
```

According to the equation developed in Chapter 11:

$$MaxClients = \frac{Total\_RAM - Shared\_RAM\_per\_Child}{Max\_Process\_Size - Shared\_RAM\_per\_Child}$$

$$MaxClients = \frac{251 - 11}{17 - 11} = 40$$

We see that we can run 40 processes, using the given memory and the two code sets in the same server.

Now consider this practical decision. Since we have recognized that the code sets are very distinct in nature and there is no significant memory sharing in place, the wise thing to do is to split the two code sets between two mod_perl servers (a single mod_perl server actually is a set of the parent process and a number of the child processes). So instead of running everything on one server, now we move the second code set onto another mod_perl server. At this point we are talking about a single machine.

Let's look at the figures again. After the split we will have 20 11-MB processes (4 MB unshared + 7 MB shared) running on one server and another 20 such processes running on the other server.

How much memory do we need now? From the above equation we derive:

$$Total\_RAM = MaxClients \times (Max\_Process\_Size - Shared\_RAM\_per\_Child) + Shared\_RAM\_per\_Child$$

Using our numbers, this works out to a total of 174 MB of memory required:

$$Total\_RAM = 2 \times \langle 20 \times (11 - 7) + 7 \rangle = 174$$

---

* 4 MB of unshared memory is a pretty typical size, especially when connecting to databases, as the database connections cannot be shared. Databases like Oracle can take even more RAM per connection on top of this.

But hey, we have 251 MB of memory! That leaves us with 77 MB of free memory. If we recalculate MaxClients, we will see that we can run almost 60 more servers:

$$MaxClients = (251 - 7 \times 2)/(11 - 7) = 59$$

So we can run about 19 more servers using the same memory size—that's almost 30 servers for each code set instead of 20. We have enlarged the server pool by half without changing the machine's hardware.

Moreover, this new setup allows us to fine-tune the two code sets—in reality the smaller code base might have a higher hit rate—so we can benefit even more.

Let's assume that, based on usage statistics, we know that the first code set is called in 70% of requests and the other is called in the remaining 30%. Now we assume that the first code set requires only 5 MB of RAM (3 MB shared + 2 MB unshared) over the basic mod_perl server size, and the second set needs 11 MB (7 MB shared + 4 MB unshared).

Let's compare this new requirement with our original 50:50 setup (here we have assigned the same number of clients for each code set).

So now the first mod_perl server running the first code set will have all its processes using 8 MB (3 MB server shared + 3 MB code shared + 2 MB code unshared), and the second server's process will each be using 14 MB of RAM (3 MB server shared + 7MB code shared + 4 MB code unshared). Given that we have a 70:30 hit relation and that we have 251 MB of available memory, we have to solve this set of equations:

$$\begin{cases} X/Y = 7/3 \\ X \times (8 - 6) + 6 + Y \times (14 - 10) + 10 = 251 \end{cases}$$

where X is the total number of processes the first code set can use and Y the second. The first equation reflects the 70:30 hit relation, and the second uses the equation for the total memory requirements for the given number of servers and the shared and unshared memory sizes.

When we solve these equations, we find that $X = 63$ and $Y = 27$. So we have a total of 90 servers—two and a half times more than in the original setup using the same memory size.

The hit-rate optimized solution and the fact that the code sets can be different in their memory requirements allowed us to run 30 more servers in total and gave us 33 more servers (63 versus 30) for the most-wanted code base, relative to the simple 50:50 split used in the first example.

Of course, if you identify more than two distinct sets of code based on your hit rate statistics, more complicated solutions may be required. You could even make more splits and run three or more mod_perl servers.

However, you shouldn't get carried away. Remember that having too many running processes doesn't necessarily mean better performance, because all of them will contend for CPU time slices. The more processes that are running, the less CPU time each gets and the slower overall performance will be. Therefore, after hitting a certain load you might want to start spreading your servers over different machines.

When you have different components running on different servers, in addition to the obvious memory saving, you gain the power to more easily troubleshoot problems that occur. It's quite possible that a small change in the server configuration to fix or improve something for one code set might completely break the second code set. For example, if you upgrade the first code set and it requires an update of some modules that both code bases rely on, there is a chance that the second code set won't work with the new versions of those modules.

SSL Functionality and a mod_perl Server

If you need SSL functionality, you can get it by adding the mod_ssl or equivalent Apache-SSL to the light frontend server (*httpd_docs*) or the heavy backend mod_perl server (*httpd_perl*). The configuration and installation instructions are given in Chapter 3.

The question is, is it a good idea to add mod_ssl to the backend mod_perl-enabled server? If your internal network is secured, or if both the frontend and backend servers are running on the same machine and you can ensure a safe communication between the processes, there is no need for encrypted traffic between them.

If this is the situation, you don't have to put mod_ssl into the already heavy mod_perl server. You will have the external traffic encrypted by the frontend server, which will proxypass the unencrypted request and response data internally. This is depicted in Figure 12-11.

Another important point is that if you put mod_ssl on the backend server, you have to tunnel back your images to it (i.e., have the backend serve the images), defeating the whole purpose of having the lightweight frontend server.

You cannot serve a secure page that includes nonsecure information. If you fetch over SSL an HTML page containing an <img> tag that fetches an image from the nonsecure server, the image is shown broken. This is true for any other nonsecure objects as well. Of course, if the generated response doesn't include any embedded objects (e.g., images) this isn't a problem.

Giving the SSL functionality to the frontend machine also simplifies configuration of mod_perl by eliminating VirtualHost duplication for SSL. mod_perl configuration files can be plenty difficult without the mod_ssl overhead.

Also, assuming that your frontend machine is underworked anyway, especially if you run a high-volume web service deploying a cluster of machines to serve requests, you

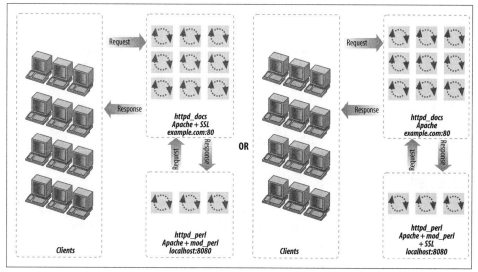

Figure 12-11. mod_proxy enabled-Apache with SSL and mod_perl-enabled Apache

will save some CPU, as it's known that SSL connections are about 100 times more CPU-intensive than non-SSL connections.

Of course, caching session keys so you don't have to set up a new symmetric key for every single connection improves the situation. If you use the shared-memory session-caching mechanism that mod_ssl supports, the overhead is actually rather small, except for the initial connection.

But then, on the other hand, why even bother to run a full-scale mod_ssl-enabled server in front? You might as well just choose a small tunnel/port-forwarding application such as Stunnel or one of the many others mentioned at *http://www.openssl. org/related/apps.html*.

Of course, if you do heavy SSL processing, ideally you should really be offloading it to a dedicated cryptography server. But this advice can be misleading, based on the current status of crypto hardware. If you use hardware, you get extra speed now, but you're locked into a proprietary solution; in six months or a year software will have caught up with whatever hardware you're using, and because software is easier to adapt, you'll have more freedom to change whatever software you're using and more control of things. So the choice is in your hands.

Uploading and Downloading Big Files

You don't want to tie up your precious mod_perl backend server children doing something as long and simple as transferring a file, especially a big one. The overhead saved by mod_perl is typically under one second, which is an enormous savings for scripts whose runtimes are under one second. However, the user won't really see any important performance benefits from mod_perl, since the upload may take up to several minutes.

If some particular script's main functionality is the uploading or downloading of big files, you probably want it to be executed on a plain Apache server under mod_cgi (i.e., performing this operation on the frontend server, if you use a dual-server setup as presented earlier).

This of course assumes that the script requires none of the functionality of the mod_ perl server, such as custom authentication handlers.

References

- Chapter 9 ("Tuning Apache and mod_perl") in *mod_perl Developer's Cookbook*, by Geoffrey Young, Paul Lindner, and Randy Kobes (Sams Publishing).
- mod_backhand, which provides load balancing for Apache: *http://www. backhand.org/mod_backhand/*.
- The High-Availability Linux Project, the definitive guide to load-balancing techniques: *http://www.linux-ha.org/*.
- lbnamed, a load-balancing name server written in Perl: *http://www.stanford.edu/ ~riepel/lbnamed/*, *http://www.stanford.edu/~riepel/lbnamed/bof.talk/*, or *http:// www.stanford.edu/~schemers/docs/lbnamed/lbnamed.html*.
- The Linux Virtual Server Project: *http://www.linuxvirtualserver.org/*.
- The latest IPFilter: *http://coombs.anu.edu.au/~avalon/*.

  This filter includes some simple load-balancing code that allows a round-robin distribution onto several machines via *ipnat*. This may be a simple solution for a few specific load problems.
- The lingerd server and all the documentation are available from *http://www. iagora.com/about/software/lingerd/*.
- The mod_proxy_add_forward Apache module, complete with instructions on how to compile it, is available from one of these URLs: *http://modules.apache.org/ search?id=124* or *http://develooper.com/code/mpaf/mod_proxy_add_forward.c* .
- Apache::Proxy::Info, a friendly mod_perl counterpart to mod_proxy_add_ forward.
- *Solaris 2.x—Tuning Your TCP/IP Stack and More*: *http://www.sean.de/Solaris/ soltune.html*.

  This page talks about the TCP/IP stack and various tricks of tuning your system to get the most out of it as a web server. While the information is for the Solaris 2.x OS, most of it will be relevant of other Unix flavors. At the end of the page, an extensive list of related literature is presented.
- *splitlog*, part of the *wwwstat* distribution, is available at *http://www.ics.uci.edu/ pub/websoft/wwwstat/*.

## CHAPTER 13

TMTOWTDI: Convenience and Habit Versus Performance

TMTOWTDI (sometimes pronounced *"tim toady"*), an acronym for "There's More Than One Way To Do It," is the main motto of Perl. In other words, you can reach the same goal (usually a working product) by coding in many different styles, using different modules and deploying the same modules in different ways.

However, when you come to the point where performance is the goal, you might have to learn what's efficient and what's not. This may mean that you will have to use an approach that you don't really like, that's less convenient, or that requires changing your coding habits.

This section is about performance trade-offs. For almost every comparison, we will provide the theoretical difference and then run benchmarks to support the theory. No matter how good the theory is, it's the numbers we get in practice that matter.

We also would like to mention that the code snippets used in the benchmarks are meant to demonstrate the points we are making and are intended to be as short and easy to understand as possible, rather than being real-world examples.

In the following benchmarks, unless stated differently, mod_perl is tested directly, and the following Apache configuration has been used:

```
MinSpareServers 10
MaxSpareServers 20
StartServers 10
MaxClients 20
MaxRequestsPerChild 10000
```

Apache::Registry PerlHandler Versus Custom PerlHandler

At some point you have to decide whether to use `Apache::Registry` or similar handlers and stick to writing scripts only for content generation, or to write pure Perl handlers.

Apache::Registry maps a request to a file and generates a package and the handler( ) subroutine to run the code contained in that file. If you use a mod_perl handler instead of Apache::Registry, you have a direct mapping from request to subroutine, without the steps in between. The steps that Apache::Registry must go through include:

1. Run the stat( ) system call on the script's filename ($r->filename).
2. Check that the file exists and is executable.
3. Generate a Perl package name based on the request's URI ($r->uri).
4. Change to the directory in which the script resides (chdir basename $r->*filename*).
5. Compare the file's last-modified time to the compiled subroutine's last modified time as stored in memory (if it has already been compiled).
6. If modified since the last compilation or not yet compiled, compile the subroutine.
7. Change back to the previous directory (chdir $old_cwd).

If you remove these steps, you cut out some overhead, plain and simple. Do you *need* to cut out that overhead? Maybe yes, maybe no: it depends on your performance requirements.

You should also take a look at the sister Apache::Registry modules (e.g., Apache::RegistryBB) that don't perform all these steps, so you can still stick to using scripts to generate the content. The greatest added value of scripts is that you don't have to modify the configuration file to add the handler configuration and restart the server for each newly written content handler.

Another alternative is the Apache::Dispatch module (covered in Appendix B), which allows you to add new handlers and run them without modifying the configuration.

Now let's run some benchmarks and compare.

We want to see the overhead that Apache::Registry adds compared to a custom handler and whether it becomes insignificant when used for heavy and time-consuming code. In order to do this we will run two benchmark sets: the first, the *light* set, will use an almost empty script that sends only a basic header and one word of content; the second will be the *heavy* set, which adds some time-consuming operation to the script and handler code.

For the light set we will use the *registry.pl* script running under Apache::Registry (see Example 13-1).

Example 13-1. benchmarks/registry.pl

```
use strict;
print "Content-type: text/plain\n\n";
print "Hello";
```

And we will use the equivalent content-generation handler, shown in Example 13-2.

Example 13-2. Benchmark/Handler.pm

```
package Benchmark::Handler;
use Apache::Constants qw(:common);

sub handler {
    $r = shift;
    $r->send_http_header('text/plain');
    $r->print("Hello");
    return OK;
}
1;
```

We will add these settings to *httpd.conf*:

```
PerlModule Benchmark::Handler
<Location /benchmark_handler>
    SetHandler perl-script
    PerlHandler Benchmark::Handler
</Location>
```

The first directive preloads and compiles the `Benchmark::Handler` module. The remaining lines tell Apache to execute the subroutine `Benchmark::Handler::handler` when a request with the relative URI *benchmark_handler* is made.

We will use the usual configuration for `Apache::Registry` scripts, where all the URIs starting with *perl* are mapped to the files residing under the *home/httpd/perl* directory:

```
Alias /perl /home/httpd/perl
<Location /perl>
    SetHandler perl-script
    PerlHandler +Apache::Registry
    Options ExecCGI
    PerlSendHeader On
</Location>
```

We will use `Apache::RegistryLoader` to preload and compile the script at server startup as well, so the benchmark is fair and only processing time is measured. To accomplish the preloading we add the following code to the *startup.pl* file:

```
use Apache::RegistryLoader ();
Apache::RegistryLoader->new->handler(
        "/perl/benchmarks/registry.pl",
  "/home/httpd/perl/benchmarks/registry.pl");
```

To create the heavy benchmark set, let's leave the preceding code examples unmodified but add some CPU-intensive processing operation (e.g., an I/O operation or a database query):

```
my $x = 100;
my $y = log ($x ** 100)  for (0..10000);
```

This code does lots of mathematical processing and is therefore very CPU-intensive.

Now we are ready to proceed with the benchmark. We will generate 5,000 requests with a concurrency level of 15. Here are the results:

```
----------------------------
    name       | avtime   rps
----------------------------
light handler  |     15   911
light registry |     21   680
----------------------------
heavy handler  |    183    81
heavy registry |    191    77
----------------------------
```

First let's compare the results from the light set. We can see that the average overhead added by Apache::Registry (compared to the custom handler) is about:

```
21 - 15 = 6 milliseconds
```

per request.

The difference in speed is about 40% (15 ms versus 21 ms). Note that this doesn't mean that the difference in real-world applications would be so big. The results of the heavy set confirm this.

In the heavy set the average processing time is almost the same for Apache::Registry and the custom handler. You can clearly see that the difference between the two is almost the same as in the light set's results—it has grown from 6 ms to 8 ms (191 ms – 183 ms). This means that the identical heavy code that has been added was running for about 168 ms (183 ms – 15 ms). However, this doesn't mean that the added code itself ran for 168 ms; it means that it took 168 ms for this code to be completed in a multiprocess environment where each process gets a time slice to use the CPU. The more processes that are running, the more time the process will have to wait to get the next time slice when it can use the CPU.

We have answered the second question as well (whether the overhead of Apache::Registry is significant when used for heavy code). You can see that when the code is not just the *hello* script, the overhead added by Apache::Registry is almost insignificant. It's not zero, though. Depending on your requirements, this 5–10 ms overhead may be tolerable. If that's the case, you may choose to use Apache::Registry.

An interesting observation is that when the server being tested runs on a very slow machine the results are completely different:

```
----------------------------
    name       | avtime   rps
----------------------------
light handler  |     50   196
light registry |    160    61
----------------------------
heavy handler  |    149    67
heavy registry |    822    12
----------------------------
```

First of all, the 6-ms difference in average processing time we saw on the fast machine when running the light set has now grown to 110 ms. This means that the few extra operations that `Apache::Registry` performs turn out to be very expensive on a slow machine.

Secondly, you can see that when the heavy set is used, the time difference is no longer close to that found in the light set, as we saw on the fast machine. We expected that the added code would take about the same time to execute in the handler and the script. Instead, we see a difference of 673 ms (822 ms – 149 ms).

The explanation lies in the fact that the difference between the machines isn't merely in the CPU speed. It's possible that there are many other things that are different—for example, the size of the processor cache. If one machine has a processor cache large enough to hold the whole handler and the other doesn't, this can be very significant, given that in our heavy benchmark set, 99.9% of the CPU activity was dedicated to running the calculation code.

This demonstrates that none of the results and conclusions made here should be taken for granted. Most likely you will see similar behavior on your machine; however, only after you have run the benchmarks and analyzed the results can you be sure of what is best for your situation. If you later happen to use a different machine, make sure you run the tests again, as they may lead to a completely different decision (as we found when we tried the same benchmark on different machines).

Apache::args Versus Apache::Request::param Versus CGI::param

`Apache::args`, `Apache::Request::param`, and `CGI::param` are the three most common ways to process input arguments in mod_perl handlers and scripts. Let's write three `Apache::Registry` scripts that use `Apache::args`, `Apache::Request::param`, and `CGI::param` to process a form's input and print it out. Notice that `Apache::args` is considered identical to `Apache::Request::param` only when you have single-valued keys. In the case of multi-valued keys (e.g., when using checkbox groups), you will have to write some extra code. If you do a simple:

```
my %params = $r->args;
```

only the last value will be stored and the rest will collapse, because that's what happens when you turn a list into a hash. Assuming that you have the following list:

```
(rules => 'Apache', rules => 'Perl', rules => 'mod_perl')
```

and assign it to a hash, the following happens:

```
$hash{rules} = 'Apache';
$hash{rules} = 'Perl';
$hash{rules} = 'mod_perl';
```

So at the end only the following pair will get stored:

```
rules => 'mod_perl'
```

With `CGI.pm` or `Apache::Request`, you can solve this by extracting the whole list by its key:

```
my @values = $q->param('rules');
```

In addition, `Apache::Request` and `CGI.pm` have many more functions that ease input processing, such as handling file uploads. However, `Apache::Request` is theoretically much faster, since its guts are implemented in C, glued to Perl using XS code.

Assuming that the only functionality you need is the parsing of key-value pairs, and assuming that every key has a single value, we will compare the almost identical scripts in Examples 13-3, 13-4, and 13-5 by trying to pass various query strings.

Example 13-3. processing_with_apache_args.pl

```
use strict;
my $r = shift;
$r->send_http_header('text/plain');

my %args = $r->args;
print join "\n", map {"$_ => $args{$_}" } keys %args;
```

Example 13-4. processing_with_apache_request.pl

```
use strict;
use Apache::Request ();
my $r = shift;
my $q = Apache::Request->new($r);
$r->send_http_header('text/plain');

my %args = map {$_ => $q->param($_) } $q->param;
print join "\n", map {"$_ => $args{$_}" } keys %args;
```

Example 13-5. processing_with_cgi_pm.pl

```
use strict;
use CGI;
my $r = shift;
my $q = new CGI;
$r->send_http_header('text/plain');

my %args = map {$_ => $q->param($_) } $q->param;
print join "\n", map {"$_ => $args{$_}" } keys %args;
```

All three scripts and the modules they use are preloaded at server startup in *startup.pl*:

```
use Apache::RegistryLoader ();
use CGI ();
CGI->compile('param');
use Apache::Request ();
```

```
# Preload registry scripts
Apache::RegistryLoader->new->handler(
                        "/perl/processing_with_cgi_pm.pl",
              "/home/httpd/perl/processing_with_cgi_pm.pl"
                      );
Apache::RegistryLoader->new->handler(
                        "/perl/processing_with_apache_request.pl",
              "/home/httpd/perl/processing_with_apache_request.pl"
                      );
Apache::RegistryLoader->new->handler(
                        "/perl/processing_with_apache_args.pl",
              "/home/httpd/perl/processing_with_apache_args.pl"
                      );
1;
```

We use four different query strings, generated by:

```
my @queries = (
    join("&", map {"$_=" . 'e' x 10} ('a'..'b')),
    join("&", map {"$_=" . 'e' x 50} ('a'..'b')),
    join("&", map {"$_=" . 'e' x 5 } ('a'..'z')),
    join("&", map {"$_=" . 'e' x 10} ('a'..'z')),
);
```

The first string is:

```
a=eeeeeeeeee&b=eeeeeeeeee
```

which is 25 characters in length and consists of two key/value pairs. The second string is also made of two key/value pairs, but the values are 50 characters long (a total of 105 characters). The third and fourth strings are each made from 26 key/value pairs, with value lengths of 5 and 10 characters respectively and total lengths of 207 and 337 characters respectively. The query_len column in the report table is one of these four total lengths.

We conduct the benchmark with a concurrency level of 50 and generate 5,000 requests for each test. The results are:

```
-------------------------------------------------
name    val_len pairs query_len |  avtime  rps
-------------------------------------------------
apreq     10      2      25     |    51    945
apreq     50      2      105    |    53    907
r_args    50      2      105    |    53    906
r_args    10      2      25     |    53    899
apreq      5     26      207    |    64    754
apreq     10     26      337    |    65    742
r_args     5     26      207    |    73    665
r_args    10     26      337    |    74    657
cgi_pm    50      2      105    |    85    573
cgi_pm    10      2      25     |    87    559
cgi_pm     5     26      207    |   188    263
cgi_pm    10     26      337    |   188    262
-------------------------------------------------
```

where apreq stands for Apache::Request::param( ), r_args stands for Apache::args( ) or $r->args( ), and cgi_pm stands for CGI::param( ).

You can see that Apache::Request::param and Apache::args have similar performance with a few key/value pairs, but the former is faster with many key/value pairs. CGI::param is significantly slower than the other two methods.

These results also suggest that the processing gets progressively slower as the number of key/value pairs grows, but longer lengths of the key/value pairs have less of a slowdown impact. To verify that, let's use the Apache::Request::param method and first test several query strings made of five key/value pairs with value lengths growing from 10 characters to 60 in steps of 10:

```
my @strings = map {'e' x (10*$_)} 1..6;
my @ae = ('a'..'e');
my @queries = ( );
for my $string (@strings) {
    push @queries, join "&", map {"$_=$string"} @ae;
}
```

The results are:

```
-----------------------------------
val_len query_len  |  avtime  rps
-----------------------------------
  10       77       |    55    877
  20      197       |    55    867
  30      257       |    56    859
  40      137       |    56    858
  50      317       |    56    857
  60      377       |    58    828
-----------------------------------
```

Indeed, the length of the value influences the speed very little, as we can see that the average processing time almost doesn't change as the length of the value grows.

Now let's use a fixed value length of 10 characters and test with a varying number of key/value pairs, from 2 to 26 in steps of 5:

```
my @az = ('a'..'z');
my @queries = map { join("&", map {"$_=" . 'e' x 10 } @az[0..$_]) }
    (1, 5, 10, 15, 20, 25);
```

The results are:

```
-----------------------------
pairs  query_len |  avtime  rps
-----------------------------
  2       25      |    53    906
  6       77      |    55    869
 12      142      |    57    838
 16      207      |    61    785
 21      272      |    64    754
 26      337      |    66    726
-----------------------------
```

Now by looking at the average processing time column, we can see that the number of key/value pairs makes a significant impact on processing speed.

Buffered Printing and Better print( ) Techniques

As you probably know, this statement:

```
local $|=1;
```

disables buffering of the currently select( )ed file handle (the default is STDOUT). Under mod_perl, the STDOUT file handle is automatically tied to the output socket. If STDOUT buffering is disabled, each print( ) call also calls ap_rflush( ) to flush Apache's output buffer.

When multiple print( ) calls are used (*bad* style in generating output), or if there are just too many of them, you will experience a degradation in performance. The severity depends on the number of print( ) calls that are made.

Many old CGI scripts were written like this:

```
print "<body bgcolor=\"black\" text=\"white\">";
print "<h1>Hello</h1>";
print "<a href=\"foo.html\">foo</a>";
print "</body>";
```

This example has multiple print( ) calls, which will cause performance degradation with $|=1. It also uses too many backslashes. This makes the code less readable, and it is more difficult to format the HTML so that it is easily readable as the script's output. The code below solves the problems:

```
print qq{
  <body bgcolor="black" text="white">
    <h1>Hello</h1>
    <a href="foo.html">foo</a>
  </body>
};
```

You can easily see the difference. Be careful, though, when printing an <html> tag. The correct way is:

```
print qq{<html>
  <head></head>
};
```

You can also try the following:

```
print qq{
  <html>
  <head></head>
};
```

but note that some older browsers expect the first characters after the headers and empty line to be <html> with *no* spaces before the opening left angle bracket. If there are any other characters, they might not accept the output as HTML might and print it as plain text. Even if this approach works with your browser, it might not work with others.

Another approach is to use the *here document* style:

```
print <<EOT;
<html>
<head></head>
EOT
```

Performance-wise, the qq{ } and here document styles compile down to exactly the same code, so there should not be any real difference between them.

Remember that the closing tag of the here document style (EOT in our example) *must* be aligned to the left side of the line, with no spaces or other characters before it and nothing but a newline after it.

Yet another technique is to pass the arguments to print( ) as a list:

```
print "<body bgcolor=\"black\" text=\"white\">",
      "<h1>Hello</h1>",
      "<a href=\"foo.html\">foo</a>",
      "</body>";
```

This technique makes fewer print( ) calls but still suffers from so-called *backslashitis* (quotation marks used in HTML need to be prefixed with a backslash). Single quotes can be used instead:

```
'<a href="foo.html">foo</a>'
```

but then how do we insert a variable? The string will need to be split again:

```
'<a href="',$foo,'.html">', $foo, '</a>'
```

This is ugly, but it's a matter of taste. We tend to use the qq operator:

```
print qq{<a href="$foo.html">$foo</a>
         Some text
         <img src="bar.png" alt="bar" width="1" height="1">
        };
```

What if you want to make fewer print( ) calls, but you don't have the output ready all at once? One approach is to buffer the output in the array and then print it all at once:

```
my @buffer = ( );
push @buffer, "<body bgcolor=\"black\" text=\"white\">";
push @buffer, "<h1>Hello</h1>";
push @buffer, "<a href=\"foo.html\">foo</a>";
push @buffer, "</body>";
print @buffer;
```

An even better technique is to pass print( ) a reference to the string. The print( ) used under Apache overloads the default CORE::print( ) and knows that it should automatically dereference any reference passed to it. Therefore, it's more efficient to pass strings by reference, as it avoids the overhead of copying.

```perl
my $buffer = "<body bgcolor=\"black\" text=\"white\">";
$buffer .= "<h1>Hello</h1>";
$buffer .= "<a href=\"foo.html\">foo</a>";
$buffer .= "</body>";
print \$buffer;
```

If you print references in this way, your code will not be backward compatible with mod_cgi, which uses the CORE::print( ) function.

Now to the benchmarks. Let's compare the printing techniques we have just discussed. The benchmark that we are going to use is shown in Example 13-6.

Example 13-6. benchmarks/print.pl

```perl
use Benchmark;
use Symbol;

my $fh = gensym;
open $fh, ">/dev/null" or die;

my @text = (
    "<!DOCTYPE HTML PUBLIC \"-//IETF//DTD HTML//EN\">\n",
    "<HTML>\n",
    "  <HEAD>\n",
    "    <TITLE>\n",
    "      Test page\n",
    "    </TITLE>\n",
    "  </HEAD>\n",
    "  <BODY BGCOLOR=\"black\" TEXT=\"white\">\n",
    "    <H1>\n",
    "      Test page \n",
    "    </H1>\n",
    "    <A HREF=\"foo.html\">foo</A>\n",
    "text line that emulates some real output\n" x 100,
    "    <HR>\n",
    "  </BODY>\n",
    "</HTML>\n",
);

my $text = join "", @text;

sub multi {
    my @copy = @text;
    my_print($_) for @copy;
}

sub single {
    my $copy = $text;
```

Example 13-6. benchmarks/print.pl (continued)

```perl
        my_print($copy);
}

sub array {
    my @copy = @text;
    my_print(@copy);
}

sub ref_arr {
    my @refs = \(@text);
    my_print(@refs);
}

sub concat {
    my $buffer;
    $buffer .= $_ for @text;
    my_print($buffer);
}

sub my_join {
    my $buffer = join '', @text;
    my_print($buffer);
}

sub my_print {
    for (@_) {
        print $fh ref($_) ? $$_ : $_;
    }
}

timethese(100_000, {
    join    => \&my_join,
    array   => \&array,
    ref_arr => \&ref_arr,
    multi   => \&multi,
    single  => \&single,
    concat  => \&concat,
});

timethese(100_000, {
    'array  /b' => sub {my $ofh=select($fh);$|=0;select($ofh); array()  },
    'array  /u' => sub {my $ofh=select($fh);$|=1;select($ofh); array()  },
    'ref_arr/b' => sub {my $ofh=select($fh);$|=0;select($ofh); ref_arr()},
    'ref_arr/u' => sub {my $ofh=select($fh);$|=1;select($ofh); ref_arr()},
    'multi  /b' => sub {my $ofh=select($fh);$|=0;select($ofh); multi()  },
    'multi  /u' => sub {my $ofh=select($fh);$|=1;select($ofh); multi()  },
    'single /b' => sub {my $ofh=select($fh);$|=0;select($ofh); single() },
    'single /u' => sub {my $ofh=select($fh);$|=1;select($ofh); single() },
    'concat /b' => sub {my $ofh=select($fh);$|=0;select($ofh); concat() },
    'concat /u' => sub {my $ofh=select($fh);$|=1;select($ofh); concat() },
    'join   /b' => sub {my $ofh=select($fh);$|=0;select($ofh); my_join()},
```

Example 13-6. benchmarks/print.pl (continued)

```
    'join    /u' => sub {my $ofh=select($fh);$|=1;select($ofh); my_join()},
});
```

Under Perl 5.6.0 on Linux, the first set of results, sorted by CPU clocks, is:

```
Benchmark: timing 100000 iterations of array, concat, multi, ref_array...
   single:  6 wallclock secs ( 5.42 usr + 0.16 sys =  5.58 CPU)
     join:  8 wallclock secs ( 8.63 usr + 0.14 sys =  8.77 CPU)
   concat: 12 wallclock secs (10.57 usr + 0.31 sys = 10.88 CPU)
  ref_arr: 14 wallclock secs (11.92 usr + 0.13 sys = 12.05 CPU)
    array: 15 wallclock secs (12.95 usr + 0.26 sys = 13.21 CPU)
    multi: 38 wallclock secs (34.94 usr + 0.25 sys = 35.19 CPU)
```

single string print is obviously the fastest; *join, concatination of string, array of references to string,* and *array of strings* are very close to each other (the results may vary according to the length of the strings); and *print call per string* is the slowest.

Now let's look at the same benchmark, where the printing was either buffered or not:

```
Benchmark: timing 100000 iterations of ...
single /b: 10 wallclock secs ( 8.34 usr + 0.23 sys =  8.57 CPU)
single /u: 10 wallclock secs ( 8.57 usr + 0.25 sys =  8.82 CPU)
join   /b: 13 wallclock secs (11.49 usr + 0.27 sys = 11.76 CPU)
join   /u: 12 wallclock secs (11.80 usr + 0.18 sys = 11.98 CPU)
concat /b: 14 wallclock secs (13.73 usr + 0.17 sys = 13.90 CPU)
concat /u: 16 wallclock secs (13.98 usr + 0.15 sys = 14.13 CPU)
ref_arr/b: 15 wallclock secs (14.95 usr + 0.20 sys = 15.15 CPU)
array  /b: 16 wallclock secs (16.06 usr + 0.23 sys = 16.29 CPU)
ref_arr/u: 18 wallclock secs (16.85 usr + 0.98 sys = 17.83 CPU)
array  /u: 19 wallclock secs (17.65 usr + 1.06 sys = 18.71 CPU)
multi  /b: 41 wallclock secs (37.89 usr + 0.28 sys = 38.17 CPU)
multi  /u: 48 wallclock secs (43.24 usr + 1.67 sys = 44.91 CPU)
```

First, we see the same picture among different printing techniques. Second, we can see that the buffered print is always faster, but only in the case where print() is called for each short string does it have a significant speed impact.

Now let's go back to the $|=1 topic. You might still decide to disable buffering, for two reasons:

- You use relatively few print() calls. You achieve this by arranging for print() statements to print multiline text, not one line per print() statement.

- You want your users to see output immediately. If you are about to produce the results of a database query that might take some time to complete, you might want users to get some feedback while they are waiting. Ask yourself whether you prefer getting the output a bit slower but steadily from the moment you press the Submit button, or having to watch the "falling stars" for a while and then getting the whole output at once, even if it's a few milliseconds faster—assuming the browser didn't time out during the wait.

An even better solution is to keep buffering enabled and call $r->rflush( ) to flush the buffers when needed. This way you can place the first part of the page you are sending in the buffer and flush it a moment before you perform a lengthy operation such as a database query. This kills two birds with the same stone: you show some of the data to the user immediately so she will see that something is actually happening, and you don't suffer from the performance hit caused by disabling buffering. Here is an example of such code:

```perl
use CGI ( );
my $r = shift;
my $q = new CGI;
print $q->header('text/html');
print $q->start_html;
print $q->p("Searching...Please wait");
$r->rflush;

# imitate a lengthy operation
for (1..5) {
    sleep 1;
}

print $q->p("Done!");
```

The script prints the beginning of the HTML document along with a nice request to wait by flushing the output buffer just before it starts the lengthy operation.

Now let's run the web benchmark and compare the performance of buffered versus unbuffered printing in the multi-printing code used in the last benchmark. We are going to use two identical handlers, the first handler having its STDOUT stream (tied to socket) unbuffered. The code appears in Example 13-7.

Example 13-7. Book/UnBuffered.pm

```perl
package Book::UnBuffered;
use Apache::Constants qw(:common);
local $|=1; # Switch off buffering.
sub handler {
    my $r = shift;
    $r->send_http_header('text/html');
    print "<!DOCTYPE HTML PUBLIC \"-//IETF//DTD HTML//EN\">\n";
    print "<html>\n";
    print "  <head>\n";
    print "    <title>\n";
    print "      Test page\n";
    print "    </title>\n";
    print "  </head>\n";
    print "  <body bgcolor=\"black\" text=\"white\">\n";
    print "    <h1> \n";
    print "      Test page \n";
    print "    </h1>\n";
    print "    <a href=\"foo.html\">foo</a>\n" for 1..100;
    print "    <hr>\n";
```

Example 13-7. Book/UnBuffered.pm (continued)

```
    print "    </body>\n";
    print "</html>\n";
    return OK;
}
1;
```

The following *httpd.conf* configuration is used:

```
##################################
### Buffered output
##################################
<Location /buffering>
    SetHandler perl-script
    PerlHandler +Book::Buffered
</Location>

##################################
### UnBuffered output
##################################
<Location /unbuffering>
    SetHandler perl-script
    PerlHandler +Book::UnBuffered
</Location>
```

Now we run the benchmark, using *ApacheBench*, with concurrency set to 50, for a total of 5,000 requests. Here are the results:

```
name        |  avtime completed failed  RPS
--------------------------------------------
unbuffering |    56      5000      0     855
buffering   |    55      5000      0     865
```

As you can see, there is not much difference when the overhead of other processing is added. The difference was more significant when we benchmarked only the Perl code. In real web requests, a few percent difference will be felt only if you unbuffer the output and print thousands of strings one at a time.

Interpolation, Concatenation, or List

Let's revisit the various approaches of munging with strings, and compare the speed of using lists of strings versus interpolation. We will add a string concatenation angle as well.

When the strings are small, it almost doesn't matter whether interpolation or a list is used (see Example 13-8).

Example 13-8. benchmarks/join.pl

```
use Benchmark;
use Symbol;
my $fh = gensym;
```

Example 13-8. benchmarks/join.pl (continued)

```
open $fh, ">/dev/null" or die;

my($one, $two, $three, $four) = ('a'..'d');

timethese(1_000_000, {
    interp => sub {
        print $fh "$one$two$three$four";
    },
    list => sub {
        print $fh $one, $two, $three, $four;
    },
    conc => sub {
        print $fh $one . $two . $three . $four;
    },
});
```

Here's the benchmarking result:

```
Benchmark: timing 1000000 iterations of conc, interp, list...
    conc:  3 wallclock secs ( 3.38 usr +  0.00 sys =  3.38 CPU)
  interp:  3 wallclock secs ( 3.45 usr + -0.01 sys =  3.44 CPU)
    list:  2 wallclock secs ( 2.58 usr +  0.00 sys =  2.58 CPU)
```

The results of the concatenation technique are very similar to those of interpolation. The list technique is a little bit faster than interpolation. However, when the strings are large, lists are significantly faster. We saw this in the previous section, and Example 13-9 presents another benchmark to increase our confidence in our conclusion. This time we use 1,000-character strings.

Example 13-9. benchmarks/join_long.pl

```
use Benchmark;
use Symbol;
my $fh = gensym;
open $fh, ">/dev/null" or die;

my($one, $two, $three, $four) = map { $_ x 1000 } ('a'..'d');

timethese(500_000, {
    interp => sub {
        print $fh "$one$two$three$four";
    },
    list => sub {
        print $fh $one, $two, $three, $four;
    },
    conc => sub {
        print $fh $one . $two . $three . $four;
    },
});
```

Here's the benchmarking result:

```
Benchmark: timing 500000 iterations of interp, list...
    conc:  5 wallclock secs ( 4.47 usr +  0.27 sys =  4.74 CPU)
  interp:  4 wallclock secs ( 4.25 usr +  0.26 sys =  4.51 CPU)
    list:  4 wallclock secs ( 2.87 usr +  0.16 sys =  3.03 CPU)
```

In this case using a list is about 30% faster than interpolation. Concatenation is a little bit slower than interpolation.

Let's look at this code:

```
$title = 'My Web Page';
print "<h1>$title</h1>";        # Interpolation (slow)
print '<h1>' . $title . '</h1>'; # Concatenation (slow)
print '<h1>', $title, '</h1>'; # List (fast for long strings)
```

When you use "<h1>$title</h1>", Perl does interpolation (since "" is an operator in Perl)—it parses the contents of the string and replaces any variables or expressions it finds with their respective values. This uses more memory and is slower than using a list. Of course, if there are no variables to interpolate it makes no difference whether you use "string" or 'string'.

Concatenation is also potentially slow, since Perl might create a temporary string, which it then prints.

Lists are fast because Perl can simply deal with each element in turn. This is true if you don't run join( ) on the list at the end to create a single string from the elements of the list. This operation might be slower than directly appending to the string whenever a new string springs into existence.

Please note that this optimization is a pure waste of time, except maybe in a few extreme cases (if you have even 5,000 concatenations to serve a request, it won't cost you more than a few milliseconds to do it the wrong way). It's a good idea to always look at the big picture when running benchmarks.

Another aspect to look at is the size of the generated code. For example, lines 3, 4, and 5 in Example 13-10 produce the same output.

Example 13-10. size_interp.pl

```
$uri = '/test';
$filename = '/test.pl';
print "uri => ", $uri, " filename => ", $filename, "\n";
print "uri => " . $uri . " filename => " . $filename . "\n";
print "uri => $uri filename => $filename\n";
1; # needed for TerseSize to report the previous line's size
```

Let's look at how many bytes each line compiles into. We will use B::TerseSize for this purpose:

```
panic% perl -MO=TerseSize size_interp.pl | grep line
size_interp.pl syntax OK
```

```
[line 1 size: 238 bytes]
[line 2 size: 241 bytes]
[line 3 size: 508 bytes]
[line 4 size: 636 bytes]
[line 5 size: 689 bytes]
```

The code in line 3, which uses a list of arguments to print( ), uses significantly less memory (508 bytes) than the code in line 4, which uses concatenation (636 bytes), and the code in line 5, which uses interpolation (689 bytes).

If there are no variables to interpolate, it's obvious that a list will use more memory then a single string. Just to confirm that, take a look at Example 13-11.

Example 13-11. size_nointerp.pl

```
print "uri => ", "uri", " filename => ", "filename", "\n";
print "uri => " . "uri" . " filename => " . "filename" . "\n";
print "uri => uri filename => filename\n";
1; # needed for TerseSize to report the previous line's size

panic% perl -MO=TerseSize size_nointerp.pl | grep line
size_nointerp.pl syntax OK
[line 1 size: 377 bytes]
[line 2 size: 165 bytes]
[line 3 size: 165 bytes]
```

Lines 2 and 3 get compiled to the same code, and its size is smaller than the code produced by line 1, which uses a list.

Keeping a Small Memory Footprint

Since mod_perl processes tend to consume a lot of memory as the number of loaded modules and scripts grows during the child's lifetime, it's important to know how to keep memory usage down. Let's see what should be kept in mind when writing code that will be executed under mod_perl.

"Bloatware" Modules

Perl IO:: modules are very convenient, but let's see what it costs to use them. The following command (Perl 5.6.1 on Linux) reveals that when we use IO we also load the IO::Handle, IO::Seekable, IO::File, IO::Pipe, IO::Socket, and IO::Dir modules. The command also shows us how big they are in terms of code lines. *wc(1)* reports how many lines of code are in each of the loaded files:

```
panic% wc -l `perl -MIO -e 'print join("\n", sort values %INC, "")'`
  124 /usr/lib/perl5/5.6.1/Carp.pm
  602 /usr/lib/perl5/5.6.1/Class/Struct.pm
  456 /usr/lib/perl5/5.6.1/Cwd.pm
  313 /usr/lib/perl5/5.6.1/Exporter.pm
  225 /usr/lib/perl5/5.6.1/Exporter/Heavy.pm
```

```
   93 /usr/lib/perl5/5.6.1/File/Spec.pm
  458 /usr/lib/perl5/5.6.1/File/Spec/Unix.pm
  115 /usr/lib/perl5/5.6.1/File/stat.pm
  414 /usr/lib/perl5/5.6.1/IO/Socket/INET.pm
  143 /usr/lib/perl5/5.6.1/IO/Socket/UNIX.pm
   52 /usr/lib/perl5/5.6.1/SelectSaver.pm
  146 /usr/lib/perl5/5.6.1/Symbol.pm
  160 /usr/lib/perl5/5.6.1/Tie/Hash.pm
   92 /usr/lib/perl5/5.6.1/base.pm
 7525 /usr/lib/perl5/5.6.1/i386-linux/Config.pm
  276 /usr/lib/perl5/5.6.1/i386-linux/Errno.pm
  222 /usr/lib/perl5/5.6.1/i386-linux/Fcntl.pm
   47 /usr/lib/perl5/5.6.1/i386-linux/IO.pm
  239 /usr/lib/perl5/5.6.1/i386-linux/IO/Dir.pm
  169 /usr/lib/perl5/5.6.1/i386-linux/IO/File.pm
  612 /usr/lib/perl5/5.6.1/i386-linux/IO/Handle.pm
  252 /usr/lib/perl5/5.6.1/i386-linux/IO/Pipe.pm
  127 /usr/lib/perl5/5.6.1/i386-linux/IO/Seekable.pm
  428 /usr/lib/perl5/5.6.1/i386-linux/IO/Socket.pm
  453 /usr/lib/perl5/5.6.1/i386-linux/Socket.pm
  129 /usr/lib/perl5/5.6.1/i386-linux/XSLoader.pm
  117 /usr/lib/perl5/5.6.1/strict.pm
   83 /usr/lib/perl5/5.6.1/vars.pm
  419 /usr/lib/perl5/5.6.1/warnings.pm
   38 /usr/lib/perl5/5.6.1/warnings/register.pm
14529 total
```

About 14,500 lines of code! If you run a trace of this test code, you will see that it also puts a big load on the machine to actually load these modules, although this is mostly irrelevant if you preload the modules at server startup.

CGI.pm suffers from the same problem:

```
panic% wc -l `perl -MCGI -le 'print for values %INC'`
  313 /usr/lib/perl5/5.6.1/Exporter.pm
  124 /usr/lib/perl5/5.6.1/Carp.pm
  117 /usr/lib/perl5/5.6.1/strict.pm
   83 /usr/lib/perl5/5.6.1/vars.pm
   38 /usr/lib/perl5/5.6.1/warnings/register.pm
  419 /usr/lib/perl5/5.6.1/warnings.pm
  225 /usr/lib/perl5/5.6.1/Exporter/Heavy.pm
 1422 /usr/lib/perl5/5.6.1/overload.pm
  303 /usr/lib/perl5/5.6.1/CGI/Util.pm
 6695 /usr/lib/perl5/5.6.1/CGI.pm
  278 /usr/lib/perl5/5.6.1/constant.pm
10017 total
```

However, judging the bloat by the number of lines is misleading, since not all the code is used in most cases. Also remember that documentation might account for a significant chunk of the lines in every module.

Since we can preload the code at server startup, we are mostly interested in the execution overhead and memory footprint. So let's look at the memory usage.

Example 13-12 is the *perlbloat.pl* script, which shows how much memory is acquired by Perl when you run some code. Now we can easily test the overhead of loading the modules in question.

Example 13-12. perlbloat.pl

```
#!/usr/bin/perl -w

use GTop ();

my $gtop = GTop->new;
my $before = $gtop->proc_mem($$)->size;

for (@ARGV) {
    if (eval "require $_") {
        eval { $_->import; };
    }
    else {
        eval $_;
        die $@ if $@;
    }
}

my $after = $gtop->proc_mem($$)->size;
print "@ARGV added " . GTop::size_string($after - $before) . "\n";
```

The script simply samples the total memory use, then evaluates the code passed to it, samples the memory again, and prints the difference.

Now let's try to load IO:

```
panic% ./perlbloat.pl 'use IO;'
use IO; added  1.3M
```

"Only" 1.3 MB of overhead. Now let's load CGI.pm (v2.79) and compile its methods:

```
panic% ./perlbloat.pl 'use CGI; CGI->compile(":cgi")'
use CGI; CGI->compile(":cgi") added 784k
```

That's almost 1 MB of extra memory per process.

Let's compare CGI.pm with its younger sibling, whose internals are implemented in C:

```
%. /perlbloat.pl 'use Apache::Request'
use Apache::Request added    36k
```

Only 36 KB this time. A significant difference, isn't it? We have compiled the :cgi group of the CGI.pm methods, because CGI.pm is written in such a way that the actual code compilation is deferred until some function is actually used. To make a fair comparison with Apache::Request, we compiled only the methods present in both.

If we compile :all CGI.pm methods, the memory bloat is much bigger:

```
panic% ./perlbloat.pl 'use CGI; CGI->compile(":all")'
use CGI; CGI->compile(":all") added  1.9M
```

The following numbers show memory sizes in KB (virtual and resident) for Perl 5.6.0 on four different operating systems. Three calls are made: without any modules, with only -MCGI, and with -MIO (never with both). The rows with -MCGI and -MIO are followed by the difference relative to raw Perl.

	OpenBSD		FreeBSD		RedHat		Linux		Solaris	
	vsz	rss	vsz	rss	vsz	rss	vsz	rss	vsz	rss
Raw Perl	736	772	832	1208	2412	980	2928	2272
w/ CGI	1220	1464	1308	1828	2972	1768	3616	3232
delta	+484	+692	+476	+620	+560	+788	+688	+960
w/ IO	2292	2580	2456	3016	4080	2868	5384	4976
delta	+1556	+1808	+1624	+1808	+1668	+1888	+2456	+2704

Which is more important: saving enough memory to allow the machine to serve a few extra concurrent clients, or using off-the-shelf modules that are proven and well understood? Debugging a reinvention of the wheel can cost a lot of development time, especially if each member of your team reinvents in a different way. In general, it is a lot cheaper to buy more memory or a bigger machine than it is to hire an extra programmer. So while it may be wise to avoid using a bloated module if you need only a few functions that you could easily code yourself, the place to look for real efficiency savings is in how you write your code.

Importing Symbols

Imported symbols act just like global variables; they can add up memory quickly. In addition to polluting the namespace, a process grows by the size of the space allocated for all the symbols it imports. The more you import (e.g., qw(:standard) versus qw(:all) with CGI.pm), the more memory will be used.

Let's say the overhead is of size *Overhead*. Now take the number of scripts in which you deploy the function method interface—let's call that *Scripts*. Finally, let's say that you have a number of processes equal to *Processes*.

You will need *Overhead × Scripts × Processes* of additional memory. Taking an insignificant *Overhead* of 10 KB and, adding in 10 *Scripts* used across 30 *Processes*, we get 10 KB × 10 × 30 = 3 MB! The 10-KB overhead becomes a very significant one.

Let's assume that we need to use strtol( ) from the POSIX package. Under Perl 5.6.1 we get:

```
panic% ./perlbloat.pl 'use POSIX (); POSIX::strtol(__PACKAGE__, 16)'
use POSIX () added  176k

panic% ./perlbloat.pl 'use POSIX; strtol(__PACKAGE__, 16)'
use POSIX added  712k
```

The first time we import no symbols, and the second time we import all the default symbols from POSIX. The difference is 536 KB worth of aliases. Now let's say 10 different Apache::Registry scripts 'use POSIX;' for strftime( ), and we have 30 mod_perl processes:

```
536KB×10×30 = 160MB
```

We have 160 MB of extra memory used. Of course, you may want to import only needed symbols:

```
panic% ./perlbloat.pl 'use POSIX qw(strtol); strtol(__PACKAGE__, 16);'
use POSIX qw(strftime) added  344k
```

Still, using strftime( ) uses 168 KB more memory. Granted, POSIX is an extreme case—usually the overhead is much smaller for a single script but becomes significant if it occurs in many scripts executed by many processes.

Here is another example, now using the widely deployed CGI.pm module. Let's compare CGI.pm's object-oriented and procedural interfaces. We'll use two scripts that generate the same output, the first (Example 13-13) using methods and the second (Example 13-14) using functions. The second script imports a few functions that are going to be used.

Example 13-13. cgi_oo.pl

```
use CGI ();
my $q = CGI->new;
print $q->header;
print $q->b("Hello");
```

Example 13-14. cgi_proc.pl

```
use CGI qw(header b);
print header( );
print b("Hello");
```

After executing each script in single server mode (-X), we can see the results with the help of Apache::Status, as explained in Chapter 9.

Here are the results of the first script:

```
Totals: 1966 bytes | 27 OPs

handler 1514 bytes | 27 OPs
exit     116 bytes |  0 OPs
```

The results of the second script are:

```
Totals: 4710 bytes | 19 OPs

handler   1117 bytes | 19 OPs
basefont   120 bytes |  0 OPs
frameset   120 bytes |  0 OPs
caption    119 bytes |  0 OPs
applet     118 bytes |  0 OPs
```

```
script    118 bytes |   0 OPs
ilayer    118 bytes |   0 OPs
header    118 bytes |   0 OPs
strike    118 bytes |   0 OPs
layer     117 bytes |   0 OPs
table     117 bytes |   0 OPs
frame     117 bytes |   0 OPs
style     117 bytes |   0 OPs
Param     117 bytes |   0 OPs
small     117 bytes |   0 OPs
embed     117 bytes |   0 OPs
font      116 bytes |   0 OPs
span      116 bytes |   0 OPs
exit      116 bytes |   0 OPs
big       115 bytes |   0 OPs
div       115 bytes |   0 OPs
sup       115 bytes |   0 OPs
Sub       115 bytes |   0 OPs
TR        114 bytes |   0 OPs
td        114 bytes |   0 OPs
Tr        114 bytes |   0 OPs
th        114 bytes |   0 OPs
b         113 bytes |   0 OPs
```

As you see, the object-oriented script uses about 2 KB of memory while the procedural interface script uses about 5 KB.

Note that the above is correct if you didn't precompile all of CGI.pm's methods at server startup. If you did, the procedural interface in the second test will take up to 18 KB, not 5 KB. That's because the entire CGI.pm namespace is inherited, and it already has all its methods compiled, so it doesn't really matter whether you attempt to import only the symbols that you need. So if you have:

```
use CGI  qw(-compile :all);
```

in the server startup script, having:

```
use CGI qw(header);
```

or:

```
use CGI qw(:all);
```

is essentially the same. All the symbols precompiled at startup will be imported, even if you request only one symbol. It seems like a bug, but it's just how CGI.pm works.

Object Methods Calls Versus Function Calls

Which form of subroutine call is more efficient: object methods or function calls? Let's look at the overhead.

The Overhead with Light Subroutines

Let's do some benchmarking. We will start by using empty methods, which will allow us to measure the real difference in the overhead each kind of call introduces. We will use the code in Example 13-15.

Example 13-15. bench_call1.pl

```
package Book::LightSub;

use strict;
use Benchmark;

sub bar { };

timethese(1_000_000, {
    method   => sub { Book::LightSub->bar()              },
    function => sub { Book::LightSub::bar('Book::LightSub');},
});
```

The two calls are equivalent, since both pass the class name as their first parameter; function does this explicitly, while method does this transparently.

Here's the benchmarking result:

```
Benchmark: timing 1000000 iterations of function, method...
  function:  2 wallclock secs ( 1.36 usr +  0.05 sys =  1.41 CPU)
    method:  3 wallclock secs ( 2.57 usr + -0.03 sys =  2.54 CPU)
```

We see that the function call is almost twice as fast as the method call: 1.41 CPU clocks compared to 2.54. Why is this? With a function call we give Perl the fully qualified function name and set up its call stack ourselves by passing in the package (class) name. With a method call Perl must work out the package (class) name for itself, then search the inheritance tree to find the required method, then set up the call stack. So in the case of a method call Perl must do a lot more work and is therefore slower.

Perl 5.6.0 and higher do better method caching than older Perl versions. Book:: LightSub->method() is a little bit faster (as it does better constant-folding magic), but not Book::LightSub->$method(). The improvement does not address the @ISA lookup that still happens in either case.

The Overhead with Heavy Subroutines

The above results don't mean that you shouldn't use methods. Generally your functions do something, and the more they do the less significant the overhead of the call itself becomes. This is because the calling time is effectively fixed and usually creates a very small overhead in comparison to the execution time of the method or function itself. This is demonstrated by the next benchmark (see Example 13-16).

Example 13-16. bench_call2.pl

```perl
package Book::HeavySub;

use strict;
use Benchmark;

sub bar {
    my $class = shift;

    my ($x, $y) = (100, 100);
    $y = log ($x ** 10)  for (0..20);
};

timethese(100_000, {
    method   => sub { Book::HeavySub->bar( )             },
    function => sub { Book::HeavySub::bar('Book::HeavySub');},
});
```

We get a very close benchmark!

```
panic% ./bench_call2.pl
function:  5 wallclock secs ( 4.42 usr +  0.02 sys =  4.44 CPU)
  method:  5 wallclock secs ( 4.66 usr +  0.00 sys =  4.66 CPU)
```

Let's make the subroutine bar even heavier, by making the for( ) loop five times longer:

```perl
sub bar {
    my $class = shift;

    my ($x, $y) = (100, 100);
    $y = log ($x ** 10) for (0..100);
};
```

The result is:

```
function: 18 wallclock secs (17.87 usr +  0.10 sys = 17.97 CPU)
  method: 19 wallclock secs (18.22 usr +  0.01 sys = 18.23 CPU)
```

You can see that in the first and second benchmarks the difference between the function and method calls is almost the same: 0.22 and 0.26 CPU clocks, respectively.

In cases where functions do very little work, the overhead might become significant. If your goal is speed you might consider using the function form, but if you write a large and complicated application, it's much better to use the method form, as it will make your code easier to develop, maintain, and debug. Saving programmer time over the life of a project may turn out to be the most significant cost factor.

Are All Methods Slower Than Functions?

Some modules' APIs are misleading—for example, CGI.pm allows you to execute its subroutines as functions or as methods. As you will see in a moment, its function form of the calls is slower than the method form because it does some voodoo behind the scenes when the function form call is used:

```
use CGI;
my $q = new CGI;
$q->param('x', 5);
my $x = $q->param('x');
```

versus:

```
use CGI qw(:standard);
param('x', 5);
my $x = param('x');
```

Let's benchmark some very light calls (see Example 13-17) and compare. We would expect the methods to be slower than functions, based on the previous benchmarks.

Example 13-17. bench_call3.pl

```
use Benchmark;

use CGI qw(:standard);
$CGI::NO_DEBUG = 1;
my $q = new CGI;
my $x;
timethese(2_000_000, {
    method   => sub {$q->param('x',5); $x = $q->param('x'); },
    function => sub {    param('x',5); $x =    param('x'); },
});
```

The benchmark is written in such a way that all initializations are done at the beginning, so that we get as accurate performance figures as possible:

```
panic% ./bench_call3.pl
function: 21 wallclock secs (19.88 usr +  0.30 sys = 20.18 CPU)
  method: 18 wallclock secs (16.72 usr +  0.24 sys = 16.96 CPU)
```

As you can see, methods are faster than functions, which seems to be wrong. The explanation lies in the way CGI.pm is implemented. CGI.pm uses some fancy tricks to make the same routine act both as a method and as a plain function. The overhead of checking whether the arguments list looks like a method invocation or not will mask the slight difference in time for the way the function was called.

If you are intrigued and want to investigate further by yourself, the subroutine you should explore is called self_or_default. The first line of this function short-circuits if you are using object methods, but the whole function is called if you are using the function-call forms. Therefore, the function-call form should be slightly slower than the object form for the CGI.pm module, which you shouldn't be using anyway if you have Apache::Request and a real templating system.

Using the Perl stat( ) Call's Cached Results

When you call stat( ) (or its variants -M, -e, etc.), the returned information is cached internally. If you need to make an additional check on the same file, assuming that it hasn't been modified, use the _ magic file handle and save the overhead an unnecessary stat( ) call. For example, when testing for existence and read permissions, you might use:

```
my $filename = "./test";
# three stat( ) calls
print "OK\n" if -e $filename and -r $filename;
my $mod_time = (-M $filename) * 24 * 60 * 60;
print "$filename was modified $mod_time seconds before startup\n";
```

or the more efficient:

```
my $filename = "./test";
# one stat( ) call
print "OK\n" if -e $filename and -r _;
my $mod_time = (-M _) * 24 * 60 * 60;
print "$filename was modified $mod_time seconds before startup\n";
```

Two stat( ) calls were saved!

If you need to stat( ) the mod_perl script that is being executed (or, in a handler, the requested filename in $r->filename), you can save this stat( ) system call by passing it $r->finfo as an argument. For example, to retrieve the user ID of the script's owner, use:

```
my $uid = (stat $r->finfo)[4];
```

During the default translation phase, Apache calls stat( ) on the script's filename, so later on we can reuse the cached stat( ) structure, assuming that it hasn't changed since the stat( ) call. Notice that in the example we do call stat( ), but this doesn't invoke the system call, since Perl resuses the cached data structure.

Furthermore, the call to $r->finfo stores its result in _ once again, so if we need more information we can do:

```
print $r->filename, " is writable" if -e $r->finfo and -w _;
```

time( ) System Call Versus $r->request_time

If you need to know the time at which the request started, you can either install PerlPostReadRequestHandler, which adjusts the special Perl variable $^T to store that time:

```
$^T = time( );
```

and subsequently use that variable in the code, or you can use $r->request_time, which stores the exact request's start time and saves the extra system call to time( ).

Printing Unmodified Files

To send a complete file from disk, without applying any modifications first, instead of:

```
my $filename = "/tmp/foo";
my $fh = Apache::gensym( );  # generate a new filehandle
open $fh, $filename or return NOT_FOUND;
print <$fh>;
close $fh;
```

it's better to write:

```
my $filename = "/tmp/foo";
my $fh = Apache::gensym( );  # generate a new filehandle
open $fh, $filename or return NOT_FOUND;
$r->send_fd($fh);
close $fh;
```

The former implementation uses more memory and it's slower, because it creates a temporary variable to read the data in and then print it out. The latter uses optimized C code to read the file and send it to the client.

Caching and Pre-Caching

In some situations, you may have data that is expensive to generate but must be created on the fly. If the data can be reused, it may be more efficient to cache it. This will save the CPU cycles that regenerating the data would incur and will improve performance (at the expense of using more memory to cache the results).

If the data set is final, it can be a good idea to generate this data set at server startup and then share it with all the child processes, thus saving both memory and time.

We'll create a calendar example similar to the ones many online services use to allow their users to choose dates for online forms or to navigate to pages specific to a particular date. Since we are talking about dynamic pages, we cannot allow the calendar to be static.

To make our explanations easier, let's assume that we are trying to build a nice navigation system for forums, but will implement only the temporal navigation. You can extend our code to add the actual forums and interface elements to change presentation modes (*index*, *thread*, *nested*) and to change forums (*perl*, *mod_perl*, *apache*).

In Figure 13-1, you can see how the calendar looks if today is May 16, 2002 and the user has just entered the site. You can see that only day numbers before this date are linked to the data for those dates. The current month appears between the previous month, April, and the next to come, June. June dates aren't linked at all, since they're in the future.

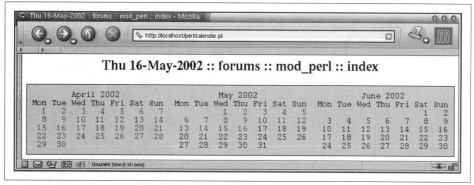

Figure 13-1. The calendar as seen on May 16, 2002

We click on April 16 and get a new calendar (see Figure 13-2), where April is shown in the middle of the two adjacent months. Again, we can see that in May not all dates are linked, since we are still in the middle of the month.

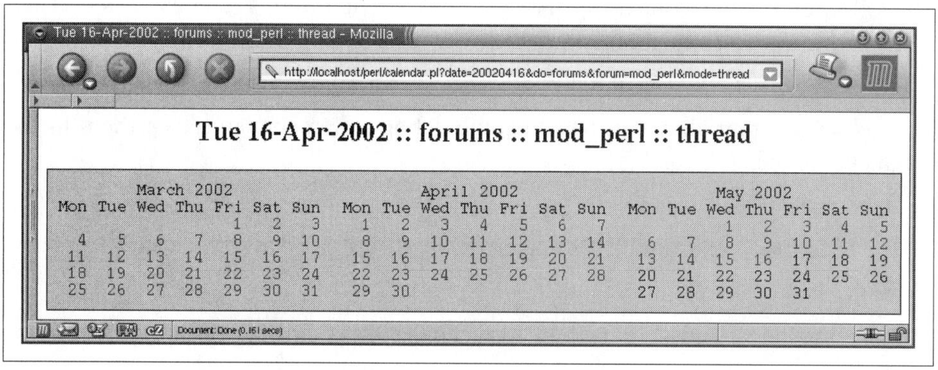

Figure 13-2. After clicking on the date April 16, 2002

In both figures you can see a title (which can be pretty much anything) that can be passed when some link in the calendar is clicked. When we go through the actual script that presents the calendar we will show this in detail.

As you can see from the figures, you can move backward and forward in time by clicking on the righthand or lefthand month. If you currently have a calendar showing Mar-Apr-May, by clicking on some day in March, you will get a calendar of Feb-Mar-Apr, and if you click on some day in May you will see Apr-May-Jun.

Most users will want to browse recent data from the forums—especially the current month and probably the previous month. Some users will want to browse older archives, but these users would be a minority.

Since the generation of the calendar is quite an expensive operation, it makes sense to generate the current and previous months' calendars at server startup and then reuse them in all the child processes. We also want to cache any other items generated during the requests.

In order to appreciate the results of the benchmark presented at the end of this section, which show the benefits of caching for this application, it's important to understand how the application works. Therefore, let's explain the code first.

First we create a new package and load `Date::Calc`:

```
package Book::Calendar;
use Date::Calc ();
```

`Date::Calc`, while a quite bloated module, is very useful for working with dates.

We have two caches, one for one-month text calendars (`%TXT_CAL_CACHE`, where we will cache the output of `Date::Calc::Calendar()`), and the other for caching the real three-month HTML calendar components:

```
my %HTML_CAL_CACHE = ();
my %TXT_CAL_CACHE = ();
```

The following variable controls the last day the current month's calendar was updated in the cache. We will explain this variable (which serves as a flag) in a moment.

```
my $CURRENT_MONTH_LAST_CACHED_DAY = 0;
```

The debug constant allows us to add some debug statements and keep them in the production code:

```
use constant DEBUG => 1;
```

All the code that is executed if `DEBUG` is true:

```
warn "foo" if DEBUG;
```

will be removed at compile time by Perl when `DEBUG` is made false (in production, for example).

This code prebuilds each month's calendar from three months back to one month forward. If this module is loaded at server startup, pre-caching will happen automatically and data will be shared between the children, so you save both memory and time. If you think that you need more months cached, just adjust this pre-caching code.

```
my ($cyear,$cmonth) = Date::Calc::Today();
for my $i (-3..1) {
    my($year, $month) =
        Date::Calc::Add_Delta_YMD($cyear, $cmonth, 1, 0, $i, 0);
    my $cal = '';
    get_html_calendar(\$cal, $year, $month);
}
```

The `get_text_calendar` function wraps a retrieval of plain-text calendars generated by `Date::Calc::Calendar()`, caches the generated months, and, if the month was already cached, immediately returns it, thus saving time and CPU cycles.

```
sub get_text_calendar{
    my($year, $month) = @_;
    unless ($TXT_CAL_CACHE{$year}{$month}) {
        $TXT_CAL_CACHE{$year}{$month} = Date::Calc::Calendar($year, $month);
        # remove extra new line at the end
        chomp $TXT_CAL_CACHE{$year}{$month};
    }
    return $TXT_CAL_CACHE{$year}{$month};
}
```

Now the main function starts.

```
sub get_html_calendar{
    my $r_calendar = shift;
    my $year    = shift || 1;
    my $month   = shift || 1;
```

get_html_calendar() is called with a reference to a final calendar and the year/month of the middle month in the calendar. Remember that the whole widget includes three months. So you call it like this, as we saw in the pre-caching code:

```
my $calendar = '';
get_html_calendar(\$calendar, $year, $month);
```

After get_html_calendar() is called, $calendar contains all the HTML needed.

Next we get the current year, month, and day, so we will know what days should be linked. In our design, only past days and today are linked.

```
my($cur_year, $cur_month, $cur_day) = Date::Calc::Today();
```

The following code decides whether the $must_update_current_month_cache flag should be set or not. It's used to solve a problem with calendars that include the current month. We cannot simply cache the current month's calendar, because on the next day it will be incorrect, since the new day will not be linked. So what we are going to do is cache this month's day and remember this day in the $CURRENT_MONTH_LAST_CACHED_DAY variable, explained later.

```
my $must_update_current_month_cache = 0;
for my $i (-1..1) {
    my($t_year, $t_month) =
        Date::Calc::Add_Delta_YMD($year, $month, 1, 0, $i, 0);
    $must_update_current_month_cache = 1
        if $t_year == $cur_year and $t_month == $cur_month
            and $CURRENT_MONTH_LAST_CACHED_DAY < $cur_day;
    last if $must_update_current_month_cache;
}
```

Now the decision logic is simple: we go through all three months in our calendar, and if any of them is the current month, we check the date when the cache was last updated for the current month (stored in the $CURRENT_MONTH_LAST_CACHED_DAY variable). If this date is less than today's date, we have to rebuild this cache entry.

```
unless (exists $HTML_CAL_CACHE{$year}{$month}
        and not $must_update_current_month_cache) {
```

So we enter the main loop where the calendar is HTMLified and linked. We enter this loop if:

1. There is no cached copy of the requested month.
2. There is a cached copy of the requested month, but it includes the current month and the next date has arrived; we need to rebuild it again, since the new day should be linked as well.

The following is the debug statement we mentioned earlier. This can help you check that the cache works and that you actually reuse it. If the constant DEBUG is set to a true value, the warning will be output every time this loop is entered.

```
warn "creating a new calendar for $year $month\n" if DEBUG;
```

When we load this module at server startup, the pre-caching code we described earlier gets executed, and we will see the following warnings (if DEBUG is true):

```
creating a new calendar for 2000 9
creating a new calendar for 2000 10
creating a new calendar for 2000 11
creating a new calendar for 2000 12
creating a new calendar for 2001 1
```

```
        my @cal = ();
```

Now we create three calendars, which will be stored in @cal:

```
for my $i (-1..1) {
    my $id = $i+1;
```

As you can see, we make a loop (-1,0,1) so we can go one month back from the requested month and one month forward in a generic way.

Now we call Date::Calc::Add_Delta_YMD() to retrieve the previous, current, or next month by providing the requested year and month, using the first date of the month. Then we add zero years, $i months, and zero days. Since $i loops through the values (-1, 0, 1), we get the previous, current, and next months:

```
my ($t_year, $t_month) =
    Date::Calc::Add_Delta_YMD($year, $month, 1, 0, $i, 0);
```

Next, we get the text calendar for a single month. It will be cached internally by get_text_calendar() if it wasn't cached already:

```
$cal[$id] = get_text_calendar($t_year, $t_month);
```

The following code determines whether the requested month is the current month (present), a month from the past, or the month in the future. That's why the decision variable has three possible values: -1, 0, and 1 (past, present, and future, respectively). We will need this flag when we decide whether a day should be linked or not.

```
my $yearmonth = sprintf("%0.4d%0.2d", $t_year, $t_month);
my $cur_yearmonth = sprintf("%0.4d%0.2d", $cur_year, $cur_month);
```

```
# tri-state: ppf (past/present/future)
my $ppf = $yearmonth <=> $cur_yearmonth;
  # If    $yearmonth == $cur_yearmonth, $ppf = 0;
  # elsif $yearmonth < $cur_yearmonth,  $ppf = -1;
  # elsif $yearmonth > $cur_yearmonth,  $ppf = 1;
```

This regex is used to substitute days in the textual calendar returned by Date::Calc::
Calendar( ) with links:

```
$cal[$id] =~ s{(\s\d|\b\d\d)\b}
             {link_days($1, $yearmonth, $ppf, $cur_day)}eg;
```

It means: "Find a space followed by a digit, or find two digits (in either case with no
adjoining digits), and replace what we've found with the result of the link_days( )
subroutine call." The e option tells Perl to execute the substitution expression—i.e.,
to call link_days( )—and the g option tells Perl to perform the substitution for every
match found in the source string. Note that word boundaries are zero-width asser-
tions (they don't match any text) and are needed to ensure that we don't match the
year digits. You can see them in the first line of the calendar:

```
          May 2002
   Mon Tue Wed Thu Fri Sat Sun
             1   2   3   4   5
    6   7   8   9  10  11  12
   13  14  15  16  17  18  19
   20  21  22  23  24  25  26
   27  28  29  30  31
```

The link_days( ) subroutine will add HTML links only to dates that aren't in the
future.

This line closes the for loop:

```
}
```

This code constructs an HTML table with three calendars and stores it in the cache.
We use <pre> ... </pre> blocks to preserve the textual layout of the calendar:

```
# cache the HTML calendar for future use
$HTML_CAL_CACHE{$year}{$month} =
qq{
 <table border="0" cellspacing="0"
  cellpadding="1" bgcolor="#000000">
    <tr>
      <td>
        <table border="0" cellspacing="0"
         cellpadding="10" bgcolor="#ccccff">
          <tr>
            <td valign="top"><pre>$cal[0]</pre></td>
            <td valign="top"><pre>$cal[1]</pre></td>
            <td valign="top"><pre>$cal[2]</pre></td>
          </tr>
        </table>
      </td>
    </tr>
```

```
    </table>
  };
```

If the $must_update_current_month_cache flag was turned on, the current month is re-processed, since a new day just started. Therefore, we update the $CURRENT_MONTH_LAST_CACHED_DAY with the current day, so that the next request in the same day will use the cached data:

```
# update the last cached day in the current month if needed
$CURRENT_MONTH_LAST_CACHED_DAY = $cur_day
    if $must_update_current_month_cache;
```

This line signals that the conditional block where the calendar was created is over:

```
  }
```

Regardless of whether the calendar is created afresh or was already cached, we provide the requested calendar component by assigning it to a variable in the caller namespace, via the reference. The goal is for just this last statement to be executed and for the cache to do the rest:

```
$$r_calendar = $HTML_CAL_CACHE{$year}{$month};

  } # end of sub calendar
```

Note that we copy the whole calendar component and don't just assign the reference to the cached value. The reason for doing this lies in the fact that this calendar component's HTML text will be adjusted to the user's environment and will render the cached entry unusable for future requests. In a moment we will get to customize_calendar( ), which adjusts the calendar for the user environment.

This is the function that was called in the second part of the regular expression:

```
sub link_days {
    my ($token, $yearmonth, $ppf, $cur_day) = @_;
```

It accepts the matched space digit or two digits. We kept the space character for days 1 to 9 so that the calendar is nicely aligned. The function is called as:

```
link_days($token, 200101, $ppf, $cur_day);
```

where the arguments are the token (e.g., ' 2' or '31' or possibly something else), the year and the month concatenated together (to be used in a link), the past/present/future month flag, and finally the current date's day, which is relevant only if we are working in the current month.

We immediately return unmodified non-days tokens and break the token into two characters in one statement. Then we set the $fill variable to a single space character if the token included days below 10, or set it to an empty string. $day actually includes the date (1–31).

```
return $token unless my($c1, $c2) = $token =~ /^(\s|\d)(\d)$/;
my ($fill, $day) = ($c1 =~ /\d/) ? ('', $c1.$c2) : ($c1, $c2) ;
```

The function is not supposed to link days in future months, or days in this month that are in the future. For days in the future the function returns the token unmodified, which renders these days as plain text with no link.

```
# don't link days in the future
return $token if $ppf == 1 or ($ppf == 0 and $day > $cur_day);
```

Finally, those tokens that reach this point get linked. The link is constructed of the [URL] placeholder, the date arguments, and the [PARAMS] placeholder. The placeholders will be replaced with real data at runtime.

```
return qq{$fill<a href="[URL]?date=$yearmonth}.
        sprintf("%0.2d", $day).
        qq{&[PARAMS]" class="nolink">$day</a>};
```

The a tag's nolink class attribute will be used by the client code to render the links with no underlining, to make the calendar more visually appealing. The nolink class must be defined in a Cascading Style Sheet (CSS). Be careful, though—this might not be a very good usability technique, since many people are used to links that are blue and underlined.

This line concludes the link_days( ) function:

```
} # end of sub link_days
```

The customize_calendar( ) subroutine takes a reference to a string of HTML (our calendar component, for example) and replaces the placeholders with the data we pass it. We do an efficient one-pass match and replace for both placeholders using the hash lookup trick. If you want to add more placeholders later, all that's needed is to add a new placeholder name to the %map hash:

```
# replace the placeholders with live data
# customize_calendar(\$calendar,$url,$params);
#######################
sub customize_calendar {
    my $r_calendar = shift;
    my $url        = shift || '';
    my $params     = shift || '';
    my %map = (
        URL    => $url,
        PARAMS => $params,
    );
    $$r_calendar =~ s/\[(\w+)\]/$map{$1}/g;

} # end of sub calendar
```

The module ends with the usual true statement to make require( ) happy:

```
1;
```

The whole Book::Calendar package is presented in Example 13-18.

Example 13-18. Book/Calendar.pm

```perl
package Book::Calendar;

use Date::Calc ();

my %HTML_CAL_CACHE = ();
my %TXT_CAL_CACHE = ();
my $CURRENT_MONTH_LAST_CACHED_DAY = 0;

use constant DEBUG => 0;

# prebuild this month's, 3 months back and 1 month forward calendars
my($cyear, $cmonth) = Date::Calc::Today();
for my $i (-3..1) {
    my($year, $month) = Date::Calc::Add_Delta_YMD($cyear, $cmonth, 1, 0, $i, 0);
    my $cal = '';
    get_html_calendar(\$cal, $year, $month); # disregard the returned calendar
}

# $cal = create_text_calendar($year, $month);
# the created calendar is cached
#####################
sub get_text_calendar {
    my($year,$month) = @_;
    unless ($TXT_CAL_CACHE{$year}{$month}) {
        $TXT_CAL_CACHE{$year}{$month} = Date::Calc::Calendar($year, $month);
        # remove extra new line at the end
        chomp $TXT_CAL_CACHE{$year}{$month};
    }
    return $TXT_CAL_CACHE{$year}{$month};
}

# get_html_calendar(\$calendar,1999,7);
#####################
sub get_html_calendar {
    my $r_calendar = shift;
    my $year   = shift || 1;
    my $month  = shift || 1;

    my($cur_year, $cur_month, $cur_day) = Date::Calc::Today();

    # should requested calendar be updated if it exists already?
    my $must_update_current_month_cache = 0;
    for my $i (-1..1) {
        my ($t_year, $t_month) =
            Date::Calc::Add_Delta_YMD($year, $month, 1, 0, $i, 0);
        $must_update_current_month_cache = 1
            if $t_year == $cur_year and $t_month == $cur_month
                and $CURRENT_MONTH_LAST_CACHED_DAY < $cur_day;
        last if $must_update_current_month_cache;
    }
```

Example 13-18. Book/Calendar.pm (continued)

```perl
    unless (exists $HTML_CAL_CACHE{$year}{$month}
            and not $must_update_current_month_cache) {

        warn "creating a new calendar for $year $month\n" if DEBUG;

        my @cal = ( );

        for my $i (-1..1) {
            my $id = $i+1;

            my ($t_year, $t_month) =
                Date::Calc::Add_Delta_YMD($year, $month, 1, 0, $i, 0);

            # link the calendar from passed month
            $cal[$id] = get_text_calendar($t_year, $t_month); # get a copy
            my $yearmonth = sprintf("%0.4d%0.2d", $t_year, $t_month);
            my $cur_yearmonth = sprintf("%0.4d%0.2d", $cur_year, $cur_month);

            # tri-state: ppf (past/present/future)
            my $ppf = $yearmonth <=> $cur_yearmonth;

            $cal[$id] =~ s{(\s\d|\b\d\d)\b}
                          {link_days($1, $yearmonth, $ppf, $cur_day)}eg;
        }

        # cache the HTML calendar for future use
        $HTML_CAL_CACHE{$year}{$month} =
        qq{
          <table border="0" cellspacing="0"
           cellpadding="1" bgcolor="#000000">
            <tr>
              <td>
                <table border="0" cellspacing="0"
                 cellpadding="10" bgcolor="#ccccff">
                  <tr>
                    <td valign="top"><pre>$cal[0]</pre></td>
                    <td valign="top"><pre>$cal[1]</pre></td>
                    <td valign="top"><pre>$cal[2]</pre></td>
                  </tr>
                </table>
              </td>
            </tr>
          </table>
        };

        $CURRENT_MONTH_LAST_CACHED_DAY = $cur_day
            if $must_update_current_month_cache;

    }

    $$r_calendar = $HTML_CAL_CACHE{$year}{$month};
```

Example 13-18. Book/Calendar.pm (continued)

```
} # end of sub calendar

#
# link_days($token,199901,1,10);
###########
sub link_days {
    my($token, $yearmonth, $ppf, $cur_day) = @_;
    # $cur_day relevant only if $ppf == 0

    # skip non-days (non (\d or \d\d) )
    return $token unless my ($c1, $c2) = $token =~ /(\s|\d)(\d)/;

    my($fill, $day) = ($c1 =~ /\d/) ? ('', $c1.$c2) : ($c1, $c2) ;

    # don't link days in the future
    return $token if $ppf == 1 or ($ppf == 0 and $day > $cur_day);

    # link the date with placeholders to be replaced later
    return qq{$fill<a href="[URL]?date=$yearmonth}.
            sprintf("%0.2d",$day).
            qq{&[PARAMS]" class="nolink">$day</a>};

} # end of sub link_days


# replace the placeholders with live data
# customize_calendar(\$calendar,$url,$params);
#######################
sub customize_calendar {
    my $r_calendar = shift;
    my $url        = shift || '';
    my $params     = shift || '';
    my %map = (
        URL    => $url,
        PARAMS => $params,
    );
    $$r_calendar =~ s/\[(\w+)\]/$map{$1}/g;

} # end of sub calendar

1;
```

Now let's review the code that actually prints the page. The script starts by the usual strict mode, and adds the two packages that we are going to use:

```
use strict;
use Date::Calc ();
use Book::Calendar ();
```

We extract the arguments via $r->args and store them in a hash:

```
my $r = shift;
my %args = $r->args;
```

Now we set the $year, $month, and $day variables by parsing the requested date (which comes from the day clicked by the user in the calendar). If the date isn't provided we use today as a starting point.

```
# extract the date or set it to be today
my ($year, $month, $day) =
    ($args{date} and $args{date} =~ /(\d{4})(\d\d)(\d\d)/)
    ? ($1, $2, $3)
    : Date::Calc::Today( );
```

Then we retrieve or use defaults for the other arguments that one might use in a forum application:

```
my $do    = $args{do}    || 'forums';
my $forum = $args{forum} || 'mod_perl';
my $mode  = $args{mode}  || 'index';
```

Next we start to generate the HTTP response, by setting the Content-Type header to text/html and sending all HTTP headers:

```
$r->send_http_header("text/html");
```

The beginning of the HTML page is generated. It includes the previously mentioned CSS for the calendar link, whose class we have called nolink. Then we start the body of the page and print the title of the page constructed from the arguments that we received or their defaults, followed by the selected or current date:

```
my $date_str = Date::Calc::Date_to_Text($year, $month, $day);

my $title = "$date_str :: $do :: $forum :: $mode";
print qq{<html>
<head>
  <title>$title</title>
  <style type="text/css">
    <!--
    a.nolink { text-decoration: none; }
    -->
  </style>
</head>
<body bgcolor="white">
<h2 align="center">$title</h2>
};
```

Now we request the calendar component for $year and $month:

```
my $calendar = '';
Book::Calendar::get_html_calendar(\$calendar, $year, $month);
```

We adjust the links to the live data by replacing the placeholders, taking the script's URI from $r->uri, and setting the paramaters that will be a part of the link:

```
my $params = "do=forums&forum=mod_perl&mode=index";
Book::Calendar::customize_calendar(\$calendar, $r->uri, $params);
```

At the end we print the calendar and finish the HTML:

```
    print $calendar;
    print qq{</body></html>};
```

The entire script is shown in Example 13-19.

Example 13-19. calendar.pl

```perl
use strict;
use Date::Calc ();
use Book::Calendar ();

my $r = shift;
my %args = $r->args;

# extract the date or set it to be today
my($year, $month, $day) =
    ($args{date} and $args{date} =~ /(\d{4})(\d\d)(\d\d)/)
    ? ($1, $2, $3)
    : Date::Calc::Today();

my $do    = $args{do}    || 'forums';
my $forum = $args{forum} || 'mod_perl';
my $mode  = $args{mode}  || 'index';

$r->send_http_header("text/html");

my $date_str = Date::Calc::Date_to_Text($year, $month, $day);

my $title = "$date_str :: $do :: $forum :: $mode";
print qq{<html>
<head>
  <title>$title</title>
  <style type="text/css">
    <!--
    a.nolink { text-decoration: none; }
    -->
  </style>
</head>
<body bgcolor="white">
<h2 align="center">$title</h2>
};

my $calendar = '';
Book::Calendar::get_html_calendar(\$calendar, $year, $month);

my $params = "do=forums&forum=mod_perl&mode=index";
Book::Calendar::customize_calendar(\$calendar, $r->uri, $params);
print $calendar;
print qq{</body></html>};
```

Now let's analyze the importance of the caching that we used in the Book::Calendar module. We will use the simple benchmark in Example 13-20 to get the average runtime under different conditions.

Example 13-20. bench_cal.pl

```perl
use strict;
use Benchmark;
use Book::Calendar;

my ($year, $month) = Date::Calc::Today();

sub calendar_cached {
    ($year, $month) = Date::Calc::Add_Delta_YMD($year, $month, 1, 0, 0, 0);
    my $calendar = '';
    Book::Calendar::get_html_calendar(\$calendar, $year, $month);
}
sub calendar_non_cached {
    ($year, $month) = Date::Calc::Add_Delta_YMD($year, $month, 1, 0, 1, 0);
    my $calendar = '';
    Book::Calendar::get_html_calendar(\$calendar, $year, $month);
}

timethese(10_000,
        {
         cached      => \&calendar_cached,
         non_cached => \&calendar_non_cached,
        });
```

We create two subroutines: calendar_cached() and calendar_non_cached(). Note that we aren't going to remove the caching code from Book::Calendar; instead, in the calendar_non_cached() function we will increment to the next month on each invocation, thus not allowing the data to be cached. In calendar_cached() we will request the same calendar all the time.

When the benchmark is executed on an unloaded machine, we get the following results:

```
panic% perl calendar_bench.pl
  Benchmark: timing 10000 iterations of cached, non_cached...
      cached:  0 wallclock secs ( 0.48 usr +  0.01 sys =  0.49 CPU)
  non_cached: 26 wallclock secs (24.93 usr +  0.56 sys = 25.49 CPU)
```

The non-cached version is about 52 times slower. On the other hand, when a pretty heavy load is created, which is a common situation for web servers, we get these results:

```
panic% perl calendar_bench.pl
  Benchmark: timing 10000 iterations of cached, non_cached...
      cached:  3 wallclock secs ( 0.52 usr +  0.00 sys =  0.52 CPU)
  non_cached: 146 wallclock secs (28.09 usr +  0.46 sys = 28.55 CPU)
```

We can see that the results of running the same benchmark on machines with different loads are very similar, because the module in question mostly needed CPU. It took six times longer to complete the same benchmark, but CPU-wise the performance is not very different from that of the unloaded machine. You should nevertheless draw your conclusions with care: if your code is not CPU-bound but I/O-bound, for example, the same benchmark on the unloaded and loaded machines will be very different.

Caching with Memoize

If you have a subroutine with simpler logic, where a returned value is solely a function of an input, you can use the Memoize module, which does the caching automatically for you. The gist of its usage is giving the name of the function to be memoize()d:

```
use Memoize;
memoize('slow_function');
slow_function(arguments);
```

Remember that in our case we had two caches: one for the text versions of the calendars and the other for HTML components. The get_text_calendar() function is responsible for populating the text calendar's cache. It depends only on inputs, so we could rewrite it as:

```
use Memoize;
memoize('get_text_calendar');
sub get_text_calendar {
    my($year,$month) = @_;
    warn "$year,$month\n" if DEBUG;
    my $cal = Date::Calc::Calendar($year, $month);
    chomp $cal;
    return $cal;
}
```

We have added another debug warning to check that the cache is actually working. If you want to test it under mod_perl, set DEBUG to a true value, start the server in single-process mode (-X), and issue requests to the calendar registry script we just discussed.

You can also control the size of the cache and do other automatic cache manipulations with Memoize. See its manpage for more information.

The get_html_calendar() subroutine cannot be memoize()d because the returned value depends on the relation between the requested date and the current date, in addition to the normal input/output relation.

Comparing Runtime Performance of Perl and C

Perl is commonly used for web scripting because it is quick and easy to write, and very easy to change. Compiled languages usually take a lot more time and effort to write and debug and can be time-consuming to change. But compiled code often runs faster (sometimes a *lot* faster) than bytecode-interpreted languages such as Perl or Java. In most projects it is programmer time that is paramount, because programmers are expensive, but some projects demand performance above all other considerations. How do we compare the performance of a Perl script to that of a C program?

We know we can use the Benchmark module to compare Perl code. There are equivalent tools for C also, but how are we going to use two different tools and keep the comparison fair? Since Perl is a glue language in addition to its own merits, we can glue the C code into Perl and then use the Benchmark module to run the benchmark.

To simplify the task, we are going to demonstrate only the fact that C is more suitable than Perl for mathematical and memory-manipulation tasks. The purpose is to show how to use the best of both worlds.

We will use a very simple task that we will implement in Perl and C: the factorial function written both recursivly and iteratively. If you have ever taken a basic programming course you will be familiar with this example.

In mathematical language, we define the factorial function as follows:

```
1! = 1
N! = N * (N-1)!
```

So if we start from 1 and go up, we get these numbers:

```
1! =               1
2! = (2)(1)        = 2
3! = (3)(2)(1)     = 6
4! = (4)(3)(2)(1) = 24
... and so on.
```

The factorial grows very fast—e.g., 10! = 3,628,800 and 12! = 4.790016e+08 (479 million)—so you can imagine that the calculation of the factorial of large numbers is a memory-intensive operation.

Now since we have a recursive definition of the solution:

```
fact(1) = 1;
fact(N) = N * fact(N-1)
```

the easiest way to implement it is to write a recursive function. In Perl we just reproduce the definition:

```
sub factorial_recursive_perl {
    return 1 if $_[0] < 2;
    return $_[0] * factorial_recursive_perl($_[0] - 1);
}
```

Computer science teaches us that while recursive functions are often easy to write they are usually slower to run than their iterative equivalents. The iterative implementation is as easy as the recursive one in our example, and it should run much faster, since there is no function-call overhead. This is the iterative algorithm to calculate fact(N):

```
result = 1
for (i = 2; i <= N; i++) {
```

```
        result *= i;
    }
```

By adjusting it to use idiomatic Perl, we get the following function:

```
sub factorial_iterative_perl {
    my $return = 1;
    $return *= $_ for 2..$_[0];
    return $return;
}
```

The implementations in C are again similar to the algorithm itself:

```
double factorial_recursive_c(int x) {
    if (x < 2)  return 1;
    return x * factorial_recursive_c(x - 1);
}

double factorial_iterative_c(int x) {
    int i;
    double result = 1;
    for (i = 2; i <= x; i++)
        result *= i;
    return result;
}
```

To jump ahead, when we run the final benchmark we get the following results:

```
Benchmark: timing 300000 iterations of iterative_c, iterative_perl,
            recursive_c, recursive_perl...
  iterative_c:  0 wallclock secs ( 0.47 usr +  0.00 sys =  0.47 CPU)
  recursive_c:  2 wallclock secs ( 1.15 usr +  0.00 sys =  1.15 CPU)
iterative_perl: 28 wallclock secs (26.34 usr +  0.00 sys = 26.34 CPU)
recursive_perl: 75 wallclock secs (74.64 usr +  0.11 sys = 74.75 CPU)
```

All functions under test were executing 100!, which is 9.33262154439441e+157 using scientific notation.

The iterative implementation is about two and a half times as fast in C and three times as fast in Perl, where function calls are more expensive. Comparing C to Perl, the iterative implementation in C is about 56 times faster than the same algorithm implemented in Perl, and in the case of the recursive algorithm, C is 65 times faster.

There are at least three approaches to embedding other languages into Perl: XS, SWIG, and Inline.pm. We will implement the C functions we've written using the XS and Inline.pm techniques in the following sections. While SWIG is easier to use than XS for simple tasks, it's not as powerful as XS and it's not bundled with Perl. If you work on code that may later be distributed on CPAN, you'd better use XS or Inline.pm.

Building Perl Extensions with XS and h2xs

Perl comes with a nifty utility called *h2xs* that builds a skeleton for a new module. It's useful whether you are going to write a module with extensions in C/C++ or just in plain Perl.

When you run this utility it creates a new directory named after the module, and a skeleton of the *Makefile.PL*, *test.pl*, *Module.xs*, *Module.pm*, *Changes*, and *MANIFEST* files. If you have a C header file, it tries to guess the XS code based on it and write the correct XS file. Depending on how complicated your interface is, it may or may not do the right thing, but it helps anyway since it creates a boilerplate (which saves quite a lot of work).

First we prepare a C source file and its header file (see Examples 13-21 and 13-22).

Example 13-21. factorial.h

```
double factorial_recursive_c(int x);
double factorial_iterative_c(int x);
```

Example 13-22. factorial.c

```
double factorial_recursive_c(int x) {
    if (x < 2)  return 1;
    return x * factorial_recursive_c(x - 1);
}

double factorial_iterative_c(int x) {
    int i;
    double result = 1;
    for (i = 2; i <= x; i++)
        result *= i;
    return result;
}
```

It's easy to get lost in directories when creating a new module; therefore, we will show the exact directory we are in, using the prompt:

```
/home/stas/dev/fact>
```

Assuming that we work in this directory, we will save both files in this working directory. Let's check:

```
/home/stas/dev/fact> find /home/stas/dev/fact -type f
/home/stas/dev/fact/factorial.c
/home/stas/dev/fact/factorial.h
```

Now we are ready to create the skeleton of the new module:

```
/home/stas/dev/fact> h2xs -n Book::Factorial -A -O -x \
  -F '-I ../..' factorial.h
Scanning typemaps...
Scanning /usr/lib/perl5/5.6.1/ExtUtils/typemap
Scanning factorial.h for functions...
Scanning factorial.h for typedefs...
Writing Book/Factorial/Factorial.pm
Writing Book/Factorial/Factorial.xs
Writing Book/Factorial/Makefile.PL
Writing Book/Factorial/README
Writing Book/Factorial/test.pl
Writing Book/Factorial/Changes
Writing Book/Factorial/MANIFEST
```

We'll explain the *h2xs* arguments we used:

- *-n Book::Factorial* specifies the name of the new module. It is also used to create the base directory (in our case, *Book/Factorial/*).

- *-A* omits all autoload facilities.

- *-O* allows us to overwrite a directory with the new module if one already exists.

- *-x* automatically generates XSUBs based on function declarations in the header file (*factorial.h* in our case).

- *-F '-I../..'* specifies where the header file is to be found. When *h2xs* runs, it changes into the newly created directory (*Book/Factorial/* in our example), so in order to see the header file, we have to tell *h2xs* to look two directories back. (You may also need to add *-F '-I.'* during the *make* stage.)

- The header file (*factorial.h* in our case) comes last.

Our next step is to copy the C file and header into the newly created directory and *cd* into it:

```
/home/stas/dev/fact> cp factorial.c factorial.h Book/Factorial/
/home/stas/dev/fact> cd Book/Factorial/
```

Since we have a really simple header file with only two function declarations, we just need to adjust *Makefile.PL* to build the *factorial.o* object file and *Factorial.o*, the actual extension library. We adjust *Makefile.PL* by adding the following line:

```
'OBJECT'              => 'Factorial.o factorial.o',
```

We fix the INC attribute to point to the current directory so the copied *include* file will be found.

Now *Makefile.PL* looks like Example 13-23 (remember that *h2xs* does most of the work for us).

Example 13-23. Makefile.PL

```
use ExtUtils::MakeMaker;
# See lib/ExtUtils/MakeMaker.pm for details of how to influence
# the contents of the Makefile that is written.
WriteMakefile(
    'NAME'            => 'Book::Factorial',
    'VERSION_FROM'    => 'Factorial.pm', # finds $VERSION
    'PREREQ_PM'       => {}, # e.g., Module::Name => 1.1
    'LIBS'            => [''], # e.g., '-lm'
    'DEFINE'          => '', # e.g., '-DHAVE_SOMETHING'
    'INC'             => '-I .', # e.g., '-I/usr/include/other'
    'OBJECT'          => 'Factorial.o factorial.o',
);
```

Now we remove parts of the default module created by *h2xs* and add the Perl functions to *Factorial.pm*, since our module mixes pure Perl and C functions. We also write some simple documentation in POD format. After we add the Perl code and documentation and do some patching, *Factorial.pm* looks like Example 13-24.

Example 13-24. Book/Factorial.pm

```perl
package Book::Factorial;

require 5.006;
use strict;

use vars   qw($VERSION);
$VERSION = '0.01';

use base qw(DynaLoader);

bootstrap Book::Factorial $VERSION;

sub factorial_recursive_perl {
    return 1 if $_[0] < 2;
    return $_[0] * factorial_recursive_perl($_[0] - 1);
}

sub factorial_iterative_perl {
    my $return = 1;
    $return *= $_ for 2..$_[0];
    return $return;
}

1;
__END__

=head1 NAME

Book::Factorial - Perl and C, Recursive and Iterative Factorial
Calculation Functions

=head1 SYNOPSIS

  use Book::Factorial;
  $input = 5;
  $result = Book::Factorial::factorial_iterative_c(  $input);
  $result = Book::Factorial::factorial_recursive_c(  $input);
  $result = Book::Factorial::factorial_iterative_perl($input);
  $result = Book::Factorial::factorial_recursive_perl($input);

=head1 DESCRIPTION

This module provides functions to calculate a factorial using
recursive and iterative algorithms, whose internal implementation are
coded in Perl and C.

=head2 EXPORTS

None.

=head1 AUTHORS

Eric Cholet <email address> and Stas Bekman <email address>
```

Example 13-24. Book/Factorial.pm (continued)

```
=head1 SEE ALSO

perl(1).

=cut
```

If you've written pure Perl modules before, you'll see that the only unusual part is the code:

```
use base qw(DynaLoader);

bootstrap Book::Factorial $VERSION;
```

The base pragma specifies that the package Book::Factorial inherits from DynaLoader. Alternatively, you can write this as:

```
require DynaLoader;
@Book::Factorial::ISA = qw(DynaLoader);
```

where @ISA is the array that's used when inheritance relations are specified.

bootstrap is the place where the C extension Factorial.o is loaded, making the C functions available as Perl subroutines.

It's very important to document the module, especially when the package's functions don't reside within the module itself. Doing so will let you and your users know what functions are available, how they should be called, and what they return.

We have written very basic documentation. Usually it's a good idea to document each method.

In our example we decided not to export any functions to the callers; therefore, you always need to prefix the functions with the package name if used outside of this module:

```
use Book::Factorial;
$result = Book::Factorial::factorial_iterative_c(5);
```

We are almost done. Let's build the *Makefile*:

```
/home/stas/dev/fact/Book/Factorial> perl Makefile.PL
Checking if your kit is complete...
Looks good
Writing Makefile for Book::Factorial
```

Next we run *make* to compile the extension and get the module ready for testing:

```
/home/stas/dev/fact/Factorial> make
```

In addition to building the extension, *make* also renders the POD documentation in *nroff* format, which will be installed as a manpage when *make install* is run.

It's now time to test that the C extension was successfully linked and can be boot-strapped. *h2xs* has already created *test.pl*, which does this basic testing:

```
/home/stas/dev/fact/Book/Factorial> make test
PERL_DL_NONLAZY=1 /usr/bin/perl -Iblib/arch -Iblib/lib
-I/usr/lib/perl5/5.6.1/i386-linux -I/usr/lib/perl5/5.6.1 test.pl
1..1
ok 1
```

As we can see, the testing phase has passed without any problems. Is that all? Not really. We actually have to test that the functions are working as well, so we extend the test suite with an exhaustive set of tests.

In product-validation terminology this is sometimes known as comparing the results from the good and the bad machine, where the good machine is known to produce a correct result. In our case the good machine is either our head or a simple calculator. We know that:

```
4! == 24
```

So we know that if the function works correctly, for a given input of 4, the output should be 24. Of course, in some cases this test is not enough to tell a good function from a broken one. The function might work correctly for some inputs but misbehave for others. You may need to come up with more elaborate tests.

The testing procedure is based on printing the number of tests to be run in the BEGIN block and, for each test, printing either *ok* or *not ok*, followed by the number of the current test. Example 13-25 is a modified *test.pl* that exercises the bootstrapping (as provided by *h2xs*), plus two C functions and two Perl functions.

Example 13-25. test.pl

```
use Test;

BEGIN { plan tests => 5; }
use Book::Factorial;
ok 1; # module loaded OK

my $input = 4;
my $correct_result = 24; # the good machine: 4! = 24
my $result = 0;
my $s = 1;

# testing iterative C version
$result = Book::Factorial::factorial_iterative_c($input);
ok $result == $correct_result;

# testing recursive C version
$result = Book::Factorial::factorial_recursive_c($input);
ok $result == $correct_result;
```

Example 13-25. test.pl (continued)

```
# testing iterative Perl version
$result = Book::Factorial::factorial_iterative_perl($input);
ok $result == $correct_result;

# testing recursive Perl version
$result = Book::Factorial::factorial_recursive_perl($input);
ok $result == $correct_result;
```

Note the magic BEGIN block, which ensures that the test reports failure if it failed to load the module.

Now we run the test again using our new *test.pl*:

```
/home/stas/dev/fact/Book/Factorial> make test
PERL_DL_NONLAZY=1 /usr/bin/perl -Iblib/arch -Iblib/lib
-I/usr/lib/perl5/5.6.1/i386-linux -I/usr/lib/perl5/5.6.1 test.pl
1..5
ok 1
ok 2
ok 3
ok 4
ok 5
```

Fortunately all the tests have passed correctly. Now all we have to do is to install the module in our filesystem and start using it. You have to be *root* to install the module into the system-wide area:

```
/home/stas/dev/fact/Book/Factorial# su
/home/stas/dev/fact/Book/Factorial# make install
Installing /usr/lib/perl5/site_perl/5.6.1/i386-linux/auto/Book/Factorial/Factorial.so
Installing /usr/lib/perl5/site_perl/5.6.1/i386-linux/auto/Book/Factorial/Factorial.bs
Installing /usr/lib/perl5/site_perl/5.6.1/i386-linux/Book/Factorial.pm
Installing /usr/lib/perl5/man/man3/Book::Factorial.3
```

That's it. Neither very complicated nor very simple. We mentioned the XS macro language earlier but didn't actually use it—this is because the code was simple, and *h2xs* wrote the *Factorial.xs* file (shown in Example 13-26) for us based on the header file we provided (*factorial.h*).

Example 13-26. Factorial.xs

```
#include "EXTERN.h"
#include "perl.h"
#include "XSUB.h"

#include <factorial.h>

MODULE = Book::Factorial        PACKAGE = Book::Factorial

double
factorial_iterative_c(x)
  int x
```

Example 13-26. Factorial.xs (continued)

```
double
factorial_recursive_c(x)
  int x
```

This file actually implements the real gluing specification. During the *make* phase it was macro-processed by the xsubpp subroutine into the C code version *Factorial.c*, which was then compiled into the *Factorial.o* object file and finally converted into the *Factorial.so* loadable object and installed in the architecture-dependent module library tree (*/usr/lib/perl5/site_perl/5.6.1/i386-linux/auto/Book/Factorial* on our machine).

When a more complicated C interface is used, the glue code might be much more involved and require knowledge of the XS language. XS is explained in the *perlxs* manpage. The following manpages might be useful too:

```
perlembed   Perl ways to embed Perl in your C or C++ application
perlapio    Perl internal I/O abstraction interface
perldebguts Perl debugging guts and tips
perlxs      Perl XS application programming interface
perlxstut   Perl XS tutorial
perlguts    Perl internal functions for those doing extensions
perlcall    Perl calling conventions from C
perlapi     Perl API listing (autogenerated)
perlintern  Perl internal functions (autogenerated)
```

The POD documentation format is explained in the *perlpod* manpage.

You may also want to read *Advanced Perl Programming*, by Sriram Srinivasan (O'Reilly), which covers XS and SWIG, and *Extending and Embedding Perl*, by Tim Jenness and Simon Cozens (Manning Publications).

The Benchmark

We are now ready to write the benchmark code. Take a look at Example 13-27.

Example 13-27. factorial_benchmark.pl

```perl
use strict;
use Benchmark;
use Book::Factorial ();

my $top = 100;

timethese(300_000, {
  recursive_perl => sub {Book::Factorial::factorial_recursive_perl($top)},
  iterative_perl => sub {Book::Factorial::factorial_iterative_perl($top)},
  recursive_c    => sub {Book::Factorial::factorial_recursive_c($top)   },
  iterative_c    => sub {Book::Factorial::factorial_iterative_c($top)   },
});
```

As you can see, this looks just like normal Perl code. The Book::Factorial module is loaded (assuming that you have installed it system-wide) and its functions are used in the test.

We showed and analyzed the results at the beginning of our discussion, but we will repeat the results here for the sake of completeness:

```
panic% ./factorial_benchmark.pl
Benchmark: timing 300000 iterations of iterative_c, iterative_perl,
        recursive_c, recursive_perl...
  iterative_c:  0 wallclock secs ( 0.47 usr +  0.00 sys =  0.47 CPU)
  recursive_c:  2 wallclock secs ( 1.15 usr +  0.00 sys =  1.15 CPU)
iterative_perl: 28 wallclock secs (26.34 usr +  0.00 sys = 26.34 CPU)
recursive_perl: 75 wallclock secs (74.64 usr +  0.11 sys = 74.75 CPU)
```

If you want to do the benchmarking after the module has been tested but before it's installed, you can use the blib pragma in the build directory:

```
panic% perl -Mblib factorial_benchmark.pl
```

Inline.pm

Using XS and SWIG may seem like a lot of time and work, especially for something as simple as our factorial benchmark. Fortunately, there is a new module called Inline.pm that makes using Perl with C almost as easy as writing Perl by itself.

Inline.pm allows you to put the source code of other programming languages directly inside your Perl script or module. It currently supports C, C++, Python, Tcl, and Java. The idea is that you can write functions, subroutines, or methods in these languages, and Inline.pm will automatically do whatever it takes to make them callable by Perl. It will analyze your code, compile it if necessary, bind the appropriate routines, and load all the required components. This means that you can simply run your code as if it were any other Perl program.

For example, the entire factorial benchmark program can be written as shown in Example 13-28.

Example 13-28. factorial_benchmark_inline.pl

```
use strict;
use Benchmark;
use Inline 'C';

my $top = 150;

timethese(500000,
    {
      recursive_perl => sub {factorial_recursive_perl($top)},
      iterative_perl => sub {factorial_iterative_perl($top)},
      recursive_c    => sub {factorial_recursive_c(  $top)},
      iterative_c    => sub {factorial_iterative_c(  $top)},
    });
```

Example 13-28. factorial_benchmark_inline.pl (continued)

```perl
sub factorial_recursive_perl {
    return 1 if $_[0] < 2;
    return $_[0] * factorial_recursive_perl($_[0] - 1);
}

sub factorial_iterative_perl {
    my $return = 1;
    $return *= $_ for 2..$_[0];
    return $return;
}

__END__

__C__

double factorial_recursive_c(int x) {
    if (x < 2)  return 1;
    return x * factorial_recursive_c(x - 1);
}

double factorial_iterative_c(int x) {
    int i;
    double result = 1;
    for (i = 2; i <= x; i++) result *= i;
    return result;
}
```

That's all there is to it. Just run this Perl program like any other, and it will work exactly as you expect. The first time you run it, `Inline.pm` takes time to compile the C code and build an executable object. On subsequent runs, `Inline.pm` will simply load the precompiled version. If you ever modify the C code, `Inline.pm` will detect that and recompile automatically for you.

The results of this benchmark should be similar to the benchmark of the XS version of `Book::Factorial`, developed in the previous section.

Example 13-29 is an example of a simple mod_perl handler using `Inline.pm` with C.

Example 13-29. Apache/Factorial.pm

```perl
package Apache::Factorial;
use strict;

use Apache::Constants qw(:common);

use Inline 'Untaint';
use Inline Config => DIRECTORY => '/tmp/Inline';
use Inline 'C';
Inline->init;

sub handler {
    my $r = shift;
```

Example 13-29. Apache/Factorial.pm (continued)

```
    $r->send_http_header('text/plain');
    printf "%3d! = %10d\n", $_, factorial($_) for 1..10;
    return OK;
}
1;

__DATA__

__C__

double factorial(int x) {
    int i;
    double result = 1;
    for (i = 2; i <= x; i++) result *= i;
    return result;
}
```

This handler will list out all of the factorial numbers between 1 and 10. The extra `Inline.pm` commands are needed because of mod_perl's unique environment requirements. It's somewhat tricky to make `Inline.pm` work with mod_perl because of the file permissions. The best approach is to force `Inline.pm` to compile the module before starting the server. In our case, we can do:

```
panic% mkdir /tmp/Inline
panic% perl -I/home/httpd/perl -MApache::Factorial \
-e 'Apache::Factorial::handler'
```

Now all we need is for the */tmp/Inline* directory to be readable by the server. That's where `Inline.pm` has built the loadable object and where it's going to read from.

`Inline.pm` is an extremely versatile tool and can be used instead of XS in almost any application. It also has features that go well beyond the capabilities of XS. Best of all, you can get an `Inline.pm` program up and running in minutes.

The `Inline.pm` distribution comes with copious documentation, including a cookbook of common C-based recipes that you can adapt to your taste. It is also actively supported by the *inline@perl.org* mailing list.

Just like with XS, you can prepare a package with *Makefile.PL* and a test suite for a distribution on CPAN. See the `Inline.pm` manpage for more details.

Perl Extensions Conclusion

We have presented two techniques to extend your Perl code with the power of other languages (the C language in particular, but `Inline.pm` lets you embed other languages as well).

If you find that some sections of your code are better written in other languages that may make them more efficient, it may be worth experimenting. Don't blindly use

Perl to solve all your problems—some problems are better solved in other languages. The more languages you know, the better.

Because Perl is so good at gluing other languages into itself, you don't necessarily have to choose between Perl and other languages to solve a problem. You can use Perl and other languages together to get the best out of them all.

References

- XS macro language resources:
  - *perlguts*, *perlxs*, and *perlxstut* manpages
  - Dean Roehrich's XS *CookBookA* and *CookBookB*: *http://search.cpan.org/search?dist=CookBookA* and *http://search.cpan.org/search?dist=CookBookB*
  - A series of articles at *PerlMonth.com* by Steven McDougall:
  - *http://world.std.com/~swmcd/steven/perl/pm/xs/intro/index.html*
  - *http://world.std.com/~swmcd/steven/perl/pm/xs/concepts.html*
  - *http://world.std.com/~swmcd/steven/perl/pm/xs/tools/index.html*
  - *http://world.std.com/~swmcd/steven/perl/pm/xs/modules/modules.html*
  - *http://world.std.com/~swmcd/steven/perl/pm/xs/nw/NW.html*
  - Chapters 18–20 in *Advanced Perl Programming*, by Sriram Srinivasan (O'Reilly)
  - *Extending and Embedding Perl*, by Tim Jenness and Simon Cozens (Manning Publications Company)
  - The *perl-xs* mailing list on *http://perl.org/* (email *perl-xs-subscribe@perl.org*)
- SWIG: *http://www.swig.org/*
- Chapter 9 ("Tuning Apache and mod_perl") in *mod_perl Developer's Cookbook*, by Geoffrey Young, Paul Lindner, and Randy Kobes (Sams Publishing).
- *Mastering Regular Expressions: Powerful Techniques for Perl and Other Tools*, Second Edition, by Jeffrey E. F. Friedl (O'Reilly)

CHAPTER 14

Defensive Measures for Performance Enhancement

If you have already worked with mod_perl, you have probably noticed that it can be difficult to keep your mod_perl processes from using a lot of memory. The less memory you have, the fewer processes you can run and the worse your server will perform, especially under a heavy load. This chapter presents several common situations that can lead to unnecessary consumption of RAM, together with preventive measures.

Controlling Your Memory Usage

When you need to control the size of your *httpd* processes, use one of the two modules, `Apache::GTopLimit` and `Apache::SizeLimit`, which kill Apache *httpd* processes when those processes grow too large or lose a big chunk of their shared memory. The two modules differ in their methods for finding out the memory usage. `Apache::GTopLimit` relies on the `libgtop` library to perform this task, so if this library can be built on your platform you can use this module. `Apache::SizeLimit` includes different methods for different platforms—you will have to check the module's manpage to figure out which platforms are supported.

Defining the Minimum Shared Memory Size Threshold

As we have already discussed, when it is first created, an Apache child process usually has a large fraction of its memory shared with its parent. During the child process's life some of its data structures are modified and a part of its memory becomes unshared (pages become "dirty"), leading to an increase in memory consumption. You will remember that the `MaxRequestsPerChild` directive allows you to specify the number of requests a child process should serve before it is killed. One way to limit the memory consumption of a process is to kill it and let Apache replace it with a newly started process, which again will have most of its memory shared with the Apache parent. The new child process will then serve requests, and eventually the cycle will be repeated.

This is a fairly crude means of limiting unshared memory, and you will probably need to tune `MaxRequestsPerChild`, eventually finding an optimum value. If, as is likely, your service is undergoing constant changes, this is an inconvenient solution. You'll have to retune this number again and again to adapt to the ever-changing code base.

You really want to set some guardian to watch the shared size and kill the process if it goes below some limit. This way, processes will not be killed unnecessarily.

To set a shared memory lower limit of 4 MB using `Apache::GTopLimit`, add the following code into the *startup.pl* file:

```
use Apache::GTopLimit;
$Apache::GTopLimit::MIN_PROCESS_SHARED_SIZE = 4096;
```

and add this line to *httpd.conf*:

```
PerlFixupHandler Apache::GTopLimit
```

Don't forget to restart the server for the changes to take effect.

Adding these lines has the effect that as soon as a child process shares less than 4 MB of memory (the corollary being that it must therefore be occupying a lot of memory with its unique pages), it will be killed after completing its current request, and, as a consequence, a new child will take its place.

If you use `Apache::SizeLimit` you can accomplish the same by adding this to *startup.pl*:

```
use Apache::SizeLimit;
$Apache::SizeLimit::MIN_SHARE_SIZE = 4096;
```

and this to *httpd.conf*:

```
PerlFixupHandler Apache::SizeLimit
```

If you want to set this limit for only some requests (presumably the ones you think are likely to cause memory to become unshared), you can register a post-processing check using the set_min_shared_size( ) function. For example:

```
use Apache::GTopLimit;
if ($need_to_limit) {
    # make sure that at least 4MB are shared
    Apache::GTopLimit->set_min_shared_size(4096);
}
```

or for `Apache::SizeLimit`:

```
use Apache::SizeLimit;
if ($need_to_limit) {
    # make sure that at least 4MB are shared
    Apache::SizeLimit->setmin(4096);
}
```

Since accessing the process information adds a little overhead, you may want to check the process size only every N times. In this case, set the $Apache::GTopLimit::

CHECK_EVERY_N_REQUESTS variable. For example, to test the size every other time, put the following in your *startup.pl* file:

```
$Apache::GTopLimit::CHECK_EVERY_N_REQUESTS = 2;
```

or, for Apache::SizeLimit:

```
$Apache::SizeLimit::CHECK_EVERY_N_REQUESTS = 2;
```

You can run the Apache::GTopLimit module in debug mode by setting:

```
PerlSetVar Apache::GTopLimit::DEBUG 1
```

in *httpd.conf*. It's important that this setting appears before the Apache::GTopLimit module is loaded.

When debug mode is turned on, the module reports in the *error_log* file the memory usage of the current process and also when it detects that at least one of the thresholds was crossed and the process is going to be killed.

Apache::SizeLimit controls the debug level via the $Apache::SizeLimit::DEBUG variable:

```
$Apache::SizeLimit::DEBUG = 1;
```

which can be modified any time, even after the module has been loaded.

Potential drawbacks of memory-sharing restrictions

In Chapter 11 we devised a formula to calculate the optimum value for the MaxClients directive when sharing is taking place. In the same section, we warned that it's very important that the system not be heavily engaged in swapping. Some systems do swap in and out every so often even if they have plenty of real memory available, and that's OK. The following discussion applies to conditions when there is hardly any free memory available.

If the system uses almost all of its real memory (including the cache), there is a danger of the parent process's memory pages being swapped out (i.e., written to a swap device). If this happens, the memory-usage reporting tools will report all those swapped out pages as nonshared, even though in reality these pages are still shared on most OSs. When these pages are getting swapped in, the sharing will be reported back to normal after a certain amount of time. If a big chunk of the memory shared with child processes is swapped out, it's most likely that Apache::SizeLimit or Apache::GTopLimit will notice that the shared memory threshold was crossed and as a result kill those processes. If many of the parent process's pages are swapped out, and the newly created child process is already starting with shared memory below the limit, it'll be killed immediately after serving a single request (assuming that the $CHECK_EVERY_N_REQUESTS variable is set to 1). This is a very bad situation that will eventually lead to a state where the system won't respond at all, as it'll be heavily engaged in the swapping process.

This effect may be less or more severe depending on the memory manager's implementation, and it certainly varies from OS to OS and between kernel versions. Therefore, you should be aware of this potential problem and simply try to avoid situations where the system needs to swap at all, by adding more memory, reducing the number of child servers, or spreading the load across more machines (if reducing the number of child servers is not an option because of the request-rate demands).

Defining the Maximum Memory Size Threshold

No less important than maximizing shared memory is restricting the absolute size of the processes. If the processes grow after each request, and if nothing restricts them from growing, you can easily run out of memory.

Again you can set the MaxRequestsPerChild directive to kill the processes after a few requests have been served. But as we explained in the previous section, this solution is not as good as one that monitors the process size and kills it only when some limit is reached.

If you have Apache::GTopLimit (described in the previous section), you can limit a process's memory usage by setting the $Apache::GTopLimit::MAX_PROCESS_SIZE directive. For example, if you want processes to be killed when they reach 10 MB, you should put the following in your *startup.pl* file:

```
$Apache::GTopLimit::MAX_PROCESS_SIZE = 10240;
```

Just as when limiting shared memory, you can set a limit for the current process using the set_max_size( ) method in your code:

```
use Apache::GTopLimit;
Apache::GTopLimit->set_max_size(10000);
```

For Apache::SizeLimit, the equivalents are:

```
use Apache::SizeLimit;
$Apache::SizeLimit::MAX_PROCESS_SIZE = 10240;
```

and:

```
use Apache::SizeLimit;
Apache::SizeLimit->setmax(10240);
```

Defining the Maximum Unshared Memory Size Threshold

Instead of setting the shared and total memory usage thresholds, you can set a single threshold that measures the amount of unshared memory by subtracting the shared memory size from the total memory size.

Both modules allow you to set the thresholds in similar ways. With Apache::GTopLimit, you can set the unshared memory threshold server-wide with:

```
$Apache::GTopLimit::MAX_PROCESS_UNSHARED_SIZE = 6144;
```

and locally for a handler with:

```
Apache::GTopLimit->set_max_unshared_size(6144);
```

If you are using Apache::SizeLimit, the corresponding settings would be:

```
$Apache::SizeLimit::MAX_UNSHARED_SIZE = 6144;
```

and:

```
Apache::SizeLimit->setmax_unshared(6144);
```

Coding for a Smaller Memory Footprint

The following sections present proactive techniques that prevent processes from growing large in the first place.

Memory Reuse

Consider the code in Example 14-1.

Example 14-1. memory_hog.pl

```
use GTop ( );
my $gtop = GTop->new;
my $proc = $gtop->proc_mem($$);
print "size before:  ", $gtop->proc_mem($$)->size( ), " B\n";
{
    my $x = 'a' x 10**7;
    print "size inside: ", $gtop->proc_mem($$)->size( ), " B\n";
}
print "size  after: ", $gtop->proc_mem($$)->size( ), " B\n";
```

When executed, it prints:

```
size before:  1830912 B
size inside: 21852160 B
size  after: 21852160 B
```

This script starts by printing the size of the memory it occupied when it was first loaded. The opening curly brace starts a new block, in which a lexical variable $x is populated with a string 10,000,000 bytes in length. The script then prints the new size of the process and exits from the block. Finally, the script again prints the size of the process.

Since the variable $x is lexical, it is destroyed at the end of the block, before the final print statement, thus releasing all the memory that it was occupying. But from the output we can clearly see that a huge chunk of memory wasn't released to the OS—the process's memory usage didn't change. Perl reuses this released memory internally. For example, let's modify the script as shown in Example 14-2.

Example 14-2. memory_hog2.pl

```
use GTop ();
my $gtop = GTop->new;
my $proc = $gtop->proc_mem($$);
print "size before : ", $gtop->proc_mem($$)->size(), " B\n";
{
    my $x = 'a' x 10**7;
    print "size inside : ", $gtop->proc_mem($$)->size(), " B\n";
}
print "size  after : ", $gtop->proc_mem($$)->size(), " B\n";
{
    my $x = 'a' x 10;
    print "size inside2: ", $gtop->proc_mem($$)->size(), " B\n";
}
print "size  after2: ", $gtop->proc_mem($$)->size(), " B\n";
```

When we execute this script, we will see the following output:

```
size before :  1835008 B
size inside : 21852160 B
size  after : 21852160 B
size inside2: 21852160 B
size  after2: 21852160 B
```

As you can see, the memory usage of this script was no more than that of the previous one.

So we have just learned that Perl programs don't return memory to the OS until they quit. If variables go out of scope, the memory they occupied is reused by Perl for newly created or growing variables.

Suppose your code does memory-intensive operations and the processes grow fast at first, but after a few requests the sizes of the processes stabilize as Perl starts to reuse the acquired memory. In this case, the wisest approach is to find this limiting size and set the upper memory limit to a slightly higher value. If you set the limit lower, processes will be killed unnecessarily and lots of redundant operations will be performed by the OS.

Big Input, Big Damage

This section demonstrates how a malicious user can bring the service down or cause problems by submitting unexpectedly big data.

Imagine that you have a guestbook script/handler, which works fine. But you've forgotten about a small nuance: you don't check the size of the submitted message. A 10 MB core file copied and pasted into the HTML textarea entry box intended for a guest's message and submitted to the server will make the server grow by at least 10 MB. (Not to mention the horrible experience users will go through when trying to view the guest book, since the contents of the binary core file will be displayed.) If your server is short of memory, after a few more submissions like this one it will start swapping, and it may be on its way to crashing once all the swap memory is exhausted.

To prevent such a thing from happening, you could check the size of the submitted argument, like this:

```
my $r = shift;
my %args = $r->args;
my $message = exists $args{message} ? $args{message} : '';
die "the message is too big"
    unless length $message > 8192; # 8KB
```

While this prevents your program from adding huge inputs into the guest book, the size of the process will grow anyway, since you have allowed the code to process the submitted form's data. The only way to really protect your server from accepting huge inputs is not to read data above some preset limit. However, you cannot safely rely on the Content-Length header, since that can easily be spoofed.

You don't have to worry about GET requests, since their data is submitted via the query string of the URI, which has a hard limit of about 8 KB.

Think about disabling file uploads if you don't use them. Remember that a user can always write an HTML form from scratch and submit it to your program for processing, which makes it easy to submit huge files. If you don't limit the size of the form input, even if your program rejects the faulty input, the data will be read in by the server and the process will grow as a result. Here is a simple example that will readily accept anything submitted by the form, including fields that you didn't create, which a malicious user may have added by mangling the original form:

```
use CGI;
my $q = CGI->new;
my %args = map {$_ => $q->param($_)} $q->params;
```

If you are using CGI.pm, you can set the maximum allowed POST size and disable file uploads using the following setting:

```
use CGI;
$CGI::POST_MAX = 1048576;  # max 1MB allowed
$CGI::DISABLE_UPLOADS = 1; # disable file uploads
```

The above setting will reject all submitted forms whose total size exceeds 1 MB. Only non–file upload inputs will be processed.

If you are using the Apache::Request module, you can disable file uploads and limit the maximum POST size by passing the appropriate arguments to the new( ) function. The following example has the same effect as the CGI.pm example shown above:

```
my $apr = Apache::Request->new($r,
                        POST_MAX        => 1048576,
                        DISABLE_UPLOADS => 1
                       );
```

Another alternative is to use the `LimitRequestBody` directive in *httpd.conf* to limit the size of the request body. This directive can be set per-server, per-directory, per-file, or per-location. The default value is 0, which means unlimited. As an example, to limit the size of the request body to 2 MB, you should add:

```
LimitRequestBody 2097152
```

The value is set in bytes (2097152 bytes = = 2 MB).

In this section, we have presented only a single example among many that can cause your server to use more memory than planned. It helps to keep an open mind and to explore what other things a creative user might try to do with your service. Don't assume users will only click where you intend them to.

Small Input, Big Damage

This section demonstrates how a small input submitted by a malicious user may hog the whole server.

Imagine an online service that allows users to create a canvas on the server side and do some fancy image processing. Among the inputs that are to be submitted by the user are the width and the height of the canvas. If the program doesn't restrict the maximum values for them, some smart user may ask your program to create a canvas of 1,000,000×1,000,000 pixels. In addition to working the CPU rather heavily, the processes that serve this request will probably eat all the available memory (including the swap space) and kill the server.

How can the user do this, if you have prepared a form with a pull-down list of possible choices? Simply by saving the form and later editing it, or by using a `GET` request. Don't forget that what you receive is merely an input from a user agent, and it can very easily be spoofed by anyone knowing how to use `LWP::UserAgent` or something equivalent. There are various techniques to prevent users from fiddling with forms, but it's much simpler to make your code check that the submitted values are acceptable and then move on.

If you do some relational database processing, you will often encounter the need to read lots of records from the database and then print them to the browser after they are formatted. Let's look at an example.

We will use `DBI` and `CGI.pm` for this example. Assume that we are already connected to the database server (refer to the `DBI` manpage for a complete reference to the `DBI` module):

```
my $q = new CGI;
my $default_hits = 10;
my $hits = int $q->param("hints") || $default_hits;

my $do_sql = "SELECT from foo LIMIT 0,$hits";
my $sth = $dbh->prepare($do_sql);
$sth->execute;
```

```
while (@row_ary = $sth->fetchrow_array) {
    # do DB accumulation into some variable
}
# print the data
...
```

In this example, the records are accumulated in the program data before they are printed. The variables that are used to store the records that matched the query will grow by the size of the data, in turn causing the *httpd* process to grow by the same amount.

Imagine a search engine interface that allows a user to choose to display 10, 50, or 100 results. What happens if the user modifies the form to ask for 1,000,000 hits? If you have a big enough database, and if you rely on the fact that the only valid choices would be 10, 50, or 100 without actually checking, your database engine may unexpectedly return a million records. Your process will grow by many megabytes, possibly eating all the available memory and swap space.

The obvious solution is to disallow arbitrary inputs for critical variables like this one. Another improvement is to avoid the accumulation of matched records in the program data. Instead, you could use DBI::bind_columns() or a similar function to print each record as it is fetched from the database. In Chapter 20 we will talk about this technique in depth.

Think Production, Not Development

Developers often use sample inputs for testing their new code. But sometimes they forget that the real inputs can be much bigger than those they used in development.

Consider code like this, which is common enough in Perl scripts:

```
{
    open IN, $file or die $!;
    local $/;
    $content = <IN>; # slurp the whole file in
    close IN;
}
```

If you know for sure that the input will always be small, the code we have presented here might be fine. But if the file is 5 MB, the child process that executes this script when serving the request will grow by that amount. Now if you have 20 children, and each one executes this code, together they will consume 20×5 MB = 100 MB of RAM! If, when the code was developed and tested, the input file was very small, this potential excessive memory usage probably went unnoticed.

Try to think about the many situations in which your code might be used. For example, it's possible that the input will originate from a source you did not envisage. Your code might behave badly as a result. To protect against this possibility, you might want to try to use other approaches to processing the file. If it has lines, perhaps you can process one line at a time instead of reading them all into a variable at once. If you need to modify the file, use a temporary file. When the processing is finished, you can overwrite the source file. Make sure that you lock the files when you modify them.

Often you just don't expect the input to grow. For example, you may want to write a birthday reminder process intended for your own personal use. If you have 100 friends and relatives about whom you want to be reminded, slurping the whole file in before processing it might be a perfectly reasonable way to approach the task.

But what happens if your friends (who know you as one who usually forgets their birthdays) are so surprised by your timely birthday greetings that they ask you to allow them to use your cool invention as well? If all 100 friends have yet another 100 friends, you could end up with 10,000 records in your database. The code may not work well with input of this size. Certainly, the answer is to rewrite the code to use a DBM file or a relational database. If you continue to store the records in a flat file and read the whole database into memory, your code will use a lot of memory and be very slow.

Passing Variables

Let's talk about passing variables to a subroutine. There are two ways to do this: you can pass a *copy* of the variable to the subroutine (this is called *passing by value*) or you can instead pass a *reference* to it (a reference is just a pointer, so the variable itself is not copied). Other things being equal, if the copy of the variable is larger than a pointer to it, it will be more efficient to pass a reference.

Let's use the example from the previous section, assuming we have no choice but to read the whole file before any data processing takes place and its size is 5 MB. Suppose you have some subroutine called process( ) that processes the data and returns it. Now say you pass $content by value and process( ) makes a copy of it in the familiar way:

```
my $content = qq{foobarfoobar};
$content = process($content);
sub process {
    my $content = shift;
    $content =~ s/foo/bar/gs;
    return $content;
}
```

You have just copied another 5 MB, and the child has grown in size by another 5 MB. Assuming 20 Apache children, you can multiply this growth again by factor of 20—now you have 200 MB of wasted RAM! This will eventually be reused, but it's still a waste. Whenever you think the variable may grow bigger than a few kilobytes, definitely pass it by reference.

There are several forms of syntax you can use to pass and use variables passed by reference. For example:

```
my $content = qq{foobarfoobar};
process(\$content);
sub process {
    my $r_content = shift;
    $$r_content =~ s/foo/bar/gs;
}
```

Here $content is populated with some data and then passed by reference to the subroutine process( ), which replaces all occurrences of the string *foo* with the string *bar*. process( ) doesn't have to return anything—the variable $content was modified directly, since process( ) took a reference to it.

If the hashes or arrays are passed by reference, their individual elements are still accessible. You don't need to dereference them:

```
$var_lr->[$index]  get $index'th element of an array via a ref
$var_hr->{$key}    get $key'th element of a hash via a ref
```

Note that if you pass the variable by reference but then dereference it to copy it to a new string, you don't gain anything, since a new chunk of memory will be acquired to make a *copy* of the original variable. The *perlref* manpage provides extensive information about working with references.

Another approach is to use the @_ array directly. Internally, Perl always passes these variables by reference and dereferences them when they are copied from the @_ array. This is an efficiency mechanism to allow you to write subroutines that take a variable passed as a value, without copying it.

```
process($content);
sub process {
  $_[0] =~ s/foo/bar/gs;
}
```

From *perldoc perlsub*:

> The array @_ is a local array, but its elements are aliases for the actual scalar parameters. In particular, if an element $_[0] is updated, the corresponding argument is updated (or an error occurs if it is not possible to update)...

Be careful when you write this kind of subroutine for use by someone else; it can be confusing. It's not obvious that a call like process($content); modifies the passed variable. Programmers (the users of your library, in this case) are used to subroutines that either modify variables passed by reference or expressly return a result, like this:

```
$content = process($content);
```

You should also be aware that if the user tries to submit a read-only value, this code won't work and you will get a runtime error. Perl will refuse to modify a read-only value:

```
$content = process("string foo");
```

Memory Leakage

It's normal for a process to grow when it processes its first few requests. They may be different requests, or the same requests processing different data. You may try to reload the same request a few times, and in many cases the process will stop growing after only the second reload. In any case, once a representative selection of requests and inputs has been executed by a process, it won't usually grow any more unless the code leaks memory. If it grows after each reload of an identical request, there is probably a memory leak.

The experience might be different if the code works with some external resource that can change between requests. For example, if the code retrieves database records matching some query, it's possible that from time to time the database will be updated and that a different number of records will match the same query the next time it is issued. Depending on the techniques you use to retrieve the data, format it, and send it to the user, the process may increase or decrease in size, reflecting the changes in the data.

The easiest way to see whether the code is leaking is to run the server in single-process mode (*httpd -X*), issuing the same request a few times to see whether the process grows after each request. If it does, you probably have a memory leak. If the code leaks 5 KB per request, then after 1,000 requests to run the leaking code, 5 MB of memory will have leaked. If in production you have 20 processes, this could possibly lead to 100 MB of leakage after a few tens of thousands of requests.

This technique to detect leakage can be misleading if you are not careful. Suppose your process first runs some clean (non-leaking) code that acquires 100 KB of memory. In an attempt to make itself more efficient, Perl doesn't give the 100 KB of memory back to the operating system. The next time the process runs *any* script, some of the 100 KB will be reused. But if this time the process runs a script that needs to acquire only 5 KB, you won't see the process grow even if the code has actually leaked these 5 KB. Now it might take 20 or more requests for the leaking script *served by the same process* before you would see that process start growing again.

A process may leak memory for several reasons: badly written system C/C++ libraries used in the *httpd* binary and badly written Perl code are the most common. Perl modules may also use C libraries, and these might leak memory as well. Also, some operating systems have been known to have problems with their memory-management functions.

If you know that you have no leaks in your code, then for detecting leaks in C/C++ libraries you should either use the technique of sampling the memory usage described above, or use C/C++ developer tools designed for this purpose. This topic is beyond the scope of this book.

The Apache::Leak module (derived from Devel::Leak) might help you to detect leaks in your code. Consider the script in Example 14-3.

Example 14-3. leaktest.pl

```
use Apache::Leak;

my $global = "FooA";

leak_test {
    $$global = 1;
    ++$global;
};
```

You do not need to be inside mod_perl to use this script. The argument to leak_ test( ) is an anonymous sub or a block, so you can just throw in any code you suspect might be leaking. The script will run the code twice. The first time, new scalar values (SVs) are created, but this does not mean the code is leaking. The second pass will give better evidence.

From the command line, the above script outputs:

```
ENTER: 1482 SVs
new c28b8 : new c2918 :
LEAVE: 1484 SVs
ENTER: 1484 SVs
new db690 : new db6a8 :
LEAVE: 1486 SVs
!!! 2 SVs leaked !!!
```

This module uses the simple approach of walking the Perl internal table of allocated SVs. It records them before entering the scope of the code under test and after leaving the scope. At the end, a comparison of the two sets is performed, sv_ dump( ) is called for anything that did not exist in the first set, and the difference in counts is reported. Note that you will see the dumps of SVs only if Perl was built with the *-DDEBUGGING* option. In our example the script will dump two SVs twice, since the same code is run twice. The volume of output is too great to be presented here.

Our example leaks because $$global = 1; creates a new global variable, FooA (with the value of 1), which will not be destroyed until this module is destroyed. Under mod_perl the module doesn't get destroyed until the process quits. When the code is run the second time, $global will contain FooB because of the increment operation at the end of the first run. Consider:

```
$foo = "AAA";
print "$foo\n";
$foo++;
print "$foo\n";
```

which prints:

```
AAA
AAB
```

So every time the code is executed, a new variable (FooC, FooD, etc.) will spring into existence.

Apache::Leak is not very user-friendly. You may want to take a look at B::LexInfo. It is possible to see something that might appear to be a leak, but is actually just a Perl optimization. Consider this code, for example:

```
sub test { my ($string) = @_;}
test("a string");
```

B::LexInfo will show you that Perl does not release the value from $string unless you undef( ) it. This is because Perl anticipates that the memory will be needed for another string, the next time the subroutine is entered. You'll see similar behavior for @array lengths, %hash keys, and scratch areas of the padlist for operations such as join( ), ., etc.

Let's look at how B::LexInfo works. The code in Example 14-4 creates a new B:: LexInfo object, then runs cvrundiff( ), which creates two snapshots of the lexical variables' padlists—one before the call to LeakTest1::test( ) and the other, in this case, after it has been called with the argument "a string". Then it calls *diff -u* to generate the difference between the snapshots.

Example 14-4. leaktest1.pl

```
package LeakTest1;
use B::LexInfo ();

sub test { my ($string) = @_;}

my $lexi = B::LexInfo->new;
my $diff = $lexi->cvrundiff('LeakTest1::test', "a string");
print $$diff;
```

In case you aren't familiar with how diff works, - at the beginning of the line means that that line was removed, + means that a line was added, and other lines are there to show the context in which the difference was found. Here is the output:

```
--- /tmp/B_LexInfo_3099.before      Tue Feb 13 20:09:52 2001
+++ /tmp/B_LexInfo_3099.after       Tue Feb 13 20:09:52 2001
@@ -2,9 +2,11 @@
   {
     'LeakTest1::test' => {
       '$string' => {
-        'TYPE' => 'NULL',
+        'TYPE' => 'PV',
+        'LEN' => 9,
         'ADDRESS' => '0x8146d80',
-        'NULL' => '0x8146d80'
+        'PV' => 'a string',
+        'CUR' => 8
       },
       '__SPECIAL__1' => {
         'TYPE' => 'NULL',
```

Perl tries to optimize the speed by keeping the memory allocated for $string, even after the variable is destroyed.

Let's run the script from Example 14-3 with B::LexInfo (see Example 14-5).

Example 14-5. leaktest2.pl

```
package LeakTest2;
use B::LexInfo ();

my $global = "FooA";

sub test {
    $$global = 1;
    ++$global;
}

my $lexi = B::LexInfo->new;
my $diff = $lexi->cvrundiff('LeakTest2::test');
print $$diff;
```

Here's the result:

```
--- /tmp/B_LexInfo_3103.before Tue Feb 13 20:12:04 2001
+++ /tmp/B_LexInfo_3103.after        Tue Feb 13 20:12:04 2001
@@ -5,7 +5,7 @@
            'TYPE' => 'PV',
            'LEN' => 5,
            'ADDRESS' => '0x80572ec',
-           'PV' => 'FooA',
+           'PV' => 'FooB',
            'CUR' => 4
        }
    }
```

We can clearly see the leakage, since the value of the PV entry has changed from one string to a different one. Compare this with the previous example, where a variable didn't exist and sprang into existence for optimization reasons. If you find this confusing, probably the best approach is to run *diff* twice when you test your code.

Now let's run the cvrundiff( ) function on this example, as shown in Example 14-6.

Example 14-6. leaktest3.pl

```
package LeakTest2;
use B::LexInfo ();

my $global = "FooA";

sub test {
    $$global = 1;
    ++$global;
}
```

Example 14-6. leaktest3.pl (continued)

```
my $lexi = B::LexInfo->new;
my $diff = $lexi->cvrundiff('LeakTest2::test');
$diff    = $lexi->cvrundiff('LeakTest2::test');
print $$diff;
```

Here's the output:

```
--- /tmp/B_LexInfo_3103.before Tue Feb 13 20:12:04 2001
+++ /tmp/B_LexInfo_3103.after      Tue Feb 13 20:12:04 2001
@@ -5,7 +5,7 @@
         'TYPE' => 'PV',
         'LEN' => 5,
         'ADDRESS' => '0x80572ec',
-        'PV' => 'FooB',
+        'PV' => 'FooC',
         'CUR' => 4
     }
  }
```

We can see the leak again, since the value of PV has changed again, from FooB to FooC. Now let's run cvrundiff( ) on the second example script, as shown in Example 14-7.

Example 14-7. leaktest4.pl

```
package LeakTest1;
use B::LexInfo ();

sub test { my ($string) = @_;}

my $lexi = B::LexInfo->new;
my $diff = $lexi->cvrundiff('LeakTest1::test', "a string");
   $diff = $lexi->cvrundiff('LeakTest1::test', "a string");
print $$diff;
```

No output is produced, since there is no difference between the second and third runs. All the data structures are allocated during the first execution, so we are sure that no memory is leaking here.

Apache::Status includes a StatusLexInfo option that can show you the internals of your code via B::LexInfo. See Chapter 21 for more information.

Conclusion

The impacts of coding style, efficiency, differences in data, potential abuse by users, and a host of other factors combine to make each web service unique. You will therefore need to consider these things carefully in the light of your unique knowledge of your system and the pointers and guidelines suggested here. In this chapter we have tried to show how a defensive and efficient coding style will make sure that your processes are reasonably small and also unlikely to grow excessively. Knowing that your processes are well behaved will give you the confidence to make the best use of the available RAM, so that you can run the maximum number of processes while ensuring that the server will be unlikely to swap.

References

- The `mod_limitipconn.c` and `Apache::LimitIPConn` Apache modules: *http://dominia.org/djao/limitipconn.html*

  These modules allow web server administrators to limit the number of simultaneous downloads permitted from a single IP address.

- Chapter 9 ("Tuning Apache and mod_perl") in *mod_perl Developer's Cookbook*, by Geoffrey Young, Paul Lindner, and Randy Kobes (Sams Publishing)

- *Advanced Perl Programming*, by Sriram Srinivasan (O'Reilly)

## CHAPTER 15

Improving Performance Through Build Options

It's important how you build mod_perl-enabled Apache. The build process influences the size of the *httpd* executable—for example, some irrelevant modules might slow down performance.

When you build Apache, it strips the debug symbols by default, so you don't have to strip them yourself. For production use, you definitely shouldn't build mod_perl with debugging options enabled. Apache and mod_perl do not add these options unless you explicitly require them. In Chapter 21 we talk about debug build options in detail.

Server Size as a Function of Compiled-in Features

You might wonder if it's better to compile in only the required modules and mod_perl hooks, or if it doesn't really matter. To answer this question, let's first make a few compilations and compare the results.

We'll build mod_perl starting with:

```
panic% perl Makefile.PL APACHE_SRC=../apache_1.3.x/src \
    DO_HTTPD=1 USE_APACI=1
```

and followed by one of these option groups, in turn:

- Default (no arguments)
- Minimum:
  ```
  APACI_ARGS='--disable-module=env, \
              --disable-module=negotiation, \
              --disable-module=status, \
              --disable-module=info, \
              --disable-module=include, \
              --disable-module=autoindex, \
              --disable-module=dir, \
              --disable-module=cgi, \
  ```

```
                --disable-module=asis, \
                --disable-module=imap, \
                --disable-module=userdir, \
                --disable-module=access, \
                --disable-module=auth'
```

- mod_perl's EVERYTHING:

```
    EVERYTHING=1
```

- mod_perl's EVERYTHING and debug:

```
    EVERYTHING=1 PERL_DEBUG=1
```

After recompiling with the arguments of each of these groups in turn, we can summarize the results as follows:

```
   Build group      httpd size (bytes)  Difference
   ---------------------------------------------------
   Minimum                892928          +     0
   Default                994316          +101388
   Everything            1044432          +151504
   Everything+Debug      1162100          +269172
```

Clearly when you strip most of the defaults, the server size is slimmer. But the savings become insignificant, because you don't multiply the added size by the number of child processes if your OS supports memory sharing. The parent process is a little bigger, but it shares these memory pages with its child processes. Of course, not all the memory will be shared, but most of it will.

This is just an example to show the maximum possible difference in size. You can't actually strip everything away, because there will be Apache modules and mod_perl options that you won't be able to work without. But as a good system administrator's rule says: "Run the absolute minimum of the applications. If you don't know or need something, disable it." Following this rule to decide on the required Apache components and disabling the unneeded default components makes you a better Apache administrator.

mod_status and ExtendedStatus On

If you build in mod_status and you also set:

```
    ExtendedStatus On
```

in *httpd.conf*, on every request Apache will perform two calls to gettimeofday(2) (or times(2), depending on your operating system). This is done so that the status report contains timing information. For highest performance, set ExtendedStatus Off (which is the default).

DYNAMIC_MODULE_LIMIT Apache Build Option

If you have no intention of using dynamically loaded modules (you probably don't if you're tuning your server for every last ounce of performance), you should add *-DDYNAMIC_MODULE_LIMIT=0* when building the server. This will save RAM that's allocated only for supporting dynamically loaded modules.

Perl Build Options

The Perl interpreter is the brain of the mod_perl server. If you can optimize Perl into doing things faster under mod_perl, you'll make the whole server faster. Generally, optimizing the Perl interpreter means enabling or disabling some build options. Let's look at a few important ones. (Note that you have to build Perl *before* you build mod_perl-enabled Apache. If you have rebuilt the Perl interpreter, make sure to rebuild mod_perl as well, or the changes won't affect mod_perl.)

You can pass build options to Perl via the *Configure* script. To specify additional C compiler flags, use the *-Accflags=...* *Configure* command-line option (e.g., *-Accflags=-DFOO* will define the C preprocessor symbol FOO.) You can also pass additional optimizer/debugger flags via *-Doptimize=...* (e.g., *-Doptimize='-O2 -march=pentium'*).

Don't enable Perl's thread support unless you need it, because some internal data structures are modified and/or extended under *ithreads/5005threads*—this may make certain things slower and could lead to extra memory usage.

You have a choice of using the native or Perl's own malloc() implementation. The default choice depends on your operating system. On some OSes the native implementation might be worse than Perl's. Unless you know which of the two is better on yours, try both and compare the benchmarks.

To build without Perl's malloc(), you can use the *Configure* command:

```
panic% sh Configure -Uusemymalloc
```

Note that:

```
-U == undefine usemymalloc (== use system malloc)
-D == define   usemymalloc (== use Perl's malloc)
```

The Linux OS still defaults to system malloc(), so you might want to configure Perl with -Dusemymalloc. Perl's malloc() is not much of an imporovement under Linux (it's about a 5–10% speed improvement according to Scott Thomason, as explained at *http://www.mlug.net/mlug-list/2000/msg00701.html*), but it makes a huge difference under Solaris (when using Sun's C compiler). Be sure also to check the *README.** file corresponding to your OS in the Perl source code distribution for specific instructions and caveats.

Architecture-Specific Compile Options

When you build Apache and Perl, you can optimize the compiled applications to take advantage of the benefits of your machine's architecture.

Everything depends on the kind of compiler that you use, the kind of CPU(s) you use, and your OS.

For example, if you use *gcc(1)*, you might want to use *-march=pentium* if you have a Pentium CPU, or *-march=pentiumpro* for PentiumPro and above.

-fomit-frame-pointer makes an extra register available but disables debugging. You can also try these options, which have been reported to improve performance: *-ffast-math*, *-malign-double*, *-funroll-all-loops*, *-fno-rtti*, and *-fno-exceptions*. See the *gcc(1)* manpage for details about these.

You may also want to change the default -O2 flag to a flag with a higher number, such as -O3. -OX (where X is a number between 1 and 6) defines a collection of various optimization flags; the higher the number, the more flags are bundled. The *gcc* manpage will tell you what flags are used for each number. Test your applications thoroughly (and run the Perl test suite!) when you change the default optimization flags, especially when you go beyond -O2. It's possible that the optimization will make the code work incorrectly and/or cause segmentation faults.

See your preferred compiler's manpage and the resources listed in the next section for detailed information about optimization.

References

- The GCC manual: *http://gcc.gnu.org/onlinedocs/*
- "Code Optimization Using the GNU C Compiler," by Rahul U Joshi: *http://www.linuxgazette.com/issue71/joshi.html*

    This article describes some of the code optimization techniques used by the GNU C Compiler, in order to give the reader a feel of what code optimization is and how it can increase the efficiency of the generated object code.

- *Using and Porting GNU CC for Version 2.8*, by Richard Stallman (Free Software Foundation). Also available online from *http://www.delorie.com/gnu/docs/gcc/gcc_toc.html* and many other locations.

- Chapter 6 of the online book *Securing and Optimizing Linux, RedHat Edition: A Hands on Guide* talks extensively about compiler flags. It is located at *http://www.linuxdoc.org/LDP/solrhe/Securing-Optimizing-Linux-RH-Edition-v1.3/gen-optim.html*. The whole book (available in different formats) can be found at *http://www.linuxdoc.org/guides.html#securing_linux*.

- More Apache and platform-specific performance-tuning notes can be found at *http://httpd.apache.org/docs/misc/perf-tuning.html*.

## CHAPTER 16

HTTP Headers for Optimal Performance

Header composition is often neglected in the CGI world. Dynamic content is dynamic, after all, so why would anybody care about HTTP headers? Because pages are generated dynamically, one might expect that pages without a Last-Modified header are fine, and that an If-Modified-Since header in the client's request can be ignored. This laissez-faire attitude is a disadvantage when you're trying to create a server that is entirely driven by dynamic components and the number of hits is significant.

If the number of hits on your server is not significant and is never going to be, then it is safe to skip this chapter. But if keeping up with the number of requests is important, learning what cache-friendliness means and how to cooperate with caches to increase the performance of the site can provide significant benefits. If Squid or mod_proxy is used in *httpd* accelerator mode (as discussed in Chapter 12), it is crucial to learn how best to cooperate with it.

In this chapter, when we refer to a section in the HTTP standard, we are using HTTP standard 1.1, which is documented in RFC 2616. The HTTP standard describes many headers. In this chapter, we discuss only the headers most relevant to caching. We divide them into three sets: date headers, content headers, and the special Vary header.

Date-Related Headers

The various headers related to when a document was created, when it was last modified, and when it should be considered stale are discussed in the following sections.

Date Header

Section 14.18 of the HTTP standard deals with the circumstances under which we must or must not send a Date header. For almost everything a normal mod_perl user does, a Date header needs to be generated. But the mod_perl programmer doesn't have to worry about this header, since the Apache server guarantees that it is always sent.

In *http_protocol.c*, the Date header is set according to $r->request_time. A mod_perl script can read, but not change, $r->request_time.

Last-Modified Header

Section 14.29 of the HTTP standard covers the Last-Modified header, which is mostly used as a *weak validator*. Here is an excerpt from the HTTP specification:

> A validator that does not always change when the resource changes is a "weak validator."
>
> One can think of a strong validator as one that changes whenever the bits of an entity changes, while a weak value changes whenever the meaning of an entity changes.

What this means is that we must decide for ourselves when a page has changed enough to warrant the Last-Modified header being updated. Suppose, for example that we have a page that contains text with a white background. If we change the background to light gray then clearly the page has changed, but if the text remains the same we would consider the semantics (meaning) of the page to be unchanged. On the other hand, if we changed the text, the semantics may well be changed. For some pages it is not quite so straightforward to decide whether the semantics have changed or not. This may be because each page comprises several components, or it might be because the page itself allows interaction that affects how it appears. In all cases, we must determine the moment in time when the semantics changed and use that moment for the Last-Modified header.

Consider for example a page that provides a text-to-GIF renderer that takes as input a font to use, background and foreground colors, and a string to render. The images embedded in the resultant page are generated on the fly, but the structure of the page is constant. Should the page be considered unchanged so long as the underlying script is unchanged, or should the page be considered to have changed with each new request?

Actually, a few more things are relevant: the semantics also change a little when we update one of the fonts that may be used or when we update the ImageMagick or equivalent image-generating program. All the factors that affect the output should be considered if we want to get it right.

In the case of a page comprised of several components, we must check when the semantics of each component last changed. Then we pick the most recent of these times. Of course, the determination of the moment of change for each component may be easy or it may be subtle.

mod_perl provides two convenient methods to deal with this header: update_mtime() and set_last_modified(). These methods and several others are unavailable in the standard mod_perl environment but are silently imported when we use Apache::File. Refer to the Apache::File manpage for more information.

The update_mtime( ) function takes Unix's time(2) (in Perl the equivalent is also the time( ) function) as its argument and sets Apache's request structure finfo.st_mtime to this value. It does so only when the argument is greater than the previously stored finfo.st_mtime.

The set_last_modified( ) function sets the outgoing Last-Modified header to the string that corresponds to the stored finfo.st_mtime. When passing a Unix time(2) to set_last_modified( ), mod_perl calls update_mtime( ) with this argument first.

The following code is an example of setting the Last-Modified header by retrieving the last-modified time from a Revision Control System (RCS)–style of date tag.

```
use Apache::File;
use Date::Parse;
$Mtime ||= Date::Parse::str2time(
    substr q$Date: 2003/05/01 21:25:17 $, 6);
$r->set_last_modified($Mtime);
```

Normally we would use the Apache::Util::parsedate function, but since it doesn't parse the RCS format, we have used the Date::Parse module instead.

Expires and Cache-Control Headers

Section 14.21 of the HTTP standard deals with the Expires header. The purpose of the Expires header is to determine a point in time after which the document should be considered out of date (stale). Don't confuse this with the very different meaning of the Last-Modified header. The Expires header is useful to avoid unnecessary validation from now until the document expires, and it helps the recipients to clean up their stored documents. Here's an excerpt from the HTTP standard:

> The presence of an Expires field does not imply that the original resource will change or cease to exist at, before, or after that time.

Think carefully before setting up a time when a resource should be regarded as stale. Most of the time we can determine an expected lifetime from "now" (that is, the time of the request). We do not recommend hardcoding the expiration date, because when we forget that we did it, and the date arrives, we will serve already expired documents that cannot be cached. If a resource really will never expire, make sure to follow the advice given by the HTTP specification:

> To mark a response as "never expires," an origin server sends an Expires date approximately one year from the time the response is sent. HTTP/1.1 servers SHOULD NOT send Expires dates more than one year in the future.

For example, to expire a document half a year from now, use the following code:

```
$r->header_out('Expires',
            HTTP::Date::time2str(time + 180*24*60*60));
```

or:

```
$r->header_out('Expires',
            Apache::Util::ht_time(time + 180*24*60*60));
```

The latter method should be faster, but it's available only under mod_perl.

A very handy alternative to this computation is available in the HTTP/1.1 cache-control mechanism. Instead of setting the Expires header, we can specify a delta value in a Cache-Control header. For example:

```
$r->header_out('Cache-Control', "max-age=" . 180*24*60*60);
```

This is much more processor-economical than the previous example because Perl computes the value only once, at compile time, and optimizes it into a constant.

As this alternative is available only in HTTP/1.1 and old cache servers may not understand this header, it may be advisable to send both headers. In this case the Cache-Control header takes precedence, so the Expires header is ignored by HTTP/1.1-compliant clients. Or we could use an if...else clause:

```
if ($r->protocol =~ /(\d\.\d)/ && $1 >= 1.1) {
    $r->header_out('Cache-Control', "max-age=" . 180*24*60*60);
}
else {
    $r->header_out('Expires',
                HTTP::Date::time2str(time + 180*24*60*60));
}
```

Again, use the Apache::Util::ht_time() alternative instead of HTTP::Date::time2str() if possible.

If the Apache server is restarted regularly (e.g., for log rotation), it might be beneficial to save the Expires header in a global variable to save the runtime computation overhead.

To avoid caching altogether, call:

```
$r->no_cache(1);
```

which sets the headers:

```
Pragma: no-cache
Cache-control: no-cache
```

This should work in most browsers.

Don't set Expires with $r->header_out if you use $r->no_cache, because header_out() takes precedence. The problem that remains is that there are broken browsers that ignore Expires headers.

Content Headers

The following sections describe the HTTP headers that specify the type and length of the content, and the version of the content being sent. Note that in this section we often use the term *message*. This term is used to describe the data that comprises the HTTP headers along with their associated content; the content is the actual page, image, file, etc.

Content-Type Header

Most CGI programmers are familiar with Content-Type. Sections 3.7, 7.2.1, and 14.17 of the HTTP specification cover the details. mod_perl has a content_type( ) method to deal with this header:

```
$r->content_type("image/png");
```

Content-Type *should* be included in every set of headers, according to the standard, and Apache will generate one if your code doesn't. It will be whatever is specified in the relevant DefaultType configuration directive, or text/plain if none is active.

Content-Length Header

According to section 14.13 of the HTTP specification, the Content-Length header is the number of octets (8-bit bytes) in the body of a message. If the length can be determined prior to sending, it can be very useful to include it. The most important reason is that KeepAlive requests (when the same connection is used to fetch more than one object from the web server) work only with responses that contain a Content-Length header. In mod_perl we can write:

```
$r->header_out('Content-Length', $length);
```

When using Apache::File, the additional set_content_length( ) method, which is slightly more efficient than the above, becomes available to the Apache class. In this case we can write:

```
$r->set_content_length($length);
```

The Content-Length header can have a significant impact on caches by invalidating cache entries, as the following extract from the specification explains:

> The response to a HEAD request MAY be cacheable in the sense that the information contained in the response MAY be used to update a previously cached entity from that resource. If the new field values indicate that the cached entity differs from the current entity (as would be indicated by a change in Content-Length, Content-MD5, ETag or Last-Modified), then the cache MUST treat the cache entry as stale.

It is important not to send an erroneous Content-Length header in a response to either a GET or a HEAD request.

Entity Tags

An entity tag (ETag) is a validator that can be used instead of, or in addition to, the Last-Modified header; it is a quoted string that can be used to identify different versions of a particular resource. An entity tag can be added to the response headers like this:

```
$r->header_out("ETag","\"$VERSION\"");
```

mod_perl offers the $r->set_etag( ) method if we have use( )ed Apache::File. However, we strongly recommend that you don't use the set_etag( ) method! set_etag( ) is meant to be used in conjunction with a static request for a file on disk that has been stat( )ed in the course of the current request. It is inappropriate and dangerous to use it for dynamic content.

By sending an entity tag we are promising the recipient that we will not send the same ETag for the same resource again unless the content is "equal" to what we are sending now.

The pros and cons of using entity tags are discussed in section 13.3 of the HTTP specification. For mod_perl programmers, that discussion can be summed up as follows.

There are strong and weak validators. Strong validators change whenever a single bit changes in the response; i.e., when anything changes, even if the meaning is unchanged. Weak validators change only when the meaning of the response changes. Strong validators are needed for caches to allow for sub-range requests. Weak validators allow more efficient caching of equivalent objects. Algorithms such as MD5 or SHA are good strong validators, but what is usually required when we want to take advantage of caching is a good weak validator.

A Last-Modified time, when used as a validator in a request, can be strong or weak, depending on a couple of rules described in section 13.3.3 of the HTTP standard. This is mostly relevant for range requests, as this quote from section 14.27 explains:

> If the client has no entity tag for an entity, but does have a Last-Modified date, it
> MAY use that date in an If-Range header.

But it is not limited to range requests. As section 13.3.1 states, the value of the Last-Modified header can also be used as a cache validator.

The fact that a Last-Modified date may be used as a strong validator can be pretty disturbing if we are in fact changing our output slightly without changing its semantics. To prevent this kind of misunderstanding between us and the cache servers in the response chain, we can send a weak validator in an ETag header. This is possible because the specification states:

> If a client wishes to perform a sub-range retrieval on a value for which it has only
> a Last-Modified time and no opaque validator, it MAY do this only if the Last-
> Modified time is strong in the sense described here.

In other words, by sending an ETag that is marked as weak, we prevent the cache server from using the Last-Modified header as a strong validator.

An ETag value is marked as a weak validator by prepending the string W/ to the quoted string; otherwise, it is strong. In Perl this would mean something like this:

```
$r->header_out('ETag',"W/\"$VERSION\"");
```

HTTP Range Requests

It is possible in web clients to interrupt the connection before the data transfer has finished. As a result, the client may have partial documents or images loaded into its memory. If the page is reentered later, it is useful to be able to request the server to return just the missing portion of the document, instead of retransferring the entire file.

There are also a number of web applications that benefit from being able to request the server to give a byte range of a document. As an example, a PDF viewer would need to be able to access individual pages by byte range—the table that defines those ranges is located at the end of the PDF file.

In practice, most of the data on the Web is represented as a byte stream and can be addressed with a byte range to retrieve a desired portion of it.

For such an exchange to happen, the server needs to let the client know that it can support byte ranges, which it does by sending the Accept-Ranges header:

```
Accept-Ranges: bytes
```

The server will send this header only for documents for which it will be able to satisfy the byte-range request—e.g., for PDF documents or images that are only partially cached and can be partially reloaded if the user interrupts the page load.

The client requests a byte range using the Range header:

```
Range: bytes=0-500,5000-
```

Because of the architecture of the byte-range request and response, the client is not limited to attempting to use byte ranges only when this header is present. If a server does not support the Range header, it will simply ignore it and send the entire document as a response.

Consider carefully which string is chosen to act as a validator. We are on our own with this decision:

```
... only the service author knows the semantics of a resource well enough to select
an appropriate cache validation mechanism, and the specification of any validator
comparison function more complex than byte-equality would open up a can of worms.
Thus, comparisons of any other headers (except Last-Modified, for compatibility with
HTTP/1.0) are never used for purposes of validating a cache entry.
```

If we are composing a message from multiple components, it may be necessary to combine some kind of version information for all these components into a single string.

If we are producing relatively large documents, or content that does not change frequently, then a strong entity tag will probably be preferred, since this will give caches a chance to transfer the document in chunks.

Content Negotiation

Content negotiation is a wonderful feature that was introduced with HTTP/1.1. Unfortunately it is not yet widely supported. Probably the most popular usage scenario for content negotiation is language negotiation for multilingual sites. Users specify in their browsers' preferences the languages they can read and order them according to their ability. When the browser sends a request to the server, among the headers it sends it also includes an Accept-Language header. The server uses the Accept-Language header to determine which of the available representations of the document best fits the user's preferences. But content negotiation is not limited to language. Quoting the specification:

> HTTP/1.1 includes the following request-header fields for enabling server-driven negotiation through description of user agent capabilities and user preferences: Accept (section 14.1), Accept-Charset (section 14.2), Accept-Encoding (section 14.3), Accept-Language (section 14.4), and User-Agent (section 14.43). However, an origin server is not limited to these dimensions and MAY vary the response based on any aspect of the request, including information outside the request-header fields or within extension header fields not defined by this specification.

The Vary Header

To signal to the recipient that content negotiation has been used to determine the best available representation for a given request, the server must include a Vary header. This tells the recipient which request headers have been used to determine the representation that is used. So an answer may be generated like this:

```
$r->header_out('Vary', join ", ",
            qw(accept accept-language accept-encoding user-agent));
```

The header of a very cool page may greet the user with something like this:

```
Hallo Harri, Dein NutScrape versteht zwar PNG aber leider kein GZIP.
```

However, this header has the side effect of being expensive for a caching proxy. As of this writing, Squid (Version 2.3.STABLE4) does not cache resources that come with a Vary header at all. So without a clever workaround, the Squid accelerator is of no use for these documents.

HTTP Requests

Section 13.11 of the specification states that the only two cacheable methods are GET and HEAD. Responses to POST requests are not cacheable, as you'll see in a moment.

GET Requests

Most mod_perl programs are written to service GET requests. The server passes the request to the mod_perl code, which composes and sends back the headers and the content body.

But there is a certain situation that needs a workaround to achieve better cacheability. We need to deal with the "?" in the relative path part of the requested URI. Section 13.9 specifies that:

> ... caches MUST NOT treat responses to such URIs as fresh unless the server provides an explicit expiration time. This specifically means that responses from HTTP/1.0 servers for such URIs SHOULD NOT be taken from a cache.

Although it is tempting to imagine that if we are using HTTP/1.1 and send an explicit expiration time we are safe, the reality is unfortunately somewhat different. It has been common for quite a long time to misconfigure cache servers so that they treat all GET requests containing a question mark as uncacheable. People even used to mark anything that contained the string "cgi-bin" as uncacheable.

To work around this bug in HEAD requests, we have stopped calling CGI directories *cgi-bin* and we have written the following handler, which lets us work with CGI-like query strings without rewriting the software (e.g., Apache::Request and CGI.pm) that deals with them:

```perl
sub handler {
    my $r = shift;
    my $uri = $r->uri;
    if ( my($u1,$u2) = $uri =~ / ^ ([^?]+?) ; ([^?]*) $ /x ) {
        $r->uri($u1);
        $r->args($u2);
    }
    elsif ( my ($u1,$u2) = $uri =~ m/^(.*?)%3[Bb](.*)$/ ) {
        # protect against old proxies that escape volens nolens
        # (see HTTP standard section 5.1.2)
        $r->uri($u1);
        $u2 =~ s/%3[Bb]/;/g;
        $u2 =~ s/%26/;/g; # &
        $u2 =~ s/%3[Dd]/=/g;
        $r->args($u2);
    }
    DECLINED;
}
```

This handler must be installed as a PerlPostReadRequestHandler.

The handler takes any request that contains one or more semicolons but *no* question mark and changes it so that the first semicolon is interpreted as a question mark and everything after that as the query string. So now we can replace the request:

```
http://example.com/query?BGCOLOR=blue;FGCOLOR=red
```

with:

```
http://example.com/query;BGCOLOR=blue;FGCOLOR=red
```

This allows the coexistence of queries from ordinary forms that are being processed by a browser alongside predefined requests for the same resource. It has one minor bug: Apache doesn't allow percent-escaped slashes in such a query string. So instead of:

```
http://example.com/query;BGCOLOR=blue;FGCOLOR=red;FONT=%2Ffont%2Fpath
```

we must use:

```
http://example.com/query;BGCOLOR=blue;FGCOLOR=red;FONT=/font/path
```

To unescape the escaped characters, use the following code:

```
s/%([0-9A-Fa-f]{2})/chr hex $1/ge;
```

Conditional GET Requests

A rather challenging request that may be received is the conditional GET, which typically means a request with an If-Modified-Since header. The HTTP specification has this to say:

> The semantics of the GET method change to a "conditional GET" if the request message includes an If-Modified-Since, If-Unmodified-Since, If-Match, If-None-Match, or If-Range header field. A conditional GET method requests that the entity be transferred only under the circumstances described by the conditional header field(s). The conditional GET method is intended to reduce unnecessary network usage by allowing cached entities to be refreshed without requiring multiple requests or transferring data already held by the client.

So how can we reduce the unnecessary network usage in such a case? mod_perl makes it easy by providing access to Apache's meets_conditions( ) function (which lives in Apache::File). The Last-Modified (and possibly ETag) headers must be set up before calling this method. If the return value of this method is anything other than OK, then this value is the one that should be returned from the handler when we have finished. Apache handles the rest for us. For example:

```
if ((my $result = $r->meets_conditions) != OK) {
    return $result;
}
#else ... go and send the response body ...
```

If we have a Squid accelerator running, it will often handle the conditionals for us, and we can enjoy its extremely fast responses for such requests by reading the *access.log* file. Just *grep* for TCP_IMS_HIT/304. However, there are circumstances under which Squid may not be allowed to use its cache. That is why the origin server (which is the server we are programming) needs to handle conditional GETs as well, even if a Squid accelerator is running.

HEAD Requests

Among the headers described thus far, the date-related ones (Date, Last-Modified, and Expires/Cache-Control) are usually easy to produce and thus should be computed for HEAD requests just the same as for GET requests.

The Content-Type and Content-Length headers should be exactly the same as would be supplied to the corresponding GET request. But since it may be expensive to compute them, they can easily be omitted, since there is nothing in the specification that requires them to be sent.

What is important is that the response to a HEAD request *must not* contain a message-body. The code in a mod_perl handler might look like this:

```
# compute the headers that are easy to compute
# currently equivalent to $r->method eq "HEAD"
if ( $r->header_only ) {
    $r->send_http_header;
    return OK;
}
```

If a Squid accelerator is being used, it will be able to handle the whole HEAD request by itself, but under some circumstances it may not be allowed to do so.

POST Requests

The response to a POST request is not cacheable, due to an underspecification in the HTTP standards. Section 13.4 does not forbid caching of responses to POST requests, but no other part of the HTTP standard explains how the caching of POST requests could be implemented, so we are in a vacuum. No existing caching servers implement the caching of POST requests (although some browsers with more aggressive caching implement their own caching of POST requests). However, this may change if someone does the groundwork of defining the semantics for cache operations on POST requests.

Note that if a Squid accelerator is being used, you should be aware that it accelerates outgoing traffic but does not bundle incoming traffic. Squid is of no benefit at all on POST requests, which could be a problem if the site receives a lot of long POST requests. Using GET instead of POST means that requests can be cached, so the possibility of using GETs should always be considered. However, unlike with POSTs, there are size limits and visibility issues that apply to GETs, so they may not be suitable in every case.

Avoiding Dealing with Headers

There is another approach to dynamic content that is possible with mod_perl. This approach is appropriate if the content changes relatively infrequently, if we expect lots of requests to retrieve the same content before it changes again, and if it is much cheaper to test whether the content needs refreshing than it is to refresh it.

In this situation, a `PerlFixupHandler` can be installed for the relevant location. This handler must test whether the content is up to date or not, returning `DECLINED` so that the Apache core can serve the content from a file if it is up to date. If the content has expired, the handler should regenerate the content into the file, update the `$r->finfo` status and *still* return `DECLINED`, which will force Apache to serve the now updated file. Updating `$r->finfo` can be achieved by calling:

```
$r->filename($file); # force update of the finfo structure
```

even if this seems redundant because the filename is the same as `$file`. This is important because otherwise Apache would use the out-of-date *finfo* when generating the response header.

References

- "Hypertext Transfer Protocol—HTTP/1.0," RFC 1945T, by T. Berners-Lee, *et al.*: *http://www.w3.org/Protocols/rfc1945/rfc1945/*

- "Hypertext Transfer Protocol—HTTP/1.1," RFC 2616, by R. Fielding, *et al.*: *http://www.w3.org/Protocols/rfc2616/rfc2616/*

- "Cachebusting—Cause and Prevention, by Martin Hamilton. *draft-hamilton-cachebusting-01*. Also available online at *http://vancouver-webpages.com/CacheNow/*.

- *Writing Apache Modules with Perl and C*, by Lincoln Stein and Doug MacEachern (O'Reilly). Selected chapters available online at *http://www.modperl.com/*.

- *mod_perl Developer's Cookbook*, by Geoffrey Young, Paul Lindner, and Randy Kobes (Sams Publishing). Selected chapters and code examples available online at *http://www.modperlcookbook.org/*.

- Prevent the browser from caching a page *http://www.pacificnet.net/~johnr/meta.html*.

  This page is an explanation of how to use the `Meta` HTML tag to prevent caching, by browser or proxy, of an individual page wherein the page in question has data that may be of a sensitive nature (as in a "form page for submittal") and the creator of the page wants to make sure that the page does not get submitted twice.

## PART III

Databases and mod_perl

Databases are used to store and retrieve data, and are commonly used with mod_perl applications. In this section, we present the following chapters:

Chapter 17, *Databases Overview*, gives an introduction to the types of databases that are available to mod_perl applications.

Chapter 18, *mod_perl Data-Sharing Techniques*, covers techniques for sharing data between processes that are unique to mod_perl.

Chapter 19, *DBM and mod_perl*, introduces you to DBM files and how mod_perl interacts with them.

Chapter 20, *Relational Databases and mod_perl*, shows you how to use `Apache::DBI` to connect to relational databases such as *mysql*.

## CHAPTER 17

Databases Overview

What's a database? We can use pretty much anything as a database, as long as it allows us to store our data and retrieve it later. There are many different kinds of databases. Some allow us to store data and retrieve it years later; others are capable of preserving data only while there is an electricity supply. Some databases are designed for fast searches, others for fast insertions. Some databases are very easy to use, while some are very complicated (you may even have to learn a whole language to know how to operate them). There are also large price differences.

When we choose a database for our application, we first need to define the requirements in detail (this is known as a *specification*). If the application is for short-term use, we probably aren't going to use an expensive, advanced database. A quick-and-dirty hack may do. If, on the other hand, we design a system for long-term use, it makes sense to take the time to find the ideal database implementation.

Databases can be of two kinds: volatile and non-volatile. These two concepts pretty much relate to the two kinds of computer memory: RAM-style memory, which usually loses all its contents when the electricity supply is cut off; and magnetic (or optical) memory, such as hard disks and compact discs, which can retain the information even without power.

Volatile Databases

We use volatile databases all the time, even if we don't think about them as real databases. These databases are usually just part of the programs we run.

In-Memory Databases in a Single Process

If, for example, we want to store the number of Perl objects that exist in our program's data, we can use a variable as a volatile database:

```
package Book::ObjectCounter;
use strict;
```

```
my $object_count = 0;
sub new {
    my $class = shift;
    $object_count++;
    return bless {}, $class;
}
sub DESTROY {
    $object_count--;
}
```

In this example, $object_count serves as a database—it stores the number of currently available objects. When a new object is created this variable increments its value, and when an object gets destroyed the value is decremented.

Now imagine a server, such as mod_perl, where the process can run for months or even years without quitting. Doing this kind of accounting is perfectly suited for the purpose, for if the process quits, all objects are lost anyway, and we probably won't care how many of them were alive when the process terminated.

Here is another example:

```
$DNS_CACHE{$dns} ||= dns_resolve($dns);
print "Hostname $dns has $DNS_CACHE{$dns} IP\n";
```

This little code snippet takes the hostname stored in $dns and checks whether we have the corresponding IP address cached in %DNS_CACHE. If not, it resolves it and caches it for later reuse. At the end, it prints out both the hostname and the corresponding IP address.

%DNS_CACHE satisfies our definition of a database. It's a volatile database, since when the program quits the data disappears. When a mod_perl process quits, the cache is lost, but there is a good chance that we won't regret the loss, since we might want to cache only the latest IP addresses anyway. Now if we want to turn this cache into a non-volatile database, we just need to tie %DNS_CACHE to a DBM file, and we will have a permanent database. We will talk about Database Management (DBM) files in Chapter 19.

In Chapter 18, we will show how you can benefit from this kind of in-process database under mod_perl. We will also show how during a single request different handlers can share data and how data can persist across many requests.

In-Memory Databases Across Multiple Processes

Sharing results is more efficient than having each child potentially waste a lot of time generating redundant data. On the other hand, the information may not be important enough, or have sufficient long-term value, to merit being stored on disk. In this scenario, Inter-Process Communication (IPC) is a useful tool to have around.

This topic is non-specific to mod_perl and big enough to fill several books on its own. A non-exhaustive list of the modules to look at includes `IPC::SysV`, `IPC::Shareable`, `IPC::Semaphore`, `IPC::ShareLite`, `Apache::Session`, and `Cache::Cache`. And of course make sure to read the `perlipc` manpage. Also refer to the books listed in the reference section at the end of this chapter.

Non-Volatile Databases

Some information is so important that you cannot afford to lose it. Consider the name and password for authenticating users. If a person registers at a site that charges a subscription fee, it would be unfortunate if his subscription details were lost the next time the web server was restarted. In this case, the information must be stored in a non-volatile way, and that usually means on disk. Several options are available, ranging from flat files to DBM files to fully-fledged relational databases. Which one you choose will depend on a number of factors, including:

- The size of each record and the volume of the data to be stored
- The number of concurrent accesses (to the server or even to the same data)
- Data complexity (do all the records fit into one row, or are there relations between different kinds of record?)
- Budget (some database implementations are great but very expensive)
- Failover and backup strategies (how important it is to avoid downtime, how soon the data must be restored in the case of a system failure)

Flat-File Databases

If we have a small amount of data, sometimes the easiest technique is to just write this data in a text file. For example, if we have a few records with a fixed number of fields we can store them in a file, having one record per row and separating the fields with a delimiter. For example:

```
Eric|Cholet|cholet@logilune.com
Doug|MacEachern|dougm@pobox.com
Stas|Bekman|stas@stason.org
```

As long as we have just a few records, we can quickly insert, edit, and remove records by reading the flat-file database line by line and adjusting things as required. We can retrieve the fields easily by using the `split` function:

```
@fields = split /\|/, $record;
```

and we can put them back using `join`:

```
$record = join '|', @fields;
```

However, we must make sure that no field uses the field separator we have chosen (| in this case), and we must lock the file if it is to be used in a multiprocess environment where many processes may try to modify the same file simultaneously. This is the case whether we are using mod_perl or not.

If we are using some flavor of Unix, the */etc/passwd* file is a perfect example of a flat-file database, since it has a fixed number of fields and most systems have a relatively small number of users.* This is an example of such a file:

```
root:x:0:0:root:/root:/bin/tcsh
bin:x:1:1:bin:/bin:
daemon:x:2:2:daemon:/sbin:
adm:x:3:4:adm:/var/adm:
lp:x:4:7:lp:/var/spool/lpd:
```

: is used to separate the various fields.

Working with flat-file databases is easy and straightforward in plain Perl. There are no special mod_perl tricks involved.

Filesystem Databases

Many people don't realize that in some cases, the filesystem can serve perfectly well as a database. In fact, you are probably using this kind of database every day on your PC—for example, if you store your MP3 files categorized by genres, artists, and albums. If we run:

```
panic% cd /data/mp3
panic% find .
```

We can see all the MP3 files that we have under */data/mp3*:

```
./Rock/Bjork/MTV Unplugged/01 - Human Behaviour.mp3
./Rock/Bjork/MTV Unplugged/02 - One Day.mp3
./Rock/Bjork/MTV Unplugged/03 - Come To Me.mp3
...
./Rock/Bjork/Europa/01 - Prologue.mp3
./Rock/Bjork/Europa/02 - Hunter.mp3
...
./Rock/Nirvana/MTV Unplugged/01 - About A Girl.mp3
./Rock/Nirvana/MTV Unplugged/02 - Come As You Are.mp3
...
./Jazz/Herbie Hancock/Head Hunters/01 - Chameleon.mp3
./Jazz/Herbie Hancock/Head Hunters/02 - Watermelon Man.mp3
```

Now if we want to query what artists we have in the Rock genre, we just need to list the files in the *Rock/* directory. Once we find out that Bjork is one of the artists in the Rock category, we can do another enquiry to find out what Bjork albums we have bought by listing the files under the *Rock/Bjork/* directory. Now if we want to see the

---

* Disregard the fact that the actual password is stored in */etc/shadow* on modern systems.

actual MP3 files from a particular album (e.g., *MTV Unplugged*), we list the files under that directory.

What if we want to find all the albums that have *MTV* in their names? We can use `ls` to give us all the albums and MP3 files:

```
panic% ls -l ./*/*/*MTV*
```

Of course, filesystem manipulation can be done from your Perl program.

Let's look at another example. If you run a site about rock groups, you might want to store images relating to different groups. Using the filesystem as a database is a perfect match. Chances are these images will be served to users via `<img>` tags, so it makes perfect sense to use the real path (`DocumentRoot` considerations aside) to the image. For example:

```
<img src="/images/rock/ACDC/cover-front.gif" alt="ACDC" ...>
<img src="/images/rock/ACDC/cover-back.gif"  alt="ACDC" ...>
```

In this example we treat *ACDC* as a record and *cover-front.gif* and *cover-back.gif* as fields. This database implementation, just like the flat-file database, has no special benefits under mod_perl, so we aren't going to expand on the idea, but it's worth keeping in mind.

DBM Databases

DBM databases are very similar to flat-file databases, but if all you need is to store the key/value pairs, they will do it much faster. Their use is much simpler, too. Perl uses `tie()` to interact with DBM databases, and you work with these files as with normal hash data structures. When you want to store a value, you just assign it to a hash tied to the DBM database, and to retrieve some data you just read from the hash.

A good example is session tracking: any user can connect to any of several mod_perl processes, and each process needs to be able to retrieve the session ID from any other process. With DBM this task is trivial. Every time a lookup is needed, tie the DBM file, get the shared lock, and look up the *session_id* there. Then retrieve the data and untie the database. Each time you want to update the session data, you tie the database, acquire an exclusive lock, update the data, and untie the database. It's probably not the fastest approach, and probably not the best one if you need to store more than a single scalar for each record, but it works quite well.

In Chapter 20 we give some important background information about DBM files and provide a few examples of how you can benefit from usingDBM files under mod_perl.

Relational Databases

Of course, the most advanced solution is a relational database. But even though it provides the best solution in many cases, it's not always the one you should pick. You don't need a sledgehammer to crack a nut, right?

Relational databases come in different implementations. Some are very expensive and provide many tools and extra features that aren't available with the cheaper and free implementations. What's important to keep in mind is that it's not necessarily the most expensive one that is the best choice in a given situation. Just as you need to choose the right database structure, you need to choose the right relational database. For example, ask yourself whether you need speed, or support for transactions, or both.

It makes sense to try to write your code in such a way that if later in the course of development you discover that your choice of relational database wasn't the best, it will be easy to switch to a different one.

mod_perl greatly helps work with relational databases, mainly because it allows persistent database connections. We'll talk extensively about relational databases and mod_perl in Chapter 20.

References

- Chapters 2 and 3 of the book *Programming the Perl DBI*, by Alligator Descartes and Tim Bunce (O'Reilly), provide a good overview of relational and nonrelational databases
- Chapter 10 of the book *Advanced Perl Programming*, by Sriram Srinivasan (O'Reilly), talks about persistence

CHAPTER 18

mod_perl Data-Sharing Techniques

In this chapter, we discuss the ways mod_perl makes it possible to share data between processes or even between different handlers.

Sharing the Read-Only Data in and Between Processes

If you need to access some data in your code that's static and will not be modified, you can save time and resources by processing the data once and caching it for later reuse. Since under mod_perl processes persist and don't get killed after each request, you can store the data in global variables and reuse it.

For example, let's assume that you have a rather expensive function, get_data( ), which returns read-only data as a hash. In your code, you can do the following:

```
...
use vars qw(%CACHE);
%CACHE = get_data( ) unless %CACHE;
my $foo = $CACHE{bar};
...
```

This code creates a global hash, %CACHE, which is undefined when the code is executed for the first time. Therefore, the get_data( ) method is called, which hopefully populates %CACHE with some data. Now you can access this data as usual.

When the code is executed for the second time within the same process, the get_data( ) method will not be called again, since %CACHE has the data already (assuming that get_data( ) returned data when it was called for the first time).

Now you can access the data without any extra retrieval overhead.

If, for example, get_data( ) returns a reference to a list, the code will look like this:

```
....
use enum qw(FIRST SECOND THIRD);
use vars qw($RA_CACHE);
```

```
$RA_CACHE = get_data() unless $RA_CACHE;
my $second = $RA_CACHE->[SECOND];
...
```

Here we use the enum pragma to create constants that we will use in accessing the array reference. In our example, FIRST equals 0, SECOND equals 1, etc. We have used the RA_ prefix to indicate that this variable includes a reference to an array. So just like with the hash from the previous example, we retrieve the data once per process, cache it, and then access it in all subsequent code re-executions (e.g., HTTP requests) without calling the heavy get_data() method.

This is all fine, but what if the retrieved data set is very big and duplicating it in all child processes would require a huge chunk of memory to be allocated? Since we assumed that the data is read-only, can we try to load it into memory only once and share it among child processes? There is a feasible solution: we can run the get_data() method during server startup and place the retrieved data into a global variable of some new package that we have created on the fly. For example, let's create a package called Book::Cache, as shown in Example 18-1.

Example 18-1. Book/Cache.pm

```
package Book::Cache;

%Book::Cache::DATA = get_data();
sub get_data {
    # some heavy code that generates/retrieves data
}
1;
```

And initialize this module from *startup.pl*:

```
use Book::Cache ();
```

Now when the child processes get spawned, this data is available for them all via a simple inclusion of the module in the handler's code:

```
use Book::Cache ();
...
$foo = $Book::Cache::DATA{bar};
...
```

Be careful, though, when accessing this data. The data structure will be shared only if none of the child processes attempts to modify it. The moment a child process modifies this data, the copy-on-write event happens and the child copies the whole data structure into its namespace, and this data structure is not shared anymore.

Sharing Data Between Various Handlers

Sometimes you want to set some data in one of the early handler phases and make it available in the latter handlers. For example, say you set some data in a TransHandler and you want the PerlHandler to be able to access it as well.

To accomodate this, Apache maintains a "notes" table (tables are implemented by the Apache::Table module) in the request record. This table is simply a list of key/value pairs. One handler can add its own key/value entry to the notes table, and later the handler for a subsequent phase can retrieve the stored data. Notes are maintained for the life of the current request and are deleted when the transaction is finished. The notes( ) method is used to manipulate the notes table, and a note set in one Apache module (e.g., mod_perl) can later be accessed in another Apache module (e.g., mod_php).

The notes( ) method accepts only non-reference scalars as its values, which makes this method unfit for storing non-scalar variables. To solve this limitation mod_perl provides a special method, called pnotes( ), that can accept any kind of data structure as its values. However, the data set by pnotes( ) is accessible only by mod_perl.

The note gets set when the key/value pair is provided. For example, let's set a scalar value with a key *foo*:

```
$r->notes("foo" => 10);
```

and a reference to a list as a value for the key *bar*:

```
$r->pnotes("bar" => [1..10]);
```

Notes can be retrieved in two ways. The first way is to ask for the value of the given key:

```
$foo = $r->notes("foo");
```

and:

```
@bar = @{ $r->pnotes("bar") || [] };
```

Note that we expect the note keyed as *bar* to be a reference to a list.

The second method is to retrieve the whole notes table, which returns a hash reference blessed into the Apache::Table class:

```
$notes = $r->notes( );
$foo   = $notes->{foo};
```

and:

```
$pnotes = $r->pnotes( );
@bar    = @{ $pnotes->{bar} || [] };
```

Apache modules can pass information to each other via the notes table. Here is an example of how a mod_perl authentication handler can pass data to a mod_php content handler:

```
package Book::Auth;
...
sub handler {
    my $r = shift;
    ...
    $r->notes('answer',42);
```

```
    ...
    }
    1;
```

The mod_php content handler can retrieve this data as follows:

```
    ...
    $answer = apache_note("answer");
    ...
```

You can use notes along with the subrequest methods `lookup_uri()` and `lookup_filename()`, too. To make it work, you need to set notes in the subrequest object. For example, if you want to call a PHP subrequest from within mod_perl and pass it a note, you can do it in the following way:

```
    my $subr = $r->lookup_uri('wizard.php');
    $subr->notes('answer' => 42);
    $subr->run;
```

As of the time of this writing you cannot access the parent request tables from a PHP handler; therefore, you must set this note for the subrequest. If the subrequest is running in the mod_perl domain, however, you can always keep the notes in the parent request notes table and access them via the `main()` method:

```
    $r->main->notes('answer');
```

Similarly to the notes, you may want or need to use the Apache environment variables table to pass the information between different handlers.

If you know what environment variables you want to set before the server starts and you know their respective values, you can use `SetEnv` and `PerlSetEnv` in *httpd.conf*, as explained in Chapter 4. These settings will always be the same for all requests.

However, if you want to change or add some of the environment variables during the processing of a request, because some other handler that will be executed later relies on them, you should use the `subprocess_env()` method.

```
    <!--#if expr="$hour > 6 && $hour < 12" -->
    Good morning!
    <!--#elif expr="$hour >= 12 && $hour <= 18" -->
    Good afternoon!
    <!--#elif expr="$hour > 18 && $hour < 22" -->
    Good evening!
    <!--#else -->
    Good night!
    <!--#endif -->
```

and you have the following code in your mod_perl handler:

```
    my $hour = (localtime)[2];
    $r->subprocess_env(hour => $hour);
```

The page will nicely greet the surfer, picking the greeting based on the current time. Of course, the greeting will be correct only for users located in the same time zone as the server, but this is just a simple example.

References

- mod_include, an Apache module that provides Server-Side Includes (SSI): *http://httpd.apache.org/docs/mod/mod_include.html*

## CHAPTER 19

DBM and mod_perl

Some of the earliest databases implemented on Unix were Database Management (DBM) files, and many are still in use today. As of this writing, the Berkeley DB is the most powerful DBM implementation. Berkeley DB is available at *http://www. sleepycat.com/*. If you need a light database with an easy API, using simple key-value pairs to store and manipulate a relatively small number of records, DBM is the solution that you should consider first.

With DBM, it is rare to read the whole database into memory. Combine this feature with the use of smart storage techniques, and DBM files can be manipulated much faster than flat files. Flat-file databases can be very slow when the number of records starts to grow into the thousands, especially for insert, update, and delete operations. Sort algorithms on flat files can also be very time-consuming.

The maximum practical size of a DBM database depends on many factors, such as your data, your hardware, and the desired response times. But as a rough guide, consider 5,000 to 10,000 records to be reasonable.

We will talk mostly about Berkeley DB Version 1.x, as it provides the best functionality while having good speed and almost no limitations. Other implementations might be faster in some cases, but they are limited either in the length of the maximum value or the total number of records.

There are a number of Perl interfaces to the major DBM implementations, such as DB_File, NDBM_File, ODBM_File, GDBM_File, and SDBM_File. The original Perl module for Berkeley DB was DB_File, which was written to interface with Berkeley DB Version 1.85. The newer Perl module for Berkeley DB is BerkeleyDB, which was written to interface with Version 2.0 and subsequent releases. Because Berkeley DB Version 2.x has a compatibility API for Version 1.85, you can (and should) build DB_File using Version 2.x of Berkeley DB, although DB_File will still support only the 1.85 functionality.

Several different indexing algorithms (known also as *access methods*) can be used with DBM implementations:

- The HASH access method gives an O(1) complexity (see sidebar) of search and update, fast insert, and delete, but a slow sort (which you have to implement yourself). HASH is used by almost all DBM implementations.

- The BTREE access method allows arbitrary key/value pairs to be stored in a sorted, balanced binary tree. This allows you to get a sorted sequence of data pairs in O(1) (see sidebar), at the expense of much slower insert, update, and delete operations than is the case with HASH. BTREE is available mostly in Berkeley DB.

- The RECNO access method is more complicated, and enables both fixed-length and variable-length flat text files to be manipulated using the same key/value pair interface as in HASH and BTREE. In this case the key will consist of a record (line) number. RECNO is available mostly in Berkeley DB.

- The QUEUE access method stores fixed-length records with logical record numbers as keys. It is designed for fast inserts at the tail and has a special cursor-consume operation that deletes and returns a record from the head of the queue. The QUEUE access method uses record-level locking. QUEUE is available only in Berkeley DB Version 3.0 and higher.

Big-O Notation

In math, complexity is expressed using *big-O* notation. For a problem of size N:

- A constant-time method is "order 1": O(1)
- A linear-time method is "order N": O(N)
- A quadratic-time method is "order N squared": O(N^2)

For example, a lookup action in a properly implemented hash of size N with random data has a complexity of O(1), because the item is located almost immediately after its hash value is calculated. However, the same action in the list of N items has a complexity of O(N), since on average you have to go through almost all the items in the list before you find what you need.

Most often you will want to use the HASH method, but there are many considerations and your choice may be dictated by your application.

In recent years, DBM databases have been extended to allow you to store more complex values, including data structures. The MLDBM module can store and restore the whole symbol table of your script, including arrays and hashes.

It is important to note that you cannot simply switch a DBM file from one storage algorithm to another. The only way to change the algorithm is to copy all the records one by one into a new DBM file, initialized according to a desired access method. You can use a script like the one shown in Example 19-1.

Example 19-1. btree2hash.pl

```perl
#!/usr/bin/perl -w

#
# This script takes as its parameters a list of Berkeley DB
# file(s) which are stored with the DB_BTREE algorithm.  It
# will back them up using the .bak extension and create
# instead DBMs with the same records but stored using the
# DB_HASH algorithm.
#
# Usage: btree2hash.pl filename(s)

use strict;
use DB_File;
use Fcntl;

# @ARGV checks
die "Usage: btree2hash.pl filename(s))\n" unless @ARGV;

for my $filename (@ARGV) {
    die "Can't find $filename: $!"
        unless -e $filename and -r _;

    # First back up the file
    rename "$filename", "$filename.btree"
        or die "can't rename $filename with $filename.btree: $!";

    # tie both DBs (db_hash is a fresh one!)
    tie my %btree , 'DB_File',"$filename.btree", O_RDWR|O_CREAT,
        0660, $DB_BTREE or die "Can't tie $filename.btree: $!";
    tie my %hash , 'DB_File',"$filename" , O_RDWR|O_CREAT,
        0660, $DB_HASH  or die "Can't tie $filename: $!";

    # copy DB
    %hash = %btree;

    # untie
    untie %btree;
    untie %hash;
}
```

Note that some DBM implementations come with other conversion utilities as well.

mod_perl and DBM

Where does mod_perl fit into the picture? If you need read-only access to a DBM file in your mod_perl code, the operation is much faster if you keep the DBM file open (tied) all the time and therefore ready to be used. We will see an example of this in a moment. This will work with dynamic (read/write) database accesses as well, but you need to use locking and data flushing to avoid data corruption.

It's possible that a process will die, for various reasons. There are a few consequences of this event.

If the program has been using external file locking and the lock is based on the existence of the lock file, the code might be aborted before it has a chance to remove the file. Therefore, the next process that tries to get a lock will wait indefinitely, since the lock file is dead and no one can remove it without manual intervention. Until this lock file is removed, services relying on this lock will stay deactivated. The requests will queue up, and at some point the whole service will become useless as all the processes wait for the lock file. Therefore, this locking technique is not recommended. Instead, an advisory flock( ) method should be used. With this method, when a process dies, the lock file will be unlocked by the operating system, no matter what.

Another issue lies in the fact that if the DBM files are modified, they have to be properly closed to ensure the integrity of the data in the database. This requires a flushing of the DBM buffers, or just untying of the database. In case the code flow is aborted before the database is flushed to disk, use Perl's END block to handle the unexpected situations, like so:

```
END { my_dbm_flush( ) }
```

Remember that under mod_perl, this will work on each request only for END blocks declared in scripts running under Apache::Registry and similar handlers. Other Perl handlers need to use the $r->register_cleanup( ) method:

```
$r->register_cleanup(\&my_dbm_flush);
```

as explained in Chapter 6.

As a rule, your application should be tested very thoroughly before you put it into production to handle important data.

Resource Locking

Database locking is required if more than one process will try to modify the data. In an environment in which there are both reading and writing processes, the reading processes should use locking as well, since it's possible for another process to modify the resource at the same moment, in which case the reading process gets corrupted data.

We distinguish between shared-access and exclusive-access locks. Before doing an operation on the DBM file, an *exclusive* lock request is issued if a read/write access is required. Otherwise, a *shared* lock is issued.

Deadlocks

First let's make sure that you know how processes work with the CPU. Each process gets a tiny CPU time slice before another process takes over. Usually operating systems use a "round robin" technique to decide which processes should get CPU slices and when. This decision is based on a simple queue, with each process that needs CPU entering the queue at the end of it. Eventually the added process moves to the head of the queue and receives a tiny allotment of CPU time, depending on the processor speed and implementation (think microseconds). After this time slice, if it is still not finished, the process moves to the end of the queue again. Figure 19-1 depicts this process. (Of course, this diagram is a simplified one; in reality various processes have different priorities, so one process may get more CPU time slices than others over the same period of time.)

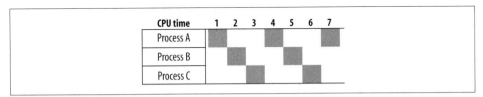

Figure 19-1. CPU time allocation

Now let's talk about the situation called *deadlock*. If two processes simultaneously try to acquire exclusive locks on two separate resources (databases), a deadlock is possible. Consider this example:

```
sub lock_foo {
    exclusive_lock('DB1');
    exclusive_lock('DB2');
}

sub lock_bar {
    exclusive_lock('DB2');
    exclusive_lock('DB1');
}
```

Suppose process A calls lock_foo( ) and process B calls lock_bar( ) at the same time. Process A locks resource DB1 and process B locks resource DB2. Now suppose process A needs to acquire a lock on DB2, and process B needs a lock on DB1. Neither of them can proceed, since they each hold the resource needed by the other. This situation is called a deadlock.

Using the same CPU-sharing diagram shown in Figure 19-1, let's imagine that process A gets an exclusive lock on DB1 at time slice 1 and process B gets an exclusive lock on DB2 at time slice 2. Then at time slice 4, process A gets the CPU back, but it cannot do anything because it's waiting for the lock on DB2 to be released. The same thing happens to process B at time slice 5. From now on, the two processes will get the CPU, try to get the lock, fail, and wait for the next chance indefinitely.

Deadlock wouldn't be a problem if lock_foo( ) and lock_bar( ) were atomic, which would mean that no other process would get access to the CPU before the whole subroutine was completed. But this never happens, because all the running processes get access to the CPU only for a few milliseconds or even microseconds at a time (called a *time slice*). It usually takes more than one CPU time slice to accomplish even a very simple operation.

For the same reason, this code shouldn't be relied on:

```
sub get_lock {
    sleep 1, until -e $lock_file;
    open LF, $lock_file or die $!;
    return 1;
}
```

The problem with this code is that the test and the action pair aren't atomic. Even if the -e test determines that the file doesn't exist, nothing prevents another process from creating the file in between the -e test and the next operation that tries to create it. Later we will see how this problem can be resolved.

Exclusive Locking Starvation

If a shared lock request is issued, it is granted immediately if the file is not locked or has another shared lock on it. If the file has an exclusive lock on it, the shared lock request is granted as soon as that lock is removed. The lock status becomes SHARED on success.

If an exclusive lock is requested, it is granted as soon as the file becomes unlocked. The lock status becomes EXCLUSIVE on success.

If the DB has a shared lock on it, a process that makes an exclusive lock request will poll until there are no reading or writing processes left. Lots of processes can successfully read the file, since they do not block each other. This means that a process that wants to write to the file may never get a chance to squeeze in, since it needs to obtain an exclusive lock.

Figure 19-2 represents a possible scenario in which everybody can read but no one can write. ("pX" represents different processes running at different times, all acquiring shared locks on the DBM file.)

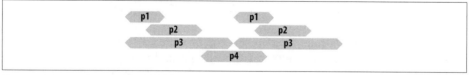

Figure 19-2. Overlapping shared locks prevent an exclusive lock

The result is a starving process that will time out the request, which will fail to update the DB. Ken Williams solved this problem with his `Tie::DB_Lock` module, discussed later in this chapter.

There are several locking wrappers for `DB_File` on CPAN right now. Each one implements locking differently and has different goals in mind. It is worth knowing the differences between them, so that you can pick the right one for your application.

Flawed Locking Methods

The suggested locking methods in the first and second editions of the book *Programming Perl* (O'Reilly) and the `DB_File` manpage (before Version 1.72, fixed in 1.73) are flawed. If you use them in an environment where more than one process can modify the DBM file, it can be corrupted. The following is an explanation of why this happens.

You cannot use a tied file's file handle for locking, since you get the file handle after the file has already been tied. It's too late to lock. The problem is that the database file is locked *after* it is opened. When the database is opened, the first 4 KB (for the Berkeley DB library, at least) are read and then cached in memory. Therefore, a process can open the database file, cache the first 4 KB, and then block while another process writes to the file. If the second process modifies the first 4 KB of the file, when the original process gets the lock it now has an inconsistent view of the database. If it writes using this view it may easily corrupt the database on disk.

This problem can be difficult to trace because it does not cause corruption every time a process has to wait for a lock. One can do quite a bit of writing to a database file without actually changing the first 4 KB. But once you suspect this problem, you can easily reproduce it by making your program modify the records in the first 4 KB of the DBM file.

It's better to resort to using the standard modules for locking than to try to invent your own.

If your DBM file is used only in the read-only mode, generally there is no need for locking at all. If you access the DBM file in read/write mode, the safest method is to tie the DBM file after acquiring an external lock and untie it before the lock is released. So to access the file in shared mode (FLOCK_SH*), follow this pseudocode:

```
flock $fh, FLOCK_SH <===== start critical section
tie...
read...
untie...
flock $fh, FLOCK_UN <===== end critical section
```

---

* The FLOCK_* constants are defined in the Fcntl module; FLOCK_SH for shared, FLOCK_EX for exclusive, and FLOCK_UN for unlock.

Similarly for the exclusive (EX) write access:

```
flock FLOCK_EX <===== start critical section
tie...
write...
sync...
untie...
flock FLOCK_UN <===== end critical section
```

You might want to save a few tie( )/untie( ) calls if the same request accesses the DBM file more than once. Be careful, though. Based on the caching effect explained above, a process can perform an atomic downgrade of an exclusive lock to a shared one without retying the file:

```
flock FLOCK_EX <===== start critical section
tie...
write...
sync...
               <===== end critical section
flock FLOCK_SH <===== start critical section
read...
untie...
flock FLOCK_UN <===== end critical section
```

because it has the updated data in its cache. By atomic, we mean it's ensured that the lock status gets changed without any other process getting exclusive access in between.

If you can ensure that one process safely upgrades a shared lock to an exclusive lock, you can save the overhead of doing the extra tie( ) and untie( ). But this operation might lead to a deadlock if two processes try to upgrade from shared to exclusive locks at the same time. Remember that in order to acquire an exclusive lock, all other processes need to release *all* locks. If your OS's locking implementation resolves this deadlock by denying one of the upgrade requests, make sure your program handles that appropriately. The process that was denied has to untie the DBM file and then ask for an exclusive lock.

A DBM file always has to be untied before the lock is released (unless you do an atomic downgrade from exclusive to shared, as we have just explained). Remember that if at any given moment a process wants to lock and access the DBM file, it has to retie this file if it was tied already. If this is not done, the integrity of the DBM file is not ensured.

To conclude, the safest method of reading from a DBM file is to lock the file before tying it, untie it before releasing the lock, and, in the case of writing, call sync( ) before untying it.

Locking Wrappers Overview

Here are the pros and cons of the DBM file-locking wrappers available from CPAN:

Tie::DB_Lock

A DB_File wrapper that creates copies of the DBM file for read access, so that you have a kind of multiversioning concurrent read system. However, updates are still serial. After each update, the read-only copies of the DBM file are recreated. Use this wrapper in situations where reads may be very lengthy and therefore the write starvation problem may occur. On the other hand, if you have big DBM files, it may create a big load on the system if the updates are quite frequent. This module is discussed in the next section.

Tie::DB_FileLock

A DB_File wrapper that has the ability to lock and unlock the database while it is being used. Avoids the tie-before-flock problem by simply retying the database when you get or drop a lock. Because of the flexibility in dropping and reacquiring the lock in the middle of a session, this can be used in a system that will work with long updates and/or reads. Refer to the Tie::DB_FileLock manpage for more information.

DB_File::Lock

An extremely lightweight DB_File wrapper that simply flocks an external lock file before tying the database and drops the lock after untying. This allows you to use the same lock file for multiple databases to avoid deadlock problems, if desired. Use this for databases where updates and reads are quick, and simple flock() locking semantics are enough. Refer to the DB_File::Lock manpage for more information.

On some operating systems (FreeBSD, for example), it is possible to lock on tie:

```
tie my %t, 'DB_File', $DBM_FILE, O_RDWR | O_EXLOCK, 0664;
```

and release the lock only by untying the file. Check if the O_EXLOCK flag is available on your operating system before you try to use this method!

Tie::DB_Lock

Tie::DB_Lock ties hashes to databases using shared and exclusive locks. This module, written by Ken Williams, solves the problems discussed earlier.

The main difference with this module is that Tie::DB_Lock copies a DBM file on read. Reading processes do not have to keep the file locked while they read it, and writing processes can still access the file while others are reading. This works best when you have lots of long-duration reading processes and a few short bursts of writing.

The drawback of this module is the heavy I/O performed when every reader makes a fresh copy of the DB. With big DBM files this can be quite a disadvantage and can slow down the server considerably.

An alternative would be to have one copy of the DBM image shared by all the reading processes. This would cut the number of files that are copied and put the responsibility of copying the read-only file on the writer, not the reader. However, some care would be required to make sure that readers are not disturbed when a new read-only copy is put into place.

Examples

Let's look at a few examples that will demonstrate the theory presented at the beginning of the chapter.

tie( )-ing Once and Forever

If you know that your code accesses the DBM file in read-only mode and you want to gain the maximum data-retrieval speed, you should tie the DBM file during server startup and register code in the child initialization stage that will tie the DBM file when the child process is spawned.

Consider the small test module in Example 19-2.

Example 19-2. Book/DBMCache.pm

```
package Book::DBMCache;

use DB_File;
use Fcntl qw(O_RDONLY O_CREAT);

use vars qw(%dbm);

sub init {
    my $filename = shift;
    tie %dbm, 'DB_File', $filename, O_RDONLY|O_CREAT,
        0660, $DB_BTREE or die "Can't tie $filename: $!";
}
1;
```

This module imports two symbols from the Fcntl package that we will use to tie the DBM file. The first one is O_RDONLY, as we want the file to be opened only for reading. It is important to note that in the case of the tie( ) interface, nothing prevents you from updating the DBM file, even if the file was tied with the O_RDONLY flag. The second flag, O_CREAT, is used just in case the DBM file wasn't found where it was expected—in this case, an empty file will be created instead, since otherwise tie( ) will fail and the code execution will be aborted.

The module specifies a global variable, %dbm, which we need to be global so that we can access it directly from outside of the Book::DBMCache module. Alternatively, we could define this variable as lexically scoped to this module and write an accessor (method), which would make the code cleaner. However, this accessor would be called every time we wanted to read some value.

When Book::DBMCache::init( ) is called with a path to the DBM file as its argument, the global variable %dbm is tied to this file. We want the tie operation to happen before the first request is made, so we do it in the ChildInitHandler code executed from *startup.pl*:

```
use Book::DBMCache;
Apache->push_handlers(PerlChildInitHandler => sub {
                        Book::DBMCache::init("/tmp/foo.db");
                    });
```

Assuming */tmp/foo.db* is already populated with data, we can now write the test script shown in Example 19-3.

Example 19-3. test_dbm.pl

```
use Book::DBMCache;
use strict;

my $r = shift;
$r->send_http_header("text/plain");

my $foo = exists $Book::DBMCache::dbm{foo} ? $Book::DBMCache::dbm{foo} : '';
print "The value of foo: [$foo]";
```

When this is executed as an Apache::Registry script (assuming the DBM file was populated with the foo, bar key/value pair), we will see the following output:

```
The value of foo: [bar]
```

There's an easy way to guarantee that a tied hash is read-only: use a subclass of the tie module you're using that prevents writing. For example, you can subclass DB_File as follows:

```
package DB_File::ReadOnly;

use strict;
require DB_File;
$DB_File::ReadOnly::ISA = qw(DB_File);

sub STORE  {}
sub DELETE {}
sub CLEAR  {}

1;
```

As you can see, the methods of the tie( ) interface that can alter the DBM file are overriden with methods that do nothing. Of course, you may want to use warn( ) or die( ) inside these methods, depending on how you want to flag writes. Any attempts to write probably should be considered serious problems.

Now you can use DB_File::ReadOnly just like you were using DB_File before, but you can be sure that the DBM file won't be modified through this interface.

Read/Write Access

This simple example will show you how to use the DBM file when you want to be able to safely modify it in addition to just reading from it. As mentioned earlier, we are running in a multiprocess environment in which more than one process might attempt to write to the file at the same time. Therefore, we need to have a lock on the DBM file before we can access it, even when doing only a read operation—we want to make sure that the retrieved data is completely valid, which might not be the case if someone is writing to the same record at the time of our read. We are going to use the DB_File::Lock module from CPAN to perform the actual locking.

The simple script shown in Example 19-4 imports the O_RDWR and O_CREAT symbols from the Fcntl module, loads the DB_File::Lock module, and sends the HTTP header as usual.

Example 19-4. read_write_lock.pl

```
use strict;
use DB_File::Lock;
use Fcntl qw(O_RDWR O_CREAT);

my $r = shift;
$r->send_http_header("text/plain");

my $dbfile = "/tmp/foo.db";
tie my %dbm, 'DB_File::Lock', $dbfile, O_RDWR|O_CREAT,
    0600, $DB_HASH, 'write';
# assign a random value
$dbm{foo} = ('a'..'z')[int rand(26)];
untie %dbm;

# read the assigned value
tie %dbm, 'DB_File::Lock', $dbfile, O_RDWR|O_CREAT,
    0600, $DB_HASH, 'read';
my $foo = exists $dbm{foo} ? $dbm{foo} : 'undefined';
untie %dbm;

print "The value of foo: [$foo]";
```

The next step is to tie the existing */tmp/foo.db* file, or create a new one if it doesn't already exist. Notice that the last argument for the tie is 'write', which tells DB_File:: Lock to obtain an exclusive (write) lock before moving on. Once the exclusive lock is acquired and the DBM file is tied, the code assigns a random letter as a value and saves the change by calling untie( ), which unlocks the DBM and closes it. It's important to stress here that in our example the section of code between the calls to tie( ) and untie( ) is called a critical section, because while we are inside of it, no other process can read from or write to the DBM file. Therefore, it's important to keep it the execution time of this section as short as possible.

The next section is similar to the first one, but this time we ask for a shared (read) lock, as we only want to read the value from the DBM file. Once the value is read, it's printed. Since the letter was picked randomly, you will see something like this:

```
The value of foo: [d]
```

then this (when reloading again):

```
The value of foo: [z]
```

and so on.

Based on this example you can build more evolved code, and of course you may choose to use other locking wrapper modules, as discussed earlier.

Storing Complex Data Structures

As mentioned earlier, you can use the MLDBM module to store complex data structures in the DBM file (which apparently accepts only a scalar as a single value). Example 19-5 shows how to do this.

Example 19-5. mldbm.pl

```perl
use strict;
use MLDBM qw(DB_File);
use DB_File;
use Data::Dumper ( );
use Fcntl qw(O_RDWR O_CREAT);

my $r = shift;
$r->send_http_header("text/plain");

my $rh = {
        bar => ['a'..'c'],
        tar => { map {$_ => $_**2 } 1..4 },
        };

my $dbfile = "/tmp/foo.db";
tie my %dbm, 'MLDBM', $dbfile, O_RDWR|O_CREAT,
    0600, $DB_HASH or die $!;
# assign a reference to a Perl datastructure
$dbm{foo} = $rh;
untie %dbm;
```

Example 19-5. mldbm.pl (continued)

```
# read the assigned value
tie %dbm, 'MLDBM', $dbfile, O_RDWR|O_CREAT,
    0600, $DB_HASH or die $!;
my $foo = exists $dbm{foo} ? $dbm{foo} : 'undefined';
untie %dbm;

print Data::Dumper::Dumper($foo);
```

As you can see, this example is very similar to the normal use of DB_File; we just use MLDBM instead, and tell it to use DB_File as an underlying DBM implementation. You can choose any other available implementation instead. If you don't specify one, SDBM_File is used.

The script creates a complicated nested data structure and stores it in the $rh scalar. Then we open the database and store this value as usual.

When we want to retrieve the stored value, we do pretty much the same thing as before. The script uses the Data::Dumper::Dumper method to print out the nested data structure. Here is what it prints:

```
$VAR1 = {
          'bar' => [
                     'a',
                     'b',
                     'c'
                   ],
          'tar' => {
                     '1' => '1',
                     '2' => '4',
                     '3' => '9',
                     '4' => '16'
                   }
        };
```

That's exactly what we inserted into the DBM file.

There is one important note, though. If you want to modify a value that is a reference to a data structure, you cannot modify it directly. You have to retrieve the value, modify it, and store it back.

For example, in the above example you cannot do:

```
tie my %dbm, 'MLDBM', $dbfile, O_RDWR|O_CREAT,
    0600, $DB_HASH or die $!;
# update the existing key
$dbm{foo}->{bar} = ['a'..'z']; # this doesn't work
untie %dbm;
```

if the key bar existed before. Instead, you should do the following:

```
tie my %dbm, 'MLDBM', $dbfile, O_RDWR|O_CREAT,
    0600, $DB_HASH or die $!;
# update the existing key
```

```
my $tmp     = $dbm{foo};
$tmp->{bar} = ['a'..'z'];
$dbm{foo}   = $tmp;        # this works
untie %dbm;
```

This limitation exists because the perl TIEHASH interface currently has no support for multidimensional ties.

By default, MLDBM uses Data::Dumper to serialize the nested data structures. You may want to use the FreezeThaw or Storable serializer instead. In fact, Storable is the preferred one. To use Storable in our example, you should do:

```
use MLDBM qw(DB_File Storable);
```

at the beginning of the script.

Refer to the MLDBM manpage to find out more information about it.

References

- Chapter 14 in *Perl Cookbook*, by Tom Christiansen and Nathan Torkington (O'Reilly)
- Chapter 17 in *Learning Perl*, Second Edition, by Randal L. Schwartz and Tom Christiansen (O'Reilly)
- Chapter 2 in *Programming the Perl DBI*, by Alligator Descartes and Tim Bunce (O'Reilly)
- The Berkeley DB web site: *http://www.sleepycat.com/*

CHAPTER 20

Relational Databases and mod_perl

Nowadays, millions of people surf the Internet. There are millions of terabytes of data lying around, and many new techniques and technologies have been invented to manipulate this data. One of these inventions is the relational database, which makes it possible to search and modify huge stores of data very quickly. The Structured Query Language (SQL) is used to access and manipulate the contents of these databases.

Let's say that you started your web services with a simple, flat-file database. Then with time your data grew big, which made the use of a flat-file database slow and inefficient. So you switched to the next simple solution—using DBM files. But your data set continued to grow, and even the DBM files didn't provide a scalable enough solution. So you finally decided to switch to the most advanced solution, a relational database.

On the other hand, it's quite possible that you had big ambitions in the first place and you decided to go with a relational database right away.

We went through both scenarios, sometimes doing the minimum development using DBM files (when we knew that the data set was small and unlikely to grow big in the short term) and sometimes developing full-blown systems with relational databases at the heart.

As we repeat many times in this book, none of our suggestions and examples should be applied without thinking. But since you're reading this chapter, the chances are that you are doing the right thing, so we are going to concentrate on the extra benefits that mod_perl provides when you use relational databases. We'll also talk about related coding techniques that will help you to improve the performance of your service.

From now on, we assume that you use the DBI module to talk to the databases. This in turn uses the unique database driver module for your database, which resides in the DBD:: namespace (for example, DBD::Oracle for Oracle and DBD::mysql for MySQL). If you stick to standard SQL, you maximize portability from one database to another. Changing to a new database server should simply be a matter of using a different database driver. You do this just by changing the data set name string ($dsn) in the DBI->connect( ) call.

Rather than writing your queries in plain SQL, you should probably use some other abstraction module on top of the DBI module. This can help to make your code more extensible and maintainable. Raw SQL coupled with DBI usually gives you the best machine performance, but sometimes time to market is what counts, so you have to make your choices. An abstraction layer with a well-thought-out API is a pleasure to work with, and future modifications to the code will be less troublesome. Several DBI abstraction solutions are available on CPAN. DBIx::Recordset, Alzabo, and Class::DBI are just a few such modules that you may want to try. Take a look at the other modules in the DBIx:: category—many of them provide some kind of wrapping and abstraction around DBI.

Persistent Database Connections with Apache::DBI

When people first started to use the Web, they found that they needed to write web interfaces to their databases, or add databases to drive their web interfaces. Whichever way you look at it, they needed to connect to the databases in order to use them.

CGI is the most widely used protocol for building such interfaces, implemented in Apache's mod_cgi and its equivalents. For working with databases, the main limitation of most implementations, including mod_cgi, is that they don't allow persistent connections to the database. For every HTTP request, the CGI script has to connect to the database, and when the request is completed the connection is closed. Depending on the relational database that you use, the time to instantiate a connection may be very fast (for example, MySQL) or very slow (for example, Oracle). If your database provides a very short connection latency, you may get away without having persistent connections. But if not, it's possible that opening a connection may consume a significant slice of the time to serve a request. It may be that if you can cut this overhead you can greatly improve the performance of your service.

Apache::DBI was written to solve this problem. When you use it with mod_perl, you have a database connection that persists for the entire life of a mod_perl process. This is possible because with mod_perl, the child process does not quit when a request has been served. When a mod_perl script needs to use a database, Apache::DBI immediately provides a valid connection (if it was already open) and your script starts doing the real work right away without having to make a database connection first.

Of course, the persistence doesn't help with any latency problems you may encounter during the actual use of the database connections. Oracle, for example, is notorious for generating a network transaction for each row returned. This slows things down if the query execution matches many rows.

You may want to read Tim Bunce's "Advanced DBI" talk, at *http://dbi.perl.org/doc/conferences/tim_1999/index.html*, which covers many techniques to reduce latency.

Apache::DBI Connections

The DBI module can make use of the Apache::DBI module. When the DBI module loads, it tests whether the environment variable $ENV{MOD_PERL} is set and whether the Apache::DBI module has already been loaded. If so, the DBI module forwards every connect( ) request to the Apache::DBI module.

When Apache::DBI gets a connect( ) request, it checks whether it already has a handle with the same connect( ) arguments. If it finds one, it checks that the connection is still valid using the ping( ) method. If this operation succeeds, the database handle is returned immediately. If there is no appropriate database handle, or if the ping( ) method fails, Apache::DBI establishes a new connection, stores the handle, and then returns the handle to the caller.

It is important to understand that the pool of connections is not shared between the processes. Each process has its own pool of connections.

When you start using Apache::DBI, there is no need to delete all the disconnect( ) statements from your code. They won't do anything, because the Apache::DBI module overloads the disconnect( ) method with an empty one. You shouldn't modify your scripts at all for use with Apache::DBI.

When to Use Apache::DBI (and When Not to Use It)

You will want to use the Apache::DBI module only if you are opening just a few database connections per process. If there are ten child processes and each opens two different connections (using different connect( ) arguments), in total there will be 20 opened and persistent connections.

This module must *not* be used if (for example) you have many users, and a unique connection (with unique connect( ) arguments) is required for each user.[*] You cannot ensure that requests from one user will be served by any particular process, and connections are not shared between the child processes, so many child processes will open a separate, persistent connection for each user. In the worst case, if you have 100 users and 50 processes, you could end up with 5,000 persistent connections, which might be largely unused. Since database servers have limitations on the maximum number of opened connections, at some point new connections will not be permitted, and eventually your service will become unavailable.

If you want to use Apache::DBI but you have both situations on one machine, at the time of writing the only solution is to run two mod_perl-enabled servers, one that uses Apache::DBI and one that does not.

---

[*] That is, database user connections. This doesn't mean that if many people register as users on your web site you shouldn't use Apache::DBI; it is only a very special case.

In mod_perl 2.0, a threaded server can be used, and this situation is much improved. Assuming that you have a single process with many threads and each unique open connection is needed by only a single thread, it's possible to have a pool of database connections that are reused by different threads.

Configuring Apache::DBI

Apache::DBI will not work unless mod_perl was built with:

```
PERL_CHILD_INIT=1 PERL_STACKED_HANDLERS=1
```

or:

```
EVERYTHING=1
```

during the `perl Makefile.PL ...` stage.

After installing this module, configuration is simple—just add a single directive to *httpd.conf*:

```
PerlModule Apache::DBI
```

Note that it is important to load this module before any other Apache*DBI module and before the DBI module itself. The best rule is just to load it first of all. You can skip preloading DBI at server startup, since Apache::DBI does that for you, but there is no harm in leaving it in, as long as Apache::DBI is loaded first.

Debugging Apache::DBI

If you are not sure whether this module is working as advertised and that your connections are actually persistent, you should enable debug mode in the *startup.pl* script, like this:

```
$Apache::DBI::DEBUG = 1;
```

Starting with Apache::DBI Version 0.84, the above setting will produce only minimal output. For a full trace, you should set:

```
$Apache::DBI::DEBUG = 2;
```

After setting the DEBUG level, you will see entries in the *error_log* file. Here is a sample of the output with a DEBUG level of 1:

```
12851 Apache::DBI new connect to
'test::localhostPrintError=1RaiseError=0AutoCommit=1'

12853 Apache::DBI new connect to
'test::localhostPrintError=1RaiseError=0AutoCommit=1'
```

When a connection is reused, Apache::DBI stays silent, so you can see when a real connect() is called. If you set the DEBUG level to 2, you'll see a more verbose output. This output was generated after two identical requests with a single server running:

```
12885 Apache::DBI need ping: yes
12885 Apache::DBI new connect to
```

```
'test::localhostPrintError=1RaiseError=0AutoCommit=1'
12885 Apache::DBI need ping: yes
12885 Apache::DBI already connected to
'test::localhostPrintError=1RaiseError=0AutoCommit=1'
```

You can see that process 12885 created a new connection on the first request and on the next request reused it, since it was using the same connect( ) argument. Moreover, you can see that the connection was validated each time with the ping( ) method.

Caveats and Troubleshooting

This section covers some of the risks and things to keep in mind when using Apache:: DBI.

Database locking risks

When you use Apache::DBI or similar persistent connections, be very careful about locking the database (LOCK TABLE ...) or single rows. MySQL threads keep tables locked until the thread ends (i.e., the connection is closed) or until the tables are explicitly unlocked. If your session dies while tables are locked, they will stay locked, as your connection to the database won't be closed. In Chapter 6 we discussed how to terminate the program cleanly if the session is aborted prematurely.

Transactions

A standard Perl script using DBI will automatically perform a rollback whenever the script exits. In the case of persistent database connections, the database handle will not be destroyed and hence no automatic rollback will occur. At first glance it even seems to be possible to handle a transaction over multiple requests, but the temptation should be avoided because different requests are handled by different mod_perl processes, and a mod_perl process does not know the state of a specific transaction that has been started by another mod_perl process.

In general, it is good practice to perform an explicit commit or rollback at the end of every script. To avoid inconsistencies in the database in case AutoCommit is Off and the script terminates prematurely without an explicit rollback, the Apache::DBI module uses a PerlCleanupHandler to issue a rollback at the end of every request.

Opening connections with different parameters

When Apache::DBI receives a connection request, before it decides to use an existing cached connection it insists that the new connection be opened in exactly the same way as the cached connection. If you have one script that sets AutoCommit and one that does not, Apache::DBI will make two different connections. So, for example, if you have limited Apache to 40 servers at most, instead of having a maximum of 40 open connections, you may end up with 80.

These two connect( ) calls will create two different connections:

```
my $dbh = DBI->connect
    ("DBI:mysql:test:localhost", '', '',
    {
      PrintError => 1, # warn( ) on errors
      RaiseError => 0, # don't die on error
      AutoCommit => 1, # commit executes immediately
    }
    ) or die "Cannot connect to database: $DBI::errstr";

my $dbh = DBI->connect
    ("DBI:mysql:test:localhost", '', '',
    {
      PrintError => 1, # warn( ) on errors
      RaiseError => 0, # don't die on error
      AutoCommit => 0, # don't commit executes immediately
    }
    ) or die "Cannot connect to database: $DBI::errstr";
```

Notice that the only difference is in the value of AutoCommit.

However, you are free to modify the handle immediately after you get it from the cache, so always initiate connections using the same parameters and set AutoCommit (or whatever) afterward. Let's rewrite the second connect( ) call to do the right thing (i.e., not to create a new connection):

```
my $dbh = DBI->connect
    ("DBI:mysql:test:localhost", '', '',
    {
      PrintError => 1, # warn( ) on errors
      RaiseError => 0, # don't die on error
      AutoCommit => 1, # commit executes immediately
    }
    ) or die "Cannot connect to database: $DBI::errstr";
$dbh->{AutoCommit} = 0; # don't commit if not asked to
```

When you aren't sure whether you're doing the right thing, turn on debug mode.

When the $dbh attribute is altered after connect( ), it affects all other handlers retrieving this database handle. Therefore, it's best to restore the modified attributes to their original values at the end of database handle usage. As of Apache::DBI Version 0.88, the caller has to do this manually. The simplest way to handle this is to localize the attributes when modifying them:

```
my $dbh = DBI->connect(...) ...
{
   local $dbh->{LongReadLen} = 40;
}
```

Here, the LongReadLen attribute overrides the value set in the connect( ) call or its default value only within the enclosing block.

The problem with this approach is that prior to Perl Version 5.8.0 it causes memory leaks. So the only clean alternative for older Perl versions is to manually restore $dbh's values:

```
my @attrs = qw(LongReadLen PrintError);
my %orig = ( );

my $dbh = DBI->connect(...) ...

# store the values away
$orig{$_} = $dbh->{$_} for @attrs;
# do local modifications
$dbh->{LongReadLen} = 40;
$dbh->{PrintError}  = 1;

# do something with the database handle
# ...

# now restore the values
$dbh->{$_} = $orig{$_} for @attrs;
```

Another thing to remember is that with some database servers it's possible to access more than one database using the same database connection. MySQL is one of those servers. It allows you to use a fully qualified table specification notation. So if there is a database *foo* with a table *test* and a database *bar* with its own table *test*, you can always use:

```
SELECT * FROM foo.test ...
```

or:

```
SELECT * FROM bar.test ...
```

No matter what database you have used in the database name string in the connect( ) call (e.g., DBI:mysql:foo:localhost), you can still access both tables by using a fully qualified syntax.

Alternatively, you can switch databases with USE foo and USE bar, but this approach seems less convenient, and therefore error-prone.

Cannot find the DBI handler

You must use DBI->connect( ) as in normal DBI usage to get your $dbh database handle. Using Apache::DBI does not eliminate the need to write proper DBI code. As the Apache::DBI manpage states, you should program as if you are not using Apache::DBI at all. Apache::DBI will override the DBI methods where necessary and return your cached connection. Any disconnect( ) calls will just be ignored.

The morning bug

The SQL server keeps a connection to the client open for a limited period of time. In the early days of Apache::DBI, everyone was bitten by the so-called *morning bug*—

every morning the first user to use the site received a "No Data Returned" message, but after that everything worked fine.

The error was caused by Apache::DBI returning an invalid connection handle (the server had closed it because of a timeout), and the script was dying on that error. The ping( ) method was introduced to solve this problem, but it didn't work properly until Apache::DBI Version 0.82 was released. In that version and after, ping( ) was called inside an eval block, which resolved the problem.

It's still possible that some DBD:: drivers don't have the ping( ) method implemented. The Apache::DBI manpage explains how to write it.

Another solution is to increase the timeout parameter when starting the database server. We usually start the MySQL server with the script *safe_mysqld*, so we modified it to use this option:

```
nohup $ledir/mysqld [snipped other options] -O wait_timeout=172800
```

The timeout value that we use is 172,800 seconds, or 48 hours. This change solves the problem, but the ping( ) method works properly in DBD::mysql as well.

Apache:DBI does not work

If Apache::DBI doesn't work, first make sure that you have it installed. Then make sure that you configured mod_perl with either:

```
PERL_CHILD_INIT=1 PERL_STACKED_HANDLERS=1
```

or:

```
EVERYTHING=1
```

Turn on debug mode using the $Apache::DBI::DEBUG variable.

Skipping connection cache during server startup

Does your error_log look like this?

```
10169 Apache::DBI PerlChildInitHandler
10169 Apache::DBI skipping connection cache during server startup
Database handle destroyed without explicit disconnect at
/usr/lib/perl5/site_perl/5.6.1/Apache/DBI.pm line 29.
```

If so, you are trying to open a database connection in the parent *httpd* process. If you do, the children will each get a copy of this handle, causing clashes when the handle is used by two processes at the same time. Each child must have its own unique connection handle.

To avoid this problem, Apache::DBI checks whether it is called during server startup. If so, the module skips the connection cache and returns immediately without a database handle.

You must use the Apache::DBI->connect_on_init( ) method (see the next section) in the startup file to preopen a connection before the child processes are spawned.

Improving Performance

Let's now talk about various techniques that allow you to boost the speed of applications that work with relational databases. A whole book could be devoted to this topic, so here we will concentrate on the techniques that apply specifically to mod_perl servers.

Preopening DBI Connections

If you are using Apache::DBI and you want to make sure that a database connection will already be open when your code is first executed within each child process after a server restart, you should use the connect_on_init( ) method in the startup file to preopen every connection that you are going to use. For example:

```
Apache::DBI->connect_on_init(
    "DBI:mysql:test:localhost", "my_username", "my_passwd",
    {
      PrintError => 1, # warn( ) on errors
      RaiseError => 0, # don't die on error
      AutoCommit => 1, # commit executes immediately
    }
);
```

For this method to work, you need to make sure that you have built mod_perl with PERL_CHILD_INIT=1 or EVERYTHING=1.

Be warned, though, that if you call connect_on_init( ) and your database is down, Apache children will be delayed at server startup, trying to connect. They won't begin serving requests until either they are connected or the connection attempt fails. Depending on your DBD driver, this can take several minutes!

Improving Speed by Skipping ping( )

If you use Apache::DBI and want to save a little bit of time, you can change how often the ping( ) method is called. The following setting in a startup file:

```
Apache::DBI->setPingTimeOut($data_source, $timeout)
```

will change this behavior. If the value of $timeout is 0, Apache:DBI will validate the database connection using the ping( ) method for every database access. This is the default. Setting $timeout to a negative value will deactivate the validation of the database handle. This can be used for drivers that do not implement the ping( ) method (but it's generally a bad idea, because you don't know if your database handle really works). Setting $timeout to a positive value will *ping* the database on access only if the previous access was more than $timeout seconds earlier.

$data_source is the same as in the connect( ) method (e.g., DBI:mysql:...).

Efficient Record-Retrieval Techniques

When working with a relational database, you'll often encounter the need to read the retrieved set of records into your program, then format and print them to the browser.

Assuming that you're already connected to the database, let's consider the following code prototype:

```
my $query = "SELECT id,fname,lname FROM test WHERE id < 10";
my $sth = $dbh->prepare($query);
$sth->execute;

my @results = ( );
while (my @row_ary  = $sth->fetchrow_array) {
    push @results, [ transform(@row_ary) ];
}
# print the output using the the data returned from the DB
```

In this example, the *httpd* process will grow by the size of the variables that have been allocated for the records that matched the query. Remember that to get the total amount of extra memory required by this technique, this growth should be multiplied by the number of child processes that your server runs—which is probably not a constant.

A better approach is not to accumulate the records, but rather to print them as they are fetched from the DB. You can use the methods $sth->bind_columns( ) and $sth->fetchrow_arrayref( ) (aliased to $sth->fetch( )) to fetch the data in the fastest possible way. Example 20-1 prints an HTML table with matched data. Now the only additional memory consumed is for an @cols array to hold temporary row values.

Example 20-1. bind_cols.pl

```
my $query = "SELECT id,fname,lname FROM test WHERE id < 10";
my @fields = qw(id fname lname);

# create a list of cols values
my @cols = ( );
@cols[0..$#fields] = ( );
$sth = $dbh->prepare($query);
$sth->execute;

# Bind perl variables to columns.
$sth->bind_columns(undef, \(@cols));
print "<table>";
print '<tr bgcolor="grey">',
    map("<th>$_</th>", @fields), "</tr>";
while ($sth->fetch) {
    print "<tr>",
        map("<td>$_</td>", @cols), "</tr>";
}
print "</table>";
```

Note that this approach doesn't tell you how many records have been matched. The workaround is to run an identical query before the code above, using SELECT count(*)... instead of SELECT * ... to get the number of matched records:

```
my $query = "SELECT count(*) FROM test WHERE id < 10";
```

This should be much faster, since you can remove any SORT BY and similar attributes.

You might think that the DBI method $sth->rows will tell you how many records will be returned, but unfortunately it will not. You can rely on a row count only after a do (for some specific operations, such as update and delete), after a non-select execute, or after fetching all the rows of a select statement.

For select statements, it is generally not possible to know how many rows will be returned except by fetching them all. Some DBD drivers will return the number of rows the application has fetched so far, but others may return -1 until all rows have been fetched. Thus, use of the rows method with select statements is not recommended.

mysql_use_result Versus mysql_store_result Attributes

Many mod_perl developers use MySQL as their preferred relational database server because of its speed. Depending on the situation, it may be possible to change the way in which the DBD::mysql driver delivers data. The two attributes mysql_use_result and mysql_store_result influence the speed and size of the processes.

You can tell the DBD::mysql driver to change the default behavior before you start to fetch the results:

```
my $sth = $dbh->prepare($query);
$sth->{"mysql_use_result"} = 1;
```

This forces the driver to use mysql_use_result rather than mysql_store_result. The former is faster and uses less memory, but it tends to block other processes, which is why mysql_store_result is the default.

Think about it in client/server terms. When you ask the server to spoon-feed you the data as you use it, the server process must buffer the data, tie up that thread, and possibly keep database locks open for a long time. So if you read a row of data and ponder it for a while, the tables you have locked are still locked, and the server is busy talking to you every so often. That is the situation with mysql_use_result.

On the other hand, if you just suck down the whole data set to the client, then the server is free to serve other requests. This improves parallelism, since rather than blocking each other by doing frequent I/O, the server and client are working at the same time. That is the situation with mysql_store_result.

As the MySQL manual suggests, you should not use mysql_use_result if you are doing a lot of processing for each row on the client side. This can tie up the server and prevent other threads from updating the tables.

If you are using some other DBD driver, check its documentation to see if it provides the flexibility of DBD::mysql in this regard.

Running Two or More Relational Databases

Sometimes you end up running many databases on the same machine. These might have very different needs. For example, one may handle user sessions (updated frequently but with tiny amounts of data), and another may contain large sets of data that are hardly ever updated. You might be able to improve performance by running two differently tuned database servers on one machine. The frequently updated database can gain a lot from fast disk access, whereas the database with mostly static data could benefit from lots of caching.

Caching prepare( ) Statements

You can also benefit from persistent connections by replacing prepare( ) with prepare_cached( ). That way you will always be sure that you have a good statement handle and you will get some caching benefit. The downside is that you are going to pay for DBI to parse your SQL and do a cache lookup every time you call prepare_cached( ). This will give a big performance boost to database servers that execute prepare( ) quite slowly (e.g., Oracle), but it might add an unnecessary overhead with servers such as MySQL that do this operation very quickly.

Be warned that some databases (e.g., PostgreSQL and Sybase) don't support caches of prepared plans. With Sybase you could open multiple connections to achieve the same result, but this is at the risk of getting deadlocks, depending on what you are trying to do!

Another pitfall to watch out for lies in the fact that prepare_cached( ) actually gives you a reference to the *same* cached statement handle, not just a similar copy. So you can't do this:

```
my $sth1 = $dbh->prepare_cached('SELECT name FROM table WHERE id=?');
my $sth2 = $dbh->prepare_cached('SELECT name FROM table WHERE id=?');
```

because $sth1 and $sth2 are now the same object! If you try to use them independently, your code will fail.

Make sure to read the DBI manpage for the complete documentation of this method and the latest updates.

DBI Debug Techniques

Sometimes the code that talks to the database server doesn't seem to work. It's important to know how to debug this code at the DBI level. Here is how this debugging can be accomplished.

To log a trace of DBI statement execution, you must set the DBI_TRACE environment variable. The PerlSetEnv DBI_TRACE directive must appear before you load Apache::DBI and DBI.

For example, if you use Apache::DBI, modify your *httpd.conf* file with:

```
PerlSetEnv DBI_TRACE "3=~/tmp/dbitrace.log"
PerlModule Apache::DBI
```

Replace 3 with the trace level you want. The traces from each request will be appended to */tmp/dbitrace.log*. Note that the logs will probably be interleaved if requests are processed concurrently.

Within your code, you can control trace generation with the trace( ) method:

```
DBI->trace($trace_level)
DBI->trace($trace_level, $trace_filename)
```

DBI trace information can be enabled for all handles using this DBI class method. To enable trace information for a specific handle, use the similar $dbh->trace method.

Using the trace option with a $dbh or $sth handle is useful to limit the trace information to the specific bit of code that you are debugging.

The trace levels are:

0   Trace disabled

1   Trace DBI method calls returning with results

2   Trace method entry with parameters and exit with results

3   As above, adding some high-level information from the driver and also adding some internal information from the DBI

4   As above, adding more detailed information from the driver and also including DBI mutex information when using threaded Perl

5+   As above, but with more and more obscure information

References

- "Introduction to Structured Query Language": *http://web.archive.org/web/20011116021648/http://w3.one.net/~jhoffman/sqltut.htm*
- "SQL for Web Nerds," by Philip Greenspun: *http://philip.greenspun.com/sql/*
- DBI-related information: *http://dbi.perl.org/*
- *Programming the Perl DBI*, by Alligator Descartes and Tim Bunce (O'Reilly)
- "DBI Examples and Performance Tuning," by Jeffrey Baker: *http://www.saturn5.com/~jwb/dbi-examples.html*
- *SQL Fundamentals*, by John J Patrick (Prentice Hall)
- *SQL in a Nutshell*, by Kevin Kline with Daniel Kline (O'Reilly)

## PART IV

Debugging and Troubleshooting

If the rest of this book is about how to use mod_perl properly, this section is about what to do when things go wrong. It contains three chapters:

Chapter 21, *Error Handling and Debugging*, explains what various errors from Apache, Perl, or mod_perl might indicate, and what you can do about them.

Chapter 22, *Troubleshooting mod_perl*, is about what you can do to fix mod_perl problems at all stages, from configuration to compilation to runtime to shutdown.

Chapter 23, *Getting Help and Online Resources*, points you to various books, online documentation, mailing lists, etc. that can help bail you out when you're really stuck.

## CHAPTER 21

Error Handling and Debugging

Every programmer needs to know how to debug his programs. It is an easy task with plain Perl: just invoke the program with the *-d* flag to invoke the debugger. Under mod_perl, however, you have to jump through a few hoops.

In this chapter we explain how to correctly handle server, program, and user errors and how to keep your user loyal to your service by displaying good error messages.

We also demonstrate how you can peek at what is going on in a mod_perl-enabled server while it is running: for example, monitoring the value of a global variable, seeing what database connections are open, tracing what modules were loaded and their paths, checking the value of @INC, and much more.

It's been said that there's always one more bug in any given program. Bugs that show symptoms during the development cycle are usually easily found. As their number diminishes, the bugs become harder to find. Subtle interactions between software components can create bugs that aren't easily reproduced. In such cases, tools and techniques that can help track down the offending code come in handy.

Warnings and Errors Explained

The Perl interpreter distinguishes between warnings and errors. *Warnings* are messages that the Perl interpreter prints to STDERR (or to Apache's error log under mod_perl). These messages indicate that Perl thinks there is a problem with your code, but they do not prevent the code from running. *Errors* are output in the same way as warnings, but the program terminates after an error. For example, errors occur if your code uses invalid syntax. If a die( ) occurs outside of any exception-handling eval, it behaves just like an error, with a message being output and program execution terminating.

For someone new to Perl programming, the warning and error messages output by Perl can be confusing and worrysome. In this section we will show you how to interpret Perl's messages, and how to track down and solve the problems that cause them.

The Importance of Warnings

Just like errors, Perl's optional warnings, if they are enabled, go to the *error_log* file. You have enabled them in your development server, haven't you? We discussed the various techniques to enable warnings in Chapters 4 and 6, but we will repeat them in this section.

The code you write lives a dual life. In the first life it is written, tested, debugged, improved, tested, debugged, rewritten, retested, and debugged again. In the second life it's just *used*.

A significant part of the script's first life is spent on the developer's machine. The second life is spent on the production server, where the code is supposed to be perfect.

When you develop the code you want all the help you can get to spot possible problems. By enabling warnings you will ensure that Perl gives you all the help it can to identify actual or potential problems in your code. Whenever you see an error or warning in the *error_log*, you *must* try to get rid of it.

But why bother, if the program runs and seems to work?

- The Perl interpreter issues warnings because it thinks that something's wrong with your code. The Perl interpreter is rarely wrong; if you ignore the warnings it provides, you may well encounter problems later, perhaps when the code is used on the production server.

- If each invocation of a script generates any superfluous warnings, it will be very hard to catch real problems. The warnings that seem important will be lost amongst the mass of "unimportant" warnings that you didn't bother to fix. All warnings are important, and all warnings can be dealt with.

On the other hand, on a production server, you really want to turn warnings off. And there are good reasons for this:

- There is no added value in having the same warning showing up, again and again, triggered by thousands of script invocations. If your code isn't very clean and generates even a single warning per script invocation, on the heavily loaded server you will end up with a huge *error_log* file in a short time.

  The warning-elimination phase is supposed to be a part of the development process and should be done before the code goes live.

- In any Perl script, not just under mod_perl, enabling runtime warnings has a performance impact.

mod_perl provides a very simple solution to handling warnings, so you should avoid enabling warnings in the scripts themselves unless you really have to. Let mod_perl control this mode globally. All you need to do is put the directive:

```
PerlWarn On
```

in *httpd.conf* on your development machine and the directive:

```
PerlWarn Off
```

on the live machine.

If there is a piece of code that generates warnings and you want to disable them only in that code, you can do that too. The Perl special variable $^W allows you to dynamically turn warnings mode on and off.

```
{
    local $^W = 0;
    # some code that generates innocuous warnings
}
```

Don't forget to localize the setting inside a block. By localizing the variable you switch warnings off only within the scope of the block and ensure that the original value of $^W is restored upon exit from the block. Without localization, the setting of $^W will affect *all* the requests handled by the Apache child process that changed this variable, for *all* the scripts it executes—not just the one that changed $^W!

Starting from Perl 5.6.0 you can use the warnings pragma:

```
{
    no warnings;
    # some code that generates innocuous warnings
}
```

The diagnostics pragma can shed more light on errors and warnings, as we will see in the following sections.

The diagnostics pragma

This pragma extends the terse diagnostics normally emitted during the compilation and runtime phases and augments them with the more verbose and endearing descriptions found in the *perldiag* manpage.

Like any other pragma, diagnostics is invoked with use, by placing:

```
use diagnostics;
```

in your program. This also turns warnings mode on for the scope of the program.

This pragma is especially useful when you are new to Perl and want a better explanation of the errors and warnings. It's also helpful when you encounter some warning you've never seen before—e.g., when a new warning has been introduced in an upgraded version of Perl.

You may not want to leave diagnostics mode on for your production server. For each warning, diagnostics mode generates about ten times more output than warnings mode. If your code generates warnings that go into the *error_log* file, with the diagnostics pragma you will use disk space much faster.

Diagnostics mode adds a large performance overhead in comparison with just having the warnings mode on. You can see the benchmark results in Chapter 9.

Curing "Internal Server Error" Problems

Say you've just installed a new script, and when you try it out you see the grey screen of death saying "Internal Server Error" (Figure 21-1). Or even worse, you've had a script running on a production server for a long time without problems, when the same grey screen starts to show up occasionally for no apparent reason.

Figure 21-1. Internal Server Error

How can you find out what the problem is, before you actually attempt to solve it?

The first problem is determining the location of the error message.

You have been coding in Perl for years, and whenever an error occurred in the past it was displayed in the same terminal window from which you started the script. But when you work with a web server, the errors do not show up in a terminal. In many cases, the server has no terminal to which to send the error messages.

Actually, the error messages don't disappear; they end up in the *error_log* file. Its location is specified by the ErrorLog directive in *httpd.conf*. The default setting is:

```
ErrorLog logs/error_log
```

where *logs/error_log* is appended to the value of the ServerRoot directive.

If you've followed the convention we've used in this book and your ServerRoot is:

```
ServerRoot /home/httpd/httpd_perl
```

the full path to the file will be */home/httpd/httpd_perl/logs/error_log*.

Whenever you see "Internal Server Error" in a browser it's time to look at this file.

There are cases when errors don't go to the *error_log* file. This can happen when the server is starting and hasn't gotten as far as opening the *error_log* file for writing before it needs to write an error message. In that case, Apache writes the messages to STDERR. If you have entered a nonexistent directory path in your ErrorLog directive in *httpd.conf*, the error message will be printed to STDERR. If the error happens when the server executes a PerlRequire, PerlModule, or other startup-time directive you might also see output sent to STDERR. If you haven't redirected Apache's STDERR, then the messages are printed to the console (tty, terminal) from which you started the server.

Note that when you're running the server in single-process mode (*httpd -X*), the usual startup message:

```
Apache/1.3.24 (Unix) mod_perl/1.26 configured
```

won't appear in the *error_log* file. Also, any startup warnings will be printed to the console, since in this mode the server redirects its STDERR stream to the *error_log* file only at a later stage.

The first problem is solved: we know where the error messages are.

The second problem is, how useful is the error message?

The usefulness of the error message depends to some extent on the programmer's coding style. An uninformative message might not help you spot and fix the error.

For example, let's take a function that opens a file passed to it as a parameter for reading. It does nothing else with the file. Here's the first version of the code:

```perl
my $r = shift;
$r->send_http_header('text/plain');

sub open_file {
    my $filename = shift;
    die "No filename passed" unless defined $filename;
    open FILE, $filename or die;
}

open_file("/tmp/test.txt");
```

Let's assume that */tmp/test.txt* doesn't exist, so the open( ) call will fail to open the file. When we call this script from our browser, the browser returns an "Internal Server Error" message and we see the following error appended to *error_log*:

```
Died at /home/httpd/perl/test.pl line 9.
```

We can use the hint Perl kindly gave to us to find where in the code die( ) was called. However, we still won't necessarily know what filename was passed to this subroutine to cause the program termination.

If we have only one function call, as in the example above, the task of finding the problematic filename is trivial. Now let's add one more open_file() function call and assume that of the two, only the file */tmp/test.txt* exists:

```
open_file("/tmp/test.txt");
open_file("/tmp/test2.txt");
```

When you execute the above call, you will see:

```
Died at /home/httpd/perl/test.pl line 9.
```

Based on this error message, can you tell what file your program failed to open? Probably not. Let's improve it by showing the name of the file that failed:

```
sub open_file {
    my $filename = shift;
    die "No filename passed" unless defined $filename;
    open FILE, $filename or die "failed to open $filename";
}

open_file("/tmp/test2.txt");
```

When we execute the above code, we see:

```
failed to open /tmp/test2.txt at
    /home/httpd/perl/test.pl line 9.
```

which obviously makes a big difference, since now we know what file we failed to open.

By the way, if you append a newline to the end of the message you pass to die(), Perl won't report the line number at which the error has happened. If you write:

```
open FILE, $filename or die "failed to open $filename\n";
```

the error message will be:

```
failed to open /tmp/test2.txt
```

which gives you very little to go on. It's very hard to debug with such uninformative error messages.

The warn() function outputs an error message in the same way as die(), but whereas die() causes program termination, execution continues normally after a warn(). Just like with die(), if you add a newline to the end of the message, the filename and the line number from which warn() was called won't be logged.

You might want to use warn() instead of die() if the failure isn't critical. Consider the following code:

```
if (open FILE, $filename) {
    # do something with the file
    close FILE;
}
else {
    warn "failed to open $filename";
}
# more code here...
```

However, unless you have a really good reason to do otherwise, you should generally die( ) when your code encounters any problem whatsoever. It can be very hard to catch a problem that manifests itself only several hundred lines after the problem was caused.

A different approach for producing useful warnings and error messages is to print the function call stack backtrace. The Carp module comes to our aid with its cluck( ) function. Consider the script in Example 21-1.

Example 21-1. warnings.pl

```
#!/usr/bin/perl -w

use strict;
use Carp ();
local $SIG{__WARN__} = \&Carp::cluck;

correct();
incorrect();

sub correct   { print_value("Perl"); }
sub incorrect { print_value(); }

sub print_value {
  my $var = shift;
  print "My value is $var\n";
}
```

Carp::cluck( ) is assigned as a warnings signal handler. Whenever a warning is triggered, this function will be called. When we execute the script, we see:

```
My value is Perl
Use of uninitialized value at ./warnings.pl line 15.
  main::print_value() called at ./warnings.pl line 11
  main::incorrect() called at ./warnings.pl line 8
My value is
```

Take a moment to understand the stack trace in the warning. The deepest calls are printed first. So the second line tells us that the warning was triggered in print_value( ) and the third line tells us that print_value( ) was called by the subroutine incorrect( ):

```
script -> incorrect() -> print_value()
```

When we look at the source code for the function incorrect( ), we see that we forgot to pass the variable to the print_value( ) function. Of course, when you write a subroutine like print_value( ), it's a good idea to check the passed arguments before starting execution. We omitted that step to contrive an easily debuggable example.

You can also call Carp::cluck( ) directly in your code, and it will produce the call-stack backtrace for you. This is usually very useful during the code development phase.

Carp::confess() is like Carp::cluck(), but it acts as a die() function (i.e., terminates the program) and prints the call-stack backtrace. The functions Carp::carp() and Carp::croak() are two other equivalents of warn() and die(), respectivily, but they report about the caller of the function in which they are used, rather the function itself.

In some cases the built-in caller() function can be useful as well, but it can be a bit cumbersome to use when you need to peek several levels up the call stack.

When using the warn() and die() functions, be aware of the following pitfall. Here the message passed to die() is printed with no problems, assuming the file *does_not_exist* actually doesn't exist:

```
panic% perl -e 'open F, "/does_not_exist" or die "cannot open the file"'
```

But now try the same code using the equivalent || operator:

```
panic% perl -e 'open F, "/does_not_exist" || die "cannot open the file"'
```

Nothing happens! The pitfall lies in the precedence of the || operator. The above call is equal to:

```
panic% perl -e 'open F, ("/does_not_exist" || die "cannot open the file")'
```

where the left part returns true, and makes this call equivalent to:

```
panic% perl -e 'open F, "/does_not_exist"'
```

So the die() part has effectively disappeared. Make sure you always use the low-precendence logical OR operator or in this situation. Alternatively, you can use parentheses, but this is less visually appealing:

```
panic% perl -e 'open(F, "/does_not_exist") || die("cannot open the file")'
```

Only the first pair of parentheses is really needed here, but to be consistent we use them through the whole statement.

Now let's return to improving the warning and error messages. The failing code reports the names of the problematic files, but we still don't know the real reason for the failure. Let's try to improve the warn() example. The -r operator tests whether the file is readable:

```
if (-r $filename) {
    open FILE, $filename;
    # do something with file
}
else {
    warn "Couldn't open $filename - doesn't exist or is not readable";
}
```

Now if we cannot read the file we do not even try to open it. But we still see a warning in *error_log*:

```
Couldn't open /tmp/test.txt - doesn't exist or is not readable
at /home/httpd/perl/test.pl line 9.
```

The warning tells us the reason for the failure, so we don't have to go to the code and check what it was trying to do with the file.

It could be quite a coding overhead to explain all the possible failure reasons that way, but why reinvent the wheel? We already have the reason for the failure stored in the $! variable. Let's go back to the open_file( ) function:

```
sub open_file {
    my $filename = shift;
    die "No filename passed" unless defined $filename;
    open FILE, $filename or die "failed to open $filename: $!";
}

open_file("/tmp/test.txt");
```

This time, if open( ) fails we see:

```
failed to open /tmp/test.txt: No such file or directory
at /home/httpd/perl/test.pl line 9.
```

Now we have all the information we need to debug these problems: we know what line of code triggered die( ), we know what file we were trying to open, and we also know the reason, provided by Perl's $! variable.

Note that there's a big difference between the following two commonly seen bits of Perl code:

```
open FILE, $filename or die "Can't open $filename: $!";
open FILE, $filename or die "Can't open $filename!";
```

The first bit is helpful; the second is just rude. Please do your part to ease human suffering, and use the first version, not the second.

To show our useful error messages in action, let's cause an error. We'll create the file */tmp/test.txt* as a different user and make sure that it isn't readable by Apache processes:

```
panic% touch /tmp/test.txt
panic% chmod 0600 /tmp/test.txt # -rw-------
```

Now when we execute the latest version of the code, we see:

```
failed to open /tmp/test.txt: Permission denied
at /home/httpd/perl/test.pl line 9.
```

Here we see a different reason: we created a file that doesn't belong to the user the server runs as (usually *nobody*). It does not have permission to read the file.

Now you can see that it's much easier to debug your code if you validate the return values of the system calls and properly code arguments to die( ) and warn( ) calls. The open( ) function is just one of the many system calls Perl provides.

Second problem solved: we now have useful error messages.

So now you can code and see error messages from mod_perl scripts and modules as easily as if they were plain Perl scripts that you execute from a shell.

Making Use of the error_log

It's a good idea to keep the *error_log* open all the time in a dedicated terminal using `tail -f`:

```
panic% tail -f /home/httpd/httpd_perl/logs/error_log
```

or `less -S`:

```
panic% less -S /home/httpd/httpd_perl/logs/error_log
```

You can use whichever one you prefer (the latter allows you to navigate around the file, search, etc.). This will ensure that you see all the errors and warnings as they happen.

Another tip is to create a shell *alias*, to make it easier to execute the above commands. In a C-style shell, use:

```
panic% alias err "tail -f /home/httpd/httpd_perl/logs/error_log"
```

In a Bourne-style shell, use:

```
panic% alias err='tail -f /home/httpd/httpd_perl/logs/error_log'
```

From now on, in the shell you set the alias in, executing:

```
panic% err
```

will execute *tail -f /home/httpd/httpd_perl/logs/error_log*. If you are using a C-style shell, put the alias into your *~/.cshrc* file or its equivalent. For setting this alias globally to all users, put it into */etc/csh.cshrc* or similar. If you are using a Bourne-style shell, the corresponding files are usually *~/.bashrc* and */etc/profile*.

Displaying Errors to Users

If you spend a lot of time browsing the Internet, you will see many error messages, ranging from generic but useless messages like "An error has happened" to the cryptic ones that no one understands. If you are developing a user-friendly system, it's important to understand that the errors are divided into at least two major groups: *user related* and *server related*. When an error happens, you want to notify either a user or a server administrator, according to the category of the error. In some cases you may want to notify both.

If you set a file-upload limit to 1 MB and a user tries to upload a file bigger than the limit, it is a user error. You should report this error to the user, explain why the error has happened, and tell the user what to do to resolve the problem. Since we are talking about the Web, the error should be sent to the user's browser. A system administrator usually doesn't care about this kind of error, and therefore probably shouldn't be notified, but it may be an indication of an attempt to compromise the server, so that may be a reason to notify the administrator.

If the user has successfully uploaded a file, but the server has failed to save this file for some reason (e.g., it ran out of free disk space), the error should be logged in *error_log* if possible and the system administrator should be notified by email, pager, or similar means. Since the user couldn't accomplish what she was trying to do, you must tell her that the operation failed. The user probably doesn't care why the operation has failed, but she would want to know how to resolve it (e.g., in the worst case, tell her to try again later). The actual reason for the error probably shouldn't be displayed—if you do, it will probably only confuse the user. Instead, you should nicely explain that something went wrong and that the system administrator has been notified and will take care of the problem as soon as possible. If the service is very mission-critical, you probably need to provide the user with some problem tracking number and a way to contact a human, so she will be able to figure out when the problem has been resolved. Alternatively, you may want to ask for the user's email address and use this to follow up on the problem.

Some applications use:

```
use CGI::Carp qw(fatalsToBrowser);
```

which sends all the errors to the browser. This module might be useful in development, if you have a problem accessing your server using an interactive session, so you can see the contents of the *error_log* file. But please don't leave this line in the production version of your code. Instead, trap the errors and decide what to do about each error separately. To trap errors, you can use the eval( ) exception-handling mechanism:*

```
eval {
    # do something
};
if ($@) {
    # decide what to do about the error stored in $@
}
```

which is equivalent to the C++/Java/other languages concept of:

```
try {
    # do something
}
catch {
    # do something about errors
}
```

There are also CPAN modules, such as Error and Exception::Class, that use the same approach but provide a special interface for doing exception handling (and also provide additional functionality).

Another technique is to assign a signal handler:

```
$SIG{__DIE__} = sub {
    print STDERR "error: ", join("\n", @_), "\n";
    exit;
};
```

---

* Notice the semicolon after the eval { } block.

When die( ) is called, this anonymous function will be invoked and the argument list to die( ) will be forwarded to it. So if later in the code you write:

```
die "good bye, cruel world";
```

the code will print to STDERR (which under mod_perl usually ends up in *error_log*):

```
error: good bye, cruel world
```

and the normal program flow will be aborted, since the handler has called exit( ).

If you don't localize this setting as:

```
local $SIG{__DIE__} = sub {...};
```

it affects the whole process. It also interferes with Perl's normal exception mechanism, shown earlier; in fact, it breaks Perl's exception handling, because a signal handler will be called before you get the chance to examine $@ after calling the eval block.

You can attempt to work around this problem by checking the value of $^S, which is true when the code is running in the eval block. If you are using Apache::Registry or a similar module, the code is always executed within an eval block, so this is not a good solution.

Since the signal handler setting is global, it's possible that some other module might try to assign its own signal handler for __DIE__, and therefore there will be a mess. The two signal handlers will conflict with each other, leading to unexpected behavior. You should avoid using this technique, and use Perl's standard eval exception-handling mechanism instead. For more information about exception handling, see *http://perl.apache.org/docs/general/perl_reference.html#Exception_Handling_for_mod_perl*.

Debugging Code in Single-Server Mode

Normally, Apache runs one parent process and several children. The parent starts new child processes as required, logs errors, kills off child processes that have served MaxRequestsPerChild, etc. But it is the child processes that serve the actual requests from web browsers. Because the multiprocess model can get in your way when you're trying to find a bug, sometimes running the server in single-process mode (with -X) is very important for testing during the development phase.

You may want to test that your application correctly handles global variables, if you have any. It is best to have as few globals as possible—ideally none—but sometimes you just can't do without them. It's hard to test globals with multiple servers executing your code, since each child has a different set of values for its global variables.

Imagine that you have a random( ) subroutine that returns a random number, and you have the following script:

```
use vars qw($num);
$num ||= random( );
print ++$num;
```

This script initializes the variable $num with a random value, then increments it on each request and prints it out. Running this script in a multiple-server environment will result in something like 1, 9, 4, 19 (a different number each time you hit the browser's reload button), since each time your script will be served by a different child. But if you run in *httpd -X* single-server mode, you will get 6, 7, 8, 9... assuming that random( ) returned 6 on the first call.

But do not get too obsessive with this mode—working in single-server mode sometimes hides problems that show up when you switch to normal (multiple-server) mode.

Consider an application that allows you to change the configuration at runtime. Let's say the script produces a form to change the background color of the page. This isn't good design, but for the sake of demonstrating the potential problem we will assume that our script doesn't write the changed background color to the disk—it simply stores it in memory, like this:

```
use CGI;
my $q = CGI->new( );
use vars qw($bgcolor);
$bgcolor ||= "white";
$bgcolor = $q->param('bgcolor') if $q->param('bgcolor');
```

where $bgcolor is set to a default "white" if it's not yet set (otherwise, the value from the previous setting is used). Now if a user request updates the color, the script updates the global variable.

So you have typed in "yellow" for the new background color, and in response, your script prints back the HTML with the background color yellow—you think that's it! If only it was so simple.

If you keep running in single-server mode you will never notice that you have a problem. However, if you run the same code in normal server mode, after you submit the color change you will get the result as expected, but when you call the same URL again (not via reload!) the chances are that you will get back the original default color (white, in this case). Only the child that processed the color-change request has its $bgcolor variable set to "yellow"; the rest still have "white". This shows that the design is incorrect—the information is stored in only one process, whereas many may be running.

Remember that children can't share information directly, except for data that they inherited from their parent when they were created and that hasn't subsequently been modified.

There are many solutions to this example problem: you could use a hidden HTML form variable for the color to be remembered, or store it in some more permanent place on the server side (a file or database), or you could use shared memory, and so on.

Note that when the server is running in single-process mode, and the response includes HTML with <img> tags, the loading of the images will take a long time for browsers that try to take an advantage of the KeepAlive feature (e.g., Netscape). These browsers try to open multiple connections and keep them open. Because there is only one server process listening, each connection has to finish before the next can start. Turn off KeepAlive in *httpd.conf* to avoid this effect. Alternatively (assuming that the image-size parameters are included, so that a browser will be able to render the rest of the page) you can press Stop after a few seconds.

In addition, you should be aware that when running with -X you will not see the status messages that the parent server normally writes to the *error_log* file ("Server started", "Server stopped", etc.). Since *httpd -X* causes the server to handle all requests itself, without forking any children, there is no controlling parent to write the status messages.

Tracing System Calls

Most Unix-style operating systems offer a "tracing utility" that intercepts and records the system calls that are called by a process and the signals that are received by a process. In this respect it is similar to gdb. The name of each system call, its arguments, and its return value are printed to STDERR or to the specified file.

The tracing utility is a useful diagnostic, instructional, and debugging tool. You can learn a lot about the underlying system while examining traces of the running programs. In the case of mod_perl, tracing improves performance by enabling us to spot and eliminate redundant system calls. It also useful in cases of problem debugging— for example, when some process hangs.

Depending on your operating system, you should have available one of the utilities *strace*, *truss*, *tusc*, *ktrace*, or similar. In this book we will use the Linux *strace* utility.

There are two ways to get a trace of the process with *strace*. One way is to tell *strace* to start the process and do the tracing on it:

```
panic% strace perl -le 'print "mod_perl rules"'
```

Another way is to tell *strace* to attach to a process that's already running:

```
panic% strace -p PID
```

Replace PID with the process number you want to check on.

Many other useful arguments are accepted by *strace*. For example, you can tell it to trace only specific system calls:

```
panic% strace -e trace=open,write,close,nanosleep \
    perl -le 'print "mod_perl rules"'
```

In this example we have asked *strace* to show us only the calls to open(), write(), close(), and nanosleep(), which reduces the output generated by strace, making it simpler to understand—providing you know what you are looking for.

The generated traces are too long (unless filtered with *trace=tag*) to be presented here completely. For example, if we ask for only the `write( )` system calls, we get the following output:

```
panic% strace -e trace=write perl -le 'print "mod_perl rules"'
write(1, "mod_perl rules\n", 15mod_perl rules
) = 15
```

The output of the Perl one-liner gets mixed with the trace, so the actual trace is:

```
write(1, "mod_perl rules\n", 15) = 15
```

Note that the newline was automatically appended because of the *-l* option on the Perl command line.

Each line in the trace contains the system call name, followed by its arguments in parentheses and its return value. In the last example, a string of 15 characters was written to `STDOUT`, whose file descriptor is 1. And we can see that they were all successfully written, since the `write( )` system call has returned a value of 15, the number of characters written.

The *strace* manpage provides a comprehensive explanation of how to interpret all parts of the traces; you may want to refer to this manpage to learn more about it.

Tracing mod_perl-Specific Perl Calls

When we are interested in mod_perl-level events, it's quite hard to use system-level tracing, both because of the system trace's verbosity and because it's hard to find the boundary between events. Therefore, we need to do mod_perl-level tracing.

To enable mod_perl debug tracing, configure mod_perl with the `PERL_TRACE` option:

```
panic% perl Makefile.PL PERL_TRACE=1 ...
```

The trace levels can then be enabled via the `MOD_PERL_TRACE` environment variable which can contain any combination of the following options.

For startup processing:

c Trace directive handling during Apache (non-mod_perl) configuration-directive handling

d Trace directive handling during mod_perl directive processing during configuration read

s Trace processing of `<Perl>` sections

For runtime processing:

h Trace Perl handler callbacks during the processing of incoming requests and during startup (`PerlChildInitHandler`)

g Trace global variable handling, interpreter construction, `END` blocks, etc.

Alternatively, setting the environment variable to all will include all the options listed above.

One way of setting this variable is by adding this directive to *httpd.conf*:

```
PerlSetEnv MOD_PERL_TRACE all
```

For example, if you want to see a trace of the PerlRequire and PerlModule directives as they are executed, use:

```
PerlSetEnv MOD_PERL_TRACE d
```

You can also use the command-line environment, setting:

```
panic% setenv MOD_PERL_TRACE all
panic% ./httpd -X
```

If running under a Bourne-style shell, you can set the environment variable for only the duration of a single command:

```
panic% MOD_PERL_TRACE=all ./httpd -X
```

If using a different shell, you should try using the *env* utility, which has a similar effect:

```
panic% env MOD_PERL_TRACE=all ./httpd -X
```

For example, if you want to trace the processing of the Apache::Reload setting during startup and you want to see what happens when the following directives are processed:

```
PerlModule Apache::Reload
PerlInitHandler Apache::Reload
PerlSetVar ReloadAll Off
PerlSetVar ReloadModules "Apache::* Book::*"
```

do:

```
panic% setenv MOD_PERL_TRACE d
panic% ./httpd -X
PerlModule: arg='Apache::Reload'
loading perl module 'Apache::Reload'...ok
loading perl module 'Apache'...ok
loading perl module 'Tie::IxHash'...not ok

init `PerlInitHandler' stack
perl_cmd_push_handlers: @PerlInitHandler, 'Apache::Reload'
pushing `Apache::Reload' into `PerlInitHandler' handlers

perl_cmd_var: 'ReloadAll' = 'Off'

perl_cmd_var: 'ReloadModules' = 'Apache::* Book::*'
```

We have removed the rest of the trace and separated the output trace into four groups, each equivalent to the appropriate setting from our configuration example. So we can see that:

```
PerlModule Apache::Reload
```

loads the Apache::Reload and Apache modules but fails to load Tie::IxHash, since we don't have it installed (which is not a fatal error in the case of Apache::Reload).

The following initializes the PerlInitHandler stack, as it wasn't yet used, and pushes Apache::Reload there:

```
PerlInitHandler Apache::Reload
```

The last two directives call perl_cmd_var() to set the Perl variables that can be retrieved in the code with dir_config(), as explained in Chapter 4:

```
PerlSetVar ReloadAll Off
PerlSetVar ReloadModules "Apache::* Book::*"
```

Now let's look at the trace of the handlers called during the execution of this code:

```
use strict;
my $r = shift;
$r->send_http_header("text/plain");
$r->print("Hello");
```

We set MOD_PERL_TRACE to trace handler calls with *h*:

```
panic% setenv MOD_PERL_TRACE h
panic% ./httpd -X &
panic% tail -f /home/httpd/httpd_perl/logs/error_log
running 1 server configured stacked handlers for /perl/test.pl...
calling &{PerlInitHandler->[0]} (1 total)
&{PerlInitHandler->[0]} returned status=0
`PerlInitHandler' push_handlers() stack is empty
PerlInitHandler handlers returned 0

running 1 server configured stacked handlers for /perl/test.pl...
calling &{PerlPostReadRequestHandler->[0]} (1 total)
&{PerlPostReadRequestHandler->[0]} returned status=0
`PerlPostReadRequestHandler' push_handlers() stack is empty
PerlPostReadRequestHandler handlers returned 0

`PerlTransHandler' push_handlers() stack is empty
PerlTransHandler handlers returned -1

`PerlInitHandler' push_handlers() stack is empty
PerlInitHandler handlers returned -1

`PerlHeaderParserHandler' push_handlers() stack is empty

`PerlAccessHandler' push_handlers() stack is empty
PerlAccessHandler handlers returned -1

`PerlTypeHandler' push_handlers() stack is empty
PerlTypeHandler handlers returned -1

running 1 server configured stacked handlers for /perl/test.pl...
calling &{PerlFixupHandler->[0]} (1 total)
registering PerlCleanupHandler
&{PerlFixupHandler->[0]} returned status=-1
```

```
`PerlFixupHandler' push_handlers() stack is empty
PerlFixupHandler handlers returned -1

running 1 server configured stacked handlers for /perl/test.pl...
calling &{PerlHandler->[0]} (1 total)
&{PerlHandler->[0]} returned status=0
`PerlHandler' push_handlers() stack is empty
PerlHandler handlers returned 0

`PerlLogHandler' push_handlers() stack is empty
PerlLogHandler handlers returned -1

running registered cleanup handlers...
perl_call: handler is a cached CV
`PerlCleanupHandler' push_handlers() stack is empty
PerlCleanupHandler handlers returned -1
```

You can see what handlers were registered to be executed during the processing of this simple script. In our configuration we had these relevant directives:

```
PerlInitHandler Apache::Reload
PerlPostReadRequestHandler  Book::ProxyRemoteAddr
PerlFixupHandler Apache::GTopLimit
```

And you can see that they were all called:

```
calling &{PerlInitHandler->[0]} (1 total)
&{PerlInitHandler->[0]} returned status=0

calling &{PerlPostReadRequestHandler->[0]} (1 total)
&{PerlPostReadRequestHandler->[0]} returned status=0

calling &{PerlFixupHandler->[0]} (1 total)
registering PerlCleanupHandler
&{PerlFixupHandler->[0]} returned status=-1
```

In addition, when Apache::GTopLimit was running, it registered a PerlCleanupHandler, which was executed at the end:

```
running registered cleanup handlers...
perl_call: handler is a cached CV
```

Since we were executing an Apache::Registry script, the PerlHandler was executed as well:

```
running 1 server configured stacked handlers for /perl/test.pl...
calling &{PerlHandler->[0]} (1 total)
&{PerlHandler->[0]} returned status=0
`PerlHandler' push_handlers() stack is empty
PerlHandler handlers returned 0
```

So if you debug your handlers, you can see what handlers were called, whether they have registered some new handlers on the fly, and what the return status from the executed handler was.

Debugging Perl Code

It's a known fact that programmers spend a lot of time debugging their code. Sometimes we spend more time debugging code than writing it. The lion's share of the time spent on debugging is spent on finding the cause of the bug and trying to reproduce the bug at will. Usually it takes little time to fix the problem once it's understood.

A typical Perl program relies on many other modules written by other developers. Hence, no matter how good your code is, often you have to deal with bugs in the code written by someone else. No matter how hard you try to avoid learning to debug, you will have to do it at some point. And the earlier you acquire the skills, the better.

There are several levels of debugging complexity. The basic level is when Perl terminates the program during the compilation phase, before it tries to run the resulting byte code. This usually happens because there are syntax errors in the code, or perhaps because a used module is missing. Sometimes it takes quite an effort to solve these problems, since code that uses Apache core modules generally won't compile when executed from the shell. Later we will learn how to solve syntax problems in mod_perl code quite easily.

Once the program compiles and starts to run, various runtime errors may happen, usually when Perl tries to interact with external resources (e.g., trying to open a file or to open a connection to a database). If the code validates whether such external resource calls succeed and aborts the program with die( ) if they do not (including a useful error message, as we explained at the beginning of the chapter), there is nothing to debug here, because the error message gives us all the needed information. These are not bugs in our code, and it's expected that they may happen. However, if the error message is incomplete (e.g., if you didn't include $! in the error message when attempting to open a file), or the program continues to run, ignoring the failed call, then you have to figure out where the badly written code is and correct it to abort on the failure, properly reporting the problem.

Of course, there are cases where a failure to do something is not fatal. For example, consider a program that tries to open a connection to a database, and it's known that the database is being stopped every so often for maintenance. Here, the program may choose to try again and again until the database becomes available and aborts itself only after a certain timeout period. In such cases we hope that the logic is properly implemented, so it won't lead to mysterious, hard-to-detect bugs.

If the running program is properly handling external resource calls, it may still be prone to internal logical errors—i.e., when the program doesn't do what you thought you had programmed it to do. These are somewhat harder to solve than simple syntax errors, especially when there is a lot of code to be inspected and reviewed, but it's just a matter of time. Perl can help a lot; typos can often be found simply by enabling warnings. For example, if you wanted to compare two numbers, but you omitted the second = character so that you had something like if ($yes = 1) instead of if ($yes == 1), with warnings enabled, Perl will warn you that you may have meant ==.

The next level is when the program does what it's expected to do most of the time, but occasionally misbehaves. Often you'll find that print( ) statements or the Perl debugger can help, but inspection of the code generally doesn't. Sometimes it's easy to debug with print( ), dumping your data structures to a log file at some point, but typing the debug messages can become very tedious. That's where the Perl debugger comes into its own.

While print( ) statements always work, running the Perl debugger for CGI-style scripts might be quite a challenge. But with the right knowledge and tools handy, the debugging process becomes much easier. Unfortunately, there is no one easy way to debug your programs, as the debugging depends entirely on your code. It can be a nightmare to debug really complex and obscure code, but as your style matures you can learn ways to write simpler code that is easier to debug. You will probably find that when you write simpler, clearer code it does not need so much debugging in the first place.

One of the most difficult cases to debug is when the process just terminates in the middle of processing a request and aborts with a "Segmentation fault" error (possibly dumping core, by creating a file called *core* in the current directory of the process that was running). Often this happens when the program tries to access a memory area that doesn't belong to it. This is something that you rarely see with plain Perl scripts, but it can easily happen if you use modules whose guts are written in C or C++ and something goes wrong with them. Occasionally you will come across a bug in mod_perl itself (mod_perl is written in C and makes extensive use of XS macros).

In the following sections we will cover a selection of problems in detail, thoroughly discussing them and presenting a few techniques to solve them.

Locating and Correcting Syntax Errors

While developing code, we sometimes make syntax errors, such as forgetting to put a comma in a list or a semicolon at the end of a statement.

Don't Skimp on the Semicolons

Even at the end of a { } block, where a semicolon is not required at the end of the last statement, it may be better to put one in: there is a chance that you will add more code later, and when you do you might forget to add the now-required semicolon. Similarly, more items might be added later to a list; unlike many other languages, Perl has no problem when you end a list with a redundant comma.

One approach to locating syntactically incorrect code is to execute the script from the shell with the *-c* flag:

```
panic% perl -c test.pl
```

This tells Perl to check the syntax but not to run the code (actually, it will execute BEGIN blocks, END blocks, and use( ) calls, because these are considered as occurring outside the execution of your program, and they can affect whether your program compiles correctly or not).*

When checking syntax in this way it's also a good idea to add the *-w* switch to enable warnings:

```
panic% perl -cw test.pl
```

If there are errors in the code, Perl will report the errors and tell you at which line numbers in your script the errors were found. For example, if we create a file *test.pl* with the contents:

```
@list = ('foo' 'bar');
```

and do syntax validation from the command line:

```
panic% perl -cw test.pl
String found where operator expected at
        test.pl line 1, near "'foo' 'bar'"
  (Missing operator before  'bar'?)
syntax error at test.pl line 1, near "'foo' 'bar'"
test.pl had compilation errors.
```

we can learn from the error message that we are missing an operator before the 'bar' string, which is of course a comma in this case. If we place the missing comma between the two strings:

```
@list = ('foo', 'bar');
```

and run the test again:

```
panic% perl -cw test.pl
Name "main::list" used only once: possible typo at test.pl line 1.
test.pl syntax OK
```

we can see that the syntax is correct now. But Perl still warns us that we have some variable that is defined but not used. Is this a bug? Yes and no—it's what we really meant in this example, but our example doesn't actually do anything, so Perl is probably right to complain.

The next step is to execute the script, since in addition to syntax errors there may be runtime errors. These are usually the errors that cause the "Internal Server Error" response when a page is requested by a client's browser. With plain CGI scripts

---

* Perl 5.6.0 has introduced a new special variable, $^C, which is set to true when Perl is run with the *-c* flag; this provides an opportunity to have some further control over BEGIN and END blocks during syntax checking.

(running under mod_cgi) it's the same as running plain Perl scripts—just execute them and see if they work.

The whole thing is quite different with scripts that use Apache::* modules. These can be used only from within the mod_perl server environment. Such scripts rely on other code, and an environment that isn't available if you attempt to execute the script from the shell. There is no Apache request object available to the code when it is executed from the shell.

If you have a problem when using Apache::* modules, you can make a request to the script from a browser and watch the errors and warnings as they are logged to the *error_log* file. Alternatively, you can use the Apache::FakeRequest module, which tries to emulate a request and makes it possible to debug some scripts outside the mod_perl environment, as we will see in the next section.

Using Apache::FakeRequest to Debug Apache Perl Modules

Apache::FakeRequest is used to set up an empty Apache request object that can be used for debugging. The Apache::FakeRequest methods just set internal variables with the same names as the methods and returns the values of the internal variables. Initial values for methods can be specified when the object is created. The print( ) method prints to STDOUT.

Subroutines for Apache constants are also defined so that you can use Apache::Constants while debugging, although the values of the constants are hardcoded rather than extracted from the Apache source code.

Example 21-2 is a very simple module that prints a brief message to the client's browser.

Example 21-2. Book/Example.pm
```
package Book::Example;
use Apache::Constants qw(OK);

sub handler {
    my $r = shift;
    $r->send_http_header('text/plain');
    print "You are OK ", $r->get_remote_host, "\n";
    return OK;
}

1;
```

You cannot debug this module unless you configure the server to run it, by calling its handler from somewhere. So, for example, you could put in *httpd.conf*:
```
    <Location /ex>
        SetHandler perl-script
        PerlHandler Book::Example
    </Location>
```

Then, after restarting the server, you could start a browser, request the location *http://localhost/ex*, and examine the output. Tedious, no?

With the help of `Apache::FakeRequest`, you can write a little script that will emulate a request and return the output (see Example 21-3).

Example 21-3. fake.pl

```perl
#!/usr/bin/perl

use Apache::FakeRequest ();
use Book::Example ();

my $r = Apache::FakeRequest->new('get_remote_host'=>'www.example.com');
Book::Example::handler($r);
```

When you execute the script from the command line, you will see the following output as the body of the response:

```
You are OK www.example.com
```

As you can see, when `Apache::FakeRequest` was initialized, we hardcoded the Apache method `get_remote_host()` with a static value.

At the time of this writing, `Apache::FakeRequest` is far from being complete, but you may still find it useful.

If while developing your code you have to switch back and forth between the normal and fake modes, you may want to start your code in this way:

```perl
use constant MOD_PERL => $ENV{MOD_PERL};

my $r;

if (MOD_PERL) {
    $r = Apache->request;
} else {
    require Apache::FakeRequest;
    $r = Apache::FakeRequest->new;
}
```

When you run from the command line, the fake request will be used; otherwise, the usual method will be used.

Using print( ) for Debugging

The universal debugging tool across nearly all platforms and programming languages is `printf()` (or equivalent output functions). This function can send data to the console, a file, an application window, and so on. In Perl we generally use the `print()` function. With an idea of where and when the bug is triggered, a developer can insert `print()` statements into the source code to examine the value of data at certain stages of execution.

However, it is rather difficult to anticipate all the possible directions a program might take and what data might cause trouble. In addition, inline debugging code tends to add bloat and degrade the performance of an application and can also make the code harder to read and maintain. Furthermore, you have to comment out or remove the debugging print( ) calls when you think that you have solved the problem, and if later you discover that you need to debug the same code again, you need at best to uncomment the debugging code lines or, at worst, to write them again from scratch.

The constant pragma helps here. You can leave some debug printings in production code, without adding extra processing overhead, by using constants. For example, while developing the code, you can define a constant DEBUG whose value is 1:

```
package Foo;
use constant DEBUG => 1;
...
warn "entering foo" if DEBUG;
...
```

The warning will be printed, since DEBUG returns true. In production you just have to turn off the constant:

```
use constant DEBUG => 0;
```

When the code is compiled with a false DEBUG value, all those statements that are to be executed if DEBUG has a true value will be removed on the fly *at compile time*, as if they never existed. This allows you to keep some of the important debug statements in the code without any adverse impact on performance.

But what if you have many different debug categories and you want to be able to turn them on and off as you need them? In this case, you need to define a constant for each category. For example:

```
use constant DEBUG_TEMPLATE => 1;
use constant DEBUG_SESSION  => 0;
use constant DEBUG_REQUEST  => 0;
```

Now if in your code you have these three debug statements:

```
warn "template" if DEBUG_TEMPLATE;
warn "session"  if DEBUG_SESSION;
warn "request"  if DEBUG_REQUEST;
```

only the first one will be executed, as it's the only one that has a condition that evaluates to true.

Let's look at a few examples where we use print( ) to debug some problem.

In one of our applications, we wrote a function that returns a date from one week ago. This function (including the code that calls it) is shown in Example 21-4.

Example 21-4. date_week_ago.pl

```
print "Content-type: text/plain\n\n";
print "A week ago the date was ",date_a_week_ago(),"\n";

# return a date one week ago as a string in format: MM/DD/YYYY
sub date_a_week_ago {

    my @month_len = (31, 28, 31, 30, 31, 30, 31, 31, 30, 31, 30, 31);
    my($day, $month, $year) = (localtime)[3..5];

    for (my $j = 0; $j < 7; $j++) {

        $day--;
        if ($day == 0) {

            $month--;
            if ($month == 0) {
                $year--;
                $month = 12;
            }

            # there are 29 days in February in a leap year
            $month_len[1] =
                ($year % 400 == 0 or ($year % 4 == 0 and $year % 100))
                    ? 29 : 28;

            # set $day to be the last day of the previous month
            $day = $month_len[$month - 1];
        }
    }

    return sprintf "%02d/%02d/%04d", $month, $day, $year+1900;
}
```

This code is pretty straightforward. We get today's date and subtract 1 from the value of the day we get, updating the month and the year on the way if boundaries are being crossed (end of month, end of year). If we do it seven times in a loop, at the end we should get a date from a week ago.

Note that since localtime( ) returns the year as a value of current_year-1900 (which means that we don't have a century boundary to worry about), if we are in the middle of the first week of the year 2000, the value of $year returned by localtime( ) will be 100 and not 0, as one might mistakenly assume. So when the code does $year-- it becomes 99, not -1. At the end, we add 1900 to get back the correct four-digit year format. (If you plan to work with years before 1900, add 1900 to $year before the for loop.)

Also note that we have to account for leap years, where there are 29 days in February. For the other months, we have prepared an array containing the month lengths. A specific year is a leap year if it is either evenly divisible by 400 or evenly divisible by

4 and not evenly divisible by 100. For example, the year 1900 was not a leap year, but the year 2000 was a leap year. Logically written:

```
print ($year % 400 == 0 or ($year % 4 == 0 and $year % 100))
          ? 'Leap' : 'Not Leap';
```

Now when we run the script and check the result, we see that something is wrong. For example, if today is 10/23/1999, we expect the above code to print 10/16/1999. In fact, it prints 09/16/1999, which means that we have lost a month. The above code is buggy!

Let's put a few debug print( ) statements in the code, near the $month variable:

```
sub date_a_week_ago {

    my @month_len = (31, 28, 31, 30, 31, 30, 31, 31, 30, 31, 30, 31);
    my($day, $month, $year) = (localtime)[3..5];
    print "[set] month : $month\n"; # DEBUG

    for (my $j = 0; $j < 7; $j++) {

        $day--;
        if ($day == 0) {

            $month--;
            if ($month == 0) {
                $year--;
                $month = 12;
            }
            print "[loop $i] month : $month\n"; # DEBUG

            # there are 29 days in February in a leap year
            $month_len[1] =
                ($year % 400 == 0 or ($year % 4 == 0 and $year % 100))
                    ? 29 : 28;

        # set $day to be the last day of the previous month
            $day = $month_len[$month - 1];
        }
    }

    return sprintf "%02d/%02d/%04d", $month, $day, $year+1900;
}
```

When we run it we see:

```
[set] month : 9
```

This is supposed to be the number of the current month (10). We have spotted a bug, since the only code that sets the $month variable consists of a call to localtime( ). So did we find a bug in Perl? Let's look at the manpage of the localtime( ) function:

```
panic% perldoc -f localtime

Converts a time as returned by the time function to a 9-element array with the time
analyzed for the local time zone.  Typically used as follows:
```

```
#  0    1      2      3      4     5      6      7      8
($sec,$min,$hour,$mday,$mon,$year,$wday,$yday,$isdst) = localtime(time);
```

All array elements are numeric, and come straight out of a struct tm. In particular
this means that $mon has the range 0..11 and $wday has the range 0..6 with Sunday as
day 0. Also, $year is the number of years since 1900, that is, $year is 123 in year
2023, and *not* simply the last two digits of the year. If you assume it is, then you
create non-Y2K-compliant programs--and you wouldn't want to do that, would you?
[more info snipped]

This reveals that if we want to count months from 1 to 12 and not 0 to 11 we are
supposed to increment the value of $month. Among other interesting facts about
localtime( ), we also see an explanation of $year, which, as we've mentioned before,
is set to the number of years since 1900.

We have found the bug in our code and learned new things about localtime( ). To
correct the above code, we just increment the month after we call localtime( ):

```
my($day, $month, $year) = (localtime)[3..5];
$month++;
```

Other places where programmers often make mistakes are conditionals and loop
statements. For example, will the block in this loop:

```
my $c = 0;
for (my $i=0; $i <= 3; $i++) {
    $c += $i;
}
```

be executed three or four times?

If we plant the print( ) debug statement:

```
my $c = 0;
for (my $i=0; $i <= 3; $i++) {
    $c += $i;
    print $i+1,"\n";
}
```

and execute it:

```
1
2
3
4
```

we see that it gets executed four times. We could have figured this out by inspecting
the code, but what happens if instead of 3, there is a variable whose value is known
only at runtime? Using debugging print( ) statements helps to determine whether to
use < or <= to get the boundary condition right.

Using idiomatic Perl makes things much easier:

```
panic% perl -le 'my $c=0; $c += $_, print $_+1 for 0..3;'
```

Here you can plainly see that the loop is executed four times.

The same goes for conditional statements. For example, assuming that $a and $b are integers, what is the value of this statement?

```
$c = $a > $b and $a < $b ? 1 : 0;
```

One might think that $c is always set to zero, since:

```
$a > $b and $a < $b
```

is a false statement no matter what the values of $a and $b are. But C$ is not set to zero—it's set to 1 (a true value) if $a > $b; otherwise, it's set to undef (a false value). The reason for this behavior lies in operator precedence. The operator and (AND) has lower precedence than the operator = (ASSIGN); therefore, Perl sees the statement like this:

```
($c = ($a > $b) ) and ( $a < $b ? 1 : 0 );
```

which is the same as:

```
if ($c = $a > $b) {
    $a < $b ? 1 : 0;
}
```

So the value assigned to $c is the result of the logical expression:

```
$a > $b
```

Adding some debug printing will reveal this problem. The solutions are, of course, either to use parentheses to explicitly express what we want:

```
$c = ($a > $b and $a < $b) ? 1 : 0;
```

or to use a higher-precedence AND operator:

```
$c = $a > $b && $a < $b ? 1 : 0;
```

Now $c is always set to 0 (as presumably we intended).[*]

Using print( ) and Data::Dumper for Debugging

Sometimes we need to peek into complex data structures, and trying to print them out can be tricky. That's where Data::Dumper comes to the rescue. For example, if we create this complex data structure:

```
$data = {
    array => [qw(apple banana clementine damson)],
    hash  => {
        food => "vegetables",
        drink => "juice",
    },
};
```

---

[*] For more traps, refer to the *perltrap* manpage.

how do we print it out? Very easily:

```
use Data::Dumper;
print Dumper $data;
```

What we get is a pretty-printed $data:

```
$VAR1 = {
          'hash' => {
                      'food' => 'vegetables',
                      'drink' => 'juice'
                    },
          'array' => [
                       'apple',
                       'banana',
                       'clementine',
                       'damson'
                     ]
        };
```

Suppose while writing this example we made a mistake and wrote:

```
array => qw(apple banana clementine damson),
```

instead of:

```
array => [qw(apple banana clementine damson)],
```

When we pretty-printed the contents of $data we would immediately see our mistake:

```
$VAR1 = {
          'banana' => 'clementine',
          'damson' => 'hash',
          'HASH(0x80cd79c)' => undef,
          'array' => 'apple'
        };
```

That's not what we want—we have spotted the bug and can easily correct it.

You can use:

```
print STDERR Dumper $data;
```

or:

```
warn Dumper $data;
```

instead of printing to STDOUT, to have all the debug messages in the *error_log* file. This makes it even easier to debug your code, since the real output (which should normally go to the browser) is not mixed up with the debug output when the code is executed under mod_perl.

The Importance of a Good, Concise Coding Style

Don't strive for elegant, clever code. Try to develop a good coding style by writing code that is concise, yet easy to understand. It's much easier to find bugs in concise, simple code, and such code tends to have fewer bugs.

The "one week ago" example from the previous section is not concise. There is a lot of redundancy in it, and as a result it is harder to debug than it needs to be. Here is a condensed version of the main loop:

```
for (0..6) {
    next if --$day;
    $year--, $month=12 unless --$month;
    $day = $month != 2
        ? $month_len[$month-1]
        : ($year % 400 == 0 or ($year % 4 == 0 and $year % 100))
            ? 29
            : 28;
}
```

This version may seem quite difficult to understand and even harder to maintain, but for those who are used to reading idiomatic Perl, part of this code is easier to understand.

Larry Wall, the author of Perl, is a linguist. He tried to define the syntax of Perl in a way that makes working in Perl much like working in English. So it's a good idea to learn Perl's coding idioms—some of them might seem odd at first, but once you get used to them, you will find it difficult to understand how you could have lived without them. We'll present just a few of the more common Perl coding idioms here.

You should try to write code that is readable and avoids redundancy. For example, it's better to write:

```
unless ($i) {...}
```

than:

```
if ($i == 0) {...}
```

if you want to just test for truth.

Use a concise, Perlish style:

```
for my $j (0..6) {...}
```

instead of the syntax used in some other languages:

```
for (my $j=0; $j<=6; $j++) {...}
```

It's much simpler to write and comprehend code like this:

```
print "something" if $debug;
```

than this:

```
if ($debug) {
    print "something";
}
```

A good style that improves understanding and readability and reduces the chances of having a bug is shown below, in the form of yet another rewrite of our "one week ago" code:

```
for (0..6) {
    $day--;
    next if $day;

    $month--;
    unless ($month){
        $year--;
        $month=12
    }

    if($month == 2){ # February
        $day = ($year % 400 == 0 or ($year % 4 == 0 and $year % 100))
            ? 29 : 28;
    } else {
        $day = $month_len[$month-1];
    }
}
```

This is a happy medium between the excessively verbose style of the first version and the very obscure second version.

After debugging this obscure code for a while, we came up with a much simpler two-liner, which is much faster and easier to understand:

```
sub date_a_week_ago {
    my($day, $month, $year) = (localtime(time-7*24*60*60))[3..5];
    return sprintf "%02d/%02d/%04d", $month+1, $day, $year+1900;
}
```

Just take the current date in seconds since *epoch* as time( ) returns, subtract a week in seconds $(7661 \times 24 \times 60 \times 60)$,[*] and feed the result to localtime( ). Voilà—we have the date of one week ago!

Why is the last version important, when the first one works just fine? Not because of performance issues (although this last one is twice as fast as the first), but because there are more chances to have a bug in the first version than there are in the last one.

Of course, instead of inventing the date_a_week_ago( ) function and spending all this time debugging it, we could have just used a standard module from CPAN to provide the same functionality (with zero debugging time). In this case, Date::Calc comes to the rescue,[†] and we will write the code as:

```
use Date::Calc;
sub date_a_week_ago {
    my($year,$month,$day) =
        Date::Calc::Add_Delta_Days(Date::Calc::Today, -7);
    return sprintf "%02d/%02d/%04d", $month, $day, $year;
}
```

---

[*] Perl folds the constants at compile time.

[†] See also Class::Date and Date::Manip.

We simply use `Date::Calc::Today()`, which returns a list of three values—year, month, and day—which are immediately fed into the function `Date::Calc::Add_Delta_Days()`. This allows us to get the date *N* days from now in either direction. We use –7 to ask for a date from one week ago. Since we are relying on this standard CPAN module, there is not much to debug here; the function has no complicated logic where one can expect bugs. In contrast, our original implementation was really difficult to understand, and it was very easy to make mistakes.

We will use this example once again to stress that it's better to use standard modules than to reinvent them.

Introduction to the Perl Debugger

As we saw earlier, it's *almost* always possible to debug code with the help of `print()`. However, it is impossible to anticipate all the possible paths of execution through a program, and difficult to know what code to suspect when trouble occurs. In addition, inline debugging code tends to add bloat and degrade the performance of an application, although most applications offer inline debugging as a compile-time option to avoid these performance hits. In any case, this information tends to be useful only to the programmer who added the `print()` statements in the first place.

Sometimes you must debug tens of thousands of lines of Perl in an application, and while you may be a very experienced Perl programmer who can understand Perl code quite well just by looking at it, no mere mortal can even begin to understand what will actually happen in such a large application until the code is running. So to begin with you just don't know where to add your trusty `print()` statements to see what is happening inside.

The most effective way to track down a bug is often to run the program inside an interactive debugger. Most programming languages have such tools available, allowing programmers to see what is happening inside an application while it is running. The basic features of any interactive debugger allow you to:

- Stop at a certain point in the code, based on a routine name or source file and line number (this point is called a *break point*).
- Stop at a certain point in the code, based on conditions such as the value of a given variable (this is called a *conditional break point*).
- Perform an action without stopping, based on the criteria above.
- View and modify the values of variables at any time.
- Provide context information such as stack traces and source views.

It takes practice to learn the most effective ways of using an interactive debugger, but the time and effort will be paid back many times in the long run.

Perl comes with an interactive debugger called *perldb*. Giving control of your Perl program to the interactive debugger is simply a matter of specifying the *-d* command-line switch. When this switch is used, Perl inserts debugging hooks into the program syntax tree, but it leaves the job of debugging to a Perl module separate from the Perl binary itself.

We will start by reviewing a few of the basic concepts and commands provided by Perl's interactive debugger. These examples are all run from the command line, independent of mod_perl, but they will still be relevant when we work within Apache.

It might be useful to keep the *perldebug* manpage handy for reference while reading this section, and for future debugging sessions on your own.

The interactive debugger will attach to the current terminal and present you with a prompt just before the first program statement is executed. For example:

```
panic% perl -d -le 'print "mod_perl rules the world"'

Loading DB routines from perl5db.pl version 1.0402

Emacs support available.

Enter h or `h h' for help.

main::(-e:1):   print "mod_perl rules the world"
  DB<1>
```

The source line shown is the line that Perl is *about* to execute. To *single step*—i.e., execute one line at a time—use the *next* command (or just *n*). Each time you enter something in the debugger, you must finish by pressing the Return key. This will cause the line to be executed, after which execution will stop and the next line to be executed (if any) will be displayed:

```
main::(-e:1):   print "mod_perl rules the world"
  DB<1> n
mod_perl rules the world
Debugged program terminated.  Use q to quit or R to restart,
use O inhibit_exit to avoid stopping after program termination,
h q, h R or h O to get additional info.
  DB<1>
```

In this case, our example code is only one line long, so we have finished interacting after the first line of code is executed. Let's try again with a slightly longer example:

```
my $word = 'mod_perl';
my @array = qw(rules the world);

print "$word @array\n";
```

Save the script in a file called *domination.pl* and run it with the *-d* switch:

```
panic% perl -d domination.pl

main::(domination.pl:1):     my $word = 'mod_perl';
  DB<1> n
main::(domination.pl:2):     my @array = qw(rules the world);
  DB<1>
```

At this point, the first line of code has been executed and the variable $word has been assigned the value mod_perl. We can check this by using the *p* (*print*) command:

```
main::(domination.pl:2):        my @array = qw(rules the world);
  DB<1> p $word
mod_perl
```

The *print* command is similar to Perl's built-in print( ) function, but it adds a trailing newline and outputs to the $DB::OUT file handle, which is normally opened on the terminal from which Perl was launched. Let's continue:

```
  DB<2> n
main::(domination.pl:4):        print "$word @array\n";
  DB<2> p @array
rulestheworld
  DB<3> n
mod_perl rules the world
Debugged program terminated.  Use q to quit or R to restart,
use O inhibit_exit to avoid stopping after program termination,
h q, h R or h O to get additional info.
```

Unfortunately, *p @array* printed rulestheworld and not rules the world, as we would prefer, but that's absolutely correct. If you print an array without expanding it first into a string it will be printed without adding the content of the $" variable (otherwise known as $LIST_SEPARATOR, if the English pragma is being used) between the elements of the array.

If you type:

```
print "@array";
```

the output will be rules the world, since the default value of the $" variable is a single space.

You should have noticed by now that there is some valuable information to the left of each executable statement:

```
main::(domination.pl:4):        print "$word @array\n";
  DB<2>
```

First is the current package name (in this case, main::). Next is the current filename and statement line number (*domination.pl* and 4, in this example). The number presented at the prompt is the command number, which can be used to recall commands from the session history, using the *!* command followed by this number. For example, *!1* would repeat the first command:

```
panic% perl -d -e0

main::(-e:1):   0
  DB<1> p $]
5.006001
  DB<2> !1
p $]5.006001
  DB<3>
```

where $] is Perl's version number. As you can see, *!1* prints the value of $],
prepended by the command that was executed.

Notice that the code given to Perl to debug (with *-e*) was 0—i.e., a statement that
does nothing. To use Perl as a calculator, and to experiment with Perl expressions, it
is common to enter *perl -de0*, and then type in expressions and *p* (*print*) their results.

Things start to get more interesting as the code gets more interesting. In the script in
Example 21-5, we've increased the number of source files and packages by including
the standard Symbol module, along with an invocation of its gensym( ) function.

Example 21-5. test_sym.pl

```
use Symbol ( );

my $sym = Symbol::gensym( );

print "$sym\n";
```

Now let's debug it:

```
panic% perl -d test_sym.pl

main::(test_sym.pl:3):     my $sym = Symbol::gensym( );
  DB<1> n
main::(test_sym.pl:5):     print "$sym\n";
  DB<1> n
GLOB(0x80c7a44)
```

Note that the debugger did not stop at the first line of the file. This is because use ...
is a compile-time statement, not a runtime statement. Also notice there was more
work going on than the debugger revealed. That's because the *next* command does
not enter subroutine calls, it *steps over*. To *step into* subroutine code, use the *step*
command (or its abbreviated form, *s*):

```
panic% perl -d test_sym.pl

main::(test_sym.pl:3):     my $sym = Symbol::gensym( );
  DB<1> s
Symbol::gensym(/usr/lib/perl5/5.6.1/Symbol.pm:86):
86:        my $name = "GEN" . $genseq++;
  DB<1>
```

Notice the source line information has changed to the Symbol::gensym package and
the *Symbol.pm* file. We can carry on by hitting the Return key at each prompt, which
causes the debugger to repeat the last *step* or *next* command. It won't repeat a *print*
command, though. The debugger will eventually return from the subroutine back to
our main program:

```
  DB<1>
Symbol::gensym(/usr/lib/perl5/5.6.1/Symbol.pm:87):
87:        my $ref = *{$genpkg . $name};
  DB<1>
```

```
Symbol::gensym(/usr/lib/perl5/5.6.1/Symbol.pm:88):
88:         delete $$genpkg{$name};
  DB<1>
Symbol::gensym(/usr/lib/perl5/5.6.1/Symbol.pm:89):
89:         $ref;
  DB<1>
main::(test_sym.pl:5):      print "$sym\n";
  DB<1>
GLOB(0x80c7a44)
```

Our line-by-line debugging approach has served us well for this small program, but imagine the time it would take to step through a large application at the same pace. There are several ways to speed up a debugging session, one of which is known as *setting a breakpoint*.

The *breakpoint* command (*b*) is used to tell the debugger to stop at a named subroutine or at any line of any file. In this example session, at the first debugger prompt we will set a breakpoint at the Symbol::gensym subroutine, telling the debugger to stop at the first line of this routine when it is called. Rather than moving along with *next* or *step*, we give the *continue* command (*c*), which tells the debugger to execute the script without stopping until it reaches a breakpoint:

```
panic% perl -d test_sym.pl

main::(test_sym.pl:3):      my $sym = Symbol::gensym();
  DB<1> b Symbol::gensym
  DB<2> c
Symbol::gensym(/usr/lib/perl5/5.6.1/Symbol.pm:86):
86:         my $name = "GEN" . $genseq++;
```

Now let's imagine we are debugging a large application where Symbol::gensym might be called from any one of several places. When the subroutine breakpoint is reached, by default the debugger does not reveal where it was called from. One way to find out this information is with the stack *Trace* command (*T*):

```
  DB<2> T
$ = Symbol::gensym() called from file `test_sym.pl' line 3
```

In this example, the call stack is only one level deep, so only that call is printed. We'll look at an example with a deeper stack later. The leftmost character reveals the context in which the subroutine was called. $ represents scalar context; in other examples you may see @, which represents list context, or ., which represents void context. In our case we called:

```
my $sym = Symbol::gensym();
```

which calls the Symbol::gensym( ) in scalar context.

Now let's make our *test_sym.pl* example a little more complex. First, we add a Book::World1 package declaration at the top of the script, so we are no longer working in the main:: package. Next, we add a subroutine named do_work( ), which invokes the familiar Symbol::gensym, along with another function called Symbol::qualify, and then returns a hash reference of the results. The do_work( ) routine is invoked inside a for loop, which will be run twice. The new version of the script is shown in Example 21-6.

Example 21-6. test_sym2.pl

```perl
package Book::World2;

use Symbol ( );

for (1, 2) {
    do_work("now");
}

sub do_work {
    my($var) = @_;

    return undef unless $var;

    my $sym  = Symbol::gensym( );
    my $qvar = Symbol::qualify($var);

    my $retval = {
        sym => $sym,
        var => $qvar,
    };

    return $retval;
}
1;
```

We'll start by setting a few breakpoints, then we'll use the *List* command (*L*) to display them:

```
panic% perl -d test_sym2.pl

Book::World2::(test_sym2.pl:5):   for (1, 2) {
  DB<1> b Symbol::qualify
  DB<2> b Symbol::gensym
  DB<3> L
/usr/lib/perl5/5.6.1/Symbol.pm:
 86:        my $name = "GEN" . $genseq++;
   break if (1)
 95:        my ($name) = @_;
   break if (1)
```

The filename and line number of the breakpoint are displayed just before the source line itself. Because both breakpoints are located in the same file, the filename is displayed only once. After the source line, we see the condition on which to stop. In this case, as the constant value 1 indicates, we will always stop at these breakpoints. Later on you'll see how to specify a condition.

As we will see, when the *continue* command is executed, the execution of the program stops at one of these breakpoints, at either line 86 or line 95 of the file */usr/lib/perl5/5.6.1/Symbol.pm*, whichever is reached first. The displayed code lines are the first line of each of the two subroutines from *Symbol.pm*. Breakpoints may be applied only to lines of runtime-executable code—you cannot, for example, put breakpoints on empty lines or comments.

In our example, the *List* command shows which lines the breakpoints were set on, but we cannot tell which breakpoint belongs to which subroutine. There are two ways to find this out. One is to run the *continue* command and, when it stops, execute the *Trace* command we saw before:

```
    DB<3> c
Symbol::gensym(/usr/lib/perl5/5.6.1/Symbol.pm:86):
86:         my $name = "GEN" . $genseq++;
    DB<3> T
$ = Symbol::gensym() called from file `test_sym2.pl' line 14
. = Book::World2::do_work('now') called from file `test_sym2.pl' line 6
```

So we see that this breakpoint belongs to Symbol::gensym. The other way is to ask for a listing of a range of lines from the code. For example, let's check which subroutine line 86 is a part of. We use the *list* (lowercase!) command (*l*), which displays parts of the code. The *list* command accepts various arguments; the one that we want to use here is a range of lines. Since the breakpoint is at line 86, let's print a few lines around that line number:

```
    DB<3> l 85-87
85          sub gensym () {
86==>b          my $name = "GEN" . $genseq++;
87:             my $ref = *{$genpkg . $name};
```

Now we know it's the gensym subroutine, and we also see the breakpoint highlighted with the ==>b markup. We could also use the name of the subroutine to display its code:

```
    DB<4> l Symbol::gensym
85          sub gensym () {
86==>b          my $name = "GEN" . $genseq++;
87:             my $ref = *{$genpkg . $name};
88:             delete $$genpkg{$name};
89:             $ref;
90          }
```

The *delete* command (*d*) is used to remove a breakpoint by specifying the line number of the breakpoint. Let's remove the first one we set:

```
    DB<5> d 95
```

The *Delete* (with a capital D) command (*D*) removes all currently installed breakpoints.

Now let's look again at the trace produced at the breakpoint:

```
    DB<3> c
Symbol::gensym(/usr/lib/perl5/5.6.1/Symbol.pm:86):
86:         my $name = "GEN" . $genseq++;
    DB<3> T
$ = Symbol::gensym( ) called from file `test_sym2.pl' line 14
. = Book::World2::do_work('now') called from file `test_sym2.pl' line 6
```

As you can see, the stack trace prints the values that are passed into the subroutine. Ah, and perhaps we've found our first bug: as we can see from the first character on the second line of output from the *Trace* command, do_work( ) was called in void context, so the return value was discarded. Let's change the for loop to check the return value of do_work( ):

```
for (1, 2) {
    my $stuff = do_work("now");
    if ($stuff) {
        print "work is done\n";
    }
}
```

In this session we will set a breakpoint at line 7 of *test_sym2.pl*, where we check the return value of do_work( ):

```
panic% perl -d test_sym2.pl

Book::World2::(test_sym2.pl:5):    for (1, 2) {
    DB<1> b 7
    DB<2> c
Book::World2::(test_sym2.pl:7):        if ($stuff) {
    DB<2>
```

Our program is still small, but already it is getting more difficult to understand the context of just one line of code. The *window* command (*w*)* will list a few lines of code that surround the current line:

```
    DB<2> w
4
5:          for (1, 2) {
6:              my $stuff = do_work("now");
7==>b           if ($stuff) {
8:                  print "work is done\n";
9               }
10          }
11
12          sub do_work {
13:             my($var) = @_;
```

The arrow points to the line that is about to be executed and also contains a b, indicating that we have set a breakpoint at this line.[†]

---

[*] In Perl 5.8.0 use *l* instead of *w*, which is used for watch-expressions.

[†] Note that breakable lines of code include a colon (:) immediately after the line number.

Now, let's take a look at the value of the $stuff variable:

```
DB<2> p $stuff
HASH(0x82b89b4)
```

That's not very useful information. Remember, the *print* command works just like the built-in print( ) function. The debugger's *x* command evaluates a given expression and pretty-prints the results:

```
DB<3> x $stuff
0  HASH(0x82b89b4)
   'sym' => GLOB(0x826a944)
      -> *Symbol::GEN0
   'var' => 'Book::World2::now'
```

Things seem to be okay. Let's double check by calling do_work( ) with a different value and print the results:

```
DB<4> x do_work('later')
0  HASH(0x82bacc8)
   'sym' => GLOB(0x818f16c)
      -> *Symbol::GEN1
   'var' => 'Book::World2::later'
```

We can see the symbol was incremented from GEN0 to GEN1 and the variable later was qualified, as expected.[*]

Now let's change the test program a little to iterate over a list of arguments held in @args and print a slightly different message (see Example 21-7).

Example 21-7. test_sym3.pl

```
package Book::World3;

use Symbol ();

my @args = qw(now later);
for my $arg (@args) {
    my $stuff = do_work($arg);
    if ($stuff) {
        print "do your work $arg\n";
    }
}

sub do_work {
    my($var) = @_;

    return undef unless $var;

    my $sym = Symbol::gensym();
    my $qvar = Symbol::qualify($var);
```

---

[*] You won't see the symbol printout with Perl 5.6.1, but it works fine with 5.005_03 or 5.8.0

Example 21-7. test_sym3.pl (continued)

```
    my $retval = {
        sym => $sym,
        var => $qvar,
    };

    return $retval;
}
1;
```

There are only two arguments in the list, so stopping to look at each one isn't too time-consuming, but consider the debugging pace if we had a large list of 100 or so entries. Fortunately, it is possible to customize breakpoints by specifying a condition. Each time a breakpoint is reached, the condition is evaluated, stopping only if the condition is true. In the session below, the *window* command shows breakable lines. The = => symbol shows us the line of code that's about to be executed.

```
panic% perl -d test_sym3.pl

Book::World3::(test_sym3.pl:5): my @args = qw(now later);
    DB<1> w
5==>        my @args = qw(now later);
6:          for my $arg (@args) {
7:              my $stuff = do_work($arg);
8:              if ($stuff) {
9:                  print "do your work $arg\n";
10              }
11          }
12
13          sub do_work {
14:             my($var) = @_;
```

We set a breakpoint at line 7 with the condition $arg eq 'later'. As we continue, the breakpoint is skipped when $arg has the value of now but not when it has the value of later:

```
    DB<1> b 7 $arg eq 'later'
    DB<2> c
do your work now
Book::World3::(test_sym3.pl:7):     my $stuff = do_work($arg);
    DB<2> n
Book::World3::(test_sym3.pl:8):     if ($stuff) {
    DB<2> x $stuff
0  HASH(0x82b90e4)
    'sym' => GLOB(0x82b9138)
        -> *Symbol::GEN1
    'var' => 'Book::World3::later'
    DB<5> c
do your work later
Debugged program terminated.  Use q to quit or R to restart,
```

You should now understand enough about the debugger to try many other features on your own, with the *perldebug* manpage by your side. Quick online help from inside the debugger is available by typing the *h* command, which will display a list of the most useful commands and a short explanation of what they do.

Some installations of Perl include a readline module that allows you to work more interactively with the debugger—for example, by pressing the up arrow to see previous commands, which can then be repeated by pressing the Return key.

Interactive Perl Debugging Under mod_cgi

Devel::ptkdb is a visual Perl debugger that uses Perl/Tk for the user interface and requires a windows system like X Windows or Windows to run.

To debug a plain Perl script with Devel::ptkdb, invoke it as:

```
panic% perl -d:ptkdb myscript.pl
```

The Tk application will be loaded. Now you can do most of the debugging you did with the command-line Perl debugger, but using a simple GUI to set/remove breakpoints, browse the code, step through it, and more.

With the help of Devel::ptkdb, you can debug your CGI scripts running under mod_cgi (we'll look at mod_perl debugging later). Be sure that the web server's Perl installation includes the Tk package. To enable the debugger, change your shebang line from:

```
#!/usr/bin/perl -Tw
```

to:

```
#!/usr/bin/perl -Twd:ptkdb
```

You can debug scripts remotely if you're using a Unix-based server and if the machine where you are writing the script has an X server. The X server can be another Unix workstation, or a Macintosh or Win32 platform with an appropriate X Windows package. You must insert the following BEGIN subroutine into your script:

```
BEGIN {
    $ENV{'DISPLAY'} = "localhost:0.0" ;
}
```

You may need to replace the *localhost* value with a real DNS or IP address if you aren't working at the machine itself. You must be sure that your web server has permission to open windows on your X server (see the *xhost* manpage for more information).

Access the web page with the browser and request the script as usual. The ptkdb window should appear on the monitor if you have correctly set the $ENV{'DISPLAY'} variable (see Figure 21-2). At this point you can start debugging your script. Be aware that the browser may time out waiting for the script to run.

To expedite debugging you may want to set your breakpoints in advance with a *.ptkdbrc* file and use the $DB::no_stop_at_start variable. For debugging web

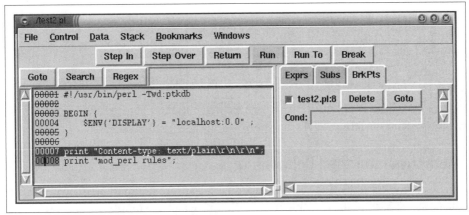

Figure 21-2. Devel::ptkdb Interactive Debugger

scripts, you may have to have the *.ptkdbrc* file installed in the server account's home directory (e.g., *~httpd*) or whatever username the web server is running under. Also try installing a *.ptkdbrc* file in the same directory as the target script.

ptkdb is available from CPAN: *http://www.perl.com/CPAN/authors/id/A/AE/AE/*.

Noninteractive Perl Debugging Under mod_perl

To debug scripts running under mod_perl noninteractively (i.e., to print the Perl execution trace), simply set the usual environment variables that control debugging.

The NonStop debugger option enables you to get some decent debugging information when running under mod_perl. For example, before starting the server:

```
panic% setenv PERL5OPT -d
panic% setenv PERLDB_OPTS \
        "NonStop=1 LineInfo=/tmp/db.out AutoTrace=1 frame=2"
```

Now watch */tmp/db.out* for *line:filename* information. This is most useful for tracking those core dumps that normally leave us guessing, even with a stack trace from gdb, which we'll discuss later. *db.out* will show you what Perl code triggered the core dump. Refer to the *perldebug* manpage for more PERLDB_OPTS options.

Say we execute a simple Apache::Registry script, *test.pl*:

```
use strict;
my $r = shift;
$r->send_http_header("text/plain");
$r->print("Hello");
```

The generated trace found in */tmp/db.out* is too long to be printed here in its entirety. We will show only the part that actually executes the handler created on the fly by Apache::Registry:

```
entering Apache::ROOT::perl::test_2epl::handler
 2:
```

```
3:
entering Apache::send_http_header
exited Apache::send_http_header
4:
entering Apache::print
exited Apache::print
exited Apache::ROOT::perl::test_2epl::handler
```

You can see how Perl executes this script—first the send_http_header( ) function is executed, then the string "Hello" is printed.

Interactive mod_perl Debugging

Now we'll look at how the interactive debugger is used in a mod_perl environment. The Apache::DB module available from CPAN provides a wrapper around perldb for debugging Perl code running under mod_perl.

The server must be run in non-forking (single-process) mode to use the interactive debugger; this mode is turned on by passing the *-X* flag to the *httpd* executable. It is convenient to use an IfDefine section around the Apache::DB configuration; the example below does this using the name PERLDB. With this setup, debugging is turned on only when starting the server with the *httpd -X -DPERLDB* command.

This configuration section should be placed before any other Perl code is pulled in, so that debugging symbols will be inserted into the syntax tree, triggered by the call to Apache::DB->init. The Apache::DB::handler can be configured using any of the Perl*Handler directives. In this case we use a PerlFixupHandler so handlers in the response phase will bring up the debugger prompt:

```
<IfDefine PERLDB>

    <Perl>
        use Apache::DB ();
        Apache::DB->init;
    </Perl>

    <Location />
        PerlFixupHandler Apache::DB
    </Location>

</IfDefine>
```

Since we have used "/" as the argument to the Location directive, the debugger will be invoked for any kind of request, but of course it will immediately quit unless there is some Perl module registered to handle these requests.

In our first example, we will debug the standard Apache::Status module, which is configured like this:

```
PerlModule Apache::Status
<Location /perl-status>
    SetHandler perl-script
```

```
    PerlHandler Apache::Status
  </Location>
```

When the server is started with the debugging flag, a notice will be printed to the console:

```
panic% ./httpd -X -DPERLDB
[notice] Apache::DB initialized in child 950
```

The debugger prompt will not be available until the first request is made (in our case, to *http://localhost/perl-status*). Once we are at the prompt, all the standard debugging commands are available. First we run *window* to get some of the context for the code being debugged, then we move to the next statement after a value has been assigned to $r, and finally we print the request URI. If no breakpoints are set, the *continue* command will give control back to Apache and the request will finish with the Apache::Status main menu showing in the browser window:

```
Loading DB routines from perl5db.pl version 1.07
Emacs support available.

Enter h or `h h' for help.

Apache::Status::handler(.../5.6.1/i386-linux/Apache/Status.pm:55):
55:            my($r) = @_;
  DB<1> w
52         }
53
54     sub handler {
55==>          my($r) = @_;
56:            Apache->request($r); #for Apache::CGI
57:            my $qs = $r->args || "";
58:            my $sub = "status_$qs";
59:            no strict 'refs';
60
61:            if($qs =~ s/^(noh_\w+).*/$1/) {
  DB<1> n
Apache::Status::handler(.../5.6.1/i386-linux/Apache/Status.pm:56):
56:            Apache->request($r); #  for Apache::CGI
  DB<1> p $r->uri
/perl-status
  DB<2> c
```

All the techniques we saw while debugging plain Perl scripts can be applied to this debugging session.

Debugging Apache::Registry scripts is somewhat different, because the handler routine does quite a bit of work before it reaches your script. In this example, we make a request for */perl/test.pl*, which consists of the code shown in Example 21-8.

Example 21-8. test.pl

```
use strict;

my $r = shift;
```

Example 21-8. test.pl (continued)

```
$r->send_http_header('text/plain');

print "mod_perl rules";
```

When a request is issued, the debugger stops at line 28 of *Apache/Registry.pm*. We set a breakpoint at line 140, which is the line that actually calls the script wrapper subroutine. The *continue* command will bring us to that line, where we can step into the script handler:

```
Apache::Registry::handler(.../5.6.1/i386-linux/Apache/Registry.pm:28):
28:        my $r = shift;
  DB<1> b 140
  DB<2> c
Apache::Registry::handler(.../5.6.1/i386-linux/Apache/Registry.pm:140):
140:             eval { &{$cv}($r, @_) } if $r->seqno;
  DB<2> s
Apache::ROOT::perl::test_2epl::handler((eval 87):3):
3:        my $r = shift;
```

Notice the funny package name—it's generated from the URI of the request, for namespace protection. The filename is not displayed, since the code was compiled via eval( ), but the print command can be used to show you $r->filename:

```
  DB<2> n
Apache::ROOT::perl::test_2epl::handler((eval 87):4):
4:        $r->send_http_header('text/plain');
  DB<2> p $r->filename
/home/httpd/perl/test.pl
```

The line number might seem off too, but the *window* command will give you a better idea of where you are:

```
  DB<4> w
1:        package Apache::ROOT::perl::test_2epl;use Apache qw(exit);
sub handler {  use strict;
2
3:        my $r = shift;
4= =>       $r->send_http_header('text/plain');
5
6:        print "mod_perl rules";
7
8         }
9         ;
```

The code from the *test.pl* file is between lines 2 and 7. The rest is the Apache::Registry magic to cache your code inside a handler subroutine.

It will always take some practice and patience when putting together debugging strategies that make effective use of the interactive debugger for various situations. Once you have a good strategy, bug squashing can actually be quite a bit of fun!

ptkdb and interactive mod_perl debugging

As we saw earlier, we can use the ptkdb visual debugger to debug CGI scripts running under mod_cgi. At the time of writing it works partially under mod_perl as well. It hangs after the first run, so you have to kill it manually every time. Hopefully it will work completely with mod_perl in the future.

However, ptkdb won't work for mod_perl using the same configuration as used in mod_cgi. We have to tweak the *Apache/DB.pm* module to use *Devel/ptkdb.pm* instead of *Apache/perl5db.pl*.

Open the file in your favorite editor and replace:

```
require 'Apache/perl5db.pl';
```

with:

```
require Devel::ptkdb;
```

Now when you use the interactive mod_perl debugger configuration from the previous section and issue a request, the ptkdb visual debugger will be loaded.

If you are debugging Apache::Registry scripts, as in the terminal debugging mode example, go to line 140 (or to whatever line number at which the eval { &{$cv}($r, @_) } if $r->seqno; statement is located) and press the *step in* button to start debugging the script itself.

Note that you can use Apache with ptkdb in plain multi-server mode; you don't have to start *httpd* with the -*X* option.

Analyzing Dumped core Files

When your application dies with the "Segmentation fault" error (generated by the default SIGSEGV signal handler) and generates a *core* file, you can analyze the *core* file using gdb or a similar debugger to find out what caused the segmentation fault (or *segfault*).

Getting Ready to Debug

To debug the *core* file, you may need to recompile Perl and mod_perl so that their executables contain debugging symbols. Usually you have to recompile only mod_perl, but if the *core* dump happens in the *libperl.so* library and you want to see the whole backtrace, you will probably want to recompile Perl as well.

For example, sometimes people send this kind of backtrace to the mod_perl list:

```
#0  0x40448aa2 in ?? ()
#1  0x40448ac9 in ?? ()
#2  0x40448bd1 in ?? ()
#3  0x4011d5d4 in ?? ()
#4  0x400fb439 in ?? ()
```

```
#5  0x400a6288 in ?? ()
#6  0x400a5e34 in ?? ()
```

This kind of trace is absolutely useless, since you cannot tell where the problem happens from just looking at machine addresses. To preserve the debug symbols and get a meaningful backtrace, recompile Perl with *-DDEBUGGING* during the *./Configure* stage (or with *-Doptimize="-g"*, which, in addition to adding the *-DDEBUGGING* option, adds the *-g* option, which allows you to debug the Perl interpreter itself).

After recompiling Perl, recompile mod_perl with `PERL_DEBUG=1` during the *perl Makefile.PL* stage. Building mod_perl with `PERL_DEBUG=1` will:

1. Add *-g* to `EXTRA_CFLAGS`, passed to your C compiler during compilation.

2. Turn on the `PERL_TRACE` option.

3. Set `PERL_DESTRUCT_LEVEL=2`.

4. Link against `libperld` if -e `$Config{archlibexp}/CORE/libperld$Config{lib_ext}` (i.e., if you've compiled perl with *-DDEBUGGING*).

During *make install*, Apache strips all the debugging symbols. To prevent this, you should use the Apache *--without-execstrip ./configure* option. So if you configure Apache via mod_perl, you should do this:

```
panic% perl Makefile.PL USE_APACI=1 \
   APACI_ARGS='--without-execstrip' [other options]
```

Alternatively, you can copy the unstripped binary manually. For example, we did this to give us an Apache binary called *httpd_perl* that contains debugging symbols:

```
panic# cp apache_1.3.24/src/httpd /home/httpd/httpd_perl/bin/httpd_perl
```

Now the software is ready for a proper debug.

Creating a Faulty Package

The next stage is to create a package that aborts abnormally with a segfault, so you will be able to reproduce the problem and exercise the debugging technique explained here. Luckily, you can download `Debug::DumpCore` from CPAN, which does a very simple thing—it segfaults when called as:

```
use Debug::DumpCore;
Debug::DumpCore::segv();
```

`Debug::DumpCore::segv()` calls a function, which calls another function, which dereferences a `NULL` pointer, which causes the segfault:

```
int *p;
p = NULL;
printf("%d", *p); // cause a segfault
```

For those unfamiliar with C programming, *p* is a pointer to a segment of memory. Setting it to `NULL` ensures that we try to read from a segment of memory to which the operating system does not allow us access, so of course dereferencing the NULL pointer through *p causes a segmentation fault. And that's what we want.

Of course, you can use Perl's CORE::dump( ) function, which causes a core dump, but you don't get the nice long trace provided by Debug::DumpCore, which on purpose calls a few other functions before causing a segfault.

Dumping the core File

Now let's dump the *core* file from within the mod_perl server. Sometimes the program aborts abnormally via the SIGSEGV signal (a segfault), but no *core* file is dumped. And without the *core* file it's hard to find the cause of the problem, unless you run the program inside gdb or another debugger in the first place. In order to get the *core* file, the application must:

- Have the same effective UID as the real UID (the same goes for GID). This is the case with mod_perl unless you modify these settings in the server configuration file.

- Be running from a directory that is writable by the process at the moment of the segmentation fault. Note that the program might change its current directory during its run, so it's possible that the *core* file will need to be dumped in a different directory from the one from which the program was started. For example when mod_perl runs an Apache::Registry script, it changes its directory to the one in which the script's source is located.

- Be started from a shell process with sufficient resource allocations for the *core* file to be dumped. You can override the default setting from within a shell script if the process is not started manually. In addition, you can use BSD::Resource to manipulate the setting from within the code as well.

  You can use *ulimit* for a Bourne-style shell and *limit* for a C-style shell to check and adjust the resource allocation. For example, inside *bash*, you may set the *core* file size to unlimited with:

      panic% ulimit -c unlimited

  or for csh:

      panic% limit coredumpsize unlimited

  For example, you can set an upper limit of 8 MB on the *core* file with:

      panic% ulimit -c 8388608

  This ensures that if the *core* file would be bigger than 8 MB, it will be not created.

You must make sure that you have enough disk space to create a big *core* file (mod_perl *core* files tend to be of a few MB in size).

Note that when you are running the program under a debugger like gdb, which traps the SIGSEGV signal, the *core* file will not be dumped. Instead, gdb allows you to examine the program stack and other things without having the *core* file.

First let's test that we get the *core* file from the command line (under *tcsh*):

```
panic% limit coredumpsize unlimited
panic% perl -MDebug::DumpCore -e 'Debug::DumpCore::segv()'
Segmentation fault (core dumped)
panic% ls -l core
-rw------- 1 stas stas 954368 Jul 31 23:52 core
```

Indeed, we can see that the *core* file was dumped. Let's write a simple script that uses Debug::DumpCore, as shown in Example 21-9.

Example 21-9. core_dump.pl

```
use strict;
use Debug::DumpCore ();
use Cwd()

my $r = shift;
$r->send_http_header("text/plain");

my $dir = getcwd;
$r->print("The core should be found at $dir/core\n");
Debug::DumpCore::segv();
```

In this script we load the Debug::DumpCore and Cwd modules. Then we acquire the request object and send the HTTP headers. Now we come to the real part—we get the current working directory, print out the location of the *core* file that we are about to dump, and finally call Debug::DumpCore::segv(), which dumps the *core* file.

Before we run the script we make sure that the shell sets the *core* file size to be unlimited, start the server in single-server mode as a non-*root* user, and generate a request to the script:

```
panic% cd /home/httpd/httpd_perl/bin
panic% limit coredumpsize unlimited
panic% ./httpd_perl -X
    # issue a request here
Segmentation fault (core dumped)
```

Our browser prints out:

```
The core should be found at /home/httpd/perl/core
```

And indeed the *core* file appears where we were told it would (remember that Apache::Registry scripts change their directory to the location of the script source):

```
panic% ls -l /home/httpd/perl/core
-rw------- 1 stas httpd 4669440 Jul 31 23:58 /home/httpd/perl/core
```

As you can see it's a 4.7 MB *core* file. Notice that mod_perl was started as user *stas*, which has write permission for the directory */home/httpd/perl*.

Analyzing the core File

First we start gdb, with the location of the mod_perl executable and the *core* file as the arguments:

```
panic% gdb /home/httpd/httpd_perl/bin/httpd_perl /home/httpd/perl/core
```

To see the backtrace, execute the *where* or *bt* commands:

```
(gdb) where
#0  0x4039f781 in crash_now_for_real (
       suicide_message=0x403a0120 "Cannot stand this life anymore")
       at DumpCore.xs:10
#1  0x4039f7a3 in crash_now (
       suicide_message=0x403a0120 "Cannot stand this life anymore",
       attempt_num=42) at DumpCore.xs:17
#2  0x4039f824 in XS_Debug__DumpCore_segv (cv=0x84ecda0)
       at DumpCore.xs:26
#3  0x401261ec in Perl_pp_entersub ()
    from /usr/lib/perl5/5.6.1/i386-linux/CORE/libperl.so
#4  0x00000001 in ?? ()
```

Notice that only the symbols from the *DumpCore.xs* file are available (plus Perl_pp_ entersub from *libperl.so*), since by default Debug::DumpCore always compiles itself with the -g flag. However, we cannot see the rest of the trace, because our Perl and mod_ perl libraries and Apache server were built without the debug symbols. We need to recompile them all with the debug symbols, as explained earlier in this chapter.

Then we repeat the process of starting the server, issuing a request, and getting the *core* file, after which we run gdb again against the executable and the dumped *core* file:

```
panic% gdb /home/httpd/httpd_perl/bin/httpd_perl /home/httpd/perl/core
```

Now we can see the whole backtrace:

```
(gdb) bt
#0  0x40448aa2 in crash_now_for_real (
       suicide_message=0x404499e0 "Cannot stand this life anymore")
       at DumpCore.xs:10
#1  0x40448ac9 in crash_now (
       suicide_message=0x404499e0 "Cannot stand this life anymore",
       attempt_num=42) at DumpCore.xs:17
#2  0x40448bd1 in XS_Debug__DumpCore_segv (my_perl=0x8133b60, cv=0x861d1fc)
       at DumpCore.xs:26
#3  0x4011d5d4 in Perl_pp_entersub (my_perl=0x8133b60) at pp_hot.c:2773
#4  0x400fb439 in Perl_runops_debug (my_perl=0x8133b60) at dump.c:1398
#5  0x400a6288 in S_call_body (my_perl=0x8133b60, myop=0xbffff160, is_eval=0)
       at perl.c:2045
#6  0x400a5e34 in Perl_call_sv (my_perl=0x8133b60, sv=0x85d696c, flags=4)
       at perl.c:1963
#7  0x0808a6e3 in perl_call_handler (sv=0x85d696c, r=0x860bf54, args=0x0)
       at mod_perl.c:1658
#8  0x080895f2 in perl_run_stacked_handlers (hook=0x8109c47 "PerlHandler",
       r=0x860bf54, handlers=0x82e5c4c) at mod_perl.c:1371
```

```
#9   0x080864d8 in perl_handler (r=0x860bf54) at mod_perl.c:897
#10  0x080d2560 in ap_invoke_handler (r=0x860bf54) at http_config.c:517
#11  0x080e6796 in process_request_internal (r=0x860bf54) at http_request.c:1308
#12  0x080e67f6 in ap_process_request (r=0x860bf54) at http_request.c:1324
#13  0x080ddba2 in child_main (child_num_arg=0) at http_main.c:4595
#14  0x080ddd4a in make_child (s=0x8127ec4, slot=0, now=1028133659)
#15  0x080ddeb1 in startup_children (number_to_start=4) at http_main.c:4792
#16  0x080de4e6 in standalone_main (argc=2, argv=0xbffff514) at http_main.c:5100
#17  0x080ded04 in main (argc=2, argv=0xbffff514) at http_main.c:5448
#18  0x40215082 in __libc_start_main () from /lib/i686/libc.so.6
```

Reading the trace from bottom to top, we can see that it starts with Apache functions, moves on to the mod_perl and then Perl functions, and finally calls functions from the Debug::DumpCore package. At the top we can see the crash_now_for_real( ) function, which was the one that caused the segmentation fault; we can also see that the faulty code was at line 10 of the *DumpCore.xs* file. And indeed, if we look at that line number we can see the reason for the segfault—the dereferencing of the NULL pointer:

```
9: int *p = NULL;
  10: printf("%d", *p); /* cause a segfault */
```

In our example, we knew what Perl script had caused the segmentation fault. In the real world, it is likely that you'll have only the *core* file, without any clue as to which handler or script has triggered it. The special *curinfo* gdb macro can help:

```
panic% gdb /home/httpd/httpd_perl/bin/httpd_perl /home/httpd/perl/core
(gdb) source mod_perl-1.xx/.gdbinit
(gdb) curinfo
9:/home/httpd/perl/core_dump.pl
```

Start the gdb debugger as before. *.gdbinit*, the file with various useful gdb macros, is located in the source tree of mod_perl. We use the gdb *source* function to load these macros, and when we run the *curinfo* macro we learn that the *core* was dumped when */home/httpd/perl/core_dump.pl* was executing the code at line 9.

These are the bits of information that are important in order to reproduce and resolve a problem: the filename and line number where the fault occurred (the faulty function is Debug::DumpCore::segv( ) in our case) and the actual line where the segmentation fault occurred (the printf("%d", *p) call in XS code). The former is important for problem reproducing, since it's possible that if the same function was called from a different script the problem wouldn't show up (not the case in our example, where using a dereferenced NULL pointer will always cause a segmentation fault).

Extracting the Backtrace Automatically

With the help of Debug::FaultAutoBT, you can try to get the backtrace extracted automatically, without any need for the *core* file. As of this writing this CPAN module is very new and doesn't work on all platforms.

To use this module we simply add the following code in the startup file:

```
use Debug::FaultAutoBT;
use File::Spec::Functions;
my $tmp_dir = File::Spec::Functions::tmpdir;
die "cannot find out a temp dir" if $tmp_dir eq '';
my $trace = Debug::FaultAutoBT->new(dir => "$tmp_dir");
$trace->ready();
```

This code tries to automatically figure out the location of the temporary directory, initializes the Debug::FaultAutoBT object with it, and finally uses the method ready() to set the signal handler, which will attempt to automatically get the backtrace. Now when we repeat the process of starting the server and issuing a request, if we look at the *error_log* file, it says:

```
SIGSEGV (Segmentation fault) in 29072
writing to the core file /tmp/core.backtrace.29072
```

And indeed the file */tmp/core.backtrace.29072* includes a backtrace similar to the one we extracted before, using the *core* file.

Hanging Processes: Detection and Diagnostics

Sometimes an *httpd* process might hang in the middle of processing a request. This may happen because of a bug in the code, such as being stuck in a while loop. Or it may be blocked in a system call, perhaps waiting indefinitely for an unavailable resource. To fix the problem, we need to learn in what circumstances the process hangs, so that we can reproduce the problem, which will allow us to uncover its cause.

Hanging Because of an Operating System Problem

Sometimes you can find a process hanging because of some kind of system problem. For example, if the processes was doing some disk I/O operation, it might get stuck in uninterruptible sleep ('D' disk wait in *ps* report, 'U' in *top*), which indicates either that something is broken in your kernel or that you're using NFS. Also, usually you find that you cannot *kill -9* this process.

Another process that cannot be killed with *kill -9* is a zombie process ('Z' disk wait in *ps* report, <defunc> in *top*), in which case the process is already dead and Apache didn't wait on it properly (of course, it can be some other process not related to Apache).

In the case of *disk wait*, you can actually get the *wait* channel from *ps* and look it up in your kernel symbol table to find out what resource it was waiting on. This might point the way to what component of the system is misbehaving, if the problem occurs frequently.

When a Process Might Hang

In Chapter 19, we discussed the concept of deadlock. This can happen when two processes are each trying to acquire locks on the resources held by the other. Neither process will release the lock it currently holds, and thus neither can acquire a lock on the second resource it desires.

This scenario is a very good candidate for code that might lead to a hanging process. Since usually the deadlock cannot be resolved without manual intervention, the two processes will hang, doing nothing and wasting system resources, while trying to acquire locks.

An infinite loop might lead to a hanging process as well. Moreover, such a loop will usually consume a lot of CPU resources and memory. You should be very careful when using while and similar loop constructs that are capable of creating endless loops.

A process relying on some external resource, for example when accessing a file over NFS, might hang if the mounted partition it tries to access is not available. Usually it takes a long time before the request times out, and in the meantime the process may hang.

There are many other reasons that a process might hang, but these are some of the most common.

Detecting Hanging Processes

It's not so easy to detect hanging processes. There is no way you can tell how long the request is taking to process by using plain system utilities such as *ps* and *top*. The reason is that each Apache process serves many requests without quitting. System utilities can tell how long the process has been running since its creation, but this information is useless in our case, since Apache processes normally run for extended periods.

However, there are a few approaches that can help to detect a hanging process. If the hanging process happens to demand lots of resources, it's quite easy to spot it by using the *top* utility. You will see the same process show up in the first few lines of the automatically refreshed report. (But often the hanging process uses few resources—e.g., when waiting for some event to happen.)

Another easy case is when some process thrashes the *error_log* file, writing millions of error messages there. Generally this process uses lots of resources and is also easily spotted by using *top*.

Two other tools that report the status of Apache processes are the mod_status module, which is usually accessed from the */server_status* location, and the Apache::VMonitor module, covered in Chapter 5.

Both tools provide counters of requests processed per Apache process. You can watch the report for a few minutes and try to spot any process with an unchanging number of processed requests and a status of W (waiting). This means that it has hung.

But if you have 50 processes, it can be quite hard to spot such a process. Apache:: Watchdog::RunAway is a hanging-processes monitor and terminator that implements this feature and could be used to solve this kind of problem. It's covered in Chapter 5.

If you have a really bad problem, where processes hang one after the other, the time will come when the number of hanging processes is equal to the value of MaxClients. This means that no more processes will be spawned. As far as the users are concerned, your server will be down. It is easy to detect this situation, attempt to resolve it, and notify the administrator using a simple *crontab* watchdog that periodically requests some very light script (see Chapter 5).

In the watchdog, you set a timeout appropriate for your service, which may be anything from a few seconds to a few minutes. If the server fails to respond before the timeout expires, the watchdog spots trouble and attempts to restart the server. After a restart an email report is sent to the administrator saying that there was a problem and whether or not the restart was successful.

If you get such reports constantly, something is wrong with your web service and you should review your code. Note that it's possible that your server is being overloaded by more requests than it can handle, so the requests are being queued and not processed for a while, which triggers the watchdog's alarm. If this is the case, you may need to add more servers or more memory, or perhaps split a single machine across a cluster of machines.

Determination of the Reason

Given the PID, there are three ways to find out where the server is hanging:

- Deploy the Perl calls-tracing mechanism. This will allow you to spot the location of the Perl code that triggers the problem.
- Use a system calls–tracing utility such as *strace*. This approach reveals low-level details about the misbehavior of some part of the system.
- Use an interactive debugger such as gdb. When the process is stuck and you don't know what it was doing just before it got stuck, using gdb you can attach to this process and print its call stack, to reveal where the last call originated. Just like with *strace*, you see the C function call trace, not the Perl high-level function calls.

Using the Perl trace

To see where an *httpd* process is spinning, the first step is to add the following to your startup file:

```
package Book::StartUp;
use Carp ();
$SIG{'USR2'} = sub {
    Carp::confess("caught SIGUSR2!");
};
```

The above code assigns a signal handler for the USR2 signal. This signal has been chosen because it's unlikely to be used by the other server components.

We can check the registered signal handlers with help of Apache::Status. Using this code, if we fetch the URL *http://localhost/perl-status?sig* we will see:

```
USR2 = \&Book::StartUp::__ANON__
```

where Book::StartUp is the name of the package declared in *startup.pl*.

After applying this server configuration, let's use the simple code in Example 21-10, where sleep(10000) will emulate a hanging process.

Example 21-10. debug/perl_trace.pl

```
local $|=1;
my $r = shift;
$r->send_http_header('text/plain');

print "[$$] Going to sleep\n";
hanging_sub();

sub hanging_sub { sleep 10000; }
```

We execute the above script as *http://localhost/perl/debug/perl_trace.pl*. In the script we use $|=1; to unbuffer the STDOUT stream and we get the PID from the $$ special variable.

Now we issue the *kill* command, using the PID we have just seen printed to the browser's window:

```
panic% kill -USR2 PID
```

and watch this showing up in the *error_log* file:

```
caught SIGUSR2!
    at /home/httpd/perl/startup/startup.pl line 32
Book::StartUp::__ANON__('USR2') called
    at /home/httpd/perl/debug/perl_trace.pl line 6
Apache::ROOT::perl::debug::perl_trace_2epl::hanging_sub() called
    at /home/httpd/perl/debug/perl_trace.pl line 5
Apache::ROOT::perl::debug::perl_trace_2epl::handler('Apache=SCALAR(0x8309d08)')
  called
    at /usr/lib/perl5/site_perl/5.6.1/i386-linux/Apache/Registry.pm
      line 140
```

```
eval {...} called
    at /usr/lib/perl5/site_perl/5.6.1/i386-linux/Apache/Registry.pm
        line 140
Apache::Registry::handler('Apache=SCALAR(0x8309d08)') called
    at PerlHandler subroutine `Apache::Registry::handler' line 0
eval {...} called
    at PerlHandler subroutine `Apache::Registry::handler' line 0
```

We can clearly see that the process "hangs" in the code executed at line 6 of the */home/httpd/perl/debug/perl_trace.pl* script, and it was called by the hanging_sub() routine defined at line 5.

Using the system calls trace

Let's write another similar mod_perl script that hangs, and deploy *strace* to find the point at which it hangs (see Example 21-11).

Example 21-11. hangme.pl

```
local $|=1;
my $r = shift;
$r->send_http_header('text/plain');

print "PID = $$\n";

my $i = 0;
while (1) {
    $i++;
    sleep 1;
}
```

The reason this simple code hangs is obvious. It never breaks from the while loop. As you can see, it prints the PID of the current process to the browser. Of course, in a real situation you cannot use the same trick—in the previous section we presented several ways to detect the runaway processes and their PIDs.

We save the above code in a file and make a request. As usual, we use $|=1; in our demonstration scripts to unbuffer STDOUT so we will immediately see the process ID. Once the script is requested, the script prints the PID and obviously hangs. So we press the Stop button, but the process continues to hang in this code. Isn't Apache supposed to detect the broken connection and abort the request? Yes and no—you will understand soon what's really happening.

First let's attach to the process and see what it's doing. We use the PID the script printed to the browser—in this case, it is 10045:

```
panic% strace -p 10045

[...truncated identical output...]
SYS_175(0, 0xbffff41c, 0xbffff39c, 0x8, 0) = 0
SYS_174(0x11, 0, 0xbffff1a0, 0x8, 0x11) = 0
SYS_175(0x2, 0xbffff39c, 0, 0x8, 0x2)   = 0
```

```
nanosleep(0xbffff308, 0xbffff308, 0x401a61b4, 0xbffff308, 0xbffff41c) = 0
time([940973834])                       = 940973834
time([940973834])                       = 940973834
[...truncated the identical output...]
```

It isn't what we expected to see, is it? These are some system calls we don't see in our little example. What we actually see is how Perl translates our code into system calls. We know that our code hangs in this snippet:

```
while (1) {
    $i++;
    sleep 1;
}
```

so these must be the system calls that represent this loop, since they are printed repeatedly.

Usually the situation is different from the one we have shown. You first detect the hanging process, then you attach to it and watch the trace of calls it does (or observe the last few system calls if the process is hanging waiting for something, as when blocking on a file-lock request). From watching the trace you figure out what it's actually doing, and probably find the corresponding lines in your Perl code. For example, let's see how one process hangs while requesting an exclusive lock on a file that is exclusively locked by another process (see Example 21-12).

Example 21-12. excl_lock.pl

```
use Fcntl qw(:flock);
use Symbol;

fork(); # child and parent do the same operation

my $fh = gensym;
open $fh, ">/tmp/lock" or die "cannot open /tmp/lock: $!";
print "$$: I'm going to obtain the lock\n";
flock $fh, LOCK_EX;
print "$$: I've got the lock\n";
sleep 30;
close $fh;
```

The code is simple. The process executing the code forks a second process, and both do the same thing: generate a unique symbol to be used as a file handle, open the lock file for writing using the generated symbol, lock the file in exclusive mode, sleep for 30 seconds (pretending to do some lengthy operation), and close the lock file, which also unlocks the file.

The gensym function is imported from the Symbol module. The Fcntl module provides us with a symbolic constant, LOCK_EX. This is imported via the :flock tag, which imports this and other flock( ) constants.

The code used by both processes is identical, so we cannot predict which one will get its hands on the lock file and succeed in locking it first. Thus, we add `print( )` statements to find the PID of the process blocking (waiting to get the lock) on a lock request.

When the above code is executed from the command line, we see that one of the processes gets the lock:

```
panic% perl ./excl_lock.pl

3038: I'm going to obtain the lock
3038: I've got the lock
3037: I'm going to obtain the lock
```

Here we see that process 3037 is blocking, so we attach to it:

```
panic% strace -p 3037

about to attach c10
flock(3, LOCK_EX
```

It's clear from the above trace that the process is waiting for an exclusive lock. The missing closing parenthesis is not a typo; it means that *strace* didn't yet receive a return status from the call.

After spending time watching the running traces of different scripts, you will learn to more easily recognize what Perl code is being executed.

Using the interactive debugger

Another way to see a trace of the running code is to use a debugger such as gdb (the GNU debugger). It's supposed to work on any platform that supports the GNU development tools. Its purpose is to allow you to see what is going on inside a program while it executes, or what it was doing at the moment it failed.

To trace the execution of a process, gdb needs to know the PID and the path to the binary that the process is executing. For Perl code, it's */usr/bin/perl* (or whatever the path to your Perl is). For *httpd* processes, it's the path to your *httpd* executable—often the binary is called *httpd*, but there's really no standard location for it.

Here are a few examples using gdb. First, let's go back to our last locking example, execute it as before, and attach to the process that didn't get the lock:

```
panic% gdb /usr/bin/perl 3037
```

After starting the debugger, we execute the *where* command to see the trace:

```
(gdb) where
#0  0x40209791 in flock () from /lib/libc.so.6
#1  0x400e8dc9 in Perl_pp_flock () at pp_sys.c:2033
#2  0x40099c56 in Perl_runops_debug () at run.c:53
#3  0x4003118c in S_run_body (oldscope=1) at perl.c:1443
#4  0x40030c7e in perl_run (my_perl=0x804bf00) at perl.c:1365
```

```
#5  0x804953e in main (argc=3, argv=0xbffffac4, env=0xbffffad4)
    at perlmain.c:52
#6  0x4018bcbe in __libc_start_main () from /lib/libc.so.6
```

That's not what we may have expected to see (i.e., a Perl stack trace). And now it's a different trace from the one we saw when we were using *strace*. Here we see the current state of the call stack, with main( ) at the bottom of the stack and flock( ) at the top.

We have to find out the place the code was called from—it's possible that the code calls flock( ) in several places, and we won't be able to locate the place in the code where the actual problem occurs without having this information. Therefore, we again use the *curinfo* macro after loading it from the *.gdbinit* file:

```
(gdb) source /usr/src/httpd_perl/mod_perl-1.25/.gdbinit
(gdb) curinfo
9:/home/httpd/perl/excl_lock.pl
```

As we can see, the program was stuck at line 9 of */home/httpd/perl/excl_lock.pl* and that's the place to look at to resolve the problem.

When you attach to a running process with gdb, the program stops executing and control of the program is passed to the debugger. You can continue the normal program run with the *continue* command or execute it step by step with the *next* and *step* commands, which you type at the gdb prompt. (*next* steps over any function calls in the source, while *step* steps into them.)

The use of C/C++ debuggers is a large topic, beyond the scope of this book. The gdb man and info pages are quite good. You might also want to check ddd (the Data Display Debugger), which provides a visual interface to gdb and other debuggers. It even knows how to debug Perl programs.

For completeness, let's see the gdb trace of the *httpd* process that's hanging in the while(1) loop of the first example in this section:

```
panic% gdb /home/httpd/httpd_perl/bin/httpd 1005

(gdb) where
#0  0x402251c1 in nanosleep () from /lib/libc.so.6
#1  0x40225158 in sleep () from /lib/libc.so.6
#2  0x4014d3a6 in Perl_pp_sleep () at pp_sys.c:4187
#3  0x400f5c56 in Perl_runops_debug () at run.c:53
#4  0x4008e088 in S_call_body (myop=0xbffff688, is_eval=0) at perl.c:1796
#5  0x4008dc4f in perl_call_sv (sv=0x82fc75c, flags=4) at perl.c:1714
#6  0x807350e in perl_call_handler (sv=0x82fc75c, r=0x8309eec, args=0x0)
    at mod_perl.c:1677
#7  0x80729cd in perl_run_stacked_handlers (hook=0x80d0db9 "PerlHandler",
    r=0x8309eec, handlers=0x82e9b64) at mod_perl.c:1396
#8  0x80701b4 in perl_handler (r=0x8309eec) at mod_perl.c:922
#9  0x809f409 in ap_invoke_handler (r=0x8309eec) at http_config.c:517
#10 0x80b3e8f in process_request_internal (r=0x8309eec) at http_request.c:1286
#11 0x80b3efa in ap_process_request (r=0x8309eec) at http_request.c:1302
```

```
#12 0x80aae60 in child_main (child_num_arg=0) at http_main.c:4205
#13 0x80ab0e8 in make_child (s=0x80eea54, slot=0, now=981621024)
    at http_main.c:4364
#14 0x80ab19c in startup_children (number_to_start=3) at http_main.c:4391
#15 0x80ab80c in standalone_main (argc=1, argv=0xbffff9e4) at http_main.c:4679
#16 0x80ac03c in main (argc=1, argv=0xbffff9e4) at http_main.c:5006
#17 0x401bbcbe in __libc_start_main () from /lib/libc.so.6
```

As before, we can see a complete trace of the last executed call. To see the line the program hangs, we use *curinfo* again:

```
(gdb) source /usr/src/httpd_perl/mod_perl-1.25/.gdbinit
(gdb) curinfo
9:/home/httpd/perl/hangme.pl
```

Indeed, the program spends most of its time at line 9:

```
7 : while (1) {
8 :     $i++;
9 :     sleep 1;
10: }
```

Since while( ) and $i++ are executed very fast, it's almost impossible to catch Perl running either of these instructions.

mod_perl gdb Debug Macros

So far we have seen only the use of the *curinfo* gdb macro. Let's explore a few more gdb macros that come with the mod_perl source and might be handy during a problem debug.

Remember that we are still stuck in the while(1) loop, and that's when we are going to run the macros (assuming of course that they were loaded as per our last example). The *longmess* macro shows us the full Perl backtrace of the current state:

```
(gdb) longmess
at /home/httpd/perl/hangme.pl line 9
Apache::ROOT::perl::hangme_2epl::handler
('Apache=SCALAR(0x82ec0ec)') called at
/usr/lib/perl5/site_perl/5.6.1/i386-linux/Apache/Registry.pm
line 143
eval {...} called at
/usr/lib/perl5/site_perl/5.6.1/i386-linux/Apache/Registry.pm
line 143
Apache::Registry::handler('Apache=SCALAR(0x82ec0ec)')
called at (eval 29) line 0
eval {...} called at (eval 29) line 0
```

So we can see that we are inside the Apache::Registry handler, which was executed via eval( ), and the program is currently executing the code on line 9 in the script */home/httpd/perl/hangme.pl*. Internally the macro uses Carp::longmess( ) to generate the trace. The *shortmess* macro is similar to *longmess*, but it prints only the top-level caller's package, via `Carp::shortmess()`:

```
(gdb) shortmess
at /usr/lib/perl5/site_perl/5.6.1/i386-linux/Apache/Registry.pm
line 143
```

Don't search for `shortmess()` or `longmess()` functions in the `Carp` manpage—you won't find them, as they aren't a part of the public API. The *caller* macro prints the package that called the last command:

```
(gdb) caller
caller = Apache::ROOT::perl::hangme_2epl
```

In our example this is the `Apache::ROOT::perl::hangme_2epl` package, which was created on the fly by `Apache::Registry`.

Other macros allow you to look at the values of variables and will probably require some level of Perl API knowledge. You may want to refer to the *perlxs*, *perlguts* and other related manpages before you proceed with these.

Useful Debug Modules

You may find the modules discussed in this section very useful while debugging your code. They will allow you to learn a lot about Perl internals.

B::Deparse

Perl optimizes many things away at compile time, which explains why Perl is so fast under mod_perl. If you want to see what code is actually executed at runtime, use the *-MO=Deparse* Perl option.

For example, if you aren't sure whether Perl will do what you expect it to, it will show you what Perl is really going to do. Consider this trap we discussed earlier:

```
open IN, "filename" || die $!;
```

This looks like perfectly valid code, and indeed it compiles without any errors, but let's see what Perl is executing:

```
panic% perl -MO=Deparse -e 'open IN, "filename" || die $!'
open IN, 'filename';
```

As you can see, the die() part was optimized away. open() is a list operator (since it accepts a list of arguments), and list operators have lower precedence than the || operator. Therefore, Perl executes the following:

```
open IN, ("filename" || die $!);
```

Since in our example we have used `"filename"`, which is a true value, the rest of the expression in the parentheses above is discarded. The code is reduced to:

```
open IN, "filename";
```

at compile time. So if the file cannot be opened for some reason, the program will never call die( ), since Perl has removed this part of the statement.

To do the right thing you should either use parentheses explicitly to specify the order of execution or use the low-precedence or operator. Both examples below will do the right thing:

```
panic% perl -MO=Deparse -e 'open(IN, "filename") || die $!'
die $! unless open IN, 'filename';
panic% perl -MO=Deparse -e 'open IN, "filename" or die $!'
die $! unless open IN, 'filename';
```

As you can see, Perl compiles both sources into exactly the same code.

Notice that if the "filename" argument is not true, the code gets compiled to this:

```
panic% perl -MO=Deparse,-p -e 'open IN, "" || die $!'
open(IN, die($!));
```

which causes the program to die($!) without any reason in $!:

```
panic% perl -e 'open IN, "" || die $!'
Died at -e line 1.
```

while if we do the right thing, we should see the reason for the open( ) failure:

```
panic% perl -e 'open IN, "" or die $!'
No such file or directory at -e line 1.
```

Also consider:

```
panic% perl -MO=Deparse,-p -e 'select MYSTD || die $!'
select(MYSTD);
```

Since select( ) always returns a true value, the right part of the expression will never be executed. Therefore, Perl optimizes it away. In the case of select( ), it always returns the currently selected file handle, and there always is one.

We have used this cool *-MO=Deparse* technique without explaining it so far. B::Deparse is a backend module for the Perl compiler that generates Perl source code, based on the internal compiled structure that Perl itself creates after parsing a program. Therefore, you may find it useful while developing and debugging your code. We will show here one more useful thing it does. See its manpage for an extensive usage manual.

When you use the *-p* option, the output also includes parentheses (even when they are not required by precedence), which can make it easy to see if Perl is parsing your expressions the way you intended. If we repeat the last example:

```
panic% perl -MO=Deparse,-p -e 'open IN, "filename" or die $!'
(open(IN, 'filename') or die($!));
```

we can see the exact execution precedence. For example, if you are writing constructor code that can serve as a class method and an instance method, so you can instantiate objects in both ways:

```
my $cool1 = PerlCool->new( );
my $cool2 = $cool1->new( );
```

and you are unsure whether you can write this:

```
package PerlCool;
sub new {
    my $self = shift;
    my $type = ref $self || $self;
    return bless {}, type;
}
```

or whether you have to put in parentheses:

```
my $type = ref ($self) || $self;
```

you can use B::Deparse to verify your assumptions:

```
panic% perl -MO=Deparse,-p -e 'ref $self || $self'
(ref($self) or $self);
```

Indeed, ref() has a higher precedence than ||, and therefore this code will do the right thing:

```
my $type = ref $self || $self;
```

On the other hand, it might confuse other readers of your code, or even yourself some time in the future, so if you are unsure about code readability, use the parentheses.

Of course, if you forget the simple mathematical operations precedences, you can ask the backend compiler to help you. This one is obvious:

```
panic% perl -MO=Deparse,-p -e 'print $a + $b * $c % $d'
print(($a + (($b * $c) % $d)));
```

This one is not so obvious:

```
panic% perl -MO=Deparse,-p -e 'print $a ** -$b ** $c'
print(($a ** (-($b ** $c))));
```

B::Deparse tells it all, but you probably shouldn't leave such a thing in your code without explicit parentheses.

Finally, let's use B::Deparse to help resolve the confusion regarding the statement we saw earlier:

```
$c = $a > $b and $a < $b ? 1 : 0;

panic% perl -MO=Deparse -e '$c = $a > $b and $a < $b ? 1 : 0;'
$a < $b ? '???' : '???' if $c = $a > $b;
-e syntax OK
```

Just as we explained earlier, the and operator has a lower precedence than the = operator. We can explicitly see this in the output of B::Deparse, which rewrites the statement in a less obscure way.

Of course, it's worth learning the precedences of the Perl operators from the *perlop* manpage so you don't have to resort to using B::Deparse.

-D Runtime Option

You can watch your code as it's being compiled and executed by Perl via the *-D* runtime option. Perl will generate different output according to the extra options (letters or numbers) specified after *-D*. You can supply one or more options at the same time. Here are the available options for Perl Version 5.6.0 (reproduced from the *perlrun* manpage):

```
    1  p  Tokenizing and parsing
    2  s  Stack snapshots
    4  l  Context (loop) stack processing
    8  t  Trace execution
   16  o  Method and overloading resolution
   32  c  String/numeric conversions
   64  P  Print preprocessor command for -P
  128  m  Memory allocation
  256  f  Format processing
  512  r  Regular expression parsing and execution
 1024  x  Syntax tree dump
 2048  u  Tainting checks
 4096  L  Memory leaks (needs -DLEAKTEST when compiling Perl)
 8192  H  Hash dump -- usurps values()
16384  X  Scratchpad allocation
32768  D  Cleaning up
65536  S  Thread synchronization
```

Let's look at some of these options. Consider this one-line example:

```
panic% perl -le '$_="yafoo"; s/foo/bar/; print'
yabar
```

which simply substitutes the string "foo" with the string "bar" in the variable $_ and prints out its value. Now let's see how Perl compiles and executes the regular expression substitution part of the code. We will use Perl's -Dr (or -D512) option:

```
panic% perl -Dr -le '$_="yafoo"; s/foo/bar/; print'
Compiling REx `foo'
size 3 first at 1
rarest char f at 0
   1: EXACT <foo>(3)
   3: END(0)
anchored `foo' at 0 (checking anchored isall) minlen 3
Omitting $` $& $' support.

EXECUTING...

Guessing start of match, REx `foo' against `yafoo'...
Found anchored substr `foo' at offset 2...
Starting position does not contradict /^/m...
Guessed: match at offset 2
Matching REx `foo' against `foo'
  Setting an EVAL scope, savestack=3
   2 <ya> <foo>            |  1:  EXACT <foo>
   5 <yafoo> <>            |  3:  END
```

```
Match successful!
yabar
Freeing REx: `foo'
```

As you can see, there are two stages: compilation and execution. During the compilation stage, Perl records the stages it should go through when matching the string, notes what length it should match for, and notes whether one of the $', $&, or $' special variables will be used.* During the execution we can see the actual process of matching. In our example the match was successful.

The trace doesn't mention the *replace* segment of the s/// construct, since it's not a part of the regular expression per se.

The -Dx (or -D1024) option tells Perl to print the syntax tree dump. We'll use some very simple code so the execution tree will not be too long to be presented here:

```
panic% perl -Dx -le 'print 12*60*60'
{
6    TYPE = leave   ===> DONE
     FLAGS = (VOID,KIDS,PARENS)
     REFCNT = 0
     {
1        TYPE = enter  ===> 2
     }
     {
2        TYPE = nextstate  ===> 3
         FLAGS = (VOID)
         LINE = 1
         PACKAGE = "main"
     }
     {
5        TYPE = print  ===> 6
         FLAGS = (VOID,KIDS)
         {
3            TYPE = pushmark  ===> 4
             FLAGS = (SCALAR)
         }
         {
4            TYPE = const  ===> 5
             FLAGS = (SCALAR)
             SV = IV(43200)
         }
     }
}
```

This code shows us the tree of opcodes after the compilation process. Each opcode is prefixed with a number, which then is used to determine the order of execution. You can see that each opcode is linked to some other opcode (a number following the == => tag). If you start from the opcode numbered 1, jump to the opcode it's linked to

---

* You should avoid using these at all, since they add a performance hit, and once used in any regular expression they will be set in every other regular expression, even if you didn't ask for them.

(2, in this example), and continue this way, you will see the execution pass of the code. Since the code might have conditional branches, Perl cannot predetermine a definite order at compile time; therefore, when you follow the execution, the numbers will not necessarily be in sequence.

Of course, internally Perl uses opcode pointers in memory, not numbers. Numbers are used in the debug printout only for our convenience.

Another interesting fact that we learn from this output is that Perl optimizes everything it can at compile time. For example, when you need to know how many seconds are in 12 hours, you could calculate it manually and use the resulting number. But, as we see from:

```
SV = IV(43200)
```

Perl has already done the calculation at compile time, so no runtime overhead occurs if you say 12*60*60 and not 43200. The former is also more self-explanatory, while the latter may require an explicit comment to tell us what it is.

Now let's bundle a few other options together and see a subroutine argument stack snapshot via *s*, context stack processing via *l*, and trace execution via *t* all at once:

```
panic% perl -Dtls -le 'print 12*60*60'
    =>
(-e:1)    const(IV(12))
    =>  IV(12)
(-e:1)    const(IV(60))
    =>  IV(12)  IV(60)
(-e:1)    multiply
    =>
(-e:1)    const(IV(720))
    =>  IV(720)
(-e:1)    const(IV(60))
    =>  IV(720)  IV(60)
(-e:1)    multiply
(-e:1)    ENTER scope 2 at op.c:6501
(-e:1)    LEAVE scope 2 at op.c:6811
(-e:0)    LEAVE scope 1 at perl.c:1319
(-e:0)    ENTER scope 1 at perl.c:1327
(-e:0)    Setting up jumplevel 0xbffff8cc, was 0x40129f40
```

You can see how Perl pushes constants 12 and 60 onto an argument stack, executes multiply( ), gets a result of 720, pushes it back onto the stack, pushes 60 again, and executes another multiplication. The tracing and argument stack options show us this information. All this happens at compile time.

In addition, we see a number of scope entering and leaving messages, which come from the context stack status report. These options might be helpful when you want to see Perl entering and leaving block scopes (loops, subroutines, files, etc.). As you can see, bundling a few options together gives very useful reports.

Since we have been using command-line execution rather than code placed in the file, Perl uses *-e* as the code's filename. Line 0 doesn't exist; it's used for special purposes.

Having finished the compilation, now we proceed to the execution part:

```
EXECUTING...

    =>
(-e:0)    enter
(-e:0)    ENTER scope 2 at pp_hot.c:1535
Entering block 0, type BLOCK
    =>
(-e:0)    nextstate
    =>
(-e:1)    pushmark
    =>  *
(-e:1)    const(IV(43200))
    =>  *  IV(43200)
(-e:1)    print
43200
    =>  SV_YES
(-e:1)    leave
Leaving block 0, type BLOCK
(-e:0)    LEAVE scope 2 at pp_hot.c:1657
(-e:0)    LEAVE scope 1 at perl.c:395
```

Here you can see what Perl does on each line of your source code. So basically the gist of this code (bolded in the example) is pushing the constant integer scalar (const(IV)) onto the execution stack, and then calling print( ). The SV_YES symbol indicates that print( ) returns a scalar value. The rest of the output consists of controlling messages, where Perl changes scopes.

Of course, as the code gets more complicated, the traces will get longer and trickier to understand. But sometimes these traces can be as indispensable as interactive debugging.

You can use the -D[letter|number] techniques from within mod_perl as well by setting the PERL5OPT environment variable. For example, using the bash shell to see the compilation and execution traces, you can start the server in this way:

```
panic% PERL5OPT=-Dt ./httpd_perl -X
```

You will see a lot of output while the server starts. Once it finishes the tracing, open the *error_log* file and issue a request to your code. The tracing output will show up in this file.

Devel::Peek and Apache::Peek

Devel::Peek is a very useful module for looking at the Perl internals. It's especially useful for debugging XS code. With Devel::Peek we can look at Perl variables' data structures. This code:

```
use Devel::Peek;
my $x = 'mod_perl rules';
Dump $x;
```

prints:

```
SV = PV(0x804c674) at 0x80571fc
  REFCNT = 1
  FLAGS = (PADBUSY,PADMY,POK,pPOK)
  PV = 0x805ce78 "mod_perl rules"\0
  CUR = 14
  LEN = 15
```

We can see that this variable is a scalar, whose reference count is 1 (there are no other variables pointing to it). Its value is the string "mod_perl rules", terminated by \0 (one more character is used for the string-terminating \0 character, which is handled behind the scenes, transparently to the user), whose length is 15 characters including the terminating \0 character. The data structure starts at 0x80571fc, and its string value is stored starting from the address 0x805ce78.

If you want to look at more complicated structures, such as a hash or an array, you should create references to them and pass the references to the Dump( ) function.

The Apache::Peek module is built for use with mod_perl's Devel::Peek, so you can use it to peek at mod_perl's code internals.

In Chapter 10 we showed a few examples where Devel::Peek and Apache::Peek have been found very useful. To learn about Perl variables' internals, refer to the *perlguts* manpage.

Devel::Symdump and Apache::Symdump

Devel::Symdump allows us to access Perl's symbol table. This package is object oriented. To instantiate an object, you should provide the name of the package to traverse. If no package is provided as an argument, the main package is used. If the object is created with new( ), Devel::Symdump analyzes only the packages that are given as arguments; if rnew( ) is used, nested modules are analyzed recursively.

Once the object is instantiated, the methods packages( ), scalars( ), arrays( ), hashes( ), functions( ), ios( ), and unknowns( ) can be used. Each method returns an array of fully qualified symbols of the specified type in all packages that are held within a Devel::Symdump object, but without the leading "$", "@", or "%". In a scalar context, they will return the number of such symbols. Unknown symbols are usually either formats or variables that don't yet have defined values.

For example:

```
require Devel::Symdump;
@packs = qw(Devel::Symdump);
$obj = Devel::Symdump->new(@packs);
print join "\n", $obj->scalars;

Devel::Symdump::rnew
Devel::Symdump::inh_tree
Devel::Symdump::_partdump
```

```
Devel::Symdump::DESTROY
...more symbols stripped
```

You may find this package useful to see what symbols are defined, traverse trees of symbols from inherited packages, and more. See the package's manpage for more information.

Apache::Symdump uses Devel::Symdump to record snapshots of the Perl symbol table in *ServerRoot/logs/symdump.$$.$n*. Here *$$* is the process ID and *$n* is incremented each time the handler is run.

To enable this module, add the following to *httpd.conf*:

```
PerlLogHandler Apache::Symdump
```

This module is useful for watching the growth of the processes and hopefully, by taking steps against the growth, reducing it. One of the reasons for process growth is the definition of new symbols. You can use the *diff* utility to compare snapshots and get an idea of what might be making a process grow. For example:

```
panic% diff -u symdump.1892.0 symdump.1892.1
```

where 1892 is PID. Normally, new symbols come from modules or scripts that were not preloaded, the Perl method cache, and so on. Let's write a simple script that uses DB_File, which wasn't preloaded (see Example 21-13).

Example 21-13. use_dbfile.pl

```
use strict;
require DB_File;
my $r = shift;
$r->send_http_header("text/plain");
$r->print("Hello $$\n");
```

If we issue a few requests and then compare two consecutive request dumps for the same process, nothing happens. That's because the module is loaded on the first request, and therefore from now on the symbol table will be the same. So in order to help Apache::Symdump to help us detect the load, we will require the module only on the second reload (see Example 21-14).

Example 21-14. use_dbfile1.pl

```
use strict;
use vars qw($loaded);
require DB_File if defined $loaded;
$loaded = 1;
my $r = shift;
$r->send_http_header("text/plain");
$r->print("Hello $$\n");
```

Running the *diff*:

```
panic% diff symdump.9909.1 symdump.9909.2 |wc -1
   301
```

reveals that there were 301 symbols defined, mostly from the DB_File and Fcntl packages. We can also see what new files were loaded, by applying *diff* on the *incdump.$$.$n* files, which dump the contents of %INC after each request:

```
panic% diff incdump.9909.1 incdump.9909.2
1a2
> /usr/lib/perl5/5.6.1/i386-linux/auto/DB_File/autosplit.ix
= /usr/lib/perl5/5.6.1/i386-linux/auto/DB_File/autosplit.ix
21a23
> DB_File.pm = /usr/lib/perl5/5.6.1/i386-linux/DB_File.pm
```

Remember that Apache::Symdump does not clean up its snapshot files, so you have to do it yourself:

```
panic% rm logs/symdump.* logs/incdump.*
```

Apache::Status also uses Devel::Symdump to allow you to inspect symbol tables through your browser.

Apache::Debug

This module sends what may be helpful debugging information to the client, rather than to the *error_log* file.

This module specifies only the dump( ) method:

```
use Apache::Debug ();
my $r = shift;
Apache::Debug::dump($r, "some comment", "another comment", ...);
```

For example, if we take this simple script:

```
use Apache::Debug ();
use Apache::Constants qw(SERVER_ERROR);
my $r = shift;
Apache::Debug::dump($r, SERVER_ERROR, "Uh Oh!");
```

it prints out the HTTP headers as received by server and various request data:

```
SERVER_ERROR

Uh Oh!

cwd=/home/httpd/perl
$r->method          : GET
$r->uri             : /perl/test.pl
$r->protocol        : HTTP/1.0
$r->path_info       :
$r->filename        : /home/httpd/perl/test.pl
$r->allow_options   : 8
$s->server_admin    : root@localhost
$s->server_hostname : localhost
$s->port            : 8000
$c->remote_host     :
$c->remote_ip       : 127.0.0.1
```

```
$c->remote_logname   :
$c->user             :
$c->auth_type        :

scalar $r->args      :

$r->args:

$r->content:

$r->headers_in:
   Accept        = image/gif, image/x-xbitmap, image/jpeg,
                   image/pjpeg, image/png, */*
   Accept-Charset = iso-8859-1,*,utf-8
   Accept-Encoding = gzip
   Accept-Language = en
   Connection     = Keep-Alive
   Host           = localhost:8000
   Pragma         = no-cache
   User-Agent     = Mozilla/4.76 [en] (X11; U; Linux 2.2.17-21mdk i686)
```

Other Debug Modules

The following are a few other modules that you may find of use, but in this book we won't delve deeply into their details:

- Apache::DumpHeaders is used to watch an HTTP transaction, looking at the client and server headers.

- Apache::DebugInfo offers the ability to monitor various bits of per-request data. Similar to Apache::DumpHeaders.

- Devel::StackTrace encapsulates the information that can be found through using the caller( ) function and provides a simple interface to this data.

- Apache::Symbol provides XS tricks to avoid a mandatory "Subroutine redefined" warning when reloading a module that contains a subroutine that is eligible for inlining. Useful during development when using Apache::Reload or Apache::StatINC to reload modules.

Looking Inside the Server

There are a number of tools that allow you look at the server internals at runtime, through a convenient web interface.

Apache::Status—Embedded Interpreter Status Information

This is a very useful module. It lets you watch what happens to the Perl part of the mod_perl server. You can watch the size of all subroutines and variables, variable dumps, lexical information, opcode trees, and more.

You shouldn't use it on a production server, as it adds quite a bit of overhead for each request.

Minimal configuration

This configuration enables the Apache::Status module with its minimum feature set. Add this to *httpd.conf*:

```
<Location /perl-status>
    SetHandler perl-script
    PerlHandler Apache::Status
</Location>
```

If you are going to use Apache::Status it's important to put it as the first module in the startup file, or in *httpd.conf*:

```
# startup.pl
use Apache::Status ();
use Apache::Registry ();
use Apache::DBI ();
```

For example, if you use Apache::DBI and you don't load Apache::Status before Apache::DBI, you will not get the Apache::DBI menu entry (which allows you to see persistent connections).

Extended configuration

There are several variables you can use to modify the behavior of Apache::Status:

PerlSetVar StatusOptionsAll On
> This single directive will enable all of the options described below.

PerlSetVar StatusDumper On
> When you are browsing symbol tables, you can view the values of your arrays, hashes, and scalars with Data::Dumper.

PerlSetVar StatusPeek On
> With this option On and the Apache::Peek module installed, functions and variables can be viewed in Devel::Peek style.

PerlSetVar StatusLexInfo On
> With this option On and the B::LexInfo module installed, subroutine lexical variable information can be viewed.

PerlSetVar StatusDeparse On
> With this option On and B::Deparse version 0.59 or higher (included in Perl 5.005_ 59+), subroutines can be "deparsed." Options can be passed to B::Deparse::new like so:
>
> ```
>     PerlSetVar StatusDeparseOptions "-p -sC"
> ```
>
> See the B::Deparse manpage for details.

PerlSetVar StatusTerse On

> With this option On, text-based optree graphs of subroutines can be displayed, thanks to B::Terse.

PerlSetVar StatusTerseSize On

> With this option On and the B::TerseSize module installed, text-based optree graphs of subroutines and their sizes can be displayed. See the B::TerseSize documentation for more info.

PerlSetVar StatusTerseSizeMainSummary On

> With this option On and the B::TerseSize module installed, a "Memory Usage" submenu will be added to the Apache::Status main menu. This option is disabled by default, as it can be rather CPU-intensive to summarize memory usage for the entire server. It is strongly suggested that this option be used only with a development server running in -X mode, as the results will be cached.
>
> Remember to preload B::TerseSize in *httpd.conf* and make sure that it's loaded after Apache::Status:
>
> ```
> PerlModule Apache::Status
> PerlModule B::Terse
> ```

PerlSetVar StatusGraph On

> When StatusDumper (see above) is enabled, another submenu, "OP Tree Graph," will be present with the dump if this configuration variable is set to On.
>
> This requires the B module (part of the Perl compiler kit) and the B::Graph module, Version 0.03 or higher, to be installed along with the dot program. dot is part of the graph-visualization toolkit from AT&T (*http://www.research.att.com/sw/tools/graphviz/*).
>
> WARNING: Some graphs may produce very large images, and some graphs may produce no image if B::Graph's output is incorrect.

There is more information about Apache::Status in its manpage.

Usage

Assuming that your mod_perl server is listening on port 81, fetch *http://www.example.com:81/perl-status*:

```
Embedded Perl version v5.6.1 for Apache/1.3.17 (Unix) mod_perl/1.25
process 9943, running since Fri Feb 9 17:48:50 2001
```

All the sections below are links when you view them through */perl-status*:

```
Perl Configuration
Loaded Modules
Inheritance Tree
Enabled mod_perl Hooks
Environment
PerlRequire'd Files
Signal Handlers
```

```
Symbol Table Dump
ISA Tree
Compiled Registry Scripts
```

Here's what these sections show:

- *Perl Configuration* is the same as the output from *perl -V* (loaded from *Config. pm*).
- *Loaded Modules* shows the loaded Perl modules.
- *Inheritance Tree* shows the inheritance tree of the loaded modules.
- *Enabled mod_perl Hooks* shows all mod_perl hooks that were enabled at compile time.
- *Environment* shows the contents of %ENV.
- *PerlRequire'd Files* displays the files that were required via PerlRequire.
- *Signal Handlers* shows the status of all signal handlers (using %SIG).
- *Symbol Table Dump* shows the symbol table dump of all packages loaded in the process—you can click through the symbols and, for example, see the values of scalars, jump to the symbol dumps of specific packages, and more.
- *ISA Tree* shows the ISA inheritance tree.
- *Compiled Registry Scripts* shows Apache::Registry, Apache::PerlRun, and other scripts compiled on the fly.

From some menus you can move deeper to peek into the internals of the server, to see the values of the global variables in the packages, to see the cached scripts and modules, and much more. Just click around.

Remember that whenever you access */perl-status* you are always inside one of the child processes, so you may not see what you expect, since this child process might have a different history of processed requests and therefore a different internal state. Sometimes when you fetch */perl-status* and look at the *Compiled Registry Scripts* section you see no listing of scripts at all. Apache::Status shows the registry scripts compiled in the *httpd* child that is serving your request for */perl-status*; if the child has not yet compiled the requested script, */perl-status* will just show you the main menu.

mod_status

The mod_status module allows a server administrator to find out how well the server is performing. An HTML page is presented that gives the current server statistics in an easily readable form. If required, given a compatible browser, this page can be automatically refreshed. Another page gives a simple machine-readable list of the current server state.

This Apache module is written in C. It is compiled by default, so all you have to do to use it is enable it in your configuration file:

```
<Location /status>
    SetHandler server-status
</Location>
```

For security reasons you will probably want to limit access to it. If you have installed Apache according to the instructions given in this book, you will find a prepared configuration section in *httpd.conf*. To enable use of the mod_status module, just uncomment it:

```
ExtendedStatus On
<Location /status>
    SetHandler server-status
    Order deny,allow
    Deny from all
    Allow from localhost
</Location>
```

You can now access server statistics by using a web browser to access the page *http://localhost/status* (as long as your server recognizes *localhost*).

The details given by mod_status are:

- The number of children serving requests
- The number of idle children
- The status of each child, the number of requests that child has performed and the total number of bytes served by the child
- The total number of accesses and the total bytes served
- The time the server was last started/restarted and for how long it has been running
- Averages giving the number of requests per second, the number of bytes served per second, and the number of bytes per request
- The current percentage of the CPU being used by each child and in total by Apache
- The current hosts and requests being processed

In Chapter 5 you can read about Apache::VMonitor, which is a more advanced sibling of mod_status.

Turning the ExtendedStatus mode on is not recommended for high-performance production sites, as it adds overhead to the request response times.

References

- *Perl Debugged*, by Peter Scott and Ed Wright (Addison Wesley). A good book on how to debug Perl code and how to code in Perl so you won't need to debug.
- *Debugging Perl: Troubleshooting for Programmers*, by Martin Brown (McGraw Hill). This book tells you pretty much everything you might want to know about Perl debugging.
- *Programming Perl*, Third Edition, by Larry Wall, Tom Christiansen, and Jon Orwant (O'Reilly). Covers Perl Versions 5.005 and 5.6.0. Chapter 20 talks in depth about the Perl debugger.
- "Cultured Perl: Debugging Perl with ease, catch the bugs before they bite," by Teodor Zlatanov: *http://www-106.ibm.com/developerworks/library/l-pl-deb.html*

  This article talks about using the Perl command-line debugger, the GUI Devel:: ptkdb, and a special Perl shell for debugging.
- *The Mythical Man-Month*, 20th Anniversary Edition, by Fred P. Brooks (Addison Wesley). A must-read for all programmers. After reading this book, you will at least learn to plan more time for the debug phase of your project.
- General software-testing techniques FAQ: *http://www.faqs.org/faqs/software-eng/ testing-faq/*.

## CHAPTER 22

Troubleshooting mod_perl

When something goes wrong, we expect the software to report the problem. But if we don't understand the meaning of the error message, we won't be able to resolve it. Therefore in this chapter we will talk about errors specific to mod_perl, as reported by a mod_perl-enabled Apache server.

Many reports are produced by Perl itself. If you find them unclear, you may want to use the `use diagnostics` pragma in your development code. With the `diagnostics` pragma, Perl provides an in-depth explanation of each reported warning and error. Note that you should remove this pragma in your production code, since it adds a runtime overhead.

Errors that may occur during the build and installation stages are covered in the respective troubleshooting sections of Chapter 3. This chapter deals with errors that may occur during the configuration and startup, code parsing and compilation, runtime, and shutdown and restart phases.

Configuration and Startup

This section covers errors you might encounter when you start the server.

libexec/libperl.so: open failed: No such file or directory

If you get this error when you start the server, it probably means that your version of Perl was itself compiled with a shared library called *libperl.so*. mod_perl detects this and links the Apache executable to the same Perl shared library. This error simply means that the shared library cannot be found by searching the paths that Apache knows about.

Make sure you have Perl installed on the machine, and that you have *libperl.so* in `<perlroot>/<version>/<architecture>/CORE` (for example, */usr/local/lib/perl5/5.6.1/ sun4-solaris/CORE*).

If the file is there but you still get the error, you should include the directory in which the file is located in the environment variable LD_LIBRARY_PATH (or the equivalent variable for your operating system). Under normal circumstances, Apache should have had the library path configured properly at compile time; if Apache was misconfigured, adding the path to LD_LIBRARY_PATH manually will help Apache find the shared library.

install_driver(Oracle) failed: Can't load '.../DBD/Oracle/Oracle.so' for module DBD::Oracle

Here's an example of the full error report that you might see:

```
install_driver(Oracle) failed: Can't load
'/usr/lib/perl5/site_perl/5.6.1/i386-linux/auto/DBD/Oracle/Oracle.so'
for module DBD::Oracle:
libclntsh.so.8.0: cannot open shared object file:
No such file or directory at
/usr/lib/perl5/5.6.1/i386-linux/DynaLoader.pm line 169.
at (eval 27) line 3
Perhaps a required shared
library or dll isn't installed where expected at
/usr/local/apache/perl/tmp.pl line 11
```

On BSD-style filesystems, LD_LIBRARY_PATH is not searched for *setuid* programs. If Apache is a *setuid* executable, you might receive this error. Therefore, the first solution is to explicitly load the library from the system-wide *ldconfig* configuration file:

```
panic# echo $ORACLE_HOME/lib >> /etc/ld.so.conf
panic# ldconfig
```

Another solution to this problem is to modify the *Makefile* file (which is created when you run *perl Makefile.PL*) as follows:

1. Search for the line LD_RUN_PATH=
2. Replace it with LD_RUN_PATH=my_oracle_home/lib

where *my_oracle_home* is, of course, the home path to your Oracle installation. In particular, the file *libclntsh.so.8.0* should exist in the *lib* subdirectory.

Then just type *make install*, and all should go well.

Note that setting LD_RUN_PATH has the effect of hardcoding the path to *my_oracle_home/lib* in the file *Oracle.so*, which is generated by DBD::Oracle. This is an efficiency mechanism, so that at runtime it doesn't have to search through LD_LIBRARY_PATH or the default directories used by *ld*.

For more information, see the *ld* manpage and the essay on LD_LIBRARY_PATH at *http://www.visi.com/~barr/ldpath.html*.

Invalid command 'PerlHandler'...

Here's an example of the full error report that you might see:

```
Syntax error on line 393 of /home/httpd/httpd_perl/conf/httpd.conf:
Invalid command 'PerlHandler', perhaps mis-spelled or
defined by a module not included in the server
configuration [FAILED]
```

You might get this error when you have a mod_perl-enabled Apache server compiled with DSO, but the mod_perl module isn't loaded. (This generally happens when it's an installed RPM or other binary package.) In this case you have to tell Apache to load mod_perl by adding the following line to your *httpd.conf* file:

```
AddModule mod_perl.c
```

You might also get this error when you try to run a non-mod_perl Apache server using the *httpd.conf* file from a mod_perl server.

RegistryLoader: Translation of uri [...] to filename failed

Here's an example of the full error report that you might see:

```
RegistryLoader: Translation of uri
    [/home/httpd/perl/test.pl] to filename failed
    [tried: /home/httpd/docs/home/httpd/perl/test.pl]
```

In this example, this means you are trying to preload a script called */perl/test.pl*, located at */home/httpd/perl/test.pl* in the filesystem. This error shows up when Apache::RegistryLoader fails to translate the URI into the corresponding filesystem path. Most failures happen when a user passes a file path (such as */home/httpd/perl/test.pl*) instead of a relative URI (such as */perl/test.pl*).

You should either provide both the URI and the filename:

```
Apache::RegistryLoader->new->handler($uri, $filename);
```

or supply a callback subroutine that will perform the URI-to-filename conversion. The callback accepts the URI as an argument and returns a filename. For example, if your mod_perl scripts reside in */home/httpd/perl-scripts/* but the base URI is */perl/*, you might do the following:

```
my $rl = Apache::RegistryLoader->new(
            trans => \&uri2filename);
$rl->handler("/perl/test.pl");

sub uri2filename{
    my $uri = shift;
    $uri =~ s:^/perl/:/perl-scripts/:;
    return Apache->server_root_relative($uri);
}
```

Here, we initialize the Apache::RegistryLoader object with the uri2filename() function that will perform the URI-to-filename translation. In this function, we just adjust the URI and return the filename based on the location of the server root. So if the server root is *home/httpd/*, the callback will return *home/httpd/perl-scripts/test.pl*—exactly what we have requested.

For more information please refer to the `Apache::RegistryLoader` manpage.

Code Parsing and Compilation

The following warnings and errors might be reported when the Perl code is compiled. This may be during the server startup phase or, if the code hasn't yet been compiled, at request time.

Value of $x will not stay shared at - line 5

This warning usually happens when scripts are run under `Apache::Registry` and similar handlers, and some function uses a lexically scoped variable that is defined outside of that function.

This warning is important and should be considered an error in most cases. The explanation of the problem and possible solutions are discussed in Chapter 6.

Value of $x may be unavailable at - line 5

Similar to the previous section, the warning may happen under `Apache::Registry` and similar handlers, and should be considered an error. The cause is discussed in the *perldiag* manpage and possible solutions in Chapter 6.

Can't locate loadable object for module ...

Here's an example of the full error report that you might see:

```
Can't locate loadable object for module Apache::Util in @INC...
```

In this particular example, it means that there is no object built for `Apache::Util`. You should build mod_perl with one of these arguments: `PERL_UTIL_API=1`, `EVERYTHING=1`, or `DYNAMIC=1`.

For similar errors, see Chapter 3. Locate the missing module and see what build-time argument enables it.

Can't locate object method "get_handlers" ...

If you see this error:

```
Can't locate object method "get_handlers" via package "Apache"
```

you need to rebuild your mod_perl with stacked handlers; that is, with `PERL_STACKED_HANDLERS=1` or with `EVERYTHING=1`.

Missing right bracket at line ...

This error usually means you really do have a syntax error. However, you might also see it because a script running under Apache::Registry is using either the __DATA__ or __END__ tokens. In Chapter 6, we explain why this problem arises when a script is run under Apache::Registry.

Can't load '.../auto/DBI/DBI.so' for module DBI

If you have the DBI module installed, this error is usually caused by binary incompatibilities. Check that all your modules were compiled with the same Perl version that mod_perl was built with. For example, Perl 5.005 and 5.004 are not binary compatible by default.

Other known causes of this problem are:

- OS distributions that ship with a broken binary Perl installation.
- The perl program and libperl.a library are somehow built with different binary compatibility flags.

The solution to these problems is to rebuild Perl and any extension modules from a fresh source tree. Read Perl's *INSTALL* document for more details.

On the Solaris OS, if you see the "Can't load DBI" or a similar error for the IO module (or whatever dynamic module mod_perl tries to pull in first), you need to reconfigure, rebuild, and reinstall Perl and any dynamic modules. When *Configure* asks for "additional LD flags," add the following flags:

```
-Xlinker --export-dynamic
```

or:

```
-Xlinker -E
```

This problem is known to be caused only by installing GNU *ld* under Solaris.

Runtime

Once you have your server up and running and most of the code working correctly, you may still encounter errors generated by your code at runtime. Some possible errors are discussed in this section.

foo ... at /dev/null line 0

Under mod_perl, you may receive a warning or an error in the *error_log* file that specifies */dev/null* as the source file and line 0 as the line number where the printing of the message was triggered. This is quite normal if the code is executed from within a handler, because there is no actual file associated with the handler. Therefore, $0 is set to */dev/null*, and that's what you see.

Segfaults When Using XML::Parser

If some processes have segmentation faults when using XML::Parser, you should use the following flags during Apache configuration:

```
--disable-rule=EXPAT
```

This should be necessary only with mod_perl Version 1.22 and lower. Starting with mod_perl Version 1.23, the EXPAT option is disabled by default.

exit signal Segmentation fault (11)

If you build mod_perl and mod_php in the same binary, you might get a segmentation fault followed by this error:

```
exit signal Segmentation fault (11)
```

The solution is to not rely on PHP's built-in MySQL support, and instead build mod_php with your local MySQL support files by adding *--with-mysql=/path/to/mysql* during *./configure*.

CGI Code Is Returned as Plain Text Instead of Being Executed

If the CGI program is not actually executed but is just returned as plain text, it means the server doesn't recognize it as a CGI script. Check your configuration files and make sure that the ExecCGI option is turned on. For example, your configuration section for Apache::Registry scripts should look like this:

```
<Location /perl>
    SetHandler perl-script
    PerlHandler Apache::Registry
    Options +ExecCGI
</Location>
```

rwrite returned -1

This error message is returned when the client breaks the connection while your script is trying to write to the client. With Apache 1.3.x, you should see the rwrite messages only if LogLevel is set to debug. (Prior to mod_perl 1.19_01, there was a bug that reported this debug message regardless of the value of the LogLevel directive.)

Generally LogLevel is either debug or info. debug logs everything, and info is the next level, which doesn't include debug messages. You shouldn't use debug mode on a production server. At the moment there is no way to prevent users from aborting connections.

Global symbol "$foo" requires explicit package name

This error message is printed when a nondeclared variable is used in the code running under the strict pragma. For example, consider the short script below, which contains a use strict; pragma and then shamelessly violates it:

```
#!/usr/bin/perl -w
use strict;
print "Content-type: text/html\n\n";
print "Hello $username";
```

Since Perl will insist that all variables are defined before being used, the program will not run and will print the error:

```
Global symbol "$username" requires
explicit package name at /home/httpd/perl/tmp.pl line 4.
```

Moreover, in certain situations (e.g., when SIG{__DIE__} is set to Carp::confess()) the entire script is printed to the *error_log* file as code that the server has tried to evaluate, so if this script is run repeatedly, the *error_log* file will grow very fast and you may run out of disk space.

This problem can easily be avoided by always declaring variables before using them. Here is the fixed version of our example:

```
#!/usr/bin/perl -w
use strict;
my $username = '';
print "Content-type: text/html\n\n";
print "Hello $username";
```

Use of uninitialized value at (eval 80) line 12

If you see this message, your code includes an undefined variable that you have used as if it was already defined and initialized. For example:

```
my $param = $q->param('test');
print $param;
```

You can fix this fairly painlessly by just specifying a default value:

```
my $param = $q->param('test') || '';
print $param;
```

In the second case, $param will always be defined, either with $q->param('test')'s return value or the default value the empty string ('' in our example).

Undefined subroutine &Apache::ROOT::perl::test_2epl:: some_function called at

This error usually happens when two scripts or handlers (Apache::Registry in this case) call a function defined in a library without a package definition, or when the two use two libraries with different content but an identical name (as passed to require( )).

Chapter 6 provides in-depth coverage of this conundrum and numerous solutions.

Callback called exit

"Callback called exit" is just a generic message when Perl encounters an unrecoverable error during perl_call_sv( ). mod_perl uses perl_call_sv( ) to invoke all handler subroutines. Such problems seem to occur far less often with Perl Version 5. 005_03 than 5.004. It shouldn't appear with Perl Version 5.6.1 and higher.

Sometimes you discover that your server is not responding and its *error_log* file has filled up the remaining space on the filesystem. When you finally get to see the contents of the *error_log* file, it includes millions of lines like this:

```
Callback called exit at -e line 33, <HTML> chunk 1.
```

This is because Perl can get very confused inside an infinite loop in your code. It doesn't necessarily mean that your code called exit( ). It's possible that Perl's malloc( ) went haywire and called croak( ), but no memory was left to properly report the error, so Perl gets stuck in a loop writing that same message to STDERR.

Perl Version 5.005 and higher is recommended for its improved *malloc.c*, and also for other features that improve the performance of mod_perl and are turned on by default.

See also the next section.

Out of memory!

If something goes really wrong with your code, Perl may die with an "Out of memory!" and/or "Callback called exit" message. Common causes of this are infinite loops, deep recursion, or calling an undefined subroutine.

If -DPERL_EMERGENCY_SBRK is defined, running out of memory need not be a fatal error: a memory pool can be allocated by using the special variable $^M. See the *perlvar* manpage for more details.

If you compile with that option and add use Apache::Debug level => 4; to your Perl code, it will allocate the $^M emergency pool and the $SIG{__DIE__} handler will call Carp::confess( ), giving you a stack trace that should reveal where the problem is. See the Apache::Resource module for the prevention of spinning *httpds*.

Note that Perl 5.005 and later have PERL_EMERGENCY_SBRK turned on by default.

Another trick is to have a startup script initialize Carp::confess( ), like this:

```
use Carp ( );
eval { Carp::confess("init") };
```

This way, when the real problem happens, Carp::confess doesn't eat memory in the emergency pool ($^M).

syntax error at /dev/null line 1, near "line arguments:"

If you see an error of this kind:

```
syntax error at /dev/null line 1, near "line arguments:"
Execution of /dev/null aborted due to compilation errors.
parse: Undefined error: 0
```

there is a chance that your *dev/null* device is broken. You can test it with:

```
panic% echo > /dev/null
```

It should silently complete the command. If it doesn't, */dev/null* is broken. Refer to your OS's manpages to learn how to restore this device. On most Unix flavors, this is how it's done:

```
panic# rm /dev/null
panic# mknod /dev/null c 1 3
panic# chmod a+rw /dev/null
```

You need to create a special file using *mknod*, for which you need to know the type and both the major and minor modes. In our case, c stands for character device, 1 is the major mode, and 3 is the minor mode. The file should be readable and writable by everybody, hence the permission mode settings (a+rw).

Shutdown and Restart

When you shut down or restart the server, you may encounter the problems presented in the following sections.

Evil Things Might Happen When Using PerlFreshRestart

Unfortunately, not all Perl modules are robust enough to survive reload. For them this is an unusual situation. PerlFreshRestart does not much more than:

```
while (my($k,$v) = each %INC) {
    delete $INC{$k};
    require $k;
}
```

Besides that, it flushes the Apache::Registry cache and empties any dynamic stacked handlers (e.g., PerlChildInitHandler).

Lots of segfaults and other problems have been reported by users who turned on PerlFreshRestart. Most of them go away when it is turned off. It doesn't mean that you shouldn't use PerlFreshRestart, if it works for you. Just beware of the dragons.

Note that if you have a mod_perl-enabled Apache built as a DSO and you restart it, the whole Perl interpreter is completely torn down (via perl_destruct()) and restarted. The value of PerlFreshRestart is irrelevent at this point.

[warn] child process 30388 did not exit, sending another SIGHUP

With Apache Version 1.3.0 and higher, mod_perl will call the perl_destruct() Perl API function during the child exit phase. This will cause proper execution of any END blocks found during server startup and will also invoke the DESTROY method on global objects that still exist.

It is possible that this operation will take a long time to finish, causing problems during a restart. If you use the *apachectl* script to restart the server, it sends the SIGHUP signal after waiting for a short while. The SIGHUP can cause problems, since it might disrupt something you need to happen during server shutdown (for example, saving data).

If you are certain that your code does not contain any END blocks or DESTROY methods to be run during child server shutdown, you can avoid the delays by setting the PERL_DESTRUCT_LEVEL environment variable to -1. Be careful, however; even if your code doesn't include any END blocks or DESTROY methods, any modules you use() might.

Processes Get Stuck on Graceful Restart

If after doing a graceful restart (e.g, by sending *kill -USR1*) you see via mod_status or Apache::VMonitor that a process is stuck in state *G* (Gracefully finishing), it means that the process is hanging in perl_destruct() while trying to clean up. If you don't need the cleanup, see the previous section on how to disable it.

CHAPTER 23

Getting Help and Online Resources

In this chapter, we propose a way to solve your mod_perl-related problems and provide starting points for information resources related to mod_perl.

If you have any problem with mod_perl itself, be it a build problem or a runtime problem, you should follow the steps below. But before you follow them, think carefully about whether the problem you are experiencing is mod_perl-related. It's quite possible that the problem is in the Perl code, SQL code, Apache itself, or something else entirely. In such cases, you should refer to other resources presented later in this chapter. Remember that although mod_perl resources might help you with many related things, they will never be as detailed as resources devoted to the topic at hand.

If you still think that the problem has something to do with mod_perl, these are the steps to follow:

1. Try to tackle the problem by yourself for a while. Check that you have the right permissions, that there is enough disk space, etc. Do sanity checks: try to remove the mod_perl source tree, unpack it again, and build from fresh.

   When trying to figure out what the problem is, always run under single-server mode (*httpd -X*) and always check the *error_log* file.

   If you still have problems, proceed to step 2.

2. Reread the documentation (or if you didn't read it yet, do it now). Try to follow the build and usage steps as explained there. This book, *Writing Apache Modules with Perl and C* (O'Reilly), and the documentation distributed with the mod_perl sources provide in-depth details on this topic. Also, make sure to read Chapter 22 thoroughly. If you are still in trouble, proceed to step 3.

3. Go to the mod_perl list archives (at *http://perl.apache.org/maillist/*) and see whether someone has already reported the same problem. If someone did, chances are that a cure to the problem has been posted to the list, be it a source

patch or a workaround. If after doing an exhaustive search you haven't come up with any solution, proceed to step 4.

Notice that sometimes doing this step before step 2 can be a good idea as well—you may happen to have encountered a well-known bug, and if that's the case doing a quick lookup in the mailing-list archives will save you time and frustration.

4. This step is the last resort. Contact the mod_perl mailing list. You should never abuse this step, and use it only when you have already been through the previous three steps. If you ask FAQ questions unnecessarily, chances are that people will not reply to you. And if you ask more FAQ questions, you might get onto people's blacklists and they will not answer your future questions even if they are relevant. Remember that all the answers that you get are coming from volunteers who, instead of having fun outdoors, try to have fun answering challenging questions. FAQ questions aren't challenging, and few people have fun answering them. See more details about mod_perl list etiquette in the next section.

It's not enough to just contact the list and ask for help. You have to provide as many details as possible. The next section covers the details you have to provide.

However, don't be afraid. The mod_perl mailing list is filled with only nice people who can provide much help and guidance, so if you can't figure something out after having followed the above steps, your question is welcome.

You cannot post to the list without first subscribing to it. To subscribe, send an email to *modperl-subscribe@perl.apache.org*. After you receive a confirmation email, you can start posting to the list. Send your emails to *modperl@perl. apache.org*.

There are other related mailing lists you might want to be on too. See the list of these and subscription instructions in the Resources section of this chapter.

How to Report Problems

When reporting a problem to the mod_perl mailing list, always send these details:

- Anything in the *error_log* file that looks suspicious and possibly related to the problem
- Output of *perl -V*
- Version of mod_perl
- Version of Apache
- Options given to mod_perl's *Makefile.PL* file
- Server configuration details
- If *make test* fails, the output of *make test TEST_VERBOSE=1*

Also check whether:

- *make test* passes 100%
- The script works under mod_cgi, if applicable

You should try to isolate the problem and send the smallest possible code snippet that reproduces the problem.

Getting the Backtrace from Core Dumps

If you get a *core* dump (segmentation fault), send a backtrace if possible. Before you try to produce it, rebuild mod_perl with:

```
panic% perl Makefile.PL PERL_DEBUG=1
```

which will:

- Add *-g* to EXTRA_CFLAGS
- Turn on PERL_TRACE
- Set PERL_DESTRUCT_LEVEL=2 (additional checks during Perl cleanup)
- Link against *libperld*, if it exists

You can read a full explanation in Chapter 21, but here is a summary of how to get a backtrace:

```
panic% cd mod_perl-1.xx
panic% gdb ../apache_1.3.xx/src/httpd
(gdb) run -X -f `pwd`/t/conf/httpd.conf -d `pwd`/t
[now make request that causes core dump]
(gdb) bt
```

In English: *cd* to the mod_perl source directory and start *gdb* with a path to the *httpd* binary, which is located in the Apache source tree. (Of course, replace *x* with real version numbers.) Next, start the *httpd* process from within *gdb* and issue a request that causes a core dump. When the code has died with the SIGSEGV signal, run *bt* to get the backtrace.

Alternatively, you can also attach to an already running process like so:

```
panic% gdb httpd <process id number>
```

If the dump is happening in *libperl*, you have to rebuild Perl with *-DDEBUGGING* enabled during the *./Configure* stage. A quick way to this is to go to your Perl source tree and run these commands:

```
panic% rm *.[oa]
panic% make LIBPERL=libperld.a
panic% cp libperld.a $Config{archlibexp}/CORE
```

where $Config{archlibexp} is:

```
% perl -V:archlibexp
```

Spinning Processes

The *gdb* attaching to the live process approach is helpful when debugging a *spinning* process. You can also get a Perl stack trace of a spinning process by installing a $SIG{USR1} handler in your code:

```
use Carp ( );
$SIG{USR1} = \&Carp::confess;
```

While the process is spinning, send it a USR1 signal:

```
panic% kill -USR1 <process id number>
```

and the Perl stack trace will be printed.

Alternatively, you can use *gdb* to find which Perl code is causing the spin:

```
panic% gdb httpd <pid of spinning process>
(gdb) where
(gdb) source mod_perl-x.xx/.gdbinit
(gdb) curinfo
```

After loading the special macros file (*.gdbinit*), you can use the *curinfo gdb* macro to figure out the file and line number in which the code stuck. Chapter 21 talks in more detail about tracing techniques.

Finally, send all these details to *modperl@perl.apache.org*.

Mailing List Etiquette

Like any community, the mod_perl mailing list has its own rules of etiquette that you would be wise to avoid violating:

- Never contact people in person to ask a question unless they have explicitly given you permission. Even if someone was kind enough to reply to a previous question, this doesn't mean he wants to be your go-to person for every subsequent problem as well. If you do this, don't be surprised if your question is ignored. Just think about how many emails these people receive daily, and you will understand the reason. Remember that this is a voluntary effort, not a technical support service.

- If a reply to your question is posted to the list and you want to follow up on it, in most cases you should keep posting to the list, so the conversation will be saved in the mailing-list archives and can later be reused by other users who seek help in the archives.

- However, if you receive a private email reply to the question, keep the conversation private, because the person who has answered you might not have wanted his answer to be seen in public. You have to respect that and not resend the reply to the list without this person's permission.

- When posting to the list, always use relevant subject lines. Don't just say "help" in the subject field of your post. Chances are that these messages will be ignored. Most of the people are interested in only specific topics, and therefore they will delete messages with unspecific subject lines without even reading them. To catch their attention, you should provide a concise, meaningful subject line.

- When replying to a message, please try to quote only relevant parts of the original post: don't overquote and don't overtrim. Refrain from replying on the top of the original message, since it makes it hard for other users to understand the conversation. Please use proper quoting delimiters, so users can easily tell your reply from the original message.

- If your English is not fluent, do not feel frightened to post. The mod_perl community includes many people for whom English is not their primary language. But please run a spell-checker before posting if you know that you tend to make many mistakes. Sometimes people post questions that are never answered simply because nobody understands the question.

- Avoid posting off-topic (not mod_perl-related) questions. If you really feel that you have to, at least let others know that the post is off-topic. The correct way to do that is to start your post's subject field with the [OT] tag.

- Avoid flaming. At least, don't flame in public—contact others in person if you really want to. Flaming people in public may hurt their feelings. They might leave the list, and all of us will lose an active (or potentially active) contributor. We try hard to make the mod_perl list a fun place to be.

- Remember that sometimes it might take days or even weeks before your question is answered, although during the working week most questions are answered within a few hours. Occasionally, questions aren't answered at all. If this is the case, you might want to post again some time later (at least one week), maybe with more information.

- Finally, use common sense when posting, and you will be fine. Online conversations needn't be any different than real-life ones; be polite and precise and everybody will be happy. Subscribing to the list and spending some time reading the posts will give you an idea of how things are done.

Resources

This section includes centralized resources that you should find useful when you work with mod_perl and related technologies, such as Apache, Perl, CGI, CVS, Squid, DBI, SQL, Security, etc.

mod_perl

- mod_perl home page: *http://perl.apache.org/*
- mod_perl documentation: *http://perl.apache.org/docs/*

- mod_perl books

  — Writing Apache Modules with Perl and C, by Lincoln Stein and Doug MacEachern (O'Reilly)

    http://www.modperl.com is the home site for this book, which is about creating web server modules using the Apache API. You absolutely must have this book if you plan to use mod_perl for anything other than speeding up plain CGI scripts. It will teach you the mod_perl API and provide lots of examples to learn from. This book is also very useful for developers who write Apache modules in C.

  — *The mod_perl Developer's Cookbook*, by Geoffrey Young, Paul Lindner, and Randy Kobes (Sams)

    http://www.modperlcookbook.org/ is the home site of this book, which will save you a lot of precious development time. It provides out-of-box solutions to pretty much any problem or challenge you may encounter while developing mod_perl applications. Every solution is followed by an in-depth discussion, helping you understand how the solution works and making it easy to adjust the provided code to your particular situation.

  — *mod_perl Pocket Reference*, by Andrew Ford (O'Reilly)

    http://www.oreilly.com/catalog/modperlpr/ is the home site of this book.

    You should probably also get the *Apache Pocket Reference*, by the same author and the same publisher: *http://www.oreilly.com/catalog/apachepr/*.

    See also Andrew's collection of reference cards for Apache and other programs: *http://www.refcards.com/*.

  — There are a few good books that cover technologies that deploy mod_perl. Among them are *Embedding Perl in HTML with Mason*, by Dave Rolsky and Ken Williams (O'Reilly), available from *http://www.masonbook.com/*; and *Running Weblogs with Slash*, by chromatic, Brian Aker, and David Krieger (O'Reilly). To see an updated list of books, please refer to *http://perl.apache. org/docs/offsite/books.html*.

mod_perl Mailing Lists

- The mod_perl mailing list

  The Apache/Perl mailing list is available for mod_perl users and developers to share ideas, solve problems, and discuss things related to mod_perl and the Apache::* modules. To subscribe to this list, send an empty email to *modperl-subscribe@perl.apache.org*. To unsubscribe, send email to *modperl-unsubscribe@perl.apache.org*. Send email to *modperl@perl.apache.org* to post to the list.

  To subscribe to the digest list, send email to *modperl-digest-subscribe@perl. apache.org*.

The searchable mod_perl mailing-list archives are available at *http://mathforum. org/epigone/modperl/*. Thanks to Ken Williams for this.

The following archives are also available:

> *http://www.geocrawler.com/lists/3/web/182/0/*
> *http://www.mail-archive.com/modperl%40apache.org/*
> *http://www.davin.ottawa.on.ca/archive/modperl/*
> *http://marc.theaimsgroup.com/?l=apache-modperl*
> *http://www.egroups.com/group/modperl/*

- The mod_perl development mailing list

  This list is for discussions about the development of the core mod_perl. To subscribe, send an empty email to *dev-subscribe@perl.apache.org*. To unsubscribe from the list, send an empty email to *dev-unsubscribe@perl.apache.org*. To get help with the list, send an empty email to *dev-help@perl.apache.org*.

  The list's searchable archives are:

  > *http://mathforum.org/epigone/modperl-dev/*
  > *http://marc.theaimsgroup.com/?l=apache-modperl-dev&r=1&w=2#apache-modperl-dev*
  > *http://www.mail-archive.com/dev%40perl.apache.org/*

- The mod_perl documentation mailing list

  This mailing list is for discussing the development of the mod_perl documentation and site. To subscribe, send an empty email to *docs-dev-subscribe@perl. apache.org*. To unsubscribe from the list, send an empty email to *docs-dev-unsubscribe@perl.apache.org*. To get help with the list, send an empty email to *docs-dev-help@perl.apache.org*.

  The list has a searchable archive at *http://mathforum.org/epigone/modperl-docs-dev/*.

- The Apache test framework development mailing list

  The *test-dev* list is the list where the Apache HTTP Test project is discussed.

  To subscribe, send an empty email to *test-dev-subscribe@httpd.apache.org*. To unsubscribe from the list, send an empty email to *test-dev-unsubscribe@httpd. apache.org*. To get help with the list, send an empty email to *test-dev-help@httpd.apache.org*.

  The list has a searchable archive at *http://www.apachelabs.org/test-dev/*.

- The advocacy mailing list

  The list for mod_perl advocacy issues, discussions about sites, etc.

  To subscribe send an empty email to *advocacy-subscribe@perl.apache.org*. To unsubscribe from the list, send an empty email to *advocacy-unsubscribe@perl. apache.org*. To get help with the list, send an empty email to *advocacy@perl. apache.org*.

The list has a searchable archive at *http://www.mail-archive.com/advocacy@perl.apache.org/*.

- The *modperl-cvs* mailing list

  The mod_perl CVS list is the list where you can watch mod_perl getting patched. No real discussions happen on this list, but if you want to know about the latest changes in the mod_perl core before everyone else, this is the list to be on.

  To subscribe, send email to *modperl-cvs-subscribe@perl.apache.org*. To unsubscribe send email to *modperl-cvs-unsubscribe@perl.apache.org*. Send email to *modperl-cvs@perl.apache.org* to post to the list.

  The list is archived at *http://marc.theaimsgroup.com/?l=apache-modperl-cvs&r=1&w=2#apache-modperl-cvs*.

Perl

The following resources are available for Perl:

- Books:
  - *Programming Perl*, Third Edition, by Larry Wall, Tom Christiansen, and Jon Orwant (O'Reilly)
  - *The Perl Cookbook*, by Tom Christiansen and Nathan Torkington (O'Reilly)
  - *Effective Perl Programming*, by Joseph Hall (Addison Wesley)
  - *Web Client Programming with Perl*, by Clinton Wong (O'Reilly)
- The Perl FAQ: *http://www.perl.com/language/faq/*
- The Perl home pages: *http://www.perl.com/* and *http://www.perl.org/*
- The Perl Journal: *http://www.tpj.com/*
- The Perl Review: *http://www.theperlreview.com/*
- Perl Monks: *http://www.perlmonks.org/*
- Searchable Perl documentation: *http://www.perldoc.com/*
- Perl Module Mechanics: *http://world.std.com/~swmcd/steven/perl/module_mechanics.html*

  This page describes the mechanics of creating, compiling, releasing, and maintaining Perl modules
- Perl news: *http://use.perl.org/*
- Searchable CPAN: *http://search.cpan.org/*
- Perl mailing lists: *http://lists.perl.org/*

Perl/CGI

The following resources are valuable for learning more about writing CGI scripts with Perl:

- *The Official Guide to CGI.pm*, by Lincoln Stein (John Wiley & Sons)
- *CGI/Perl Cookbook*, by Craig Patchett and Matthew Wright (John Wiley & Sons)
- *CGI Programming with Perl*, Second Edition, by Scott Guelich, Shishir Gundavaram, and Gunther Birznieks (O'Reilly)

Here are some resources on the Web you might find useful:

Answers to Some Troublesome Perl and Perl/CGI Questions
  http://stason.org/TULARC/webmaster/myfaq.html

Idiot's Guide to CGI Programming
  http://www.webdeveloper.com/cgi-perl/cgi_idiots_guide_to_perl.html

WWW Security FAQ
  http://www.w3.org/Security/Faq/www-security-faq.html

CGI/Perl Taint Mode FAQ
  http://www.gunther.web66.com/FAQS/taintmode.html (by Gunther Birznieks)

cgi-list Mailing List
  Send email to *majordomo@jann.com* with body:

```
subscribe cgi-list
```

CGI Newsgroup
  comp.infosystems.www.authoring.cgi

Apache

The following resources are useful for learning more about Apache:

- Apache Software Foundation home: *http://www.apache.org/*
- Apache *httpd* server: *http://httpd.apache.org/*
- Apache mailing lists: *http://www.apache.org/foundation/mailinglists.html* contains a comprehensive list of all Apache projects' mailing lists
- Apache quick reference card: *http://www.refcards.com/* (other reference cards are also available from this link)
- The Apache FAQ: *http://httpd.apache.org/docs/misc/FAQ.html*
- Apache server documentation: *http://httpd.apache.org/docs/* for 1.3.xx, *http://httpd.apache.org/docs-2.0/* for 2.0
- Apache handlers in C: *http://httpd.apache.org/docs/handler.html*
- mod_rewrite Guide: *http://www.engelschall.com/pw/apache/rewriteguide/*
- Security

- — "Security and Apache: An Essential Primer," by Ken Coar: *http://linuxplanet. com/linuxplanet/print/1527/*
- — "Using Apache with Suexec on Linux," by Ken Coar: *http://linuxplanet.com/ linuxplanet/print/1445/*
- The Unix *chroot* jail facility
  - — "How to 'chroot' an Apache tree with Linux and Solaris": *http://penguin. epfl.ch/chroot.html*
  - — "Installing and Securing the Apache Webserver with SSL," by Dale Cod- dington: *http://online.securityfocus.com/infocus/1356/*
  - — "How to break out of a chroot( ) jail": *http://www.bpfh.net/simes/computing/ chroot-break.html*
- The FreeBSD jail facility:
  - — Jails: Confining the omnipotent root," by Paul-Henning Kamp and Robert N. M. Watson: *http://docs.freebsd.org/44doc/papers/jail/jail.html*
  - — Chapter 12 of FreeBSD Developers' Handbook, by Evan Sarmiento: *http:// www.freebsd.org/doc/en_US.ISO8859-1/books/developers-handbook/jail.html*
- mod_throttle_access: *http://www.fremen.org/apache/*
- Books:
  - — *How to Set Up and Maintain a Web Site: The Guide for Information Provid- ers*, Second Edition, by Lincoln Stein (Addison Wesley)
  - — *Apache: The Definitive Guide*, Second Edition, by Ben Laurie and Peter Lau- rie (O'Reilly)
  - — *Apache Server for Dummies*, by Ken Coar (IDE)

DBI and SQL

The following resources are useful for questions on DBI and SQL:

- Introduction to Structured Query Language: *http://www.dbbm.fiocruz.br/class/ Lecture/d17/sql/jhoffman/sqltut.html*
- "SQL for Web Nerds," by Philip Greenspun: *http://www.arsdigita.com/books/sql/*
- DBI Examples and Performance Tuning, by Jeffery Baker: *http://www.saturn5.com/ ~jwb/dbi-examples.html*
- DBI home page: *http://dbi.perl.org/*
- DBI mailing-list information: *http://www.fugue.com/dbi/*
- DBI mailing-list archives: *http://www.bitmechanic.com/mail-archives/dbi-users/* and *http://www.xray.mpe.mpg.de/mailing-lists/dbi/*

Squid

- Home page: *http://www.squid-cache.org/*
- FAQ: *http://www.squid-cache.org/Doc/FAQ/FAQ.html*
- Users guide: *http://www.squid-cache.org/Doc/Users-Guide/*
- Mailing lists: *http://www.squid-cache.org/mailing-lists.html*

CVS

- CVS instructions for access to the mod_perl repository: *http://perl.apache.org/contribute/cvs_howto.html*
- Open source development with CVS: *http://cvsbook.red-bean.com/*
- Online documents: *http://www.cvshome.org/docs/*
- CVS quick reference card: *http://www.refcards.com/about/cvs.html*

Performance and Scalability

- "Techniques and Technologies for Scaling Internet Services" mailing list: *scalable@arctic.org*. Subscribe by sending a message to *scalable-subscribe@arctic.org*.
- "Solaris 2.x—Tuning Your TCP/IP Stack and More": *http://www.sean.de/Solaris/tune.html*

  This page talks about the TCP/IP stack and various tricks of tuning your system to get the most out of it as a web server. While the information is for the Solaris 2.x OS, most of it is relevant to other Unix flavors. At the end, an extensive list of related literature is presented.

Web Security

- *Web Security: A Step-by-Step Reference Guide*, by Lincoln Stein (Addison Wesley)
- *Web Security and Electronic Commerce*, by Simpson Garfinkle with Gene Spafford (O'Reilly)
- Chapter 13 of *Apache: The Definitive Guide*, Second Edition, by Ben Laurie and Peter Laurie (O'Reilly) talks extensively about the Apache configuration process

mod_perl 2.0

The majority of this book covers mod_perl 1.x, which was the stable version of mod_perl at the time of this writing. However, the exciting rewrite of mod_perl, Version 2.0, is near release and deserves special attention in this book. Although it may be some time before mod_perl programmers have completely embraced mod_perl 2.0, it's clearly the direction that mod_perl is taking.

Chapter 24, *mod_perl 2.0: Installation and Configuration*, gives an introduction to Apache 2.0 and mod_perl 2.0, and shows you how to install and configure it.

Chapter 25, *Programming for mod_perl 2.0*, covers the new handlers in mod_perl 2.0 and how they are designed to be used.

mod_perl 2.0: Installation and Configuration

Since Doug MacEachern introduced mod_perl 1.0* in 1996, he has had to tweak it with every change in Apache and Perl, while maintaining compatibility with the older versions. These rewrites have led to very complex source code, with hundreds of #ifdefs and workarounds for various incompatibilities in older Perl and Apache versions.

Apache 2.0, however, is based on a new threads design, requiring that mod_perl be based on a thread-safe Perl interpreter. Perl 5.6.0 was the first Perl version to support internal thread-safety across multiple interpreters. Since Perl 5.6.0 and Apache 2.0 are the very minimum requirements for the newest version of mod_perl, backward compatibility was no longer a concern, so this seemed like a good time to start from scratch. mod_perl 2.0 was the result: a leaner, more efficient mod_perl that's streamlined for Apache 2.0.

mod_perl 2.0 includes a mechanism for building the Perl interface to the Apache API automatically, allowing us to easily adjust mod_perl 2.0 to the ever-changing Apache 2.0 API during its development period. Another important feature is the Apache::Test framework, which was originally developed for mod_perl 2.0 but then was adopted by Apache 2.0 developers to test the core server features and third-party modules. Moreover the tests written using the Apache::Test framework could be run with Apache 1.0 and 2.0, assuming that both supported the same features.

Many other interesting changes have already happened to mod_perl in Version 2.0, and more will be developed in the future. Some of these will be covered in this chapter, and some you will discover on your own while reading mod_perl documentation.

At the time of this writing, mod_perl 2.0 is considered beta when used with the *prefork* Multi-Processing Model module (MPM) and alpha when used with a threaded

---

* Here and in the rest of this and the next chapter we refer to the mod_perl 1.x series as mod_perl 1.0 and to 2.0.x as mod_perl 2.0 to keep things simple. Similarly, we call the Apache 1.3.x series Apache 1.3 and the 2.0.x series Apache 2.0.

MPM. It is likely that Perl 5.8.0+ will be required for mod_perl 2.0 to move past alpha with threaded MPMs. Also, the Apache 2.0 API hasn't yet been finalized, so it's possible that certain examples in this chapter may require modifications once production versions of Apache 2.0 and mod_perl 2.0 are released.

In this chapter, we'll first discuss the new features in Apache 2.0, Perl 5.6 and later, and mod_perl 2.0 (in that order). Then we'll cover the installation and configuration of mod_perl 2.0. Details on the new functionality implemented in mod_perl 2.0 are provided in Chapter 25.

What's New in Apache 2.0

Whereas Apache 1.2 and 1.3 were based on the NCSA *httpd* code base, Apache 2.0 rewrote big chunks of the 1.3 code base, mainly to support numerous new features and enhancements. Here are the most important new features:

Apache Portable Runtime (APR)

> The APR presents a standard API for writing portable client and server applications, covering file I/O, logging, shared memory, threads, managing child processes, and many other functionalities needed for developing the Apache core and third-party modules in a portable and efficient way. One important effect is that it significantly simplifies the code that uses the APR, making it much easier to review and understand the Apache code, and increasing the number of revealed bugs and contributed patches.

> The APR uses the concept of memory pools, which significantly simplifies the memory-management code and reduces the possibility of memory leaks (which always haunt C programmers).

I/O filtering

> Apache 2.0 allows multiple modules to filter both the request and the response. Now one module can pipe its output to another module as if it were being sent directly from the TCP stream. The same mechanism works with the generated response.

> With I/O filtering in place, simple filters (e.g., data compression and decompression) can easily be implemented, and complex filters (e.g., SSL) can now be implemented without needing to modify the the server code (unlike with Apache 1.3).

> To make the filtering mechanism efficient and avoid unnecessary copying, the *bucket brigades* model was used, as follows.

> A bucket represents a chunk of data. Buckets linked together comprise a brigade. Each bucket in a brigade can be modified, removed, and replaced with another bucket. The goal is to minimize the data copying where possible. Buckets come in different types: files, data blocks, end-of-stream indicators, pools, etc. You don't need to know anything about the internal representation of a bucket in order to manipulate it.

The stream of data is represented by bucket brigades. When a filter is called, it gets passed the brigade that was the output of the previous filter. This brigade is then manipulated by the filter (e.g., by modifying some buckets) and passed to the next filter in the stack.

Figure 24-1 depicts an imaginary bucket brigade. The figure shows that after the presented bucket brigade has passed through several filters, some buckets were removed, some were modified, and some were added. Of course, the handler that gets the brigade doesn't know the history of the brigade; it can only see the existing buckets in the brigade. We will see bucket brigades in use when discussing protocol handlers and filters.

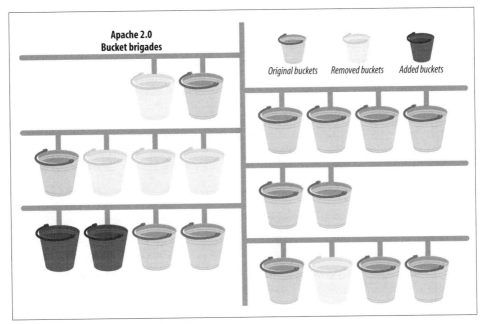

Figure 24-1. Imaginary bucket brigade

Multi-Processing Model modules (MPMs)

In the previous Apache generation, the same code base was trying to manage incoming requests for different platforms, which led to scalability problems on certain (mostly non-Unix) platforms. This also led to an undesired complexity of the code.

Apache 2.0 introduces the concept of MPMs, whose main responsibility is to map the incoming requests to either threads, processes, or a threads/processes hybrid. Now it's possible to write different processing modules specific to various platforms. For example, Apache 2.0 on Windows is much more efficient and maintainable now, since it uses *mpm_winnt*, which deploys native Windows features.

Here is a partial list of the major MPMs available as of this writing:

prefork

The *prefork* MPM implements Apache 1.3's preforking model, in which each request is handled by a different forked child process.

worker

The *worker* MPM implements a hybrid multi-process/multi-threaded approach based on the *pthreads* standard.

mpmt_os2, netware, winnt, and beos

These MPMs also implement the hybrid multi-process/multi-threaded model, like *worker*, but unlike *worker*, each is based on the native OS thread implementations, while *worker* uses the *pthread* library available on Unix.

On platforms that support more than one MPM, it's possible to switch the used MPMs as the need changes. For example, on Unix it's possible to start with a preforked module, then migrate to a more efficient threaded MPM as demand grows and the code matures (assuming that the code base is capable of running in the threaded environment).

New hook scheme

In Apache 2.0 it's possible to dynamically register functions for each Apache hook, with more than one function registered per hook. Moreover, when adding new functions, you can specify where the new function should be added—for example, a function can be inserted between two already registered functions, or in front of them.

Protocol modules

The previous Apache generation could speak only the HTTP protocol. Apache 2. 0 has introduced a "server framework" architecture, making it possible to plug in handlers for protocols other than HTTP. The protocol module design also abstracts the transport layer, so protocols such as SSL can be hooked into the server without requiring modifications to the Apache source code. This allows Apache to be extended much further than in the past, making it possible to add support for protocols such as FTP, NNTP, POP3, RPC flavors, and the like. The main advantage is that protocol plug-ins can take advantage of Apache's portability, process/thread management, configuration mechanism, and plug-in API.

GNU Autoconf-based configuration

Apache 2.0 uses the ubiquitous GNU *Autoconf* for its configuration process, to make the configuration process more portable.

Parsed configuration tree

Apache 2.0 makes the parsed configuration tree available at runtime, so modules needing to read the configuration data (e.g., mod_info) don't have to re-parse the configuration file, but can reuse the parsed tree.

All these new features boost Apache's performance, scalability, and flexibility. The APR helps the overall performance by doing lots of platform-specific optimizations in the APR internals and giving the developer the already greatly optimized API.

The I/O layering helps performance too, since now modules don't need to waste memory and CPU cycles to manually store the data in shared memory or *pnotes* in order to pass the data to another module (e.g., to provide *gzip* compression for outgoing data).

And, of course, an important impact of these features is the simplification and added flexibility for the core and third-party Apache module developers.

What's New in Perl 5.6.0–5.8.0

As mentioned earlier, Perl 5.6.0 is the minimum requirement for mod_perl 2.0. However, certain new features work only with Perl 5.8.0 and higher.

The following are the important changes in the recent Perl versions that had an impact on mod_perl. For a complete list of changes, see the appropriate *perldelta* manpage. The 5.6 generation of Perl introduced the following features:

- The beginnings of support for running multiple interpreters concurrently in different threads. In conjunction with the perl_clone( ) API call, which can be used to selectively duplicate the state of any given interpreter, it is possible to compile a piece of code once in an interpreter, clone that interpreter one or more times, and run all the resulting interpreters in distinct threads. See the *perlembed* and *perl561delta* manpages.

- The core support for declaring subroutine attributes, which is used by mod_perl 2.0's method handlers (with the : method attribute). See the *attributes* manpage.

- The warnings pragma, which allows programmers to force the code to be super clean, via the setting:

      use warnings FATAL => 'all';

  which will abort any code that generates warnings. This pragma also allows fine control over what warnings should be reported. See the *perllexwarn* manpage.

- Certain CORE:: functions can now be overridden via the CORE::GLOBAL:: namespace. For example, mod_perl now can override exit( ) globally by defining CORE::GLOBAL::exit. So when exit( ) is called, CORE::GLOBAL::exit( ) gets invoked. Note that you can still use CORE::exit( ) to get the original behavior. See the *perlsub* manpage.

- The XSLoader extension as a simpler alternative to DynaLoader. See the *XSLoader* manpage.

- Large-file support. If you have filesystems that support files larger than 2 GB), you may now also be able to create and access them from Perl. See the *perl561delta* manpage.

- Multiple performance enhancements. See the *perl561delta* manpage.
- Numerous memory leaks were fixed. See the *perl561delta* manpage.
- Improved security features: more potentially unsafe operations taint their results for improved security. See the *perlsec* and *perl561delta* manpages.
- Perl is now available on new platforms: GNU/Hurd, Rhapsody/Darwin, and EPOC.

Overall, multiple bugs and problems were fixed in Perl 5.6.1, so if you plan on running the 5.6 generation, you should run at least 5.6.1. It is possible that when this book is released 5.6.2 will be out, which will then incorporate the bug fixes from Perl 5.8.0.

Perl 5.8.0 has introduced the following features:

- The experimental PerlIO layer, introduced in 5.6.0, has been stabilized and become the default I/O layer in 5.8.0. Now the I/O stream can be filtered through multiple I/O layers. See the *perlapio* and *perliol* manpages.

  For example, this allows mod_perl to interoperate with the APR I/O layer and even use the APR I/O layer in Perl code. See the *APR::PerlIO* manpage.

  Another example of using this new feature is the extension of the open( ) functionality to create anonymous temporary files via:

  ```
  open my $fh, "+>", undef or die $!;
  ```

  That is a literal undef( ), not an undefined value. See the open( ) entry in the *perlfunc* manpage.
- More keywords are now overridable via CORE::GLOBAL::. See the *perlsub* manpage.
- The signal handling in Perl has been notoriously unsafe because signals have been able to arrive at inopportune moments, leaving Perl in an inconsistent state. Now Perl delays signal handling until it is safe.
- File::Temp was added to allow creation of temporary files and directories in an easy, portable, and secure way. See the *File::Temp* manpage.
- A new command-line option, *-t*, is available. It is the little brother of *-T*: instead of dying on taint violations, lexical warnings are given. This is meant only as a temporary debugging aid while securing the code of old legacy applications. It is *not* a substitute for *-T*. See the *perlrun* manpage.
- A new special variable, ${^TAINT}, was introduced. It indicates whether taint mode is enabled. See the *perlvar* manpage.
- Thread implementation is much improved since 5.6.0. The Perl interpreter should now be completely thread-safe, and 5.8.0 marks the arrival of the threads module, which allows Perl programs to work with threads (creating them, sharing variables, etc.).
- Much better support for Unicode has been added.

- Numerous bugs and memory leaks have been fixed. For example, now you can localize the tied `Apache::DBI` database handles without leaking memory.

- Perl is now available on new platforms: AtheOS, Mac OS Classic, MinGW, NCR MP-RAS, NonStop-UX, NetWare, and UTS. Also, the following platforms are again supported: BeOS, DYNIX/ptx, POSIX-BC, VM/ESA, and z/OS (OS/390).

What's New in mod_perl 2.0

The new features introduced by Apache 2.0 and the Perl 5.6 and 5.8 generations provide the base of the new mod_perl 2.0 features. In addition, mod_perl 2.0 reimplements itself from scratch, providing such new features as a new build and testing framework. Let's look at the major changes since mod_perl 1.0.

Thread Support

In order to adapt to the Apache 2.0 threads architecture (for threaded MPMs), mod_perl 2.0 needs to use thread-safe Perl interpreters, also known as *ithreads* (interpreter threads). This mechanism is enabled at compile time and ensures that each Perl interpreter instance is reentrant—that is, multiple Perl interpreters can be used concurrently within the same process without locking, as each instance has its own copy of any mutable data (symbol tables, stacks, etc.). This of course requires that each Perl interpreter instance is accessed by only one thread at any given time.

The first mod_perl generation has only a single `PerlInterpreter`, which is constructed by the parent process, then inherited across the forks to child processes. mod_perl 2.0 has a configurable number of `PerlInterpreters` and two classes of interpreters, parent and clone. A *parent* is like in mod_perl 1.0, where the main interpreter created at startup time compiles any preloaded Perl code. A *clone* is created from the parent using the Perl API `perl_clone()` function. At request time, parent interpreters are used only for making more clones, as the clones are the interpreters that actually handle requests. Care is taken by Perl to copy only mutable data, which means that no runtime locking is required and read-only data such as the syntax tree is shared from the parent, which should reduce the overall mod_perl memory footprint.

Rather than creating a `PerlInterperter` for each thread, by default mod_perl creates a pool of interpreters. The pool mechanism helps cut down memory usage a great deal. As already mentioned, the syntax tree is shared between all cloned interpreters. If your server is serving more than just mod_perl requests, having a smaller number of `PerlInterpreters` than the number of threads will clearly cut down on memory usage. Finally, perhaps the biggest win is memory reuse: as calls are made into Perl subroutines, memory allocations are made for variables when they are used for the first time. Subsequent use of variables may allocate more memory; e.g., if a scalar variable needs to hold a longer string than it did before, or an array has new elements added. As an optimization, Perl hangs onto these allocations, even though their values go out of scope. mod_perl 2.0 has much better control over which PerlInterpreters are used for incoming requests. The interpreters are stored in two linked lists, one for available interpreters and another for busy ones. When needed to handle a request, one interpreter is taken from the head of the available list, and it's put back at the head of the same list when it's done. This means that if, for example, you have ten interpreters configured to be cloned at startup time, but no more than five are ever used concurrently, those five continue to reuse Perl's allocations, while the other five remain much smaller, but ready to go if the need arises.

The interpreters pool mechanism has been abstracted into an API known as *tipool* (thread item pool). This pool, currently used to manage a pool of PerlInterpreter objects, can be used to manage any data structure in which you wish to have a smaller number of items than the number of configured threads.

It's important to notice that the Perl ithreads implementation ensures that Perl code is thread-safe, at least with respect to the Apache threads in which it is running. However, it does not ensure that functions and extensions that call into third-party C/C++ libraries are thread-safe. In the case of non–thread-safe extensions, if it is not possible to fix those routines, care needs to be taken to serialize calls into such functions (either at the XS or Perl level). See Perl 5.8.0's *perlthrtut* manpage.

Note that while Perl data is thread-private unless explicitly shared and threads themselves are separate execution threads, the threads can affect process-scope state, affecting all the threads. For example, if one thread does chdir("/tmp"), the current working directory of all threads is now */tmp*. While each thread can correct its current working directory by storing the original value, there are functions whose process-scope changes cannot be undone. For example, chroot( ) changes the root directory of all threads, and this change is not reversible. Refer to the *perlthrtut* manpage for more information.

Perl Interface to the APR and Apache APIs

As we mentioned earlier, Apache 2.0 uses two APIs:

- The Apache Portable Runtime (APR) API, which implements a portable and efficient API to generically work with files, threads, processes, shared memory, etc.
- The Apache API, which handles issues specific to the web server

mod_perl 2.0 provides its own very flexible special-purpose XS code generator, which is capable of doing things none of the existing generators can handle. It's possible that in the future this generator will be generalized and used for other projects of a high complexity.

This generator creates the Perl glue code for the public APR and Apache APIs, almost without a need for any extra code (just a few thin wrappers to make the API more Perlish).

Since APR can be used outside of Apache, the Perl APR:: modules can be used outside of Apache as well.

Other New Features

In addition to the already mentioned new features in mod_perl 2.0, the following are of major importance:

- Apache 2.0 protocol modules are supported. Later we will see an example of a protocol module running on top of mod_perl 2.0.

- mod_perl 2.0 provides a very simple-to-use interface to the Apache filtering API; this is of great interest because in mod_perl 1.0 the Apache::Filter and Apache:: OutputChain modules, used for filtering, had to go to great lengths to implement filtering and couldn't be used for filtering output generated by non-Perl modules. Moreover, incoming-stream filtering has now become possible. We will discuss filtering and see a few examples later on.

- A feature-full and flexible Apache::Test framework was developed especially for mod_perl testing. While intended to test the core mod_perl features, it is also used by third-party module writers to easily test their modules. Moreover, Apache::Test was adopted by Apache and is currently used to test the Apache 1.3, 2.0, and other ASF projects. Anything that runs on top of Apache can be tested with Apache:: Test, whether the target is written in Perl, C, PHP, etc.

- The support of the new MPMs makes mod_perl 2.0 able to scale better on a wider range of platforms. For example, if you've happened to try mod_perl 1.0 on Win32 you probably know that parallel requests had to be serialized—i.e., only a single request could be processed at a time, rendering the Win32 platform unusable with mod_perl as a heavy production service. Thanks to the new Apache MPM design, mod_perl 2.0 can now efficiently process parallel requests on Win32 platforms (using its native *win32* MPM).

Improved and More Flexible Configuration

mod_perl 2.0 provides new configuration directives for the newly added features and improves upon existing ones. For example, the PerlOptions directive provides fine-grained configuration for what were compile-time only options in the first mod_perl generation. The Perl*FilterHandler directives provide a much simpler Apache filtering API, hiding most of the details underneath. We will talk in detail about these and other options in the section "Configuring mod_perl 2.0."

The new Apache::Directive module provides a Perl interface to the Apache configuration tree, which is another new feature in Apache 2.0.

Optimizations

The rewrite of mod_perl gives us a chance to build a smarter, stronger, and faster implementation based on lessons learned over the years since mod_perl was introduced. There are some optimizations that can be made in the mod_perl source code, some that can be made in the Perl space by optimizing its syntax tree, and some that are a combination of both.

Installing mod_perl 2.0

Since as of this writing mod_perl 2.0 hasn't yet been released, the installation instructions may change a bit, but the basics should be the same. Always refer to the mod_perl documentation for the correct information.

Installing from Source

First download the latest stable sources of Apache 2.0, mod_perl 2.0, and Perl 5.8.0.[*] Remember that mod_perl 1.0 works only with Apache 1.3, and mod_perl 2.0 requires Apache 2.0. You can get the sources from:

- mod_perl 2.0—*http://perl.apache.org/dist/*
- Apache 2.0—*http://httpd.apache.org/dist/*
- Perl 5.8.0—*http://cpan.org/src/*

You can always find the most up-to-date download information at *http://perl.apache.org/ download/*.

Next, build Apache 2.0:

1. Extract the source (as usual, replace *x* with the correct version number):

       panic% tar -xzvf httpd-2.0.xx

   If you don't have GNU *tar(1)*, use the appropriate tools and flags to extract the source.

2. Configure:

       panic% cd httpd-2.0.xx
       panic% ./configure --prefix=/home/httpd/httpd-2.0 --with-mpm=prefork

   Adjust the *--prefix* option to the directory where you want Apache 2.0 to be installed. If you want to use a different MPM, adjust the *--with-mpm* option. The easiest way to find all of the configuration options for Apache 2.0 is to run:

       panic% ./configure --help

3. Finally, build and install:

       panic% make && make install

---

[*] Perl 5.6.1 can be used with *prefork*, but if you build from source why not go for the best?

If you don't have Perl 5.6.0 or higher installed, or you need to rebuild it because you want to enable certain compile-time features or you want to run one of the threaded MPMs, which require Perl 5.8.0, build Perl (we will assume that you build Perl 5.8.0):

1. Extract the source:

   ```
   panic% tar -xzvf perl-5.8.0.tar.gz
   ```

2. Configure:

   ```
   panic% cd perl-5.8.0
   panic% ./Configure -des -Dprefix=$HOME/perl/perl-5.8.0 -Dusethreads
   ```

   This configuration accepts all the defaults suggested by the *Configure* script and produces a terse output. The *-Dusethreads* option enables Perl ithreads. The *-Dprefix* option specifies a custom installation directory, which you may want to adjust. For example, you may decide to install it in the default location provided by Perl, which is */usr/local* under most systems.

   For a complete list of configuration options and for information on installation on non-Unix systems, refer to the *INSTALL* document.

3. Now build, test, and install Perl:

   ```
   panic% make && make test && make install
   ```

Before proceeding with the installation of mod_perl 2.0, it's advisable to install at least the LWP package into your newly installed Perl distribution so that you can fully test mod_perl 2.0 later. You can use CPAN.pm to accomplish that:

```
panic% $HOME/perl/perl-5.8.0/bin/perl -MCPAN -e 'install("LWP")'
```

Now that you have Perl 5.8.0 and Apache 2.0 installed, you can proceed with the mod_perl 2.0 installation:

1. Extract the source:

   ```
   panic% tar -xzvf mod_perl-2.0.x.tar.gz
   ```

2. Remember the nightmare number of options for mod_perl 1.0? You need only two options to build mod_perl 2.0. If you need more control, read *install.pod* in the source mod_perl distribution or online at *http://perl.apache.org/docs/2.0/user/*. Configure:

   ```
   panic% cd mod_perl-2.0.x
   panic% perl Makefile.PL MP_AP_PREFIX=/home/stas/httpd/prefork \
       MP_INST_APACHE2=1
   ```

   The *MP_AP_PREFIX* option specifies the base directory of the installed Apache 2.0, under which the *include/* directory with Apache C header files can be found. For example, if you have installed Apache 2.0 in the directory *\Apache2* on Win32, you should use:

   ```
   MP_AP_PREFIX=\Apache2
   ```

   The *MP_INST_APACHE2* option is needed only if you have mod_perl 1.0 installed under the same Perl tree. You can remove this option if you don't have or don't plan to install mod_perl 1.0.

3. Now build, test, and install mod_perl 2.0:

```
panic% make && make test && make install
```

On Win32 you have to use *nmake* instead of *make*, and the *&&* chaining doesn't work on all Win32 platforms, so instead you should do:

```
C:\modperl-2.0\> nmake
C:\modperl-2.0\> nmake test
C:\modperl-2.0\> nmake install
```

Installing Binaries

Apache 2.0 binaries can be obtained from *http://httpd.apache.org/dist/binaries/*.

Perl 5.6.1 or 5.8.0 binaries can be obtained from *http://cpan.org/ports/index.html*.

For mod_perl 2.0, as of this writing only the binaries for the Win32 platform are available, kindly prepared and maintained by Randy Kobes. Once mod_perl 2.0 is released, various OS distributions will provide binary versions for their platforms.

If you are not on a Win32 platform you can safely skip to the next section.

There are two ways of obtaining a binary mod_perl 2.0 package for Win32:

PPM

> The first, for ActivePerl users, is through PPM, which assumes you already have ActivePerl (build 6xx or later), available from *http://www.activestate.com/*, and a Win32 Apache 2.0 binary, available from *http://www.apache.org/dist/httpd/binaries/win32/*. In installing this, you may find it convenient when transcribing any Unix-oriented documentation to choose installation directories that do not have spaces in their names (e.g., *C:\Apache2*).
>
> After installing Perl and Apache 2.0, you can then install mod_perl 2.0 via the PPM utility. ActiveState does not maintain mod_perl in its PPM repository, so you must get it from somewhere else. One way is simply to do:
>
> ```
> C:\> ppm install http://theoryx5.uwinnipeg.ca/ppmpackages/mod_perl-2.ppd
> ```
>
> Another way, which will be useful if you plan on installing additional Apache modules, is to set the repository within the PPM shell utility as follows (the lines are broken here for readability):
>
> ```
> PPM> set repository theoryx5
>      http://theoryx5.uwinnipeg.ca/cgi-bin/ppmserver?urn:/PPMServer
> ```
>
> or, for PPM3:
>
> ```
> PPM> rep add theoryx5
>      http://theoryx5.uwinnipeg.ca/cgi-bin/ppmserver?urn:/PPMServer
> ```
>
> mod_perl 2.0 can then be installed as:
>
> ```
> PPM> install mod_perl-2
> ```
>
> This will install the necessary modules under an *Apache2/* subdirectory in your Perl tree, so as not to disturb an existing *Apache/* directory from mod_perl 1.0.

See the next section for instructions on how to add this directory to the `@INC` path for searching for modules.

The mod_perl PPM package also includes the necessary Apache DLL *mod_perl.so*; a post-installation script that will offer to copy this file to your *Apache2* modules directory (e.g., *C:\Apache2\modules*) should be run. If this is not done, you can get the file *mod_perl-2.tar.gz* from *http://theoryx5.uwinnipeg.ca/ppmpackages/ x86/*. This file, when unpacked, contains *mod_perl.so* in the top-level directory.

Note that the mod_perl package available from this site will always use the latest mod_perl sources compiled against the latest official Apache release; depending on changes made in Apache, you may or may not be able to use an earlier Apache binary. However, in the Apache Win32 world it is a particularly good idea to use the latest version, for bug and security fixes.

Apache/mod_perl binary

At *ftp://theoryx5.uwinnipeg.ca/pub/other/* you can find an archive called *Apache2. tar.gz* containing a binary version of Apache 2.0 with mod_perl 2.0. This archive unpacks into an *Apache2* directory, underneath which is a *blib* subdirectory containing the necessary mod_perl files (enabled with a `PerlSwitches` directive in *httpd.conf*). Some editing of *httpd.conf* will be necessary to reflect the location of the installed directory. See the *Apache2.readme* file for further information.

This package, which is updated periodically, is compiled against recent CVS sources of Apache 2.0 and mod_perl 2.0. As such, it may contain features, and bugs, not present in the current official releases. Also for this reason, these may not be binary-compatible with other versions of Apache 2.0/mod_perl 2.0.

Apache/mod_perl/Perl 5.8 binary distribution

Because mod_perl 2.0 works best with Perl 5.8 in threaded environments such as Apache 2.0 with the *win32* MPM, there is a package including Perl 5.8, Apache 2.0, and mod_perl 2.0. To get this, look for the *perl-5.8-win32-bin.tar.gz* package at *ftp://theoryx5.uwinnipeg.ca/pub/other/*, and extract it to *C:*, which will give you an *Apache2* directory containing the Apache 2.0 installation along with mod_perl 2.0, and a *Perl* directory containing the Perl installation (you should add this *Perl* directory to your path).

Configuring mod_perl 2.0

Similar to mod_perl 1.0, in order to use mod_perl 2.0 a few configuration settings should be added to *httpd.conf*. They are quite similar to the 1.0 settings, but some directives were renamed and new directives were added.

Enabling mod_perl

To enable mod_perl as a DSO, add this to *httpd.conf*:

```
LoadModule perl_module modules/mod_perl.so
```

This setting specifies the location of the mod_perl module relative to the ServerRoot setting, so you should put it somewhere after ServerRoot is specified.

Win32 users need to make sure that the path to the Perl binary (e.g., *C:\Perl\bin*) is in the PATH environment variable. You could also add the directive:

```
LoadFile "/Path/to/your/Perl/bin/perl5x.dll"
```

to *httpd.conf* to load your Perl DLL, before loading *mod_perl.so*.

Accessing the mod_perl 2.0 Modules

To prevent you from inadvertently loading mod_perl 1.0 modules, mod_perl 2.0 Perl modules are installed into dedicated directories under *Apache2/*. The Apache2 module prepends the locations of the mod_perl 2.0 libraries to @INC: @INC is the same as the core @INC, but with *Apache2/* prepended. This module has to be loaded just after mod_perl has been enabled. This can be accomplished with:

```
use Apache2 ();
```

in the startup file. If you don't use a startup file, you can add:

```
PerlModule Apache2
```

to *httpd.conf*, due to the order in which the PerlRequire and PerlModule directives are processed.

Startup File

Next, a startup file with Perl code usually is loaded:

```
PerlRequire "/home/httpd/httpd-2.0/perl/startup.pl"
```

It's used to adjust Perl module search paths in @INC, preload commonly used modules, precompile constants, etc. A typical *startup.pl* file for mod_perl 2.0 is shown in Example 24-1.

Example 24-1. startup.pl

```
use Apache2 ();

use lib qw(/home/httpd/perl);

# enable if the mod_perl 1.0 compatibility is needed
# use Apache::compat ();

# preload all mp2 modules
# use ModPerl::MethodLookup;
# ModPerl::MethodLookup::preload_all_modules();

use ModPerl::Util (); #for CORE::GLOBAL::exit
```

Example 24-1. startup.pl (continued)

```
use Apache::RequestRec ();
use Apache::RequestIO ();
use Apache::RequestUtil ();

use Apache::Server ();
use Apache::ServerUtil ();
use Apache::Connection ();
use Apache::Log ();

use APR::Table ();

use ModPerl::Registry ();

use Apache::Const -compile => ':common';
use APR::Const -compile => ':common';

1;
```

In this file the `Apache2` module is loaded, so the 2.0 modules will be found. Afterwards, `@INC` is adjusted to include nonstandard directories with Perl modules:

```
use lib qw(/home/httpd/perl);
```

If you need to use the backward-compatibility layer, to get 1.0 modules that haven't yet been ported to work with mod_perl 2.0, load `Apache::compat`:

```
use Apache::compat ();
```

Next, preload the commonly used mod_perl 2.0 modules and precompile the common constants. You can preload all mod_perl 2.0 modules by uncommenting the following two lines:

```
use ModPerl::MethodLookup;
ModPerl::MethodLookup::preload_all_modules();
```

Finally, the *startup.pl* file must be terminated with `1;`.

Perl's Command-Line Switches

Now you can pass Perl's command-line switches in *httpd.conf* by using the `PerlSwitches` directive, instead of using complicated workarounds.

For example, to enable warnings and taint checking, add:

```
PerlSwitches -wT
```

The *-I* command-line switch can be used to adjust `@INC` values:

```
PerlSwitches -I/home/stas/modperl
```

For example, you can use that technique to set different `@INC` values for different virtual hosts, as we will see later.

mod_perl 2.0 Core Handlers

mod_perl 2.0 provides two types of core handlers: modperl and perl-script.

modperl

modperl is configured as:

```
SetHandler modperl
```

This is the bare mod_perl handler type, which just calls the Perl*Handler's callback function. If you don't need the features provided by the perl-script handler, with the modperl handler, you can gain even more performance. (This handler isn't available in mod_perl 1.0.)

Unless the Perl*Handler callback running under the modperl handler is configured with:

```
PerlOptions +SetupEnv
```

or calls:

```
$r->subprocess_env;
```

in a void context (which has the same effect as PerlOptions +SetupEnv for the handler that called it), only the following environment variables are accessible via %ENV:

- MOD_PERL and GATEWAY_INTERFACE (always)
- PATH and TZ (if you had them defined in the shell or *httpd.conf*)

Therefore, if you don't want to add the overhead of populating %ENV when you simply want to pass some configuration variables from *httpd.conf*, consider using PerlSetVar and PerlAddVar instead of PerlSetEnv and PerlPassEnv.

perl-script

perl-script is configured as:

```
SetHandler perl-script
```

Most mod_perl handlers use the perl-script handler. Here are a few things to note:

- PerlOptions +GlobalRequest is in effect unless:
  ```
  PerlOptions -GlobalRequest
  ```
  is specified.
- PerlOptions +SetupEnv is in effect unless:
  ```
  PerlOptions -SetupEnv
  ```
  is specified.
- STDOUT and STDOUT get tied to the request object $r, which makes it possible to read from STDIN and print directly to STDOUT via print( ), instead of having to use implicit calls like $r->print( ).

- Several special global Perl variables are saved before the handler is called and restored afterward (as in mod_perl 1.0). These include %ENV, @INC, $/, and STDOUT's $| and END blocks.

A simple response handler example

Let's demonstrate the differences between the modperl and perl-script core handlers. Example 24-2 represents a simple mod_perl response handler that prints out the environment variables as seen by it.

Example 24-2. Apache/PrintEnv1.pm

```
package Apache::PrintEnv1;

use strict;
use warnings;

use Apache::RequestRec (); # for $r->content_type

use Apache::Const -compile => 'OK';

sub handler {
    my $r = shift;

    $r->content_type('text/plain');
    for (sort keys %ENV){
        print "$_ => $ENV{$_}\n";
    }

    return Apache::OK;
}

1;
```

This is the required configuration for the perl-script handler:

```
PerlModule Apache::PrintEnv1
<Location /print_env1>
    SetHandler perl-script
    PerlResponseHandler Apache::PrintEnv1
</Location>
```

Now issue a request to *http://localhost/print_env1*, and you should see all the environment variables printed out.

The same response handler, adjusted to work with the modperl core handler, is shown in Example 24-3.

Example 24-3. Apache/PrintEnv2.pm

```perl
package Apache::PrintEnv2;

use strict;
use warnings;

use Apache::RequestRec (); # for $r->content_type
use Apache::RequestIO (); # for $r->print

use Apache::Const -compile => 'OK';

sub handler {
    my $r = shift;

    $r->content_type('text/plain');
    $r->subprocess_env;
    for (sort keys %ENV){
        $r->print("$_ => $ENV{$_}\n");
    }

    return Apache::OK;
}

1;
```

The configuration now will look like this:

```
PerlModule Apache::PrintEnv2
<Location /print_env2>
    SetHandler modperl
    PerlResponseHandler Apache::PrintEnv2
</Location>
```

Apache::PrintEnv2 cannot use print( ), so it uses $r->print( ) to generate a response. Under the modperl core handler, %ENV is not populated by default; therefore, subprocess_env( ) is called in a void context. Alternatively, we could configure this section to do:

```
PerlOptions +SetupEnv
```

If you issue a request to *http://localhost/print_env2*, you should see all the environment variables printed out as with *http://localhost/print_env1*.

PerlOptions Directive

The PerlOptions directive provides fine-grained configuration for what were compile-time–only options in the first mod_perl generation. It also provides control over what class of PerlInterpreter is used for a <VirtualHost> or location configured with <Location>, <Directory>, etc.

Options are enabled by prepending + and disabled with -. The options are discussed in the following sections.

Enable

On by default; can be used to disable mod_perl for a given <VirtualHost>. For example:

```
<VirtualHost ...>
    PerlOptions -Enable
</VirtualHost>
```

Clone

Share the parent Perl interpreter, but give the <VirtualHost> its own interpreter pool. For example, should you wish to fine-tune interpreter pools for a given virtual host:

```
<VirtualHost ...>
    PerlOptions +Clone
    PerlInterpStart 2
    PerlInterpMax 2
</VirtualHost>
```

This might be worthwhile in the case where certain hosts have their own sets of large modules, used only in each host. Tuning each host to have its own pool means that the hosts will continue to reuse the Perl allocations in their specific modules.

When cloning a Perl interpreter, to inherit the parent Perl interpreter's PerlSwitches, use:

```
<VirtualHost ...>
    ...
    PerlSwitches +inherit
</VirtualHost>
```

Parent

Create a new parent Perl interpreter for the given <VirtualHost> and give it its own interpreter pool (implies the Clone option).

A common problem with mod_perl 1.0 was that the namespace was shared by all code within the process. Consider two developers using the same server, each of whom wants to run a different version of a module with the same name. This example will create two parent Perl interpreters, one for each <VirtualHost>, each with its own namespace and pointing to a different path in @INC:

```
<VirtualHost ...>
    ServerName dev1
    PerlOptions +Parent
    PerlSwitches -Mblib=/home/dev1/lib/perl
</VirtualHost>

<VirtualHost ...>
    ServerName dev2
```

```
        PerlOptions +Parent
        PerlSwitches -Mblib=/home/dev2/lib/perl
    </VirtualHost>
```

Perl*Handler

Disable specific Perl*Handlers (all compiled-in handlers are enabled by default). The option name is derived from the Perl*Handler name, by stripping the Perl and Handler parts of the word. So PerlLogHandler becomes Log, which can be used to disable PerlLogHandler:

```
    PerlOptions -Log
```

Suppose one of the hosts does not want to allow users to configure PerlAuthenHandler, PerlAuthzHandler, PerlAccessHandler, and <Perl> sections:

```
    <VirtualHost ...>
        PerlOptions -Authen -Authz -Access -Sections
    </VirtualHost>
```

Or maybe it doesn't want users to configure anything but the response handler:

```
    <VirtualHost ...>
        PerlOptions None +Response
    </VirtualHost>
```

AutoLoad

Resolve Perl*Handlers at startup time; loads the modules from disk if they're not already loaded.

In mod_perl 1.0, configured Perl*Handlers that are not fully qualified subroutine names are resolved at request time, loading the handler module from disk if needed. In mod_perl 2.0, configured Perl*Handlers are resolved at startup time. By default, modules are not auto-loaded during startup-time resolution. It is possible to enable this feature with:

```
    PerlOptions +Autoload
```

Consider this configuration:

```
    PerlResponseHandler Apache::Magick
```

In this case, Apache::Magick is the package name, and the subroutine name will default to handler. If the Apache::Magick module is not already loaded, PerlOptions +Autoload will attempt to pull it in at startup time. With this option enabled you don't have to explicitly load the handler modules. For example, you don't need to add:

```
    PerlModule Apache::Magick
```

GlobalRequest

Set up the global Apache::RequestRec object for use with Apache->request. This setting is needed, for example, if you use CGI.pm to process the incoming request.

This setting is enabled by default for sections configured as:

```
<Location ...>
    SetHandler perl-script
    ...
</Location>
```

And can be disabled with:

```
<Location ...>
    SetHandler perl-script
    PerlOptions -GlobalRequest
    ...
</Location>
```

ParseHeaders

Scan output for HTTP headers. This option provides the same functionality as mod_perl 1.0's `PerlSendHeaders` option, but it's more robust. It usually must be enabled for registry scripts that send the HTTP header with:

```
print "Content-type: text/html\n\n";
```

MergeHandlers

Turn on merging of `Perl*Handler` arrays. For example, with this setting:

```
PerlFixupHandler Apache::FixupA

<Location /inside>
    PerlFixupHandler Apache::FixupB
</Location>
```

a request for *inside* runs only `Apache::FixupB` (mod_perl 1.0 behavior). But with this configuration:

```
PerlFixupHandler Apache::FixupA

<Location /inside>
    PerlOptions +MergeHandlers
    PerlFixupHandler Apache::FixupB
</Location>
```

a request for *inside* will run both the `Apache::FixupA` and `Apache::FixupB` handlers.

SetupEnv

Set up environment variables for each request, à la mod_cgi.

When this option is enabled, mod_perl fiddles with the environment to make it appear as if the code is called under the mod_cgi handler. For example, the `$ENV{QUERY_STRING}` environment variable is initialized with the contents of `Apache::args()`, and the value returned by `Apache::server_hostname()` is put into `$ENV{SERVER_NAME}`.

Those who have moved to the mod_perl API no longer need this extra %ENV population and can gain by disabling it, since %ENV population is expensive. Code using the CGI.pm module requires PerlOptions +SetupEnv because that module relies on a properly populated CGI environment table.

This option is enabled by default for sections configured as:

```
<Location ...>
    SetHandler perl-script
    ...
</Location>
```

Since this option adds an overhead to each request, if you don't need this functionality you can turn it off for a certain section:

```
<Location ...>
    SetHandler perl-script
    PerlOptions -SetupEnv
    ...
</Location>
```

or globally affect the whole server:

```
PerlOptions -SetupEnv
<Location ...>
    ...
</Location>
```

It can still be enabled for sections that need this functionality.

When this option is disabled you can still read environment variables set by you. For example, when you use the following configuration:

```
PerlOptions -SetupEnv
<Location /perl>
  PerlSetEnv TEST hi
  SetHandler perl-script
  PerlHandler ModPerl::Registry
  Options +ExecCGI
</Location>
```

and you issue a request for setupenvoff.pl from Example 24-4.

Example 24-4. setupenvoff.pl

```
use Data::Dumper;
my $r = Apache->request();
$r->send_http_header('text/plain');
print Dumper(\%ENV);
```

you should see something like this:

```
$VAR1 = {
          'GATEWAY_INTERFACE' => 'CGI-Perl/1.1',
          'MOD_PERL' => 'mod_perl/2.0.1',
          'PATH' => '/bin:/usr/bin',
          'TEST' => 'hi'
        };
```

Notice that we got the value of the environment variable TEST.

Thread-Mode–Specific Directives

The following directives are enabled only in a threaded MPM mod_perl:

PerlInterpStart

The number of interpreters to clone at startup time.

PerlInterpMax

If all running interpreters are in use, mod_perl will clone new interpreters to handle the request, up until this number of interpreters is reached. When PerlInterpMax is reached, mod_perl will block until an interpreter becomes available.

PerlInterpMinSpare

The minimum number of available interpreters this parameter will clone before a request comes in.

PerlInterpMaxSpare

mod_perl will throttle down the number of interpreters to this number as those in use become available.

PerlInterpMaxRequests

The maximum number of requests an interpreter should serve. The interpreter is destroyed and replaced with a fresh clone when this number is reached.

PerlInterpScope

As mentioned, when a request in a threaded MPM is handled by mod_perl, an interpreter must be pulled from the interpreter pool. The interpreter is then available only to the thread that selected it, until it is released back into the interpreter pool. By default, an interpreter will be held for the lifetime of the request, equivalent to this configuration:

```
PerlInterpScope request
```

For example, if a PerlAccessHandler is configured, an interpreter will be selected before it is run and not released until after the logging phase.

Interpreters will be shared across subrequests by default; however, it is possible to configure the interpreter scope to be per subrequest on a per-directory basis:

```
PerlInterpScope subrequest
```

With this configuration, an autoindex-generated page, for example, would select an interpreter for each item in the listing that is configured with a `Perl*Handler`.

It is also possible to configure the scope to be per handler:

```
PerlInterpScope handler
```

With this configuration, an interpreter will be selected before `PerlAccessHandlers` are run and put back immediately afterwards, before Apache moves on to the authentication phase. If a `PerlFixupHandler` is configured further down the chain, another interpreter will be selected and again put back afterwards, before `PerlResponseHandler` is run.

For protocol handlers, the interpreter is held for the lifetime of the connection. However, a C protocol module (e.g., mod_ftp) might hook into mod_perl and provide a request_rec record. In this case, the default scope is that of the request (the download of one file). Should a mod_perl handler want to maintain state for the lifetime of an FTP connection, it is possible to do so on a per-`<VirtualHost>` basis:

```
PerlInterpScope connection
```

Retrieving Server Startup Options

The *httpd* server startup options can be retrieved using `Apache::exists_config_define( )`. For example, to check if the server was started in single-process mode:

```
panic% httpd -DONE_PROCESS
```

use the following code:

```
if (Apache::exists_config_define("ONE_PROCESS")) {
    print "Running in a single process mode";
}
```

Resources

For up-to-date documentation on mod_perl 2.0, see:

http://perl.apache.org/docs/2.0/

## CHAPTER 25

Programming for mod_perl 2.0

In this chapter, we discuss how to migrate services from mod_perl 1.0 to 2.0, and how to make the new services based on mod_perl 2.0 backward compatible with mod_perl 1.0 (if possible). We also cover all the new Perl*Handlers in mod_perl 2.0.

Migrating to and Programming with mod_perl 2.0

In mod_perl 2.0, several configuration directives were renamed or removed. Several APIs also were changed, renamed, removed, or moved to new packages. Certain functions, while staying exactly the same as in mod_perl 1.0, now reside in different packages. Before using them, you need to find and load the new packages.

Since mod_perl 2.0 hasn't yet been released as of this writing, it's possible that certain things will change after the book is published. If something doesn't work as explained here, please refer to the documentation in the mod_perl distribution or the online version at *http://perl.apache.org/docs/2.0/* for the updated documentation.

The Shortest Migration Path

mod_perl 2.0 provides two backward-compatibility layers: one for the configuration files and the other for the code. If you are concerned about preserving backward compatibility with mod_perl 1.0, or are just experimenting with mod_perl 2.0 while continuing to run mod_perl 1.0 on your production server, simply enable the code-compatibility layer by adding:

```
use Apache2;
use Apache::compat;
```

at the top of your startup file. Backward compatibility of the configuration is enabled by default.

Migrating Configuration Files

To migrate the configuration files to mod_perl 2.0 syntax, you may need to make certain adjustments. Several configuration directives are deprecated in 2.0 but are still available for backward compatibility with mod_perl 1.0. If you don't need backward compatibility, consider using the directives that have replaced them.

PerlHandler

PerlHandler has been replaced with PerlResponseHandler.

PerlSendHeader

PerlSendHeader has been replaced with the PerlOptions +/-ParseHeaders directive:

```
PerlSendHeader On  => PerlOptions +ParseHeaders
PerlSendHeader Off => PerlOptions -ParseHeaders
```

PerlSetupEnv

PerlSetupEnv has been replaced with the PerlOptions +/-SetupEnv directive:

```
PerlSetupEnv On  => PerlOptions +SetupEnv
PerlSetupEnv Off => PerlOptions -SetupEnv
```

PerlTaintCheck

Taint mode can now be turned on with:

```
PerlSwitches -T
```

As with standard Perl, taint mode is disabled by default. Once enabled, taint mode cannot be turned off.

PerlWarn

Warnings now can be enabled globally with:

```
PerlSwitches -w
```

PerlFreshRestart

PerlFreshRestart is a mod_perl 1.0 legacy option and doesn't exist in mod_perl 2.0. A full tear-down and startup of interpreters is done on restart.

If you need to use the same *httpd.conf* file for 1.0 and 2.0, use:

```
<IfDefine !MODPERL2>
    PerlFreshRestart On
</IfDefine>
```

Code Porting

mod_perl 2.0 is trying hard to be backward compatible with mod_perl 1.0. However, some things (mostly APIs) have changed. To gain complete compatibility with 1.0 while running under 2.0, you should load the compatibility module as early as possible:

```
use Apache::compat;
```

at server startup. Unless there are forgotten things or bugs, your code should work without any changes under the 2.0 series.

However, if you don't have a good reason to keep 1.0 compatibility, you should try to remove the compatibility layer and adjust your code to work under 2.0 without it. This will improve performance. The online mod_perl documentation includes a document (*http://perl.apache.org/docs/2.0/user/porting/compat.html*) that explains what APIs have changed and what new APIs should be used instead.

If you have mod_perl 1.0 and 2.0 installed on the same system and the two use the same Perl libraries directory (e.g., */usr/lib/perl5*), to use mod_perl 2.0 make sure to first load the Apache2 module, which will perform the necessary adjustments to @INC:

```
use Apache2; # if you have 1.0 and 2.0 installed
use Apache::compat;
```

So if before loading Apache2.pm the @INC array consisted of:

```
/usr/lib/perl5/5.8.0/i686-linux-thread-multi
/usr/lib/perl5/5.8.0
/usr/lib/perl5/site_perl/5.8.0/i686-linux-thread-multi
/usr/lib/perl5/site_perl/5.8.0
/usr/lib/perl5/site_perl
.
```

it will now look like this:

```
/usr/lib/perl5/site_perl/5.8.0/i686-linux-thread-multi/Apache2
/usr/lib/perl5/5.8.0/i686-linux-thread-multi
/usr/lib/perl5/5.8.0
/usr/lib/perl5/site_perl/5.8.0/i686-linux-thread-multi
/usr/lib/perl5/site_perl/5.8.0
/usr/lib/perl5/site_perl
.
```

Notice that a new directory was appended to the search path. If, for example, the code attempts to load Apache::Server and there are two versions of this module under */usr/lib/perl5/site_perl/*:

```
5.8.0/i686-linux-thread-multi/Apache/Server.pm
  5.8.0/i686-linux-thread-multi/Apache2/Apache/Server.pm
```

the mod_perl 2.0 version will be loaded first, because the directory *5.8.0/i686-linux-thread-multi/Apache2* comes before the directory *5.8.0/i686-linux-thread-multi* in @INC.

Finally, mod_perl 2.0 has all its methods spread across many modules. To use these methods, you first have to load the modules containing them. The ModPerl::MethodLookup module can be used to figure out what modules need to be loaded. For example, if you try to use:

```
$r->construct_url();
```

and mod_perl complains that it can't find the construct_url() method, you can ask ModPerl::MethodLookup:

```
panic% perl -MApache2 -MModPerl::MethodLookup -e print_method construct_url
```

This will print:

```
to use method 'construct_url' add:
        use Apache::URI ();
```

Another useful feature provided by ModPerl::MethodLookup is the preload_all_modules() function, which preloads all mod_perl 2.0 modules. This is useful when you start to port your mod_perl 1.0 code (though preferrably avoided in the production environment to save memory). You can simply add the following snippet to your *startup.pl* file:

```
use ModPerl::MethodLookup;
ModPerl::MethodLookup::preload_all_modules();
```

ModPerl::Registry Family

In mod_perl 2.0, Apache::Registry and friends (Apache::PerlRun, Apache::RegistryNG, etc.) have migrated into the ModPerl:: namespace. The new family is based on the idea of Apache::RegistryNG from mod_perl 1.0, where you can customize pretty much all the functionality by providing your own hooks. The functionality of the Apache::Registry, Apache::RegistryBB, and Apache::PerlRun modules hasn't changed from the user's perspective, except for the namespace. All these modules are now derived from the ModPerl::RegistryCooker class. So if you want to change the functionality of any of the existing subclasses, or you want to "cook" your own registry module, it can be done easily. Refer to the ModPerl::RegistryCooker manpage for more information.

Here is a typical registry section configuration in mod_perl 2.0:

```
Alias /perl/ /home/httpd/perl/
<Location /perl>
    SetHandler perl-script
    PerlResponseHandler ModPerl::Registry
    Options +ExecCGI
    PerlOptions +ParseHeaders
</Location>
```

As we explained earlier, the ParseHeaders option is needed if the headers are being sent via print() (i.e., without using the mod_perl API) and comes as a replacement for the PerlSendHeader option in mod_perl 1.0.

Example 25-1 shows a simple registry script that prints the environment variables.

Example 25-1. print_env.pl

```
print "Content-type: text/plain\n\n";
for (sort keys %ENV){
    print "$_ => $ENV{$_}\n";
}
```

Save the file in */home/httpd/perl/print_env.pl* and make it executable:

```
panic% chmod 0700 /home/stas/modperl/mod_perl_rules1.pl
```

Now issue a request to *http://localhost/perl/print_env.pl*, and you should see all the environment variables printed out.

One currently outstanding issue with the registry family is the issue with chdir( ). mod_perl 1.0 registry modules always performed cdhir( )s to the directory of the script, so scripts could require modules relative to the directory of the script. Since mod_perl 2.0 may run in a threaded environment, the registry scripts can no longer call chdir( ), because when one thread performs a chdir( ) it affects the whole process—all other threads will see that new directory when calling Cwd::cwd( ), which will wreak havoc. As of this writing, the registry modules can't handle this problem (they simply don't chdir( ) to the script's directory); however, a satisfying solution will be provided by the time mod_perl 2.0 is released.

Method Handlers

In mod_perl 1.0, method handlers had to be specified by using the ($$) prototype:

```
package Eagle;
@ISA = qw(Bird);

sub handler ($$) {
    my($class, $r) = @_;
    ...;
}
```

Starting with Perl Version 5.6, you can use subroutine attributes, and that's what mod_perl 2.0 does instead of conventional prototypes:

```
package Eagle;
@ISA = qw(Bird);

sub handler : method {
    my($class, $r) = @_;
    ...;
}
```

See the *attributes* manpage.

mod_perl 2.0 doesn't support the ($$) prototypes, mainly because several callbacks in 2.0 have more arguments than $r, so the ($$) prototype doesn't make sense any more. Therefore, if you want your code to work with both mod_perl generations, you should use the subroutine attributes.

Apache::StatINC Replacement

Apache::StatINC has been replaced by Apache::Reload, which works for both mod_perl generations. To migrate to Apache::Reload, simply replace:

```
PerlInitHandler Apache::StatINC
```

with:

```
PerlInitHandler Apache::Reload
```

Apache::Reload also provides some extra functionality, covered in the module's manpage.

New Apache Phases and Corresponding Perl*Handlers

Because the majority of the Apache phases supported by mod_perl haven't changed since mod_perl 1.0, in this chapter we will discuss only those phases and corresponding handlers that were added or changed in mod_perl 2.0.

Figure 25-1 depicts the Apache 2.0 server cycle. You can see the mod_perl phases PerlOpenLogsHandler, PerlPostConfigHandler, and PerlChildInitHandler, which we will discuss shortly. Later, we will zoom into the connection cycle depicted in Figure 25-2, which will expose other mod_perl handlers.

Apache 2.0 starts by parsing the configuration file. After the configuration file is parsed, any PerlOpenLogsHandler handlers are executed. After that, any PerlPostConfigHandler handlers are run. When the *post_config* phase is finished the server immediately restarts, to make sure that it can survive graceful restarts after starting to serve the clients.

When the restart is completed, Apache 2.0 spawns the workers that will do the actual work. Depending on the MPM used, these can be threads, processes, or a mixture of both. For example, the *worker* MPM spawns a number of processes, each running a number of threads. When each child process is started PerlChildInitHandlers are executed. Notice that they are run for each starting process, not thread.

From that moment on each working process (or thread) processes connections until it's killed by the server or the server is shut down. When the server is shut down, any registered PerlChildExitHandlers are executed.

Example 25-2 demonstrates all the startup phases.

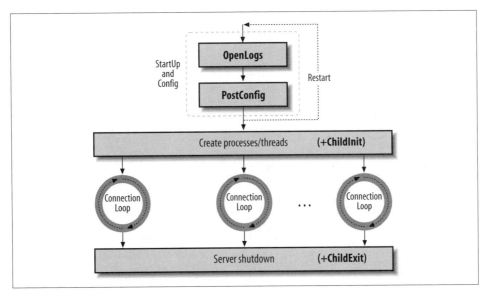

Figure 25-1. Apache 2.0 server lifecycle

Example 25-2. Book/StartupLog.pm

```
package Book::StartupLog;

use strict;
use warnings;

use Apache::Log ();
use Apache::ServerUtil ();

use File::Spec::Functions;

use Apache::Const -compile => 'OK';

my $log_file = catfile "logs", "startup_log";
my $log_fh;

sub open_logs {
    my($conf_pool, $log_pool, $temp_pool, $s) = @_;
    my $log_path = Apache::server_root_relative($conf_pool, $log_file);

    $s->warn("opening the log file: $log_path");
    open $log_fh, ">>$log_path" or die "can't open $log_path: $!";
    my $oldfh = select($log_fh); $| = 1; select($oldfh);

    say("process $$ is born to reproduce");
    return Apache::OK;
}

sub post_config {
    my($conf_pool, $log_pool, $temp_pool, $s) = @_;
```

Example 25-2. Book/StartupLog.pm (continued)

```perl
        say("configuration is completed");
        return Apache::OK;
}

sub child_exit {
    my($child_pool, $s) = @_;
    say("process $$ now exits");
    return Apache::OK;
}

sub child_init {
    my($child_pool, $s) = @_;
    say("process $$ is born to serve");
    return Apache::OK;
}

sub say {
    my($caller) = (caller(1))[3] =~ /([^:]+)$/;
    if (defined $log_fh) {
        printf $log_fh "[%s] - %-11s: %s\n",
            scalar(localtime), $caller, $_[0];
    }
    else {
        # when the log file is not open
        warn __PACKAGE__ . " says: $_[0]\n";
    }
}

END {
    say("process $$ is shutdown\n");
}

1;
```

Here's the *httpd.conf* configuration section:

```
PerlModule              Book::StartupLog
PerlOpenLogsHandler     Book::StartupLog::open_logs
PerlPostConfigHandler   Book::StartupLog::post_config
PerlChildInitHandler    Book::StartupLog::child_init
PerlChildExitHandler    Book::StartupLog::child_exit
```

When we perform a server startup followed by a shutdown, the *logs/startup_log* is created, if it didn't exist already (it shares the same directory with *error_log* and other standard log files), and each stage appends to it its log information. So when we perform:

```
panic% bin/apachectl start && bin/apachectl stop
```

the following is logged to *logs/startup_log*:

```
[Thu Mar  6 15:57:08 2003] - open_logs  : process 21823 is born to reproduce
[Thu Mar  6 15:57:08 2003] - post_config: configuration is completed
[Thu Mar  6 15:57:09 2003] - END        : process 21823 is shutdown
```

```
[Thu Mar  6 15:57:10 2003] - open_logs  : process 21825 is born to reproduce
[Thu Mar  6 15:57:10 2003] - post_config: configuration is completed
[Thu Mar  6 15:57:11 2003] - child_init : process 21830 is born to serve
[Thu Mar  6 15:57:11 2003] - child_init : process 21831 is born to serve
[Thu Mar  6 15:57:11 2003] - child_init : process 21832 is born to serve
[Thu Mar  6 15:57:11 2003] - child_init : process 21833 is born to serve
[Thu Mar  6 15:57:12 2003] - child_exit : process 21833 now exits
[Thu Mar  6 15:57:12 2003] - child_exit : process 21832 now exits
[Thu Mar  6 15:57:12 2003] - child_exit : process 21831 now exits
[Thu Mar  6 15:57:12 2003] - child_exit : process 21830 now exits
[Thu Mar  6 15:57:12 2003] - END        : process 21825 is shutdown
```

First, we can clearly see that Apache always restarts itself after the first *post_config* phase is over. The logs show that the *post_config* phase is preceded by the *open_logs* phase. Only after Apache has restarted itself and has completed the *open_logs* and *post_config* phases again is the *child_init* phase run for each child process. In our example we had the setting StartServers=4; therefore, you can see that four child processes were started.

Finally, you can see that on server shutdown, the *child_exit* phase is run for each child process and the END { } block is executed by the parent process only.

Apache also specifies the *pre_config* phase, which is executed before the configuration files are parsed, but this is of no use to mod_perl, because mod_perl is loaded only during the configuration phase.

Now let's discuss each of the mentioned startup handlers and their implementation in the Book::StartupLog module in detail.

Server Configuration and Startup Phases

open_logs, configured with PerlOpenLogsHandler, and *post_config*, configured with PerlPostConfigHandler, are the two new phases available during server startup.

PerlOpenLogsHandler

The *open_logs* phase happens just before the *post_config* phase.

Handlers registered by PerlOpenLogsHandler are usually used for opening module-specific log files (e.g., *httpd* core and mod_ssl open their log files during this phase).

At this stage the STDERR stream is not yet redirected to *error_log*, and therefore any messages to that stream will be printed to the console from which the server is starting (if one exists).

The PerlOpenLogsHandler directive may appear in the main configuration files and within <VirtualHost> sections.

Apache will continue executing all handlers registered for this phase until the first handler returns something other than Apache::OK or Apache::DECLINED.

As we saw in the Book::StartupLog::open_logs handler, the *open_logs* phase handlers accept four arguments: the configuration pool,[*] the logging streams pool, the temporary pool, and the server object:

```
sub open_logs {
    my($conf_pool, $log_pool, $temp_pool, $s) = @_;
    my $log_path = Apache::server_root_relative($conf_pool, $log_file);

    $s->warn("opening the log file: $log_path");
    open $log_fh, ">>$log_path" or die "can't open $log_path: $!";
    my $oldfh = select($log_fh); $| = 1; select($oldfh);

    say("process $$ is born to reproduce");
    return Apache::OK;
}
```

In our example the handler uses the Apache::server_root_relative( ) function to set the full path to the log file, which is then opened for appending and set to unbuffered mode. Finally, it logs the fact that it's running in the parent process.

As you've seen in this example, this handler is configured by adding the following to *httpd.conf*:

```
PerlOpenLogsHandler Book::StartupLog::open_logs
```

PerlPostConfigHandler

The *post_config* phase happens right after Apache has processed the configuration files, before any child processes are spawned (which happens at the *child_init* phase).

This phase can be used for initializing things to be shared between all child processes. You can do the same in the startup file, but in the *post_config* phase you have access to a complete configuration tree.

The *post_config* phase is very similar to the *open_logs* phase. The PerlPostConfigHandler directive may appear in the main configuration files and within <VirtualHost> sections. Apache will run all registered handlers for this phase until a handler returns something other than Apache::OK or Apache::DECLINED. This phase's handlers receive the same four arguments as the *open_logs* phase's handlers. From our example:

```
sub post_config {
    my($conf_pool, $log_pool, $temp_pool, $s) = @_;
    say("configuration is completed");
    return Apache::OK;
}
```

This example handler just logs that the configuration was completed and returns right away.

---

[*] Pools are used by Apache for memory-handling functions. You can make use of them from the Perl space, too.

This handler is configured by adding the following to *httpd.conf*:

```
PerlOpenLogsHandler Book::StartupLog::post_config
```

PerlChildInitHandler

The *child_init* phase happens immediately after a child process is spawned. Each child process (not a thread!) will run the hooks of this phase only once in its lifetime.

In the *prefork* MPM this phase is useful for initializing any data structures that should be private to each process. For example, Apache::DBI preopens database connections during this phase, and Apache::Resource sets the process's resource limits.

The PerlChildInitHandler directive should appear in the top-level server configuration file. All PerlChildInitHandlers will be executed, disregarding their return values (although mod_perl expects a return value, so returning Apache::OK is a good idea).

In the Book::StartupLog example we used the child_init() handler:

```
sub child_init {
    my($child_pool, $s) = @_;
    say("process $$ is born to serve");
    return Apache::OK;
}
```

The child_init() handler accepts two arguments: the child process pool and the server object. The example handler logs the PID of the child process in which it's run and returns.

This handler is configured by adding the following to *httpd.conf*:

```
PerlOpenLogsHandler Book::StartupLog::child_init
```

PerlChildExitHandler

The *child_exit* phase is executed before the child process exits. Notice that it happens only when the process exits, not when the thread exits (assuming that you are using a threaded MPM).

The PerlChildExitHandler directive should appear in the top-level server configuration file. mod_perl will run all registered PerlChildExitHandler handlers for this phase until a handler returns something other than Apache::OK or Apache::DECLINED.

In the Book::StartupLog example we used the child_exit() handler:

```
sub child_exit {
    my($child_pool, $s) = @_;
    say("process $$ now exits");
    return Apache::OK;
}
```

The child_exit() handler accepts two arguments: the child process pool and the server object. The example handler logs the PID of the child process in which it's run and returns.

As you saw in the example, this handler is configured by adding the following to *httpd.conf*:

```
PerlOpenLogsHandler Book::StartupLog::child_exit
```

Connection Phases

Since Apache 2.0 makes it possible to implement protocols other than HTTP, the connection phases *pre_connection*, configured with `PerlPreConnectionHandler`, and *process_connection*, configured with `PerlProcessConnectionHandler`, were added. The *pre_connection* phase is used for runtime adjustments of things for each connection—for example, mod_ssl uses the *pre_connection* phase to add the SSL filters if `SSLEngine On` is configured, regardless of whether the protocol is HTTP, FTP, NNTP, etc. The *process_connection* phase is used to implement various protocols, usually those similar to HTTP. The HTTP protocol itself is handled like any other protocol; internally it runs the request handlers similar to Apache 1.3.

When a connection is issued by a client, it's first run through the `PerlPreConnection-Handler` and then passed to the `PerlProcessConnectionHandler`, which generates the response. When `PerlProcessConnectionHandler` is reading data from the client, it can be filtered by connection input filters. The generated response can also be filtered though connection output filters. Filters are usually used for modifying the data flowing though them, but they can be used for other purposes as well (e.g., logging interesting information). Figure 25-2 depicts the connection cycle and the data flow and highlights which handlers are available to mod_perl 2.0.

Now let's discuss the `PerlPreConnectionHandler` and `PerlProcessConnectionHandler` handlers in detail.

PerlPreConnectionHandler

The *pre_connection* phase happens just after the server accepts the connection, but before it is handed off to a protocol module to be served. It gives modules an opportunity to modify the connection as soon as possible and insert filters if needed. The core server uses this phase to set up the connection record based on the type of connection that is being used. mod_perl itself uses this phase to register the connection input and output filters.

In mod_perl 1.0, during code development `Apache::Reload` was used to automatically reload Perl modules modified since the last request. It was invoked during *post_read_request*, the first HTTP request's phase. In mod_perl 2.0, *pre_connection* is the earliest phase, so if we want to make sure that all modified Perl modules are reloaded for any protocols and their phases, it's best to set the scope of the Perl interpreter to the lifetime of the connection via:

```
PerlInterpScope connection
```

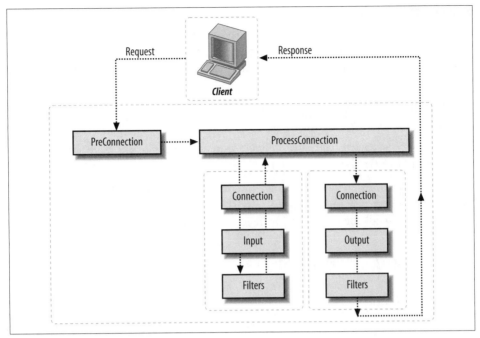

Figure 25-2. Apache 2.0 connection cycle

and invoke the `Apache::Reload` handler during the *pre_connection* phase. However, this development-time advantage can become a disadvantage in production—for example, if a connection handled by the HTTP protocol is configured as `KeepAlive` and there are several requests coming on the same connection (one handled by mod_perl and the others by the default image handler), the Perl interpreter won't be available to other threads while the images are being served.

Apache will continue executing all handlers registered for this phase until the first handler returns something other than `Apache::OK` or `Apache::DECLINED`.

The `PerlPreConnectionHandler` directive may appear in the main configuration files and within `<VirtualHost>` sections.

A *pre_connection* handler accepts a connection record and a socket object as its arguments:

```
sub handler {
    my ($c, $socket) = @_;
    # ...
    return Apache::OK;
}
```

PerlProcessConnectionHandler

The *process_connection* phase is used to process incoming connections. Only protocol modules should assign handlers for this phase, as it gives them an opportunity to replace the standard HTTP processing with processing for some other protocol (e.g., POP3, FTP, etc.).

Apache will continue executing all handlers registered for this phase until the first handler returns something other than Apache::DECLINED.

The PerlProcessConnectionHandler directive may appear in the main configuration files and within <VirtualHost> sections.

The *process_connection* handler can be written in two ways. The first way is to manipulate bucket brigades, in a way very similar to the filters. The second, simpler way is to bypass all the filters and to read from and write to the connection socket directly.

A *process_connection* handler accepts a connection record object as its only argument:

```
sub handler {
    my ($c) = @_;
    # ...
    return Apache::OK;
}
```

Now let's look at two examples of connection handlers. The first uses the connection socket to read and write the data, and the second uses bucket brigades to accomplish the same thing and allow the connection filters to do their work.

Socket-based protocol module. To demonstrate the workings of a protocol module, we'll take a look at the Book::Eliza module, which sends the data read from the client as input to Chatbot::Eliza, which in turn implements a mock Rogerian psychotherapist and forwards the response from the psychotherapist back to the client. In this module we will use the implementation that works directly with the connection socket and therefore bypasses any connection filters.

A protocol handler is configured using the PerlProcessConnectionHandler directive, and we will use the Listen and <VirtualHost> directives to bind to the nonstandard port 8084:

```
Listen 8084
<VirtualHost _default_:8084>
    PerlModule                 Book::Eliza
    PerlProcessConnectionHandler Book::Eliza
</VirtualHost>
```

Book::Eliza is then enabled when starting Apache:

```
panic% httpd
```

And we give it a whirl:

```
panic% telnet localhost 8084
Trying 127.0.0.1...
Connected to localhost (127.0.0.1).
Escape character is '^]'.
Hello Eliza
How do you do. Please state your problem.

How are you?
Oh, I?

Why do I have core dumped?
You say Why do you have core dumped?

I feel like writing some tests today, you?
I'm not sure I understand you fully.

Good bye, Eliza
Does talking about this bother you?

Connection closed by foreign host.
```

The code is shown in Example 25-3.

Example 25-3. Book/Eliza.pm

```perl
package Book::Eliza;

use strict;
use warnings FATAL => 'all';

use Apache::Connection ();
use APR::Socket ();

require Chatbot::Eliza;

use Apache::Const -compile => 'OK';

use constant BUFF_LEN => 1024;

my $eliza = new Chatbot::Eliza;

sub handler {
    my $c = shift;
    my $socket = $c->client_socket;

    my $buff;
    my $last = 0;
    while (1) {
        my($rlen, $wlen);
        $rlen = BUFF_LEN;
        $socket->recv($buff, $rlen);
        last if $rlen <= 0;
```

Example 25-3. Book/Eliza.pm (continued)

```
            # \r is sent instead of \n if the client is talking over telnet
            $buff =~ s/[\r\n]*$//;
            $last++ if $buff =~ /good bye/i;
            $buff = $eliza->transform( $buff ) . "\n\n";
            $socket->send($buff, length $buff);
            last if $last;
        }

    Apache::OK;
}
1;
```

The example handler starts with the standard package declaration and, of course, use
strict;. As with all Perl*Handlers, the subroutine name defaults to handler. However, in the case of a protocol handler, the first argument is not a request_rec, but a
conn_rec blessed into the Apache::Connection class. We have direct access to the client socket via Apache::Connection's client_socket() method, which returns an
object blessed into the APR::Socket class.

Inside the read/send loop, the handler attempts to read BUFF_LEN bytes from the client socket into the $buff buffer. The $rlen parameter will be set to the number of
bytes actually read. The APR::Socket::recv() method returns an APR status value,
but we need only check the read length to break out of the loop if it is less than or
equal to 0 bytes. The handler also breaks the loop after processing an input including the "good bye" string.

Otherwise, if the handler receives some data, it sends this data to the $eliza object
(which represents the psychotherapist), whose returned text is then sent back to the
client with the APR::Socket::send() method. When the read/print loop is finished
the handler returns Apache::OK, telling Apache to terminate the connection. As mentioned earlier, since this handler is working directly with the connection socket, no
filters can be applied.

Bucket brigade–based protocol module. Now let's look at the same module, but this time
implemented by manipulating bucket brigades. It runs its output through a connection output filter that turns all uppercase characters into their lowercase equivalents.

The following configuration defines a <VirtualHost> listening on port 8085 that
enables the Book::Eliza2 connection handler, which will run its output through the
Book::Eliza2::lowercase_filter filter:

```
Listen 8085
<VirtualHost _default_:8085>
    PerlModule                    Book::Eliza2
    PerlProcessConnectionHandler Book::Eliza2
    PerlOutputFilterHandler      Book::Eliza2::lowercase_filter
</VirtualHost>
```

As before, we start the *httpd* server:

```
panic% httpd
```

and try the new connection handler in action:

```
panic% telnet localhost 8085
Trying 127.0.0.1...
Connected to localhost.localdomain (127.0.0.1).
Escape character is '^]'.
Hello Eliza!
hi. what seems to be your problem?

Problem? I don't have any problems ;)
does that trouble you?

Not at all, I don't like problems.
i'm not sure i understand you fully.

I said that I don't like problems.
that is interesting. please continue.

You are boring :(
does it please you to believe i am boring?

Yes, yes!
please tell me some more about this.

Good bye!
i'm not sure i understand you fully.

Connection closed by foreign host.
```

As you can see, the response, which normally is a mix of upper- and lowercase words, now is all in lowercase, because of the output filter. The implementation of the connection and the filter handlers is shown in Example 25-4.

Example 25-4. Book/Eliza2.pm

```perl
package Book::Eliza2;

use strict;
use warnings FATAL => 'all';

use Apache::Connection ();
use APR::Bucket ();
use APR::Brigade ();
use APR::Util ();

require Chatbot::Eliza;

use APR::Const -compile => qw(SUCCESS EOF);
use Apache::Const -compile => qw(OK MODE_GETLINE);

my $eliza = new Chatbot::Eliza;
```

Example 25-4. Book/Eliza2.pm (continued)

```perl
sub handler {
    my $c = shift;

    my $bb_in  = APR::Brigade->new($c->pool, $c->bucket_alloc);
    my $bb_out = APR::Brigade->new($c->pool, $c->bucket_alloc);
    my $last = 0;

    while (1) {
        my $rv = $c->input_filters->get_brigade($bb_in,
                                                 Apache::MODE_GETLINE);

        if ($rv != APR::SUCCESS or $bb_in->empty) {
            my $error = APR::strerror($rv);
            unless ($rv == APR::EOF) {
                warn "[eliza] get_brigade: $error\n";
            }
            $bb_in->destroy;
            last;
        }

        while (!$bb_in->empty) {
            my $bucket = $bb_in->first;

            $bucket->remove;

            if ($bucket->is_eos) {
                $bb_out->insert_tail($bucket);
                last;
            }

            my $data;
            my $status = $bucket->read($data);
            return $status unless $status == APR::SUCCESS;

            if ($data) {
                $data =~ s/[\r\n]*$//;
                $last++ if $data =~ /good bye/i;
                $data = $eliza->transform( $data ) . "\n\n";
                $bucket = APR::Bucket->new($data);
            }

            $bb_out->insert_tail($bucket);
        }

        my $b = APR::Bucket::flush_create($c->bucket_alloc);
        $bb_out->insert_tail($b);
        $c->output_filters->pass_brigade($bb_out);
        last if $last;
    }

    Apache::OK;
}
```

Example 25-4. Book/Eliza2.pm (continued)

```
use base qw(Apache::Filter);
use constant BUFF_LEN => 1024;

sub lowercase_filter : FilterConnectionHandler {
    my $filter = shift;

    while ($filter->read(my $buffer, BUFF_LEN)) {
        $filter->print(lc $buffer);
    }

    return Apache::OK;
}

1;
```

For the purpose of explaining how this connection handler works, we are going to simplify the handler. The whole handler can be represented by the following pseudocode:

```
while ($bb_in = get_brigade()) {
    while ($bucket_in = $bb_in->get_bucket()) {
        my $data = $bucket_in->read();
        $data = transform($data);
        $bucket_out = new_bucket($data);

        $bb_out->insert_tail($bucket_out);
    }
    $bb_out->insert_tail($flush_bucket);
    pass_brigade($bb_out);
}
```

The handler receives the incoming data via bucket bridages, one at a time, in a loop. It then processes each brigade, by retrieving the buckets contained in it, reading in the data, transforming that data, creating new buckets using the transformed data, and attaching them to the outgoing brigade. When all the buckets from the incoming bucket brigade are transformed and attached to the outgoing bucket brigade, a flush bucket is created and added as the last bucket, so when the outgoing bucket brigade is passed out to the outgoing connection filters, it will be sent to the client right away, not buffered.

If you look at the complete handler, the loop is terminated when one of the following conditions occurs: an error happens, the end-of-stream bucket has been seen (i.e., there's no more input at the connection), or the received data contains the string "good bye". As you saw in the demonstration, we used the string "good bye" to terminate our shrink's session.

We will skip the filter discussion here, since we are going to talk in depth about filters in the following sections. All you need to know at this stage is that the data sent from the connection handler is filtered by the outgoing filter, which transforms it to be all lowercase.

HTTP Request Phases

The HTTP request phases themselves have not changed from mod_perl 1.0, except the PerlHandler directive has been renamed PerlResponseHandler to better match the corresponding Apache phase name (*response*).

The only difference is that now it's possible to register HTTP request input and output filters, so PerlResponseHandler will filter its input and output through them. Figure 25-3 depicts the HTTP request cycle, which should be familiar to mod_perl 1.0 users, with the new addition of the request filters. From the diagram you can also see that the request filters are stacked on top of the connection filters. The request input filters filter only a request body, and the request output filters filter only a response body. Request and response headers can be accessed and modified using the $r-> headers_in, $r->headers_out, and other methods.

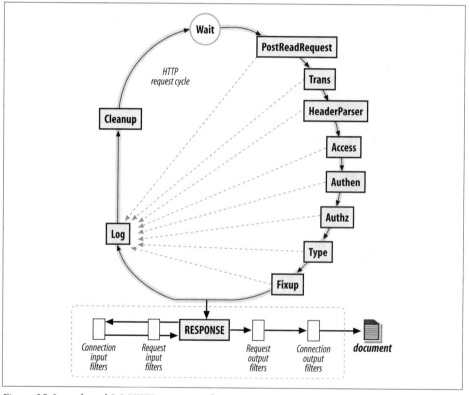

Figure 25-3. mod_perl 2.0 HTTP request cycle

I/O Filtering

Now let's talk about a totally new feature of mod_perl 2.0: input/output filtering.

As of this writing the mod_perl filtering API hasn't been finalized, and it's possible that it will change by the time the production version of mod_perl 2.0 is released. However, most concepts presented here won't change, and you should find the discussion and the examples useful for understanding how filters work. For the most up-to-date documentation, refer to *http://perl.apache.org/docs/2.0/user/handlers/filters.html*.

I/O Filtering Concepts

Before introducing the mod_perl filtering API, there are several important concepts to understand.

Two methods for manipulating data

As discussed in the last chapter, Apache 2.0 considers all incoming and outgoing data as chunks of information, disregarding their kind and source or storage methods. These data chunks are stored in buckets, which form bucket brigades. Input and output filters massage the data in the bucket brigades.

mod_perl 2.0 filters can directly manipulate the bucket brigades or use the simplified streaming interface, where the filter object acts like a file handle, which can be read from and printed to.

Even though you don't have to work with bucket brigades directly, since you can write filters using the simplified, streaming filter interface (which works with bucket brigades behind the scenes), it's still important to understand bucket brigades. For example, you need to know that an output filter will be invoked as many times as the number of bucket brigades sent from an upstream filter or a content handler, and that the end-of-stream indicator (EOS) is sometimes sent in a separate bucket brigade, so it shouldn't be a surprise if the filter is invoked even though no real data went through.

You will also need to understand how to manipulate bucket brigades if you plan to implement protocol modules, as you have seen earlier in this chapter.

HTTP request versus connection filters

HTTP request filters are applied when Apache serves an HTTP request.

HTTP request input filters get invoked on the body of the HTTP request only if the body is consumed by the content handler. HTTP request headers are not passed through the HTTP request input filters.

HTTP response output filters get invoked on the body of the HTTP response, if the content handler has generated one. HTTP response headers are not passed through the HTTP response output filters.

Connection-level filters are applied at the connection level.

A connection may be configured to serve one or more HTTP requests, or handle other protocols. Connection filters see all the incoming and outgoing data. If an HTTP request is served, connection filters can modify the HTTP headers and the body of the request and response. Of course, if a different protocol is served over the connection (e.g., IMAP), the data could have a completely different pattern than the HTTP protocol (headers and body).

Apache supports several other filter types that mod_perl 2.0 may support in the future.

Multiple invocations of filter handlers

Unlike other Apache handlers, filter handlers may get invoked more than once during the same request. Filters get invoked as many times as the number of bucket brigades sent from the upstream filter or content provider.

For example, if a content-generation handler sends a string, and then forces a flush, following with more data:

```
# assuming buffered STDOUT ($|==0)
$r->print("foo");
$r->rflush;
$r->print("bar");
```

Apache will generate one bucket brigade with two buckets (there are several types of buckets that contain data—one of them is *transient*):

```
bucket type        data
---------------------
1st    transient   foo
2nd    flush
```

and send it to the filter chain. Then, assuming that no more data was sent after print("bar"), it will create a last bucket brigade containing data:

```
bucket type        data
---------------------
1st    transient   bar
```

and send it to the filter chain. Finally it'll send yet another bucket brigade with the EOS bucket indicating that no more will be data sent:

```
bucket type        data
---------------------
1st    eos
```

In our example the filter will be invoked three times. Notice that sometimes the EOS bucket comes attached to the last bucket brigade with data and sometimes in its own bucket brigade. This should be transparent to the filter logic, as we will see shortly.

A user may install an upstream filter, and that filter may decide to insert extra bucket brigades or collect all the data in all bucket brigades passing through it and send it all down in one brigade. What's important to remember when coding a filter is to never assume that the filter is always going to be invoked once, or a fixed number of times. You can't make assumptions about the way the data is going to come in. Therefore, a typical filter handler may need to split its logic into three parts, as depicted in Figure 25-4.

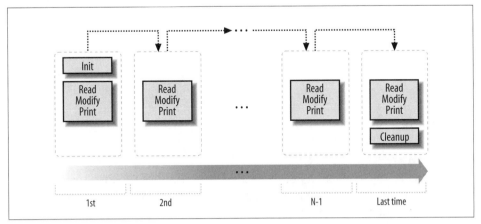

Figure 25-4. mod_perl 2.0 filter logic

Jumping ahead, we will show some pseudocode that represents all three parts. This is what a typical filter looks like:

```
sub handler {
    my $filter = shift;

    # runs on first invocation
    unless ($filter->ctx) {
        init($filter);
        $filter->ctx(1);
    }

    # runs on all invocations
    process($filter);

    # runs on the last invocation
    if ($filter->seen_eos) {
        finalize($filter);
    }

    return Apache::OK;
}
sub init     { ... }
sub process  { ... }
sub finalize { ... }
```

Let's examine the parts of this pseudofilter:

1. Initialization

During the initialization, the filter runs all the code that should be performed only once across multiple invocations of the filter (during a single request). The filter context is used to accomplish this task. For each new request, the filter context is created before the filter is called for the first time, and it's destroyed at the end of the request. When the filter is invoked for the first time, `$filter->ctx` returns undef and the custom function init( ) is called:

```
unless ($filter->ctx) {
    init($filter);
    $filter->ctx(1);
}
```

This function can, for example, retrieve some configuration data set in *httpd.conf* or initialize some data structure to its default value. To make sure that init( ) won't be called on the following invocations, we must set the filter context before the first invocation is completed:

```
$filter->ctx(1);
```

In practice, the context is not just served as a flag, but used to store real data. For example, the following filter handler counts the number of times it was invoked during a single request:

```
sub handler {
    my $filter = shift;

    my $ctx = $filter->ctx;
    $ctx->{invoked}++;
    $filter->ctx($ctx);
    warn "filter was invoked $ctx->{invoked} times\n";

    return Apache::DECLINED;
}
```

Since this filter handler doesn't consume the data from the upstream filter, it's important that this handler returns Apache::DECLINED, so that mod_perl will pass the bucket brigades to the next filter. If this handler returns Apache::OK, the data will simply be lost.

2. Processing

The next part:

```
process($filter);
```

is unconditionally invoked on every filter invocation. This is where the incoming data is read, modified, and sent out to the next filter in the filter chain. Here is an example that lowers the case of the characters passing through:

```
use constant READ_SIZE  => 1024;
sub process {
    my $filter = shift;
    while ($filter->read(my $data, READ_SIZE)) {
```

```
        $filter->print(lc $data);
    }
}
```

Here the filter operates on only a single bucket brigade. Since it manipulates every character separately, the logic is really simple.

In more complicated filters, the filters may need to buffer data first before the transformation can be applied. For example, if the filter operates on HTML tokens (e.g., `<img src="me.jpg">`), it's possible that one brigade will include the beginning of the token (`<img `) and the remainder of the token (`src="me.jpg" >`) will come in the next bucket brigade (on the next filter invocation). In certain cases it may involve more than two bucket brigades to get the whole token, and the filter will have to store the remainder of the unprocessed data in the filter context and then reuse it in the next invocation. Another good example is a filter that performs data compression (compression usually is effective only when applied to relatively big chunks of data)—if a single bucket brigade doesn't contain enough data, the filter may need to buffer the data in the filter context until it collects enough of it.

1. Finalization

   Finally, some filters need to know when they are invoked for the last time, in order to perform various cleanups and/or flush any remaining data. As mentioned earlier, Apache indicates this event by a special end-of-stream token, represented by a bucket of type EOS. If the filter is using the streaming interface, rather than manipulating the bucket brigades directly, it can check whether this is the last time it's invoked using the `$filter->seen_eos` method:

   ```
   if ($filter->seen_eos) {
       finalize($filter);
   }
   ```

   This check should be done at the end of the filter handler, because sometimes the EOS token comes attached to the tail of data (the last invocation gets both the data and the EOS token) and sometimes it comes all alone (the last invocation gets only the EOS token). So if this test is performed at the beginning of the handler and the EOS bucket was sent in together with the data, the EOS event may be missed and the filter won't function properly.

   Filters that directly manipulate bucket brigades have to look for a bucket whose type is EOS for the same reason.

Some filters may need to deploy all three parts of the described logic. Others will need to do only initialization and processing, or processing and finalization, while the simplest filters might perform only the normal processing (as we saw in the example of the filter handler that lowers the case of the characters going through it).

Blocking calls

All filters (excluding the core filter that reads from the network and the core filter that writes to it) block at least once when invoked. Depending on whether it's an input or an output filter, the blocking happens when the bucket brigade is requested from the upstream filter or when the bucket brigade is passed to the next filter.

Input and output filters differ in the ways they acquire the bucket brigades (which include the data that they filter). Although the difference can't be seen when a streaming API is used, it's important to understand how things work underneath.

When an input filter is invoked, it first asks the upstream filter for the next bucket brigade (using the get_brigade( ) call). That upstream filter in turn asks for the bucket brigade from the next upstream filter in the chain, and so on, until the last filter that reads from the network (called core_in) is reached. The core_in filter reads, using a socket, a portion of the incoming data from the network, processes it, and sends it to its downstream filter, which processes the data and sends it to its downstream filter, and so on, until it reaches the very first filter that asked for the data. (In reality, some other handler triggers the request for the bucket brigade (e.g., the HTTP response handler or a protocol module), but for our discussion it's good enough to assume that it's the first filter that issues the get_brigade( ) call.)

Figure 25-5 depicts a typical input filter chain data flow, in addition to the program control flow. The arrows show when the control is switched from one filter to another, and the black-headed arrows show the actual data flow. The diagram includes some pseudocode, both in Perl for the mod_perl filters and in C for the internal Apache filters. You don't have to understand C to understand this diagram. What's important to understand is that when input filters are invoked they first call each other via the get_brigade( ) call and then block (notice the brick walls in the diagram), waiting for the call to return. When this call returns, all upstream filters have already completed their filtering tasks.

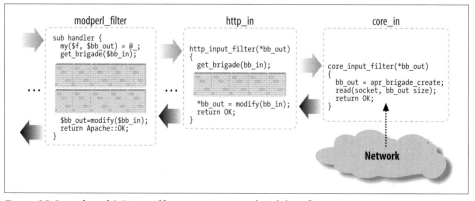

Figure 25-5. mod_perl 2.0 input filter program control and data flow

As mentioned earlier, the streaming interface hides these details; however, the first call to $filter->read( ) will block, as underneath it performs the get_brigade( ) call.

Figure 25-5 shows a part of the actual input filter chain for an HTTP request. The ... shows that there are more filters in between the mod_perl filter and http_in.

Now let's look at what happens in the output filter chain. The first filter acquires the bucket brigades containing the response data from the content handler (or another protocol handler if we aren't talking HTTP), then it applies any modifications and passes the data to the next filter (using the pass_brigade( ) call), which in turn applies its modifications and sends the bucket brigade to the next filter, and so on, all the way down to the last filter (called core), which writes the data to the network, via the socket to which the client is listening. Even though the output filters don't have to wait to acquire the bucket brigade (since the upstream filter passes it to them as an argument), they still block in a similar fashion to input filters, because they have to wait for the pass_brigade( ) call to return.

Figure 25-6 depicts a typical output filter chain data flow in addition to the program control flow. As in the input filter chain diagram, the arrows show the program control flow, and the black-headed arrows show the data flow. Again, the diagram uses Perl pseudocode for the mod_perl filter and C pseudocode for the Apache filters, and the brick walls represent the blocking. The diagram shows only part of the real HTTP response filter chain; ... stands for the omitted filters.

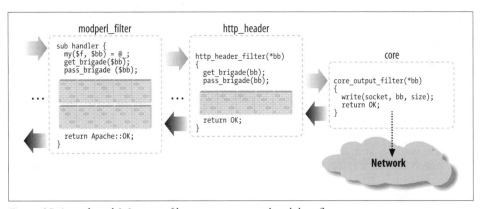

Figure 25-6. mod_perl 2.0 output filter program control and data flow

Filter Configuration

HTTP request filter handlers are declared using the FilterRequestHandler attribute. Consider the following request input and output filter skeletons:

```
package Book::FilterRequestFoo;
use base qw(Apache::Filter);
```

```
sub input  : FilterRequestHandler {
    my($filter, $bb, $mode, $block, $readbytes) = @_;
    #...
}

sub output : FilterRequestHandler {
    my($filter, $bb) = @_;
    #...
}

1;
```

If the attribute is not specified, the default `FilterRequestHandler` attribute is assumed. Filters specifying subroutine attributes must subclass `Apache::Filter`.

The request filters are usually configured in the `<Location>` or equivalent sections:

```
PerlModule Book::FilterRequestFoo
PerlModule Book::NiceResponse
<Location /filter_foo>
    SetHandler modperl
    PerlResponseHandler     Book::NiceResponse
    PerlInputFilterHandler  Book::FilterRequestFoo::input
    PerlOutputFilterHandler Book::FilterRequestFoo::output
</Location>
```

Now we have the request input and output filters configured.

The connection filter handler uses the `FilterConnectionHandler` attribute. Here is a similar example for the connection input and output filters:

```
package Book::FilterConnectionBar;
use base qw(Apache::Filter);

sub input  : FilterConnectionHandler {
    my($filter, $bb, $mode, $block, $readbytes) = @_;
    #...
}

sub output : FilterConnectionHandler {
    my($filter, $bb) = @_;
    #...
}

1;
```

This time the configuration must be done outside the `<Location>` or equivalent sections, usually within the `<VirtualHost>` section or the global server configuration:

```
Listen 8005
<VirtualHost _default_:8005>
    PerlModule Book::FilterConnectionBar
    PerlModule Book::NiceResponse

    PerlInputFilterHandler  Book::FilterConnectionBar::input
    PerlOutputFilterHandler Book::FilterConnectionBar::output
```

```
<Location />
    SetHandler modperl
    PerlResponseHandler Book::NiceResponse
</Location>

</VirtualHost>
```

This accomplishes the configuration of the connection input and output filters.

Input Filters

We looked at how input filters call each other in Figure 25-5. Now let's look at some examples of input filters.

Bucket brigade–based connection input filter

Let's say that we want to test how our handlers behave when they are requested as HEAD requests rather than GET requests. We can alter the request headers at the incoming connection level transparently to all handlers.

This example's filter handler looks for data like:

```
GET /perl/test.pl HTTP/1.1
```

and turns it into:

```
HEAD /perl/test.pl HTTP/1.1
```

The input filter handler that does that by directly manipulating the bucket brigades is shown in Example 25-5.

Example 25-5. Book/InputFilterGET2HEAD.pm

```
package Book::InputFilterGET2HEAD;

use strict;
use warnings;

use base qw(Apache::Filter);

use APR::Brigade ();
use APR::Bucket ();

use Apache::Const -compile => 'OK';
use APR::Const    -compile => ':common';

sub handler : FilterConnectionHandler {
    my($filter, $bb, $mode, $block, $readbytes) = @_;

    return Apache::DECLINED if $filter->ctx;

    my $rv = $filter->next->get_brigade($bb, $mode, $block, $readbytes);
    return $rv unless $rv == APR::SUCCESS;
```

Example 25-5. Book/InputFilterGET2HEAD.pm (continued)

```
    for (my $b = $bb->first; $b; $b = $bb->next($b)) {
        my $data;
        my $status = $b->read($data);
        return $status unless $status == APR::SUCCESS;
        warn("data: $data\n");

        if ($data and $data =~ s|^GET|HEAD|) {
            my $bn = APR::Bucket->new($data);
            $b->insert_after($bn);
            $b->remove; # no longer needed
            $filter->ctx(1); # flag that that we have done the job
            last;
        }
    }

    Apache::OK;
}
1;
```

The filter handler is called for each bucket brigade, which in turn includes buckets with data. The basic task of any input filter handler is to request the bucket brigade from the upstream filter, and return it to the downstream filter using the second argument, $bb. It's important to remember that you can call methods on this argument, but you shouldn't assign to this argument, or the chain will be broken. You have two techniques to choose from to retrieve, modify, and return bucket brigades:

- Create a new, empty bucket brigade, $ctx_bb, pass it to the upstream filter via get_brigade( ), and wait for this call to return. When it returns, $ctx_bb is populated with buckets. Now the filter should move the bucket from $ctx_bb to $bb, on the way modifying the buckets if needed. Once the buckets are moved, and the filter returns, the downstream filter will receive the populated bucket brigade.

- Pass $bb to get_brigade( ) to the upstream filter, so it will be populated with buckets. Once get_brigade( ) returns, the filter can go through the buckets and modify them in place, or it can do nothing and just return (in which case, the downstream filter will receive the bucket brigade unmodified).

Both techniques allow addition and removal of buckets, although the second technique is more efficient since it doesn't have the overhead of creating the new brigade and moving the bucket from one brigade to another. In this example we have chosen to use the second technique; in the next example we will see the first technique.

Our filter has to perform the substitution of only one HTTP header (which normally resides in one bucket), so we have to make sure that no other data gets mangled (e.g., there could be POSTed data that may match /^GET/ in one of the buckets). We use $filter->ctx as a flag here. When it's undefined, the filter knows that it hasn't done the required substitution; once it completes the job, it sets the context to 1.

To optimize the speed, the filter immediately returns Apache::DECLINED when it's invoked after the substitution job has been done:

```
return Apache::DECLINED if $filter->ctx;
```

mod_perl then calls get_brigade( ) internally, which passes the bucket brigade to the downstream filter. Alternatively, the filter could do:

```
my $rv = $filter->next->get_brigade($bb, $mode, $block, $readbytes);
return $rv unless $rv == APR::SUCCESS;
return Apache::OK if $filter->ctx;
```

but this is a bit less efficient.

If the job hasn't yet been done, the filter calls get_brigade(), which populates the $bb bucket brigade. Next, the filter steps through the buckets, looking for the bucket that matches the regex /^GET/. If it finds it, a new bucket is created with the modified data s/^GET/HEAD/, and that bucket is inserted in place of the old bucket. In our example, we insert the new bucket after the bucket that we have just modified and immediately remove the bucket that we don't need any more:

```
$b->insert_after($bn);
$b->remove; # no longer needed
```

Finally, we set the context to 1, so we know not to apply the substitution on the following data and break from the for loop.

The handler returns Apache::OK, indicating that everything was fine. The downstream filter will receive the bucket brigade with one bucket modified.

Now let's check that the handler works properly. Consider the response handler shown in Example 25-6.

Example 25-6. Book/RequestType.pm

```
package Book::RequestType;

use strict;
use warnings;

use Apache::RequestIO ();
use Apache::RequestRec ();
use Apache::Response ();

use Apache::Const -compile => 'OK';

sub handler {
    my $r = shift;

    $r->content_type('text/plain');
    my $response = "the request type was " . $r->method;
    $r->set_content_length(length $response);
    $r->print($response);
```

Example 25-6. Book/RequestType.pm (continued)

```
    Apache::OK;
}

1;
```

This handler returns to the client the request type it has issued. In the case of the HEAD request, Apache will discard the response body, but it will still set the correct Content-Length header, which will be 24 in case of a GET request and 25 for HEAD. Therefore, if this response handler is configured as:

```
Listen 8005
<VirtualHost _default_:8005>
    <Location />
        SetHandler modperl
        PerlResponseHandler +Book::RequestType
    </Location>
</VirtualHost>
```

and a GET request is issued to /:

```
panic% perl -MLWP::UserAgent -le \
'$r = LWP::UserAgent->new( )->get("http://localhost:8005/"); \
print $r->headers->content_length . ": ". $r->content'
24: the request type was GET
```

the response's body is:

```
the request type was GET
```

and the Content-Length header is set to 24.

However, if we enable the Book::InputFilterGET2HEAD input connection filter:

```
Listen 8005
<VirtualHost _default_:8005>
    PerlInputFilterHandler +Book::InputFilterGET2HEAD

    <Location />
        SetHandler modperl
        PerlResponseHandler +Book::RequestType
    </Location>
</VirtualHost>
```

and issue the same GET request, we get only:

```
25:
```

which means that the body was discarded by Apache, because our filter turned the GET request into a HEAD request. If Apache wasn't discarding the body of responses to HEAD requests, the response would be:

```
the request type was HEAD
```

That's why the content length is reported as 25 and not 24, as in the real GET request.

Bucket brigade–based HTTP request input filter

Let's look at the request input filter that lowers the case of the text in the request's body, Book::InputRequestFilterLC (shown in Example 25-7).

Example 25-7. Book/InputRequestFilterLC.pm

```
package Book::InputRequestFilterLC;

use strict;
use warnings;

use base qw(Apache::Filter);

use Apache::Connection ();
use APR::Brigade ();
use APR::Bucket ();

use Apache::Const -compile => 'OK';
use APR::Const    -compile => ':common';

sub handler : FilterRequestHandler {
    my($filter, $bb, $mode, $block, $readbytes) = @_;

    my $c = $filter->c;
    my $bb_ctx = APR::Brigade->new($c->pool, $c->bucket_alloc);
    my $rv = $filter->next->get_brigade($bb_ctx, $mode, $block, $readbytes);
    return $rv unless $rv == APR::SUCCESS;

    while (!$bb_ctx->empty) {
        my $b = $bb_ctx->first;

        $b->remove;

        if ($b->is_eos) {
            $bb->insert_tail($b);
            last;
        }

        my $data;
        my $status = $b->read($data);
        return $status unless $status == APR::SUCCESS;

        $b = APR::Bucket->new(lc $data) if $data;

        $bb->insert_tail($b);
    }

    Apache::OK;
}

1;
```

As promised, in this filter handler we have used the first technique of bucket-brigade modification. The handler creates a temporary bucket brigade (ctx_bb), populates it with data using get_brigade( ), and then moves buckets from it to the bucket brigade $bb, which is then retrieved by the downstream filter when our handler returns.

This filter doesn't need to know whether it was invoked for the first time with this request or whether it has already done something. It's a stateless handler, since it has to lowercase everything that passes through it. Notice that this filter can't be used as a connection filter for HTTP requests, since it will invalidate the incoming request headers. For example, the first header line:

```
GET /perl/TEST.pl HTTP/1.1
```

will become:

```
get /perl/test.pl http/1.1
```

which messes up the request method, the URL, and the protocol.

Now if we use the Book::Dump response handler we developed earlier in this chapter, which dumps the query string and the content body as a response, and configure the server as follows:

```
<Location /lc_input>
    SetHandler modperl
    PerlResponseHandler     +Book::Dump
    PerlInputFilterHandler +Book::InputRequestFilterLC
</Location>
```

when issuing a POST request:

```
panic% echo "mOd_pErl RuLeS" | POST 'http://localhost:8002/lc_input?FoO=1&BAR=2'
```

we get a response like this:

```
args:
FoO=1&BAR=2
content:
mod_perl rules
```

We can see that our filter lowercased the POSTed body before the content handler received it, and the query string wasn't changed.

Stream-based HTTP request input filter

Let's now look at the same filter implemented using the stream-based filtering API (see Example 25-8).

Example 25-8. Book/InputRequestFilterLC2.pm

```
package Book::InputRequestFilterLC2;

use strict;
use warnings;
```

Example 25-8. Book/InputRequestFilterLC2.pm (continued)

```perl
use base qw(Apache::Filter);

use Apache::Const -compile => 'OK';

use constant BUFF_LEN => 1024;

sub handler : FilterRequestHandler {
    my $filter = shift;

    while ($filter->read(my $buffer, BUFF_LEN)) {
        $filter->print(lc $buffer);
    }

    Apache::OK;
}
1;
```

You've probably asked yourself why we had to go through the bucket-brigade filters when all this can be done so much more easily. The reason is that we wanted you to understand how the filters work underneath, which will help you when you need to debug filters or optimize their speed. Also, in certain cases a bucket-brigade filter may be more efficient than a stream-based one. For example, if the filter applies a transformation to selected buckets, certain buckets may contain open file handles or pipes, rather than real data. When you call read( ) the buckets will be forced to read in that data, but if you don't want to modify these buckets, you can pass them as they are and let Apache use a faster technique for sending data from the file handles or pipes.

The logic is very simple here: the filter reads in a loop and prints the modified data, which at some point (when the internal mod_perl buffer is full or when the filter returns) will be sent to the next filter.

read( ) populates $buffer to a maximum of BUFF_LEN characters (1,024 in our example). Assuming that the current bucket brigade contains 2,050 characters, read( ) will get the first 1,024 characters, then 1,024 characters more, and finally the remaining two characters. Notice that even though the response handler may have sent more than 2,050 characters, every filter invocation operates on a single bucket brigade, so you have to wait for the next invocation to get more input. In one of the earlier examples, we showed that you can force the generation of several bucket brigades in the content handler by using rflush( ). For example:

```perl
$r->print("string");
$r->rflush( );
$r->print("another string");
```

It's possible to get more than one bucket brigade from the same filter handler invocation only if the filter is not using the streaming interface—simply call get_brigade( ) as many times as needed or until the EOS token is received.

The configuration section is pretty much identical:

```
<Location /lc_input2>
    SetHandler modperl
    PerlResponseHandler    +Book::Dump
    PerlInputFilterHandler +Book::InputRequestFilterLC2
</Location>
```

When issuing a POST request:

```
% echo "mOd_pErl RuLeS" | POST 'http://localhost:8002/lc_input2?FoO=1&BAR=2'
```

we get a response like this:

```
args:
FoO=1&BAR=2
content:
mod_perl rules
```

Again, we can see that our filter lowercased the POSTed body before the content handler received it. The query string wasn't changed.

Output Filters

Earlier, in Figure 25-6, we saw how output filters call each other. Now let's look at some examples of output filters.

Stream-based HTTP request output filter

The PerlOutputFilterHandler handler registers and configures output filters.

The example of a stream-based output filter that we are going to present is simpler than the one that directly manipulates bucket brigades, although internally the stream-based interface is still manipulating the bucket brigades.

Book::FilterROT13 implements the simple Caesar-cypher encryption that replaces each English letter with the one 13 places forward or back along the alphabet, so that "mod_perl 2.0 rules!" becomes "zbq_crey 2.0 ehyrf!". Since the English alphabet consists of 26 letters, the ROT13 encryption is self-inverse, so the same code can be used for encoding and decoding. In our example, Book::FilterROT13 reads portions of the output generated by some previous handler, rotates the characters and sends them downstream.

The first argument to the filter handler is an Apache::Filter object, which as of this writing provides two methods, read( ) and print( ). The read( ) method reads a chunk of the output stream into the given buffer, returning the number of characters read. An optional size argument may be given to specify the maximum size to read into the buffer. If omitted, an arbitrary number of characters (which depends on the size of the bucket brigade sent by the upstream filter or handler) will fill the buffer. The print() method passes data down to the next filter. This filter is shown in Example 25-9.

Example 25-9. Book/FilterROT13.pm

```perl
package Book::FilterROT13;

use strict;

use Apache::RequestRec ();
use Apache::RequestIO ();
use Apache::Filter ();

use Apache::Const -compile => 'OK';

use constant BUFF_LEN => 1024;

sub handler {
    my $filter = shift;

    while ($filter->read(my $buffer, BUFF_LEN)) {
        $buffer =~ tr/A-Za-z/N-ZA-Mn-za-m/;
        $filter->print($buffer);
    }

    return Apache::OK;
}
1;
```

Let's say that we want to encrypt the output of the registry scripts accessed through a */perl-rot13* location using the ROT13 algorithm. The following configuration section accomplishes that:

```
PerlModule Book::FilterROT13
Alias /perl-rot13/ /home/httpd/perl/
<Location /perl-rot13>
    SetHandler perl-script
    PerlResponseHandler ModPerl::Registry
    PerlOutputFilterHandler Book::FilterROT13
    Options +ExecCGI
    #PerlOptions +ParseHeaders
</Location>
```

Now that you know how to write input and output filters, you can write a pair of filters that decode ROT13 input before the request processing starts and then encode the generated response back to ROT13 on the way back to the client.

The request output filter can be used as the connection output filter as well. However, HTTP headers will then look invalid to standard HTTP user agents. The client should expect the data to come encoded as ROT13 and decode it before using it. Writing such a client in Perl should be a trivial task.

Another stream-based HTTP request output filter

Let's look at another example of an HTTP request output filter—but first, let's develop a response handler that sends two lines of output: the numerals 1234567890 and the English alphabet in a single string. This handler is shown in Example 25-10.

Example 25-10. Book/SendAlphaNum.pm

```perl
package Book::SendAlphaNum;

use strict;
use warnings;

use Apache::RequestRec ();
use Apache::RequestIO ();

use Apache::Const -compile => qw(OK);

sub handler {
    my $r = shift;

    $r->content_type('text/plain');

    $r->print(1..9, "0\n");
    $r->print('a'..'z', "\n");

    Apache::OK;
}
1;
```

The purpose of our filter handler is to reverse every line of the response body, preserving the newline characters in their places. Since we want to reverse characters only in the response body, without breaking the HTTP headers, we will use an HTTP request output filter.

The first filter implementation (Example 25-11) uses the stream-based filtering API.

Example 25-11. Book/FilterReverse1.pm

```perl
package Book::FilterReverse1;

use strict;
use warnings;

use base qw(Apache::Filter);

use Apache::Const -compile => qw(OK);

use constant BUFF_LEN => 1024;

sub handler : FilterRequestHandler {
    my $filter = shift;
```

Example 25-11. Book/FilterReverse1.pm (continued)

```
    while ($filter->read(my $buffer, BUFF_LEN)) {
        for (split "\n", $buffer) {
            $filter->print(scalar reverse $_);
            $filter->print("\n");
        }
    }

    Apache::OK;
}
1;
```

Next, we add the following configuration to *httpd.conf*:

```
    PerlModule Book::FilterReverse1
    PerlModule Book::SendAlphaNum
    <Location /reverse1>
        SetHandler modperl
        PerlResponseHandler     Book::SendAlphaNum
        PerlOutputFilterHandler Book::FilterReverse1
    </Location>
```

Now when a request to */reverse1* is made, the response handler `Book::SendAlphaNum::` `handler( )` sends:

```
    1234567890
    abcdefghijklmnopqrstuvwxyz
```

as a response and the output filter handler `Book::FilterReverse1::handler` reverses the lines, so the client gets:

```
    0987654321
    zyxwvutsrqponmlkjihgfedcba
```

The `Apache::Filter` module loads the `read( )` and `print( )` methods that encapsulate the stream-based filtering interface.

The reversing filter is quite simple: in the loop it reads the data in the `readline( )` mode in chunks up to the buffer length (1,024 in our example), then it prints each line reversed while preserving the newline control characters at the end of each line. Behind the scenes, `$filter->read( )` retrieves the incoming brigade and gets the data from it, and `$filter->print( )` appends to the new brigade, which is then sent to the next filter in the stack. `read( )` breaks the `while` loop when the brigade is emptied or the EOS token is received.

So as not to distract the reader from the purpose of the example, we've used oversimplified code that won't correctly handle input lines that are longer than 1,024 characters or use a different line-termination token (it could be "\n", "\r", or "\r\n", depending on the platform). Moreover, a single line may be split across two or even more bucket brigades, so we have to store the unprocessed string in the filter context so that it can be used in the following invocations. So here is an example of a more complete handler, which does takes care of these issues:

```
sub handler {
    my $f = shift;

    my $leftover = $f->ctx;
    while ($f->read(my $buffer, BUFF_LEN)) {
        $buffer = $leftover . $buffer if defined $leftover;
        $leftover = undef;
        while ($buffer =~ /([^\r\n]*)([\r\n]*)/g) {
            $leftover = $1, last unless $2;
            $f->print(scalar(reverse $1), $2);
        }
    }

    if ($f->seen_eos) {
        $f->print(scalar reverse $leftover) if defined $leftover;
    }
    else {
        $f->ctx($leftover) if defined $leftover;
    }

    return Apache::OK;
}
```

The handler uses the $leftover variable to store unprocessed data as long as it fails
to assemble a complete line or there is an incomplete line following the newline
token. On the next handler invocation, this data is then prepended to the next chunk
that is read. When the filter is invoked for the last time, it unconditionally reverses
and flushes any remaining data.

Bucket brigade-based HTTP request output filter

The filter implementation in Example 25-12 uses the bucket brigades API to accomplish exactly the same task as the filter in Example 25-11.

Example 25-12. Book/FilterReverse2.pm

```
package Book::FilterReverse2;

use strict;
use warnings;

use base qw(Apache::Filter);

use APR::Brigade ();
use APR::Bucket ();

use Apache::Const -compile => 'OK';
use APR::Const -compile => ':common';

sub handler : FilterRequestHandler {
    my($filter, $bb) = @_;
```

Example 25-12. Book/FilterReverse2.pm (continued)

```perl
    my $c = $filter->c;
    my $bb_ctx = APR::Brigade->new($c->pool, $c->bucket_alloc);

    while (!$bb->empty) {
        my $bucket = $bb->first;

        $bucket->remove;

        if ($bucket->is_eos) {
            $bb_ctx->insert_tail($bucket);
            last;
        }

        my $data;
        my $status = $bucket->read($data);
        return $status unless $status == APR::SUCCESS;

        if ($data) {
            $data = join "",
                map {scalar(reverse $_), "\n"} split "\n", $data;
            $bucket = APR::Bucket->new($data);
        }

        $bb_ctx->insert_tail($bucket);
    }

    my $rv = $filter->next->pass_brigade($bb_ctx);
    return $rv unless $rv == APR::SUCCESS;

    Apache::OK;
}
1;
```

Here's the corresponding configuration:

```
    PerlModule Book::FilterReverse2
    PerlModule Book::SendAlphaNum
    <Location /reverse2>
        SetHandler modperl
        PerlResponseHandler     Book::SendAlphaNum
        PerlOutputFilterHandler Book::FilterReverse2
    </Location>
```

Now when a request to *reverse2* is made, the client gets:

```
    0987654321
    zyxwvutsrqponmlkjihgfedcba
```

as expected.

The bucket brigades output filter version is just a bit more complicated than the stream-based one. The handler receives the incoming bucket brigade $bb as its second argument. Because when it is completed, the handler must pass a brigade to the next filter in the stack, we create a new bucket brigade, into which we put the modified buckets and which eventually we pass to the next filter.

The core of the handler is in removing buckets from the head of the bucket brigade $bb one at a time, reading the data from each bucket, reversing the data, and then putting it into a newly created bucket, which is inserted at the end of the new bucket brigade. If we see a bucket that designates the end of the stream, we insert that bucket at the tail of the new bucket brigade and break the loop. Finally, we pass the created brigade with modified data to the next filter and return.

As in the original version of Book::FilterReverse1::handler, this filter is not smart enough to handle incomplete lines. The trivial exercise of making the filter foolproof by porting a better matching rule and using the $leftover buffer from the previous section is left to the reader.

## PART VI

Appendixes

This book has six appendixes:

Appendix A, *mod_perl Recipes*, is a mini-cookbook for mod_perl. Look here before reinventing the wheel; it's possible that someone else has saved you the hassle.

Appendix B, *Apache Perl Modules*, is a listing of the Apache:: modules for use with mod_perl.

Appendix C, *ISPs Providing mod_perl Services*, is for Internet Service Providers who provide mod_perl support on their servers.

Appendix D, *The Template Toolkit*, is a tutorial on the Template Toolkit, a powerful templating system based on mod_perl.

Appendix E, *The AxKit XML Application Server*, is a tutorial on AxKit, an XML application server based on mod_perl.

Appendix F, *HTTP Status Codes*, is a listing of HTTP status codes.

mod_perl Recipes

This appendix acts as a mini-cookbook for mod_perl. As we've mentioned many times in this book, the mod_perl mailing list is a terrific resource for anyone working with mod_perl. Many very useful code snippets and neat techniques have been posted to the mod_perl mailing list. In this appendix, we present the techniques that you will find most useful in your day-to-day mod_perl programming.

Emulating the Authentication Mechanism

You can authenticate users with your own mechanism (instead of the standard one) but still make Apache think that the user was authenticated by the standard mechanism. Set the username with:

```
$r->connection->user('username');
```

Now you can use this information, for example, during logging, so that you can have your "username" passed as if it was transmitted to Apache through HTTP authentication.

Reusing Data from POST Requests

What happens if you need to access the POSTed data more than once. For example, suppose you need to reuse it in subsequent handlers of the same request? POSTed data comes directly from the socket, and at the low level data can be read from a socket only once. You have to store it to make it available for reuse.

But what do you do with large multipart file uploads? Because POSTed data is not all read in one clump, it's a problem that's not easy to solve in a general way. A transparent way to do this is to switch the request method from POST to GET and store the POST data in the query string. The handler in Example A-1 does exactly that.

Example A-1. Apache/POST2GET.pm

```
package Apache::POST2GET;
use Apache::Constants qw(M_GET OK DECLINED);

sub handler {
    my $r = shift;
    return DECLINED unless $r->method eq "POST";
    $r->args(scalar $r->content);
    $r->method('GET');
    $r->method_number(M_GET);
    $r->headers_in->unset('Content-length');
    return OK;
}
1;
```

In *httpd.conf* add:

```
PerlInitHandler Apache::POST2GET
```

or even this:

```
<Limit POST>
    PerlInitHandler Apache::POST2GET
</Limit>
```

to save a few more cycles. This ensures that the handler will be called only for POST requests.

Be aware that this will work only if the POSTed data doesn't exceed the maximum allowed size for GET requests. The default maximum size is 8,190 bytes, but it can be lowered using the LimitRequestLine configuration directive.

Effectively, this trick turns the POST request into a GET request internally. Now when a module such as CGI.pm or Apache::Request parses the client data, it can do so more than once, since $r->args doesn't go away (unless you make it go away by resetting it).

If you are using Apache::Request, it solves this problem for you with its instance( ) class method, which allows Apache::Request to be a singleton. This means that whenever you call Apache::Request->instance( ) within a single request, you always get the same Apache::Request object back.

Redirecting POST Requests

Under mod_cgi, it's not easy to redirect POST requests to another location. With mod_perl, however, you can easily redirect POST requests. All you have to do is read in the content, set the method to GET, populate args( ) with the content to be forwarded, and finally do the redirect, as shown in Example A-2.

Example A-2. redirect.pl

```
use Apache::Constants qw(M_GET);
my $r = shift;
my $content = $r->content;
$r->method("GET");
$r->method_number(M_GET);
$r->headers_in->unset("Content-length");
$r->args($content);
$r->internal_redirect_handler("/new/url");
```

In this example we use `internal_redirect_handler( )`, but you can use any other kind of redirect with this technique.

Redirecting While Maintaining Environment Variables

Let's say you have a module that sets some environment variables. Redirecting most likely tells the web browser to fetch the new page. This makes it a totally new request, so no environment variables are preserved.

However, if you're using `internal_redirect( )`, you can make the environment variables visible in the subprocess via `subprocess_env( )`. The only nuance is that the %ENV keys will be prefixed with REDIRECT_. For example, `$ENV{CONTENT_LENGTH}` will become:

```
$r->subprocess_env->{REDIRECT_CONTENT_LENGTH};
```

Handling Cookies

Unless you use a module such as CGI::Cookie or Apache::Cookie, you need to handle cookies yourself. Cookies are accessed via the `$ENV{HTTP_COOKIE}` environment variable. You can print the raw cookie string as `$ENV{HTTP_COOKIE}`. Here is a fairly well-known bit of code to take cookie values and put them into a hash:

```
sub get_cookies {
    # cookies are separated by a semicolon and a space, this will
    # split them and return a hash of cookies
    my @rawCookies = split /; /, $ENV{'HTTP_COOKIE'};
    my %cookies;

    foreach (@rawCookies){
        my($key, $val) = split /=/, $_;
        $cookies{$key} = $val;
    }

    return %cookies;
}
```

And here's a slimmer version:

```
sub get_cookies {
    map { split /=/, $_, 2 } split /; /, $ENV{'HTTP_COOKIE'};
}
```

Sending Multiple Cookies with the mod_perl API

Given that you have prepared your cookies in @cookies, the following code will submit all the cookies:

```
for (@cookies) {
    $r->headers_out->add('Set-Cookie' => $_);
}
```

Sending Cookies in REDIRECT Responses

You should use err_headers_out( ), not headers_out( ), when you want to send cookies in a REDIRECT response or in any other non-2XX response. The difference between headers_out( ) and err_headers_out( ) is that the latter prints even on error and persists across internal redirects (so the headers printed for ErrorDocument handlers will have them). Example A-3 shows a cookie being sent in a REDIRECT.

Example A-3. redirect_cookie.pl

```
use Apache::Constants qw(REDIRECT OK);
my $r = shift;
# prepare the cookie in $cookie
$r->err_headers_out->add('Set-Cookie' => $cookie);
$r->headers_out->set(Location => $location);
$r->status(REDIRECT);
$r->send_http_header;
return OK;
```

CGI::params in the mod_perlish Way

Assuming that all your variables are single key-value pairs, you can retrieve request parameters in a way similar to using CGI::params with this technique:

```
my $r = shift;  # or $r = Apache->request
my %params = $r->method eq 'POST' ? $r->content : $r->args;
```

Also take a look at Apache::Request, which has the same API as CGI.pm for extracting and setting request parameters but is significantly faster, since it's implemented in C.

Sending Email from mod_perl

There is nothing special about sending email from mod_perl, it's just that we do it a lot. There are a few important issues. The most widely used approach is starting a *sendmail* process and piping the headers and the body to it. The problem is that *sendmail* is a very heavy process, and it makes mod_perl processes less efficient.

If you don't want your process to wait until delivery is complete, you can tell *sendmail* not to deliver the email straight away, but to either do it in the background or just queue the job until the next queue run. This can significantly reduce the delay for the mod_perl process, which would otherwise have to wait for the *sendmail* process to complete. You can specify this for all deliveries in *sendmail.cf*, or for individual email messages on each invocation on the *sendmail* command line. Here are the options:

-odb
> Deliver in the background

-odq
> Queue only

-odd
> Queue, and also defer the DNS/NIS lookups

The current trend is to move away from `sendmail` and switch to using lighter mail delivery programs such as `qmail` or `postfix`. You should check the manpage of your favorite mailer application for equivalents to the configuration presented for *sendmail*.

Alternatively, you may want to use `Net::SMTP` to send your mail without calling an extra process. The main disadvantage of using `Net::SMTP` is that it might fail to deliver the mail because the destination peer server might be down. It can also be very slow, in which case the mod_perl application will do nothing while it waits for the mail to be sent.

mod_rewrite in Perl

mod_rewrite provides virtually any functionality you can think of for manipulating URLs. Because of its highly generalized nature and use of complex regular expressions, it is not easy to use and has a high learning curve.

With the help of `PerlTransHandler`, which is invoked at the beginning of request processing, we can easily implement everything mod_rewrite does in Perl. For example, if we need to perform a redirect based on the query string and URI, we can use the following handler:

```
package Apache::MyRedirect;
use Apache::Constants qw(OK REDIRECT);
use constant DEFAULT_URI => 'http://www.example.org';
```

```
sub handler {
    my $r    = shift;
    my %args = $r->args;
    my $path = $r->uri;

    my $uri = (($args{'uri'}) ? $args{'uri'} : DEFAULT_URI) . $path;

    $r->header_out->add('Location' => $uri);
    $r->status(REDIRECT);
    $r->send_http_header;

    return OK;
}
1;
```

Set it up in *httpd.conf* as:

```
PerlTransHandler Apache::MyRedirect
```

The code consists of four parts: retrieving the request data, deciding what to do based on this data, setting the headers and the status code, and issuing the redirect.

So if a client submits the following request:

```
http://www.example.com/news/?uri=http://www2.example.com/
```

the $uri parameter is set to http://www2.example.com/news/, and the request will be redirected to that URI.

Let's look at another example. Suppose you want to make this translation before a content handler is invoked:

```
/articles/10/index.html  =>  /articles/index.html?id=10
```

The TransHandler shown in Example A-4 will do that for you.

Example A-4. Book/Trans.pm

```
package Book::Trans;
use Apache::Constants qw(:common);
sub handler {
    my $r = shift;
    my $uri = $r->uri;
    my($id) = ($uri =~ m|^/articles/(.*?)/|);
    $r->uri("/articles/index.html");
    $r->args("id=$id");
    return DECLINED;
}
1;
```

To configure this handler, add these lines to *httpd.conf*:

```
PerlModule Book::Trans
PerlTransHandler Book::Trans
```

The handler code retrieves the request object and the URI. Then it retrieves the *id*, using the regular expression. Finally, it sets the new value of the URI and the arguments string. The handler returns DECLINED so the default Apache TransHandler will take care of URI-to-filename remapping.

Notice the technique to set the arguments. By the time the Apache request object has been created, arguments are handled in a separate slot, so you cannot just push them into the original URI. Therefore, the args( ) method should be used.

Setting PerlHandler Based on MIME Type

It's very easy to implement a dispatching module based on the MIME type of the request—that is, for different content handlers to be called for different MIME types. Example A-5 shows such a dispatcher.

Example A-5. Book/MimeTypeDispatch.pm

```
package Book::MimeTypeDispatch;
use Apache::Constants qw(DECLINED);

my %mime_types = (
    'text/html'  => \&HTML::Template::handler,
    'text/plain' => \&Book::Text::handler,
);

sub handler {
    my $r = shift;
    if (my $h = $mime_types{$r->content_type}) {
        $r->push_handlers(PerlHandler => $h);
        $r->handler('perl-script');
    }
    return DECLINED;
}
1;
__END__
```

This should be done with PerlFixupHandler, so we add this line in *httpd.conf*:

```
PerlFixupHandler Book::MimeTypeDispatch
```

After declaring the package name and importing constants, we set a translation table of MIME types and the corresponding handlers to be called. Then comes the handler, where the request object is retrieved. If the request object's MIME type is found in our translation table, we set the handler that should handle this request; otherwise, we do nothing. At the end we return DECLINED so another fixup handler can take over.

Singleton Database Handles

Let's say we have an object we want to be able to access anywhere in the code, without making it a global variable or passing it as an argument to functions. The singleton design pattern helps here. Rather than implementing this pattern from scratch, we will use Class::Singleton.

For example, if we have a class Book::DBIHandle that returns an instance of the opened database connection handle, we can use it in the TransHandler phase's handler (see Example A-6).

Example A-6. Book/TransHandler.pm

```
package Book::TransHandler;

use Book::DBIHandle;
use Apache::Constants qw(:common);

sub handler {
    my $r = shift;
    my $dbh = Book::DBIHandle->instance->dbh;
    $dbh->do("show tables");
    # ...
    return OK;
}
1;
```

We can then use the same database handle in the content-generation phase (see Example A-7).

Example A-7. Book/ContentHandler.pm

```
package Book::ContentHandler;

use Book::DBIHandle;
use Apache::Constants qw(:common);

sub handler {
    my $r = shift;
    my $dbh = Book::DBIHandle->instance->dbh;
    $dbh->do("select from foo...");
    # ...
    return OK;
}
1;
```

In *httpd.conf*, use the following setup for the TransHandler and content-generation phases:

```
PerlTransHandler +Book::TransHandler
<Location /dbihandle>
    SetHandler perl-script
```

```
        PerlHandler +Book::ContentHandler
    </Location>
```

This specifies that Book::TransHandler should be used as the PerlTransHandler, and
Book::ContentHandler should be used as a content-generation handler. We use the +
prefix to preload both modules at server startup, in order to improve memory sharing between the processes (as explained in Chapter 10).

Book::DBIHandle, shown in Example A-8, is a simple subclass of Class::Singleton
that is used by both handlers.

Example A-8. Book/DBIHandle.pm

```perl
package Book::DBIHandle;

use strict;
use warnings;

use DBI;

use Class::Singleton;
@Book::DBIHandle::ISA = qw(Class::Singleton);

sub _new_instance {
    my($class, $args) = @_;

    my $self = DBI->connect($args->{dsn},    $args->{user},
                            $args->{passwd}, $args->{options})
        or die "Cannot connect to database: $DBI::errstr";

    return bless $self, $class;
}

sub dbh {
    my $self = shift;
    return $$self;
}
1;
```

Book::DBIHandle inherits the instance( ) method from Class::Singleton and overrides its _new_instance( ) method. _new_instance( ) accepts the connect( ) arguments and opens the connection using these arguments. The _new_instance( )
method will be called only the first time the instance( ) method is called.

We have used a reference to a scalar ($dbh) for the Book::DBIHandle objects. There-
fore, we need to dereference the objects when we want to access the database handle
in the code. The dbh( ) method does this for us.

Since each child process must have a unique database connection, we initialize the
database handle during the PerlChildInit phase, similar to DBI::connect_on_init( ).
See Example A-9.

Example A-9. Book/ChildInitHandler.pm

```perl
package Book::ChildInitHandler;

use strict;
use Book::DBIHandle;
use Apache;

sub handler {
    my $s = Apache->server;

    my $dbh = Book::DBIHandle->instance(
        { dsn    => $s->dir_config('DATABASE_DSN'),
          user   => $s->dir_config('DATABASE_USER'),
          passwd => $s->dir_config('DATABASE_PASSWD'),
          options => {
              AutoCommit => 0,
              RaiseError => 1,
              PrintError => 0,
              ChopBlanks => 1,
          },
        }
    );

    $s->log_error("$$: Book::DBIHandle object allocated, handle=$dbh");
}
1;
```

Here, the instance( ) method is called for the first time, so its arguments are passed to the new _new_instance( ) method. _new_instance( ) initializes the database connection.

httpd.conf needs to be adjusted to enable the new ChildInitHandler:

```
PerlSetVar DATABASE_DSN    "DBI:mysql:test::localhost"
PerlSetVar DATABASE_USER   "foo"
PerlSetVar DATABASE_PASSWD "bar"

PerlChildInitHandler +Book::ChildInitHandler
```

Terminating a Child Process on Request Completion

If you want to terminate the child process upon completion of processing the current request, use the child_terminate( ) method anywhere in the code:

```
$r->child_terminate;
```

Apache won't actually terminate the child until everything it needs to do is done and the connection is closed.

References

- *mod_perl Developer's Cookbook*, by Geoffrey Young, Paul Lindner, and Randy Kobes (Sams Publishing). Selected chapters and code examples available online from *http://www.modperlcookbook.org/*.
- For more information about signal handling, refer to the *perlipc* manpage
- GET and POST request methods are explained in section 9 of RFC 2068, "Hypertext Transfer Protocol—HTTP/1.1"
- Cookies
  - RFC 2965 specifies the HTTP State Management Mechanism, which describes three new headers, Cookie, Cookie2, and Set-Cookie2, that carry state information between participating origin servers and user agents
  - The cookie specification can be viewed at *http://home.netscape.com/newsref/std/cookie_spec.html*
  - BCP 44, RFC 2964, "Use of HTTP State Management," is an important adjunct to the cookie specification itself
  - Cookie Central (*http://www.cookiecentral.com/*) is another good resource for information about cookies
- "Design Patterns: Singletons," by Brian D. Foy (*The Perl Review*, Volume 0, Issue 1), available at *http://www.theperlreview.com/*.

APPENDIX B
Apache Perl Modules

Many third-party modules have been written to extend mod_perl's core functionality. They may be distributed with the mod_perl source code, or they may be available from CPAN. In this chapter we will attempt to group these modules based on their functionality. Some modules will be discussed in depth, but others will be touched on only briefly.

Since most of these modules are continually evolving, the moment this book is published much of the information in it will be out of date. For this reason, you should refer to the modules' manpages when you start using them; that's where you will find the most up-to-date documentation.

We will consider modules in the following groups:

Development
    Modules used mainly during the development process

Debugging
    Modules that assist in code debugging

Control and monitoring
    Modules to help you monitor the production server and take care of any problems as soon as they appear

Server configuration
    Modules used in server configuration

Authentication
    Modules used to facilitate authentication

Authorization
    Modules used to facilitate authorization

Access
    Modules used during the access-verification phase

Type handlers
    Modules used as `PerlTypeHandlers`

Trans handlers
Modules used as `PerlTransHandlers`

Fixup Handlers
Modules used as `PerlFixupHandlers`

Generic content-generation phase
Generic modules that assist during the content-generation phase

Application-specific content generation phase
Non–general-purpose content generators

Database
Database-specific modules

Toolkits and framework for content generation and other phases
Mostly large toolkits and frameworks built on top of mod_perl

Output filters and layering
Modules that filter output from the content generation stage

Logging-phase handlers
Modules that assist during the logging stage

Core Apache
Modules that interface with core mod_perl

Miscellaneous
Modules that don't fit into any of the above categories

Development-Stage Modules

The following modules are mainly useful during the code-development cycle. Some of them can also be useful in the production environment.

Apache::Reload—Automatically Reload Changed Modules

`Apache::Reload` is used to make specific modules reload themselves when they have changed. It's also very useful for mod_perl module development.

Covered in Chapter 6.

Available from CPAN. See the module manpage for more information.

Apache::PerlVINC—Allow Module Versioning in <Location> and <VirtualHost> blocks

This module makes it possible to have different @INC values for different `<VirtualHost>`s, `<Location>`s, and equivalent configuration blocks.

Suppose two versions of Apache::Status are being hacked on the same server. In this configuration:

```
PerlModule Apache::PerlVINC

<Location /status-dev/perl>
    SetHandler        perl-script
    PerlHandler       Apache::Status

    PerlINC           /home/httpd/dev/lib
    PerlFixupHandler  Apache::PerlVINC
    PerlVersion       Apache/Status.pm
</Location>

<Location /status/perl>
    SetHandler        perl-script
    PerlHandler       Apache::Status

    PerlINC           /home/httpd/prod/lib
    PerlFixupHandler  Apache::PerlVINC
    PerlVersion       Apache/Status.pm
</Location>
```

Apache::PerlVINC is loaded and then two different locations are specified for the same handler Apache::Status, whose development version resides in */home/httpd/dev/lib* and production version in */home/httpd/prod/lib*.

If a request for */status/perl* is issued (the latter configuration section), the fixup handler will internally do:

```
delete $INC{"Apache/Status.pm"};
unshift @INC, "/home/httpd/prod/lib";
require Apache::Status;
```

which will load the production version of the module, which will in turn be used to process the request.

If on the other hand the request is for */status-dev/perl* (the former configuration section), a different path (*/home/httpd/dev/lib*) will be prepended to @INC:

```
delete $INC{"Apache/Status.pm"};
unshift @INC, "/home/httpd/dev/lib";
require Apache::Status;
```

It's important to be aware that a changed @INC is effective only inside the <Location> block or a similar configuration directive. Apache::PerlVINC subclasses the PerlRequire directive, marking the file to be reloaded by the fixup handler, using the value of PerlINC for @INC. That's local to the fixup handler, so you won't actually see @INC changed in your script.

Additionally, modules with different versions can be unloaded at the end of the request, using the PerlCleanupHandler:

```
<Location /status/perl>
    SetHandler          perl-script
    PerlHandler         Apache::Status

    PerlINC             /home/httpd/prod/lib
    PerlFixupHandler    Apache::PerlVINC
    PerlCleanupHandler  Apache::PerlVINC
    PerlVersion         Apache/Status.pm
</Location>
```

Also note that `PerlVersion` affects things differently depending on where it is placed. If it is placed inside a `<Location>` or a similar block section, the files will be reloaded only on requests to that location. If it is placed in a server section, all requests to the server or virtual hosts will have these files reloaded.

As you can guess, this module slows down the response time because it reloads some modules on a per-request basis. Hence, this module should be used only in a development environment, not in production.

If you need to do the same in production, a few techniques are suggested in Chapter 4.

Available from CPAN. See the module manpage for more information.

Apache::DProf—Hook Devel::DProf into mod_perl

Covered in Chapter 9.

Available from CPAN. See the module manpage for more information.

Apache::SmallProf—Hook Devel::SmallProf into mod_perl

Covered in Chapter 9.

Available from CPAN. See the module manpage for more information.

Apache::FakeRequest—Fake Request Object for Debugging

Covered in Chapter 21.

Available from CPAN. See the module manpage for more information.

Apache::test—Facilitate Testing of Apache::* Modules

This module helps authors of `Apache::*` modules write test suites that can query a running Apache server with mod_perl and their modules loaded into it. Its functionality is generally separated into: (a) methods that go in a *Makefile.PL* file to configure, start, and stop the server; and (b) methods that go into one of the test scripts to make HTTP queries and manage the results.

Supplied with the mod_perl distribution. See the module manpage for more information.

Modules to Aid Debugging

The following modules are used mainly when something is not working properly and needs to be debugged. Unless your bug is very hard to reproduce and the production environment is required to reproduce the conditions that will trigger the bug, these modules should not be used in production.

Apache::DB—Hooks for the Interactive Perl Debugger

Allows developers to interactively debug mod_perl.

Covered in Chapter 9.

Available from CPAN. See the module manpage for more information.

Apache::Debug—Utilities for Debugging Embedded Perl Code

Covered in Chapter 21.

Supplied with the mod_perl distribution. See the module manpage for more information.

Apache::DebugInfo—Send Debug Information to Client

Available from CPAN. See the module manpage for more information.

Apache::Leak—Module for Tracking Memory Leaks in mod_perl Code

Covered in Chapter 14.

Supplied with the mod_perl distribution. See the module manpage for more information.

Apache::Peek—A Data Debugging Tool for the XS Programmer

Covered in Chapter 10.

Available from CPAN. See the module manpage for more information.

Apache::Symbol—Avoid the Mandatory 'Subroutine Redefined' Warning

Supplied with the mod_perl distribution. See the module manpage for more information.

Apache::Symdump—Symbol Table Snapshots

Covered in Chapter 21.

Supplied with the mod_perl distribution. See the module manpage for more information.

Control and Monitoring Modules

Apache::Watchdog::RunAway—Hanging Processes Monitor and Terminator

Covered in Chapter 5.

Available from CPAN. See the module manpage for more information.

Apache::VMonitor—Visual System and Apache Server Monitor

Covered in Chapter 5.

Available from CPAN. See the module manpage for more information.

Apache::SizeLimit—Limit Apache httpd Processes

This module allows you to kill off Apache processes if they grow too large or if they share too little of their memory. It's similar to `Apache::GTopLimit`.

Covered in Chapter 14.

Supplied with the mod_perl distribution. See the module manpage for more information.

Apache::GTopLimit—Limit Apache httpd Processes

This module allows you to kill off Apache processes if they grow too large or if they share too little of their memory. It's similar to `Apache::SizeLimit`.

Covered in Chapter 14.

Available from CPAN. See the module manpage for more information.

Apache::TimedRedirect—Redirect URLs for a Given Time Period

Apache::TimedRedirect is a mod_perl TransHandler module that allows the configuration of a timed redirect. In other words, if a user enters a web site and the URI matches a regex *and* it is within a certain time period she will be redirected somewhere else.

This was first created to *politely* redirect visitors away from database-driven sections of a web site while the databases were being refreshed.

Available from CPAN. See the module manpage for more information.

Apache::Resource—Limit Resources Used by httpd Children

Apache::Resource uses the BSD::Resource module, which uses the C function setrlimit() to set limits on system resources such as memory and CPU usage.

Covered in Chapter 5.

Supplied with the mod_perl distribution. See the module manpage for more information.

Apache::Status—Embedded Interpreter Status Information

The Apache::Status module provides various information about the status of the Perl interpreter embedded in the server.

Covered in Chapter 21.

Available from CPAN. See the module manpage for more information.

Server Configuration Modules

Apache::ModuleConfig—Interface to Configuration API

Supplied with the mod_perl distribution. See the module manpage for more information.

Apache::PerlSections—Utilities for Working with <Perl> Sections

Apache::PerlSections configures Apache entirely in Perl.

Covered in Chapter 4.

Supplied with the mod_perl distribution. See the module manpage for more information.

Apache::httpd_conf—Generate an httpd.conf File

The Apache::httpd_conf module will generate a tiny *httpd.conf* file, which pulls itself back in via a <Perl> section. Any additional arguments passed to the write() method will be added to the generated *httpd.conf* file and will override those defaults set in the <Perl> section. This module is handy mostly for starting *httpd* servers to test mod_perl scripts and modules.

Supplied with the mod_perl distribution. See the module manpage for more information.

Apache::src—Methods for Locating and Parsing Bits of Apache Source Code

This module provides methods for locating and parsing bits of Apache source code. For example:

```
my $src = Apache::src->new;
my $v = $src->httpd_version;
```

returns the server version. And:

```
my $dir = $src->dir;
-d $dir or die "can't stat $dir $!\n";
```

returns the top level directory where source files are located and then tests whether it can read it.

The main() method will return the location of *httpd.h*:

```
-e join "/", $src->main, "httpd.h" or die "can't stat httpd.h\n";
```

Other methods are available from this module.

Supplied with the mod_perl distribution. See the module manpage for more information.

Apache::ConfigFile—Parse an Apache-Style httpd.conf Configuration File

This module parses *httpd.conf*, or any compatible configuration file, and provides methods for accessing the values from the parsed file.

Available from CPAN. See the module manpage for more information.

Authentication-Phase Modules

The following modules make it easier to handle the authentication phase:

```
AuthenCache      Cache authentication credentials
AuthCookie       Authentication and authorization via cookies
AuthDigest       Authentication and authorization via digest scheme
AuthenDBI        Authenticate via Perl's DBI
AuthenIMAP       Authentication via an IMAP server
AuthenPasswdSrv  External authentication server
AuthenPasswd     Authenticate against /etc/passwd
AuthLDAP         LDAP authentication module
AuthPerLDAP      LDAP authentication module (PerLDAP)
AuthenNIS        NIS authentication
AuthNISPlus      NIS Plus authentication/authorization
AuthenSmb        Authenticate against an NT server
AuthenURL        Authenticate via another URL
DBILogin         Authenticate to backend database
PHLogin          Authenticate via a PH database
```

All available from CPAN. See the module manpages for more information.

Authorization-Phase Modules

The following modules make it easier to handle the authorization phase:

```
AuthCookie       Authentication and authorization via cookies
AuthzDBI         Group authorization via Perl's DBI
AuthzNIS         NIS authorization
AuthzPasswd      Authorize against /etc/passwd
```

All available from CPAN. See the module manpages for more information.

Access-Phase Modules

The following modules are used during the access request phase:

```
AccessLimitNum  Limit user access by the number of requests
RobotLimit      Limit the access of robots
```

Available from CPAN. See the module manpages for more information.

Stonehenge::Throttle—Limit Bandwith Consumption by IP Address

http://www.stonehenge.com/merlyn/LinuxMag/col17.html

The source code to Stonehenge::Throttle is available from *http://www.stonehenge.com/merlyn/LinuxMag/col17.listing.txt*.

Type Handlers

Apache::MimeXML—mod_perl Mime Encoding Sniffer for XML Files

This module is an XML content-type sniffer. It reads the encoding attribute in the XML declaration and returns an appropriate content-type heading. If no encoding declaration is found it returns *utf-8* or *utf-16*, depending on the specific encoding.

Available from CPAN. See the module manpage for more information.

Apache::MIMEMapper—Associates File Extensions with PerlHandlers

Apache::MIMEMapper extends the core AddHandler directive to allow you to dispatch different PerlHandlers based on the file extension of the requested resource.

Available from CPAN. See the module manpage for more information.

Trans Handlers

Apache::AddHostPath—Adds Some or All of the Hostname and Port to the URI

This module transforms the requested URI based on the hostname and port number from the HTTP request header. It allows you to manage an arbitrary number of domains and subdomains all pointing to the same document root but for which you want a combination of shared and distinct files.

Essentially the module implements Apache's URI-translation phase by attempting to use some or all of the URL hostname and port number as the base of the URI. It simply does file and directory existence tests on a series of URIs (from most-specific to least-specific) and sets the URI to the most specific match.

For example, if the request is:

```
URL: http://www.example.org:8080/index.html
URI: /index.html
```

Apache::AddHostPath would go through the following list of possible paths and set the new URI based on the first match that passes a -f or -d existence test:

```
$docRoot/org/example/www/8080/index.html
$docRoot/org/example/www/index.html
$docRoot/org/example/index.html
$docRoot/org/index.html
$docRoot/index.html
```

Available from CPAN. See the module manpage for more information.

Apache::ProxyPass—implement ProxyPass in Perl

This module implements the Apache mod_proxy module in Perl. Based on Apache::ProxyPassThru.

Available from CPAN. See the module manpage for more information.

Apache::ProxyPassThru—Skeleton for Vanilla Proxy

This module uses *libwww-perl* as its web client, feeding the response back into the Apache API request_rec structure. PerlHandler will be invoked only if the request is a proxy request; otherwise, your normal server configuration will handle the request.

If used with the Apache::DumpHeaders module it lets you view the headers from another site you are accessing.

Available from CPAN. See the module manpage for more information.

Apache::Throttle—Speed-Based Content Negotiation

Apache::Throttle is a package designed to allow Apache web servers to negotiate content based on the speed of the connection. Its primary purpose is to transparently send smaller (lower resolution/quality) images to users with slow Internet connections, but it can also be used for many other purposes.

Available from CPAN. See the module manpage for more information.

Apache::TransLDAP—Trans Handler Example

This module is an example of how you can create a trans handler. This particular example translates from a user's virtual directory on the server to the labeledURI attribute for the given user.

Available from CPAN. See the module manpage for more information.

Fixup Handlers

Apache::RefererBlock—Block Request Based Upon "Referer" Header

`Apache::RefererBlock` will examine each request. If the MIME type of the requested file is one of those listed in `RefBlockMimeTypes`, it will check the request's `Referer` header. If the referrer starts with one of the strings listed in `RefBlockAllowed`, access is granted. Otherwise, if there's a `RefBlockRedirect` directive for the referrer, a redirect is issued. If not, a "Forbidden" (403) error is returned.

Available from CPAN. See the module manpage for more information.

Apache::Usertrack—Emulate the mod_usertrack Apache Module

As of this writing no documentation is available.

Available from CPAN.

Generic Content-Generation Modules

These modules extend mod_perl functionality during the content-generation phase. Some of them can also be used during earlier phases.

Apache::Registry and Apache::PerlRun

These two modules allow mod_cgi Perl scripts to run unaltered under mod_perl. They are covered throughout the book, mainly in Chapters 6 and 13.

See also the related `Apache::RegistryNG` and `Apache::RegistryBB` modules.

Supplied with the mod_perl distribution. See the module manpage for more information.

Apache::RegistryNG—Apache::Registry New Generation

`Apache::RegistryNG` is almost the same as `Apache::Registry`, except that it uses filenames instead of URIs for namespaces. It also uses an object-oriented interface.

```
PerlModule Apache::RegistryNG
<Location /perl>
  SetHandler perl-script
  PerlHandler Apache::RegistryNG->handler
</Location>
```

The usage is just the same as `Apache::Registry`.

Apache::RegistryNG inherits from Apache::PerlRun, but the handler( ) is overriden. Apart from the handler( ), the rest of Apache::PerlRun contains all the functionality of Apache::Registry, broken down into several subclassable methods. These methods are used by Apache::RegistryNG to implement the exact same functionality as Apache::Registry, using the Apache::PerlRun methods.

There is no compelling reason to use Apache::RegistryNG over Apache::Registry, unless you want to add to or change the functionality of the existing Registry.pm. For example, Apache::RegistryBB is another subclass that skips the stat( ) call, Option +ExecCGI, and other checks performed by Apache::Registry on each request.

Supplied with the mod_perl distribution. See the module manpage for more information.

Apache::RegistryBB—Apache::Registry Bare Bones

This works just like Apache::Registry, but it does not test the *x* bit (-x file test for executable mode), compiles the file only once (no stat( ) call is made for each request), skips the OPT_EXECCGI checks, and does not chdir( ) into the script's parent directory. It uses the object-oriented interface.

Configuration:

```
PerlModule Apache::RegistryBB
<Location /perl>
    SetHandler perl-script
    PerlHandler Apache::RegistryBB->handler
</Location>
```

The usage is just the same as Apache::Registry.

Supplied with the mod_perl distribution. See the module manpage for more information.

Apache::Request (libapreq)—Generic Apache Request Library

This package contains modules for manipulating client request data via the Apache API with Perl and C. Functionality includes:

- Parsing *application/x-www-form-urlencoded* data
- Parsing *multipart/form* data
- Parsing HTTP cookies

The Perl modules are simply a thin XS layer on top of *libapreq*, making them a lighter and faster alternative to CGI.pm and CGI::Cookie. See the Apache::Request and Apache::Cookie documentation for more details and *eg/perl/* for examples.

`Apache::Request` and *libapreq* are tied tightly to the Apache API, to which there is no access in a process running under mod_cgi.

This module is mentioned in Chapters 6 and 13.

Available from CPAN. See the module manpage for more information.

Apache::Dispatch—Call PerlHandlers with the Ease of Registry Scripts

`Apache::Dispatch` translates `$r->uri` into a class and method and runs it as a `PerlHandler`. Basically, this allows you to call `PerlHandlers` as you would Registry scripts, without having to load your *httpd.conf* file with a lot of <Location > tags.

Available from CPAN. See the module manpage for more information.

Application-Specific Content-Generation Modules

Apache::AutoIndex—Perl Replacement for the mod_autoindex and mod_dir Apache Modules

This module can completely replace the mod_dir and mod_autoindex standard directory-handling modules shipped with Apache.

Available from CPAN. See the module manpage for more information.

Apache::WAP::AutoIndex—WAP Demonstration Module

This is a simple module to demonstrate the use of `CGI::WML` to create a WML (wireless) file browser using mod_perl. It was written to accompany an article in the *Perl Journal* (Issue 20).

Available from CPAN. See the module manpage for more information.

Apache::WAP::MailPeek—Demonstrate Use of WML Delivery

This is a simple module to demonstrate the use of delivery of WML with mod_perl. It was written to accompany an article in the *Perl Journal* (Issue number 20).

Available from CPAN. See the module manpage for more information.

Apache::Archive—Expose Archive Files Through the Apache Web Server

Apache::Archive is a mod_perl extension that allows the Apache HTTP server to expose *.tar* and *.tar.gz* archives on the fly. When a client requests such an archive file, the server will return a page displaying information about the file that allows the user to view or download individual files from within the archive.

Available from CPAN. See the module manpage for more information.

Apache::Gateway—Implement a Gateway

The Apache::Gateway module implements a gateway using LWP with assorted optional features. From the HTTP/1.1 draft, a gateway is:

> [a] server which acts as an intermediary for some other server.
> Unlike a proxy, a gateway receives requests as if it were the origin
> server for the requested resource; the requesting client may not be
> aware that it is communicating with a gateway.

Features:

- Standard gateway features implemented using LWP
- Automatic failover with mirrored instances
- Multiplexing
- Pattern-dependent gatewaying
- FTP directory gatewaying
- Timestamp correction

Available from CPAN. See the module manpage for more information.

Apache::NNTPGateway—NNTP Interface for a mod_perl-Enabled Apache Web Server.

Available from CPAN. See the module manpage for more information.

Apache::PrettyPerl—Syntax Highlighting for Perl Files

An Apache mod_perl PerlHandler that outputs color syntax-highlighted Perl files in the client's browser.

Available from CPAN. See the module manpage for more information.

Apache::PrettyText—Reformat .txt Files for Client Display

Dynamically formats *.txt* files so they look nicer in the client's browser.

Available from CPAN. See the module manpage for more information.

Apache::RandomLocation—Random File Display

Given a list of locations in ConfigFile, this module will instruct the browser to redirect to one of them. The locations in ConfigFile are listed one per line, with lines beginning with # being ignored. How the redirection is handled depends on the variable Type.

Available from CPAN. See the module manpage for more information.

Apache::Stage—Manage a Staging Directory

A staging directory is a place where the author of an HTML document checks the look and feel of the document before it's uploaded to the final location. A staging place doesn't need to be a separate server or a mirror of the "real" tree, or even a tree of symbolic links. A sparse directory tree that holds nothing but the staged files will do.

Apache::Stage implements a staging directory that needs a minimum of space. By default, the path for the per-user staging directory is hardcoded as:

```
/STAGE/any-user-name
```

The code respects proper internal and external redirects for any documents that are not in the staging directory tree. This means that all graphics are displayed as they will be when the staged files have been published. The following table provides an example structure:

```
Location            Redirect-to Comment
------------------- ----------- ---------------------------
/STAGE/u1/          /           Homepage. Internal Redirect.
/STAGE/u2/dir1      /dir1/      Really /dir1/index.html
/STAGE/u3/dir2      /dir2/      Directory has no index.html
                                Options Indexes is off, thus
                                "Forbidden"
/STAGE/u4/dir2/foo /dir2/foo    Internal redirect.
/STAGE/u5/bar       -           Exists really, no redirect
                                necessary
/STAGE/u6           -           Fails unless location exists
```

The entries described in *SYNOPSIS* in *access.conf* or an equivalent place define the name of the staging directory, the name of an internal location that catches the exception when a document is not in the staging directory, and the regular expression that transforms the staging URI into the corresponding public URI.

With this setup only ErrorDocuments 403 and 404 will be served by Apache::Stage. If you need coexistence with different ErrorDocument handlers, you will either have to disable them for */STAGE* or integrate the code of Apache::Stage into an if/else branch based on the path.

Available from CPAN. See the module manpage for more information.

Apache::Roaming—A mod_perl Handler for Roaming Profiles

With `Apache::Roaming` you can use your Apache web server as a Netscape Roaming Access server. This allows users to store Netscape Communicator 4.5+ preferences, bookmarks, address books, cookies, etc., on the server so that they can use (and update) the same settings from any Netscape Communicator 4.5+ browser that can access the server.

Available from CPAN. See the module manpage for more information.

Apache::Backhand—Write mod_backhand Functions in Perl

`Apache::Backhand` ties mod_perl together with mod_backhand, in two major ways. First, the `Apache::Backhand` module itself provides access to the global and shared state information provided by mod_backhand (most notably server stats). Second, the byPerl C function (which is not part of the `Apache::Backhand` module but is distributed with it) allows you to write candidacy functions in Perl.

Available from CPAN. See the module manpage for more information.

Database Modules

Apache::DBI—Initiate a Persistent Database Connection

Covered in Chapter 20.

Available from CPAN. See the module manpage for more information.

Apache::OWA—Oracle's PL/SQL Web Toolkit for Apache

This module makes it possible to run scripts written using Oracle's PL/SQL Web Toolkit under Apache.

Available from CPAN. See the module manpage for more information.

Apache::Sybase::CTlib—Persistent CTlib Connection Management for Apache

Available from CPAN. See the module manpage for more information.

Toolkits and Frameworks for Content-Generation and Other Phases

Apache::ASP—Active Server Pages for Apache with mod_perl

Apache::ASP provides an Active Server Pages port to the Apache web server with Perl scripting *only* and enables developing of dynamic web applications with session management and embedded Perl code. There are also many powerful extensions, including XML taglibs, XSLT rendering, and new events not originally part of the ASP API.

Available from CPAN. See the module manpage for more information.

Apache::AxKit—XML Toolkit for mod_perl

AxKit is a suite of tools for the Apache *httpd* server running mod_perl. It provides developers with extremely flexible options for delivering XML to all kinds of browsers, from hand-held systems to Braille readers to ordinary browsers. All this can be achieved using nothing but W3C standards, although the plug-in architecture provides the hooks for developers to write their own stylesheet systems, should they so desire. Two non-W3C stylesheet systems are included as examples.

The toolkit provides intelligent caching, which ensures that if any parameters in the display of the XML file change, the cache is overwritten. The toolkit also provides hooks for DOM-based stylesheets to cascade. This allows (for example) the initial stylesheet to provide menu items and a table of contents, while the final stylesheet formats the finished file to the desired look. It's also possible to provide multiple language support this way.

AxKit and its documentation are available from *http://www.axkit.org/*.

HTML::Embperl—Embed Perl into HTML

Embperl gives you the power to embed Perl code in your HTML documents and the ability to build your web site out of small, reusable objects in an object-oriented style. You can also take advantage of all the standard Perl modules (including DBI for database access) and use their functionality to easily include their output in your web pages.

Embperl has several features that are especially useful for creating HTML, including dynamic tables, form-field processing, URL escaping/unescaping, session handling, and more.

Embperl is a server-side tool, which means that it's browser-independent. It can run in various ways: under mod_perl, as a CGI script, or offline.

For database access, there is a module called `DBIx::Recordset` that works well with Embperl and simplifies creating web pages with database content.

Available from CPAN. See the module manpage for more information.

Apache::EmbperlChain—Process Embedded Perl in HTML in the OutputChain

Uses `Apache::OutputChain` to filter the output of content generators through `Apache::Embperl`.

Available from CPAN. See the module manpage for more information.

Apache::ePerl—Embedded Perl 5 Language

ePerl interprets an ASCII file that contains Perl program statements by replacing any Perl code it finds with the result of evaluating that code (which may be chunks of HTML, or could be nothing) and passing through the plain ASCII text untouched. It can be used in various ways: as a standalone Unix filter or as an integrated Perl module for general file-generation tasks and as a powerful web-server scripting language for dynamic HTML page programming.

Available from CPAN. See the module manpage for more information.

Apache::iNcom—E-Commerce Framework

`Apache::iNcom` is an e-commerce framework. It is not a ready-to-run merchant system. It integrates the different components needed for e-commerce into a coherent whole.

The primary design goals of the framework are flexibility and security. Most merchant systems will make assumptions about the structure of your catalog data and your customer data, or about how your order process works. Most also impose severe restrictions on how the programmer will interface with your electronic catalog. These are precisely the kinds of constraints that `Apache::iNcom` is designed to avoid.

`Apache::iNcom` provides the following infrastructure:

- Session management
- Cart management
- Input validation
- Order management

- User management
- Easy database access
- Internationalization
- Error handling

Most of the base functionality of `Apache::iNcom` is realized by using standard well-known modules such as `DBI` for generic SQL database access, `HTML::Embperl` for dynamic page generation, `Apache::Session` for session management, `mod_perl` for Apache integration, and `Locale::Maketext` for localization.

Here are its assumptions:

- Data is held in a SQL database that supports transactions.
- The user interface is presented using HTML.
- Sessions are managed through cookies.

Available from CPAN. See the module manpage for more information.

Apache::Mason—Perl-Based Web Site Development and Delivery System

`Apache::Mason` allows web pages and sites to be constructed from shared, reusable building blocks called *components*. Components contain a mixture of Perl and HTML and can call each other and pass values back and forth like subroutines. Components increase modularity and eliminate repetitive work: common design elements (headers, footers, menus, logos) can be extracted into their own components, so that they need be changed only once to affect the whole site.

Other `Mason` features include powerful filtering and templating facilities, an HTML/data-caching model, and a web-based site-previewing utility.

Available from CPAN and *http://www.masonhq.com/*. See the module manpage for more information.

Apache::PageKit—Web Applications Framework

`Apache::PageKit` is a web applications framework that is based on mod_perl. This framework is distinguished from others (such as `Embperl` and `Mason`) by providing a clear separation of programming, content, and presentation. It does this by implementing a Model/View/Content/Controller (MVCC) design paradigm:

- Model is implemented by user-supplied Perl classes
- View is a set of HTML templates
- Content is a set of XML files
- Controller is `PageKit`

This allows programmers, designers, and content editors to work independently, using clean, well-defined interfaces.

Apache::PageKit provides the following features:

- Component-based architecture
- Language localization
- Session management
- Input validation
- Sticky HTML forms
- Authentication
- Co-branding
- Automatic dispatching of URIs
- Easy error handling

Available from CPAN. See the module manpage for more information.

Template Toolkit—Template Processing System

The Template Toolkit is a collection of modules that implements a fast, flexible, powerful, and extensible template processing system. It was originally designed for generating dynamic web content, but it can be used equally well for processing any other kind of text-based documents (HTML, XML, POD, PostScript, LaTeX, etc.).

It can be used as a standalone Perl module or embedded within an Apache/mod_perl server for generating highly configurable dynamic web content. A number of Perl scripts are also provided that can greatly simplify the process of creating and managing static web content and other offline document systems.

The Apache::Template module provides a simple mod_perl interface to the Template Toolkit.

Available from CPAN. It's covered in Appendix D and at *http://tt2.org/*.

Output Filters and Layering Modules

Apache::OutputChain—Chain Stacked Perl Handlers

Apache::OutputChain was written to explore the possibilities of stacked handlers in mod_perl. It ties STDOUT to an object that catches the output and makes it easy to build a chain of modules that work on the output data stream.

Examples of modules that are built using this idea are Apache::SSIChain, Apache::GzipChain, and Apache::EmbperlChain—the first processes the SSIs in the stream, the second compresses the output on the fly, and the last provides Embperl processing.

The syntax is like this:

```
<Files *.html>
    SetHandler perl-script
    PerlHandler Apache::OutputChain Apache::SSIChain Apache::PassHtml
</Files>
```

The modules are listed in *reverse* order of their execution—here the Apache::
PassHtml module simply collects a file's content and sends it to STDOUT, and then it's
processed by Apache::SSIChain, which sends its output to STDOUT again. Then it's
processed by Apache::OutputChain, which finally sends the result to the browser.

An alternative to this approach is Apache::Filter, which has a more natural *forward*
configuration order and is easier to interface with other modules.

Apache::OutputChain works with Apache::Registry as well. For example:

```
Alias /foo /home/httpd/perl/foo
<Location /foo>
    SetHandler "perl-script"
    Options +ExecCGI
    PerlHandler Apache::OutputChain Apache::GzipChain Apache::Registry
</Location>
```

It's really a regular Apache::Registry setup, except for the added modules in the
PerlHandler line.

Available from CPAN. See the module manpage for more information.

Apache::Clean—mod_perl Interface Into HTML::Clean

Apache::Clean uses HTML::Clean to tidy up large, messy HTML, saving bandwidth. It
is particularly useful with Apache::Compress for maximum size reduction.

Available from CPAN. See the module manpage for more information.

Apache::Filter—Alter the Output of Previous Handlers

In the following configuration:

```
<Files ~ "*\.fltr">
    SetHandler perl-script
    PerlSetVar Filter On
    PerlHandler Filter1 Filter2 Filter3
</Files>
```

each of the handlers Filter1, Filter2, and Filter3 will make a call to $r->filter_
input( ), which will return a file handle. For Filter1, the file handle points to the
requested file. For Filter2, the file handle contains whatever Filter1 wrote to
STDOUT. For Filter3, it contains whatever Filter2 wrote to STDOUT. The output of
Filter3 goes directly to the browser.

Available from CPAN. See the module manpage for more information.

Apache::GzipChain—Compress HTML (or Anything) in the OutputChain

Covered in Chapter 13.

Available from CPAN. See the module manpage for more information.

Apache::PassFile—Send File via OutputChain

See Apache::GzipChain. It's a part of the same package as Apache::GzipChain.

Apache::Gzip—Auto-Compress Web Files with gzip

Similar to Apache::GzipChain but works with Apache::Filter.

This configuration:

```
PerlModule Apache::Filter
<Files ~ "*\.html">
    SetHandler perl-script
    PerlSetVar Filter On
    PerlHandler Apache::Gzip
</Files>
```

will send all the *.html* files compressed if the client accepts the compressed input.

And this one:

```
PerlModule Apache::Filter
Alias /home/http/perl /perl
<Location /perl>
    SetHandler perl-script
    PerlSetVar Filter On
    PerlHandler Apache::RegistryFilter Apache::Gzip
</Location>
```

will compess the output of the Apache::Registry scripts. Note that you should use Apache::RegistryFilter instead of Apache::Registry for this to work.

You can use as many filters as you want:

```
PerlModule Apache::Filter
<Files ~ "*\.fltr">
    SetHandler perl-script
    PerlSetVar Filter On
    PerlHandler Filter1 Filter2 Apache::Gzip
</Files>
```

You can test that it works by either looking at the size of the response in the *access.log* file or by telnet:

```
panic% telnet localhost 8000
Trying 127.0.0.1
Connected to 127.0.0.1
```

```
Escape character is '^]'.
GET /perl/test.pl HTTP 1.1
Accept-Encoding: gzip
User-Agent: Mozilla
```

You will get the data compressed if it's configured correctly.

Apache::Compress—Auto-Compress Web Files with gzip

This module lets you send the content of an HTTP response as *gzip*-compressed data. Certain browsers (e.g., Netscape and IE) can request content compression via the Content-Encoding header. This can speed things up if you're sending large files to your users through slow connections.

Browsers that don't request *gzip*ped data will receive uncompressed data.

This module is compatibile with Apache::Filter, so you can compress the output of other content generators.

Available from CPAN. See the module manpage for more information.

Apache::Layer—Layer Content Tree Over One or More Others

This module is designed to allow multiple content trees to be layered on top of each other within the Apache server.

Available from CPAN. See the module manpage for more information.

Apache::Sandwich—Layered Document (Sandwich) Maker

The Apache::Sandwich module allows you to add per-directory custom "header" and "footer" content to a given URI. Works only with GET requests. Output of combined parts is forced to *text/html*. The handler for the sandwiched document is specified by the SandwichHandler configuration variable. If it is not set, default-handler is used.

The basic concept is that the concatenation of the header and footer parts with the sandwiched file in between constitutes a complete valid HTML document.

Available from CPAN. See the module manpage for more information.

Apache::SimpleReplace—Simple Template Framework

Apache::SimpleReplace provides a simple way to insert content within an established template for uniform content delivery. While the end result is similar to Apache::Sandwich, Apache::SimpleReplace offers two main advantages:

- It does not use separate header and footer files, easing the pain of maintaining syntactically correct HTML in separate files.

- It is `Apache::Filter` aware, so it can both accept content from other content handlers and pass its changes on to others later in the chain.

Available from CPAN. See the module manpage for more information.

Apache::SSI—Implement Server-Side Includes in Perl

`Apache::SSI` implements the functionality of mod_include for handling server-parsed HTML documents. It runs under Apache's mod_perl.

There are two main reasons you might want to use this module: you can subclass it to implement your own custom SSI directives, and you can parse the output of other mod_perl handlers or send the SSI output through another handler (use `Apache::Filter` to do this).

Available from CPAN. See the module manpage for more information.

Logging-Phase Handlers

Apache::RedirectLogFix—Correct Status While Logging

Because of the way mod_perl handles redirects, the status code is not properly logged. The `Apache::RedirectLogFix` module works around this bug until mod_perl can deal with this. All you have to do is to enable it in the *httpd.conf* file.

```
PerlLogHandler Apache::RedirectLogFix
```

For example, you will have to use it when doing:

```
$r->status(304);
```

and do some manual header sending, like this:

```
$r->status(304);
$r->send_http_header();
```

Available from the mod_perl distribution. See the module manpage for more information.

Apache::DBILogConfig—Logs Access Information in a DBI Database

This module replicates the functionality of the standard Apache module mod_log_config but logs information in a DBI-compatible database instead of a file.

Available from CPAN. See the module manpage for more information.

Apache::DBILogger—Tracks What's Being Transferred in a DBI Database

This module tracks what's being transferred by the Apache web server in SQL database (everything with a DBI/DBD driver). This allows you to get statistics (of almost everything) without having to parse the log files (as with the `Apache::Traffic` module, but using a "real" database, and with a lot more logged information).

After installation, follow the instructions in the synopsis and restart the server. The statistics are then available in the database.

Available from CPAN. See the module manpage for more information.

Apache::DumpHeaders—Watch HTTP Transaction via Headers

This module is used to watch an HTTP transaction, looking at the client and server headers. With `Apache::ProxyPassThru` configured, you can watch your browser talk to any server, not just the one that is using this module.

Available from CPAN. See the module manpage for more information.

Apache::Traffic—Track Hits and Bytes Transferred on a Per-User Basis

This module tracks the total number of hits and bytes transferred per day by the Apache web server, on a per-user basis. This allows for real-time statistics without having to parse the log files.

After installation, add this to your server's *httpd.conf* file:

```
PerlLogHandler  Apache::Traffic
```

and restart the server. The statistics will then be available through the traffic script, which is included in the distribution.

Available from CPAN. See the module manpage for more information.

Core Apache Modules

Apache::Module—Interface to Apache C Module Structures

This module provides an interface to the list of Apache modules configured with your *httpd* server and their `module *` structures.

Available from CPAN. See the module manpage for more information.

Apache::ShowRequest—Show Phases and Module Participation

Part of the Apache::Module package. This module allows you to see the all phases of the request and what modules are participating in each of the phases.

Available from CPAN. See the module manpage for more information.

Apache::SubProcess—Interface to Apache Subprocess API

The output of system( ), exec( ), and open(PIPE,"|program") calls will not be sent to the browser unless your Perl interpreter was configured with sfio.

One workaround is to use backticks:

```
print `command here`;
```

But a cleaner solution is provided by the Apache::SubProcess module. It overrides the exec( ) and system( ) calls with calls that work correctly under mod_perl.

Let's look at a few examples. This example overrides the built-in system( ) function and sends the output to the browser:

```
use Apache::SubProcess qw(system);
my $r = shift;
$r->send_http_header('text/plain');

system "/bin/echo hi there";
```

This example overrides the built-in exec( ) function and sends the output to the browser. As you can guess, the print statement after the exec( ) call will never be executed.

```
use Apache::SubProcess qw(exec);
my $r = shift;
$r->send_http_header('text/plain');

exec "/usr/bin/cal";

print "NOT REACHED\n";
```

The env( ) function sets an environment variable that can be seen by the main process and subprocesses, then it executes the /bin/env program via call_exec( ). The main code spawns a process, and tells it to execute the env( ) function. This call returns an output file handle from the spawned child process. Finally, it takes the output generated by the child process and sends it to the browser via send_fd( ), which expects the file handle as an argument:

```
use Apache::SubProcess ();
my $r = shift;
$r->send_http_header('text/plain');
```

```
my $efh = $r->spawn_child(\&env);
$r->send_fd($efh);

sub env {
    my $fh = shift;
    $fh->subprocess_env(HELLO => 'world');
    $fh->filename("/bin/env");
    $fh->call_exec;
}
```

This example is very similar to the previous example, but it shows how you can pass arguments to the external process. It passes the string to print as a banner via a subprocess:

```
use Apache::SubProcess ();
my $r = shift;
$r->send_http_header('text/plain');

my $fh = $r->spawn_child(\&banner);
$r->send_fd($fh);

sub banner {
    my $fh = shift;
    # /usr/games/banner on many Unices
    $fh->filename("/usr/bin/banner");
    $fh->args("-w40+Hello%20World");
    $fh->call_exec;
}
```

The last example shows how you can have full access to the STDIN, STDOUT, and STDERR streams of the spawned subprocess, so that you can pipe data to a program and send its output to the browser:

```
use Apache::SubProcess ();
my $r = shift;
$r->send_http_header('text/plain');

use vars qw($string);
$string = "hello world";
my($out, $in, $err) = $r->spawn_child(\&echo);
print $out $string;
$r->send_fd($in);

sub echo {
    my $fh = shift;
    $fh->subprocess_env(CONTENT_LENGTH => length $string);
    $fh->filename("/tmp/pecho");
    $fh->call_exec;
}
```

The echo( ) function is similar to the earlier example's env( ) function. /tmp/pecho is as follows:

```
#!/usr/bin/perl
read STDIN, $buf, $ENV{CONTENT_LENGTH};
print "STDIN: '$buf' ($ENV{CONTENT_LENGTH})\n";
```

In the last example, a string is defined as a global variable, so its length could be calculated in the echo( ) function. The subprocess reads from STDIN, to which the main process writes the string ("hello world"). It reads only the number of bytes specified by the CONTENT_LENGTH environment variable. Finally, the external program prints the data that it read to STDOUT, and the main program intercepts it and sends it to the client's socket (i.e., to the browser).

This module is also discussed in Chapter 10.

Available from CPAN. See the module manpage for more information.

Apache::Connection—Interface to the Apache conn_rec Data Structure

This module provides the Perl interface to the conn_rec data structure, which includes various records unique to each connection, such as the state of a connection, server and base server records, child number, etc. See *include/httpd.h* for a complete description of this data structure.

Supplied with the mod_perl distribution. See the module manpage for more information.

Apache::Constants—Constants Defined in httpd.h

Server constants (OK, DENIED, NOT_FOUND, etc.) used by Apache modules are defined in *httpd.h* and other header files. This module gives Perl access to those constants.

Supplied with the mod_perl distribution. See the module manpage for more information.

Apache::ExtUtils—Utilities for Apache C/Perl Glue

Supplied with the mod_perl distribution. See the module manpage for more information.

Apache::File—Advanced Functions for Manipulating Files on the Server Side

Apache::File does two things. First, it provides an object-oriented interface to file handles, similar to Perl's standard IO::File class. While the Apache::File module does not provide all the functionality of IO::File, its methods are approximately twice as fast as the equivalent IO::File methods. Secondly, when you use Apache::File, it adds to the Apache class several new methods that provide support for handling files under the HTTP/1.1 protocol.

Supplied with the mod_perl distribution. See the module manpage for more information.

Apache::Log—Interface to Apache Logging

The `Apache::Log` module provides an interface to Apache's `ap_log_error()` and `ap_log_rerror()` routines.

Supplied with the mod_perl distribution. See the module manpage for more information.

Apache::LogFile—Interface to Apache's Logging Routines

The `PerlLogFile` directive from this package can be used to hook a Perl file handle to a piped logger or to a file open for appending. If the first character of the filename is a "|", the file handle is opened as a pipe to the given program. The file or program can be relative to the `ServerRoot`.

So if *httpd.conf* contains these settings:

```
PerlModule Apache::LogFile
PerlLogFile |perl/mylogger.pl My::Logger
```

in your code you can log to the `My::Logger` file handle:

```
print My::Logger "a message to the Log"
```

and it'll be piped through the *perl/mylogger.pl* script.

Available from CPAN. See the module manpage for more information.

Apache::Scoreboard—Perl Interface to Apache's scoreboard.h

Apache keeps track of server activity in a structure known as the scoreboard. There is a slot in the scoreboard for each child server, containing information such as status, access count, bytes served, and CPU time. This information is also used by mod_status to provide server statistics in a human-readable form.

Available from CPAN. See the module manpage for more information.

Apache::Server—Perl Interface to the Apache server_rec Struct

The `Apache::Server` class contains information about the server's configuration. Using this class it's possible to retrieve any data set in *httpd.conf* and `<Perl>` sections.

Supplied with the mod_perl distribution. See the module manpage for more information.

Apache::Table—Perl Interface to the Apache Table Struct

This module provides tied interfaces to Apache data structures. By using it you can add, merge, and clear entries in *headers_in*, *headers_out*, *err_headers_out*, *notes*, *dir_config*, and *subprocess_env*.

Supplied with the mod_perl distribution. See the module manpage for more information.

Apache::URI—URI Component Parsing and Unparsing

This module provides an interface to the Apache util_uri module and the uri_components structure. The available methods are: parsed_uri( ), parse( ), unparse( ), scheme( ), hostinfo( ), user( ), password( ), hostname( ), port( ), path( ), rpath( ), query( ), and fragment( ).

Supplied with the mod_perl distribution. See the module manpage for more information.

Apache::Util—Perl Interface to Apache C Utility Functions

This module provides a Perl interface to some of the C utility functions available in Apache. The same functionality is avaliable in *libwww-perl*, but the C versions are faster: escape_html( ), escape_uri( ), unescape_uri( ), unescape_uri_info( ), parsedate( ), ht_time( ), size_string( ), and validate_password( ).

Supplied with the mod_perl distribution. See the module manpage for more information.

Other Miscellaneous Modules

Apache::Session—Maintain Session State Across HTTP Requests

This module provides mod_perl with a mechanism for storing persistent user data in a global hash, which is independent of the underlying storage mechanism. Currently it supports storage in standard files, DBM files, or a relational database using DBI. Read the manpage of the mechanism you want to use for a complete reference.

Apache::Session provides persistence to a data structure. The data structure has an ID number, and you can retrieve it by using the ID number. In the case of Apache, you would store the ID number in a cookie or the URL to associate it with one browser, but how you handle the ID is completely up to you. The flow of things is generally:

```
Tie a session to Apache::Session.
Get the ID number.
Store the ID number in a cookie.
End of Request 1.

(time passes)

Get the cookie.
Restore your hash using the ID number in the cookie.
Use whatever data you put in the hash.
End of Request 2.
```

Using Apache::Session is easy: simply tie a hash to the session object, put any data structure into the hash, and the data you put in automatically persists until the next invocation. Example B-1 is an example that uses cookies to track the user's session.

Example B-1. session.pl

```perl
# pull in the required packages
use Apache::Session::MySQL;
use Apache;

use strict;

# read in the cookie if this is an old session
my $r = Apache->request;
my $cookie = $r->header_in('Cookie');
$cookie =~ s/SESSION_ID=(\w+)/$1/;

# create a session object based on the cookie we got from the
# browser, or a new session if we got no cookie
my %session;
eval {
    tie %session, 'Apache::Session::MySQL', $cookie,
        {DataSource => 'dbi:mysql:sessions',
         UserName    => $db_user,
         Password    => $db_pass,
         LockDataSource => 'dbi:mysql:sessions',
         LockUserName   => $db_user,
         LockPassword   => $db_pass,
        };
};
if ($@) {
    # could be a database problem
    die "Couldn't tie session: $@";
}

# might be a new session, so let's give them their cookie back
my $session_cookie = "SESSION_ID=$session{_session_id};";
$r->header_out("Set-Cookie" => $session_cookie);
```

After %session is tied, you can put anything but file handles and code references into $session{_session_id};, and it will still be there when the user invokes the next page.

It is possible to write an Apache authentication handler using Apache::Session. You can put your authentication token into the session. When a user invokes a page, you open his session, check to see if he has a valid token, and authenticate or forbid based on that.

An alternative to Apache::Session is Apache::ASP, which has session-tracking abilities. HTML::Embperl hooks into Apache::Session for you.

Available from CPAN. See the module manpage for more information.

Apache::RequestNotes—Easy, Consistent Access to Cookie and Form Data Across Each Request Phase

Apache::RequestNotes provides a simple interface allowing all phases of the request cycle access to cookie or form input parameters in a consistent manner. Behind the scenes, it uses *libapreq* (Apache::Request) functions to parse request data and puts references to the data in pnotes( ).

Once the request is past the PerlInitHandler phase, all other phases can have access to form input and cookie data without parsing it themselves. This relieves some strain, especially when the GET or POST data is required by numerous handlers along the way.

Available from CPAN. See the module manpage for more information.

Apache::Cookie—HTTP Cookies Class

The Apache::Cookie module is a Perl interface to the cookie routines in *libapreq*. The interface is based on the CGI::Cookie module.

Available from CPAN. See the module manpage for more information.

Apache::Icon—Look Up Icon Images

This module rips out the icon guts of mod_autoindex and provides a Perl interface for looking up icon images. The motivation is to piggy-back the existing AddIcon and related directives for mapping file extensions and names to icons, while keeping things as small and fast as mod_autoindex does.

Available from CPAN. See the module manpage for more information.

Apache::Include—Utilities for mod_perl/mod_include Integration

The `Apache::Include` module provides a handler, making it simple to include `Apache::Registry` scripts with the mod_include Perl directive.

`Apache::Registry` scripts can also be used in mod_include-parsed documents using a *virtual include*.

The `virtual( )` method may be called to include the output of a given URI in your Perl scripts. For example:

```
use Apache::Include ();
print "Content-type: text/html\n\n";

print "before include\n";
my $uri = "/perl/env.pl";
Apache::Include->virtual($uri);
print "after include\n";
```

The output of the perl CGI script located at */perl/env.pl* will be inserted between the "before include" and "after include" strings and printed to the client.

Supplied with the mod_perl distribution. See the module manpage for more information.

Apache::Language—Perl Transparent Language Support for Apache Modules and mod_perl Scripts

The goal of this module is to provide a simple way for mod_perl module writers to include support for multiple language requests.

An `Apache::Language` object acts like a language-aware hash. It stores key/language/value triplets. Using the `Accept-Language` header field sent by the web client, it can choose the most appropriate language for the client. Its usage is transparent to the client.

Available from CPAN. See the module manpage for more information.

Apache::Mmap—Perl Interface to the mmap(2) System Call

The `Apache::Mmap` module lets you use `mmap` to map in a file as a Perl variable rather than reading the file into dynamically allocated memory. It works only if your OS supports Unix or POSIX.1b `mmap( )`. `Apache::Mmap` can be used just like `Mmap` under mod_perl.

Available from CPAN. See the module manpage for more information.

Apache::GD::Graph—Generate Graphs in an Apache Handler

The primary purpose of this module is to provide a very easy-to-use, lightweight, and fast charting capability for static pages, dynamic pages, and CGI scripts, with the chart-creation process abstracted and placed on any server.

Available from CPAN. See the module manpage for more information.

Apache::Motd—Provide motd (Message of the Day) Functionality to a Web Server

This module provides an alternative and more efficient method of notifying your web users of potential downtime or problems affecting your web server and web services.

Available from CPAN. See the module manpage for more information.

Apache::ParseLog—Object-Oriented Perl Extension for Parsing Apache Log Files

Apache::ParseLog provides an easy way to parse the Apache log files, using object-oriented constructs. The module is flexible, and the data it generates can be used for your own applications (CGI scripts, simple text-only report generators, feeding an RDBMS, data for Perl/Tk-based GUI applications, etc.).

Available from CPAN. See the module manpage for more information.

Apache::RegistryLoader—Compile Apache::Registry Scripts at Server Startup

Covered in Chapter 13.

Supplied with the mod_perl distribution. See the module manpage for more information.

Apache::SIG—Override Apache Signal Handlers with Perl's Signal Handlers

Covered in Chapter 6.

Supplied with the mod_perl distribution. See the module manpage for more information.

Apache::TempFile—Allocate Temporary Filenames for the Duration of a Request

This module provides unique paths for temporary files and ensures that they are removed when the current request is completed.

Available from CPAN. See the module manpage for more information.

Xmms—Perl Interface to the xmms Media Player

A collection of Perl interfaces for the *xmms* media player. Includes a module that allows you to control *xmms* from the browser. mod_perl generates a page with an index of available MP3 files and control buttons. You click on the links and *xmms* plays the files for you.

Available from CPAN. See the module manpage for more information.

Module::Use—Log and Load Used Perl Modules

`Module::Use` records the modules used over the course of the Perl interpreter's lifetime. If the logging module is able, the old logs are read and frequently used modules are loaded automatically.

For example, if configured as:

```
<Perl>
    use Module::Use (Counting, Logger => "Debug");
</Perl>

PerlChildExitHandler Module::Use
```

it will record the used modules only when the child exists, logging everything (debug level).

APPENDIX C

ISPs Providing mod_perl Services

This appendix proposes a few techniques for deploying mod_perl on ISP machines. Therefore, it's mostly relevant to ISP technical teams and ISP users who need to convince their providers to provide them with mod_perl services.

There are at least four different scenarios for deploying mod_perl-enabled Apache servers that ISPs may consider:

- Users sharing a single web server
- Users sharing a single machine
- Giving each user a separate machine
- Giving each user a virtual machine

This appendix covers each of those scenarios.

Users Sharing a Single Web Server

An ISP cannot let users run their code under mod_perl on the main server. There are many reasons for this. Here are just a few to consider:

Memory usage
> One user may deprive other users of memory. A careless user's code might leak memory due to sloppy programming. A user may use a lot of memory simply by loading a lot of modules. If one user's service is very popular and gets a lot of traffic, there will be more Apache children running for that service, so it's possible for that user to unintentionally consume most of the available memory even if she has a very small, well-written code base with no memory leaks.

Other resources
> It's not only memory that is shared between all users. Other important resources, such as CPU, the number of open files, the total number of processes (currently there is no easy way to control the number of mod_perl processes dedicated to each user), and process priority are all shared as well. Intentionally

or not, users may interfere with each other by consuming any or all of these resources.

File security

All users run code on the server with the same permissions (i.e., the same UID and GID). Any user who can write code for execution by the web server can read any files that are readable by the web server, no matter which user owns them. Similarly, any user who can write code for the web server can write any files that are writable by the web server, no matter which user owns them. Currently, it is not possible to run the suEXEC and cgiwrap extensions under mod_perl, and as mod_perl processes don't normally quit after servicing a request they cannot modify their UIDs and GIDs from request to request.

Potential system compromise via user's code running on the web server

One of the possible solutions here is to use the *chroot(1)* or *jail(8)* mechanisms, which allow you to run subsystems isolated from the main system. So if a subsystem gets compromised, the whole system is still safe.

Security of database connections

It's possible to hijack other users' DBI connections, and since all users can read each other's code, database usernames and passwords are visible to every user.

With all the problems described above, it's unwise to let users run their code under mod_perl on a shared server, unless they trust each other and follow strict guidelines to avoid interfering with each other's files and scripts (both of which are unlikely).

Note that there is no reason for an ISP not to run mod_perl applications that they control themselves. The dangers are only when they allow users to write their own mod_perl code. For example, an ISP might provide its users with value-added services such as guest books, hit counters, etc., that run under mod_perl. If the ISP provides code and data, which are not directly accessible by the users, they can still benefit from the performance gains offered by mod_perl.

mod_perl 2.0 improves the situation, since it allows a pool of Perl interpreters to be dedicated to a single virtual host. It is possible to set the UIDs and GIDs of these interpreters to be those of the user for which the virtual host is configured, so users can operate within their own protected spaces and are unable to interfere with other users.

Users Sharing a Single Machine

A better approach is to give each user a dedicated web server, still running on the same machine.

Now each server can run under its owners' permissions, thus protecting users from each other. Unfortunately, this doesn't address the other considerations raised in the previous setup approach. In Chapter 14 we discussed various techniques of limiting resource usage, but users will be able to override those limitations from within their code and you will have to trust your users not to do that.

Also, this scenario introduces a new problem. If an ISP uses named virtual hosts (all using the same IP address), what differs between users is the port to which their servers listen. The main frontend server will dispatch the requests to the various users' backend servers based on the port given to each user. If users are allowed to modify their parts of the server's *httpd.conf* file, it's possible that user A could adjust the server configuration to listen to the same port that user B's server is supposed to be listening to. User A's Apache server cannot bind to the same port while user B's server is running, but if the machine is rebooted at some point, it's possible that user A could take over the port allocated to user B. Now all the traffic that was supposed to go to user B will go to user A's server instead. User B's server will fail to start at all. Of course, ugly things like this will quickly be discovered, but not before some damage has been done.

If you have chosen this server-sharing technique, you must provide your clients with:

- Shutdown and startup scripts installed together with the rest of your daemon startup scripts (e.g., */etc/rc.d* directory), so that when you reboot your machine the users' servers will be properly shut down and restarted. Of course, you should make sure that the server will start under the UID of the user to whom it belongs.

- Rewrite rules in the frontend server. Since users cannot bind to port 80 in this scenario, they must bind to ports above 1024. The frontend server should rewrite each request to the correct backend server.

- Dedicated ports for each user. You must also ensure that users will use only the ports they are given. You can either trust your users or use special tools that ensure that. One such tool is called *cbs*; its documentation can be found at *http://www.epita.fr/~flav/cbs/doc/html*.

Giving Each User a Separate Machine (Colocation)

A much better and simpler (but costly) solution is *colocation*. Let the users hook their (or your) standalone machines into your network, and forget about the issues raised in the previously suggested setups. Of course, either the users or you will have to undertake all the system administration. Many ISPs make sure only that the machine is up and running and delegate the rest of the system-administration chores to their users.

Giving Each User a Virtual Machine

If users cannot afford dedicated machines, it's possible to provide each user with a virtual machine, assuming that you have a very powerful server that can run a few virtual machines on the same hardware.

There are a number of virtual-machine technologies, both commercial and open source. Here are some of them:

- The User-Mode Linux kernel gives you a virtual machine that may have different hardware and software virtual resources than the physical computer. Disk storage for the virtual machine is entirely contained inside a single file on the physical machine. You can assign your virtual machine only the hardware access you want it to have. With properly limited access, nothing you do on the virtual machine can change or damage your real computer or its software.

  If you want to completely protect one user from another and yourself from your users, this is yet another alternative to the solutions suggested at the beginning of this chapter.

  For more information, visit the home page of the project at *http://user-mode-linux.sourceforge.net/*.

- VMWare technology allows you to run a few instances of the same or different operating systems on the same machine. This technology comes in both open source and commercial flavors. The open source version is at *http://savannah.nongnu.org/projects/plex86/*. The commercial version is at *http://www.vmware.com/*.

  VMWare will allow you to run a separate OS for each of your clients on the same machine, assuming that you have enough hardware resources.

- freeVSD (*http://www.freevsd.org/*) is an open source project that enables ISPs to securely partition their physical servers into many virtual servers, each capable of running popular hosting applications such as Apache, *sendmail*, and MySQL.

- The S/390 IBM server is a great solution for huge ISPs, as it allows them to run hundreds of mod_perl servers while having only one box to maintain. The main drawback is its very high price. For more information, see *http://www.s390.ibm.com/linux/vif/*.

The Template Toolkit

This appendix provides an introduction to the Template Toolkit, a fast, flexible, powerful, and extensible template processing system written in Perl.* It is ideally suited for use in creating highly customized static and dynamic web pages and for building Perl-based web applications. This appendix explains how to get the best out of the Template Toolkit under mod_perl (although the Template Toolkit is in no way limited to use under mod_perl). All the example code is available for download from this book's web site (*http://www.modperl.com/*).

This appendix's goal is to give you a flavor of what the Template Toolkit can do for you and your web sites. It is by no means comprehensive, and you're strongly urged to consult the copious documentation that is bundled with the Perl modules or available for browsing online at the Template Toolkit web site: *http://template-toolkit.org/*.

Fetching and Installing the Template Toolkit

You can fetch the Template Toolkit from any CPAN site. It can be found at the following URL: *http://www.cpan.org/modules/by-module/Template/*.

Once you've unzipped and untarred the distribution, installation proceeds via the usual route. For example:

```
panic% perl Makefile.PL
panic% make
panic% make test
panic% su
panic# make install
```

---

* There are also some optional components written in C for speed, but you don't need to use them if you're looking for a pure Perl solution.

Alternately, you can use the CPAN.pm module to install it. Full details on installation can be found in the *INSTALL* file in the distribution directory. There is also a *README* file that is worth at least a passing glance.

Overview

The Template Toolkit is a collection of Perl modules, scripts, and other useful bits and pieces that collectively implement a powerful template processing system for generating and manipulating content. It scans through source documents looking for special directives embedded in the text. These act as instructions to the processor to perform certain tasks.

A simple directive might just insert the value of a variable:

```
<a href="[% home %]">Home</a>
```

or perhaps include and process another template:

```
[% INCLUDE header
     title = 'A Dark and Stormy Night'
%]
```

More complex directives may make use of the powerful language constructs that the Template Toolkit provides. For example:

```
<h3>[% users.size %] users currently logged in:</h3>
<ul>
[% FOREACH user = users %]
   [%# 'loop' is a reference to the FOREACH iterator -%]
   <li>[% loop.count %]/[% loop.size %]:
       <a href="[% user.home %]">[% user.name %]</a>
   [% IF user.about %]
       <p>[% user.about %]</p>
   [% END %]
   [% INCLUDE userinfo %]
   </li>
[% END %]
</ul>
```

Chances are that you can work out what most of the above is doing without too much explanation. That's the general idea—to keep the templates as simple and general as possible. It allows you to get a broad overview of what's going on without too much detail getting in the way.

We'll come back to this example later on and explain a little more about what's going on.

Typical Uses

A typical use of the Template Toolkit is as an offline tool for generating static web pages from source templates. This alone can be invaluable as a way of consistently adding standard headers, footers, menus, or other presentation elements to all of the pages in a web site.

The *ttree* utility, distributed as part of the toolkit, can be used to automatically process an entire directory tree of files in this way. Rather than creating and maintaining web pages directly, you write your pages as source templates and use *ttree* to run them through the Template Toolkit and publish them to a new location, ready to be viewed or accessed by your web server. During this process, any directives embedded within the templates are interpreted accordingly to build up the final HTML content. This can be then be combined automatically with any other standard page elements or layout templates before the output is written to the destination file.

You can also use the Template Toolkit in CGI scripts and mod_perl handlers for generating dynamic web content. The Template module provides a simple programming-level interface to the template processing engine and allows you to cleanly separate your application code from presentation logic and layout. It provides a rich set of bindings between Perl data and code in the backend and template variables in the frontend. That means you can call into templates from your Perl code and also call into Perl code from your templates. You can freely pass all kinds of Perl data between the front- and backends, in the form of scalars, hashes, lists, subroutines, and object references, allowing you to hide all manner of internal complexity behind a simple data interface. This makes it easy for you to perform all sorts of technical wizardry in your templates, without having to directly expose or embed any of the Perl code that makes it happen.

The Template Toolkit includes a number of standard plug-in modules that provide various useful add-on functionalities. These include modules for creating HTML tables; fetching CGI parameters; parsing and processing XML, POD, and LaTeX; accessing databases via DBI; manipulating dates; processing URLs; and generating graphics, to name just a few. It's also trivially easy to load and use other existing Perl modules. If CPAN doesn't have what you're looking for, you can always implement your own custom functionality as a Perl module, which can then be loaded into the Template Toolkit for use and reuse as required.

This approach makes your code and your templates much easier to develop and maintain. If the people working on Perl application code are different from those who develop the HTML pages, it allows them to work on their separate areas without getting in each other's way. Even if you're the one doing all the work, it allows you to better separate the tasks and wear just one hat at a time. When you're wearing your application developer's hat, you can concentrate on the Perl code and making it work right. When you're wearing your web page designer's hat, you can concentrate on the HTML markup and making it look good.

It also makes your backend code and your frontend templates more reusable. You can have the same backend code running behind multiple sets of frontend templates, ideal for creating different versions of the same web site localized to spoken languages or customized to different users' requirements. You can also reuse the same set of templates in front of different backend applications, CGI scripts, and mod_perl handlers. Common elements such as headers, footers, and menus can be encoded as templates and then shared between your static pages generated via *ttree* and your dynamic pages generated online. The result is that you get a consistent user interface and presentation style for all your pages, regardless of how they're generated.

Template Toolkit Language

The Template Toolkit implements a general-purpose *presentation* language rather than a general-purpose *programming* language. What that means is that for general programming tasks, building backend applications, database access, and so on, you should continue to use Perl and the many fine modules available for use with it.

The strength of the Template Toolkit language is in building the frontend—that is, the HTML that presents the output of an application or displays the content of an XML file, the results of a database query, the collection of snapshots of your pet camel, or whatever it is that you're trying to do. It has many constructs that are familiar in programming languages, such as the use of variables (GET, SET, DEFAULT), conditional clauses (IF, UNLESS, ELSIF, ELSE, etc.), loops (FOREACH, WHILE, SWITCH, CASE), and exception handling (TRY, THROW, CATCH). However, these are generally intended to be used from the perspective of layout logic; that is, controlling how the output looks, not what the underlying application actually does. To compliment these basic operations, there are also various directives more specifically oriented to gluing chunks of content together (PROCESS, INCLUDE, INSERT, WRAPPER, BLOCK), for providing useful content-manipulation tools (FILTER, MACRO), and for the loading of external modules (USE) by which the toolkit can easily and quickly be extended.

Although we are focusing on HTML in particular, it is worth pointing out that the Template Toolkit is actually language-neutral. It operates on text files (although it can be used to generate binary files such as images or PDF documents), and as such, it doesn't really care what kind of text you're generating, be it HTML, XML, LaTeX, PostScript, or an Apache *httpd.conf* configuration file.

Simple Template Example

So without further ado, let's see what a typical template looks like:

```
[% PROCESS header title="Some Interesting Links" %]

<p>
Here are some interesting links:
<ul>
[% FOREACH link = weblinks %]
   <li><a href="[% link.url %]">[% link.title %]</a></li>
```

```
[% END %]
</ul>
</p>

[% PROCESS footer %]
```

The first thing to note is that template directives are embedded within [% and %]. You can change these values, along with several dozen other configuration options, but we'll stick with the defaults for now. The directives within those tags are instructions to the template processor. They can contain references to variables (e.g., [% link.url %]) or language constructs that typically begin with an uppercase word and may have additional arguments (e.g., [% PROCESS footer %]). Anything else outside the tags is plain text and is passed through unaltered.

The example shows the PROCESS directive being used to pull in a *header* template at the top of the page and a *footer* template at the bottom. The *header* and *footer* templates can have their own directives embedded within them and will be processed accordingly. You can pass arguments when calling PROCESS, just as you might when calling a subroutine in Perl. This is shown in the first line, where we set a value for the title variable.

By default, variables are global, and if you change title in one template, the new value will apply in any other templates that reference it. The INCLUDE directive goes a little further to make arguments more local, giving you better protection from accidentally changing a variable with global consequences. Separate variable namespaces can also be used to avoid collisions between variables of the same name (e.g., page.title versus book.title).

In the middle of the example, we see the FOREACH directive. This defines the start of a repeated block that continues until the END directive two lines below. Loops, conditionals, and other blocks can be combined in any way and nested indefinitely. In this case, we're setting the link variable to alias each item in the list referenced by the weblinks variable. We print the url and title for each item, with some appropriate HTML markup to display them formatted as an HTML bullet list.

The *dot* (.) operator is used to access data items within data items, and it tries to do the right thing according to the data type. For example, each item in the list could be a reference to a hash array, in which case link.url would be equivalent to the Perl code $link->{url}, or it could be an object against which methods can be called, such as $link->url( ). The dotted notation hides the specifics of your backend code so that you don't have to know or care about the specifics of the implementation. Thus, you can change your data from hash arrays to objects at some later date and slot them straight in without making any changes to the templates.

Let's now go back to our earlier example and see if we can make sense of it:

```
<h3>[% users.size %] users currently logged in:</h3>
<ul>
[% FOREACH user = users %]
```

```
[%# 'loop' is a reference to the FOREACH iterator -%]
<li>[% loop.count %]/[% loop.size %]:
    <a href="[% user.home %]">[% user.name %]</a>
[% IF user.about %]
    <p>[% user.about %]</p>
[% END %]
[% INCLUDE userinfo %]
</li>
[% END %]
</ul>
```

Anything outside a [% ... %] directive—in this case, various HTML fragments that are building a list of users currently logged in to our fictional system—is passed through intact.

The various constructs that we meet inside the directives are:

users

> We're assuming here that the users variable contains a reference to a list of users. In fact, it might also be a reference to a subroutine that generates a list of users on demand, but that's a backend implementation detail we're quite rightly not concerned with here. The Template Toolkit does the right thing to access a list or call a subroutine to return a list, so we don't have to worry about such things.
>
> The users themselves (i.e., the items in the users list) can be references to hash arrays, or maybe references to objects. Again, the Template Toolkit hides the implementation details and does the right thing when the time comes.

users.size

> There are a number of "virtual methods" you can call on basic Perl data types. Here, the .size virtual method returns the number of items in the users list.

FOREACH user = users

> The FOREACH directive defines a block of template code up to the corresponding END directive and processes it repeatedly for each item in the users list. For each iteration, the user variable is set to reference the current item in the list.

loop

> The loop variable is set automatically within a FOREACH block to reference a special object (an iterator) that controls the loop. You can call various methods in this object, such as loop.count to return the current iteration (from 1 to n) and loop.size to return the size of the list (in this case, the same as users.size).

user

> The user variable references each item in the users list in turn. This can be a reference to a hash array or an object, but we don't care which. Again, these details are sensibly hidden from view. We just want the home part of user, and we're not too worried about where it comes from or what has to be done to fetch it.

IF user.about

> The IF directive defines a block that gets processed if the condition evaluates to some true value. Here we're simply testing to see if user.about is defined. As you might expect, you can combine IF with ELSIF and ELSE and also use UNLESS.

INCLUDE userinfo

> The INCLUDE directive is used here to process and include the output of an external template called *userinfo*. The INCLUDE_PATH configuration option can be used to specify where external templates can be found, so you can avoid hardcoding any absolute paths in the templates. All the variables currently defined are visible within the *userinfo* template, allowing it to access [% user.whatever %] to correctly reference the current user in the FOREACH loop.

> We've created this separate *userinfo* template and can assume it generates a nice table showing some interesting information about the current user. When you have simple, self-contained elements like this, it's often a good idea to move them out into separate template files. For one thing, the example is easier to read without large chunks of HTML obstructing the high-level view. A more important benefit is that we can now reuse this component in any other template where we need to display the same table of information about a user.

Now that you're familiar with what templates look like, let's move on to see how we go about processing them.

Processing Templates

In addition to the *ttree* script mentioned earlier, *tpage* is distributed with the Template Toolkit for no-frills simple template processing.

You might use it like this:

```
panic% tpage myfile.tt2 > myfile.html
```

or:

```
panic% tpage src/myfile.html > dest/myfile.html
```

It is extremely useful as a command-line tool to process a template without having to write any Perl code. However, for most uses, be it an offline script, CGI application, or mod_perl handler, you'll want to hook the Template module into your Perl code.

To see how we would go about this, let us first take one of our earlier examples and save it in a file called *example.html* (see Example D-1).

Example D-1. example1/example.html

```
[% PROCESS header title="Some Interesting Links" %]

<p>
Here are some interesting links:
<ul>
```

Example D-1. example1/example.html (continued)

```
[% FOREACH link = weblinks %]
    <li><a href="[% link.url %]">[% link.title %]</a></li>
[% END %]
</ul>
</p>

[% PROCESS footer %]
```

We're referencing two external templates, *header* and *footer*, so we'll have to create them, too. See Examples D-2 and D-3.

Example D-2. example1/header

```
<html>
<head>
<title>[% title %]</title>
</head>

<body bgcolor="#ffffff">

<h1>[% title %]</h1>
```

Example D-3. example1/footer

```
<div align="center">
[% copyright %]
</div>

</body>
</html>
```

Now we can write a simple Perl script to process *example.html*, as shown in Example D-4.:

Example D-4. example1/process_template.pl

```perl
#!/usr/bin/perl

use strict;
use warnings;
use Template;

# create template processor
my $tt = Template->new( );

# define data
my $data = {
  copyright => '&copy; 2002 Andy Wardley',
  weblinks  => [
      {
        url   => 'http://perl.apache.org/',
        title => 'Apache/mod_perl',
      },
      {
```

Example D-4. example1/process_template.pl (continued)

```
        url   => 'http://tt2.org/',
        title => 'Template Toolkit',
      },
      # ...and so on...
  ]
};

# process template - output to STDOUT by default
$tt->process('example.html', $data)
    || die $tt->error();
```

After loading the Template module (use Template;) we create a Template object via the new( ) constructor method. You can specify all sorts of options, either as a list of named arguments or by reference to a hash array. If, for example, you want to put your templates in a different directory (the default is the current working directory), then you might do something like this:

```
    my $tt = Template->new( INCLUDE_PATH => 'templates' );
```

A more complete example might look like this:

```
    my $tt = Template->new({
        INCLUDE_PATH => [ '/home/stas/web/tt2/templates',
                          '/usr/local/tt2/templates',
                        ],
        PRE_PROCESS  => 'header',
        POST_PROCESS => 'footer',
        INTERPOLATE  => 1,
        POST_CHOMP   => 1,
    });
```

The Template::Manual::Config manpage has full details on the various different configuration options and what they do.

Once you've created a Template object, you can call the process( ) method to process a template. The first argument specifies the template by name (relative to one of the INCLUDE_PATH directories) or as a reference to a file handle or scalar containing the template text. The second optional argument is a reference to a hash array of data that defines the template variables. A third optional argument can also be provided to indicate where the output should be directed, specified as a filename, file handle, reference to a scalar, or object that implements a print( ) method (e.g., an Apache request object $r). By default, the generated output is sent directly to STDOUT.

This is what it looks like:

```
    <html>
    <head>
    <title>Some Interesting Links</title>
    </head>

    <body bgcolor="#ffffff">
```

```
<h1>Some Interesting Links</h1>

<p>
Here are some interesting links:
<ul>
    <li><a href="http://perl.apache.org/">Apache/mod_perl</a></li>
    <li><a href="http://tt2.org/">Template Toolkit</a></li>
</ul>
</p>

<div align="center">
&copy; 2002 Andy Wardley
</div>

</body>
</html>
```

The external templates (*header* and *footer*) have been pulled into place and the title reference in the header and copyright in the *footer* have been correctly resolved. The body of the document is built from the data passed in as weblinks.

Apache/mod_perl Handler

There isn't much to change between the implementation of a Perl CGI script such as the example above and the equivalent Apache/mod_perl handler.

The great advantage of using mod_perl is that it allows you to keep a Template object persistent in memory. The main benefit of this is that Perl can parse and compile all the Template Toolkit code and all your application code once when the server starts, rather than repeating it for each request. The other important benefit is that the Template object will cache previously used templates in a compiled state, from which they can be redeployed extremely quickly. A call to process a template becomes as efficient as a call to a precompiled Perl subroutine (which is indeed how it is implemented under the hood), bringing you runtime machine efficiency as well as the development-time human efficiency and convenience of using a template-driven presentation system.

Example D-5 shows a typical mod_perl handler roughly equivalent to the earlier Perl script.

Example D-5. Apache/MyTemplate.pm

```
package Apache::MyTemplate;

use strict;
use Apache::Constants qw( :common );
use Template;
use vars qw( $TT );
```

Example D-5. Apache/MyTemplate.pm (continued)

```perl
sub handler {
  my $r = shift;

  # create or reuse existing Template object
  $TT ||= Template->new({
      INCLUDE_PATH => '/usr/local/tt2/templates',
  });

  my $data = {
      uri => $r->uri,
      copyright => '&copy; 2002 Andy Wardley',
      weblinks => [
          {
            url   => 'http://perl.apache.org/',
            title => 'Apache/mod_perl',
          },
          {
            url   => 'http://tt2.org/',
            title => 'Template Toolkit',
          },
      ],
      # ...and so on...
  };

  $r->content_type('text/html');
  $r->send_http_header;

  $TT->process('example.html', $data, $r) || do {
      $r->log_reason($TT->error());
      return SERVER_ERROR;
  };

  return OK;
}
1;
```

You need to adjust the value of INCLUDE_PATH to point to the directory where *header*, *example.html*, and *footer* were created.

Here's the configuration section for the *httpd.conf* file:

```
PerlModule Apache::MyTemplate
<Location /example2>
  SetHandler perl-script
  PerlHandler Apache::MyTemplate
</Location>
```

Of course, it's not particularly useful to have the template name hardcoded as it is here, but it illustrates the principle. You can implement whatever kind of strategy you like for mapping requests onto templates, using the filename, path information, or pretty much anything else that takes your fancy. No doubt you can already spot numerous other enhancements that you might make to your own handlers.

Figure D-1 shows what you should expect when issuing a request to /example2.

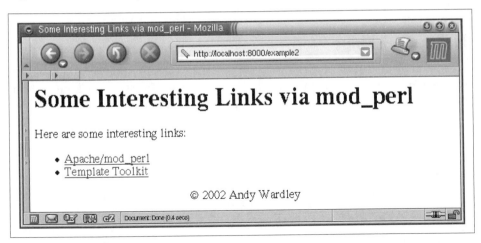

Figure D-1. A sample response

Apache::Template Module

If you're not looking to do anything too adventurous in terms of application process-ing in your handler, the `Apache::Template` module might be all you need to start pro-cessing templates from within an Apache/mod_perl server.

Adding something like the following to your *httpd.conf* file is enough to engage the Template Toolkit to automatically process template files as they are served:

```
PerlModule Apache::Template

# set various configuration options, e.g.
TT2IncludePath /usr/local/tt2/templates
TT2PreProcess  header
TT2PostProcess footer

<Files *.tt2>
  SetHandler  perl-script
  PerlHandler Apache::Template
</Files>
```

We'll come back to `Apache::Template` in the next section. For further examples and guidance on using the module, see the `Apache::Template` documentation.

Hangman Application

In this section we're going to develop a web application based on the classic hang-man example from the O'Reilly book *Writing Apache Modules with Perl and C*. Most of the game logic is borrowed intact or with minor modifications. However, when it comes to generating the HTML pages to return to the client, the script calls on the Template Toolkit to perform the task.

Hangman CGI Script

The first implementation shows a simple all-in-one CGI script that gets the job done quickly and easily. Following that, we'll look at how it can be adapted into a Template Toolkit plug-in and subsequently deployed under mod_perl.

Here's how the CGI script begins:

```
#!/usr/bin/perl
#
# hangman1.pl
#
# This variation of the classic hangman game implements
# the game logic at the start of the CGI script to
# define a game state.  It then processes an all-in-one
# template to generate the HTML page.
#
# The 'state' variable maintains the state of the game.
# It contains the following:
#    word     => the unknown word
#    guessed  => list of the guessed letters
#    gameno   => the number of words the user has tried
#    won      => the number of times the user guessed correctly
#    total    => the total number of incorrect guesses
#    left     => the number of tries the user has left on this turn
#

use IO::File ();
use CGI qw(:standard);
use Template;

use strict;
use constant URL   => '/cgi-bin/hangman1.pl';
use constant ICONS => '/icons/hangman';
use constant WORDS => '/usr/games/hangman-words';
use constant TRIES => 6;
```

Nothing too taxing here. We provide some sensible comments, load the Perl modules we're going to use (including the Template module, of course), and define some constants.

Next comes the core application logic:

```
# retrieve the state
my $state = get_state();

# reinitialize if we need to
$state = initialize($state) if !$state or param('restart');

# process the current guess, if any
my ($message, $status) = process_guess(param('guess') || '', $state );
```

We first call the get_state( ) subroutine to restore any current game state from the CGI parameters. We'll see the definition of that subroutine a little later. For now, all we need to know is that it might return undef, indicating that there isn't any current state. In this case, or if the restart CGI parameter is set, we need to call initialize( ) to set the state to contain some sensible starting values.

Then we call process_guess( ) to process any pending guess. We pass the value of the guess CGI parameter or an empty string if not defined, and also a reference to the $state hash array. The subroutine returns a message and a status value that indicates the current state of play.

Now that we've got the application processing out of the way, we can set about generating some output. To do this, we create a Template object and call its process( ) method, specifying a template to process and a hash reference containing template variables:

```
# create a Template object
my $tt = Template->new( );

# define Template variables
my $vars = {
    url     => URL,
    icons   => ICONS,
    tries   => TRIES,
    title   => 'Template Toolkit Hangman #1',
    state   => $state,
    status  => $status,
    message => $message,
    wordmap => \&wordmap,
};

# process the main template at the end of this file
$tt->process(*DATA, $vars) || die $tt->error( );
```

In this example we're going to define the main template in the __DATA__ section of the CGI script itself. The Template process( ) methods allows a file handle such as *DATA to be specified in place of a template name and will read the content and process it accordingly. Doing this allows us to separate the game logic written in Perl from the presentation template that generates the HTML page, with the benefit of being able to keep everything self-contained in a single file.

That's the main body of the Perl code. Before we look at the template defined at the end of the file, let's look at the subroutine definitions.

The get_state( ) subroutine reads the values of a number of CGI parameters and populates them into the $state hash, which it then returns:

```
sub get_state {
    return undef unless param( );
    my $state = { };
    foreach (qw(word gameno left won total guessed)) {
        $state->{$_} = param($_);
    }
```

```
        return $state;
    }
```

The initialize subroutine is called to start a new game. It picks a new random word and updates the existing $state hash or creates a new one:

```
sub initialize {
    my $state = shift || { };

    # pick a word, any word
    my $list = IO::File->new(WORDS)
        || die "Couldn't open ${\WORDS}: $!\n";
    my $word;
    rand($.) < 1 && ($word = $_) while <$list>;
    chomp $word;

    # setup state
    $state->{word}    = $word;
    $state->{left}    = TRIES;
    $state->{guessed} = '';
    $state->{gameno} += 1;
    $state->{won}    += 0;
    $state->{total}  += 0;
    return $state;
}
```

The process_guess( ) subroutine contains the core of the game logic. It processes the guess passed as the first argument and updates the current state passed as the second. It returns two values: a message for displaying to the user and a status flag indicating the current state of play.

```
sub process_guess {
    my($guess, $state) = @_;

    # lose immediately if user has no more guesses left
    return ('', 'lost') unless $state->{left} > 0;

    my %guessed = map { $_ => 1 } $state->{guessed} =~ /(.)/g;
    my %letters = map { $_ => 1 } $state->{word} =~ /(.)/g;

    # return immediately if user has already guessed the word
    return ('', 'won') unless grep(!$guessed{$_}, keys %letters);

    # do nothing more if no guess
    return ('', 'continue') unless $guess;

    # This section processes individual letter guesses
    $guess = lc $guess;
    return ("Not a valid letter or word!", 'error')
        unless $guess =~ /^[a-z]+$/;
    return ("You already guessed that letter!", 'error')
        if $guessed{$guess};

    # This section is called when the user guesses the whole word
    if (length($guess) > 1 and $guess ne $state->{word}) {
```

```
        $state->{total} += $state->{left};
        return ( qq{Loser!  The word was "$state->{word}."}, 'lost')
    }

    # update the list of guesses
    foreach ($guess =~ /(.)/g) { $guessed{$_}++; }
    $state->{ guessed } = join '', sort keys %guessed;

    # correct guess -- word completely filled in
    unless (grep(!$guessed{$_}, keys %letters)) {
        $state->{won}++;
        return (qq{Bingola!  The word was "$state->{word}."}, 'won');
    }

    # incorrect guess
    if (!$letters{$guess}) {
        $state->{total}++;
        $state->{left}--;
        # user out of turns
        return (qq{The jig is up!  The word was "$state->{word}".}, 'lost')
            if $state->{left} <= 0;
        # user still has some turns
        return ('Wrong guess!', 'continue');
    }

    # correct guess but word still incomplete
    return (qq{Good guess!}, 'continue');

}
```

In addition to these subroutines that are called from Perl, we also define wordmap( ) and bind it by reference to the corresponding wordmap template argument. This allows it to be called from within the template.

```
sub wordmap {
    my($word, $guessed) = @_;
        my %guessed = map { $_ => 1 } $guessed =~ /(.)/g;
        join '', map { $guessed{$_} ? "$_ " : '_ ' } $word =~ /(.)/g;
}
```

The subroutine expects to be passed the current word and a string containing the letters previously guessed. It returns a string representing the word with only the guessed letters shown and the others blanked out.

At the end of the script, we have the template that is processed to generate the HTML output. Notice that it follows the __DATA__ marker, which Perl will automatically bind to the *DATA file handle that we passed as the first argument to the process( ) method.[*]

---

[*] The drawback of using the __DATA__ marker is that you cannot run this script under Apache::Registry, as we explained in Chapter 6. However, the script can be easily converted into a mod_perl handler, which has no problems with the __DATA__ marker.

In the opening segment, we first define the content type and general HTML headers. This is followed by a directive that defines a particular format for displaying floating-point numbers, done by means of a standard format plug-in loaded via the USE directive. We then go on to calculate the number of tries remaining and the current game averages, storing them in a hash array named average:

```
__DATA__
Content-type: text/html

<!DOCTYPE HTML PUBLIC "-//W3C//DTD HTML 3.2 Final//EN">
<html>
<head>
  <title>[% title %]</title>
</head>

<body onload="if (document.gf) document.gf.guess.focus()">
[%
    # define a format for displaying averages
    USE format('%2.3f');

    # how many guesses left to go?
    tries_left = tries - state.left

    # calculate current averages
    average = {
      current = state.total / state.gameno
      overall = state.gameno > 1
        ? ( state.total - (tries - state.left)) / (state.gameno - 1)
        : 0
    }
%]
```

This next section displays the game title and the appropriate image for the number of tries left. It then generates a table to display the current game averages. Note that the format is now used to display the floating-point averages to a fixed precision.

```
<h1>[% title %]</h1>

<img src="[% icons %]/h[% tries_left %].gif"
     align="left" alt="[[% tries_left %] tries left]" />

<table width="100%">
<tr>
  <td><b>Word #: [% state.gameno %]</b></td>
  <td><b>Guessed: [% state.guessed %]</b></td>
</tr>
<tr>
  <td><b>Won: [% state.won %]</b></td>
  <td><b>Current average: [% format(average.current) %]</b></td>
  <td><b>Overall average: [% format(average.overall) %]</b></td>
</tr>
</table>
```

This is where we display the current word with unguessed letters blanked out. We're using the `wordmap` variable, which results in a call back to our `wordmap` subroutine. We pass the current word and string of guessed letters as arguments:

```
<h2>Word: [% wordmap(state.word, state.guessed) %]</h2>
```

Is there a message to display? If so, this code makes it stand out as a red level-2 heading; otherwise, it does nothing.

```
[% IF message -%]
<h2><font color="red">[% message %]</font></h2>
[% END %]
```

Now we can generate the input form:

```
<form method="post" action="[% url %]" name="gf"
      enctype="application/x-www-form-urlencoded">

[% FOREACH var = [ 'word' 'gameno' 'left'
                   'won' 'total' 'guessed' ]
-%]
<input type="hidden" name="[% var %]" value="[% state.$var %]" />
[% END %]
```

We're taking the simple approach and using hidden form variables to maintain the state of the game between requests. The FOREACH loop shown above generates these fields for each of `state.word`, `state.gameno`, `state.left`, `state.won`, `state.total`, and `state.guessed`. Rather than spelling out each one, it uses an interpolated variable, `state.$var`. The leading `$` means that the value of the `var` variable is used to specify the intended item in `state`. In Perl, this would be just like writing `$state->{ $var }`.

```
[% IF status == 'won' or status == 'lost' %]
    Do you want to play again?
    <input type="submit" name="restart" value="Another game" />
[% ELSE %]
    Your guess: <input type="text" name="guess" />
    <input type="submit" name=".submit" value="Guess" />
[% END %]

</form>
```

If the current game status is "won" or "lost", the game is over and we generate a button allowing the player to start a new game. Otherwise, it's business as usual and we generate an input field for the guess before closing up the form.

Finally, we have the page footer to add some trailing text and tidy up everything nicely:

```
<br clear="all">
<hr />

<a href="[% url %]">Home</a>
```

```
<p>
  <cite style="fontsize: 10pt">graphics courtesy Andy Wardley</cite>
</p>

</body>
</html>
```

And that's it! We now have a self-contained CGI script that can be installed and run from a *cgi-bin* directory with little or no configuration required (see Figure D-2).

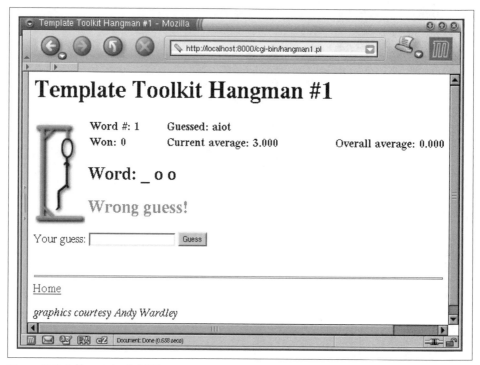

Figure D-2. Self-contained CGI hangman

Hangman with Modular Templates

Perhaps the biggest limitation of the previous example is that the presentation template isn't at all modular. In this example, we're going to split the one large template into a number of smaller ones placed in separate files. This makes the main template much simpler and easier to follow. It also allows each of the individual template components to be updated in isolation. If you want to change the display of the game averages, for example, then you just need to edit the *status* template and can leave everything else as it is.

We're also going to use a standard *html/page* template, provided as part of the Template Toolkit, to generate the required container elements to make a valid HTML page. The default location for these templates is */usr/local/tt2/templates*. You will also need to define the directory in which you're going to put the hangman templates. So, to the top of the previous script, we can add the following constant definitions (tailor them to your local values, of course):

```
use constant TEMPLATES => '/home/stas/templates/hangman2';
use constant SHARED    => '/usr/local/tt2/templates';
```

Then, when we create the Template object, we specify these directories as a list reference for the INCLUDE_PATH option:

```
# create a Template object
my $tt = Template->new({
    INCLUDE_PATH => [ TEMPLATES, SHARED ],
});
```

The rest of the script remains the same, with exception of the template specified in the __DATA__ section. This can now be written as:

```
__DATA__
Content-type: text/html

[% WRAPPER html/page
      html.head.title  = title
      html.body.onload = 'if (document.gf) document.gf.guess.focus()'
%]

[% PROCESS header %]

[% IF status == 'won' or status == 'lost';
      PROCESS restart;
   ELSE;
      PROCESS guess;
   END
%]

[% PROCESS footer %]

[% END %]
```

We've moved the *header*, the *footer*, and the two different variants of the form out into separate templates. The entire page is enclosed within a WRAPPER block, which generates the required <html>, <head>, and <body> tags to wrap around the page using the standard *html/page* template.

The external *header* and *footer* templates are shown in Examples D-6 and D-7. According to the value of TEMPLATES set above, these should be located in */home/stas/templates/hangman*.

Example D-6. hangman2/templates/header

```
<h1>[% title %]</h1>

[% # how many guesses left to go?
   tries_left = tries - state.left
```

Example D-6. hangman2/templates/header (continued)

```
%]

[%# display the appropriate image -%]
<img src="[% icons %]/h[% tries_left %].gif"
     align="left" alt="[[% tries_left %] tries left]" />

[% # display the game averages
   PROCESS status
%]
```

Example D-7. hangman2/templates/footer

```
<br clear="all">
<hr />

<a href="[% url %]">Home</a>

<p>
  <cite style="fontsize: 10pt">graphics courtesy Andy Wardley</cite>
</p>
```

Hangman Plug-in

To take our example a stage further, we're going to convert this simple application into a Template Toolkit plug-in module. A plug-in is just like any other Perl module, except that it lives in a special namespace (Template::Plugin::*) and gets passed a reference to a special variable, the context, when its new( ) constructor is called. Plug-ins can be loaded and used via the USE directive. Here's what the module looks like:[*]

```
#-------------------------------------------------------------------
# Template::Plugin::Games::Hangman
#
# Implementation of the classic hangman game written as a
# plug-in module for the Template Toolkit.
#
# Written by Andy Wardley.
#-------------------------------------------------------------------

package Template::Plugin::Games::Hangman;

use strict;
use Template::Plugin;
use Template::Exception;
use IO::File ();
use CGI;

use base qw( Template::Plugin );
```

---

[*] The code assumes that Perl 5.6.0 or higher is used. If you are using an older version, use the vars pragma instead of our.

```
our $URL    = '/cgi-bin/hangman';
our $ICONS  = '/icons/hangman';
our $WORDS  = '/usr/games/hangman-words';
our $TRIES  = 6;
our @STATE  = qw( word gameno left won total guessed );
```

The start of the module is very similar to the CGI script. In this case we're defining everything to be in the Template::Plugin::Games::Hangman namespace and specifying that it is a subclass of the Template::Plugin module.

```
sub new {
    my($class, $context, $config) = @_;

    # create plugin object
    my $self = bless {
        cgi      => CGI->new(),
        url      => $config->{ url   } || $URL,
        icons    => $config->{ icons } || $ICONS,
        words    => $config->{ words } || $WORDS,
        tries    => $config->{ tries } || $TRIES,
        _context => $context,
    }, $class;

    # restore current game or start new game
    $self->restore() || $self->init();

    return $self;
}
```

When the plug-in is loaded via a USE directive, the new() constructor method is called. The first (zeroth) argument is the calling class name, Template::Plugin:: Games::Hangman->new($context, $config), passed as a reference to a context object through which you can access the functionality of the Template Toolkit. The second argument is a reference to a hash array of any configuration items specified with the USE directive.

This method defines an object, $self, using values defined in the $config hash or the defaults specified in the appropriate package variables. It then calls the restore() method and, if restore() doesn't return a true value, the init() method. Here are the definitions of those methods:

```
sub restore {
    my $self = shift;
    my $cgi  = $self->{ cgi };
    return undef if !$cgi->param();
    $self->{ $_ } = $cgi->param($_) foreach @STATE;
    return undef if $cgi->param('restart');
    return $self;
}

sub init {
    my $self = shift;
```

```
    # pick a word, any word
    my $list = IO::File->new($WORDS)
        || die "failed to open '$WORDS' : $!\n";
    my $word;
    rand($.) < 1 && ($word = $_) while <$list>;
    chomp $word;

    $self->{ word    }  = $word;
    $self->{ left    }  = $self->{ tries };
    $self->{ guessed }  = '';
    $self->{ gameno  } += 1;
    $self->{ won     } += 0;
    $self->{ total   } += 0;
    return $self;
}
```

They are just like their counterparts in the earlier CGI script, with a few minor exceptions. A CGI object is defined in $self->{ cgi } rather than using imported subroutines, and operations are performed on $self rather than on a $state hash array passed as an argument.

The guess( ) method is also very similar to the process_guess( ) subroutine in the CGI script:

```
sub guess {
    my $self  = shift;
    my $cgi   = $self->{ cgi };
    my $guess = $cgi->param('guess') || return;

    # lose immediately if user out of guesses
    return $self->state('lost')
        unless $self->{ left } > 0;

    my %guessed = map { $_ => 1 } $self->{ guessed } =~ /(.)/g;
    my %letters = map { $_ => 1 } $self->{ word    } =~ /(.)/g;

    # return immediately if user has already guessed the word
    return $self->state('won')
        unless grep(! $guessed{ $_ }, keys %letters);

    # do nothing more if no guess
    return $self->state('continue') unless $guess;

    # process individual letter guesses
    $guess = lc $guess;
    return $self->state(continue => 'Not a valid letter or word!')
        unless $guess =~ /^[a-z]+$/;
    return $self->state(continue => 'You already guessed that letter!')
        if $guessed{$guess};

    # handle the user guessing the whole word
    if (length($guess) > 1 and $guess ne $self->{word}) {
        $self->{ total } += $self->{ left };
        return $self->state(lost => "You lose.  The word was $self->{word}.");
    }
```

```
# update the list of guesses and word map
foreach ($guess =~ /(.)/g) { $guessed{$_}++; }
$self->{ guessed } = join '', sort keys %guessed;

# correct guess -- word completely filled in
unless (grep(!$guessed{$_}, keys %letters)) {
    $self->{ won }++;
    return $self->state(won => qq{You got it!  The word was "$self->{word}".});
}

# incorrect guess
if (!$letters{$guess}) {
    $self->{total}++;
    $self->{left}--;
    return $self->state(lost =>
        qq{No dice, dude! The word was "$self->{word}".})
            if $self->{left} <= 0;
    return $self->state(continue => 'Wrong guess!');
}

# correct guess but word still incomplete
return $self->state(continue => 'Good guess!');
}
```

As a matter of convenience, we also provide the state( ) method, to retrieve the current state (when called without arguments) or set both state and message (when called with one or more arguments):

```
sub state {
    my $self = shift;
    if (@_) {
        $self->{ state   } = shift;
        $self->{ message } = join('', @_);
    }
    else {
        return $self->{ state };
    }
}
```

We also define averages( ) and wordmap( ) as object methods:

```
sub averages {
    my $self = shift;
    return {
        current => $self->{ total } / $self->{ gameno },
        overall => $self->{ gameno } > 1
            ? ($self->{ total } + $self->{ left } - $self->{ tries })
            / ($self->{ gameno } - 1)
            : 0
    };
}

sub wordmap {
    my $self = shift;
    my %guessed = map { $_ => 1 } $self->{ guessed } =~ /(.)/g;
```

```
            join ' ', map { $guessed{$_} ? "$_ " : '_ ' }
                $self->{ word } =~ /(.)/g;
    }
```

We can also encode the high-level game logic in a method:

```
    sub play {
        my $self = shift;

        # process any current guess
        $self->guess();

        # determine which form to use based on state
        my $form = (exists $self->{ state } &&
                        $self->{ state } =~ /^won|lost$/)
            ? 'restart' : 'guess';

        # process the three templates: header, form and footer
        $self->{ _context }->include([ 'header', $form, 'footer' ]);
    }
```

The play( ) method calls guess( ) to process a guess and then calls on the context object that we previously saved in _context to process three templates: the *header* template, the form relevant to the current game state, and the *footer* template.

The script that uses this plug-in can now be made even simpler, as shown in Example D-8.

Example D-8. hangman3.pl

```
#!/usr/bin/perl
#
# hangman3.pl
#
# CGI script using Template Toolkit Hangman plug-in.
#

use strict;
use Template;

# may need to tell Perl where to find plug-in module
use lib qw( /usr/local/tt2/hangman/hangman3/perl5lib );

use constant TEMPLATES => '/home/stas/templates/hangman3';
use constant SHARED    => '/usr/local/tt2/templates';
use constant URL       => '/cgi-bin/hangman3.pl';
use constant ICONS     => '/icons/hangman';
use constant WORDS     => '/usr/games/hangman-words';

# create a Template object
my $tt = Template->new({
    INCLUDE_PATH => [ TEMPLATES, SHARED ],
});
```

Example D-8. hangman3.pl (continued)

```
# define Template variables
my $vars = {
    url   => URL,
    icons => ICONS,
    words => WORDS,
    title => 'Template Toolkit Hangman #3',
};

# process the main template
$tt->process(*DATA, $vars)
    || die $tt->error();
```

Other than creating a Template object and defining variables, we don't need to do any special processing relevant to the hangman application. That is now handled entirely by the plug-in.

The template defined in the __DATA__ section can be made to look very similar to the earlier example. In this case, we're loading the plug-in (Games.Hangman, corresponding to Template::Plugin::Games::Hangman) and aliasing the object returned from new( ) to the hangman variable. We manually call the guess( ) method and PROCESS external templates according to the game state:

```
__DATA__
Content-type: text/html

[% WRAPPER html/page
        html.head.title = title
        html.body.onload = 'if (document.gf) document.gf.guess.focus()';

    TRY;
        # load the hangman plug-in
        USE hangman = Games.Hangman(
            words = words
            icons = icons
            url   = url
        );

        # process a guess
        CALL hangman.guess;

        # print header showing game averages
        PROCESS header;

        # process the right form according to game state
        IF hangman.state == 'won'
        OR hangman.state == 'lost';
            PROCESS restart;
        ELSE;
            PROCESS guess;
        END;
```

```
          # now print the footer
          PROCESS footer;
     CATCH;
          # and if any of that goes wrong...
          CLEAR;
          PROCESS error;
     END;
   END
%]
```

One other enhancement we've made is to enclose the body in a TRY block. If the plug-in init( ) method fails to open the words file, it reports the error via die( ). The TRY directive allows this error to be caught and handled in the corresponding CATCH block. This clears any output generated in the TRY block before the error occured and processes an *error* template instead to report the error in a nice manner.

The template in this example controls the overall flow of the game logic. If you prefer, you can simply call the play( ) method and have the plug-in take control. It handles all the flow control for you, processing the guess and then making calls back into the Template Toolkit to process the *header*, relevant form, and *footer* templates.

```
__DATA__
Content-type: text/html

[%  #Template Toolkit Hangman #4
      WRAPPER html/page
      html.head.title  = title
      html.body.onload = 'if (document.gf) document.gf.guess.focus( )';

      TRY;
          USE hangman = Games.Hangman(
              words = words
              icons = icons
              url   = url
          );
          hangman.play;

      CATCH;
          CLEAR;
          PROCESS error;
      END;
   END
%]
```

The complete set of templates that go with this final example are presented in Examples D-9 through D-15.

Example D-9. hangman3/templates/header

```
<h1>[% title %]</h1>

[% # how many guesses left to go?
   tries_left = hangman.tries - hangman.left
%]

[%# display the appropriate image -%]
<img src="[% hangman.icons %]/h[% tries_left %].gif"
     align="left" alt="[[% tries_left %] tries left]" />

[% PROCESS status %]
```

Example D-10. hangman3/templates/status

```
[% # define a format for displaying averages
   USE format('%2.3f');
   average = hangman.averages;
%]

<table width="100%">
<tr>
  <td><b>Word #: [% hangman.gameno %]</b></td>
  <td><b>Guessed: [% hangman.guessed %]</b></td>
</tr>
<tr>
  <td><b>Won: [% hangman.won %]</b></td>
  <td><b>Current average: [% format(average.current) %]</b></td>
  <td><b>Overall average: [% format(average.overall) %]</b></td>
</tr>
</table>

<h2>Word: [% hangman.wordmap %]</h2>

[% IF hangman.message -%]
<h2><font color="red">[% hangman.message %]</font></h2>
[% END %]
```

Example D-11. hangman3/templates/guess

```
<form method="post" action="[% hangman.url %]"
      enctype="application/x-www-form-urlencoded" name="gf">
  Your guess: <input type="text" name="guess" />
  <input type="submit" name=".submit" value="Guess" />
  [% PROCESS state %]
</form>
```

Example D-12. hangman3/templates/restart

```
<form method="post" action="[% hangman.url %]"
      enctype="application/x-www-form-urlencoded">
  Do you want to play again?
  <input type="submit" name="restart" value="Another game" />
  [% PROCESS state %]
</form>
```

Example D-13. hangman3/templates/state

```
[% FOREACH var = [ 'word' 'gameno' 'left' 'won' 'total' 'guessed' ] -%]
<input type="hidden" name="[% var %]" value="[% hangman.$var %]" />
[% END %]
```

Example D-14. hangman3/templates/footer

```
<br clear="all">
<hr />
<a href="[% hangman.url %]">Home</a>
<p>
  <cite style="fontsize: 10pt">graphics courtesy Andy Wardley</cite>
</p>
```

Example D-15. hangman3/templates/error

```
<h3>Hangman Offline</h3>
<p>
Hangman is unfortunately offline at present, reporting sick with
the following lame excuse:
<ul>
<li><b>[[% error.type %]]</b> [% error.info %]</li>
</ul>
</p>
```

Self-Contained Hangman Template

One of the benefits of writing the hangman application as a plug-in is that you no longer need to write a CGI script at all. You can load and use the plug-in from any template, which you can process via a generic CGI script, a mod_perl handler, or perhaps the Apache::Template module.

Here's an example of a self-contained template using the hangman plug-in. All we need to do is to hardcode some variable values at the start of the template:

```
[%  title = 'Template Toolkit Hangman #5'
    url   = '/tt2/hangman.html'
    words = '/usr/games/hangman-words'
    icons = '/icons/hangman';
```

```
    WRAPPER html/page
        html.head.title  = title
        html.body.onload = 'if (document.gf) document.gf.guess.focus()';

        TRY;
            USE hangman = Games.Hangman(
                words = words
                icons = icons
                url   = url
            );
            hangman.play;
        CATCH;
            CLEAR;
            PROCESS error;
        END;
    END
%]
```

If you're using Apache::Template to run the application, you can define these variables in the Apache *httpd.conf* file:

```
PerlModule        Apache::Template

TT2IncludePath    /usr/local/tt2/hangman/hangman3/templates
TT2IncludePath    /usr/local/tt2/templates
TT2Variable       title  "Template Toolkit Hangman #5"
TT2Variable       words  /usr/games/hangman-words
TT2Variable       icons  /icons/hangman
TT2Params         uri

<Location /tt2/hangman.html>
    SetHandler      perl-script
    PerlHandler     Apache::Template
</Location>
```

Our three variables, title, words, and icons, are defined using the TT2Variable directive. In addition, we use TT2Params to instruct Apache::Template to make the request URI available as the uri template variable. We previously used url to denote the URL of the hangman application, so we need to make one small change to the template. Using this dynamic uri variable should mean that the value will remain correct even if the application is moved to a new URL. The template should now look like this:

```
[%
    # ...etc...

    USE hangman = Games.Hangman(
        words   = words
        icons   = icons
        url     = uri      # now use 'uri' not 'url'
    );

    # ...etc...
%]
```

The game in Figure D-3 is for you to complete.

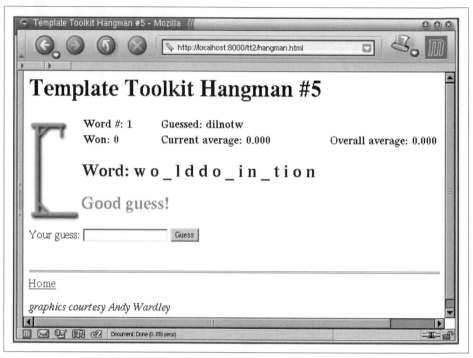

Figure D-3. White to play and mate in three moves

References

This chapter deals with a lot of code, some of which was included in listings and some of which was not because it was too long. You can get all the code and configuration files from *http://modperlbook.org/*.

- Template Toolkit home: *http://www.template-toolkit.org/*
- Template Toolkit documentation: *http://www.template-toolkit.org/docs.html*
- If you have any questions related to the Template Toolkit that the module documentation can't immediately answer, you might like to post them to the Template Toolkit mailing list. To subscribe, send an email to *templatesrequest@template-toolkit.org* with the message "subscribe" in the body or use the web form located at *http://www.template-toolkit.org/mailman/listinfo/templates/*.

The AxKit XML Application Server

AxKit is an XML application server written using the mod_perl framework. At its core, AxKit provides the developer with many ways to set up server-side XML transformations. This allows you to rapidly develop sites that use XML, allowing delivery of the same content in different formats. It also allows you to change the layout of your site very easily, due to the forced separation of content from presentation.

This appendix gives an overview of the ways you can put AxKit to use on your mod_perl-enabled server. It is not a complete description of all the capabilities of AxKit. For more detailed information, please take a look at the documentation provided on the AxKit web site at *http://axkit.org/*. Commercial support and consultancy services for AxKit also are available at this site.

There are a number of benefits of using XML for content delivery:

- Perhaps the most obvious benefit is the longevity of your data. XML is a format that is going to be around for a very long time, and if you use XML, your data (the content of your site) can be processed using standard tools for multiple platforms and languages for years to come.

- If you use XSLT as a templating solution, you can pick from a number of different implementations. This allows you to easily switch between tools that best suit your task at hand.

- XSLT takes a fundamentally different approach to templating than almost every other Perl templating solution. Rather than focusing on "sandwiching" the data into the template at various positions, XSLT transforms a tree representation of your data into another tree. This not only makes the output (in the case of HTML) less prone to mismatched tags, but it also makes chained processing, in which the output of one transformation becomes the input of another, a lot simpler and faster.

Installing and Configuring AxKit

There are many configuration options that allow you to customize your AxKit installation, but in this section we aim to get you started as quickly and simply as possible. This appendix assumes you already have mod_perl and Apache installed and working. See Chapter 3 if this is not the case. This section does not cover installing AxKit on Win32 systems, for which there is an ActiveState package at *ftp://theoryx5. uwinnipeg.ca/pub/other/ppd/*.

First download the latest version of AxKit, which you can get either from your local CPAN archive or from the AxKit download directory at *http://axkit.org/*. Then type the following:

```
panic% gunzip -c AxKit-x.xx.tar.gz | tar xvf -
panic% cd AxKit-x.xx.tar.gz
panic% perl Makefile.PL
panic% make
panic% make test
panic% su
panic# make install
```

If Perl's *Makefile.PL* warns you about missing modules, notably XML::XPath, make a note of the missing modules and install them from CPAN. AxKit will run without the missing modules, but without XML::XPath it will be impossible to run the examples in this appendix.*

Now we need to add some simple options to the very end of our *httpd.conf* file:

```
PerlModule AxKit
SetHandler perl-script
PerlHandler AxKit
AxDebugLevel 10
PerlSetVar AxXPSInterpolate 1
```

This configuration makes it look as though AxKit will deliver all of your files, but don't worry: if it doesn't detect XML at the URL you supply, it will let *httpd* deliver the content. If you're still concerned, put all but the first configuration directive in a <Location> section. Note that the first line, PerlModule AxKit, must appear in *httpd. conf* outside of any runtime configuration blocks. Otherwise, Apache cannot see the AxKit configuration directives and you will get errors when you try to start *httpd*.

Now, assuming you have XML::XPath installed (try *perl -MXML::XPath -e0* on the command line to check), restart Apache. You are now ready to begin publishing transformed XML with AxKit!

---

* AxKit is very flexible in how it lets you transform the XML on the server, and there are many modules you can plug in to AxKit to allow you to do these transformations. For this reason, the AxKit installation does not mandate any particular modules to use. Instead, it will simply suggest modules that might help when you install AxKit.

Your First AxKit Page

Now we're going to see how AxKit works, by transforming an XML file containing data about Camelids (note the dubious Perl reference) into HTML.

First you will need a sample XML file. Open the text editor of your choice and type the code shown in Example E-1.

Example E-1. firstxml.xml

```
<?xml version="1.0"?>
<dromedaries>
  <species name="Camel">
    <humps>1 or 2</humps>
    <disposition>Cranky</disposition>
  </species>
  <species name="Llama">
    <humps>1</humps>
    <disposition>Aloof</disposition>
  </species>
  <species name="Alpaca">
    <humps>(see Llama)</humps>
    <disposition>Friendly</disposition>
  </species>
</dromedaries>
```

Save this file in your web server document root (e.g., */home/httpd/httpd_perl/htdocs/*) as *firstxml.xml*.

Now we need a stylesheet to transform the XML to HTML. For this first example we are going to use XPathScript, an XML transformation language specific to AxKit. Later we will give a brief introduction to XSLT.

Create a new file and type the code shown in Example E-2.

Example E-2. firstxml.xps

```
<%
$t->{'humps'}{pre} = "<td>";
$t->{'humps'}{post} = "</td>";
$t->{'disposition'}{pre} = "<td>";
$t->{'disposition'}{post} = "</td>";
$t->{'species'}{pre} = "<tr><td>{\@name}</td>";
$t->{'species'}{post} = "</tr>";
%>
<html>
<head>
<title>Know Your Dromedaries</title>
</head>
<body>
  <table border="1">
    <tr><th>Species</th>
        <th>No. of Humps</th>
```

Example E-2. firstxml.xps (continued)

```
        <th>Disposition</th></tr>
    <%= apply_templates('/dromedaries/species') %>
  </table>
</body>
</html>
```

Save this file as *firstxml.xps*.

Now to get the original file, *firstxml.xml*, to be transformed on the server by *text.xps*, we need to somehow associate that file with the stylesheet. Under AxKit there are a number of ways to do that, with varying flexibility. The simplest way is to edit your *firstxml.xml* file and, immediately after the `<?xml version="1.0"?>` declaration, add the following:

```
<?xml-stylesheet href="firstxml.xps"
                 type="application/x-xpathscript"?>
```

Now assuming the files are both in the same directory under your *httpd* document root, you should be able to make a request for *text.xml* and see server-side transformed XML in your browser. Now try changing the source XML file, and watch AxKit detect the change next time you load the file in the browser.

If Something Goes Wrong

If you don't see HTML in your browser but instead get the source XML, you will need to check your error log. (In Internet Explorer you will see a tree-based representation of the XML, and in Mozilla, Netscape, or Opera you will see all the text of the document joined together.)

AxKit sends out varying amounts of debug information depending on the value of AxDebugLevel (which we set to the maximum value of 10). If you can't decipher the contents of the error log, contact the AxKit user's mailing list at *axkit-users@axkit.org* with details of your problem.

How it Works?

The stylesheet above specifies how the various tags work. The ASP `<% %>` syntax delimits Perl code from HTML. You can execute any code within the stylesheet.

In this example, we use the special XPathScript $t hash reference, which specifies the names of tags and how they should be output to the browser. There are several options for the second level of the hash, and here we see two of those options: pre and post. pre and post specify (respectfully) what appears before the tag and what appears after it. These values in $t take effect only when we call the apply_templates() function, which iterates over the nodes in the XML, executing the matching values in $t.

XPath

One of the key specifications being used in XML technologies is XPath. This is a little language used within other languages for selecting nodes within an XML document (just as regular expressions is a language of its own within Perl). The initial appearance of an XPath is similar to that of a Unix directory path. In Example E-2 we can see the XPath */dromedaries/species*, which starts at the root of the document, finds the *dromedaries* root element, then finds the species *children* of the *dromedaries* element. Note that unlike Unix directory paths, XPaths can match multiple nodes; so in the case above, we select all of the *species* elements in the document.

Documenting all of XPath here would take up many pages. The grammar for XPath allows many constructs of a full programming language, such as functions, string literals, and Boolean expressions. What's important to know is that the syntax we are using to find nodes in our XML documents is not just something invented for AxKit!

Dynamic Content

AxKit has a flexible tool called *eXtensible Server Pages* (XSP) for creating XML from various data sources such as relational databases, cookies, and form parameters. This technology was originally invented by the Apache Cocoon team, and AxKit shares their syntax. This allows easier migration of projects to and from Cocoon. (Cocoon allows you to embed Java code in your XSP, similar to how AxKit allows you to embed Perl code.)

XSP is an XML-based syntax that uses namespaces to provide extensibility. In many ways, this is like the Cold Fusion model of using tags to provide dynamic functionality. One of the advantages of using XSP is that it is impossible to generate invalid XML, which makes it ideal for use in an XML framework such as AxKit. Another is that the tags can hide complex functionality, allowing the XSP tags to be added by designers and freeing programmers to perform more complex and more cost-effective tasks.

The XSP framework allows you to design new tags, or use ones provided already by others on CPAN. These extra tags are called *taglibs*. By using taglibs instead of embedding Perl code in your XSP page, you can further build on AxKit's separation of content from presentation by separating out logic too. And creating new taglibs is almost trivial using AxKit's `TagLibHelper` module, which hides all the details for you.

In the examples below, we are going to show some code that embeds Perl code in the XSP pages. This is not a recommended practice, due to the ease with which you can extract functionality into tag libraries. However, it is more obvious to Perl programmers what is going on this way and provides a good introduction to the technology.

Handling Form Parameters

The AxKit::XSP::Param taglib allows you to easily read form and query string parameters within an XSP page. The following example shows how a page can submit back to itself. To allow this to work, add the following to your *httpd.conf* file:

```
AxAddXSPTaglib AxKit::XSP::Param
```

The XSP page is shown in Example E-3.

Example E-3. paramtaglib.xsp

```
<xsp:page
 xmlns:xsp="http://apache.org/xsp/core/v1"
 xmlns:param="http://axkit.org/NS/xsp/param/v1"
 language="Perl"
>
<page>
  <xsp:logic>
  if (<param:name/>) {
    <xsp:content>
     Your name is: <param:name/>
    </xsp:content>
  }
  else {
    <xsp:content>
      <form>
        Enter your name: <input type="text" name="name" />
        <input type="submit"/>
      </form>
    </xsp:content>
  }
  </xsp:logic>
</page>
</xsp:page>
```

The most significant thing about this example is how we freely mix XML tags with our Perl code, and the XSP processor figures out the right thing to do depending on the context. The only requirement is that the XSP page itself must be valid XML. That is, the following would generate an error:

```
<xsp:logic>
my $page = <param:page/>;
if ($page < 3) { # ERROR: less-than is a reserved character in XML
 ...
}
</xsp:logic>
```

We need to convert this to valid XML before XSP can handle it. There are a number of ways to do so. The simplest is just to reverse the expression to if (3 > $page), because the greater-than sign is valid within an XML text section. Another way is to encode the less-than sign as <, which will be familiar to HTML authors.

The other thing to notice is the `<xsp:logic>` and `<xsp:content>` tags. The former defines a section of Perl code, while the latter allows you to go back to processing the contents as XML output. Also note that the `<xsp:content>` tag is not always needed. Because the XSP engine inherently understands XML, you can omit the `<xsp:content>` tag when the immediate child would be an element, rather than text. For example, the following example requires the `<xsp:content>` tag:

```
<xsp:logic>
if (<param:name/>) {
  # xsp:content needed
  <xsp:content>
  Your name is: <param:name/>
  </xsp:content>
}
</xsp:logic>
```

But if you rewrote it like this, it wouldn't, because of the surrounding non-XSP tag:

```
<xsp:logic>
if (<param:name/>) {
  # no xsp:content tag needed
  <p>Your name is: <param:name/></p>
}
</xsp:logic>
```

Note that the initial example, when processed by only the XSP engine, will output the following XML:

```
<page>
  <form>
    Enter your name: <input type="text" name="name" />
    <input type="submit"/>
  </form>
</page>
```

This needs to be processed with XSLT or XPathScript to be reasonably viewable in a browser. However, the point is that you can reuse the above page as either HTML or WML just by applying different stylesheets.

Handling Cookies

`AxKit::XSP::Cookie` is a taglib interface to `Apache::Cookie` (part of the *libapreq* package). The following example demonstrates both retrieving and setting a cookie from within XSP. In order for this to run, the following option needs to be added to your *httpd.conf* file:

```
AxAddXSPTaglib AxKit::XSP::Cookie
```

The XSP page is shown in Example E-4.

Example E-4. cookietaglib.xsp

```
<xsp:page
 xmlns:xsp="http://apache.org/xsp/core/v1"
 xmlns:cookie="http://axkit.org/NS/xsp/cookie/v1"
 language="Perl"
>
<page>
  <xsp:logic>
  my $value;
  if ($value = <cookie:fetch name="count"/>) {
    $value++;
  }
  else {
    $value = 1;
  }
  </xsp:logic>
  <cookie:create name="count">
    <cookie:value><xsp:expr>$value</xsp:expr></cookie:value>
  </cookie:create>
  <p>Cookie value: <xsp:expr>$value</xsp:expr></p>
</page>
</xsp:page>
```

This page introduces the concept of XSP *expressions*, using the <xsp:expr> tag. In XSP, everything that returns a value is an expression of some sort. In the last two examples, we have used a taglib tag within a Perl if( ) statement. These tags are both expressions, even though they don't use the <xsp:expr> syntax. In XSP, everything understands its context and tries to do the right thing. The following three examples will all work as expected:

```
<cookie:value>3</cookie:value>

<cookie:value><xsp:expr>2 + 1</xsp:expr></cookie:value>

<cookie:value><param:cookie_value/></cookie:value>
```

We see this as an extension of how Perl works—the idea of "Do What I Mean," or DWIM.

Sending Email

With the AxKit::XSP::Sendmail taglib, it is very simple to send email from an XSP page. This taglib combines email-address verification, using the Email::Valid module, with email sending, using the Mail::Sendmail module (which will either interface to an SMTP server or use the *sendmail* executable directly). Again, to allow usage of this taglib, the following line must be added to *httpd.conf*:

```
AxAddXSPTaglib AxKit::XSP::Sendmail
```

Then sending email from XSP is as simple as what's shown in Example E-5.

Example E-5. sendmailtaglib.xsp

```
<xsp:page
 xmlns:xsp="http://apache.org/xsp/core/v1"
 xmlns:param="http://axkit.org/NS/xsp/param/v1"
 xmlns:mail="http://axkit.org/NS/xsp/sendmail/v1"
 language="Perl"
>
<page>
  <xsp:logic>
  if (!<param:email/>) {
    <p>You forgot to supply an email address!</p>
  }
  else {
    my $to;
    if (<param:subopt/> eq "sub") {
      $to = "axkit-users-subscribe@axkit.org";
    }
    elsif (<param:subopt/> eq "unsub") {
      $to = "axkit-users-unsubscribe@axkit.org";
    }
    <mail:send-mail>
     <mail:from><param:user_email/></mail:from>
     <mail:to><xsp:expr>$to</xsp:expr></mail:to>
     <mail:body>
      Subscribe or Unsubscribe <param:user_email/>
     </mail:body>
    </mail:send-mail>
    <p>(un)subscription request sent</p>
  }
  </xsp:logic>
</page>
</xsp:page>
```

The only thing missing here is some sort of error handling. When the *sendmail* taglib detects an error (either in an email address or in sending the email), it throws an exception.

Handling Exceptions

The exception taglib, AxKit::XSP::Exception, is used to catch exceptions. The syntax is very simple: rather than allowing different types of exceptions, it is currently a very simple try/catch block. To use the exceptions taglib, the following has to be added to *httpd.conf*:

```
AxAddXSPTaglib AxKit::XSP::Exception
```

Then you can implement form validation using exceptions, as Example E-6 demonstrates.

Example E-6. exceptiontaglib.xsp

```
<xsp:page
 xmlns:xsp="http://apache.org/xsp/core/v1"
 xmlns:param="http://axkit.org/NS/xsp/param/v1"
 xmlns:except="http://axkit.org/NS/xsp/exception/v1"
 language="Perl"
>
<page>
 # form validation:
 <except:try>
  <xsp:logic>
  if (((<param:number/> > 10) || (0 > <param:number/>)) {
    die "Number must be between 0 and 10";
  }
  if (!<param:name/>) {
    die "You must supply a name";
  }
  # Now do something with the params
  </xsp:logic>
  <p>Values saved successfully!</p>
  <except:catch>
   <p>Sorry, the values you entered were
      incorrect: <except:message/></p>
  </except:catch>
 </except:try>
</page>
</xsp:page>
```

The exact same try/catch (and message) tags can be used for *sendmail* and for ESQL (discussed in a moment).

Utilities Taglib

The AxKit::XSP::Util taglib includes some utility methods for including XML from the filesystem, from a URI, or as the return value from an expression. (Normally an expression would be rendered as plain text, so a "<" character would be encoded as "<".) The AxKit utilities taglib is a direct copy of the Cocoon utilities taglib, and as such uses the same namespace as the Cocoon Util taglib, http://apache.org/xsp/util/v1.

Executing SQL

Perhaps the most interesting taglib of all is the ESQL taglib, which allows you to execute SQL queries against a DBI-compatible database and provides access to the column return values as strings, scalars, numbers, dates, or even as XML. (Returning XML requires the utilities taglib.) Like the *sendmail* taglib, the ESQL taglib throws exceptions when an error occurs.

One point of interest about the ESQL taglib is that it is a direct copy of the Cocoon ESQL taglib. There are only a few minor differences between the two, such as how columns of different types are returned and how errors are trapped.* Having nearly identical taglibs helps you to port projects to or from Cocoon. As with all the other taglibs, ESQL requires the addition of the following to your *httpd.conf* file:

```
AxAddXSPTaglib AxKit::XSP::ESQL
```

Example E-7 uses ESQL to read data from an address-book table. This page demonstrates that it is possible to reuse the same code for both our list of addresses and viewing a single address in detail.

Example E-7. esqltaglib.xsp

```
<xsp:page
 language="Perl"
 xmlns:xsp="http://apache.org/xsp/core/v1"
 xmlns:esql="http://apache.org/xsp/SQL/v2"
 xmlns:except="http://axkit.org/NS/xsp/exception/v1"
 xmlns:param="http://axkit.org/NS/xsp/param/v1"
 indent-result="no"
>
<addresses>
 <esql:connection>
  <esql:driver>Pg</esql:driver>
  <esql:dburl>dbname=phonebook</esql:dburl>
  <esql:username>postgres</esql:username>
  <esql:password></esql:password>
  <except:try>
  <esql:execute-query>
   <xsp:logic>
   if (<param:address_id/>) {
    <esql:query>
     SELECT * FROM address WHERE id =
     <esql:parameter><param:address_id/></esql:parameter>
    </esql:query>
   }
   else {
    <esql:query>
     SELECT * FROM address
    </esql:query>
   }
   </xsp:logic>
   <esql:results>
    <esql:row-results>
     <address>
      <esql:get-columns/>
     </address>
    </esql:row-results>
   </esql:results>
  </esql:execute-query>
```

---

* In Cocoon there are ESQL tags for trapping errors, whereas AxKit uses exceptions.

Example E-7. esqltaglib.xsp (continued)

```
  <except:catch>
   Error Occured: <except:message/>
  </except:catch>
  </except:try>
 </esql:connection>
</addresses>
</xsp:page>
```

The result of running the above through the XSP processor is:

```
<addresses>
 <address>
  <id>2</id>
  <last_name>Sergeant</last_name>
  <first_name>Matt</first_name>
  <title>Mr</title>
  <company>AxKit.com Ltd</company>
  <email>matt@axkit.com</email>
  <classification_id>1</classification_id>
 </address>
</addresses>
```

More XPathScript Details

XPathScript aims to provide the power and flexibility of XSLT as an XML transformation language, without the restriction of XSLT's XML-based syntax. Unlike XSLT, which has special modes for outputting in text, XML, and HTML, XPathScript outputs only plain text. This makes it a lot easier than XSLT for people coming from a Perl background to learn. However, XPathScript is not a W3C specification, despite being based on XPath, which is a W3C recommendation.

XPathScript follows the basic ASP syntax for introducing code and outputting code to the browser: use <% %> to introduce Perl code, and <%= %> to output a value.

The XPathScript API

Along with the code delimiters, XPathScript provides stylesheet developers with a full API for accessing and transforming the source XML file. This API can be used in conjunction with the delimiters listed above to provide a stylesheet language that is as powerful as XSLT, yet supports all the features of a full programming language such as Perl. (Other implementations, such as Python or Java, also are possible.)

Extracting values

A simple example to get us started is to use the API to bring in the title from a DocBook article. A DocBook article title looks like this:

```
<article>
<artheader>
  <title>XPathScript - A Viable Alternative to XSLT?</title>
  ...
```

The XPath expression to retrieve the text in the <title> element is:

```
/article/artheader/title/text( )
```

Putting all this together to make this text into the HTML title, we get the following XPathScript stylesheet:

```
<html>
<head>
 <title><%= findvalue("/article/artheader/title") %></title>
</head>
<body>
  This was a DocBook Article.
  We're only extracting the title for now!
<p>
The title was: <%= findvalue("/article/artheader/title") %>
</body>
</html>
```

Again, we see the XPath syntax being used to find the nodes in the document, along with the function findvalue( ). Similarly, a list of nodes can be extracted (and thus looped over) using the findnodes( ) function:

```
...
<%
for my $sect1 (findnodes("/article/sect1")) {
  print $sect1->findvalue("title"), "<br>\n";
  for my $sect2 ($sect1->findnodes("sect2")) {
    print " + ", $sect2->findvalue("title"), "<br>\n";
    for my $sect3 ($sect2->findnodes("sect3")) {
      print " + + ", $sect3->findvalue("title"), "<br>\n";
    }
  }
}
%>
...
```

Here we see how we can apply the find* functions to individual nodes as methods, which makes the node the context node to search from. That is, $node-> findnodes("title") finds <title> child nodes of $node.

Declarative templates

We saw declarative templates earlier in this appendix, in the "Your First AxKit Page" section. The $t hash is the key to declarative templates. The apply_templates( ) function iterates over the nodes of your XML file, applying the templates defined in the $t hash reference as it meets matching tags. This is the most important feature of

XpathScript, because it allows you to define the appearance of individual tags without having to do your own iteration logic. We call this *declarative templating*.

The keys of $t are the names of the elements, including namespace prefixes where appropriate. When `apply_templates( )` is called, XPathScript tries to find a member of $t that matches the element name.

The following subkeys define the transformation:

pre
> Output to occur before the tag

post
> Output to occur after the tag

prechildren
> Output to occur before the children of this tag are written

postchildren
> Output to occur after the children of this tag are written

prechild
> Output to occur before every child element of this tag

postchild
> Output to occur after every child element of this tag

showtag
> Set to a false value (generally zero) to disable rendering of the tag itself

testcode
> Code to execute upon visiting this tag

More details about XPathScript can be found on the AxKit web site, at *http://axkit. org/*.

XSLT

One of the most important technologies to come out of the W3C is eXtensible Stylesheet Language Transformations (XSLT). XSLT provides a way to transform one type of XML document into another using a language written entirely in XML. XSLT works by allowing developers to create one or more template rules that are applied to the various elements in the source document to produce a second, transformed document.

While the basic concept behind XSLT is quite simple (apply these rules to the elements that match these conditions), the finer points of writing good XSLT stylesheets is a huge topic that we could never hope to cover here. We will instead provide a small example that illustrates the basic XSLT syntax.

First, though, we need to configure AxKit to transform XML documents using an XSLT processor. For this example, we will assume that you already have the

GNOME XSLT library (*libxml2* and *libxslt*, available at *http://xmlsoft.org/*) and its associated Perl modules (XML::LibXML and XML::LibXSLT) installed on your server.

Adding this line to your *httpd.conf* file tells AxKit to process all XML documents with a stylesheet processing instruction whose type is "text/xsl" with the LibXSLT language module:

```
AxAddStyleMap text/xsl Apache::AxKit::Language::LibXSLT
```

Anatomy of an XSLT Stylesheet

All XSLT stylesheets contain the following:

- An XML declaration (optional)
- An <xsl:stylesheet> element as the document's root element
- Zero or more template rules

Consider the following bare-bones stylesheet:

```
<?xml version="1.0"?>
<xsl:stylesheet
  xmlns:xsl="http://www.w3.org/1999/XSL/Transform"
  version="1.0">
  <xsl:template match="/">
    <!-- the content for the output document contained here -->
  </xsl:template>
</xsl:stylesheet>
```

Note that the root template (defined by the match="/" attribute) will be called without regard for the contents of the XML document being processed. As such, this is the best place to put the top-level elements that we want to include in the output of each and every document being transformed with this stylesheet.

Template Rules and Recursion

Let's take our basic stylesheet and extend it to allow us to transform the DocBook XML document presented in Example E-8 into HTML.

Example E-8. camelhistory.xml

```
<?xml version="1.0"?>
<book>
<title>Camels: An Historical Perspective</title>
<chapter>
  <title>Chapter One</title>
  <para>
    It was a dark and <emphasis>stormy</emphasis> night...
  </para>
</chapter>
</book>
```

First we need to alter the root template of our stylesheet:

```
<xsl:template match="/">
  <html>
    <head><xsl:copy-of select="/book/title"/></head>
    <body>
      <xsl:apply-templates/>
    </body>
  </html>
</xsl:template>
```

Here we have created the top-level structure of our output document and copied over the book's `<title>` element into the `<head>` element of our HTML page. The `<xsl:apply-templates/>` element tells the XSLT processor to pass on the entire contents of the current element (in this case the `<book>` element, since it is the root-level element in the source document) for further processing.

Now we need to create template rules for the other elements in the document:

```
<xsl:template match="chapter">
  <div class="chapter">
    <xsl:attribute name="id">chapter_id<xsl:number
    value="position( )" format="A"/></xsl:attribute>
    <xsl:apply-templates/>
  </div>
</xsl:template>
<xsl:template match="para">
  <p><xsl:apply-templates/></p>
</xsl:template>
```

Here we see more examples of recursive processing. The `<para>` and `<chapter>` elements are transformed into `<div>` and `<p>` elements, and the contents of those elements are passed along for further processing. Note also that the XPath expressions used within the template rules are evaluated in the context of the current element being processed. XSLT also maintains what is called the "current node list," which is the list of nodes being processed. In the example above, this is the list of all chapter elements. This is an example of XSLT using "least surprise".

While this sort of recursive processing is extremely powerful, it can also be quite a performance hit[*] and is necessary only for those cases where the current element contains other elements that need to be processed. If we know that a particular element will not contain any other elements, we need to return only that element's text value.

```
<xsl:template match="emphasis">
  <em><xsl:value-of select="."/></em>
</xsl:template>
<xsl:template match="chapter/title">
  <h2><xsl:value-of select="."/></h2>
```

---

[*] Although, since XSLT engines tend to be written in C, they are still very fast (often faster than most compiled Perl templating solutions).

```
  </xsl:template>
  <xsl:template match="book/title">
    <h1><xsl:value-of select="."/></h1>
  </xsl:template>
  </xsl:stylesheet>
```

Look closely at the last two template elements. Both match a <title> element, but one defines the rule for handling titles whose parent is a book element, while the other handles the chapter titles. In fact, any valid XPath expression, XSLT function call, or combination of the two can be used to define the match rule for a template element.

Finally, we need only save our stylesheet as *docbook-snippet.xsl*. Once our source document is associated with this stylesheet (see the section titled "Putting Everything Together" later in this appendix), we can point our browser to *camelhistory.xml*, and we'll see the output generated by the code in Example E-9.

Example E-9. camelhistory.html

```
<?xml version="1.0"?>
<html>
  <head>
    <title>Camels: An Historical Perspective</title>
  </head>
  <body>
    <h1>Camels: An Historical Perspective</h1>
    <div class="chapter" id="Chapter One">
      <h2>Chapter One</h2>
      <p>
          It was a dark and <em>stormy</em> night...
      </p>
    </div>
  </body>
</html>
```

The entire stylesheet is rendered in Example E-10.

Example E-10. docbook-snippet.xsl

```
<?xml version="1.0"?>
<xsl:stylesheet
  xmlns:xsl="http://www.w3.org/1999/XSL/Transform"
  version="1.0">

  <xsl:template match="/">
    <html>
      <head><xsl:copy-of select="/book/title"/></head>
      <body>
        <xsl:apply-templates/>
      </body>
    </html>
  </xsl:template>
```

Example E-10. docbook-snippet.xsl (continued)

```
<xsl:template match="chapter">
 <div class="chapter">
   <xsl:attribute name="id">chapter_id<xsl:number
   value="position()" format="A"/></xsl:attribute>
   <xsl:apply-templates/>
 </div>
</xsl:template>
<xsl:template match="para">
 <p><xsl:apply-templates/></p>
</xsl:template>

<xsl:template match="emphasis">
 <em><xsl:value-of select="."/></em>
</xsl:template>
<xsl:template match="chapter/title">
 <h2><xsl:value-of select="."/></h2>
</xsl:template>
<xsl:template match="book/title">
 <h1><xsl:value-of select="."/></h1>
</xsl:template>
</xsl:stylesheet>
```

Learning More

We have only scratched the surface of how XSLT can be used to transform XML documents. For more information, see the following resources:

- The XSLT specification: *http://www.w3.org/TR/xslt/*
- Miloslav Nic's XSLT reference: *http://www.zvon.org/xxl/XSLTreference/Output/index.html*
- Jeni Tennison's XSLT FAQ: *http://www.jenitennison.com/xslt/index.html*

Putting Everything Together

The last key piece to AxKit is how everything is tied together. We have a clean separation of logic, presentation, and content, but we've only briefly introduced using processing instructions for setting up the way a file gets processed through the AxKit engine. A generally better and more scalable way to work is to use the AxKit configuration directives to specify how to process files through the system.

Before introducing the configuration directives in detail, it is worth looking at how the W3C sees the evolving web of new media types. The HTML 4.0 specification defines eight media types:

screen
> The default media type, for normal web browsers.

tty
> For *tty*-based devices (e.g., the Lynx web browser).

printer

For printers requesting content directly (rather than for printable versions of a HTML page). Also for PDF or other paginated content.

handheld

For handheld devices. You need to distinguish between WAP, cHTML, and other handheld formats using styles, because the W3C did not make this distinction when it defined the media types.

braille

For braille interpreters.

tv

For devices with a TV-based browser, such as Microsoft's WebTV and Sega's Dreamcast.

projection

For projectors or presentations.

aural

For devices that can convert the output to spoken words, such as VoiceXML.

AxKit allows you to plug in modules that can detect these different media types, so you can deliver the same content in different ways. For finer control, you can use named stylesheets. In named stylesheets, you might have a printable page output to the *screen* media type. Named stylesheets are seen on many magazine sites (e.g., *http://take23.org/*) for displaying multi-page articles.

For example, to map all files with the extension *.dkb* to a DocBook stylesheet, you would use the following directives:

```
<Files *.dkb>
AxAddProcessor text/xsl /stylesheet/docbook.xsl
</Files>
```

Now if you wanted to display those DocBook files on WebTV as well as ordinary web browsers, but you wanted to use a different stylesheet for WebTV, you would use:

```
<Files *.dkb>
  <AxMediaType tv>
    AxAddProcessor text/xsl /stylesheets/docbook_tv.xsl
  </AxMediaType>
  <AxMediaType screen>
    AxAddProcessor text/xsl /stylesheets/docbook_screen.xsl
  </AxMediaType>
</Files>
```

Now let's extend that to chained transformations. Let's say you want to build up a table of contents the same way in both views. One way you can do it is to modularize the stylesheet. However, it's also possible to chain transformations in AxKit, simply by defining more than one processor for a particular resource:

```
<Files *.dkb>
  AxAddProcessor text/xsl /stylesheets/docbook_toc.xsl
  <AxMediaType tv>
    AxAddProcessor text/xsl /stylesheets/docbook_tv.xsl
  </AxMediaType>
  <AxMediaType screen>
    AxAddProcessor text/xsl /stylesheets/docbook_screen.xsl
  </AxMediaType>
</Files>
```

Now the TV-based browsers will see the DocBook files transformed by *docbook_toc.xsl*, with the output of that transformation processed by *docbook_tv.xsl*.

This is exactly how we would build up an application using XSP:

```
<Files *.xsp>
  AxAddProcessor application/x-xsp .
  <AxMediaType tv>
    AxAddProcessor text/xsl /stylesheets/page2tv.xsl
  </AxMediaType>
  <AxMediaType screen>
    AxAddProcessor text/xsl /stylesheets/page2html.xsl
  </AxMediaType>
</Files>
```

This resolves the earlier issue we had where the XSP did not output HTML, but something entirely different. Now we can see why—because this way we can build dynamic web applications that work easily on different devices!

There are four other configuration directives similar to AxAddProcessor. They take two additional parameters: one that specifies a particular way to examine the file being processed and one to facilitate the match. The directives are:

AxAddRootProcessor

Takes a root element name to match the first (root) element in the XML document. For example:

```
AxAddRootProcessor text/xsl article.xsl article
```

processes all XML files with a root element of <article> with the *article.xsl* stylesheet.

AxAddDocTypeProcessor

Processes XML documents with the given XML public identifier.

AxAddDTDProcessor

Processes all XML documents that use the DTD given as the third option.

AxAddURIProcessor

Processes all resources at the matching URI (which is a Perl regex).

This option was added for two reasons: because the <LocationMatch> directive is not allowed in an *.htaccess* file, and because the built-in Apache regular expressions are not powerful enough—for example, they cannot do negative matches.

Finally, the <AxStyleName> block allows you to specify named stylesheets. An example that implements printable/default views of a document might be:

```
<AxMediaType screen>
  <AxStyleName #default>
    AxAddProcessor text/xsl /styles/article_html.xsl
  </AxStyleName>
  <AxStyleName printable>
    AxAddProcessor text/xsl /styles/article_html_print.xsl
  </AxStyleName>
</AxMediaType>
```

By mixing the various embedded tags, it is possible to build up a very feature-rich site map of how your files get processed.

More Reasons to Use AxKit

Hopefully this will have whetted your appetite to play with AxKit. If you still need convincing, here are some extra things AxKit can do:

- AxKit can work with filter-aware modules and, instead of XSP, use other templating systems (such as Mason) to produce XML structures that will be styled on the fly after being passed to AxKit.

- XSLT, XSP, and XPathScript aren't the only possible processors. You can fairly easily create a new type of processor (such as a graph-outputting processor that would transform XML into charts, or rasterize some SVG).

- Apache configuration isn't the only way to control AxKit. You can create a ConfigReader that reads the configuration from another system, such as an XML file on disk.

- There are ways to choose stylesheets on the fly—for instance, to allow people to see the site with the design they prefer, based on cookies or a query string.

- AxKit has an intelligent and powerful caching system that can be controlled in various ways or replaced by a custom cache if needed.

- You don't need to fetch the initial content from the filesystem. The Provider interface allows you to return data from wherever Perl can get it (e.g., a content-management system).

For more information, help, support, and community chat, please visit the web site at *http://axkit.org/* and join in the discussions on the mailing lists, where you will find like minded people building a range of solutions.

APPENDIX F

HTTP Status Codes

The HyperText Transfer Protocol (HTTP) is an application-level protocol for distributed, collaborative, hypermedia information systems. It is a generic, stateless protocol that can be used for many tasks (e.g., name servers and distributed object management systems) beyond its use for hypertext through extension of its request methods, error codes, and headers. An important feature of HTTP is the typing and negotiation of data representation, which allows systems to be built independently of the data being transferred.

HTTP/1.0 is described in RFC 1945. HTTP/1.1 is the latest version of the specification, and as of this writing HTTP/1.1 is covered in RFC 2616.

Only a small subset of HTTP response codes usually is used when writing mod_perl applications, but sometimes you need to know others as well. We will list the codes here. Their names are fairly self-explanatory, but you can find extended explanations in the appropriate RFC (see section 9 in RFC 1945 and section 10 in RFC 2616). You can always find the latest links to these RFCs at the World Wide Web Consortium's site, *http://www.w3.org/Protocols/*.

While HTTP/1.1 is widely supported, HTTP/1.0 still remains the mainstream standard. Therefore, we will supply a summary for each version, including the corresponding Apache constants.

In mod_perl, these constants can be accessed via the Apache::Constants package (e.g., to access the HTTP_OK constant, use Apache::Constants::HTTP_OK). See the Apache:: Constants manpage for more information.

HTTP/1.0 Status Codes

```
Successful 2xx:

200 HTTP_OK
201 HTTP_CREATED
```

```
202 HTTP_ACCEPTED
204 HTTP_NO_CONTENT

Redirection 3xx:

300 HTTP_MOVED_PERMANENTLY
301 HTTP_MOVED_TEMPORARILY
302 HTTP_SEE_OTHER
304 HTTP_NOT_MODIFIED

Client Error 4xx:

400 HTTP_BAD_REQUEST
401 HTTP_UNAUTHORIZED
403 HTTP_FORBIDDEN
404 HTTP_NOT_FOUND

Server Error 5xx:

500 HTTP_INTERNAL_SERVER_ERROR
501 HTTP_NOT_IMPLEMENTED
502 HTTP_BAD_GATEWAY
503 HTTP_SERVICE_UNAVAILABLE
```

HTTP/1.1 Status Codes

```
Informational 1xx:

100 HTTP_CONTINUE
101 HTTP_SWITCHING_PROTOCOLS

Successful 2xx:

200 HTTP_OK
201 HTTP_CREATED
202 HTTP_ACCEPTED
203 HTTP_NON_AUTHORITATIVE
204 HTTP_NO_CONTENT
205 HTTP_RESET_CONTENT
206 HTTP_PARTIAL_CONTENT

Redirection 3xx:

300 HTTP_MULTIPLE_CHOICES
301 HTTP_MOVED_PERMANENTLY
302 HTTP_MOVED_TEMPORARILY
303 HTTP_SEE_OTHER
304 HTTP_NOT_MODIFIED
305 HTTP_USE_PROXY
306
307 HTTP_TEMPORARY_REDIRECT
```

```
Client Error 4xx:

400 HTTP_BAD_REQUEST
401 HTTP_UNAUTHORIZED
402 HTTP_PAYMENT_REQUIRED
403 HTTP_FORBIDDEN
404 HTTP_NOT_FOUND
405 HTTP_METHOD_NOT_ALLOWED
406 HTTP_NOT_ACCEPTABLE
407 HTTP_PROXY_AUTHENTICATION_REQUIRED
408 HTTP_REQUEST_TIMEOUT
409 HTTP_CONFLICT
410 HTTP_GONE
411 HTTP_LENGTH_REQUIRED
412 HTTP_PRECONDITION_FAILED
413 HTTP_REQUEST_ENTITY_TOO_LARGE
414 HTTP_REQUEST_URI_TOO_LARGE
415 HTTP_UNSUPPORTED_MEDIA_TYPE
416 HTTP_RANGE_NOT_SATISFIABLE
417 HTTP_EXPECTATION_FAILED

Server Error 5xx:

500 HTTP_INTERNAL_SERVER_ERROR
501 HTTP_NOT_IMPLEMENTED
502 HTTP_BAD_GATEWAY
503 HTTP_SERVICE_UNAVAILABLE
504 HTTP_GATEWAY_TIME_OUT
505 HTTP_VERSION_NOT_SUPPORTED
```

References

All the information related to web protocols can be found at the World Wide Web Consortium's site, *http://www.w3.org/Protocols/*.

There are many mirrors of the RFCs all around the world. One of the good starting points is *http://www.rfc-editor.org/*.

Index

We'd like to hear your suggestions for improving our indexes. Send email to *index@oreilly.com.*

Apache (*continued*)
   configuration directives, 94, 100
   configuration files, 93
      <Directory> section, 95, 96
      <Files> section, 95, 97
      <FilesMatch> section, 100
      <Location> section, 95, 98
      merging Options directives, 100
      merging sections, 99
      subgrouping sections, 99
   core modules, 765, 789–794
   exit( ) function, 234
   hooks, new scheme, 688
   installation
      local installation, 83
      nonstandard, 84
      nonstandard with CPAN.pm, 86
   I/O filtering, 686
   mod_cgi, 10–13
      forking, 13
   mod_perl enabled, running as suExec, 90
   mod_proxy module
      buffering, 431–433
      overview, 427–429
      ProxyPass directive, 429
      ProxyPassReverse directive, 430
      security issues, 431
   modules, overview, 22
   MPMs, 687
   new features in 2.0, 686
   phases, mod_perl 2.0 support, 714
   protocol modules, 688
   request processing, 20–22
   requests, serving, 95
   resources, 680
   source code distribution, obtaining, 26
   start procedure, 139
   starting, 94
      multi-process mode, 146
      single-process mode, 146
   starting/stopping, online
         information, 215
   stopping/restarting, 149–151
   termination/restart, optimization, 151
Apache API, Perl interface, 692
APache AutoConf-style Interface
      (APACI), 44
APache eXtension Support (APXS), 44
Apache Modules Registry web site, 23, 24
Apache Performance Notes web site, 402

Apache server
   building
      separately from mod_perl, 64
      static build, 64
   DSOs, when to use, 66
   installing, changing default directory, 65
Apache test framework develoment mailing
      list, 678
Apache Toolbox, 91
Apache web site, 41
Apache::AddHostPath module, 773
Apache::Archive module, 778
Apache::args module, compared to
         Apache::Request::param and
         CGI::param, 457–461
Apache::ASP module, 781
Apache::AutoIndex module, 777
Apache::AxKit module, 781
Apache::Backhand module, 780
ApacheBench utility, 324–326
Apache::Clean module, 785
Apache::compat module, 709
Apache::Compress module, 787
Apache::ConfigFile module, 772
Apache::Connection module, 792
Apache::Constants module, 792
Apache::Cookie module, 796
   replacing CGI::Cookie, 256
apachectl script, 29, 153
   server monitoring, 196–199
   server reboot and, 159
   starting/stopping server, 30
Apache::DB module, 768
   locating code errors, 220–226
   mod_perl debugging, 628–630
Apache::DBI module, 780
   configuration, 573
   connect( ) requests and, 572
   connection cache, skipping at
         startup, 577
   connections, 572
      opening with different
            parameters, 574
      preopening, 578
   database connections and, 571–577
   databases, locking risks, 574
   DBI handler, 576
   DBI module and, 364, 572
   debugging, 573
   disconnect( ) statements, 572

AxAddURIProcessor directive, 854
AxKit
  configuration, 836
  cookies, 841
  debugging, 838
  dynamic content, 839–846
  ESQL taglib, 844
  features, 855
  forms, parameters, 840
  installation, 836
  missing modules, 836
  page creation, 837–839
  stylesheets, 838
  utilities taglib, 844
  XPath and, 839
  XSLT and, 848
    stylesheets, 849
    templates, 849–852
  XSP and, 839
AxKit::XSP::Cookie module, 841

B

backtrace
  macros for, 645
  obtaining, 635
    automatically, 636
B::Deparse module, 646–648
BEGIN blocks, 240
benchmarking scripts, 19
benchmarks
  ApacheBench, 324–326
  Apache::Recorder, 328
  Apache::Registry, 456
  buffered compared to unbuffered
    printing, 466
  caching data compared to
    regenerating, 492
  characteristics of, 324
  creating new modules, 503
  httperf, 326
  http_load, 327
  HTTP::Monkeywrench, 328
  HTTP::RecordedSession, 328
  HTTP::WebTest, 328
  Perl code, 328–333
  print( ) function, 463
  string manipulation, 468
  string manipulation modules, 459
  subroutines, 476–477

usefulness of, 323
  (see also performance)
BenchWeb web site, 347
beos MPM, 688
Berkeley DB, 555
BerkeleyDB module, 555
big-O notation, 556
binaries, mod_perl installation, 696
#!/bin/perl directive, 243
B::LexInfo module, memory leaks and, 521
blocking calls
  I/O filtering, 734–735
  zombie processes and, 375
Boa server, 413
body (HTTP), 4
bottlenecks
  avoiding, 321
  detection, 321
braille media type, 853
breakpoints, perldb, 620–625
  listing, 621
  removing, 622
browsers
  creating, 295–302
  Mosaic, 3
BSD::Resource::getrusage, 335
bt command, 635
BTREE access method, DBM, 556
bucket brigades
  blocking calls, 734
  connection input filters, 737–740
  HTTP request output filter, 748–750
  invoking filter handlers, 730
  I/O filtering, 729
  manipulation techniques, 738
  protocol modules and, 724
  request input filters, 741–742
  stream-based HTTP request input
    filters, 742–744
buffered printing, 461–467
  disabling, reasons to, 465
buffers (DBM), flushing, 558
building
  Apache server, separately from mod_
    perl, 64
  httpd_docs, 410
  httpd_perl, 411
  manual method, 62
  mod_perl, 27

configuration (*continued*)
    Apache::DBI module, 573
    Apache::ReadConfig module, 129
    Apache::Status, 657
    Apache::Status module, 336
    Apache::VMonitor module, 187
    Apache::Watchdog::RunAway
        module, 210
    AxKit, 836
    by directory (Apache), 93
    debugging, 137
    development tier (server
        implementation), 180
    DSO support,
        advantages/disadvantages, 45
    FAQ, 144
    file browser module, 300
    httpd_docs, 411
    httpd_perl, 412
    information reporting, 140
    I/O filters, 735–737
    Makefile.PL, 46–50
    MaxClients directive, 383–388
    MaxRequestsPerChild directive, 388
    method handlers, 115
    mod_auth_dbm and mod_auth_db
        issues, 90
    mod_cgi module, 10
    mod_perl
        aliases, 102–103
        enabling mod_perl, 697
        improvements, 693
        modperl handler, 700
        module access, 698
        overview, 101
        Perl command-line switches, 699
        PerlOptions directive, 702–707
        perl-script handler, 700
        startup files, 698
    multiple server instances, 45
    name-based virtual hosts
        backend server, 441
        frontend server, 440
    openssl, 70
    parameters, 46–50
    performance, information resources, 145
    section, constructing, 124–129
    prior to installation, 43–46
    production tier (server
        implementation), 182
    saving, 136

    scripts directory, 34
    server
        Perl and, 123–137
        validating syntax, 137
    Squid server, 419–424
    staging tier (server implementation), 182
    troubleshooting, 662–665
    two server approach
        servers, 411
        source, 410
    on Unix, 29
    validating, 154
    virtual hosts, 439
configuration directives, 100
    Apache, 94
    scope, 138
Configuration file, preparing for manual
        build, 63
configuration files
    Apache, 93
    creating, 263–268
    creating in Perl, 130
    creating/including separate, 101
    <Directory> section, 95, 96
    dynamically updating, 271–278
    <Files> section, 95, 97, 101
    <FilesMatch> section, 100
    HTTP headers and, 293
    <Location> section, 95, 98
        overriding, 106
    <Location/perl> section, 104
    migrating mod_perl 1.0 to 2.0, 710
    migration compatibility, 709
    Options directives, merging, 100
    package naming and, 263
    reloading, 268–271
        dynamic configuration files, 262–278
    sections
        creating subgroups, 99
        merging, 99
configuration parameters
    supplying from file, 53
    upgrading servers, 53
configuration variables, options for
        defining, 263
Configuration.custom file, 55
conflicts, hardware, 321
connect( ) method, Apache::DBI module
        and, 572
connection input filter, 737–740
connection phases, 720

plug-in modules, converting from CGI
        script, 824–832
port forwarding
    information web site, 216
    upgrading servers with, 166
port numbers, publishing, 140
port-based virtual hosts, 439
porting (see migration)
POST method
    HTML forms, 7
    REQUEST_METHOD environment
        variable, 13
POST requests, 539
    redirecting, 754
    reusing data, 753
post_config phase, 717, 718
post-processing handler, terminating child
        processes, 235
post-read-request (Apache request
        processing), 20
pragmas
    constant, print( ) call debugging and, 608
    strict, importance of, 218
    vars, global variables and, 224
    warnings, 244, 587
preallocating memory, 369
pre-caching data, 480–494
pre_config phase, 717
pre_connection phase, 720
--prefix option, 65
prefork MPM, 688
preloaded modules, memory and, 349
preloading
    modules, server startup, 359
    registry scripts, server startup, 362
prepare( ) statements, performance and, 581
PREP_HTTPD configuration parameter, 47
presentation languages, Template
        Toolkit, 807
print( ) function, 238
    debugging code, 607–612
        Data::Dumper, 612
    HTTP response headers and, 291
    performance techniques, 461–467
print command, 618
printers, as media type, 853
printf( ) function, 239
printing
    arrays, 618
    files, perfomance tip, 480

formatting output, 239
function call stack backtrace, 591
<html> tags, 461
    performance techniques, 461–467
process_connection phase, 720, 722
processes
    child, lifespan, 13
    forking, 13, 372
        detaching, 374
    hanging
        detecting, 638
        diagnosing with interactive
            debugger, 643–645
        diagnosing with Perl trace, 640–641
        diagnosing with system calls
            trace, 641–643
        OS problems, 637
        reasons for, 638
        tracking and terminating, 210–212
    memory consumption, 333–335
    parent, 13
        identifying, 153
    PIDs
        determining, 148
        identifying, 152
    resource usage, 383
    resources, limiting number serving, 213
    size considerations, 406
    spinning, mod_perl mailing list, 675
    zombie processes, 374
production tier (server implementation)
    configuration package, 182
    overview, 179
program flow, aborting, 235
programming languages, combining with Perl
        code, 504–506
programming style
    coding idioms, 613–616
    error messages and, 589
    poor practices, 14
    semicolons, importance of, 604
    (see also coding)
projection media type, 853
protocol modules
    Apache, 688
    principles of operation, 722–727
protocols, stateless, 4
prototyping, modules, 45
proxy (mod_proxy module),
        overview, 427–429

subroutines
  breakpoints, 622
  callbacks, activating, 50
  code profiling, 340
    Devel::DProf, 340–344
    Devel::SmallProf, 344–347
  coding errors and, 220–226
  debugging, stepping into, 619
  exporting, configuration files and, 265
  handler( ), 109
  memory usage, determining, 339
  performance, 476–477
  saving as libraries, 222
  variables, passing to, 517–518
  (see also functions), 475
suExec, running mod_perl Apache as, 90
sv_dump( ) function, 520
swap files, memory swapping,
    disadvantages, 207
swap memory, 205
swap partition, 205
swapping (memory pages), 206, 320
  disadvantages, 207
  effects of, 384
SWIG web site, 507
switches, command-line, mod_perl
    configuration, 699
symbol table, accessing, 653–655
symbolic links
  coding considerations, 249
  creating, 160
  libgdbm errors, 57
symbols, imported, memory
    considerations, 473–475
SymLinksIfOwnerMatch, 399
syntax
  errors, debugging, 604–606
  functions, documentation, 218
  starting Apache server, 94
  stopping server, 159
  subroutine references, 50
  validating
    server configuration, 137
    startup file, 122
  verification, <Perl> sections, 132–135
syntax error at /dev/null line 1, near "line
    arguments:" message, 670
--sysconfdir option, 84
syslog, 205
system( ) function, 240
  executing correctly, 381

system calls
  sending output to browser, 240
  tracing, 598
system calls trace, diagnosing hanging
    processes, 641–643
system requirements
  dumping core files, 633
  memory, mod_perl, 16
  mod_perl installation, 25
SysV
  init system, server rebooting and, 158

T

-T option, validating server
    configuration, 154
-t option, validating server
    configuration, 154
-T switch, 245
$^T variable, 242
taglibs
  AxKit
    ESQL taglib, 844
    utilities, 844
    XSP framework, 839
taint checking, 142
taint mode, 245
  mod_perl 2.0, 710
tar files, mod_perl, installing on multiple
    machines, 76
tar utility, unpacking source code, 27
telnet, testing mod_perl status, 87
Template module, Template Toolkit, 806
Template Toolkit, 784
  Apache::Template module, 815
  CGI scripts, 806
  conditional clauses, 807
  directives, 807
    constructs, 809
  downloading, 804
  example template, 807
  exception handling, 807
  FOREACH directive, 808
  hangman application, 815
    CGI script, 816–822
    modular templates, 822
    plug-in module conversion, 824–832
    self-contained template, 832–834
  header template, 808
  INCLUDE directive, 808
  installation, 804
  languages, 807

About the Authors

Stas Bekman is the author of *The mod_perl Guide*, the open source document that is the basis for this book. Stas is a member of the Apache Software Foundation and is a frequent speaker at the O'Reilly Open Source Conference.

Eric Cholet is a member of the Apache Software Foundation and the Paris Perl Mongers. He is technical director of Logilune, a Paris-based company that he co-founded in 1987, and is a speaker at the O'Reilly Open Source Conference.

Colophon

Our look is the result of reader comments, our own experimentation, and feedback from distribution channels. Distinctive covers complement our distinctive approach to technical topics, breathing personality and life into potentially dry subjects.

The animal on the cover of *Practical mod_perl* is a Thoroughbred horse. The Thoroughbred, also called the English running horse, originated in England from crossbreeding an Arabian horse and a Turkish horse to create the fastest racing horse in the world. One of the swiftest of all creatures and the fastest of horses, the Thoroughbred can maintain speeds of up to 45 miles per hour for more than a mile. This makes the Thoroughbred best-suited for racing, as well as for polo.

Thoroughbreds average 16 hands and 1,100 pounds in size. They have a leggy appearance, complemented by a long, light neck. Their heads are proportionate to their bodies, and their wide foreheads are often adorned with white markings. In addition to their strong physical characteristics, Thoroughbreds' personalities are noted for their strength, courage, determination, and will. However, due to their breeding, they also tend to be racy and nervous.

The integrity of the breed is closely maintained through stud documentation. Since 1977, every foal registered in the American Stud Book must be blood-typed to prove its origins.

Linley Dolby was the production editor, and Rachel Wheeler was the copyeditor for *Practical mod_perl*. Sada Preisch and Jane Ellin proofread the book, and Claire Cloutier provided quality control. Tom Dinse wrote the index. Derek Di Matteo, Matt Hutchinson, and Jamie Peppard provided production assistance.

Ellie Volckhausen designed the cover of this book, based on a series design by Edie Freedman. The cover image is a 19th-century engraving from the Dover Pictorial Archive. Emma Colby produced the cover layout with QuarkXPress 4.1 using Adobe's ITC Garamond font.

Bret Kerr designed the interior layout, based on a series design by David Futato. This book was converted by Linda Mui and Andrew Savikas to FrameMaker 5.5.6 with a format conversion tool created by Erik Ray, Jason McIntosh, Neil Walls, and Mike Sierra that uses Perl and XML technologies. The text font is Linotype Birka; the heading font is Adobe Myriad Condensed; and the code font is LucasFont's TheSans Mono Condensed. The illustrations that appear in the book were produced by Robert Romano and Jessamyn Read using Macromedia FreeHand 9 and Adobe Photoshop 6. This colophon was written by Linley Dolby.

Other Titles Available from O'Reilly

Perl

Learning Perl, 3rd Edition

By Randal Schwartz & Tom Phoenix
3rd Edition July 2001
330 pages, ISBN 0-596-00132-0

Learning Perl is the quintessential tutorial for the Perl programming language. The third edition has not only been updated to Perl Version 5.6, but has also been rewritten from the ground up to reflect the needs of programmers learning Perl today. Other books may teach you to program in Perl, but this book will turn you into a Perl programmer.

Mastering Regular Expressions, 2nd Edition

By Jeffrey E. F. Friedl
2nd Edition July 2002
484 pages, ISBN 0-596-00289-0

Written by an expert in the topic, this book shows programmers not only how to use regular expressions, but how to think in regular expressions. Updated with a wealth of new material, the second edition explains how to use regular expressions to code complex and subtle text processing that you never imagined could be automated. Included are such key topics as avoiding common errors and optimizing expressions. The book covers many new features added to Perl—a language well endowed with regular expressions—as well as other languages such as Java, Python, and Visual Basic that include support for this powerful tool.

Embedding Perl in HTML with Mason

By Dave Rolsky & Ken Williams
1st Edition October 2002
320 pages, ISBN 0-596-00225-4

Mason, a Perl-based templating system, is becoming more and more popular as a tool for building websites and managing other dynamic collections. While using Mason is not difficult, creating Mason-based sites can be tricky, and this concise book helps you navigate around the obstacles. The book covers the most recent release of Mason, 1.10, which has many new features including line number reporting based on source files, sub-requests, and simplified use as a CGII. It also explores using Mason for dynamic generation of XML documents.

Perl & XML

By Erik T. Ray & Jason McIntosh
1st Edition April 2002
224 pages, ISBN 0-596-00205-X

Perl & XML is aimed at Perl programmers who need to work with XML documents and data. This book gives a complete, comprehensive tour of the landscape of Perl and XML, making sense of the myriad of modules, terminology, and techniques. The last two chapters of Perl and XML give complete examples of XML applications, pulling together all the tools at your disposal.

Mastering Perl/Tk

By Steve Lidie & Nancy Walsh
1st Edition January 2002
768 pages, ISBN 1-56592-716-8

Beginners and seasoned Perl/Tk programmers alike will find *Mastering Perl/Tk* to be the definitive book on creating graphical user interfaces with Perl/Tk. After a fast-moving tutorial, the book goes into detail on creating custom widgets, working with bindings and callbacks, IPC techniques, and examples using many of the non-standard add-on widgets for Perl/Tk (including Tix widgets). Every Perl/Tk programmer will need this book.

Perl Cookbook

By Tom Christiansen &
Nathan Torkington
1st Edition August 1998
794 pages, ISBN 1-56592-243-3

The *Perl Cookbook* is a comprehensive collection of problems, solutions, and practical examples for anyone programming in Perl. You'll find hundreds of rigorously reviewed Perl "recipes" for manipulating strings, numbers, dates, arrays, and hashes; pattern matching and text substitutions; references, data structures, objects, and classes; signals and exceptions; and much more.

O'REILLY®

To order: *800-998-9938* • *order@oreilly.com* • *www.oreilly.com*
Online editions of most O'Reilly titles are available by subscription at *safari.oreilly.com*
Also available at most retail and online bookstores.

Perl

Computer Science & Perl Programming: Best of The Perl Journal

Edited by Jon Orwant
1st Edition, November 2002
758 pages, ISBN 0-596-00310-2

The first of three volumes from the archives of *The Perl Journal* that O'Reilly has exclusive rights to distribute, this book is a compilation of the best from TPJ: 71 articles providing a comprehensive tour of how experts implement computer science concepts in the real world, with code walkthroughs, case studies, and explanations of difficult techniques that can't be found in any other book.

Web, Graphics & Perl/Tk: Best of the Perl Journal

Edited by Jon Orwant
1st Edition March 2003
480 pages, ISBN 0-596-00311-0

Web, Graphics & Perl/Tk is the second volume of The Best of the Perl Journal, compiled and re-edited by the original editor and publisher of *The Perl Journal*, Jon Orwant. In this series, we've taken the very best (and still relevant) articles published in TPJ over its five years of publication and immortalized them into three volumes.

Perl & LWP

By Sean M. Burke
1st Edition, June 2002
464 pages, 0-596-00178-9

This comprehensive guide to LWP and its applications comes with many practical examples. Topics include programmatically fetching web pages, submitting forms, using various techniques for HTML parsing, handling cookies, and authentication. With the knowledge in Perl & LWP, you can automate any task on the Web, from checking the prices of items at online stores to bidding at auctions automatically.

Perl Graphics Programming

By Shawn Wallace
1st Edition, December 2002
478 pages, 0-596-00219-X

This insightful volume focuses on scripting programs that enable programmers to manipulate graphics for the Web. The book also helps demystify the manipulation of graphics formats for web newcomers with a practical, resource-like approach. While most of the examples use Perl as a scripting language, the concepts are applicable to any programming language. The book documents ways to use several powerful Perl modules for generating graphics, including GD, PerlMagick, and GIMP.

Programming Web Services with Perl

By Randy J. Ray & Scott Guelich
1st Edition December 2002
486 pages, ISBN 0-596-00206-8

O'Reilly presents another Perl first: *Programming Web Services with Perl*. Like most O'Reilly books, it cuts through the hype on web services and concentrates on the useful and practical. It shows how to use Perl to create web services, introducing the major web service standards (XML-RPC, SOAP, WSDL, UDDI) and how to implement Perl servers and clients using these standards. Moving beyond the basics, the book offers solutions to the problems of security, authentication, and scalability.

O'REILLY®

To order: *800-998-9938* • *order@oreilly.com* • *www.oreilly.com*
Online editions of most O'Reilly titles are available by subscription at *safari.oreilly.com*
Also available at most retail and online bookstores.

How to stay in touch with O'Reilly

1. Visit our award-winning web site

http://www.oreilly.com/

★ "Top 100 Sites on the Web"—PC Magazine
★ CIO Magazine's Web Business 50 Awards

Our web site contains a library of comprehensive product information (including book excerpts and tables of contents), downloadable software, background articles, interviews with technology leaders, links to relevant sites, book cover art, and more. File us in your bookmarks or favorites!

2. Join our email mailing lists

Sign up to get email announcements of new books and conferences, special offers, and O'Reilly Network technology newsletters at:

http://elists.oreilly.com

It's easy to customize your free elists subscription so you'll get exactly the O'Reilly news you want.

3. Get examples from our books

To find example files for a book, go to:

http://www.oreilly.com/catalog

select the book, and follow the "Examples" link.

4. Work with us

Check out our web site for current employment opportunities:

http://jobs.oreilly.com/

5. Register your book

Register your book at:

http://register.oreilly.com

6. Contact us

O'Reilly & Associates, Inc.
1005 Gravenstein Hwy North
Sebastopol, CA 95472 USA
TEL: 707-827-7000 or 800-998-9938
       (6am to 5pm PST)
FAX: 707-829-0104

order@oreilly.com
For answers to problems regarding your order or our products. To place a book order online visit:

http://www.oreilly.com/order_new/

catalog@oreilly.com
To request a copy of our latest catalog.

booktech@oreilly.com
For book content technical questions or corrections.

corporate@oreilly.com
For educational, library, government, and corporate sales.

proposals@oreilly.com
To submit new book proposals to our editors and product managers.

international@oreilly.com
For information about our international distributors or translation queries. For a list of our distributors outside of North America check out:

http://international.oreilly.com/distributors.html

adoption@oreilly.com
For information about academic use of O'Reilly books, visit:

http://academic.oreilly.com

O'REILLY®

To order: *800-998-9938* • *order@oreilly.com* • *www.oreilly.com*
Online editions of most O'Reilly titles are available by subscription at *safari.oreilly.com*
Also available at most retail and online bookstores.